HANDBOOK OF RESPONSE TO INTERVENTION AND MULTI-TIERED SYSTEMS OF SUPPORT

Of the many issues facing special education (and general education) today, it is difficult to imagine one more important or timely than response to intervention (RTI). Almost overnight RTI has become standard practice across the nation. Unfortunately, RTI remains ill-defined, falls far short of its evidence-based practice goal, is almost invariably misused, and often results in more harm than good. Nevertheless, as a conceptual framework RTI has great potential for ensuring that students with disabilities receive appropriate, evidence-based instruction.

The mission of this handbook is to present a comprehensive and integrated discussion of response to intervention (RTI) and its relation to multi-tiered systems of support (MTSS) in both special education and general education. Although the two terms are currently used interchangeably, distinct differences exist between them. Therefore, chapters are dedicated to distinguishing the two concepts—RTI and MTSS—and describing each one's unique role in both general and special education. In addition, the authors recommend a third term, Multi-Tiered Instruction, to differentiate the practices related to the purpose of the specific intervention.

Paige C. Pullen is a Research Professor and Literacy Initiatives Officer at the University of Florida with faculty appointments in the Lastinger Center for Learning and the School of Special Education, School Psychology, and Early Childhood Studies.

Michael J. Kennedy is an Associate Professor of special education in the Curry School of Education at the University of Virginia and Co-Editor of the *Journal of Special Education Technology*.

HANDBOOK OF RESPONSE TO INTERVENTION AND MULTI-TIERED SYSTEMS OF SUPPORT

Edited by
Paige C. Pullen and
Michael J. Kennedy

Routledge
Taylor & Francis Group

NEW YORK AND LONDON

First published 2019
by Routledge
711 Third Avenue, New York, NY 10017

and by Routledge
2 Park Square, Milton Park, Abingdon, Oxon, OX14 4RN

Routledge is an imprint of the Taylor & Francis Group, an informa business

© 2019 Taylor & Francis

Library of Congress Cataloging-in-Publication Data
Names: Pullen, Paige C., editor. | Kennedy, Michael J., 1959– editor.
Title: Handbook of response to intervention and multi-tiered systems
of support / edited by Paige C. Pullen and Michael J. Kennedy.
Description: New York, NY : Routledge, 2018. | Includes
bibliographical references and index.
Identifiers: LCCN 2018015254| ISBN 9780415626033 (hbk : alk. paper) |
ISBN 9780415626040 (pbk : alk. paper) | ISBN 9780203102954 (ebk)
Subjects: LCSH: Response to intervention (Learning disabled children) |
Student assistance programs. | Learning disabled children—Education.
Classification: LCC LC4704 .H366 2018 | DDC 371.92—dc23
LC record available at https://lccn.loc.gov/2018015254

ISBN: 978-0-415-62603-3 (hbk)
ISBN: 978-0-415-62604-0 (pbk)
ISBN: 978-0-203-10295-4 (ebk)

Typeset in Bembo and Stone Sans
by Florence Production Ltd, Stoodleigh, Devon, UK

CONTENTS

Contents

ABOUT THE EDITORS

Paige C. Pullen

Dr. Paige C. Pullen is a Research Professor and Literacy Initiatives Manager at the University of Florida with faculty appointments in the Lastinger Center for Learning and the School of Special Education, School Psychology, and Early Childhood Studies. Previously, Dr. Pullen spent 12 years as an elementary and special education teacher and 16 years at the University of Virginia, where she held appointments in the Curry School of Education and the School of Medicine. Pullen has been recognized as an outstanding teacher at UVA, receiving the 2011 Seven Society Outstanding Mentor Award and the 2010 Outstanding Professor of the Year at Curry. She has served as Publications Chair for the Division for Learning Disabilities of the Council for Exceptional Children and as President of the Virginia Council for Exceptional Children. Dr. Pullen is a member of several editorial boards and since 2010 has served as the Editor-in-Chief of *Exceptionality*, and she is co-editor of the *Handbook of Special Education*. Dr. Pullen's research has focused primarily on implementing effective interventions for children with or at risk for learning disabilities, especially in the area of reading. She has worked with colleagues from the UVA School of Medicine to provide effective health and educational services to children with disabilities not only at UVA but in rural Southwest Virginia and, most notably, in Lusaka, Zambia and Gaborone, Botswana in Africa.

Michael J. Kennedy

Michael J. Kennedy is an Associate Professor of Special Education in the Curry School of Education at the University of Virginia (UVA). He is also Co-Editor of the *Journal of Special Education Technology*. Prior to earning his Ph.D. at the University of Kansas (KU) in 2011 under the mentorship of Dr. Don Deshler, Kennedy was a high-school special education teacher for six years. He also taught three years at the elementary level. Kennedy's research addresses the intersection of teacher quality, literacy instruction, and multimedia. In 2013, Kennedy received one of the inaugural Early Career Research and Development grants from the National Center for Special Education Research (NCSER) within the Institute for Education Sciences (IES). Since 2011, Kennedy has published over 50 scholarly works, including 40 peer-reviewed articles and made over 100 presentations at various professional conferences. He is a contributing author to the High Leverage Practices (HLPs) for special education created by CEC and the

CEEDAR center. His core innovation, Content Acquisition Podcasts (CAPs) are used by teachers and students all around the world to receive professional development and evidence-based vocabulary instruction. Kennedy has received various honors and recognition for his work, including the Early Career Research Award from AERA's Instructional Technology SIG, the University of Virginia's Alumni Board of Trustees All University Teaching Award, Publication of the Year from the Teacher Education Division of CEC, and Dissertation of the Year by KU's School of Education.

CONTRIBUTORS

Ana D'Abreu, Texas A&M University
Stephanie Al Otaiba, Southern Methodist University
Dimitris Anastasiou, Southern Illinois University
Kristen E. Ashworth, College of Charleston
Jeanmarie Badar, Johnson Elementary School
Amber Benedict, University of Florida
Sarah A. Benz, University of Texas at Austin
Bonnie Billingsley, Virginia Tech University
Mary T. Brownell, University of Florida
Heather M. Campbell, St. Olaf College
David Chard, Southern Methodist University
Siuman Chung, Universiteit Leiden
Nathan H. Clemens, University of Texas at Austin
Daniel Cohen, University of Alabama
Sarah Conoyer, Southern Illinois University
Jean Crockett, University of Florida
Amy Elleman, Middle Tennessee State University
Christine Espin, Universiteit Leiden
K. B. Flannery, University of Oregon
Anne Foegen, Iowa State University
Suzanne R. Forsyth, University of Texas at Austin
Douglas Fuchs, Vanderbilt University
Lynn S. Fuchs, Vanderbilt University
Jennifer Gilbert, Vanderbilt University
Vivian E. Gonsalves, University of Florida
Daniel P. Hallahan, University of Virginia
Keith C. Herman, University of Missouri
Asha K. Jitendra, University of California
Francesca Jones, Southern Methodist University
James M. Kauffman, University of Virginia
Michael J. Kennedy, University of Virginia

Jade Kestian, Texas A&M University
Jennifer Krawec, University of Miami
Holly B. Lane, University of Florida
Kathleen Lynne Lane, University of Kansas
Erica S. Lembke, University of Missouri
Dawn Levy, Southern Methodist University
Ben Lignugaris/Kraft, Utah State University
Nicole Lute, Vanderbilt University
Nancy Mamlin, North Carolina Central University
Joshua Marbach, Texas A&M University
Linda H. Mason, George Mason University
M. McGrath Kato, University of Oregon
James McLeskey, University of Florida
Holly Mariah Menzies, California State University
Ahmarlay Myint, Texas A&M University
Wendy Peia Oakes, Arizona State University
Sarah Owens, University of Missouri
Samuel Patton III, Vanderbilt University
Corey Peltier, University of Oklahoma
Peng Peng, University of Nebraska
C. Pinkney, Portland State University
Sarah R. Powell, University of Texas at Austin
Paige C. Pullen, University of Florida
Wendy M. Reinke, University of Missouri
Brenna Rivas, Southern Methodist University
Wesley Sims, Witchita State University
Kalin Stewart, University of North Carolina
Elizabeth Stevens, University of Texas at Austin
Jessica Swain-Bradway, University of Oregon
Wilhelmina van Dijk, University of Florida
Sharon Vaughn, University of Texas at Austin
Meagan Walsh, Vanderbilt University
Jeanne Wanzek, Vanderbilt University
Oscar Widales-Benitez, University of California
Andrew L. Wiley, Kent State University
Kelly J. Williams, Indiana University
Mitchell L. Yell, University of South Carolina
Loulee Yen Haga, Vanderbilt University

FOREWORD

Daniel P. Hallahan

I'm honored to write a foreword to this handbook. Admittedly, given the variable time-frame of chapter submissions, which is typical for an edited volume of this size, I was unable to read each of the chapters in detail. However, my cursory read, together with the volume's extensive range of topics covered, cohesion and logical organization, and top-shelf authors, attest to its being a significant contribution to addressing issues pertaining to RTI and MTSS.

For me, among other things, the book has begun to help clarify the difference between RTI and MTSS. I've had more than passing familiarity with RTI, but having often seen the two terms used interchangeably, I wasn't sure whether they, indeed, are the same. Or are there arcane features to MTSS that make it distinct from RTI? As it turns out, apparently neither is the case. RTI does differ from MTSS. And the distinction between RTI and MTSS seems *relatively* straightforward. Several authors in this volume state and other sources (e.g., Center on Response to Intervention) authenticate that a growing consensus considers MTSS an umbrella term that includes RTI, which focuses mainly but not entirely on academics, and Positive Behavioral Interventions and Supports (PBIS), which focuses on behavior problems.

At the same time, however, MTSS has also begun to stand for creating a school culture that specifically links RTI and PBIS in an integrated support system that includes academics and behavior (Bohanon, Goodman, and McIntosh, n. d.). This expansion of the MTSS definition does make it more difficult for me to understand exactly what MTSS means now or in the future. Thus, my comments concentrate on RTI.

Researchers, policymakers, and practitioners have championed RTI for two distinct purposes: instruction (RTI-Instruction) or identification (RTI-Identification). As far as I can tell from my reading of the literature, RTI-Instruction preceded RTI-Identification. Regardless, I'll first address RTI-Instruction.

RTI-Instruction

RTI as a means of guiding instruction has few critics. Not only have most researchers and practitioners found its logic unassailable, but the historical roots of RTI-Instruction run deep in special education practices. In many ways, we can conceptualize RTI-Instruction as following the long-standing special education practice of adjusting instruction based on the response of the learner. Numerous examples exist of special education's allegiance to an evidence-based approach to teaching in which instruction is guided by the learner's response to that instruction. I note just a few.

The paradigm of teaching–assessing–teaching was the backbone of the "precision teaching" (PT) model *promulgated* by Ogden Lindsley (1964; 1972). I emphasize *promulgated* because Lindsley insisted that he did not develop PT, but that he "founded and coached it" (Lindsley, 1990, p. 10) based on having teachers attune their instruction to children's correct or incorrect responses. The intricacies of PT's measurement protocols are too elaborate to discuss here, but apropos our discussion, a principal tenet is that, if a student is not learning, then instruction needs to be changed. Thus, the student's performance determines the "correct" teaching strategy. In fact, Lindsley's mantra, "the student knows best," was given birth by an amusing exchange with B. F. Skinner:

> When I was a graduate student, I trained a rat whose behavior did not extinguish exactly as the charts in Skinner's (1938) book had shown. My rat at first had responded much more rapidly when his responding was no longer reinforced. The rapid responding went on for about 30 minutes, at which time the rat stopped abruptly. I took the cumulative record of the rat's unusual extinction to Dr. Skinner and asked him how this had happened. How could the rat do this when the book showed a very different gradual extinction curve? Skinner answered, "In this case, the book is wrong! The rat knows best! That's why we still have him in the experiment!"
>
> *(Lindsley, 1990, p. 12)*

Curriculum-based measurement (CBM) is another example of a special education procedure reliant on measuring student learning for the purpose of then modifying instructional strategies, if needed (Deno, 1985). Similar to RTI, CBM has also had an assessment as well as an instructional purpose. Interestingly, whereas for RTI, the instructional focus preceded its assessment focus, for CBM the assessment focus preceded its use as an instructional tool. Deno's original idea was for CBM to replace the use of standardized achievement tests: "such [standardized achievement] tests are relatively unimportant in the day-to-day decision making of the classroom teacher" (Deno, 1985, p. 220).

Inherent in RTI-Instruction is the idea that students should be taught at a level of difficulty consonant with their grade level. If a student is not succeeding at one tier (e.g., Tier 1), then he or she moves to a level at his or her current level of performance but with more intensive instruction (e.g., Tier 2). This process iterates when deciding whether a student should move from Tier 2 to Tier 3. Likewise, if a student does well at Tier 2 or Tier 3, he or she moves back to Tier 1 or Tier 2, respectively. This recursive decision-making process can be viewed as compatible with the Soviet psychologist, Lev Vygotsky's (1978) influential theory of the zone of proximal development (ZPD). ZPD dictates that the difficulty level of instruction should be guided by what the learner can do *without instruction* and then can do *after* instruction. In other words, the teacher's goal is to find the "sweet spot" that challenges the child with material that is within reach based on the child's ability level, but not so easily learned that the task is boring or a waste of instructional time.

We can view RTI-Instruction as consisting of successive transition decision points—whether to move the student from one tier to the next, up or down—with each decision based, in part, on a consideration of the student's ZPD. I say, "in part" because Vygotsky's ZPD focuses on the level of difficulty of the material to be learned whereas RTI-Instruction puts at least as much attention on the level of intensity of the instruction. And the instructional intensity increases from Tiers 1 to 2 to 3 based on such things as smaller group size, duration of instruction, use of reinforcement (Pullen and Hallahan, 2015).

RTI-Identification

Prior to the 2004 reauthorization of the Individuals with Disabilities Education Act (IDEA; renamed the Individuals with Disabilities Education *Improvement* Act), students with learning disabilities were typically identified or diagnosed on the basis of a significant discrepancy between cognitive abilities (as measured by an intelligence test) and academic achievement. However, IDEA 2004 *required* states to permit the use of what we know today as RTI and *forbade* states from requiring districts to use the old standard of the discrepancy model in identifying students with learning disabilities.

As I've already noted, it's difficult to find critics of RTI as an instructional paradigm. However, for RTI-Identification, that's not the case. Undeniably, the criticisms have not stemmed the tide of states implementing RTI-Identification. At the same time, several researchers have cautioned against RTI-Identification. Most important, research does not support its use at-scale as a state-wide policy. In addition, there are other criticisms, summarized by Reynolds and Shaywitz (2009):

1. Criteria are unclear for validating the "R" in RTI—how to decide who is a non-responder;
2. Research is insufficient for the federal government to provide sufficient guidance for how to implement RTI, which leads to wide variation in how it is put into operation;
3. Highly intelligent students with poor word-level skills in reading often receive the necessary reading instruction but are shortchanged in exposure to topics at their ability level (e.g., novel studies, higher level content instruction).

The last point gets to the heart of the question of what *is* a learning disability? As Reynolds and Shaywitz (2009) assert:

> This represents a fundamental alteration in the concept of disability and cuts out the very roots basic to the concept of an LD as an unexpected difficulty in learning intrinsic to the child. Dating back over a century when the most common LD, dyslexia, was first described (Morgan, 1896), the core concept has been unexpected achievement levels in relation to ability—not to teaching methods.
>
> *(p. 46)*

For my part, I remain unconvinced that RTI-Identification serves the field of learning disabilities well. In a rush to replace IQ-achievement discrepancy, the field has latched onto an approach—RTI-Identification—that is fraught with problems, ranging from (a) a dearth of evidence of its impact (except perhaps to result in fewer students identified as LD), to (b) problems of implementation at scale, to (c) undermining the fundamental understanding of what constitutes LD.

With respect to (a) it's important to note that, after steadily rising for the better part of three decades, the prevalence of students identified to receive special education as LD has reversed course from 2006 to the present (Pullen, 2017). This period of declining prevalence corresponds to the advancement of RTI-Identification. With respect to (b), the variability of prevalence rates of LD from state-to-state has increased since the rise of RTI-Identification (Pullen and Ashworth, 2018). With respect to (c) although in the minority of researchers, practitioners, and policymakers, I continue to embrace the concept that an inherent discrepancy between expected and actual achievement is fundamental to the definition of LD. Originally, I was "bitten by the bug" of RTI-Identification as an antidote to the statistical problems of IQ-achievement discrepancy. Over the past couple years, however, I've realized that RTI also has several significant shortcomings. Given misgivings about RTI-Identification, I think the best course is to focus on the *concept LD as an ability-achievement discrepancy*. I've not come across any reasons for discrediting the conceptualization of LD as such a discrepancy.

In conclusion, achievement-discrepancy is problematic, but its problems are not conceptual, they are statistical. Given the progress in statistics since the original idea of Discrepancy, which had some flaws, it would seem that statisticians if they put their minds to it, could come up with a reliable and practical method of measuring ability-achievement discrepancy.

References

Bohanon, H., Goodman, S., and McIntosh, K. (n. d.). Integrating academic and behavior supports with an RTI framework, Part 1: General overview. RTI Action Network (National Center on Learning Disabilities). Retrieved from: www.rtinetwork.org/learn/behavior-supports/integrating-behavior-and-academic-supports-general-overview.

Deno, S. L. (1985). Curriculum-based measurement: The emerging alternative. *Exceptional Children, 52,* 219–232.

Lindsley, O. R. (1964). Direct measurement and prosthesis of retarded behavior. *Journal of Education, 147,* 62–81.

Lindsley, O. R. (1972). From Skinner to precision teaching: The child knows best. In J. B. Jordan and L. S. Robbins (Eds.), *Let's try doing something else kind of thing.* (pp. 1–12). Arlington, VA: Council for Exceptional Children.

Lindsley, O. R. (1990). Precision teaching: By teachers for children. *Teaching Exceptional Children, 22*(3), 10–15.

Morgan, W. P. (1896). A case of congenital word blindness. *The British Medical Journal, 11,* 1378.

Pullen, P. C. (2017). Prevalence of learning disabilities from parental and professional perspectives: A comparison of the data from the National Surveys of Children's Health and the Office of Special Education's Reports to Congress. *Journal of Learning Disabilities,* 50, 701–711. DOI: 10.1177/0022219416659447.

Pullen, P. C. and Hallahan, D. P. (2015). What is special education? In B. D. Bateman, J. W. Lloyd, and M. Tankersley (Eds.), *Understanding special education issues: Who, where, what, when, how & why.* (pp. 36–50). New York: Routledge.

Pullen, P. C., van Dijk, W., Gonsalvez, V., Ashworth, K. A., and Lane, H. B. (in press). Response to intervention and multi-tiered systems of support: How do they differ and how are they the same, if at all? In Pullen, P. C. and M. J. Kennedy (Eds.), *The handbook of response to intervention multi-tiered systems of support.* New York: Routledge.

Reynolds, C. R. and Shaywitz, S. E. (2009). Response to intervention: Ready or not? Or, from wait-to-fail to watch-them-fail. *School Psychology Quarterly, 24,* 130–145.

Skinner, B. F. (1938). *Behavior of organisms.* Oxford, UK: Appleton-Century.

Vygotsky, L.S. (1978). *Mind in society.* Cambridge, MA: Harvard University Press.

SECTION I

Trends and Issues in RTI and MTSS

INTRODUCTION
TO SECTION I

Paige C. Pullen

The chapters in this section address many of the trends and issues in Response to Intervention and Multi-Tiered Systems of Support. RTI has a long history, while MTSS is relatively new to the field. Perhaps one of the most controversial topics within this work is the terms RTI and MTSS, along with how each are implemented in schools. All of the authors in the section, and in the volume for that matter, use RTI in various ways, sometimes distinguishing between MTSS and RTI, other times using the terms synonymously. In Chapter 1, "Response to Intervention and Multi-Tiered Systems of Support: How Do They Differ and How Are They the Same, If at All," my colleagues (Wilhelmina van Dijk, Vivian E. Gonsalves, Holly B. Lane, and Kristen E. Ashworth) and I clarify some of the terms used to refer to the various *purposes of instruction* across multiple tiers. We took this approach to address the terms that are confusing within the field among top professionals in special education and school psychology. Even with the clarification of terms, we need to further distinguish between the various ways in which RTI is being implemented in schools. We posit that RTI (Response to Intervention) should remain as it is intended in IDEIA for the identification of disabilities. A new term for the multiple tiers of support that do not lead to identification should be identified. Distinguishing between these purposes via a new term may eliminate RTI as being a road block to students being identified for special education services.

In Chapter 2, "RTI: Controversies and Solutions," Kauffman, Badar, and Wiley discuss the barriers to RTI implementation and provide recommendations for identifying a systematic approach to RTI. Interestingly, Kauffman and colleagues also point out that RTI and MTSS "may be distinctively different or be functional equivalents" (this volume, p. 17). Likewise, they suggest that RTI is similar to the pre-referral strategies that were implemented in the 1970s to eliminate false positive identifications of children with disabilities. The tiers within RTI frameworks are similar to the Continuum of Alternative Placements, which is still mandated in IDEA 2004, with Tier 1 representing the general education classroom placement (see also Kauffman, Hallahan, Pullen, and Badar, 2018). Kauffman and colleagues make recommendations related to the changes in the law (i.e., IDEA), suggesting that fundamental changes would be regressing rather than progressing.

In order to maintain special education as "special," teachers should use multi-tiered instruction following the guidelines Yell describes in Chapter 3, "Response to Intervention, Multi-Tiered Systems of Support, and Federal Law: Analysis and Commentary." Yell provides an excellent description of how RTI became part of the process for identifying students with LD, noting that it isn't required, but that schools cannot rely on the discrepancy formula for identification. He also mentions early intervening services and that RTI cannot be used to delay evaluating student for special education services. Yell points out that the "only mention of response to instruction language is in the section of the identification of students with LD" (p. 29). He provides four recommendations to ensure that LEAs are implementing RTI in a legally acceptable manner.

In Chapter 4, "Politics and Science in the RTI Time: On the Classification and Identification of Learning Disabilities," Anastasiou examines the role of science and politics in learning disabilities (LD) classification and identification. He identifies four major issues in LD classification: (a) the categorical versus a dimensional approach, (b) a dysfunctional versus severity model, (c) the heterogeneity of LD, and (d) treatment non-responsiveness. Anastosiou then outlines a recommendation for future reauthorizations of IDEA, including an alternative to LD identification using cognitive processing and academic assessments.

Finally, Kathleen Lynne Lane and her colleagues (Wendy Peia Oakes, and Holly Mariah Menzies) describe models of prevention and screening in Chapter 5, "Comprehensive, Integrated, Three-Tiered (Ci3T) Models of Prevention: The Role of Systematic Screening to Inform Instruction." Specifically, they address various prevention models that focus on collaboration and address both students' academic and behavioral needs. They promote a school-wide system for proactive interventions to alleviate the need for more intensive intervention, particularly as they relate to behavior.

1

RTI AND MTSS: RESPONSE TO INTERVENTION AND MULTI-TIERED SYSTEMS OF SUPPORT

How Do They Differ and How Are They the Same, If at All?

Paige C. Pullen, Wilhelmina van Dijk, Vivian E. Gonsalves, Holly B. Lane, and Kristen E. Ashworth

RTI and MTSS: Are They the Same or Different?

What is the difference between Response to Intervention (RTI) and Multi-Tiered Systems of Support (MTSS)? Some researchers and academics use these two terms interchangeably, while others contend that they have different meanings. As Hallahan points out in the foreword of this volume, the terms MTSS and RTI mean different things to different people, and little consensus exists about a clear distinction between the two. In this chapter, we offer an alternative view, in an attempt to clarify the meaning of RTI and MTSS and provide a lexicon of these terms.

Response to Intervention (RTI)

Before we clarify the differences between RTI and MTSS, we must address the variation within RTI. Just as we see researchers and practitioners using interchangeable definitions between RTI and MTSS, we also see them referring to interchangeable purposes for RTI: (a) improving instruction for students who are falling behind and (b) identifying exceptional students for special education under the category Specific Learning Disability.

History of RTI

According to Vaughn and Fuchs (2003), the origins of RTI as an approach to identify students as having a learning disability (LD) come from a 1982 National Research Council study (Heller,

Holtzman, and Messick, 1982). Around this time, psychologists began examining the validity of students' identification for special education services (Vaughn and Fuchs, 2003). This validation was partly motivated by evidence suggesting test scores alone were inefficient to distinguish between students with learning disabilities and low achieving students (e.g., Ysseldyke, Algozzine, Shinn, and McGue, 1982). Moreover, it became clear that chance and the specific measure used influenced the magnitude of the difference between actual and expected performance of students disproportionally (e.g., Macmann and Barnett, 1985). To countermand these psychometric issues around classifying students for special education services, Heller et al. proposed criteria related to the quality of instruction and the students' response to the instruction to determine if students placed in special education indeed had a disability or if their academic failure was a result of ineffective instruction. That is, had the student actually been exposed to high-quality, evidence-based instruction? As such, the primary purpose of early RTI work was to establish a framework that could be used to identify students with disabilities. Specifically, psychologists wanted to replace the IQ-achievement discrepancy model in an effort to eliminate the predominant "wait to fail" approach in identifying students with LD, as well as the overrepresentation of certain subgroups (Ysseldyke and Marston, 1999).

As a result, prior to the widespread adoption of multi-tiered models, practitioners used pre-referral interventions in the 1980s as a method for determining whether a student should be evaluated for special education. Among the flaws of this approach was that teachers seldom viewed the suggested interventions as helpful for more than the one student being considered for referral (Gersten and Dimino, 2006). Around the turn of the last century, researchers began to examine a treatment validity model as a way to reconceptualize the process for identifying students with LD (Fuchs and Fuchs, 1998; Fuchs, Fuchs, and Speece, 2002). Some versions of this multi-phased model, which employs curriculum-based measurement as a tool for careful progress monitoring, included a phase in which the added value of special education must be demonstrated to justify placement. This requirement for success in special education led to problems, including both false positives and false negatives.

Among the early advocates of RTI were researchers who studied beginning reading interventionists and school psychologists with a behavioral orientation (Fuchs, Mock, Morgan, and Young, 2003). These two groups have different perspectives on the realization of RTI, which has contributed to the confusion surrounding the model. School psychologists, for example, focused more on the problem-solving aspect of the model that could overturn the discrepancy model, while reading researchers advocated for a standardized treatment protocol with validated interventions (Fuchs et al., 2003). Today, RTI is just as likely to be applied to instruction and intervention for students falling behind academically, without the purpose of identification for special education services.

Definitions and Characteristics of RTI

We can conceptualize RTI as (a) focusing on how students respond to intervention, (b) using careful progress monitoring procedures, (c) including multiple tiers of instruction, and (d) using a problem-solving approach (Fuchs and Fuchs, 2006). According to Fuchs et al. (2003), the general process for RTI included several key steps. The process began with the provision of "generally effective" instruction by the classroom teacher, and student progress was monitored. For students who did not respond, additional or different instruction was provided, and progress continued to be monitored. Finally, those students who still did not respond qualified for special education placement or formal evaluation for special education. Most RTI systems reflect this process by using three *tiers* of instruction that increase in intensity (e.g., group size, duration, and frequency). Tier 1 for a given academic area consists of evidence-based core instruction provided in the general education classroom to all students. Tier 2 includes instruction provided to students who have not responded to the first tier and who need additional support to learn the content. Students in the second tier generally receive instruction in small groups, and this instruction is provided in addition to Tier 1. Finally, Tier 3 includes instruction provided to students who have not responded to Tier 2 instruction. Tier 3 is more intensive and often involves one-on-one instruction. Generally, Tier 3 instruction is provided in addition to Tier 1 instruction.

In some school districts, poor performance in Tier 3 results in referral for special education; in others, Tier 3 *is* special education—in other words, referral for special education results from poor performance in Tier 2. In this model, the purpose of RTI is to ensure students receive evidence-based instruction prior to being referred for special education services. Judgments about students' progress are made with consideration of how well they respond to the intensive instruction provided, hence the name Response to *Intervention*.

A second purpose for the implementation of RTI is Response to *Instruction*. The focus of this model is on the student's academic performance rather than identification for special education services. In this model, the three tiers are still in place; however, students are typically assigned to each tier using the results of universal screening, or school-wide brief assessments, conducted to evaluate which students may be at risk of academic failure. All students receive Tier 1 instruction in the general education classroom. Based on the formative assessments, students identified as performing below a specified benchmark move to Tier 2, and students who are significantly below the benchmark proceed to Tier 3. Students may move between tiers during the school year depending on their progress and their response to a particular type of instruction. Schools that adopt this Response to *Instruction* approach are sometimes referred to as "all level schools" (Balu et al., 2015), because the tiers comprise the overall instruction delivered within the school. The Response to Instruction model is designed around the belief that high-quality interventions, delivered with fidelity, can reduce the number of students who are not successful. This model is much more in line with the multi-tiered systems of support philosophy outlined later in this chapter.

To illustrate the difference between Response to *Intervention* and Response to *Instruction*, suppose a student is not making adequate progress in Tier 1 (or core instruction) and, therefore, is placed in Tier 2 for additional instruction for 20 minutes per day, 3 days per week. Progress monitoring data show that, with this minimal added support, the student is able to progress as expected for his grade level. Within Response to *Intervention* model, after the first analysis of data, this student responds to the Tier 2 intervention and, therefore, is not referred for special education evaluation; and he may even be placed back into Tier 1. Within the Response to *Instruction* model, this student can receive Tier 2 supports for as long as needed, because this is the level needed for success. Another difference between the two models lies in the role of the professional providing the instruction. Balu and colleagues (2015) conducted an extensive review of RTI models in schools and found that general education teachers and paraprofessionals tend to be responsible for most of the instruction in schools that implement a Response to *Instruction* model, whereas the Response to *Intervention* schools use more specialized staff, such as reading specialists or special educators, to deliver instruction in Tiers 2 and 3.

What Are Multi-Tiered Systems of Support (MTSS)?

Multi-Tiered Systems of Support (MTSS) is a general education service delivery model in which all students' individual academic and behavioral needs are supported (Harlacher, Sakelaris, and Kattelman, 2014). One of the earliest known uses of the term "multi-tiered systems of support" was as part of an effort by the State of Kansas to reduce confusion about a state initiative to shift from standard RTI to school-wide RTI (Sailor, 2008), and the meaning of the term has evolved as its use has spread. MTSS models typically involve multiple systems to deliver individualized academic interventions (i.e., what would be considered Response to *Instruction*) and systems for addressing individual behavior needs (such as Positive Behavioral Interventions and Supports [PBIS]). Schools and districts implementing MTSS operate from a problem-solving approach, and their MTSS include increasingly intensive tiers of instruction and intervention combined with a comprehensive and objective assessment system. Underlying this continuum of services is the assumption that preventing students from developing academic or behavioral difficulties during the elementary years is more advantageous than trying to remediate these difficulties later on in their school careers (Bradley, Danielson, and Doolittle, 2005; Harn, Basaraba, Chard, and Fritz, 2015; Torgesen, 2000).

A Problem-Solving Framework

In addition to MTSS having multiple, progressively more intensive, tiers of instruction, and a comprehensive assessment system, it is usually implemented within the context of a problem-solving model (PSM) (Harlacher et al., 2014). The success of the PSM depends on the quality of the data collection system and the willingness of all members not only to consider problems at the student level, but also at the system level. For example, if data show that only 63% of the students make adequate progress in Tier 1, the PSM should lead to more focus on adapting and improving core instruction, and less on providing Tier 2 instruction for the remaining 37% of the students. On the other hand, if core instruction is as it should be and only about 5% of students struggle in Tier 1, the focus should be almost exclusively on constructing individual intervention plans. The data collection system needs to consist of four elements: (a) screening data to identify students at-risk for academic or behavioral failure, (b) diagnostic data to pinpoint specific areas of difficulty, (c) formative assessment data to monitor progress, and (d) implementation fidelity data to ensure instruction is delivered as intended.

The first step in the PSM is to state the problem in objective and measurable terms that illustrate the difference between the current performance and grade level expectations of an individual student or group of students. Then, the team uses diagnostic assessment data to determine the underlying cause of any discrepancy between performance and expectations. The causes could be the results of student performance, instructional, curricular, or environmental factors. A well-functioning MTSS model in a school allows consideration of all possible factors. After a most likely cause is determined, members of the team establish a plan to address the deficit and monitor the success of this plan by measuring progress and fidelity. Finally, after a set time, the plan is evaluated and adaptations are made as needed by following the same steps.

A Model for School-Wide Reform

The purpose of MTSS is to create a school-wide culture in which involved parties adjust supports at every level based on current student data to provide the appropriate level of support immediately, to prevent severe problems from arising (Harlacher et al., 2014). This culture of providing adaptive supports emanates from the belief that most students can learn grade level material if they are given the right amount of evidence-based supports (academic or behavioral), as determined through an iterative problem-solving approach based on the collection of formative data (Harlacher et al., 2014).

Many of these principal elements of MTSS are comparable to those of RTI. In fact, as Sugai and Horner (2009) assert, "RTI provides an excellent umbrella of guiding principles for improved assessment and intervention decision making" (p. 234). MTSS, however, is much more comprehensive than RTI. As Harlacher et al. (2014) state, "MTSS is more than just a process of providing interventions to a small group of students. Rather, it is a school reform model and with it comes a new way of thinking and doing business in education" (p. 24).

Finally, implementation of successful MTSS depends on strong support from administrators (Harlacher et al., 2014). A supportive district leadership is vital, for example, for the allocation and distribution of funds in order to provide foundational supports such as data-based decision-making systems, training opportunities, technical assistance, and communicative systems (Freeman, Miller, and Newcomer, 2015).

Discussion

In a large proportion of the professional literature, RTI has become synonymous with the academic portion of MTSS (see for example, Freeman et al., 2015), and as we noted above, many researchers now state that RTI has two functions: to identify students with LD *and* to serve as a primary intervention framework (e.g., Gersten and Dimino, 2006). To reiterate, according to IDEA (2004), the purpose of RTI is to identify students who qualify for special education purposes under the Specific Learning Disabilities category when their unexpected underperformance is not due to a lack of effective instruction. Implementing MTSS with a focus on academic performance can provide schools with the necessary quality instruction that prevents academic failure.

In sum, RTI and MTSS are, at least in practice, different. However, some researchers and practitioners continue to use the terms interchangeably. The goal of this chapter is to help clarify these differences and to identify a lexicon of terms used for tiered instructional supports: Response to *Instruction*, Response to *Intervention*, and MTSS.

In practice, the *purpose* of the tiered instruction and/or intervention often drives the term that is used. Response to *Instruction* is typically implemented in general education classrooms and does not lead to placement or evaluation for special education services. Instructional specialists (e.g., reading specialists, special education teachers) implement interventions within a Response to *Intervention* framework as part of the identification process for special education. Most but not all RTI programs focus on academics rather than behavior. The purpose, then, of RTI programs is either (a) to provide extra supports to students falling behind their peers or (b) to function as part of the process for special education identification. The purpose of MTSS, as implemented currently, is a school-wide model to prevent both academic and behavioral failure. Some schools and districts, however, use MTSS as an umbrella term that encompasses all of their tiered services, including those used for the identification of special education services.

References

Balu, R., Zhu, P., Doolittle, F., Schiller, E., Jenkins, J., and Gersten, R. (2015). Evaluation of response to intervention practices for elementary school reading (NCEE 2016–4000). Washington, DC: National Center for Educational Evaluation and Regional Assistance, Institute of Education Sciences, U.S. Department of Education.

Bradley, R., Danielson, L., and Doolittle, J. (2005). Response to intervention. *Journal of Learning Disabilities*, 38, 8–13.

Freeman, R., Miller, D., and Newcomer, L. (2015). Integration of academic and behavioral MTSS at the district level using implementation science. *Learning Disabilities: A Contemporary Journal*, 13(1), 59–72.

Fuchs, L. S., and Fuchs, D. (1998). Treatment validity: A unifying concept for reconceptualizing the identification of learning disabilities. *Learning Disabilities Research & Practice*, 13, 204–219.

Fuchs, D., and Fuchs, L. S. (2006). Introduction to response to intervention: What, why, and how valid is it? *Reading Research Quarterly*, 41(1), 93–99.

Fuchs, L. S., Fuchs, D., and Speece, D. L. (2002). Treatment validity as a unifying construct for identifying learning disabilities. *Learning Disability Quarterly*, 25(1), 33–45.

Fuchs, D., Mock, D., Morgan, P. L., and Young, C. L. (2003). Responsiveness to intervention: Definitions, evidence, and implications for the learning disabilities construct. *Learning Disabilities Research & Practice*, 18(3), 157–171.

Gersten, R., and Dimino, J. A. (2006). RTI (response to intervention): Rethinking special education for students with reading difficulties (yet again). *Reading Research Quarterly*, 41(1), 99–108.

Harlacher, J. E., Sakelaris, T. L., and Kattelman, N. M. (2014). *Practitioner's guide to curriculum-based evaluation in reading*. New York: Springer.

Harn, B., Basaraba, D., Chard, D., and Fritz, R. (2015). The impact of schoolwide prevention efforts: Lessons learned from implementing independent academic and behavior support systems. *Learning Disabilities: A Contemporary Journal*, 13(1), 30–20.

Heller, K. A., Holtzman, W. H., and Messick, S. (Eds.). (1982). *Placing children in special education: A strategy for equity*. Washington, DC: National Academy Press. Retrieved from: www.nap.edu/catalog/9440/placing-children-in-special-education-a-strategy-for-equity.

Individuals with Disabilities Education Improvement Act, U.S.C. 20 §1400 et seq. (2004)

Macmann, G. M., and Barnett, D. W. (1985). Discrepancy score analysis: A computer simulation of classification stability. *Journal of Psychoeducational Assessment*, 3(4), 363–375.

Sailor, W. (2008). Access to the general curriculum: Systems change or tinker some more? *Research and Practice for Persons with Severe Disabilities*, 34(1), 249–257.

Sugai, G., and Horner, R. H. (2009). Responsiveness-to-intervention and school-wide positive behavior supports: Intergration of Multi-tiered system approaches. *Exceptionality*, 17(4), 223–237. doi: 10.1080/09362830903235375.

Torgesen, J. K. (2000). Individual differences in response to early interventions in reading: The lingering problem of treatment resisters. *Learning Disabilities Research and Practice*, 15, 55–64.

Vaughn, S. R., and Fuchs, L. S. (2003). Redefining learning disabilities as inadequate response to treatment: Rationale and assumptions. *Learning Disabilities Research and Practice*, 18(3), 137–146.

Ysseldyke, J. E., Algozzine, B., Shinn, M. R., and McGue, M. (1982). Similarities and differences between low achievers and students classified learning disabled. *The Journal of Special Education*, 16(1), 73–85.

Ysseldyke, J. E., and Marston, D. (1999). Origins of categorical special education services in schools and a rationale for changing them. In D. Reschly, W. Tilly, and J. Grimes (Eds.), *Special education in transition* (pp. 1–18). Longmont, CO: Sopris West.

2

RTI

Controversies and Solutions

James M. Kauffman, Jeanmarie Badar, and Andrew L. Wiley

Universal public education has always been a difficult, challenging matter (Urban and Wagoner, 2009; Wagoner, 2004). From the days of the founding fathers to the present, educating the masses—the general education offered to all—has presented problems peculiar to the era in which it was to be implemented. When education was offered only to the elite, and when general education excluded those who were thought not to be able to benefit from it, the education of children with disabilities was not a pressing public issue. However, as education became more literally universal, special education for those at the statistical margins of ability became a necessary consideration.

As John Lewis stated in his preface to what was probably the first special education textbook, the primary problem of special education "is found in the fact of variability among children to be educated" (Horn, 1924, pp. 6–7). That basic problem has not changed in the century following Lewis's observation. The problem has always been the appropriate response of public education to particular variations in students, and it likely always will be.

Diversities and Special Education

Understanding any special education framework requires understanding of diversities and how they differ. For many years, it was customary for public schools in the United States to respond to difference (diversity) in parentage with strict "racial" segregation. That kind of legal segregation was struck down in 1954 by the U.S. Supreme Court in its ruling in *Brown v. Board of Education of Topeka*. Discrimination against people because of their ancestry remains a serious problem in the USA. Unfortunately, disability has often been lumped in with other forms of diversity, including ancestry, as if it has similar implications for education. Although the comparison of ancestry to disability for purposes of education has long been made in efforts to promote inclusion and disparage—and attempt to dismantle—the continuum of alternative placements (e.g., Stainback and Stainback, 1991), comparison of diversity of ancestry to diversity of ability is illogical. The comparison of "race" to disability is nonsensical because the implications for education of the two kinds of diversity (ancestry and disability) are completely different.

The social justice issue regarding access to education for diversity in parentage is that education should be the same regardless of ancestry, whereas the social justice issue regarding access to education for diversity in disability is that education should be different from the

11

typical, depending on the disability of the individual (see Kauffman and Landrum, 2009; Kauffman and Lloyd, 1995; Zigmond and Kloo, 2017). As a group, people with disabilities may, indeed, be considered a "suspect class" under the law, in that people with disabilities have historically been subject to discrimination (including denial of a free and appropriate public education), but the law calls for their treatment as individuals, some of whom should receive treatment that others do not.

If we begin with the assumption that ancestry does not equal ability or disability in the things that are to be taught in universal general education, then the essential special education issue is how to accommodate or respond appropriately to differences in learning, not differences in ancestry, religion, age, sex, or other forms of diversity. Then, the central issue is variability (variance) in learning ability and how best to respond to that particular kind of variance.

Statistical Distributions and the Nature of Learning

Unfortunately, thinking about problems of general and special education has tended to be remarkably shallow with reference to statistics. Many individuals have called for general and special education that "works" without considering what happens to statistical distributions of achievement when education "works" (see Kauffman, 1990, 2010; Kauffman and Lloyd, 2017). Figuring out what happens when education "works" is relatively simple and straightforward, but dealing with the implications is not. B. F. Skinner (1950) noted long ago that animal organisms (including human students) vary in *rate* of learning—that rate is the essential datum of a science of learning. Physicist Richard Feynman wrote: "in education you increase differences. If someone's good at something, you try to develop his ability, which results in differences, or inequalities" (Feynman, 1985, p. 281).

Learning rates vary not only between students but within an individual. Some students learn certain things very quickly and other things very slowly. In fact, noting differences in an individual student's rate of learning in different academic skills is a foundational concept in traditional special education. A student may learn math at a typical rate but learn to read at a rate far behind that of his age peers. This may mean, in a two-tiered (general and special education) system, the student attends a general education math class but a special education class for subjects in which reading is a more critical skill. If the system has more than two tiers, then a student may be at different levels or tiers for different academic subjects.

Another important reality is that rates of learning likely vary over time in any given subject. Rates of learning in a particular skill area or academic subject are likely not constant over a person's life span. A child may learn a particular skill at one rate as a first grader but at a much different rate (either slower or faster) as an eighth grader. That is, rate of learning may vary considerably with age. Thus, *average* rates for individuals are an important consideration. Nevertheless, it is important to understand that average rates differ considerably between individuals, that some individuals' average rates of learning are much higher or lower than others.

The implications of *rate* of learning for education, general and special, is education that "works" (i.e., is effective) increases the variance among students, precisely the opposite of closing gaps between achievement of faster and slower learners (see Ceci and Papierno, 2005; Kauffman, 2011, 2015; Kauffman and Lloyd, 2017). With really good instruction for each individual, a group of learners becomes more heterogeneous, not more homogeneous. The absolute size of percentiles below the median become smaller, and the absolute size of percentiles above the median become larger. Given that the left tail of the curve cannot be detached from zero and the distance between zero and the highest achievement increases, the standard deviation becomes larger. The distribution becomes somewhat flatter (mesokurtic, if not platykurtic) not peaked (leptokurtic). Naturally, this befuddles those who think really good education will result in fewer students falling below a given standard. The inevitable result of better education for all learners is greater heterogeneity, a widening of achievement gaps, and a positive skewing of the distribution, given that learners differ in *rate* of learning. Wider gaps are inevitable as a mathematical function (see Kaufman, 2015; Kauffman and Lloyd, 2017) and can be predicted based on mathematical theory, and that function has also been found the reality of universal interventions with children (see Ceci and Papierno, 2005).

Also important is evaluating interventions' effects on a distribution's shape or skew. A positive skew means that more cases (in our discussion, students) fall below the mean than above. A greater percentage of students improve but, nonetheless, fall below the mean (50% always remain below the median, although individuals can "bunch up" or "scrunch up" near the median, or lower percentile, but below it). Thus, any effort to reform education such that *all* students (or even *more*) meet a given criterion set by comparison to a mean or median is bound to fail unless the faster learners are held back—their education is worse (less effective, does not "work" as well) than that of slower learners or an intervention is available only to or useable only by the slower learners. As long as *rate* is the datum of a science of learning and mathematical principles remain operative, that is the reality, although it is a difficult reality for many to accept (see especially Kauffman, 2015; Kauffman and Lloyd, 2017).

If, however, students do not differ in *rate* of learning but learning is an *additive* process, then learning means adding a *constant* amount of learning to a student's current achievement. That is, if learning means increasing achievement by a constant amount, then gaps can be narrowed (but never completely closed) if the constant is the same for all groups compared. That is, the relative gap is narrowed, even though the absolute gap remains the same. Over a period of time—and the larger the absolute gap the longer the time needed to narrow it (e.g., adding a constant of 2 to scores of 10 and 20 will eventually result in 40 and 50, and the gap that was once 2 × is then 1.25 ×). However, achieving this relative narrowing in the example given requires 15 additions of the constant.

The only way to completely close a gap between scores if learning is additive is to add a larger constant to the lower score (e.g., adding a constant of 3 to 10 and a constant of 2 to 20 closes the gap at 40, requiring 11 additions of the constants). After the gap is closed, if the process of addition that closed the gap continues, then the gap again widens with successive additions, the formerly lower quantity now becoming increasingly larger than the formerly higher quantity.

We also point out that seemingly small differences in parts of distributions can result in differences involving hundreds or thousands of individuals, depending on the samples or populations. For example, small differences in the tails of distributions can result in disproportionality without differences in means (see Gladwell, 1997). A seemingly small skew or other change in a distribution or a cut point in one may be of great importance in evaluating the effects of a policy (Kauffman and Lloyd, 2017).

Of course, it is possible to argue that these quantitative functions do not apply to education and that a different set of assumptions or model is required to understand the effects of teaching and learning. Some critics of special education devalue or dismiss quantitative measures, except when they are questioning the effectiveness of special education, at which time quantitative measures (e.g., test scores, rates of graduation, employment, incarceration) are temporarily considered valid and meaningful (e.g., Collins, Connor, Ferri, Gallagher, and Samson, 2016). If they mean what they say, then many of these same critics would object to the suggestion that their reform alternatives to traditional special education be similarly evaluated using quantitative data or quantitative student outcomes (e.g., Baaglieri, Valle, Connor, and Gallagher, 2010). This sort of biased and inconsistent reasoning may stem from the moral absolutism underlying the most extreme anti-special education belief systems (for discussion, see Kauffman et al., 2016; Wiley, 2015); regardless, such biases and inconsistencies ought to raise red flags when critics of special education claim that quantitative functions do not apply to teaching and learning. A similar claim is that statistical distributions do not actually exist in nature; rather, they are socio-political constructions designed to oppress certain groups of people. True, scientific findings and observations can be and have been distorted and misappropriated for malicious purposes. Denying reality (statistical or otherwise) is not likely a good solution to this serious problem; the denial of scientific findings and methods can also lead, intentionally or unintentionally, to widespread injustice and harm. In any case, from a quantitative perspective learning may be a combination of rates and additions.

Statistical or mathematical formulas for calculating the effects we have explained here may be intimidating to those of us who are not mathematically literate, but the basic concepts of variability and effects of interventions on distributions are easily understood by most individuals with a college degree. Regardless, the mathematical functions we described apply to education and have their predicted effects on student learning. The quantitative phenomena we have presented so far may help educators and policy makers decide how to allocate or target resources—find the best way to use resources to try to accomplish a given outcome, which may be trying to close gaps or see them in a different way (Ceci and Papierno, 2005). An undeniable assumption of anyone who argues that there are gaps in learning is that learning can be quantified (i.e., a "gap" implies quantification), and denial of a quantitative implication merely renders the argument about gaps incoherent. Also important is understanding that although the phenomena under discussion are quantitative, the decisions related to the quantitative realities are not. That is, variability and distributions clearly are quantitative, but deciding what is best to do about them is not.

Importance of Statistical Phenomena for RTI

These statistical matters are of great importance for evaluating response to intervention (RTI) because measurement is an integral part of judging the success of any system, framework, or plan for providing general and special education (i.e., typical instruction and atypical instruction to learners with atypical educational needs). Discerning success from failure depends on understanding statistical phenomena, including basic mathematical principles related to academic progress or success of particular groups of learners (subsets of the population). This is particularly important when a plan (such as RTI) proposes to address the population of *all* students, not just those comprising a smaller sample or subset. It is important because evaluating the effects of any system or framework for delivering effective instruction to *all* students requires understanding *population* variance as well as variation in individuals and subsets of the population.

Aside from the effects of effective instruction on statistical distributions if there are differences in rate or level of achievement or learning, the fact of variability among learners' achievement is a serious problem. The history of special education for students with disabilities (and we henceforth consider special education as that addressing those with disabilities, excluding for present purposes those with exceptionally high abilities alone) is, most fundamentally, the ways in which such variability has been approached. In the early decades of the field of special education, slower learners were taught in special classes and schools, and the slowest learners were simply not in any classroom. Students' learning rates were judged by teachers and school administrators with relatively little accountability or questions asked about their judgment.

That is, the teacher was the arbiter—in the language of a U. S. President, the "decider" of need for special education. Furthermore, progress of individual students, not comparison of means, was the unit of analysis or the basis of evaluation. Judgment about students' progress (rate and level of achievement) in a curriculum was and is the issue.

Teacher Judgment

By the late 1970s, serious questions about teachers' judgments that students should be referred for evaluation of their eligibility for special education became common, likely because of increases in such referrals. Increases might have been anticipated as an effect of Public Law 94–142. By the early 1980s, only about half the number of children estimated to have disabilities when the law was passed in 1975 had been identified for special education (Kauffman, 1983). That is, nearly 4 million children estimated to have "handicaps" or disabilities in the mid-1970s had not been evaluated for possible eligibility for special education by 1980—or had been evaluated and found ineligible, which is improbable if, as some argued, referral was tantamount to placement in special education (i.e., a large majority of those referred were found eligible and placed; see Algozzine, Christenson, and Ysseldyke, 1982). Teachers who referred students were not much concerned about the effects of interventions on populations or distributions (i.e., educational policy). They were concerned primarily because the student's academic performance compared unfavorably to that of other students (see Gerber, 1984; Lloyd, Kauffman, Landrum, and Roe, 1991).

In the late 1970s and the decade of the 1980s, new policy mandates (or guidelines) required teachers to try alternatives to referral before referring a student. "Pre-referral" strategies and "teacher assistance teams" were invented to help forestall needless referrals (e.g., Chalfant, Pysh, and Moultrie, 1979). The assumption was that many teachers mistakenly attributed failure to learn to students' characteristics rather than to the inadequacy of their instruction or behavior management. That is, teachers were poor judges of their students' needs for special education. The thinking was that if a teacher assistance team (TAT) helped them implement better ways of addressing the child's problem(s) (i.e., pre-referral strategies, PRS), then they could often avoid the need to refer the student for evaluation. Part of the enthusiasm for PRS and TAT may have been generated by school psychologists' feelings of being overburdened or overwhelmed by referrals for evaluation. Part of it may have been a function of beliefs that most children referred were found eligible for special education, and that this had to indicate many false positives.

Moreover, skeptics began questioning the value of special education. To some extent, this skepticism may have been a reaction to the devaluation (or even demonization) of special education and the growing feeling that poor children and minorities were too often referred. In any case, whether any of these or other factors or combinations of them accounted for the concern, PRS and TAT were intended to decrease the likelihood that students responsive to good instruction would be referred for evaluation for their eligibility for special education.

Another reason for the popularity of PRS and TAT was, as we mentioned earlier, distrust of teachers' judgments (see Gerber, 2005; Gerber and Semmel, 1984). In essence, PRS demanded that teachers' judgments be questioned or at least double-checked to see that teachers were, in fact, employing strategies assumed to be effective but not getting the expected response. Only if they had been observed to have tried and failed with strategies recommended by other personnel (e.g., other teachers, school psychologist, principal) could a teacher make a referral deemed fully legitimate.

Pre-Referral and Tiered Education

Some have questioned the essential difference between PRS and response to intervention (e.g., Kauffman, Bruce, and Lloyd, 2012). Hoover and Love (2011) explained differences between PRS and RTI, but some essential similarities remain. For example, according to Hoover and Love, RTI involves more levels or tiers of instruction (usually three rather than two), is typically a whole school approach (rather than a classroom-by-classroom approach, although PRS could be implemented school-wide), and ostensibly requires curricula and methods of instruction that are research-based (and although "evidence-based" or "research-based" is often fudged, even in RTI, the assumption of such empirical support for curricula and instruction could have been made in PRS).

RTI might be considered an elaboration of PRS, a more systematic application of the basic ideas behind PRS. Actually, it might be considered in some sense an elaboration of the notion of special education, adding a third tier to the two-tiered division of general and special education. One possible way of looking at public education is that it was once characterized as having only a single tier—general education. Students were in school or were not; there were no special provisions for those who failed in or 'fell out' of general education. Special education was added as a second tier for those students whose learning needs were not adequately or appropriately met by *general* education. Special education is special because it is different in specific, identifiable ways from the general education that meets the learning needs of most students. However, after special education was mandated by federal law, it was treated as a mistake from which public education could recover only by adding a more rigorous referral process (PRS) or more tiers (RTI, multi-tiered system of supports [MTSS], positive behavioral interventions and supports [PBIS], or another plan with more than two levels or tiers). Always in question has been truly *special* education—what makes special education special (e.g., Scruggs and Mastropieri, 2015), how special instruction differs from typical instruction (e.g., Pullen and Hallahan, 2015; Zigmond and Kloo, 2017), and the entitlement of students to different and effective instruction and to procedures and protections offered by the Individuals with Disabilities Education Act (IDEA). In question also has been whether a tier of instruction or intervention that differs in any way from general education constitutes a 'sort of' special education, or whether special education refers only to the most different or most individualized tier or tiers.

PRS and RTI became ways of avoiding or forestalling determination of eligibility for special education, but they were soon included with or surpassed by other multi-tiered systems with three or more levels or tiers. With RTI and the claim that general education, properly tiered, could become general education made appropriate for all, RTI's suggestion of multiple tiers morphed into a plan for full inclusion. That is, tiered education, some argued (see SWIFT schools, 2016), obviated the need for educating any student in a separate, dedicated place. Rather than 'dedicated,' 'segregated' is the derogation preferred by proponents of full inclusion, intimating that disability and parentage are similar forms of diversity (Gliona, Gonzales, and Jacobson, 2005).

Ultimately, the question of whether and how any intervention framework affects distributions (mitigates or multiplies the challenges associated with statistical distributions/variability in student learning) is empirical. However, in the absence of convincing data (which may be extraordinarily difficult to obtain in the case of changes in distributions), we may be wise to base decisions regarding research and policy on the statistical-mathematical theories presented here and in Kauffman and Lloyd (2017). We use the word "theory" here to mean the best explanation of observations, not speculation. In the scientific sense, a theory is an assumed reality based on repeated observations and explanations thereof. Theories can be used to speculate or predict what will happen under various conditions if the theory is valid—if the theory is reliable and consistent with reality. For example, one might use logic or theories to predict what would happen to the 'seams' or decision points in various forms of tiered education, given that certain assumptions are made about RTI or other forms of tiered education.

RTI and Other Forms of Tiered Education

An important issue is the essential nature—the umbrella concept—of RTI. RTI and MTSS, for example, may be distinctively different or be functional equivalents. The relationships among RTI, MTSS, PBIS, and other tiered systems said to enable general education to be all-inclusive is a legitimate concern of practitioners and researchers. A quotation from a letter of the federal Office of Special Education and Rehabilitative Services dated October 23, 2015 might provide clarification of how these systems are seen by the federal government:

> For those students who may need additional academic and behavioral supports to succeed in a general education environment, schools may choose to implement a multi-tiered system of supports (MTSS), such as response to intervention (RTI) or positive behavioral interventions and supports (PBIS). MTSS is a schoolwide approach that addresses the needs of all students, including struggling learners and students with disabilities, and integrates assessment and intervention within a multi-level instructional and behavioral system to maximize student achievement and reduce problem behaviors.

This paragraph from the letter clearly indicates that RTI and other tiered forms of education known by different acronyms are not really distinctively different in the opinion of the government official writing the letter. Special education with more than two tiers has essentially the same purpose regardless of what it is called.

Tiers and the Problems of Special Education

Combined with the SWIFT schools statement that "all means all," the paragraph of the letter quoted above clearly implies that full inclusion (providing effective education to all students in one setting) is possible or achievable. Tiers done well may be terrific policy and practice, but our best guess is that relatively few teachers have the sophistication in assessment and instruction needed to make the reality of tiered education match the rhetoric of full inclusion (e.g., Sailor and McCart, 2014). We say this in part because special education has historically been unable to instill in teachers and other personnel the level of sophistication in skills needed to make the traditional two tiers work consistently and as well as hoped or intended. The reasons that train-ing and implementation have fallen short in the traditional two-tiered system are complex; however, logic dictates that adding "tiers" (beyond the traditional two) inevitably increases the complexity and challenges, particularly if *full inclusion* (all students taught in one place) is the goal.

Moreover, in our view, a major impediment to improving instruction has been and continues to be misunderstanding of the unavoidable problems of providing "tiered" or "special" education *of any kind.* At the center of special education's unavoidable problems is the problem of *judgment,* that is, making decisions about who, what, where, and how within any number of tiers (Bateman, 1994; Bateman, Lloyd, and Tankersley, 2005). Adding tiers multiplies the judgments that have been the primary problem of special education; that is, as the number of tiers increases, so do all of the problems for which special education has been criticized or found wanting: *sorting, labeling, stigma, arbitrary criteria for identification, false identification, disproportionality, waiting to see students fail before intervening, high cost, failure to cure disabilities or eliminate gaps, different curriculum.* That is, the greater number of tiers, the greater the probability of all of these problems. This is not difficult to understand. Determining the tier that is most appropriate for a given student requires that students be sorted by what they need to learn or can do, not randomly assigning them to tiers. Someone must make decisions about students' tiers, and the decisions will be imperfect, just as they are with two tiers, general and special education. With such decisions—called "sorting," an unavoidable decision process—all the other problems follow.

Consequently, like traditional special education, MTSS will be subjected to "cheap shots"—criticism for problems that can only be avoided by avoiding tiered or special or differentiated education altogether. Judgment of who needs special education can be avoided only by pretending that no degree or type of learning difference warrants access to atypical services or supports (Kauffman, Anastasiou, and Maag, 2016).

Having more than two tiers (the traditional general and special education, and we henceforth mean by "tiered education" three or more tiers) is rational. Extra tiers allow prevention of the need for more intensive intervention, but they do not guarantee prevention (see Kauffman, 1999, 2014). If prevention is to be practiced, not merely talked about, then educators must step in at the first sign of difficulty, label the problem, and intervene to prevent the problem from becoming worse. A label is required to talk about a problem. Extra tiers do not address special education's *core, unavoidable* problems. Trying to make tiers work is admirable, but logical skepticism about them as alternatives to two tiers is reasonable.

Tiers as Frameworks

Advocates of tiered education faced with criticism or skepticism often claim they are suggesting only a framework, a way of describing an array of interventions and resources, not a way of sorting and labeling students. Careful thinking about language and how it works, however, leads to the conclusion that individuals are always sorted and labeled, directly or indirectly, by the resources they use or do not use. Regardless of the framework in question, something may be done well or poorly. Even if a framework is implemented well, it is likely to be criticized because of its high cost in dollars and effort. Any framework for providing special (atypical) instruction or supports to students with disabilities will be criticized by those who, for ideological or other reasons, misunderstand or ignore the educational implications of exceptionality and, as we have discussed, the unavoidable problems of responding effectively and appropriately to the full range of individual learning differences (e.g., Ferri, 2012). Furthermore, no one will be able to avoid all mistakes, and mistakes inevitably draw criticism.

The law known as the IDEA is another framework, not an intervention, but it is now considered "outdated" by some. It has never worked flawlessly in the years since it became law in 1975. Probably, no law or policy will work flawlessly, so there are always points of attack. Critics have long complained that the law is costly, accompanied by onerous regulations, and has not had its intended effects. Tiered education such as RTI and MTSS are frameworks created more recently than the IDEA. Still, one law review regarding special education services for students with emotional and behavioral disorders concluded:

> The purposes and premises underlying the IDEA are precisely those that ought to animate any approach to ensuring a more positive future for children with social, emotional and behavioral difficulties. We would do well by these children—

and our society—to devote our attention and our resources to ensuring that they are fully realized.

(Cannon, Gregory, and Waterstone, 2013, p. 497)

Tiers and the IDEA

Educators have observed that the IDEA regulations may not apply to tiers higher than one but still not reaching the level of special education. Individual education programs (IEPs), parental involvement, formal evaluation—all requiring paperwork that plagues educators when implementing the IDEA—is side-stepped if a student is called a "struggling learner" or "at risk" rather than a "child with a disability." Furthermore, if all students are kept in general education, then the IDEA's required least restrictive environment (LRE) and continuum of alternative placements (CAP) are completely avoided because the student is assumed to be in the LRE *and* receiving all needed services, regardless of whether either is actually true.

Lines that separate special from general education have become increasingly blurred as RTI has been implemented (Fuchs, Fuchs, and Stecker, 2010). Mere exposure to content or instruction does not necessarily mean the material ostensibly being taught is accessible to students (Fuchs, Fuchs, Compton, Wehby, Schumacher, Gersten, and Jordan, 2015). Teachers often fail to make appropriate adaptations of instruction for students who are having difficulty (Fuchs and Fuchs, 2016). Even assuming that teachers implement RTI as planned, expectations that most general education teachers can manage the task seem unrealistic:

> We believe it is naive to expect that generalists will be crosstrained to teach skillfully to an academically diverse class of 28 children (Tier 1); to implement with fidelity a validated protocol to three to six students, some with behavior problems, while collecting and reviewing data on their progress (Tier 2); and to use data-based individualization (see the following) with the most difficult-to-teach children. (Tier 3)
>
> *(Fuchs and Fuchs, 2016, p. 229)*

Implementation of standard, validated protocols short of requirements of the IDEA may well be a good idea, but several caveats should be kept in mind. First, the expectation that general education teachers can do it all (i.e., teach all children well) is in our estimation not only naïve but abusive (see Kauffman and Badar, 2016). Second, if Tier 3 is special education, as Fuchs and Fuchs (2016) suggest, then funding for other tiers should in no way be allowed to diminish funding for Tier 3. Third, even if RTI or another tiered plan of education is implemented well, all of the practical issues of implementation apply.

Practical Issues in Implementing Tiered Education

Practical matters are critically important for traditional special and general education as well as any tiered system (see Kauffman, 2016; Kauffman, Anastasiou, and Maag, 2016; Kauffman, Anastasiou, Badar, Travers, and Wiley, 2016; Kauffman and Badar, 2016). Possible questions about RTI or any other tiered system of education include the following, which is not an exhaustive list:

1. Who makes the decision about the level or tier in which a student is placed?
2. If a team of individuals makes the decision and the classroom teacher objects, how is such disagreement handled?

3. Who decides, and what are the implications for curriculum and instruction as well as the teacher's judgment, that the methods used by the teacher are research-based?
4. How long must a particular intervention be implemented before it is judged to be successful or unsuccessful?
5. How much response to an intervention must a student make to be judged to have been responsive to it?
6. How responsive must a student be to an intervention (e.g., an intervention implemented in Tier 2) to be judged ready for a lower tier (e.g., to be better off in Tier 1)?
7. In what tier is instruction judged to be special education?
8. If no tier is judged to be special education, then in what tier or tiers do the special education law and regulations apply?
9. If no tier is judged to be special education, then are no students actually identified as needing special education, just different resources?
10. If students are judged to need special education, then how are they identified?
11. Are any resources, and if so which ones, identified as special education?
12. If some resources are considered to constitute special education, then how is the decision made that a particular student does or does not need them?
13. By whom and where are different levels are to be implemented, especially in the lower grades?
14. How will students develop close relationships with teachers and peers if they often have different teachers and peer groups, depending on their instructional needs in different areas?
15. What special and intensive instruction will students with special needs actually receive if they have the same general education teacher for all classes?
16. How are resources of money and personnel distributed among the tiers?
17. If resources are evenly divided among the tiers, then what are the implications for special education?
18. If resources identified for special education are disproportionately spent in attempts to keep students from needing a higher tier, then what is to prevent the highest tier from becoming a true dumping ground—a tier in which students are given comparatively little in the way of supports?
19. If greater resources are provided to higher tiers such that the highest tier receives the greatest resources, how is this a more equitable division of resources than the traditional two-tiered, general and special education system?
20. How many tiers are needed to provide effective resources and interventions for literally all students, such that none is excluded or poorly taught?
21. If tiers higher than the first carry no stigma, then why and how will this occur?
22. If a certain tier or tiers are designated as the equivalent of special education, then how will stigma be reduced by having more than two tiers?
23. Will no student be allowed to be in a single tier for all instruction?
24. If a student is in a single tier for all of his or her education, then what is the value of the other tiers for that student?
25. If a student is in the tier considered special education for all academic instruction, must that instruction be delivered in a general education classroom, and, if so, then how will the instruction be delivered effectively without distraction of students receiving instruction in other tiers and with legal guarantees of the IDEA, and how is this different from full inclusion?

26. If a student is in the tier considered special education for all academic instruction and that instruction is delivered in a separate, dedicated environment, not the general education classroom, then how is the structure different from the traditional two tiers of general and special education for that student?

Possible Solutions

Clarifying the Law and Implementing It with Greater Expertise

One possible solution to questions about tiered education is to decide what level(s) or tier(s) constitute special education so that practitioners know when the IDEA regulations apply and when they do not. Another issue is whether funds allocated to special education can be used in "non-special education" tiers. To the extent that money allocated for special education is used in tiers lower than special education, the funding for special education would seem to us to be diminished. It raises the question of the extent to which such allocation of funding increases the likelihood that special education is seen as a "dumping ground" that is not worthy of protected funds. Perhaps a more honest approach would be to designate funding specifically for special education *and* for funds spent on prevention. Allowing states or localities to determine whether to spend funds designated for special education on students not yet identified as eligible for special education appears to us to be a withdrawal of federal guarantees. In our opinion, prevention is vitally important, though it should not come at the expense of students with disabilities.

Prevention of any kind of disability is costly; so is educating students who already have disabilities. If funding for attempts to prevent disabilities is provided by using the funding for those who already have disabilities, then administrators should say so clearly. Those responsible for avoiding requests of additional funds specifically for prevention should, in our opinion, explain as clearly as possible to all stake-holders—especially parents of children with disabilities—what is being done.

Some may claim that special education as traditionally practiced with two tiers is a kind of "shell game" with only two places or cups. Under current law (the IDEA), the purported shell game is used to fool other people or disguise what is actually happening. The "other people" to be tricked may be parents or government officials. For example, parents might be told their child is receiving special instruction when that is not the case, or they might be told "I know you think your child has a learning disability, but she is not actually eligible for special education according to the law, so we can't provide the special education you want" when that is not true. A disproportionate number of children of color might be falsely identified as having disabilities, and special education is being used as a tool of racial segregation but the schools deny it, or, conversely, disproportionate numbers of children of color may be identified as needing special education but the charge of racial segregation is false. Adding a third or fourth tier does not add clarity to the "game" of complying with the law. More helpful, in our opinion, would be clarifying and improving implementation of the IDEA such that it is less likely to be used to fool anyone.

A possible solution is not changing the law but putting greater emphasis on better implementation. This might be, as Cannon et al. (2014) suggested, "a solution hiding in plain sight" for students with all categories of disabilities. If this solution is pursued, it would likely require changes in the nature of teacher training. It may well require a return to two older ideas about the nature of special education. First, a reconstruction of special education—radical reform, perhaps—in the foundation of special education, founding it unequivocally on a science of instruction (Engelmann, 1997; Engelmann and Carnine, 2011; Kauffman, 2011; Kauffman, Anastasiou, and Maag, 2016). Second, becoming a special educator may require not only special graduate training in a science of instruction and application of that science to teaching students with disabilities but also prior training in general education and a minimum number of years of successful experience as a general education teacher. These changes may represent a return to previous practices, but to us they seem progressive, not regressive.

Changing the Law

Another possible solution to the problems of possible conflict between proponents of more traditional special education and tiered education is changing the law under which special education is regulated. This seems highly likely for at least two reasons. First, the IDEA is now closer to 60 years old than to the 6-year-old law when Kauffman and Hallahan (1981) published the *Handbook of Special Education* in its first version. Second, condemnation of special education's necessary functions, arguments that separate special education does not work, and suggestions that general and special education should be merged have been common for decades (Kauffman, Anastasiou, and Maag, 2016). Inclusion is now the preferred focus of educating students with disabilities, not improvement of the instruction offered by special educators.

The IDEA has been reauthorized several times since its first enactment as Public Law 94–142 in 1975 (the most recent reauthorization as of this writing being 2004, actually called the Individuals with Disabilities Education Improvement Act, IDEIA). In the opinion of some, perhaps of many, is that nearly half a century after it was passed, it is time for dramatic, transformational change.

Change is a particularly attractive prospect for many people, and politicians often appeal to the idea that the different (whatever they propose) is going to be good. In fact, some might even suggest that change itself is important—not that things change in a particular direction, simply that things change. To them, change represents progress. This was one of the great appeals—something or someone different—of the Donald Trump presidential candidacy of 2016. But sometimes change is regressive, such that we are returned to an earlier era (see King, 2016 for commentary on how change has reversed and could again reverse civil rights).

Furthermore, change is particularly attractive when it seems to preserve an important part of the past, yet undercuts real progress. Regressive change is sometimes promoted with attractive language and deceptive, empty promises. A lie repeated often enough, particularly if it is something people want to believe, can be perceived as a truth. Some statements are partly true or mostly true, as fact checkers have noted (see Snopes.com; see also Washington Post fact checker, Glenn Kessler, who awards varying numbers of "Pinocchios" for statements depending on their level of falsehood). Change can be difficult to evaluate because the proposed change is good under some circumstances but not under others. The change could be either progressive or regressive, depending on circumstances.

We are not the first to observe that reasonably intelligent people can hold strong beliefs in things neither empirical evidence nor logical thinking support (e.g., Foxx and Mulick, 2016; Specter, 2009; Storr, 2014). We also note that fragments of truth mixed with falsehood, often lead to myths and that mixing truth with falsehood makes countering a myth extraordinarily difficult (Kauffman and Pullen, 1996).

One way in which the law might be changed to make it more contemporary and attractive to the public is to argue that the requirements and regulations of the IDEA are both outdated and unneeded and that all children should be included in general education. Further, it could be argued, special education, to the extent needed, can be provided effectively within general education classrooms. 'Improvement' in the law could become 'Inclusive,' retaining the IDEIA and insisting that inclusive schools are improved schools for students with disabilities. This could well become the line of argument, the story told, the myth made (see Anastasiou, Gregory, and Kauffman, 2018).

Controversies in special education, including RTI and other forms of tiered education could make interesting news copy (Kauffman, 1999–2000). Zigmond and Kloo (2017) have commented on how "non-special" special education has become and that some people now believe that all learning diversity, no matter how great, can be accommodated successfully in general education. Although, individualization has been the cornerstone of special education, some argue that it is time to reconsider that idea in favor of adopting rules that apply to groups of students. This legal approach fits nicely with inclusion of all students in tiers of general education in which all students in a given tier are educated according to a standard protocol. The tier then becomes the extent of individualization—every student has a personalized profile of tiers (i.e., different tiers for different areas of learning).

Individualization has always been a problem, however. First, schools must deliver educational services to thousands upon thousands of children. The most efficient way to do that is to set standards for everyone and make few exceptions. Special education runs contrary to the norms of general education, therefore, in quite fundamental ways. (Czapanskiy, 2016, p. 33)

In this version of special education, the law is simplified and, it could be argued, treats *all* children equally. This could be argued as fair because a school need only have certain resources to which *all* students have access if they need them. In our opinion, that change would be regressive, not progressive.

References

Algozzine, B., Christenson, S., and Ysseldyke, J. E. (1982). Probabilities associated with the referral to placement process. *Teacher Education and Special Education, 5*(3), 19–23.

Anastasiou, D., Gregory, M., and Kauffman, J. M. (2018). Commentary on Article 24 of the CRPD: The right to education. In I. Bantekas, M. Stein, and D. Anastasiou (Eds.), *Commentary on the UN Convention on the Rights of Persons with Disabilities* (pp. 656–704). New York, NY: Oxford University Press.

Baglieri, S., Valle, J. W., Connor, D. J., and Gallagher, D. J. (2010). Disability studies in education: The need for a plurality of perspectives on disability. *Remedial and Special Education, 32*, 267–278.

Bateman, B. D. (1994). Who, how, and where: Special education's issues in perpetuity. *Journal of Special Education, 27*, 509–520.

Bateman, B. D., Lloyd, J. W., and Tankersley, M. (Eds.). *Enduring issues in special education: Personal perspectives*. New York: Routledge.

Cannon, Y., Gregory, M., and Waterstone, J. (2013). A solution hiding in plain sight: Special education and better outcomes for students with social, emotional, and behavioral challenges. *Fordham Urban Law Journal, 41*, 403–497.

Ceci, S. J., and Papierno, P. B. (2005). The rhetoric and reality of gap closing. *American Psychologist, 60*, 149–160.

Chalfant, J. C., Pysh, M. V., and Moultrie, R. (1979). Teacher assistance teams: A model for within-building problem solving. *Learning Disability Quarterly, 2*, 85–96.

Collins, K. M., Connor, D., Ferri, B., Gallagher, D., and Samson, J. F. (2016). Dangerous assumptions and unspoken limitations: A disability studies in education response to Morgan, Farkas, Hillemeier, Mattison, Maczuga, Li, and Cook (2015). *Multiple Voices for Ethnically Diverse Exceptional Learners, 16*(1), 4–16.

Czapanskiy, K. S. (2016). Kids and rules: Challenging individualization in special education. *Journal of Law and Education, 45*(1), 1–38.

Engelmann, S. (1997). Theory of mastery and acceleration. In J. W. Lloyd, E. J. Kameenui, and D. Chard (Eds.), *Issues in educating students with disabilities* (pp. 177–195). Mahwah, NJ: Erlbaum.

Engelmann, S., and Carnine, D. (2011). *Could John Stuart Mill have saved our schools?* Verona, WI: Attainment.

Feynman, R. P. (1985). *"Surely your joking, Mr. Feynman!" Adventures of a curious character*. New York: Norton.

Foxx, R. M., and Mulick, J. A. (Eds). (2016). *Controversial therapies for autism and intellectual disabilities* (2nd ed). New York: Routledge.

Fuchs, D., and Fuchs, L. S. (2016). Responsiveness-to-intervention: A "systems" approach to instructional adaptation. *Theory Into Practice, 55*, 225–233.

Fuchs, L. S., Fuchs, D., Compton, D. L., Wehby, J., Schumacher, R. F., Gersten, R., and Jordan, N. C. (2015). Inclusion versus specialized intervention for very-low-performing students: What does access mean in an era of academic challenge? *Exceptional Children, 81*, 134–157. doi: 10.1177/00144029 14551743.

Fuchs, D., Fuchs, L. S., and Stecker, P. M. (2010). The "blurring" of special education in a new continuum of general education placements and services. *Exceptional Children, 76*, 301–323. doi.org/10.1177/001440291007600304

Gerber, M. M. (2005). Teachers are still the test: Limitations of response to instruction strategies for identifying children with learning disabilities. *Journal of Learning Disabilities, 38*, 516–524.

Gerber, M. M., and Semmel, M. I. (1984). Teacher as imperfect test: Reconceptualizing the referral process. *Educational Psychologist, 19*, 137–148.

Gladwell, M. (1997, May 19). The sports taboo: Why blacks are like boys and whites are like girls. *The New Yorker*, 50–55.

Gliona, M. F., Gonzales, A. K., and Jacobson, E. S. (2005). Dedicated, not segregated: Suggested changes in thinking about instructional environments and in the language of special education. In J. M. Kauffman and D. P. Hallahan (Eds.), *The illusion of full inclusion: A comprehensive critique of a current special education bandwagon* (2nd ed.) (pp. 135–146). Austin, TX: Pro-Ed.

Hoover, J. J., and Love, E. (2011). Supporting school-based response to intervention: A practitioner's model. *Teaching Exceptional Children, 43*(3), 40–48.

Horn, J. L. (1924). *The education of exceptional children: A consideration of public school problems and policies in the field of differential education.* New York: Century.

Kauffman, J. M. (1983). From the editor: On the missing millions. *Exceptional Education Quarterly, 3*(4), viii–ix.

Kauffman, J. M. (1990, April). *What happens when special education works? The sociopolitical context of research in the 1990s.* Invited address, Special Education Special Interest Group, American Educational Research Association Meeting, Boston, MA.

Kauffman, J. M. (1999–2000). The special education story: Obituary, accident report, conversion experience, reincarnation, or none of the above? *Exceptionality, 8*(1), 61–71. doi: 10.1207/S15327 035EX0801_6.

Kauffman, J. M. (2010). *The tragicomedy of public education: Laughing and crying, thinking and fixing.* Verona, WI: Attainment.

Kauffman, J. M. (2011). *Toward a science of education: The battle between rogue and real science.* Verona, WI: Attainment.

Kauffman, J. M. (2015). Opinion on recent developments and the future of special education. *Remedial and Special Education, 36*, 9–13. doi: 10.1177/0741932514543653.

Kauffman, J. M. (2016). Anxiety about the future of special education for students with emotional and behavioral disorders. *Journal of Modern Education Review, 6*, 357–363. doi: 10.15431/jmer(2155-7993)/05.06.2016/.

Kauffman, J. M., Anastasiou, D., Badar, J., Travers, T. C., and Wiley, A. L. (2016). Inclusive education moving forward. In J. P. Bakken F. E. Obiakorri (Eds.), *Advances in special education, Vol. 32—General and special education in an age of change: Roles of professionals involved* (pp. 153–177). Bingley, UK: Emerald.

Kauffman, J. M., Anastasiou, D., and Maag, J. W. (2016). Special education at the crossroad: An identity crisis and the need for a scientific reconstruction. *Exceptionality, 26*, 1–17. doi.org/10.1080/09362835.2016.1238380.

Kauffman, J. M., and Badar, J. (2016). It's instruction over place—not the other way around! *Phi Delta Kappan, 98*(4), 55–59. doi: 10.1177/0031721716681778.

Kauffman, J. M., Bruce, A., and Lloyd, J. W. (2012). Response to intervention (RTI) and students with EBD. In J. P. Bakken, F. E. Obiakor, and A. Rotatori (Eds.), *Advances in special education, Vol. 23—Behavioral disorders: Current perspectives and issues* (pp. 107–127). Bingley, UK: Emerald.

Kauffman, J. M., and Landrum, T. J. (2009). Politics, civil rights, and disproportional identification of students with emotional and behavioral disorders. *Exceptionality, 17,* 177–188.

Kauffman, J. M., and Lloyd, J. W. (1995). A sense of place: The importance of placement issues in contemporary special education. In J. M. Kauffman, J. W., Lloyd, D. P. Hallahan, and T. A. Astuto (Eds.), *Issues in educational placement: Students with emotional and behavioral disorders* (pp. 3–19). Mahwah, NJ: Lawrence Erlbaum Associates.

Kauffman, J. M., and Lloyd, J. W. (2017). Statistics, data, and special education decisions: Basic links to realities. In J. M. Kauffman, D. P. Hallahan, and P. C. Pullen (Eds.), *Handbook of special education* (2nd ed.) (pp. 29–39). New York: Taylor & Francis.

Kauffman, J. M., and Pullen, P. L. (1996). Eight myths about special education. *Focus on Exceptional Children, 28*(5), 1–12.

King, C. I. (2016, October 1). A Trump victory may lead to reconstruction of the racist past. *Washington Post,* A15.

Lloyd, J. W., Kauffman, J. M., Landrum, T. J., and Roe, D. L. (1991). Why do teachers refer pupils for special education? An analysis of referral records. *Exceptionality, 2,* 115–126. doi: 10.1080/09362839 109524774

Pullen, P. C., and Hallahan, D. P. (2015). What is special instruction? In. B. D. Bateman, J. W. Lloyd, and M. Tankersley (Eds.), *Enduring issues in special education: Personal perspectives* (pp. 37–51). New York: Routledge.

Sailor, W. S., and McCart, A. B. (2014). Stars in alignment. *Research and Practice for Persons with Severe Disabilities, 39*(1), 55–64.

Scruggs, T. E., and Mastropieri, M. A. (2015). What makes special education special? In. B. D. Bateman, J. W. Lloyd, and M. Takersley (Eds.), *Enduring issues in special education: Personal perspectives* (pp. 22–36). New York: Routledge.

Skinner, B. F. (1950). Are theories of learning necessary? *Psychological Review, 57,* 193–216.

Specter, M. (2009). *Denialism: How irrational thinking hinders scientific progress, harms the planet, and threatens our lives.* New York: Penguin.

Stainback, W., and Stainback, S. (1991). A rationale for integration and restructuring: A synopsis. In J. W. Lloyd, N. N. Singh, and A. C. Repp (Eds.), *The regular education initiative: Alternative perspectives on concepts, issues, and models* (pp. 225–239). Sycamore, IL: Sycarmore.

Storr, W. (2014). *The Unpersuadables: Adventures with the enemies of science.* New York: Overlook.

SWIFT schools [schoolwide integrated framework for transformation] (2016). Website downloaded September 27, 2016 from swiftschools.org.

Urban, W. J., and Wagoner, J. L., Jr. (2009). *American education: A history* (4th ed.). New York: Routledge.

Wagoner, J. L., Jr. (2004). *Jefferson and education.* Chapel Hill, NC: University of North Carolina Press.

Wiley, A. L. (2015). Place values: What moral psychology can tell us about the full inclusion debate in special education. In. B. D. Bateman, J. W. Lloyd, and M. Tankersley (Eds.), *Enduring issues in special education: Personal perspectives* (pp. 231–250). New York: Routledge.

Zigmond, N., and Kloo, A. (2017). General and special education are (and should be) different. In J. M. Kauffman, D. P. Hallahan, and P. C. Pullen (Eds.), *Handbook of special education* (2nd ed.) (pp. 249–262). New York: Routledge.

3

RESPONSE TO INTERVENTION, MULTI-TIERED SYSTEMS OF SUPPORT, AND FEDERAL LAW

Analysis and Commentary

Mitchell L. Yell

Response to intervention (RTI), now more frequently referred to as multi-tiered systems of support (MTSS), are school-wide systems that consist of multiple tiers of instructional and behavioral supports provided to students who are not succeeding in general education. Such systems usually have three or four tiers that increase the intensity of academic and behavioral support to students in the higher tiers. The goals of RTI and MTSS systems are to identify students with learning and behavioral challenges who are not succeeding in the general education setting and move them to a tier in which they are provided the type and degree of support they need to succeed. In this chapter I address RTI/MTSS systems and federal law. First, I examine the legal basis of RTI and MTSS in the Individuals with Disabilities Education Act (IDEA). Second, I explain guidance issued from the Office of Special Education and Rehabilitative Services (OSERS) and the Office of Special Education Programs (OSEP) in the U.S Department of Education. Third, I address the Child Find requirements of the IDEA and how school personnel and officials may inadvertently violate the IDEA if they use their RTI/MTSS system in an inappropriate manner. Fourth, I review RTI/MTSS in the 2015 reauthorization of the Elementary and Secondary Education Act (ESEA), which was titled the Every Student Succeeds Act (ESSA). Finally, I offer guidelines on how school district personnel can develop and implement RTI/MTSS systems that comport with federal law.

RTI/MTSS may also be a matter of state education law. An examination of state law is beyond the scope of this chapter, but I encourage readers to consult their state laws. State laws can be located on the following websites: Cornell Law by Source: State at www.law.cornell.edu/states/listing.html or at FindLaw: State resources at www.findlaw.com/casecode/.

RTI/MTSS and the IDEA

Before the IDEA was reauthorized in the Individuals with Disabilities Education Improvement Act of 2004, two influential reports, the President's Commission on Excellence in Special

Education and the Thomas B. Fordham Foundation and Progressive Policy Institute's report *Rethinking Special Education for a New Century*, were issued. Both reports made recommendations to Congress regarding important issues in reauthorization. Complete coverage of these reports, which were comprehensive and included many recommendations, is beyond the scope of this chapter to review. Nevertheless, both of these reports addressed the importance of (a) adopting the sort of school-wide systems that we now call RTI or MTSS and (b) abandoning the so-called discrepancy formula to determine if a student had a learning disability (LD) in favor of adopting a system based on a student's response to evidence-based interventions. I next briefly review pertinent sections of the reports.

RTI/MTSS, the President's Commission, and the Fordham Foundation/Progressive Policy Institute Reports

In October 2001, President George W. Bush appointed a commission to make recommendations to Congress on reauthorizing the IDEA. The commission, which was created by executive order, was chaired by Terry Branstad, the former governor of Iowa. The commission held 13 public hearings in cities throughout the nation and heard testimony from hundreds of individuals including experts in special education, educational finance, administrators, teachers, educational researchers, parents, and students with disabilities who either testified before the commission or submitted written comments. The commission's written report, which was titled *A New Era: Revitalizing Special Education for Children and Their Families*, was issued on July 1, 2002. The purpose of the Commission's report was to begin a dialogue about needed reforms to the IDEA prior to the reauthorization.

Almost a year earlier, in November 2000, the Thomas B. Fordham Foundation, a conservative think tank in Washington DC that supports research, publications, and projects of national significance in elementary and secondary education reform, and the Progressive Policy Institute, a liberal Washington DC think tank that defines and promotes progressive politics for America in the twenty-first century, commissioned a set of papers and sponsored a conference to examine special education in America prior to the reauthorization of the IDEA.

In May 2001 the Foundation and the Institute published a series of reports, entitled *Rethinking Special Education for a New Century* (Finn, Rotherham, and Hokanson, 2001). The purpose of the reports, which were edited by Chester Finn and Charles Hokanson of the Thomas B. Fordham Foundation and Andrew Rotherham of the Progressive Policy Institute, was to begin a discussion about special education that would influence congress and the administration in the forthcoming reauthorization of the IDEA.

Both reports contained a number of recommendations that were to guide Congress during reauthorization of the IDEA. Interestingly, the President's Commission Report and the Fordham Foundation reports had strikingly similar proposals regarding the category of learning disabilities and the importance of schools intervening early for students with learning and behavior problems to prevent school failure and obviate their need for special education services.

In the President's Commission Report, the IDEA's eligibility process for determining the existence of a specific learning disability, which usually relied on calculating a discrepancy formula, was derided as overly complex and lacking validity. These problems lead to "thousands of children being misidentified every year, while many others are not identified early enough or at all" (p. 8). The Commission made three major recommendations to improve the LD eligibility process. First, the IDEA should emphasize early identification of academic and behavioral problems through screening. When young children are identified as having educational problems, educators must intervene aggressively using research-based strategies and procedures. According to the Commission, too often special education used a "wait to fail" model to identify children in need of special help. That is; schools did not assess students for eligibility in special education until students had failed in school for a year or two. The Commission members believed that by relying on the "wait to fail" model instead of stressing prevention and early intervention, students with disabilities often did not get the help they needed early enough to benefit from the programming. The commission, therefore, stressed the importance of adopting a special education model that was based on prevention, early and accurate identification, and aggressive intervention using research-based strategies and procedures. Moreover, such a model would include universal screening of young children, which the commission members believed would lead to better outcomes and results for all students because the system would identify those children who were most at risk for later achievement and behavioral problems, so school personnel could implement research-based early intervening programs. These recommendations clearly were very similar to RTI/MTSS systems.

Second, the Commission recommended that the IDEA's identification and eligibility process should be simplified. The current system was found to be overly cumbersome, time consuming, and expensive. Additionally, the Commission stressed that the purpose of the assessment should be to drive instruction rather than merely to serve a gate-keeping function. As part of their assessment recommendations, the Commission recommended that Congress eliminate the regulatory requirement regarding the use of the IQ-Achievement discrepancy model to identify students with learning disabilities. One of the Commission members, Wade Horn, memorably stated that "I would like to encourage this commission to drive a stake through the heart of this over reliance on the use of the discrepancy model for determining for determining the kinds of children that need services" (p. 25).

Third, special education should incorporate models during the identification and assessment process that are based on response to intervention and progress monitoring. The commission found that many students "who are placed into special education are essentially instructional casualties and many students who do not learn to read or who do poor academically is that the instruction they received was not research-based." According to the Commission, such students do not have disabilities; rather they have not been taught using procedures and strategies that work and when they fail to learn they are referred to special education. The problem is not the student; therefore, it is inappropriate instruction. To address this problem, the Commission recommended that the IDEA be modified so that students' response to scientifically-based instruction becomes part of the criteria for determining the existence of LD and other high-incidence disabilities. Such a model would be designed to identify students who are having academic or behavior problems when these problems first become apparent and then matching evidenced-based instruction to their educational needs. Additionally, these models would use progress-monitoring systems to track how students were responding to interventions, so that the intensity of the interventions can be increased when students fail to respond.

Although the reports issued by the Fordham Foundation were considerably longer and contained more detail than the report of the President's Commission, many of the final recommendations were similar. First, the Fordham Foundation report cited one of the major policy failures in education as being the failure to identify and address students' preventable and remediable learning and behavior problems before they became intractable problems. The prevention problem, which was very similar to the President's Commission warnings about education relying on the wait to fail model, was particularly acute in the area of learning disabilities, which according to the Fordham report "continues to focus on the identification and remediation of learning problems after they have grown severe" (p. 339). Thus, a principle that the Foundation report suggested guide federal policy makers in the reauthorization of the IDEA was that the law should focus on prevention and early intervention using research-based practices.

Second, a chapter in the final Fordham report, *Rethinking Learning Disabilities* (Lyons et al. 2001) decried the use of the discrepancy formula when used as the primary criterion to determine whether a student had a specific learning disability. Following a thorough review of the literature and research on the LD identification process, Lyon and his colleagues made a number of recommendations to guide the Congressional reauthorization process. The recommendations were based on the following assumptions: (a) the discrepancy formula method for determining whether a student has a LD had serious scientific and educational problems and should not be used for making eligibility decisions, (b) the instructional methods used by teachers of students with LD often are of limited effectiveness because they are not started until a students' problems are already very serious and difficult to remediate, and (c) early intervention and prevention strategies could ameliorate the serious academic problems of many students who eventually are served in special education. Lyons et al., noted that reliance on a discrepancy formula, which was "fraught with psychometric, statistical, and conceptual problems" (p. 266), harmed more children than it helped because it essentially required the use of a "wait-to-fail" model in which a child had to endure two or three years of school failure before he or she would receive special education interventions. Such practices had "devastating, lifelong consequences" for a child (p. 266) and should be replaced by the use of research-based prevention and early intervention efforts. Moreover, the authors suggested that the discrepancy formula be jettisoned in favor of "consideration of a student's response to well-designed and well-implemented early intervention" for identification of LD (p. 279).

Lyons et al., also recommended that Congress should allow school-based teams to consider a student's response to well-designed and well-implemented research-based instruction as part of the LD identification process and that the more complex assessments should be reserved for students who had not responded to these procedures. Moreover, the authors stated that school districts should use evidence-based early intervention and prevention programs with students who are not responding to instruction as soon as academic problems appear. The authors argued that by implementing school-wide early intervention programs, school personnel could significantly reduce the number of students who are later identified as LD and who would require intensive long term special education programs throughout their school careers. The authors also noted that without early and effective intervention, "the poor first-grade reader almost invariably becomes a poor middle school reader, high school reader, and adult reader. In short children who get off to a poor start in reading rarely catch up. While 'we wait—they fail' " (p. 270).

The reports of the President's Commission and the Fordham Foundation were very influential in the drafting of the IDEA reauthorization legislation. Of the many recommendations made in these report, the recommendations regarding the LD discrepancy formula and the importance of early intervention were to be included in the new law.

RTI and IDEA Reauthorization

When the IDEIA was signed into law by President Bush, it included major changes in the ways that school districts (a) determine eligibility for the category of LD and (b) spend a portion of their IDEA funds on schoolwide early intervening and prevention services. It is important to note that the only mention of response to instruction language is in the section of the identification of students with LD (IDEA, 20 U.S.C. § 1414[b][6]).

This part of the law prohibits states from requiring that school districts use a discrepancy formula to identify students with LD. Instead, school districts "may use a process that determines if the child responds to scientific, research-based intervention" (IDEA, 20 U.S.C. § 1414[b][6][B]). Thus, the IDEA permits school districts, also referred to as local educational agencies (LEAs), to use either a discrepancy formula, a response to intervention system, or a combination of both methods to determine if a student has a LD. The regulations issued by the Department of Education further clarified that when determining the existence of a LD, state educational agencies (SEAs) may (a) permit or prohibit the use of a severe discrepancy, (b) permit or require the use of RTI, or (c) permit or require the use of an alternative research-based procedures (34 C.F.R. § 300.307[a]).

In 2006, the U.S. Department of Education further emphasized the role of RTI in determining the existence of a learning disability:

> Consensus reports and empirical synthesis indicate a need for major changes in the approach to identifying children with (specific learning disabilities). Models that incorporate RTI represent a shift in special education toward goals of better achievement and improved behavioral outcomes for children with (specific learning disabilities) because the children who are identified under such models are most likely to require special education and related services.
>
> *(71 Fed. Reg. 46,647, 2006)*

The U.S. Department of Education also noted that in SEAs and LEAs that use an RTI process to identify students with LD, the evaluation process must still use a variety of assessment tools and strategies and must not rely on any single criterion for determining eligibility. In fact, the Director of the Office of Special Education Programs (OSEP) wrote that "An RTI process does not replace the need for a comprehensive evaluation, and the results of an RTI process may be one component of the information reviewed" (Letter to Zirkel, 2007). Thus, RTI must not be the only factor in making the determination of eligibility but must be part of a full and individualized evaluation. Nonetheless, the inclusion of RTI in the IDEA "reflects the (U.S. Department of Education's) position on the identification of children with SLD and our support for models that focus on assessments that are related to instruction and promote intervention for identified children" (U.S. Department of Education, 2006).

Three points are important to an understanding of RTI and the IDEA with respect to evaluation of eligibility for special education. First, determining eligibility of students with LD is the only context within the IDEA that RTI is mentioned. Using RTI for eligibility determination is not required for determination of any other disability area (e.g., emotional disturbance, other health impaired). Certainly, a student's IEP team may use data collected from a school's RTI process as information for developing a student's individualized education program (IEP) but using RTI to determine eligibility in other categories is a matter of state law and not the IDEA (Letter to Brekken, 2010). Second, if in a schoolwide RTI system a particular assessment is used to screen all students in the school, written parental permission is not needed to conduct the assessment, even if the data is used prior to the eligibility or IEP process for a student with disabilities (Letter to Torres, 2009). Third, according to Zirkel and Thomas (2010), 12 states required the use of RTI in their evaluation processes. Of these twelve, only a few states have extended the RTI eligibility language beyond the category of LD. However, state law should be consulted to determine if there are additional requirements regarding the use of RTI in eligibility determination.

A second change that was especially significant, and directly related to the findings and recommendations of the President's Commission and the Fordham report recommendations regarding prevention and early intervention, was the addition of early intervening services (EIS) to the section in the IDEA regarding the ways that a local education agency (LEA) may spend their IDEA funds (IDEA 20 U.S.C. § 613(a)(2)(C)). Early intervening services are coordinated, structured, academic and behavioral supports provided to at-risk students. The purpose of EIS is to identify students who are at risk for developing academic and behavioral problems while they are still in general education settings, and then to address these problems by delivering interventions in a systematic manner by using research-based academic and behavioral interventions along with progress monitoring systems. The regulations implementing EIS allow school districts to use up to 15% of its IDEA Part B grants to:

> develop and implement coordinated, early intervening services, which may include interagency financing structures, for students in kindergarten through grade 12 (with a particular emphasis on students in kindergarten through grade three) who are not currently identified as needing special education or related services, but who need additional academic and behavioral support to succeed in a general education environment.
>
> *(34 C.F.R. § 300.226[a])*

When implementing EIS, school districts may carry out activities including (a) professional development activities for teachers and other school staff to enable them to deliver scientifically based academic and behavioral interventions, and (b) providing educational and behavioral evaluations, services, and supports, including scientifically based literacy instruction. Additionally, school district officials who use IDEA funds for early intervening services must describe the services that they are providing to general education students in a report to the respective state educational agencies (SEAs). Furthermore, the district officials must report on the number of students who are served in its early intervening services and the number of students in the services who were eventually found eligible for special education services.

The advantages of early intervening services include (a) identifying students early in their school careers using a risk rather than a deficit model, (b) emphasizing research-based practices in intervention, and (c) focusing on student outcomes rather than services received (Fuchs and Vaughn, 2012; Lane, Menzies, Ennis, and Oakes, 2015). Although RTI systems are included in neither the IDEA's statutory nor regulatory language, the Office of Special Education and Rehabilitative Services (OSERS) has recognized that EIS funds may be used to support RTI as long as the funds are used for services provided to students without disabilities who need additional academic or behavioral support (U.S. Department of Education, 2007). So, for example, in a three-tier school-wide RTI system EIS funds could not be used for tier one activities, because such activities typically support all students in general education and special education, thus violating the prohibition against using EIS funds for students in special education. However, EIS funds could be used to support tier two activities (e.g., academic and behavioral supports provided to a small group of students who were at risk for developing serious academic and behavioral problems) and tier three activities (e.g., intensive interventions for students with serious academic or behavioral needs) as long as the students in these tiers were not in special education programs (U.S. Department of Education, 2008).

Although the reference to RTI in the IDEA is limited to a single instance—SEAs and LEAs may use a student's response to research-based interventions in determining his or her eligibility in the category of learning disabilities—OSEP has issued policy guidance letters that address RTI/MTSS in the much broader context of schoolwide interventions used with all students.

RTI/MTSS and OSEP

Officials of departments and agencies within the federal government often issue statements or letters that offer guidance regarding particular areas of law. For example, OSERS and OSEP in the U.S Department of Education have frequently issued such documents to superintendents of public schools that provide the official's interpretation of how to appropriately implement the IDEA. These guidance documents, which may be issued as question and answer documents, memoranda, or Dear Colleague Letters (DCLs), are essentially open letters that provide information on meeting particular obligations under a law and offer members of the public information about their rights under the laws that the agency enforces (Office of Management and Budget, 2007). The U.S. Department of Education has issued many such guidance documents. These open letters do not create law; neither do they add requirements to existing law; rather, they inform recipients about how the particular agency will evaluate compliance to legal obligations under the law by covered entities. Readers should note that many of these guidance documents can be found on the U.S. Department of Education's website at www2.ed.gov/policy/speced/guid/idea/.

In the past few years OSEP have issued guidance documents that have addressed the use of RTI/MTSS systems of a schoolwide basis as well as on the more limited mention in the IDEA. For example, in a document entitled "Questions and Answers on RTI and EIS," (U.S. Department of Education, 2007), OSEP officials wrote that EIS could be used to support an RTI system. OSEP officials also noted that although the U.S. Department of Education did not endorse any particular RTI model, the following core characteristics were at the basis of all RTI systems:

- Students receive high quality research-based instruction in their general education setting;
- continuous monitoring of student performance;
- all students are screened for academic and behavioral problems; and
- multiple levels (tiers) of instruction that are progressively more intense, based on the student's response to instruction.

(p. 14)

Officials at OSEP also wrote that "The No Child Left Behind Act and IDEA call on educational practitioners to use scientifically based research to guide their decisions about which interventions to implement" (p. 15). They also reiterated that EIS funds could also be used to pay professional development activities and academic and behavioral evaluations, services, and supports. It is certainly understandable that officials at OSEP support an RTI/MTSS system to identify at-risk children and provide them with more intensive research-based interventions because it is consistent with the goal of EIS, which is "to reduce the need to label children as disabled in order to address the learning and behavioral needs of such children" (20 U.S.C. 1401 [c][5][F]). RTI/MTSS systems are also consistent with the recommendations of both the President's Commission and Fordham Foundations reports on the importance of the law emphasizing prevention, intervention, and moving away from the wait-to-fail model of identifying children for appropriate services.

On August 1, 2016 OSERS and OSEP issued a joint DCL that addressed the importance of implementing a multi-tiered behavioral framework. In the DCL, Sue Swenson, the Acting Assistant Director of OSERS, and Ruth Ryder, the Acting Director of OSEP, wrote that "implementing evidence-based, multi-tiered behavioral frameworks can help improve overall school climate, school safety, and academic achievement for all children, including children with disabilities" (p. 8). Specifically, the letter recognized that:

> behavioral supports are most effectively organized within a multi-tiered behavioral framework that provides instruction and clear behavioral expectations for all children, targeted intervention for small groups not experiencing success, and individualized supports and services for those needing the most intensive support.
>
> *(p. 8)*

The DCL writers also acknowledged that the U.S. Department of Education has provided support to RTI/MTSS by funding centers such as the OSEP Technical Assistance Center on Positive Behavioral Interventions and Supports (www.pbis.org) and the National Center of Response to Intervention (www.rti4success.org) and by disseminating tools and resources to SEA and LEAs.

RTI/MTSS is included in the IDEA and embraced by OSERS and OSEP. Nonetheless, if school district personnel implement RTI/MTSS systems, and they fail to adhere to the Child Find requirements of the IDEA, they may find they have inadvertently violated the law.

RTI/MTSS and the Child Find Requirement of the IDEA

The IDEA and its implementing regulations require that SEAs must ensure that all students with disabilities, from birth to age 21, residing in the state who are in need of special education and related services or are suspected of having disabilities and needing special education are identified, located, and evaluated (20 U.S.C. § 1414[a][1][A]; 34 C.F.R. § 300.220). These Child Find requirements constitute an affirmative duty, because LEAs must have policies and procedures in place to find these students; LEAs must not wait for parents to request that a school district identify and evaluate their child with disabilities because it is the LEA's responsibility. When students are identified in Child Find, the LEA is required to determine whether they have a disability under the IDEA. Child Find is triggered when LEA personnel have reason to suspect that a student has a disability covered under the IDEA, and that the student may need special education.

If school district officials fail to meet the IDEAs Child Find requirements, they may deprive children of a FAPE (Yell, 2016). This is potentially a very serious violation of the IDEA and could possibly result in a district having to pay compensatory education, tuition reimbursement, and attorneys' fees (Tatgenhorst, Norlin, and Gorn, 2014). Failing to adhere to Child Find when school district personnel are aware that a student with academic or behavioral problems may have a disability but fail to refer the student for a special education evaluation can be a critical error (Yell, 2016; Zirkel, 2015). When Child Find disputes go to litigation, hearing officers and judges will generally focus on the following two issues: (a) Did school district personnel have reason to suspect that a student may be eligible for services under the IDEA and (b) Did the school district meet its evaluation obligation under the IDEA within a reasonable period of time (Zirkel, 2015).

When students who may qualify for special education services are located through a LEA's Child Find process, these students should be referred for special education evaluation.

In addition to locating a student who may need special education through a Child Find process, a student's parents or school personnel may also initiate a request for an evaluation to determine if the student has an IDEA disability. Additionally, before an evaluation can be conducted, a student's parents or guardians must give their informed written consent to conduct the evaluation. After written consent is received, the evaluation must be conducted in a timely manner. The IDEA requires the initial special education evaluation must be conducted within 60 days of receiving parental consent to conduct the evaluation (IDEA, 20 U.S.C. § 614(a)(1)(C)(i)(I)). In cases in which SEA establish timelines, schools within that state must follow those guidelines.

RTI/MTSS is a school-wide approach that addresses the academic and behavioral needs of all students. The goal of the RTI process is to identify students at risk for school failure and then provide evidence-based procedures and progress monitoring procedures to adjust the intensity and nature of those interventions (U.S. Department of Education, 2011). The RTI system, because a general education tool that helps identify at-risk students, provides interventions in general education settings, and monitors the progress of all students (U.S. Department of Education, 2007). The ultimate goal is to successfully ameliorate a student's academic and behavioral problems before a referral to special education is necessary.

Unfortunately, there is an inherent tension between RTI and Child Find (Walsh, 2008, 2016). This is because the purpose of RTI is to slow down LEA referrals to special education whereas the purpose of Child Find is to locate, identify, and evaluate as soon as LEA personnel have reason to suspect that a student has a disability covered under the IDEA, and because of that disability the child may need special education services (Walsh, 2016).

When an RTI/MTSS system is implemented with the IDEA legal framework, the system should support and inform the Child Find process because when a student continues to struggle academically or behaviorally, data from the LEA's progress monitoring system can be used to support a referral of the student to special education (Tatgenhorst, et al., 2014). The RTI/MTSS system leads to more accurate referrals by ensuring that only students who truly need special education services receive those services and those students who struggle academically and behaviorally, but are not disabled under the IDEA, receive appropriate services in general education through the RTI/MTSS system (Tatgenhorst, 2014; Yell, 2016). In this sense the LEA's use of RTI/MTSS process compliments the IDEA's Child Find process, because it helps to identify students who have IDEA disabilities and should be referred for special education evaluation.

Unfortunately, in 2011, concerns that LEAs were not using RTI systems in this manner but were instead using RTI to delay and deny students' evaluations for special education led Melody Musgrove, then the director of OSEP, to write a memorandum to all state directors of special education informing them that inappropriate use of RTI/MTSS could be a violation of the Child Find and evaluation mandates of the IDEA. In the memorandum, Musgrove wrote that "the use of RTI strategies cannot be used to delay or deny the provision of a full and individual evaluation . . . to a child suspected of having a disability under [the IDEA]" (p. 3). Musgrove also noted that after it is determined that a student may have a disability, a special education evaluation should be conducted expeditiously.

A case out of the federal district court for the western district of Texas, *El Paso Independent School District* v. *Richard R.* (2008; hereafter El Paso ISD) illustrated the potential problems that may occur when an RTI/MTSS system is used in such a way that it delays or denies special education evaluation. Although the case did not involve an actual RTI/MTSS system, the findings of the court can easily be understood in light of the inappropriate use of RTI/MTSS. In this case, the El Paso ISD had repeatedly referred a student with learning and behavior problems for additional interventions in the LEA's general education classroom rather than evaluating the student for special education services. The parents requested that a special education evaluation be conducted. When the district continued to refer their child for additional interventions in general education, rather than evaluate for special education services, the parents filed for a due process hearing.

At the hearing level, the state education hearing officer ruled that the LEA had violated child find requirements because the LEA's Student Teacher Assessment Team (STAT) repeatedly referred the student for additional interventions in general education; the STAT had devolved from a body meant to "provide support and intervention" to "an obstacle to parents who want to access the special education referrals" (p. 18). The hearing officer wrote that the STAT process, which consisted of a team of school-based personnel who suggested interventions in the general education setting prior to referral, "while a mandatory district requirement, is not a prerequisite to conducting a special education evaluation" (p. 18). The hearing officer also noted that after a parent makes a request for a special education evaluation, the LEA should begin the special education evaluation process while at the same time providing intervention strategies through the STAT process.

The El Paso Independent School District appealed the hearing officer's decision to the District Court of West Texas. The district court judge affirmed the hearing officer's decision and used a two-part test to determine whether the LEA was in compliance with its Child Find responsibilities. The first part of the test involved an examination of whether the LEA had reason to suspect that the student had a disability, and whether there was reason to suspect that special education services might be needed to address that disability. The judge noted, because the first part of the test was answered in the affirmative, then the court would move to the second part of the test, which involved determining if the LEA evaluated the student within a reasonable time after having notice that the student's academic and behavior problems were likely to indicate a disability.

Officials in the El Paso School District stated that the school's STAT had delayed starting the special education evaluation process because the team needed time to implement intervention strategies in the general education setting. The district court judge was not impressed by this argument, finding that "one of the factors used to measure whether a local educational agency has met its IDEA responsibility to provide a FAPE is whether the accommodations accorded to the student demonstrate positive academic benefits" (*El Paso Independent School District*, 2008, p. 22). The facts in this case showed that the student in question had failed the Texas Assessment of Knowledge and Skills (TAKS), a statewide achievement test, for three years in a row and continued to display significant academic difficulties in reading, math, and science despite the district's implementation of intervention strategies in the general education setting. According to the hearing officer, these should have been "clear signals that an evaluation was necessary and appropriate" (p. 22) because the general education interventions that had been used over the past three years had been shown to be ineffective in helping the student achieve passing scores on the TAKS. The district court judge found that faced with three years of repeated failure, a special education evaluation should have been conducted.

The district court then turned to the second prong of the court's Child Find inquiry to determine if the LEA had evaluated the student within a reasonable time after suspecting the student might have a disability. The district court in this case pointed to other federal courts that had developed standards varying from a delay of 6 months (*A. W. v. Jersey City Public Schools*, 2007) to a delay of 12 months (*O. F. ex rel. N.S. v. Chester Upland School District*, 2002) from the time that a child's parents had informed a school district that the child was experiencing difficulties or the point at which school officials had reason to suspect a child had a disability.

After the passage of this amount of time, therefore, a LEA should schedule a special education evaluation; if it does not, this could be a Child Find violation. In the *El Paso* case the court ruled that the 13 months that passed between the request for evaluation and the school's offer of evaluation was unreasonable.

Finally, the court adopted the hearing officer's finding that the IDEA "gives the parent a right to seek an evaluation and overrides local district policy concerning intervention procedures. . . . In those instances where the STAT committee impedes the exercise of rights guaranteed by federal law, those practices violate the IDEA" (p. 18). The decision in El Paso ISD and the OSEP memorandum should serve as a warning to LEA officials not to use an RTI/MTSS system to delay or deny a special education evaluation when a student's performance indicates such a need, as this could be found to violate the IDEA.

Tatgenhorst et al. (2014) asserted that the key to LEAs balancing the Child Find requirements of the IDEA and RTI/MTSS is the LEA's appropriate monitoring use of progress monitoring data. That is, when the data indicate that a student is continuing to struggle academically or behaviorally despite the implementation of evidence-based interventions in the RTI/MTSS system, that is a strong indication that a student may need to be referred to special education. Similarly, if the data shows academic or behavioral improvement, that is an indication that the research-based interventions are proving to be successful.

It is also critical that LEA personnel understand that, if a student's parents refer their child for a special education evaluation, there are only two appropriate responses from the LEA. First, LEA officials could agree to conduct a special education evaluation, obtain the parents' written consent, conduct an evaluation, and give the parents a copy of their procedural safeguards. Second, LEA officials could decide not to conduct a special education evaluation, give the student's parents a prior written notice (PWN) form that describes the LEA personnel's reason for refusing to conduct the evaluation, and provide the parents with a copy of their procedural safeguards. Of course, the student's parents could request a due process hearing or file a state complaint, thereby taking legal action against the LEA for refusing to evaluate their child. It is not appropriate for LEA personnel to tell parents that their child is still in the LEA's RTI/MTSS system and that an evaluation will not be conducted until the process is completed. That is not a legally defensible position and may violate the Child Find requirements of the IDEA. If the RTI/MTSS data does show that a student is making progress, and the data used is legitimate and correctly interpreted, however, that could be cited as part of the reason behind a LEA's position list in the PWN, if the decision is not to evaluate a student.

RTI/MTSS and the Every Student Succeeds Act of 2015

On December 10, 2015 President Obama signed the Every Student Succeeds Act (ESSA). The law, which was a reauthorization of the Elementary and Secondary Education Act, replaced the No Child Left Behind Act. Although LEAs are not required to implement RTI/MTSS systems, SEAs and LEAs have great flexibility to adopt such systems to improve academic and behavioral programming. The ESSA defines MTSS as "a comprehensive continuum of evidence-based systematic practices to support a rapid response to students' needs, with regular observations to facilitate data-based instructional decision making" (20 U.S.C. § 8802 [33]). Moreover, the law addresses the importance of professional development to prepare teachers of students who are at risk for developing academic and behavioral problems, students with disabilities, other teachers and instructional staff to address the instructional and academic needs of their students, including positive behavioral interventions and supports (PBIS) and MTSS systems. Additionally, the ESSA allows LEAs to use federal monies to support PBIS and MTSS. Although SEAs are still developing plans to implement the ESSA, it is likely with the law's emphasis on PBIS and RTI/MTSS, the use of such systems in LEAs will only increase.

Recommendations

Federal law does not require that LEAs adopt and use RTI/MTSS systems. Rather, the only mention in federal law is in the IDEA, which allows a LEA to use a process that determines if a child responds to scientific, research-based intervention as part of the LD eligibility process. Additionally, the ESSA does allow federal funds to be expended on RTI/MTSS and PBIS systems. Unfortunately, the improper use of RTI/MTSS systems can result in a violation of the IDEA. The following guidelines are offered to ensure that RTI/MTSS is implemented in a legally correct manner.

Recommendation 1: Provide Ongoing Professional Development to Ensure that School District Administrators, Teachers, and Staff Understand Their Responsibilities under the IDEA

If an LEA implements an RTI/MTSS system, it is important that school personnel do not inadvertently violate the Child Find provisions of the IDEA by delaying or denying a special education evaluation when school personnel believe a student may have a disability and need special education. Because laws are amended, LEAs should ensure that school administrators, teachers, and staff are kept abreast of all applicable state and federal laws regarding RTI/MTSS.

SEAs and LEAs, therefore, should provide frequent and systematic professional development opportunities to school personnel on the IDEA and other federal and state education laws.

Recommendation 2: Develop an RTI System Based on Best Practices

The use of schoolwide RTI/MTSS systems is a relatively new development in education. Nonetheless, there is a growing body of evidence on how LEAs should structure and implement RTI/MTSS systems and tools and resources to assist LEA personnel with implementation. For example, OSEP currently funds the Technical Assistance Center on Positive Behavioral Interventions and Supports (www.pbis.org) and the American Institutes of Research maintains the Center of Response to Intervention (www.rti4success.org). The mission of these centers is to provide information and technical support to SEAs and LEAs.

Recommendation 3: Use Instructional Practices that are Based on Evidence and Research

Well-functioning RTI/MTSS systems are based on school-wide, multilevel instructional and behavioral programming for preventing school failure based on evidence-based instructional and behavioral interventions. The likelihood of student success in RTI/MTSS is increased if such systems are grounded in evidence-based practices.

Recommendation 4: Adopt and Use Research-Based Progress Monitoring Systems

When LEA personnel use RTI/MTSS, they need to rely on meaningful data to monitor student progress and make decisions. An LEA's multidisciplinary team can then use this information to determine if a student is responding to intervention in the general education setting; and if they are not, the student may be moved to a tier involving more intensive support. If a student is failing to respond to instruction in the intensive tiers, the team can use these data to determine if a student should be referred for special education services.

Summary

Prior to the reauthorization of the IDEA in 2004, two influential reports were issued that make recommendations to Congress to improve the special education law. These two reports, authored by the President's Commission on Excellence in Education and the Thomas B. Fordham Foundation and Progressive Policy Institute included many recommendations, but two in particular became an impetus for developing RTI. One suggestion was that Congress change the emphasis on LD eligibility from a wait to fail model to a more proactive model in which school personnel would determine how children responded to scientific, research-based instruction. In the IDEA reauthorization congress changed the law to prohibit state educational agencies from requiring that local school districts use a discrepancy formula to identify students with LDs. Instead, states were allowed to require, or at least permit, school districts to adopt an identification method in which students' response to research-based instruction was used to determine if students had LDs. A second suggestion made in the reports was to require LEAs to intervene early in the school careers of students with learning and behavior problems to prevent school failure and obviate their need for special education services. This suggestion influenced Congress to allow LEAs to use 15% of their IDEA funds to provide early intervening services to students who were at risk of developing academic or behavior problems.

In the past few years, however, the U.S. Department of Education has recognized that RTI/MTSS has become a nationwide movement toward making systematic changes in SEA and LEAs that improve the education of all students. The goal behind RTI/MTSS is that, by identifying students who are at risk of academic failure early in their school years and then providing increasing intensities of research-based instruction and progress monitoring, educators can prevent academic failure. The ESSA allows federal funds to be used to develop systems based on MTSS. Nevertheless, LEAs that adopt and implement such models must be aware of their responsibilities under the IDEA and ensure that they do not violate the Child Find and evaluation requirements of the law by using RTI/MTSS systems to delay or deny evaluations for special education eligibility.

References

71 Fed. Reg. 46,647 (2006).

A.W. v. Jersey City Public Schools, 486 F.3d 791 (3d Cir. 2007).

El Paso Independent School District v. Richard R. 50 IDELR 256 (W.D. 2008).

Finn, C.E., Rotherham, A. J., and Hokanson, C.R. (2001). *Rethinking special education for a new century*. Washington, DC: Thomas B. Fordham Foundation and Progressive Policy Institute. Available from www.ppionline.org/documents/SpecialEd_complete_volume.pdf.

Fuchs, L.S. and Vaughn, S.R. (2012). Responsiveness-to-intervention: A decade later. *Journal of Learning Disabilities, 45*, 195–203.

Individuals with Disabilities Education Act, 20 U.S.C. § 1400 *et seq.*

Individuals with Disabilities Education Act Regulations, 34 C.F.R § 300 *et seq.*

Lane, K.L., Menzies, H.M., Ennis, R.P., and Oakes, W.P (2015). *Supporting behavior for school success: A step-by-step guide to key strategies*. New York, NY: Guildford.

Letter to Brekken, 56 IDELR 80 (OSEP 2010).

Letter to Torres, 53 IDELR 333 (OSEP 2009).

Letter to Zirkel, 47 IDELR 106 (2007).

Lyon, G. R., Fletcher, J. M., Shaywitz, S. E., Shaywitz, B. A., Torgeson, J. A., Wood, F. B., Shulte, A., and Olson, R. (2001). Rethinking learning disabilities. In C. E. Finn, A. J. Rotherham, and C. R. Hokanson, (Eds.), *Rethinking special education for a new century.* Washington, DC: Thomas B. Fordham Foundation and Progressive Policy Institute. Available from www.ppionline.org/documents/SpecialEd_complete_volume.pdf.

O. F. ex rel. N.S. v. Chester Upland School District, 246. F. Supp. 2d 409 (E.D. Pa. 2002).

Office of Management and Budget (2007, January 25). Final bulletin for agency good guidance practices. 72 Fed. Reg. 3432.

President's Commission on Excellence in Special Education. (2001). A new era: Revitalizing special education for children and their families. Retrieved from www2.ed.gov/inits/commissionsboards/whspecialeducation/reports/index.html.

Tagenhorst, A., Norlin, J.W., and Gorn, S. (2014). *What do I do when . . . The answer book on special education law* (6th ed.). Palm Beach Gardens, FL: LRP Publications.

U.S. Department of Education, Analysis of Comments and Changes to 2006 IDEA Part B Regulations, 71 Fed. Reg. 46647 (U.S. Department of Education, 2006).

U.S. Department of Education, Office of Special Education Programs, *Memorandum to Chief State School Officers and State Directors of Special Education*, 51 IDELR 49 (2008).

U.S. Department of Education, Office of Special Education and Rehabilitative Services (2007). Questions and Answers on Response to Intervention (RTI) and Early Intervening Services (EIS), 47 IDELR 196 (OSERS 2007).

Walsh, J (2008). *Walsh's word: Balance tension between child find and RTI.* Palm Beach Gardens, FL: LPR Publications.

Walsh, J. (2016, November). Lessons learned from 2016 cases: Year in review. Keynote Presentation at the Tri-State Regional Special Education Law Conference: Omaha, NE.

Yell, M.L. (2016). *The law and special education* (4th ed.). Upper Saddle River, NJ: Pearson.

Zirkel, P.A. (2015, November). The "red flags" for child find under the IDEA: Separating the law from the lore. *Exceptionality, 23*, 192–209.

Zirkel, P.A. and Thomas, L.B. (2010). State laws and guidelines for implementing RTI. *Teaching Exceptional Children, 43* (1), 60–73.

4

POLITICS AND SCIENCE IN THE RTI TIME

On the Classification and Identification of Learning Disabilities

Dimitris Anastasiou

The Promise of RTI

The promise of the Response-to-Intervention (RTI) idea for achieving excellence and social justice in education is great, and the systemic approach to a national education system for prevention and early intervention to address learning difficulties and other risk factors before those evolve into learning disabilities (LD) is promising. A multi-tiered system of support (MTSS) that encompasses instructional quality, universal screening, data-based pre-referral procedures, progress monitoring, and the intensity of support in tiers of instructional needs can help schools and educators to be proactive. All of these ideas included in the RTI framework have had the potential to enrich the scope of special education in the US, which justifiably pursues an individualized approach to disabilities and special educational needs (Hornsby, 2015; Salend, 2011). RTI and MTSS, if properly applied, could offer an institutional and early response to categories of learning needs (e.g., garden-variety poor readers, English Language Learners). Systemic approaches can complement a distinct, flexible, and high-quality special education system (Fuchs, Fuchs, and Stecker, 2010; Kauffman, Anastasiou, and Maag, 2017). That said, the appreciation of the core ideas of RTI and MTSS must not succumb to unconditional love. Leaving aside legal and procedural issues such as considerable variability in RTI forms, I focus here on the issues related to RTI classification and identification.

RTI and LD: Science and Politics in a Love–Hate Relationship

20 years ago, Kavale and Forness (1998) identified a political dimension to the LD field. Indeed, politics, as form of advocacy, played an important and positive role in the creation of the LD field, and political forces have coupled science to the ongoing evolvement of the LD concept (Kauffman, Hallahan, and Lloyd, 1998; Kavale and Forness, 1998). Furthermore, the history of the contemporary LD field has been fraught with disagreements about issues such as the conceptualization, classification, definition, and operationalization of the LD construct, which has mixed up science and politics (Colker, 2013; Kavale and Forness, 1998; Fletcher, Lyon,

Fuchs, and Barnes, 2007; Fletcher, Stuebing, Morris, and Lyon, 2013). Although the role of politics in the LD field is unavoidable and legitimate (Kauffman, Hallahan, Lloyd, 1998; Sleeter, 1998), problems occur when politics and ideology come to the fore at the expense of analytical and rational thinking and decision-making (Kauffman, Hallahan, and Lloyd, 1998; Kavale and Forness, 1998).

Many things have changed in the LD field since the inception of RTI, but the role of politics remains crucial. Both politics and science have played a significant role in the adoption, formulation, and implementation of RTI policies. For example, in the early days of the RTI movement, the increase of more than 200% in the identification of students with LD fueled speculation about the overidentification and/or misidentification of these students and led the topic to become a highly economic and political issue (Lyon et al., 2001). Another issue concerned the reported patterns of over-representation of African-American and minority students in special education categories. The culprit was supposed to be the IQ discrepancy method of identification. However, the best evidence today has shown that other structural factors (such as socioeconomic disadvantages and school achievement), and not racial discrimination, explain better the seemingly higher percentages or over-representation of African-American and minority students in special education (Anastasiou, Morgan, Farkas, and Wiley, 2017; Kauffman and Anastasiou, in press; Morgan et al., 2016).

Apart from the scientific problems associated with IQ dependency and the validity of IQ tests, the aforementioned political issues played an important role in the advent of RTI (President's Commission on Excellence in Special Education, 2002; Vaughn, Linan-Thompson, and Hickman, 2003). Arguably, the adoption of RTI in the reauthorization of the Individuals with Disabilities Education Act (IDEA, 2004) and the push towards RTI in the IDEA Regulations (2006) were political selections that signified a political discontinuity over other alternative proposals for smoother transitions that would signify political business as usual. The alternative proposals included improvements in diagnostic specificity and sensitivity and reinforcement of the consistency of states' identification criteria, probably in combination with systemic RTI approaches (Bradley, Danielson, and Hallahan, 2002; Kavale and Forness, 2000; Kavale, Holdnack, and Mostert, 2005; Scruggs and Mastopieri, 2002). Moreover, "RTI politics" refers to an agenda-setting process that influences the salience of topics in the LD field. In general, part of the RTI movement seems to have been locked in a long love–hate relationship with the LD construct. In this relationship, there is space for both scientific inquiry and politics.

RTI: Functions of Science and Legitimation

It is true that part of the scientific LD community gave birth to the RTI movement. Scientific inquiry has also provided innovative techniques and intervention models for reading, math, and written language. Effective or promising innovative interventions, such as phonological processing training, the self-regulated strategy development (SRSD) model, and the collaborative strategic reading (CSR) model, are related to both the RTI framework and the LD field (Lyon and Weiser, 2013). Creating new "entities" such as intervention models, methods, techniques, tools, and technologies, and positively changing the reality of students with LD and those at risk serves as one of the two main functions of an applied scientific field, that of *instrumental function* (Hacking, 1983; Lewontin, 1992). Intervention success is a pragmatic criterion for evaluating philosophies, theories, models, concepts, policies, and practices (Bunge, 2012; Hacking, 1983).

A second but more complicated function of science is that of explanation through representations (e.g., philosophies, theories, models, and concepts). Scientific inquiry in LD tries to explain phenomena such as problems in reading, spelling, writing, and math, and includes the conceptualization and classification of those problems. Lewontin (1992) observed that even when scientists are not able to change the material mode of human existence, they constantly try to explain why things are the way they are.

Disconnections between the explanatory (i.e., concepts) and instrumental levels (i.e., diagnostic practice) can provide new insights. A disconnect between the conceptual and practice levels can be considered findings that readers display discrepancy between achievement and IQ (Ach_IQ discrepancy) and that poor readers without such a discrepancy indicated similar profiles for phonological processing, which is critical to reading and spelling development (Fletcher et al., 1994; Hoskyn and Swanson, 2000; Stanovich and Siegel, 1994; *cf.* Badian, 1994; Fuchs, Fuchs, Mathes, and Lipsey, 2000; Kudo, Lussier, and Swanson, 2015). Both low-IQ and IQ-discrepant readers, when IQ is outside the very low range associated with intellectual disabilities, showed a phonological-core deficit, despite their differences on measures of vocabulary and syntax (Hoskyn and Swanson, 2000). It is also possible that both groups benefit similarly from phonological skills training irrelevant of their IQ level (Stuebing, Barth, Molfese, Weiss, and Fletcher, 2009; Vellutino, Scanlon, Small, and Fanuele, 2006); however, the evidence for a similar treatment response is mixed (D. Fuchs and Young, 2006). The above findings undermine the *scientific legitimacy* of the Ach_IQ discrepancy and raise questions about its utility as an identification and classification method for reading (decoding) disability (Stanovich, 1991; 2000). Even for reading disability – not the entire LD umbrella – the evidence is far from incontrovertible. For example, Badian (1994) found that orthographic processing and rapid numbers-naming performance of children with an Ach_IQ discrepancy was lower than among age-matched garden-variety poor readers. Moreover, in a meta-analysis, Kudo, Lussier, and Swanson (2015) found that IQ and other cognitive processing measures (verbal working memory, visual–spatial memory, executive processing, and short-term memory) significantly contributed to group effect size differences between children with and without reading disability.

The *explanatory scientific function* is complicated, as it includes a great deal of representation (e.g., theory, models, and concepts) and semantic mediation, which is vulnerable to language ambiguity. Hence, the explanatory function is not immunized by the social and political beliefs of researchers, especially in the absence of adequate data and clear empirical evidence (French, 2007; Lewontin, 1992). Lewontin (1992) noted an overlap between the scientific explanation function and the *function of legitimation of a social practice* and/or political decision. As he stated, "[scientific] explanations of how the world really works serve another purpose, one in which there has been a remarkable success, irrespective of the practical truth of scientific claims. The purpose is that of legitimation" (p. 5). Scientific institutions and scientists are embedded into society; they are influenced by political and social forces and can act as legitimizing agents. In addition, science "is a human productive activity that takes time and money, and so is guided by and directed by those forces in the world that have control over money and time" (Lewontin, 1992, p. 3). Stanovich (2000, pp. 409–410) explicitly recognized that the undermined scientific legitimacy of the Ach_IQ discrepancy method of classifying and treating two groups with problems in basic reading (learners with Ach_IQ discrepancy and low achieving students without a discrepancy) did not automatically dictate a different identification practice. The decline of the Ach_IQ discrepancy method could have suggested either the need to search for a different method of classifying reading problems (Stanovich, 2000) or to improve the identification process for increasing diagnostic specificity and the consistency of state criteria (Kavale, Holdnack, and Mostert, 2005; Scruggs and Mastropieri, 2002). Moreover, the irrelevance of IQ to the method of identification or the definition of reading disability (Siegel,

1989) says nothing to us about the relevance of other cognitive processing measures to reading comprehension, writing, and math problems (Johnson, Humphrey, Mellard, Woods, and Swanson, 2010; Scruggs and Mastropieri, 2002). Even in basic reading, Callinan, Theiler and Cunningham (2015) provided some evidence that a cognitive deficit framework for three cognitive skills (phonological processing, naming speed, and verbal memory) could successfully predict and sort 77–82% of students into discrepancy-defined LD and low-achievement groups.

The legitimation of a practice or policy has not only conceptual implications but also economic and political consequences. It is linked to funding, which is a hard material reality in research activity. Indeed, federal agencies such as the Office of Special Education Programs (US Department of Education), the Institute of Educational Sciences (US Department of Education), and the National Institutes of Health (Department of Health and Human Services), and state education agencies have funded RTI research and guidance projects with millions of dollars over the last decade to promote RTI. Undoubtedly, this has influenced the orientation of research activities and productivity in the LD field towards an RTI and MTSS direction. In addition, it has affected the object of research at the intervention level; for example, a large portion of reading interventions are less oriented towards the needs of students with serious reading and spelling problems, sometimes in the name of prevention and early intervention.

Science and Legitimation in the "R" and "I" of RTI

Today, it seems that the potential of the available curricula and interventions based on phonics and phonological skills instruction to effect positive change in the educational landscape may have been overestimated in the 1990s and early 2000s. An unduly optimistic attitude towards the practical impact of instructional interventions was expanded from basic reading to include other learning areas (e.g., reading comprehension, spelling, writing, and math). Furthermore, the existence of some *treatment-resistors* or *non-responders* in Tier 2 or Tier 3 interventions, even in well-controlled and small-scale reading interventions with high treatment fidelity, shows that the expected "R" (response) in the RTI theory may have been overestimated across learning areas and age groups (Al Otaiba and Fuchs, 2006; Al Otaiba, Wagner, and Miller, 2014).

In addition, the limited research and rather disappointing findings on instructional changes in Tier 1 (general education) in the RTI time shows that the role of "I" (instruction quality and effectiveness) has been grossly underestimated in practice, despite its vital importance in RTI theory (Spear-Swerling and Cheesman, 2012). During the policy formulation period, Fuchs and Fuchs (2006) emphasized the theoretical connection of RTI policy with "Reading First, a major component of No Child Left Behind (2002), which requires schools to use scientific knowledge to guide [the] selection of core curricula" (p. 94). D. Fuchs and Deshler underline that, "All districts or states should establish a vetting process to help teachers and administrators distinguish good bets [that is, evidence-based instructional procedures and curricula] from bad ones" (2007, p. 132). However, they admitted that "few [districts and states] have thought seriously about how to establish such a vetting process" (p. 132) to select scientific core curricula. School-level studies with principals or teachers have also revealed that few things have changed in the "I" at Tier 1 regarding a core instruction towards evidence-based curricula and procedures (Printy and Wiliams, 2015; Regan, Berkeley, Hughes, and Brady, 2015). Spear-Swerling and Cheesman (2012) found that most general and special educators in their study were unfamiliar with research-based instructional approaches and interventions (such as multisensory structured language programs, fluency intervention programs, reciprocal teaching, and peer-assisted learning strategies), which were named in their questionnaire. Moreover, many study participants had particular difficulty with content knowledge, and especially with application knowledge, such as giving examples of appropriate words for various phonics activities. Their findings illustrated the real-world situation in the most well researched area, that of basic reading in the RTI time.

The above examples about the "R" and "I" issues are meant to clarify further the roles of the legitimation of RTI practices and the sociopolitical forces affecting law and policy decision making; these have filled the void of knowledge concerning the implementation of RTI on a large scale. Pogrow (1996) has raised concerns about poorly defined policies that cannot be made to work consistently. This is what has happened for both the "R" and "I" in RTI on the larger scale. The paradox of RTI research is that a rich body of literature supports it, yet it lacks large-scale studies apart from the one by Balu and colleagues (2015). We must recall that the starting point of the challenge to address the Ach_IQ discrepancy method was large-scale observations about the unreliability of state- and district-level identification criteria (Cone and Wilson, 1981; Finlan, 1992; Haight, Patriarca, and Burns, 2002; Reschly and Hosp, 2004). RTI must not escape this same large-scale yardstick.

Unless we realize the explanatory function of RTI at the factual-evidence level and its legitimation (ideological) function as a policy practice, it will be very difficult to map the difficulties and loopholes associated with RTI practice and to find a solution to the current "wicked problem" of LD classification. For Rittel and Webber (1973), a wicked problem is one whose definition is elusive and for which a definitive solution is lacking. Unlike well-defined problems, some wicked problems lead to societal problems.

Nevertheless, the recognition of problems with LD classification cannot justify the intense anti-scientific claims and trends in special education (Kauffman, Anastasiou, and Maag, 2017). Contrary to postmodern views, in a truly scientific inquiry, sociopolitical factors cannot arbitrarily create scientific "facts" irrelevant of evidence and external reality; this is an admirable aspect of the scientific method. However, sociopolitical factors can intervene in the orientation of scientific inquiry, influencing what science investigates and affecting the content of beliefs within a scientific community (Anastasiou and Kauffman, 2013). The remedy for the LD field is not less science, but rather more and better science. In other words, we need to foster fewer (pre)scientific ideologies or efforts toward policy legitimation by strengthening our levels of scientific inquiry and explanation.

On the Classification of Learning Disabilities

Scientific inquiry has raised several issues about the LD classification, and construct *per se.* However, past political and legal decisions, and current discourse in LD issues, have not been made only in the terrain of "pure science." Below is a brief consideration of four of the major issues in the classification of learning disabilities.

Dimensional versus Categorical Classification

Between 1970 and 1985 (the solidification period of the LD concept, according to Hallahan, Pullen, and Ward (2013)), there was a consensus that the concept of "specific reading disability" could be operationalized by the Ach_IQ discrepancy, and that there is a category of readers/learners separate from typically developing readers/learners and garden-variety poor readers/learners. Studies conducted by Rutter and Yule in the early 1970s might have played a role in promoting this view. Rutter and Yule (1975) identified a "hump" in the lower tail of the distribution of reading accuracy (and reading comprehension) scores, which led to the hypothesis of a distinct reading disability group, that is, a group of children "that constitutes more than just the lower end of a normal distribution in that its frequency significantly exceeds that predicted on statistical grounds" (p. 194). This group of readers was defined in IQ-discrepancy terms and represented a portion between about 3.5 and 6% for the distribution of reading accuracy scores. The IQ-discrepant group was also found to differ from a group of poor readers with a non-discrepant low IQs in terms of constructional difficulties, clumsiness, and educational prognosis. However, the "hump" finding at the lower end of the reading distribution was not replicated in other studies (Rodgers, 1983; Share, McGee, McKenzie, Williams, and Silva, 1987; Shaywitz, Escobar, Shaywitz, Fletcher, and Makuch, 1992). In addition, findings that readers with Ach_IQ discrepancy and poor readers had similar cognitive profiles regarding word recognition skills undermined the traditional view of a separate and distinct category of readers with a discrepant IQ (Fletcher et al., 1994; Hoskyn and Swanson, 2000; Stanovich and Siegel, 1994). This evidence was far from conclusive because other research has supported the view of a category of readers with discrepant IQs with a distinct cognitive profile (Badian, 1994; Fuchs et al., 2000; Kudo, Lussier, and Swanson, 2015). However, several questions have been raised about the social and educational utility of a categorical classification of reading difficulties featuring two categories of low-achieving readers, those with and those without a discrepant IQ (Elliott and Grigorenko, 2014; Fletcher, 2012; Fletcher et al., 2013).

That said, the negative findings about a bimodal distribution of reading ability with a distinct peak (hump) in the lower end could be a suggestive, but definitely not conclusive, criterion for the existence of a distinct group with reading disability and/or dyslexia (Meehl, 1995). In general, bimodality *per se* provides a weak criterion for testing categorical models (Beauchaine, 2007; Rutter and Yule, 1975). The absence of a bimodal distribution is inadequate evidence for inferring the absence of a latent category, such as reading disability and/or dyslexia. As O'Brien, Wolf and Lovett (2012) argued, "even if distributions are not bimodal, they can still contain two distinct subgroups" (p. 18), those with and those without cognitive and neurological deficits.

Outside the LD field, the main evidence for several mental disorders as discrete entities with putative specific causes comes from multiple statistical techniques used to determine whether these disorders show continuity or discontinuity with normality, or "typical behavior." Taxometric studies have been used in search of a taxon. A taxon is an underlying class, such as a disability category, distinct from typical behavioral functioning and other disabilities—part of a wider taxonomic system of disabilities. Taxometrics refers to a set of interrelated empirical procedures for discerning classes/categories/types from continua, identifying the latent structure of psychological constructs, and establishing defining indicators of identified categories (Beauchaine, 2007; Meehl, 1995, 2004; Meehl and Golden, 1982; Schmidt, Kotov, and Joiner, 2004). In physical medicine, the term "gold standard" has been used to describe any method of evaluation based on known discrete pathognomic characteristics and underlying causal mechanisms that are known to be excellent indicators of a true disease status (Faraone and Tsuang, 1994). The problem is that there is no gold standard criterion in LD for confirming the validity of symptoms as markers of a discrete latent trait. This is also true for *all* mind-related disabilities, mental disorders in behavioral psychopathology, and for some diseases in physical medicine (Beauchaine, 2007; Coghill and Sonuga-Barke, 2012). "In other words, there is no way of knowing a priori which indicators will mark a taxon, if one is present" (Beauchaine, 2007, p. 662). Indeed, the phenotypes in literacy difficulties are not well-defined. This is obvious if we compare the conceptualization of dyslexia as a single-dimensional reading disability versus a two-dimensional reading and spelling disability, as defined by the International Dyslexia Association (2002) and Lyon, Shaywitz, and Shaywitz (2003), or as a three-dimensional disability in the areas of reading decoding, reading fluency, and spelling, as defined by the

Diagnostic and Statistical Manual of Mental Disorders (*DSM*) (American Psychiatric Association, 2013, p. 67). It is noteworthy that a determination of the right phenotypes (a set of behavioral signs and criteria) is important in the search for a taxon in different forms of LD, and it can have practical implications for diagnosis and treatment. Given the lack of a gold standard criterion, a rational basis for inferring the existence of a taxonic entity could lie within the pattern of associations among the presumed phenotypic indicators (problematic behaviors) of the conjectured taxon (Meehl, 1995). Where a taxon is present, there should be an abrupt change in the strength of associations among manifest variables as a function of the severity of symptoms or low performance. Such abrupt changes in the structure of data (e.g., slopes, covariances, and eigenvalues) may indicate latent subgroups within a larger distribution of scores, and this can be consistent with a categorical model of a hypothetical disability (Beauchaine, 2007; Coghill and Sonuga-Barke, 2012; Meehl and Yonce, 1994, 1996; Ruscio, Haslam, and Ruscio, 2006). When there is no such abrupt change, a dimensional model would be favored provisionally, and when the results are ambiguous, judgment should be withheld (Coghill and Sonuga-Barke, 2012; Meehl, 2004; Ruscio, Haslam, and Ruscio, 2006). Given the relevant problem of a poorly defined phenotype, the examination of several patterns of variables is very important for investigating the existence of a taxon. In my view, the search for a taxon in the case of the latent construct of dyslexia should include at least the three variables of word-reading accuracy, reading fluency, and spelling. From a statistical, clinical, developmental, prognosis, and treatment perspective, spelling is an important indicator because: (1) it is highly correlated with word identification and reading fluency; (2) for clinicians and traditional wisdom in the field, severe spelling difficulties have been used as part of the signs pattern of dyslexia and a prognostic factor (Miles, 1993, 2006); (3) misspellings and reading fluency problems are apparent in well-treated adolescents and adults with dyslexia; (4) spelling scaffolds reading and vice versa; and (5) both skills are mutually reinforced by instruction and remediation. Given that reading is not inherently wired into the brain, we should also look at several cognitive and linguistic skills involved in reading acquisition when trying to find a taxon of dyslexia (Liu et al., 2017). It would be completely against scientific principles not to (Nicolson, 2016). A strict reading domain specificity and an assumed Fodorian *informational encapsulation* notion (Stanovich, 2000) does not precisely correspond to the richness of findings at cognitive and biological levels (neurobiological research includes neuroimaging research and genetics). Remediation is also imperative for embracing spelling interventions for the majority of children with dyslexia, and the findings from treatment responses show resistance to conventionally appropriate phonological processing (phonics and phonological awareness) training for a significant portion of young children with severe reading and spelling difficulties. In brief, the quest for a taxon in basic reading must have a broader phenotype as its starting point, embracing key literacy variables rather than a single-dimensional reading recognition phenotype. The first variable candidate outside the reading domain of word recognition and reading fluency for this taxonic search must be spelling.

To my knowledge, no one to date has undertaken the ambitious task of applying taxometrics to evaluate the taxonicity of LD constructs (e.g., dyslexia, reading comprehension disability, writing disability, and math disability) as a class separate from typically developing individuals' literacy or math skills. Nevertheless, O'Brien, Wolf and Lovett (2012), using taxometric classification techniques to examine heterogeneity within individuals with developmental dyslexia aged 6–8, found support for two separate subtypes of dyslexia, with and without phonological deficits. Moreover, the nonphonologically dyslexic subtype showed significant difficulty with naming speed and reading fluency.

Further taxonomic approaches are needed in the LD field, but it should be underlined that the dimensional issue is not unique to LD. In psychiatry, there has been a long-running discussion about dimensionality and whether the *DSM* and International Classification of Diseases diagnostic taxonomy systems should include a classification based on behavioral dimensions, rather than separate categories. Empirical evidence shows a categorical classification for some mental disorders, but not for others (Coghill and Sonuga-Barke, 2012). In addition, there is ongoing discussion about how to combine the categorical and dimensional perspectives, or how best to implement dimensional approaches within the used categorical classification systems (Läge, Egli, Riedel, Strauss, and Möller, 2011).

A Dysfunctional versus Severity Model

The possibility of a dimensional learning disability has precedents in physical medicine in the cases of hypertension and obesity. Both conditions are considered genuine health problems, but neither is taxonic in nature. In both cases, the dividing line between the normal and harmful states is controversial, and the cutoffs are somewhat arbitrary, as they "have changed over time as understanding of the risk associated with each has been refined" (Coghill and Sonuga-Barke, 2012, p. 484). However, the validity of obesity and hypertension concepts as genuine disorders and health problems is rarely questioned (Coghill and Sonuga-Barke, 2012; Ellis, 1984; Rayner and Pollatsek, 1989).

If we identify taxonic boundaries in LD forms, it would be imperative to specify as precisely as possible the diagnostic thresholds for their classification (Coghill and Sonuga-Barke, 2012). Due to the measurement error of psychometric tests, confidence intervals are also necessary for diagnoses (Fletcher et al., 2013; Miciak, Fletcher, and Stuebing, 2016). In addition, clear taxonic boundaries can imply an atypical dysfunctional model, rather than a deficit model at the brain or genetic levels.

To date, the scientific quest for a discrete reading disability category has failed to emerge, but a closer inspection of this limited research literature (Rodgers, 1983; Share et al., 1987; Shaywitz et al., 1992) shows two fundamental flaws in previous efforts: (a) the kind of research conducted has featured an unsophisticated focus on bimodality, which is unlikely to reveal a discrete category; however, a taxonic search would have the advantage of looking for abrupt changes across the continuum, thus avoiding arbitrary decisions related to cut scores, and (b) the putative markers for a taxon have been limited to reading recognition ability, without including spelling (which can reveal an encoding deficit) or a wider pattern of difficulties on which clinical practice has traditionally focused (Miles, 1993, 2006; Nicolson, 2016).

Due to the limited, unsatisfactory, and inconclusive research in this area, claims about the dimensionality of dyslexia (Fletcher, 2012; Fletcher et al., 2013; Miciak, Fletcher, and Stuebing, 2016) or other LD forms should be addressed with great caution. It is noteworthy that recent genetic research has shown a differential genetic etiology of reading difficulties as a function of IQ and a greater genetic influence for children with higher IQs (Wadsworth, Olson, and DeFries, 2010). Furthermore, reading disability is more genetically based in children from higher socioeconomic status (SES) families than among children from lower SES families (Friend, DeFries, and Olson, 2008). Peterson and Pennington (2015) commented, "together, these results suggest that advantaged children with strong cognitive abilities are likely to be good readers unless they have specific genetic risk factors for poor decoding. There are myriad reasons why other children will struggle with reading" (p. 285). Thus, behavioral genetic findings are not so compatible with the dimensional hypothesis of dyslexia, even when the disability is exclusively defined within the reading domain, ruling out spelling.

If some LD forms (e.g., reading comprehension disability) come to be proved dimensional, the continuous model of obesity and hypertension would be very useful. In developmental disabilities, intellectual disability provides another example. Intellectual disability (ID) is typically defined using a two-dimensional severity model, as it requires: (a) deficits in the intellectual functioning dimension and (b) deficits in the adaptive behavior dimension, as expressed in conceptual, social, and practical adaptive skills (American Association on Intellectual and Developmental Disabilities, 2002; American Psychiatric Association, 2013). Both the historical addition of the dimension of adaptive skills in the definition of ID and the shift towards more severe diagnostic thresholds can be informative for the LD field. The statistical problems and stability issues related to cutoff points and the intersection of two distributions as we move toward the lower end (e.g., from an IQ lower than 85 on a standardized measure to an IQ lower than 70), are likely to be greater. However, the decision to make the current upper IQ limit of "intellectual disability" has been made based on *social and conceptual grounds*. It is also quite probable that the correlation between word identification and spelling should be at a level similar to that of intellectual and adaptive skills. The history lessons of ID can offer valuable insight to the LD field.

In a severity (or deficit) model, diagnostic thresholds are somewhat arbitrary and controversial. In this case, decisions about diagnostic thresholds should serve students performing at or below the 10th percentile, the students who are the traditional focus of special education. That said, much of the intervention research on reading has focused on students who perform below the 25th percentile, while math research has focused on students performing below the 10th percentile (Geary, 2013). It is important to note that some estimate that the incidence of math disabilities may be as common as those of reading disabilities, about 7% (Geary, 2013). Focusing on a larger portion of low-achieving students may be convenient for researchers hoping to find significant gains, but it could be also an indicator of the mismatch between intervention research and the traditionally served LD population in special education, for whom the reported prevalence rates are 5–7% of the North American school-age population.

Heterogeneity of LD

Historically, reading disability has not been equated with the LD concept, which is a broader term covering a heterogeneous group of serious and harmful learning problems. There is also a consensus that LD is not the same as reading disability, even if reading disability has a high prevalence rate among the forms of LD. LD is a multifaceted concept that includes several types of learning problems in basic reading (accuracy and fluency), reading comprehension, mathematics (calculation and reasoning), and written expression (Bradley, Danielson, and Hallahan, 2002; Lyon et al., 2001; Mastropieri and Scruggs, 2005; Scruggs and Mastropieri, 2002). For decades, this has been clearly reflected in the federal definition of a learning disability (US Office of Education, 1968). Snowling and Hulme (2012) have argued that word recognition and reading comprehension represent different classes of reading disorders. In addition, O'Brien, Wolf, and Lovett (2012) found support for two separate subtypes of dyslexia, those with and those without phonological deficits.

Treatment Nonresponsiveness

In physical medicine, psychiatry, and special education, the process of making diagnoses is an inverse procedure. Based on signs and symptoms, we go backwards to identify a disease, disorder, and/or disability. In physical medicine we may go from the effects to underlying causal mechanisms, but in psychiatry and special education this is not feasible because there are no reliable biomarkers of mental disorders and disabilities; only behavioral and partially subjective symptoms are currently available (Bunge, 2013). Across disciplines, the diagnostic process aims to identify the causes of symptoms and, if possible, to suggest mitigations and solutions. This truth seems to have been forgotten in our field, which is stuck in the dead-end pursuit of trying to prove that the "rival" identification method has low reliability, diagnostic specificity, and sensitivity. Apparently, this is part of the scientific, intellectual game, but from a pragmatic point of view, when a method is dominant and rising, their advocates have the burden of providing evidence that it works well as a method for LD identification and underlying classification while also serving students with LD early and effectively on a large scale; after all, this was the great promise of RTI. In short, advocates of RTI as an identification method need to provide positive evidence, not just negative evidence.

The concept at the heart of the suggestion about using RTI as the main LD identification method is the "treatment nonresponsiveness" approach, which is a mutation of the initial notion of "treatment validity" within school practice. The latter refers to the frequent monitoring of responsiveness to instruction and the matching of instructional treatment to a student's responsiveness (Fuchs and Fuchs, 1998; Fuchs, Fuchs, and Speece, 2002; Gresham, 2002). At the outcome of this process, the "treatment-resistors" or "non-responders" in Tier 2 or 3 interventions can be eventually identified as having LD, after excluding other possible disabilities that can cause learning problems factors, such as sensory impairment and/or intellectual disability. However, in large-scale practice, the initial notion of "treatment validity" has mutated into a nonresponsiveness to interventions. That said, some have suggested using nonresponsiveness as the basic criterion for LD identification and special education eligibility, without using cognitive processing measures at all (Fletcher et al., 2013; Fletcher and Miciak, 2016; Miciak, Fletcher, and Stuebing, 2016).

Undoubtedly, monitoring students' progress through curriculum-based measurements (CBMs) and other formative tools, along with matching instruction-responsiveness, is a great idea, especially for the development of an effective intervention plan. This can also help with the diagnostic process by offering valuable data about learning rates and academic growth, evaluating treatment effectiveness, somehow informing instructional designing, and ruling out the possibility of an inadequate instruction (Fuchs and Fuchs, 1998; Fuchs et al., 2002). Nevertheless, there are several conceptual problems with the nonresponsiveness approach. Fuchs, Fuchs, and Speece (2002), when discussing the "treatment validity" notion, used the analogy of an endocrinologist who monitors a child's physical growth in terms of height at one point in time and growth velocity over time. We could add examples from physical medicine about the monitoring of medical parameters (risk factors) over time, such as a person's blood pressure, heart rate, and respiratory rate. There are also examples of the more specialized and intensive monitoring of people with diabetes mellitus suffering from high levels of blood glucose. Nonetheless, the emphasis on treatment monitoring and the purpose of diagnosis should not be confounded. Monitoring is basically about useful general outcome indicators for health or education, whereas diagnosis/identification is basically a quest for the causes behind the symptoms. That said, the problem is that a diagnostic causal model for LD and other disabilities is not feasible at present. Both the notion of a discrepancy between achievement and IQ, and the notion behind a "pattern of cognitive strengths and weaknesses" imitate the causal diagnostic models of other disciplines (not just medicine) by either looking for "unexpected underachievement" or searching for an imbalanced pattern that could imply a cognitive deficit or dysfunction. Both are also "top-down" approaches at great risk of being inaccurate or wrong.

To break the identification deadlock, LD diagnostic schemes need to be reconceptualized based on an integrated cognitive academic (ICA) model that includes assessments of academic skills, the cognitive processing skills necessary for intervention planning, taking nonresponsiveness and ecological factors into account. Several researchers (Berninger and May, 2011; Callinan, Theiler, and Cunningham 2015; D. Fuchs, Hale, and Kearns, 2011; Hale et al., 2010; Hale, Wycoff, and Fiorello, 2011) have argued for the importance of a cognitive processing perspective among LD identification practices. D. Fuchs, Hale, and Kearns (2011) suggested that "practitioners go beyond typical RTI assessment data documenting responsiveness/unresponsiveness to conduct comprehensive evaluations of these most difficult-to-teach students and to include in their evaluations carefully chosen cognitive measures" (p. 99).

In the ICA model, cognitive processing assessments are specific to an academic area of a suspected disability and selected for their evidence-based role in the development of an academic ability. Specifically, an ICA model, apart from the primary evaluation of an academic performance area, can include assessments of specific cognitive skills such as the following: (1) phonological processing, rapid automatized naming and verbal working memory for reading accuracy and fluency, (2) phonological processing, orthographic processing, and morphological awareness for spelling, (3) listening comprehension and verbal working memory for reading comprehension, (4) verbal working memory, executive functions (e.g., inhibition, planning, switching) and verbal fluency for writing, and (5) verbal, numerical and visuospatial working memory and executive functions (e.g., inhibition, rapid automatic switching) for arithmetic calculation and mathematics reasoning. This list is not intended to be exhaustive, but provides a minimum listing of cognitive assessments for which there is adequate evidence about cognitive and linguistic processes which may be involved in several LD forms (Altemeier, Abbott, and Berninger, 2008; Berninger and May, 2011; Bull and Kerry, 2014; Bull and Scerif, 2001; Filippetti and Richaud, 2015; Peng and D. Fuchs, 2016; Peng, Namkung, Barnes, and Sun, 2016; Toll et al., 2011). The list of cognitive assessments is open and can be updated in light of scientific advances and corroborated evidence. For example, improvements in the specificity of latent (theoretical) constructs, and better correspondence between behavioral tasks and latent constructs such as executive skills could increase the specificity, sensitivity and reliability of the ICA model.

There are several advantages to this framework: (1) An ICA model is focused on the academic problem. It is a bottom-up identification approach based on the best scientific evidence and knowledge accumulated in the LD field and can be updated and revised as needed; it is not another top-down model based on intuition or dubious non-experimental theoretical perspectives that "put the cart before the horse," and may include irrelevant cognitive skills. (2) It corresponds to the critical element of intrinsic dysfunction/deficit, which is an essential part of the federal definition of LD (Lyon et al., 2001). (3) It bridges the gap between science and diagnostic practice and is compatible with the importance of the cognitive level for both the scientific understanding and the treatment of LD and other developmental disorders (see, for further analysis, Frith, 1997; Morton, 2004). (4) It bridges the diagnostic gap between an individual child's academic behavior and the intervention method, providing educated guesses based on scientific knowledge and clinical experience about the next step in instructional planning. It also allows for progress monitoring to initiate modifications to instructional plans. (5) It is useful for consultations, because it can provide a link between the behavioral and cognitive levels and provide an evidence-based explanation of a child's difficulties that is valuable to teachers, parents, and children. (6) It directly connects the diagnostic practice with ongoing scientific inquiry in the field, thus it is useful for communication between researchers and practitioners. Further, it can facilitate a "virtuous circle" in which research informs practice, and practice informs research and theory (Snowling and Hulme, 2012). Finally, (7) it can have a face validity for policy makers and the public.

On the contrary, the nonresponsiveness approach to LD identification departs entirely from a diagnostic causal paradigm, because it negates *a priori* identification. Apparently, the "treatment validity" approach can identify "a failure to thrive" in an adequate way (Fuchs and Fuchs, 1998), but it cannot provide a research-informed reason for why a student performs as he or she does (Berninger and May, 2011). "A failure to thrive," as an assumed explanation, is a tautology, saying that the child fails simply because he or she has failed; this is not so useful for teachers, parents, and children. Some appear to reject any attempt to measure cognitive abilities; not just a pattern of strengths and weaknesses. For example, Fletcher and Miciak (2016) argued, "A cognitive deficit does not indicate 'why' a child has a learning problem; it is also possible that the learning problem causes the cognitive processing problem" (p. 3). This controversial claim downgrades much of the corroborated evidence for the role of phonology in reading provided by longitudinal studies and experimental or quasi-experimental interventional studies. For example, it overlooks "evidence from longitudinal studies showing that poor phonological (and more generally language) skills predict poor reading skills several years ahead, well before reading instruction" (Ramus, 2014, p. 3372).

By exclusively assessing and monitoring academic performance, one cannot explain why an intervention plan has failed. By watching a child fail without conducting relevant cognitive assessments, one cannot have any real idea about the instructional components needed for the next step of the intervention process. In essence, after a student fails to achieve an appropriate level of performance and/or rate of improvement, teachers are totally disarmed, and the next intervention step – probably toward special education – becomes a blind date. In this case, instructional planning can be based only on teachers' experience and professional wisdom, both of which are valuable, yet not enough. Moreover, the narrow "nonresponsiveness" approach seems to support *de facto* the idea that the degree of intervention intensity is the only reason behind nonresponsiveness, disregarding the larger strategic issues related to the kind, quality, and appropriateness of an intervention plan and instructions. To conclude, the nonresponsiveness approach, as a mutated version of the "treatment validity" notion, deemphasizes the quest for educated guesses in the presence of a LD in favor of solely using nonresponsiveness as the basic criterion for determining special education eligibility (Ihori and Olvera, 2015). It represents an unfruitful interaction among the LD concept, scientific inquiry, diagnostic practice, and instructional planning.

The Elephant in the Room: Politics in LD Classification

Politics sometimes comes to the fore at the expense of careful analytical thinking in the discourse on LD classification issues. The "elephant in the room" (politics) should not be overlooked, as it constantly operates and influences these issues. In the missing links of scientific inquiry and contradicted findings, the management of the four issues addressed in the previous section is problematic. It is marked by an unfruitful discourse at the intersection of ideology, politics, and science that has the following characteristics:

Narrow Focus

The *narrowness of the terrain and scope of the discussion* is a common problem in the field. As Ramus (2014) observed, it is quite odd that categorical versus dimensional classification is presented as a problem unique to the LD construct. Needless to say, this is a central scientific matter surrounding *all* mental disorders and mind-related disabilities. Thus, the current state of evidence shows that not all classified mental disorders represent a true taxon. In their review, Coghill and Sonuga-Barke (2012) summarized empirical findings from taxometric studies and found that the evidence supports a categorical classification for disorders such as schizotypy (observable risk factors for schizophrenia), melancholic/endogenous depression, mixed anxiety depression disorder, autism spectrum disorder (across the spectrum), anxiety sensitivity, and antisocial behavior. Instead, the evidence supports a latent dimensional structure, rather than a categorical structure for disorders such as attention deficit hyperactivity disorder (ADHD), post-traumatic stress disorder, and non-melancholic depression (Coghill and Sonuga-Barke, 2012). It seems that most disorders probably reflect behavioral extremes along continuously distributed traits; identifying those that are categorically distributed is important for clinical science (Beauchaine, 2007).

Arguments against LD constructs are sometimes based on misleading and sweeping statements about the construct validity of LD as separate distinct categories across all areas of the LD umbrella. However, taxometric investigations in the field to date have been very limited. Given the knowns and unknowns in the field, an *absence of evidence* due to a lack of evidence should not be equated with the *evidence of absence* (negative evidence) that can only be documented via strong and replicating evidence from rigorous studies (Ramus, 2014).

Overstatements

There is ample and compelling evidence for the role of phonological processing in reading and spelling acquisition provided from several sources across several alphabetic (transparent or opaque) orthographies. The phonological theory remains the most compelling explanation for reading (decoding) and spelling (encoding) problems and explains the role of phonology in reading and spelling, which is one of most important findings in the contemporary psycho-educational research (Pennington, 2012; Stanovich, 2000). In addition, it is important to keep in mind that phonological processing is a set of teachable skills that act as self-teaching mechanism and enables learners to acquire greater reading proficiency levels independently and to enlarge their orthographic lexicons (Share, 1995, 1999).

Although one can give fair credit to the phonological theory of reading problems, we should be cautious about related overstatements used as political weapons for the radical reconceptualization of LD, usually ahead of IDEA reauthorizations. In a policy report that reflected the euphoria of phonological-core theory around the turn of the century, Lyon and colleagues (2001) stated, "We estimate that the number of children who are typically identified as poor readers and served through either special education or compensatory education programs could be reduced by up to 70 percent through early identification and prevention programs" (p. 260). Consider also the following statement, "I recommend operating school-wide RTI models without having any separate special education classrooms" (Sailor, 2009, p. 123). Sailor also estimated that the changes in LD identification "weakened the disability frame as a basis for education policy" (2009, p. 30).

Progress has occurred across research specialties over the last two decades, which shows that, although the deficit in the phonological-core theory of dyslexia is prominent, a multiple deficit hypothesis, including subtle auditory and visual deficits, does a better job of explaining the accumulated evidence across specialties and may constitute a better framework for the treatment of reading and spelling problems (Kibby, Lee, and Dyer, 2014; Pennington, 2012; Ramus, 2004; Ramus et al., 2003). That said, a basic problem with the theories about subtle deficits in auditory, visual, or motor brain-related areas is that they cannot easily and/or effectively be translated into effective practices (Snowling and Hulme, 2012; Strong et al., 2011).

Despite the optimistic political predictions around the turn of the century, a large-scale federal study that compared the outcomes for students "just below" and "just above" the cut-off point of eligibility for tiered intervention failed to provide evidence for gains in reading interventions in the RTI context (Balu et al., 2015). Specifically, the researchers stated, "For those students just below the school-determined eligibility cut point in Grade 1, assignment to receive reading interventions did not improve reading outcomes; it produced negative impacts" (Balu et al., 2015, p. 1).

Balu and colleagues (2015) underlined the great difference between small-scale controlled studies and large-scale studies of RTI. They noted, "in contrast to more controlled studies of RTI that have relied on non-classroom teaching staff to provide intervention services, the current study included intervention services provided by whoever was designated by schools to provide these services" (p. 76). In my view, the evidence for the failure of RTI does not indicate a failure of phonological processing training (including phonics) and other evidence-based practices, but instead indicates the difficulty of implementing a poorly defined reform like RTI on a large scale. Gerber (2005) has warned, "research on practice is not the same as practice," because "research by its nature seeks to control unwanted sources of variance" (p. 521). Pogrow (1996), too, argued that "large-scale change reflects properties that are often diametrically opposed to those in effect in small-scale research" (p. 659). We have already discussed the mutation of the "treatment validity" notion into a nonresponsiveness approach in which the essential and most demanding characteristics (e.g., the kinds and quality of instructional programs and CBMs) have been faded out and only the formal characteristics, such as the intensity of the degree of interventions, have remained. This can make policy ideas lose their initial meaning, while they keep their form.

Furthermore, we should be cautious about exaggerated statements on the power of phonological processing training or other evidence-based practices to change radically and positively the educational landscape. In the real world of teaching, there are serious implementation issues, and quality instruction in Tier 1 has been grossly neglected on the large scale (Spear-Swerling and Cheesman, 2012). Not surprisingly, Balu and colleagues (2015) identified the following plausible factors for the negative impacts on RTI: "(1) false or incorrect identification of students for intervention, (2) mismatch between reading intervention and the instructional needs of students near the cut point, and (3) poor alignment between reading intervention and core reading instruction" (p. 17).

Shrinking the Content of the LD Domain

The notion of LD refers to an umbrella of heterogeneous conditions, despite adequate intelligence, opportunity, and instruction. As outlined in the federal definition, LD is comprised of disabilities in any one or a combination of seven skill areas: (1) basic reading (decoding and fluency), (2) reading comprehension, (3) written expression, (4) arithmetic calculations, (5) mathematics reasoning, (6) listening, and (7) speaking. There is little evidence to indicate that the causal mechanisms are the same across these LD forms, so treating them as separate disorders makes sense (Lyon et al., 2001).

Given the heterogeneity of LD, the sweeping replacement of the Ach_IQ discrepancy method of identification in the LD areas of reading comprehension, writing, and mathematics, apart from basic reading disability, was never justified on serious research grounds. We have already noted that RTI policy was based on a dominant "policy reading model," which arbitrarily extended into areas that arguably require higher-order thinking skills. In this "reading policy model," concepts and inferences from the reading (decoding) disability area tend to be applied to the whole LD domain (Mastropieri and Scruggs, 2005; Scruggs and Mastropieri, 2002).

Policy-oriented reports and manuals (e.g., American Psychiatric Association, 2000; Lyon et al., 2001) and authors (e.g., Fletcher et al., 2007) have taken for granted that about 80–90% of students with LD demonstrate significant difficulty with reading. However, there is little empirical research to support this contention. A well-cited source for this claim is Lerner (1989). Indeed, she reported, "In fact, for about 80 percent of learning disabled students, the primary academic problem is in reading" (p. 328), but no study was cited to support her claim. Evidence from two surveys (Kavale and Reese, 1992; Kirk and Elkins, 1975) shows a more complicated picture. For example, Kirk and Elkins (1975) reported, "80 percent of the emphasis was on remedial reading. . .followed by arithmetic (52.5%), then by spelling (45%), and then by language (43.5%)" (p. 34), not that 80% of LD students had a reading disability. In addition, they reported that reading as primary emphasis was 61.5%, arithmetic 29%, and language and spelling 23% and 24%, respectively. Similarly, Kavale and Reese (1992) found that 66% of the reasons for referrals in academic areas among Iowa's LD population were tied to reading, followed by math (35%), writing (25%) language (17%), and spelling (16%). They also found that reading (73%) was the primary focus area, followed by math (43%), written expression (38%), spelling (17%), and oral expression (9%). In addition, Mayes and Calhoun's (2007) clinical sample found that the most common LD type was written expression either alone (50%), or in combination with other LD areas (42%).

All in all, the evidence about the prevalence of different LD types is far from inconclusive, yet the bigger picture of academic difficulties seems to be more complicated than the typical reported percentage of 80–90% for either reading difficulties and/or reading disabilities. Rigorous studies about the frequency and coexistence of LD types are still needed. Shrinking the content of LD to a single area of basic reading is not only a conceptual but also a research, and policy problem. For example, math and written expression problems have long been neglected in LD research (Mayes and Calhoun, 2007). Any shrinkage of the LD domain when designing LD policies is misleading. Finally, a policy model that frames policy for the whole LD domain based only on reading terms can have detrimental consequences for practice.

Eroding the "D" in the LD Concept

If a LD construct (e.g., dyslexia) is distributed discretely, the identification of the proper diagnostic thresholds can be important for our understanding of its etiology and can advance prevention and intervention programs (Beauchaine, 2007). However, if some LD forms are identified as dimensional, the artificially designated diagnostic thresholds should be enough low to correspond to atypical, harmful, and deficit/dysfunctional elements of the concept. Despite this, some scholars have suggested employing low thresholds (corresponding to high cut-off scores) for LD identification such as achievement or instructional response below the 25th percentile (Fletcher et al., 2013; Miciak, Fletcher, and Stuebing, 2016). In my view, such a classification undermines the concept of disability within the LD field. In addition, if we take higher cut-off points (e.g., below the 25th percentile), then the number of false positives would increase. As Kauffman and Lloyd (2017) argued, when "the criterion for identification is moved from more extreme or obvious to less extreme or obvious cases, a greater number of cases will be included, and more cases will be found at the margins of the cut point." Just because when we move closer to the central tendency of a distribution of scores, we are going to have a greater number of students (Kauffman and Lloyd, 2017).

Like all developmental disabilities, LD encompasses atypical and harmful conditions that constitute predicaments for learners. For example, a reading disability and/or dyslexia is potentially harmful because of the pervasiveness of reading and writing in our contemporary world. Such a severe restriction of one's reading and writing ability can be traumatic and affect individuals throughout their lives, even though the impact will depend on the severity of the condition, the person's resilience, and the effectiveness of remediation efforts.

The "atypical" refers to a statistical distribution of varied abilities, and specifically to a relatively low proportion of the school-age population (5–7% according to reported prevalence rates) who face such a condition in a given time period. "Harmfulness" is caused either by a mind-related dysfunction or deficit. A deficit and/or dysfunction can refer to factually scientific concepts compatible with neurobiological and genetic evidence (Wakefield, 2007). At present, it is uncertain whether the several LD forms have to do with a dysfunction relating to a categorical classification, or with a deficit relating to a dimensional classification. In the case of dyslexia, the deficit or dysfunction element may refer to an underlying causal mechanism that restricts a person's ability to read and spell. Both the atypical and deficit/dysfunction elements could be observed and be measurable. The predicament dimension in the LD is experiential-subjective in nature, and the harmful element refers to intersubjective judgments relative to cultural and social values, including the social importance of literacy in our print-rich societies. The four conceptual elements of dysfunction/deficit, atypical, harmful, and predicament can apply to other developmental disabilities (intellectual disabilities, speech and language impairments, autism spectrum disorders, ADHD) and to emotional or behavioral disorders (EBD) as well. This brief delineation here is based on previous multidimensional analyses of the disability concept (Anastasiou and Kauffman, 2011, 2012, 2013; Anastasiou, Kauffman, and Michail, 2016; Wakefield, 2007).

Based on the notions outlined above, Miciak, Fletcher, and Stuebing (2016) suggest shifting "the identification process towards an evaluation of risk and/or probability of academic difficulty, rather than an actuarial process aimed at identifying the right children" (p. 425); this seems to be incompatible with the disability concept itself. Lowering the diagnostic thresholds required for someone to be identified as having a particular LD can fundamentally erode a core aspect of the disability concept in LD.

Concluding Remarks

Without disregarding the scientific roots of several issues in the LD field, the dominant discourse on LD identification and underlying classification includes problematic political characteristics that can affect policy decision-making in preparation for the next IDEA reauthorization bill. The main challenge to a scientifically viable classification of LD is a research program aimed at showing whether classification criteria can separate LD types from a non-disability, a specific LD type from other LD forms (heterogeneity), and provide a scientific explanation about key behavioral signs (e.g., significant deficits in reading decoding, reading fluency, spelling, reading comprehension, writing, arithmetic calculations, and mathematics reasoning) for each type based on sound scientific evidence. Diagnostic specificity, sensitivity, and reliability are related issues, but the pursuit of a valid LD classification should have priority. In this quest, it is imperative that we avoid eroding the "D" element of LD.

Softening the disability element and shifting the focus of attention from the "hard" disability issues to "softer" issues appears to be a general trend in contemporary special education (e.g., EBD and bullying) (Kauffman, 2015). This neutralizing trend may have sociopolitical influences and practical implications. Against cynical and pessimistic views, special education, as a field, should continue to serve primarily the lowest portion of school learners, recognizing that even in the most ideal societies, disabilities are unavoidable (Anastasiou and Kauffman, 2013). We should persevere in identifying early and reliably those students with disabilities, serving primarily the "weakest of the weak." Special education research must be reoriented towards effective treatments for learners with serious literacy and math difficulties whose performance is in the very lowest (5–10%) percentiles. In addition, we need an ICA model that includes key academic and cognitive assessments for each disability area and that constitutes a bottom-up, self-corrected approach based on the best evidence and open to scientific knowledge accumulation.

The LD field, like the broader special education field, seems to be at a crossroads (Kauffman, Anastasiou, and Maag, 2017). We should enhance science and restrict the role of post-evidence politics. Carnap's (1950) principle of total evidence requires that all relevant information should be included in our concepts, theories, and models. This is also critical for the viability and development of the LD field. Avoiding conceptual conservatism, a "refurbishment without rejection" attitude (Chimisso, 2015) toward elements of the RTI framework and LD concepts is also necessary. In the RTI and/or MTSS time, special education should be the third tier with a discrete and visible functional role serving students with disabilities. A second tier should also have a distinct role serving low-achieving students at risk for developing disabilities. More than three tiers (four or an indefinite number of tiers) without *specific* functional roles are conceptually problematic, systemically chaotic, and convey political expediencies (Fuchs et al., 2010).

The "refurbishment without rejection" approach can also apply to the LD construct. As Fletcher, Stuebing, Morris, and Lyon (2013) have argued, oral expression and listening comprehension are not areas of academic achievement and should be addressed as impairments of oral language. There is no conceptual or empirical reason to dictate that these two domains be part of the LD construct (Fletcher et al., 2007, 2013). However, we should also acknowledge that evidence indicates that listening comprehension is highly correlated with reading comprehension, and thus may be a useful assessment component when evaluating a suspected LD in reading comprehension (Christopher et al., 2016; Hoover and Gough, 1990; Pennington and Bishop, 2009; Snowling and Hulme, 2012).[1]

Note

1. I am grateful to Achilles N. Bardos and James M. Kauffman for reading earlier drafts of the manuscript and offering valuable comments and suggestions.

References

Al Otaiba, S. and Fuchs, D. (2006). Who are the young children for whom best practices in reading are ineffective? An experimental and longitudinal study. *Journal of Learning Disabilities, 39,* 414–431.

Al Otaiba, S., Wagner, R. K., and Miller, B. (2014). Waiting to fail redux: Understanding response to intervention. *Learning Disability Quarterly, 37,* 129–133. doi: 10.1177/0731948714525622.

Altemeier, L. E., Abbott, L. A., and Berninger, V. W. (2008). Executive functions for reading and writing in typical literacy development and dyslexia. *Journal of Clinical and Experimental Neuropsychology, 30,* 588–606. doi: 10.1080/13803390701562818.

American Psychiatric Association. (2000). *Diagnostic and statistical manual of mental disorders,* 4th ed., Text Revision. Washington, DC: Author.

American Psychiatric Association. (2013). *Diagnostic and statistical manual of mental disorders,* 5th ed. Washington, DC: Author.

Anastasiou, D. and Kauffman, J. M. (2011). A social constructionist approach to disability: Implications for special education. *Exceptional Children, 77,* 367–384. doi: 10.1177/001440291107700307.

Anastasiou, D. and Kauffman, J. M. (2012). Disability as cultural difference. *Remedial and Special Education, 33,* 139–149. doi: 10.1177/0741932510383163.

Anastasiou, D. and Kauffman, J. M. (2013). The social model of disability: Dichotomy between impairment and disability. *Journal of Medicine and Philosophy*, *38*, 441–459. doi: 10.1093/jmp/jht026.

Anastasiou, D., Kauffman, J. M., and Michail, D. (2016). Disability in multicultural theory: Conceptual and social justice issues. *Journal of Disability Policy Studies*, *27*, 3–12. doi: 10.1177/1044207314558595.

Anastasiou, D., Morgan, P. L., Farkas, G., and Wiley, A. L. (2017). Minority disproportionate representation in special education: Politics and evidence, issues and implications. In J. M. Kauffman, D. P. Hallahan, and P. C. Pullen (Eds.), *Handbook of special education* (2nd ed.) (pp. 897–910). New York: Routledge.

Badian, N. A. (1994). Do dyslexic and other poor readers differ in reading-related cognitive skills? *Reading and Writing: An Interdisciplinary Journal*, *6*, 45–63. doi: 10.1007/BF01027277.

Balu, R., Zhu, P. Doolittle, F., Schiller, E., Jenkins, J., and Gersten, G. (2015, November). Evaluation of Response to Intervention Practices for Elementary School Reading (NCEE 2016–4000). Washington, DC: National Center for Education Evaluation and Regional Assistance. Institute of Education Sciences, U.S. Department of Education.

Batsche, G., Elliott, J., Graden, J., Grimes, J., Kovaleski, J., Prasse, D., Reschly, D., Schrag, J., and Tilly III, W.D. (2006). *Response to intervention policy considerations and implementation.* Alexandria, VA: National Association of State Directors of Special Education.

Beauchaine, T. P. (2007). Brief taxometrics primer. *Journal of Clinical Child and Adolescent Psychology*, *36*, 654–676. doi: 10.1080/15374410701662840.

Berninger, V. W. and May, M. O. (2011). Evidence-based diagnosis and treatment for specific learning disabilities involving impairments in written and/or oral language. *Journal of Learning Disabilities*, *44*, 167–183. doi: 10.1177/0022219410391189.

Bradley, R., Danielson, L., and Hallahan, D. P. (2002). Specific learning disabilities: Building consensus for identification and classification. In Bradley, R., Danielson, L., and Hallahan, D. P. (Eds.), *Identification of learning disabilities: Research to practice* (pp. 791–804). Mahwah, NJ: Lawrence Erlbaum.

Bull, R. and Kerry L. (2014). Executive functioning and mathematics achievement. *Child Development Perspectives*, *8*, 36–41. doi: 10.1111/cdep.12059.

Bull, R. and Scerif, G. (2001). Executive functioning as a predictor of children's mathematics ability: Inhibition, switching, and working memory. *Developmental Neuropsychology*, *19*, 273–293. doi: 10.1207/S15326942DN1903_3.

Bunge, M. (2012). *Evaluating philosophies*. Dordrecht: Springer.

Bunge, M. (2013). *Medical philosophy: Conceptual issues in medicine*. Hackensack, NJ: World Scientific.

Callinan, S., Theiler, S., and Cunningham, E. (2015). Identifying learning disabilities through a cognitive deficit framework: Can verbal memory deficits explain similarities between learning disabled and low achievement students? *Journal of Learning Disabilities*, *48*, 271–280. doi: 10.1177/0022219413497587.

Carnap, R. (1950). *Logical foundations of probability*. Chicago, IL: University of Chicago Press.

Christopher, M. E., Keenan, J. M., Hulslander, J., DeFries, J. C., Miyake, A., Wadsworth S. J., Willcutt, E., Pennington, B., and Olson, R. K. (2016). The genetic and environmental etiologies of the relations between cognitive skills and components of reading ability. *Journal of Experimental Psychology: General*, *145*(4), 451–66. doi: 10.1037/xge0000146.

Chimisso, C. (2015). Narrative and epistemology: Georges Canguilhem's concept of scientific ideology. *Studies in History and Philosophy of Science*, *4*, 64–73. doi: 10.1016/j.shpsa.2015.08.016.

Coghill, D. and Sonuga-Barke, E. J. S. (2012). Annual research review: Categories versus dimensions in the classification and conceptualisation of child and adolescent mental disorders – implications of recent empirical study. *Journal of Child Psychology and Psychiatry*, *53*, 469–489. doi:10.1111/j.1469-7610.2011.02511.x.

Colker, R. (2013). Politics trump science: The collision between No Child Left Behind and the Individuals with Disabilities Education Act. *Journal of Law and Education*, *42*, 585–631.

Cone, T. E. and Wilson, L. R. (1981). Quantifying a severe discrepancy: A critical analysis. *Learning Disability Quarterly*, *4*, 358–379. doi: 10.2307/1510737.

Elliot, J. G. and Grigorenko, E. L. (2014). *The dyslexia debate*. New York: Cambridge University Press.

Ellis, A. (1984). *Reading, writing and dyslexia: A cognitive analysis*. London: Lawrence Erlbam.

Faraone, S. V. and Tsuang, M. T. (1994). Measuring diagnostic accuracy in the absence of a "gold standard." *The American Journal of Psychiatry*, *151*, 650–657. doi: 10.1176/ajp.151.5.650.

Filippetti, V. A. and Richaud, M. C. (2015). Do executive functions predict written composition? Effects beyond age, verbal intelligence and reading comprehension. *Acta Neuropsychologica*, *13*, 331–349. doi:10.5604/17307503.1187493.

Finlan, T. G. (1992). Do state methods of quantifying a severe discrepancy result in fewer students with learning disabilities? *Learning Disability Quarterly, 15*, 129–135. doi: 10.2307/1511014.

Fletcher, J. M. (2012). Classification and identification of learning disabilities. In B. Y. L. Wong and D. L. Butler (Eds.), *Learning about learning disabilities* (4th ed., pp. 1–25). Amsterdam: Elsevier Academic Press.

Fletcher, J. M., Lyon, G. R., Fuchs, L. S. and Barnes, M. A. (2007). *Learning disabilities: From identification to intervention.* New York, NY: Guilford Press.

Fletcher, J. M. and Miciak, J. (2016). Comprehensive cognitive assessments are not necessary for the identification and treatment of learning disabilities. *Archives of Clinical Neuropsychology* Advance online publication, 1–6.

Fletcher, J. M., Shaywitz, S. E., Shankweiler, D., Katz, L., Liberman, I., Stuebing, K., Francis, D. J., Fowler, A., and Shaywitz, B. A. (1994). Cognitive profiles of reading disability: Comparisons of discrepancy and low achievement definitions. *Journal of Educational Psychology, 86*, 6–23. doi: 10.1037/0022-0663.86.1.6.

Fletcher, J. M., Stuebing, K. K., Morris, R. D., and Lyon, G. R. (2013). Classification and definition of learning disabilities: A hybrid model. In H. L. Swanson and K. Harris (Eds.), *Handbook of learning disabilities* (2nd ed., pp. 33–50). New York: Guilford Press.

Friend, A., DeFries, J. C., and Olson, R. K. (2008). Parental education moderates genetic influences on reading disability. *Psychological Science, 11*, 1124–1130. doi: 10.1111/j.1467-9280.2008.02213.x.

Frith, U. (1997). Brain, mind and behaviour in dyslexia. In C. Hulme and M. Snowling (Eds.), *Dyslexia: Biology, Cognition and intervention* (pp. 1–19). London: Whurr.

Fuchs, D. and Deshler, D. D. (2007). What we need to know about responsiveness to intervention (and shouldn't be afraid to ask). *Learning Disabilities Research & Practice, 22*(2), 129–136.

Fuchs, D. and Fuchs, L.S. (2016). Responsiveness-to-intervention: A "systems" approach to adaptive instruction. *Theory into Practice, 55*, 225–233. doi: 10.1080/00405841.2016.1184536.

Fuchs, D., Fuchs, L. S., Mathes, P. G. and Lipsey, M. W. (2000). Reading differences between low-achieving students with and without learning disabilities: A meta-analysis. In R. Gersten, E. P. Schiller, and S. Vaughn (Eds.). *Contemporary special education research* (pp. 81–104). Mahwah, NJ: Erlbaum.

Fuchs, D., Fuchs, L. S., and Stecker, P. M. (2010). The "blurring" of special education in a new continuum of general education placements and services. *Exceptional Children, 76*, 301–323. doi.org/10.1177/001440291007600304.

Fuchs, D., Hale, J. B., and Kearns, D. M. (2011). On the importance of a cognitive processing perspective: An introduction. *Journal of Learning Disabilities, 44*, 99–104. doi: 10.1177/0022219411400019.

Fuchs, D. and Young, C. L. (2006). On the irrelevance of intelligence in predicting responsiveness to reading instruction. *Exceptional Children, 73*, 8–30.

Fuchs, L. S. and Fuchs, D. (2002). Treatment validity: A unifying construct for reconceptualizing the identification of learning disabilities. *Learning Disabilities Research & Practice, 13*, 204–219.

Fuchs, L. S. and Fuchs, D. (2006). Introduction to response to intervention. *Reading Research Quarterly, 41*, 93–99.

Fuchs, L. S., Fuchs, D., and Speece, D. L. (2002). Treatment validity as a unifying construct for identifying learning disabilities. *Learning Disability Quarterly, 25*, 33–45. doi: 10.2307/1511189.

Geary, D. C. (2013). Learning disabilities in mathematics: Recent advances. In H. L. Swanson, K. R. Harris, and S. Graham (Eds.), *Handbook of learning disabilities* (2nd ed., pp. 239–255). New York: The Guilford Press.

Gerber, M. M. (2005). Teachers are still the test: Limitations of response to instruction strategies for identifying children with learning disabilities. *Journal of Learning Disabilities, 38*, 516–523. doi: 10.1177/00222194050380060701.

Gresham, F. M. (2002). Responsiveness to intervention: An alternative approach to the identification of learning disabilities. In R. Bradley, L. Danielson, and D. Hallahan (Eds.), *Identification of learning disabilities: Research to practice* (pp. 467–519). Mahwah, NJ: Lawrence Erlbaum.

Hacking, I. (1983). *Representing and intervening: Introductory topics in the philosophy of natural science.* New York: Cambridge University Press.

Haight, S. L., Patriarca, L. A., and Burns, M. K. (2002). A statewide analysis of eligibility criteria and procedures for determining learning disabilities. *Learning Disabilities: A Multidisciplinary Journal, 11*, 39–46.

Hale, J. B., Wycoff, K. L., and Fiorello, C. A. (2011). RTI and cognitive hypothesis testing for identification and intervention of specific learning disabilities: The best of both worlds. In D. P.

Flanagan, and V. C. Alfonso (Eds.), *Essentials of specific learning disability identification* (pp. 173–202). Hoboken, NJ: Wiley.

Hale, J., Alfonso, V., Berninger, V., Bracken, B., Christo, C., Clark, E., and Yalof, J. (2010). Critical issues in response-to-intervention, comprehensive evaluation, and specific learning disabilities identification and intervention: An expert white paper consensus. *Learning Disability Quarterly, 33,* 223–236. doi: 10.1177/073194871003300310.

Hallahan, D., Pullen, P. C., and Ward, D. (2013). *A brief history of the field of learning disabilities.* In H. L. Swanson, K. R. Harris and S. Graham, *Handbook of learning disabilities* (2nd ed., pp. 15–32). New York: The Guilford Press.

Hoover, W. A. and Gough, P. B. (1990). The simple view of reading. *Reading and Writing: An Interdisciplinary Journal, 2,* 127–160. doi:10.1007/BF00401799.

Hornsby, G. (2015). Inclusive special education: Development of a new theory for the education of children with special educational needs and disabilities. *British Journal of Special Education, 42,* 234–256. doi: 10.1111/1467-8578.12101.

Hoskyn, M. and Swanson, H. L. (2000). Cognitive processing of low achievers and children with reading disabilities: A selective meta-analytic review of the published literature. *School Psychology Review, 29,* 102–119.

Ihori, D. and Olvera, P. (2015). Discrepancies, responses, and patterns: selecting a method of assessment for specific learning disabilities. *Contemporary School Psychology, 19,* 1–11. doi:10.1007/s40688-014-0042-6.

Individuals with Disabilities Education Act Regulations, 34 C.F.R. § 300 *et seq.*

Johnson, E. S., Humphrey, M., Mellard, D. F., Woods, K., and Swanson, H. L. (2010). Cognitive processing deficits and students with specific learning disabilities: A selective meta-analysis of the literature. *Learning Disability Quarterly, 33,* 3–18.

Kauffman, J. M. (2015). The "B" in EBD is not just for bullying. *Journal of Research in Special Educational Needs, 15,* 167–175. doi: 10.1111/1471-3802.12102.

Kauffman, J. M. and Anastasiou, D. (in press). On cultural politics in special education: Is much of it justifiable? *Journal of Disability Policy Studies.*

Kauffman, J. M., Anastasiou, D., and Maag, J. W. (2017). Special education at the crossroads: A crisis of identity and the need for a scientific reconstruction. *Exceptionality, 25*(2), 139–155. Doi: 10.1080/09362835.2016.

Kauffman, J. M., Hallahan, D. P., and Lloyd, J. W. (1998). Politics, science, and the future of learning disabilities. *Learning Disability Quarterly, 21,* 276–280.

Kauffman, J. M. and Lloyd, J. W. (2017). Statistics, data, and special educational decisions: Basic links to realities. In J. M. Kauffman, D. P. Hallahan, and P. C. Pullen (Eds.), *Handbook of special education* (2nd ed.) (pp. 29–39). New York: Routledge.

Kavale, K. A. and Forness, S. R. (1998). The politics of learning disabilities. *Learning Disability Quarterly, 21,* 245–273. doi: 10.2307/1511172.

Kavale, K. A. and Forness, S. R. (2000). What definitions of learning disability say and don't say: A critical analysis. *Journal of Learning Disabilities, 33,* 239–256.

Kavale, K. A., Holdnack, J. A., and Mostert, M. P. (2005). Responsiveness to intervention and the identification of specific learning disability: A critique and alternative proposal. *Learning Disability Quarterly, 29,* 113–127.

Kavale, K. A. and Reese, J. H. (1992). The character of learning disabilities: An Iowa profile. *Learning Disability Quarterly, 15,* 74–94. doi: 10.2307/1511010.

Kibby, M. Y. Lee, S. E., and Dyer, S. M. (2014). Reading performance is predicted by more than phonological processing. *Frontiers in Psychology, 19*(5), 1–7. doi: 10.3389/fpsyg.2014.00960.

Kirk, S. A. and Elkins, J. (1975). Characteristics of children enrolled in the child service demonstration centers. *Journal of Learning Disabilities, 8*(10), 31–38. doi:10.1177/002221947500801006.

Kudo, M. F., Lussier, C. M., and Swanson, H. L. (2015). Reading disabilities in children: A selective meta-analysis of the cognitive literature. *Research in Developmental Disabilities, 40,* 51-62. doi: 10.1016/j.ridd.2015.01.002.

Läge, D., Egli, S., Riedel, M., Strauss, A., and Möller, H.-J. (2011). Combining the categorical and the dimensional perspective in a diagnostic map of psychotic disorders. *European Archives of Psychiatry & Clinical Neuroscience, 261,* 3–10. doi: 10.1007/s00406-010-0125-y.

Lerner, J. W. (1989). Educational interventions in learning disabilities. *Journal of the American Academy of Child and Adolescent Psychiatry, 28,* 326–331. doi: 10.1097/00004583-198905000-00004.

Lewontin, R. (1992). *The doctrine of DNA: Biology as ideology*. London: Penguin Books.

Liu, Y., Georgiou, G., Zhang, Y., Li, H., Liu, H., Song, S., Kang, C., Shi, B., Liang, W., Pan, J., and Shu, H. (2017). Contribution of cognitive and linguistic skills to word-reading accuracy and fluency in Chinese. *International Journal of Educational Research, 82*, 75–90.

Lyon, G. R., Fletcher, J. M., Shaywitz, S. E., Shaywitz, B. A., Wood, F. B., and Schulte, A (2001). Rethinking learning disabilities. In C. E. Finn, A. J. Rotherham, and C. R. Hokanson (Eds.), *Rethinking special education for a new century* (pp. 259–287). Washington, DC: Thomas B. Fordham Foundation and Progressive Policy Institute.

Lyon, G. R., Shaywitz, S. E., and Shaywitz, B. A. (2003). A definition of dyslexia. *Annals of Dyslexia, 53*, 1–14. doi: 10.1007/s11881-003-0001-9.

Lyon, G. R., and Weiser, B. L. (2013). The state of the science in Learning disabilities: Research Impact on the field from 2001 to 2011. In H. L Swanson, K. Harris, and S. Graham (Eds.), *Handbook of learning disabilities*, (2nd ed., pp. 118–151). New York: Guildford Press.

Mastropieri, M. A. and Scruggs, T. E. (2005). Feasibility and consequences of response to intervention: Examination of the issues and scientific evidence as a model for the identification of individuals with learning disabilities. *Journal of Learning Disabilities, 38*, 525–531. doi: 10.1177/00222194050380060801.

Mayes, S. D. and Calhoun, S. L. (2007). Challenging the assumptions about the frequency and coexistence of learning disability types. *School Psychology International, 28*, 437–448. doi: 10.1177/0143034307084134.

Meehl, P. E. (1995). Bootstraps taxometrics: Solving the classification problem in psychopathology. *American Psychologist, 50*, 11–25. doi: 10.1037/0003-066X.50.4.266.

Meehl, P. E. (2004). What's in a taxon? *Journal of Abnormal Psychology, 113*, 39–43. doi: 10.1037/0021-843X.113.1.

Meehl, P. E. and Golden, R. (1982). Taxometric methods. In P. Kendall and J. Butcher (Eds.), *Handbook of research methods in clinical psychology* (pp. 127–181). New York: Wiley.

Meehl, P. E. and Yonce, L. J. (1994) Taxometric analysis: I. Detecting taxonicity with two quantitative indicators using means above and below a sliding cut (MAMBAC procedure). *Psychological Reports, 74*, 1059–1274.

Meehl, P. E. and Yonce, L. J. (1996). Taxometric analysis: II. Detecting taxonicity using covariance of two quantitative indicators in successive intervals of a third indicator (MAXCOV procedure). *Psychological Reports, 78*, 1091–1227.

Miciak, J., Fletcher, J. M., and Stuebing, K. K. (2016). Accuracy and validity methods for identifying learning disabilities in a response-to-intervention service delivery framework. In S. R. Jimerson, Burns, M. K., and VanDerHeyden, A. M. (Eds.), *Handbook of response to intervention: The science and practice of multi-tiered systems of support* (2nd ed.) (pp. 421–440). New York: Springer.

Miciak, J., Fletcher, J. M., Stuebing, K. K., Vaughn, S., and Tolar, T. D. (2014). Patterns of cognitive strengths and weaknesses: Identification rates, agreement, and validity for learning disabilities identification. *School Psychology Quarterly, 29*, 21–37. doi: 10.1037/spq0000037.

Miles, T. R. (1993). *Dyslexia: The pattern of difficulties*. London: Whurr.

Miles, T. R. (2006). *Fifty years in dyslexia research*. Chichester, UK: Wiley.

Morgan, P. L., Farkas, G. Cook, M., Strassfeld, N. M., Hillemeier, M. M., Pun, W. H., and Schussler, D. L. (2016). Are Black children disproportionally represented in special education? A best-evidence synthesis. *Exceptional Children, 83*, 181–198.

Morton, J. (2004). *Understanding developmental disorders: A causal modelling approach*. Malden, MA: Blackwell.

Nicolson, R. (2016). Developmental dyslexia. In J. Elliott and R. Nicolson (Eds.), *Dyslexia: Developing the debate* (pp. 5–72). London: Bloomsbury.

O'Brien, B. A. Wolf, M., and Lovett, M. W. (2012). A taxometric investigation of developmental dyslexia subtypes. *Dyslexia, 18,* 16–39. doi: 10.1002/dys.1431.

Peng, P. and Fuchs, D. (2016). A meta-analysis of working memory deficits in children with learning difficulties: Is there a difference between and numerical domain? *Journal of Learning Disabilities, 49*, 3–20. doi: 10.1177/0022219414521667.

Peng, P., Namkung, J., Barnes, M., and Sun, C. (2016). A meta-analysis of mathematics and working memory: Moderating effects of working memory domain, type of mathematics skill, and sample characteristics. *Journal of Educational Psychology, 108*, 455–473. doi: 10.1037/edu0000079.

Pennington, B. F. (2012). Developmental dyslexia. *The Lancet, 379*, 1997–2007.

Pennington, B. F. and Bishop, D. V. M. (2009). Relations among speech, language, and reading disorders. *Annual Review of Psychology, 60*, 283–306. doi: 10.1146/annurev.psych.60.110707.163548.

Peterson, R. L. and Pennington, B. F. (2015). Developmental dyslexia. *Annual Review of Clinical Psychology*, *11*, 283–307. doi: 10.1146/annurev-clinpsy-032814-112842.

Printy, S. M. and Wiliams, S. M. (2015). Principal's decisions: Implementing response to intervention. *Educational Policy*, *29*, 179–205. doi: 10.1177/0895904814556757.

Pogrow, S. (1996). Reforming the wannabe reformers: Why education reforms almost always end up making things worse. *The Phi Delta Kappan*, 77, 656–663.

President's Commission on Excellence in Special Education (2002). *A new era: Revitalizing special education for children and their families*. Washington, DC: United States Department of Education, Author.

Ramus, F. (2004). Neurobiology of dyslexia: A reinterpretation of the data. *Trends in Neurosciences*, *27*, 720–726. doi: 10.1016/j.tins.2004.10.004.

Ramus, F. (2014). Should there really be a 'dyslexic debate'? Book review. *Brain, 2014, 137*, 3371–3374. doi: 10.1093/brain/awu295.

Ramus, F., Rosen, S., Dakin, S. C., Day, B. L. Castellote, J. M., White, S., and Frith U. (2003). Theories of developmental dyslexia: Insights from a multiple case study of dyslexic adults. *Brain*, *126*, 841–865. doi: https://doi.org/10.1093/brain/awg076.

Rayner, K. and Pollatsek, A. (1989). *The psychology of reading*. Upper Saddle River, NJ: Prentice Hall.

Regan, K. S. Berkeley, S. L., Hughes, M., and Brady, K. K. (2015). Understanding practitioner perceptions of responsiveness to intervention. *Learning Disability Quarterly*, *38*, 234–247. doi: 10.1177/07319487 15580437.

Reschly, D. J. and Hosp, J. L. (2004). State LD identification policies and practices. *Learning Disability Quarterly*, *27*, 197–213.

Rittel, H. W. J. and Webber, M. W. (1973). Dilemmas in a general theory of planning. *Policy Science*, *4*, 155–169. doi: 10.1007/BF01405730.

Rodgers, B. (1983). The identification and prevalence of specific reading retardation. *British Journal of Educational Psychology*, *53*, 369–373. doi: 10.1111/j.2044-8279.1983.tb02570.x.

Ruscio, J., Haslam, N., and Ruscio, A. M. (2006). *Introduction to the taxometric method: A practical guide*. Mahwah, NJ: Lawrence Erlbaum.

Rutter, M. and Yule, W. J. (1975). The concept of specific reading retardation. *Journal of Child Psychology and Psychiatry*, *16*, 181–197. doi: 10.1111/j.1469-7610.1975.tb01269.x.

Sailor, W. (2009). *Making RTI work: How smart schools are reforming education through schoolwide response to intervention*. San Francisco, CA: Jossey-Bass.

Salend, S. J. (2011). *Creating inclusive classrooms: Effective and reflective practices* (7th ed.). Boston, MA: Pearson.

Schmidt, N. B., Kotov, R., and Joiner, T. E. (2004). *Taxometrics: Toward a new diagnostic scheme for psychopathology*. Washington, DC: American Psychological Association.

Share, D. L. (1995). Phonological recoding and self-teaching: Sine qua non of reading acquisition. *Cognition*, *55*, 151–218. doi: 10.1016/0010-0277(94)00645-2.

Share, D. L. (1999). Phonological recoding and orthographic learning: A direct test of the self-teaching hypothesis. *Journal of Experimental Child Psychology*, *72*, 95–129. doi: 10.1006/jecp.1998.2481.

Share, D. L., McGee R., McKenzie D., Williams S. M., and Silva P. A. (1987). Further evidence relating to the distinction between specific reading retardation and general reading backwardness. *British Journal of Developmental Psychology*, *5*,35–44. doi: 10.1111/j.2044-835X.1987.tb01039.x.

Siegel, L. S. (1989). IQ is irrelevant to the definition of learning disabilities. *Journal of Learning Disabilities*, *22*, 469–478, 486. doi: 10.1177/002221948902200803.

Scruggs, T. E. and Mastropieri, M. A. (2002). On babies and bathwater: Addressing the problems of identification of learning disabilities. *Learning Disability Quarterly*, *25*, 155–168. doi: 10.2307/1511299.

Shaywitz, S., Escobar, M., Shaywitz, B., Fletcher, J., and Makuch, R. (1992). Evidence that dyslexia may represent the lower tail of a normal distribution of reading ability. *New England Journal of Medicine*, *326*, 145–150. doi: 10.1056/NEJM199201163260301.

Sleeter, C. E. (1998). Yes, learning disabilities is political; What isn't? *Learning Disability Quarterly*, *21*, 289–296. doi: 10.2307/1511175.

Snowling, M. J. and Hulme, C. (2012). Children's reading impairments: From theory to practice. *Japanese Psychological Research*, *55*, 186–202. doi: 10.1111/j.1468-5884.2012.00541.

Spear-Swerling, L. and Cheesman, E. (2012). Teachers' knowledge base for implementing response-to-intervention models in reading. *Reading & Writing*, *25*, 1691–1723. doi: 10.1007/s11145-011-9338-3.

Stanovich, K. E. (1991). Discrepancy definitions of reading disability: Has intelligence led us astray? *Reading Research Quarterly*, *26*, 7–29. doi: 10.2307/747729.

Stanovich, K. E. (2000). *Progress in understanding reading: Scientific foundations and new frontiers*. New York: The Guilford Press.

Stanovich, K. E. and Siegel, L. S. (1994). The phenotypic performance profile of reading-disabled children: A regression-based test of the phonological-core variable-difference model. *Journal of Educational Psychology, 86*, 24–53. doi: 10.1037//0022-0663.86.1.24.

Stuebing, K. K., Barth, A. E., Molfese, P. J., Weiss, B., and Fletcher, J. M. (2009). IQ is not strongly related to response to reading instruction: A meta-analytic interpretation. *Exceptional Children, 76*, 31–51.

Stuebing, K. K., Fletcher, J. M., LeDoux, J. M. G., Lyon, R., Shaywitz, S.E., and Shaywitz, B. A. (2002). Validity of IQ-discrepancy classifications of reading disabilities: A meta-analysis. *American Educational Research Journal, 39*, 469–518. doi: 10.3102/00028312039002469.

Strong, G. K., Torgerson, C. J., Torgerson, D., and Hulme, C. (2011). A systematic meta-analytic review of evidence for the effectiveness of the "Fast forWord" language intervention program. *Journal of Child Psychology and Psychiatry, 52*, 224–235. doi: 10.1111/j.1469-7610.2010.02329.x.

Swanson, H. L. and Hoskyn, M. (1998). Experimental intervention research on students with learning disabilities: A meta-analysis of treatment outcomes. *Review of Educational Research, 68*, 277–321. doi: 10.3102/00346543068003277.

Toll, S. W. M., Van der Ven, S. H. G., Kroesbergen, E. H., and Van Luit, J. E. H. (20011) Executive functions as predictors of math learning disabilities. *Journal of Learning Disabilities, 44*, 521–532. doi: 10.1177/0022219410387302.

U.S. Office of Education. (1968). *First annual report of the National Advisory Committee on Handicapped Children*. Washington, DC: U.S. Department of Health, Education and Welfare.

Vaughn, S., Linan-Thompson, S., and Hickman, P. (2003). Response to instruction as a means of identifying students with reading/learning disabilities. *Exceptional Children, 69*, 391–409.

Vellutino, F. R., Scanlon, D. M., Small, S., and Fanuele, D. P. (2006). Response to Intervention as a vehicle for distinguishing between children with and without reading disabilities: Evidence for the role of kindergarten and first-grade interventions. *Journal of Learning Disabilities, 39*, 157–169. doi: 10.1177/00222194060390020401.

Wadsworth, S. J., Olson, R. K., and Defries, J. C. (2010). Differential genetic etiology of reading difficulties as a function of IQ: An update. *Behavior Genetics, 40*, 751–758. doi: 10.1007/s10519-010-9349-x.

Wakefield, J. C. (2007). The concept of mental disorder: Diagnostic implications of the harmful dysfunction analysis. *World Psychiatry, 6*, 149–156.

5

COMPREHENSIVE, INTEGRATED, THREE-TIERED (CI3T) MODELS OF PREVENTION

The Role of Systematic Screening to Inform Instruction

Kathleen Lynne Lane, Wendy Peia Oakes, and
Holly Mariah Menzies

In the last 20 years school systems across the country have shifted to a systems-level perspective for meeting students' academic, behavioral, and social skill needs. Historically, educators often viewed challenges as within-child deficits and subscribed to reactive approaches for meeting students' needs. Typically, the practice involved waiting for challenges to present themselves (e.g., acting out behavior, falling behind in reading performance) and then responding with reactive, consequence-based approaches. With the introduction of tiered systems of supports, focus has shifted to proactive, antecedent-based, data-informed approaches to meet students' multiple needs (Horner and Sugai, 2015).

Theoretically grounded in applied behavior analysis – a science in which behavioral principles are used to shape and sustain socially significant behaviors (Baer, Wolf, and Risely, 1968), well-constructed tiered systems hold particular benefit for many students, including those with and at-risk for emotional and behavioral disorders (EBD; Walker, Forness, and Lane, 2014). This is important given point prevalence estimates suggest approximately 20% of school age youth experience mild-to-severe EBD, which includes externalizing (e.g., noncompliance, aggression) and internalizing (e.g., anxious, social withdrawal) behaviors (Forness, Freeman, Paparella, Kauffman, and Walker, 2012). In addition to struggling behaviorally, these students also experience academic and social challenges manifesting as splintered academic skills, social isolation, strained relationships, school failure, and so on (Farmer et al., 2013; Wagner et al., 2006). While many individuals believe students with these and other challenging behaviors will be supported by special education services, this is simply not the case, as less than 1% of students receive special education supports for emotional disturbances (ED; Individuals with Disabilities Education Improvement Act [IDEA], 2004). Given the vast majority of students with EBD will receive their K-12 education under the tutelage of the general education community, it is imperative general *and* special education teachers acquire knowledge and confidence needed to work collaboratively in meeting this formidable charge (Lane, Oakes, Lusk, Cantwell, and Schatschneider, 2016).

We offer this chapter for individuals such as school-site leaders, professional development and technical assistance providers, and researchers committed to meeting students' multiple needs within efficient, data-informed tiered systems of supports. Such systems offer a cascade of supports: primary prevention (Tier 1) efforts for all students, secondary (Tier 2) practices for some students, and tertiary (Tier 3) practices reserved for a few students with intensive intervention needs. We describe Comprehensive, Integrated, Three-Tiered (Ci3T) models of prevention, a collaborative framework for educators to address students' academic, behavioral, and social skill needs in an integrated fashion using a data-informed process for instruction. Specifically, the goal is to create collaborative, efficient, effective systems-level approaches comprised of evidence-based practices to not only prevent learning and behavioral challenges from occurring, but also respond efficiently when such challenges arise. We focus on the role of behavior screening data and how these data can be used to inform (a) primary prevention (Tier 1) efforts; (b) low-intensity, teacher-delivered supports; and (c) secondary (Tier 2) and tertiary (Tier 3) supports for students.

Comprehensive, Integrated, Three-Tiered (Ci3T) Model of Prevention Described

As school-based inquiry continues to shift away from viewing learning and behavioral challenges as within-child deficits and relying heavily on reactive approaches to address identified concerns, the focus on systems-level, proactive approaches has led to new – and at times controversial – ways of meeting students' needs. In the late 1990's, tiered systems were modeled by response to intervention (RTI; Fuchs, Fuchs, and Compton, 2010) and positive behavior interventions and supports (PBIS; Horner and Sugai, 2015) frameworks. Recognizing the integrated natured of learning and behavioral challenges, new frameworks such as Multi-tiered System of Supports (MTSS) were introduced, blending RTI for reading and math with PBIS. As part of this structure, schools and districts often moved through a training model in which the system choice decided the order of their consecutive training process: MTSS for reading, MTSS for math, or MTSS for behavior. An unintended consequence of MTSS models was that school systems did not move through all components of the consecutive and accumulative training process as conceptualized, and often reached a point where there was no longer time or resources available to "address behavior." Another model featuring systematic approaches to addressing the integrated nature of students' needs in a comprehensive manner is a Ci3T model of prevention. The Ci3T model blend RTI practices for reading and math, PBIS, as well as the teaching of validated socio-emotional skills curricula. The Ci3T model is designed, implemented, and evaluated as one unified system, intended to support students' academic, behavioral, and socio-emotional needs in an integrated manner through a concurrent training process.

The Ci3T model of prevention contains the same core features as other tiered systems. For example, the model includes a cascade of supports with primary (Tier 1) prevention efforts for all students, secondary (Tier 2) prevention efforts for some students, and tertiary (Tier 3) prevention efforts reserved for a few students with the most intensive intervention needs (Lane, Oakes, Lusk et al., 2016). Each level of prevention is comprised of evidence-based strategies, practice, and programs. The model is heavily data-informed: monitoring treatment integrity of Tier 1, 2, and 3 efforts to ensure they are implemented as intended, assessing social validity regularly to inform professional learning and potential revisions each year, and monitoring student performance to determine responsiveness.

At this time, randomized control trials (RCTs) exploring the feasibility and efficacy of these integrated models have not been conducted. However, RCTs of many features constituting these models have been conducted and disseminated. To illustrate, RCTs of core reading programs (Fuchs et al., 2010), RTI for reading at the secondary school level (Vaughn and Fletcher, 2012), PBIS (Bradshaw, Waasdorp, and Leaf, 2012), and a range of social skills curricula (e.g., Positive Action; Snyder et al., 2010) offer evidence of implementation fidelity and changes in student performance on a range of outcome measures (e.g., reading skill, office discipline referrals, suspensions). Backed by empirical evidence, the commitment to comprehensive, integrated models with graduated supports is quickly becoming a national priority. Many local, state, and national leaders recognize the utility and efficacy of these systems, noting the importance of students graduating with strong academic skills as well as behavioral and social skills needed to be college and career ready (McIntosh and Goodman, 2016; Watson, 2015; Yudin, 2014). Designing, implementing, and evaluating Ci3T models is one way in which the research community is partnering with practitioners to meet this priority.

As part of the design process, each school establishes a Ci3T leadership team inclusive of an administrator with decision-making authority, one to two general education teachers, a special education teacher, one to two other members (e.g., school psychologist, behavior specialist, counselor, and/or reading specialists), a parent, and a student. Ci3T leadership teams work through an explicit six-part training process to develop a Ci3T Blueprint defining primary, secondary, and tertiary prevention efforts (see Lane, Oakes, Cantwell, and Royer, 2016).

Primary Prevention Efforts

As part of primary prevention efforts, Ci3T Blueprints have a Primary (Tier 1) Prevention Plan where teams establish: a purpose statement; mission statement; stakeholder (students, faculty and staff, parents, and administrators) roles and responsibilities for three domains: academic, behavior, and social; as well as detailed procedures for teaching, monitoring, and reinforcing the plan with all stakeholder groups.

In terms of the academic domain, students are often expected to arrive on time, participate in all instructional tasks, and meet expectations to facilitate positive, productive, safe learning environments. Faculty and staff responsibilities frequently include implementing core academic curriculum (e.g., validated reading programs such as Reading Street™; Pearson Education) with integrity (e.g., 90 min uninterrupted instruction four days per week, consistently implemented according to curriculum guidelines); low-intensity, teacher-delivered strategies to support engagement and minimize disruption (e.g., precorrection, instructional choice, and increased opportunities to respond); complete screening tools and formative assessments according to district or school timelines; and use data to inform instruction (e.g., constructing learning groups, determining frequency of progress monitoring, and selecting appropriate instructional materials). Parents' responsibilities typically include supporting attendance policies and school engagement. Administrators' responsibilities often include providing high quality professional learning offerings, scheduling dedicated planning time as part of professional learning communities, and consistent and visible support of Ci3T plan implementation and evaluation procedures.

In the behavioral domain, stakeholders subscribe to a PBIS framework. Expectations are developed using a data-informed approach where all faculty and staff are invited to complete the School-wide Expectation Survey for Specific Settings (SESSS; Lane, Oakes, and Menzies,

2010). This approach ensures expectations represent those behaviors the majority of faculty and staff express are important for student success. These expectations are taught to all stakeholders. Students receive multiple opportunities to practice with feedback and receive reinforcement (e.g., PBIS tickets paired with behavior specific praise, formal and informal teaching of expectations) for meeting expectations with a goal of teaching behaviors likely to solicit naturally occurring reinforcers (e.g., smiles, the good feeling that comes with completing assessments, and enjoying social times with friends). In addition, Ci3T leadership teams develop clearly articulated reactive plans in which rule infractions are operationally defined, as are guidelines for how challenging behaviors are managed in classrooms and by school-site administrators. As part of reactive plans, all teachers learn explicit strategies for preventing and responding to challenging behaviors (e.g., responding with empathy and interrupting the acting-out cycle; Colvin and Scott, 2014). As with the academic domain, stakeholder roles and responsibilities are defined to support implementation.

In terms of the social domain, Ci3T leadership teams work with district decision makers to select and install a validated school-wide social skills curriculum (e.g., Connect with Kids; Connect with Kids Network, 2016; Social Skills Improvement System Intervention Guide; Elliott and Gresham, 2008b) to support students in developing self-determined behaviors as part of their social-emotional learning. Ci3T leadership teams learn about reputable sources of information such as the U.S. Department of Education's What Works Clearinghouse, Substance Abuse and Mental Health Services Administration (SAMHSA), and Collaborative for Academic, Social, and Emotional Learning (CASEL) to inform their selections. Several factors impact curricular decisions: goals, populations of students served, available monetary resources, professional learning required, and so on. Once the decision is made, again stakeholder roles and responsibilities are defined to support implementation. For example, Ci3T leadership teams clearly articulate teaching schedules (e.g., one 30 min weekly lesson lead by general education teachers) to ensure students have equitable access to the curriculum.

Ci3T Blueprints then define specific procedures for teaching primary (Tier 1) intervention components, procedures for reinforcing, and procedures for monitoring. When establishing these procedures for all stakeholders (faculty and staff, students, parents, and community members), the intent is to teach primary prevention efforts in a comprehensive, integrated fashion. Equal priority is placed on addressing academic, behavior, and social domains to ensure students receive the full set of skills and experiences to achieve success within and beyond the school setting. Procedures for teaching, reinforcing, and monitoring are necessary for not only ensuring integrity of Tier 1 efforts and being responsive to stakeholder opinions (social validity), but also to inform the use of secondary and tertiary prevention efforts.

Secondary and Tertiary Prevention Efforts

In addition to establishing clear parameters for primary prevention efforts, Ci3T leadership teams develop secondary (Tier 2) and tertiary (Tier 3) prevention plans organized using tiered intervention grids. These grids list in detail the full scope of supports available for students requiring more than primary prevention efforts have to offer (Lane, Oakes, Ennis, and Hirsch, 2014). Grids include: (a) name of the available strategy, practice, or program; (b) a description of logistics (e.g., who is doing what to whom, and in what context); (c) entry criteria, objective methods for determining for whom the intervention may hold benefit (e.g., specific scores on screening tools and other data sources); (d) data to assess outcomes (e.g., treatment integrity, social validity, and measures to monitor students' progress); and (e) exit criteria for deciding when to fade the supplemental support or move to more intensive intervention efforts.

The intent of intervention grids is to support transparent communication amongst all stakeholders showing the full scope of supports available – including enrichment opportunities (Lane, Oakes, Cantwell et al., 2016). When designing intervention grids, an emphasis is placed on offering socially valid, researched-based practices, programs, and strategies likely to yield desired changes in student performance, provided they are implemented with integrity (Cook and Tankersley, 2013). Part of closing achievement gaps between various groups of students is closing gaps in access to the full scope of supports needed to attain socially significant goals (e.g., learning how to read, developing self-determined behaviors; Shogren, Wehmeyer, and Lane, 2016).

The Role of Systematic Screening in Ci3T Models of Prevention for Behavior Challenges

Within Ci3T models of prevention, multiple data sources are used together to inform instruction. For example, practitioners measure the degree to which each level of prevention (Tiers 1, 2, and 3) is implemented as designed – that is, with integrity. Treatment integrity data are necessary for drawing accurate conclusions regarding student outcomes and can also be useful in informing professional learning offerings (Lane, Carter, Jenkins, Dwiggins, and Germer, 2015). Just as it is important to measure treatment integrity of Tier 2 and Tier 3 interventions, it is also important to measure the integrity of primary prevention efforts. It would be unwise to suggest a student required Tier 2 or Tier 3 supports with insufficient evidence to indicate Tier 1 efforts are in place as designed. Similarly, social validity is an important metric to assess at each level of prevention. Evidence suggests schools' mean social validity scores during Ci3T training actually predict treatment integrity during initial implementation (Lane, Kalberg, Bruhn, Driscoll, Wehby, and Elliott, 2009) which may be used to inform professional learning efforts during the first year of implementation. Fortunately, there are a number of validated tools for use in measuring treatment integrity and social validity available at Positive Behavior Intervention and Support Office of Special Education Programs (OSEP) Technical Assistance Center (www.pbis.org) and Ci3T model of prevention (www.ci3t.org) websites.

In addition to measuring treatment integrity and social validity, systematic screening data play a critical role in data-informed decision-making within all tiered systems. Ideally such models involve reliable, valid academic and behavior screening tools in addition to other regularly collected data sources (e.g., attendance, office discipline referrals [ODR]). However, in this chapter we focus on the utility of behavior screening data. Like academic screening tools, behavior screenings are completed three times per year: fall, winter, and spring. However, there are two main differences between academic and behavior screening tools. First, behavior screenings do not require any student time. They are typically teacher-completed ratings, with each teacher independently rating each student in their class. At the elementary level, the rater is the homeroom teacher and in secondary schools, leadership teams designate one period during which ratings are completed (see Lane, Menzies, Oakes, and Kalberg, 2012, and Oakes, Lane, and Ennis, 2016 for logistics). Second, fall time points for behavior screenings typically occur 4–6 weeks after the onset of the school year; unlike academic screenings that can be completed immediately after students return from summer break.

Fortunately, there are now several validated screening tools available for use from preschool through high school, with the greatest range of options for elementary school use. Commercially available and free-access tools are available, such as: Behavior Assessment System for Children 3rd Edition: Behavioral & Emotional Screening System (BASC-3: BESS; Kamphaus and Reynolds, 2015), Social, Academic, and Emotional Behavior Risk Screener© (SAEBRS; Kilgus, Chafouleas,

Riley-Tillman, and von der Embse, 2013); Social Skills Improvement System - Performance Screening Guide (SSiS-PSG; Elliott and Gresham, 2008a); Strengths and Difficulties Questionnaire (SDQ; Goodman, 2001); Student Risk Screening Scale (SRSS; Drummond, 1994); Student Risk Screening Scale – Internalizing and Externalizing (SRSS-IE; Drummond, 1994; Lane and Menzies, 2009); and Systematic Screening for Behavior Disorders (SSBD; Walker, Severson, and Feil, 2014). There are volumes written on each screening tool, offering psychometric evidence as well as practical applications. We refer the interested readers to Oakes, Lane, Cantwell, and Royer (2017) and ci3t.org for additional information.

In this chapter we use the SRSS-IE to illustrate how behavior screening data can be used to inform (a) primary (Tier 1) prevention efforts; (b) low-intensity, teacher-delivered supports, and (c) Tier 2 and Tier 3 supports according to students' needs (Lane and Walker, 2015). We select this tool as it is a widely used, free-access tool available for use from kindergarten through twelfth grades, thus an option for schools regardless of resources. The SRSS-IE includes 12 items, each rated by teachers on a 4-point, Likert-type scale yielding two subscale scores: SRSS-E to detect externalizing behaviors and the SRSS-I to detect internalizing behaviors. Using cut scores established for elementary-age (Lane, Oakes, Swogger et al., 2015) and secondary-age (Lane, Oakes, Cantwell et al., 2016) youth, students are placed into one of three risk categories on each subscale score: low, moderate, and high.

Screening and Primary (Tier 1) Prevention Efforts

After completing any screening time point (fall, winter, and spring), Ci3T leadership teams begin by checking the accuracy of the data collected. For example, they answer important questions such as: Were the screening procedures conducted as planned (procedural integrity)? Did all teachers complete the screenings on their assigned class of students? If teachers were absent for an extended period of time, did another rater screen those students? Were all students screened and data saved?

After ensuring the accuracy and completeness of data collected, the next step is to examine the percentage of students placing into the low-, moderate-, and high-risk categories as defined by the screening tools' technical manual or published evidence. For example, in Figure 5.1, hypothetical data are presented for fall administrations of the SRSS-IE for an elementary school. In fall 2016, 65% of students scored into the low risk category on the SRSS-E (externalizing), 25% in the moderate-risk category, and 10% in the high-risk category. During the same administration, 55% of students scored in the low-risk category on the SRSS-I (internalizing), 35% in the moderate-risk category, and 10% in the high-risk category. When interpreting this first time point of fall data, it is necessary to also examine treatment integrity data to accurately interpret screening data.

Nationally, approximately 80% of students are expected to respond to primary (Tier 1) prevention efforts when implemented with integrity (Sugai and Horner, 2015). When less than 80% of students score within the low-risk category on the selected screener (which is the case for both SRSS-E and SRSS-I fall data presented), Tier 1 is targeted for improvement. In examining teachers' self-reported data during the fall semester (examining integrity during the semester as a whole; $M = 75\%$; $SD = 9.50$) as well as treatment integrity data collected during direct observation sessions by a trained observer ($M = 70\%$; $SD = 9.31$) and teacher ($M = 73\%$; $SD = 10.25$), it appears treatment integrity of Tier 1 practices has yet to achieved a desired goal of 80%. In this case, Ci3T leadership teams would support implementation efforts by revisiting procedures for teaching and reinforcing of Tier 1 components. In the illustration provided, fall 2017 suggest Tier 1 efforts were more successfully implemented in the second

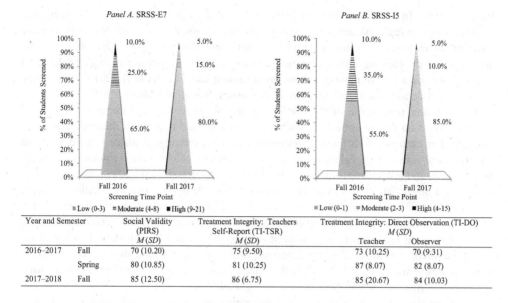

Year and Semester		Social Validity (PIRS) M (SD)	Treatment Integrity: Teachers Self-Report (TI-TSR) M (SD)	Treatment Integrity: Direct Observation (TI-DO) M (SD)	
				Teacher	Observer
2016–2017	Fall	70 (10.20)	75 (9.50)	73 (10.25)	70 (9.31)
	Spring	80 (10.85)	81 (10.25)	87 (8.07)	82 (8.07)
2017–2018	Fall	85 (12.50)	86 (6.75)	85 (20.67)	84 (10.03)

Figure 5.1 Example of Student Risk Screening Scale – Internalizing and Externalizing (SRSS-IE) data for one elementary school comparing fall times points for externalizing (Panel A; 7 items) and internalizing (Panel B; 5 items) subscales. Social validity mean scores are reported for Primary Intervention Rating Scale (PIRS; Lane et al., 2009) and treatment integrity mean scores for Teacher Self-Report and direct observations (Lane, 2009).

Adapted from Oakes et al. (2017).

year and the percentage of students' scoring in the low-risk categories on the SRSS-E and SRSS-I increased to 80% and 85%, respectfully.

Effective Ci3T leadership teams establish screening structures such as sending out prompts when scheduled screening windows open, conducting regular checks to ensure all teachers have completed the screenings and data are saved before the screening window closes. Once data are collected Ci3T teams use established procedures for sharing aggregated data with the school as a whole. Teachers and Ci3T leadership teams examine student-level data along with other data (e.g., academic screening, office discipline referrals, and attendance) to inform the use of low-intensity, teacher-level supports and – when needed – Tier 2 and Tier 3 supports for students.

We emphasize it is not possible to accurately interpret screening data in the absence of treatment integrity data. Too often, school personnel may be tempted to move forward with Tier 2 and Tier 3 practices for large numbers of students (which can strain available resources and not result in desired improvements for students), when it may be more appropriate to shore up implementation of Tier 1 efforts or empower teachers with low-intensity supports, embedded as part of instruction.

Screening and Low-Intensity, Teacher-Delivered Supports
Planning for Using Screening

As part of Tier 1 implementation, teachers commit to using low-intensity, PBIS strategies to increase student engagement and minimize disruption. Examples of these strategies are: behavior specific praise, increasing students' opportunities to respond, precorrection, active supervision, and instructional choice to name a few (Lane, Menzies, Ennis, and Oakes, 2015; Stormont and

Reinke, 2009). In instances when teachers have more than 20% of students in a given class with moderate or high-risk status on behavior screening tools, it is often effective and resource efficient to empower teachers in utilizing these research-based strategies. This can be accomplished by offering high-quality professional learning opportunities (e.g., professional learning sessions, access to practice guides, book studies; Lane, Carter et al., 2013) that include coaching and performance feedback (Briere, Simonsen, Sugai, and Myers, 2015).

Incorporating regular use of these effective, feasible strategies into instruction can yield positive returns on this investment of teacher time to learn and implement these strategies with integrity. For example, with focused professional learning offerings available from district and state technical assistance providers, teachers can learn a series of low-intensity strategies to create positive, safe, and productive learning environments (Horner and Sugai, 2015). As discussed by Horner and Sugai (2015), it is important to look for simple – yet powerful – shifts in teacher behavior that will yield desired changes in student performance. Too often, this important step of focusing on teacher-delivered, low-intensity strategies is overlooked and decision makers are quick to move to other more student-specific supports such as Check-in/Check-out (CICO; Crone, Hawken, and Horner, 2010) or functional assessment-based interventions (FABI; Umbreit, Ferro, Liaupsin, and Lane, 2007). While these are excellent, evidence-based practices, in many instances – particularly when there are multiple students in a given context (e.g., English and language arts block, seventh period science) presenting with moderate-risk behavior patterns – more intentional use of low-intensity, teacher-delivered supports may be effective for increasing engagement and minimizing disruption for individual students and the class as a whole (e.g., Lane, Royer et al., 2015). Yet, when Tier 1 practices and low-intensity, teacher-delivered supports are all in place with integrity and students are still struggling, screening data are used to connect students with evidence-based strategies such as CICO (Tier 2) and FABI (Tier 3).

Screening and Secondary (Tier 2) and Tertiary (Tier 3) Prevention

As described previously, the Ci3T Blueprint includes a secondary (Tier 2) intervention grid and a tertiary (Tier 3) intervention grid, each of which contains a full listing of available options at the school site. Ci3T leadership teams develop these grids to organize all available resources, including enrichment and remediation efforts to create structures for transparent communication and equitable access of available supports for students with targeted (Tier 2) and intensive (Tier 3) intervention needs (Lane, Oakes et al., 2014).

Intervention grids facilitate communication between all stakeholders: educators, parents, students, and community members, showing not only the strategies, practices, and programs available, but how they can be accessed. This is particularly important to support districts' commitment to academic excellence and equity. Rather than relying on referrals by teachers, parents, or other individuals, screening data become the mechanism by which students are connected to more intensive intervention efforts in addition to primary prevention efforts. Three times each year, screening data are analyzed in conjunction with other schoolwide data collected on all students to determine an appropriate educational response, which may help narrow achievement gaps by reducing the potential of special education placement bias (Sullivan and Bal, 2013) and by responding at the first sign of concern.

Tier 2 and 3 intervention grids are important components of schools' Ci3T Blueprints that define *additive* supports, not intended to replace Tier 1 components, but to enhance them. As mentioned, grids include a description of the essential components for decision making: (a) name and description of each available support (not the name of the person delivering the support, but what they actually do); (b) entry criteria with data sources and cut scores (also referred to as inclusion criteria); (c) established progress monitoring tools (including treatment integrity and social validity data as well as student performance); and (d) exit criteria with data sources and cut scores denoting when support is no longer required (either because was effective in achieving goals, or because a more intensive intervention effort is needed).

We refer interested readers to Lane, Oakes, Cantwell et al. (2016) for additional information on how to design, implement, and evaluate Tier 2 and Tier 3 interventions using intervention grids as a structure. Multiple illustrations are also available on ci3t.org. In brief, we encourage the following considerations when using data to inform intervention efforts for students requiring more than primary prevention efforts.

First, use multiple sources of data to inform intervention efforts rather than relying on just one measure. For example, as illustrated above, it will be important to assess and use treatment integrity data to understand the extent to which any Tier 1, 2, or 3 effort is actually in place. Measures for monitoring these important constructs are named for each support listed on the intervention grids (see example in Figure 5.2). Similarly, it is important to examine students' attendance data as well as academic and behavior screening data to fully inform intervention efforts. We would not want to say a student has Tier 2 needs without first knowing answers to questions such as: Are primary prevention efforts in place (treatment integrity)? Is the student attending school regularly to have benefit of primary prevention efforts consistently (attendance)? Does the student have behavioral excesses or deficits that could be impeding their instructional experience (behavior screening)? Is the student's academic performance meeting expected benchmarks (academic screening)? Given the interrelated nature of academic, behavioral, and social skills, it is important to consider these multiple sources of information for the most complete initial picture of student access and performance.

Second, we respectfully point out screening data are not intended to label or exclude students. There are no Tier 2 or Tier 3 students; instead, there are students with Tier 2 and Tier 3 needs. These needs fluctuate over time and in various contexts. For example, students

Support	Description	School-wide Data: Entry Criteria	Data to Monitor Progress	Exit Criteria
Check–In, Check-Out (CICO) (Behavior Education Program [BEP]; Crone, Hawken, & Horner, 2010)	Participating students check in and out with a mentor each day on targeted goals. During check-in, students pick up their daily progress report that they take to each class for feedback on their progress in meeting the school-wide Ci3T model expectations.	**Behavior:** ☐ SRSS-E7 score: Moderate (4-8) ☐ SRSS-I5 score: Moderate (2-3) or ☐ SRSS-E7 score: High (9-21) ☐ SRSS-I5 score: High (4-15) or ☐ 2 or more office discipline referrals (ODR) in a 5-week period or ☐ 2 or more tardies or absences per quarter AND/OR **Academic:** ☐ Progress report: 1 or more course failures ☐ Progress report: Targeted for Growth, academic learning behaviors	**Student measures:** Daily progress reports **Treatment integrity:** Coach completes component checklist of all BEP steps each day (daily and weekly percentage of completion computed) **Social Validity:** Teacher: Intervention Rating Profile-15 (IRP-15; Witt & Elliott, adapted) Student: Children's Intervention Rating Profile (CIRP; Witt & Elliott, 1985, adapted)	SRSS-E7 score: Low (0-3) SRSS-I5 score: Low (0-1) With 8 weeks of data, student has made their CICO goal 90% of the time and there have not been any office discipline referrals. The teacher is then contacted for their opinion about if exiting is appropriate or if CICO should continue.

Figure 5.2 Example of one support listed on an elementary school's Tier 2 Intervention Grid. SRSS-E7 = Student Risk Screening Scale – Externalizing, 7 items. SRSS-I5 = Student Risk Screening Scale – Internalizing, 5 items. Ci3T = comprehensive, integrated, three-tiered.
Source: ci3t.org.

might need a CICO intervention to support the initial transition from elementary to middle school, a self-monitoring intervention to increase engagement during block scheduling days that feature longer than usual instructional periods, social skills groups of varying duration to support students with common concerns (e.g., school related anxiety, making friends), or an intensive reading intervention to support the high school students continuing to build reading comprehension skills. The intent is to use reliable, valid data to inform intervention efforts with a focus on efficient resource allocations.

Third, successfully installing Tier 2 and Tier 3 supports will involve considerations such as scheduling collaboration time between educators and other school-site personnel (e.g., social workers, school psychologists), a master schedule with dedicated time for interventions to occur, and refining job responsibilities allowing for time for the most skillful instructors to assist students with the greatest needs (e.g., school counselors to work with students with the most pronounced social skills needs, teachers well-trained in current reading practices to plan and deliver intensive reading instruction).

Educational Implications: Potential Benefits of Ci3T Models

The Ci3T model of prevention is a data-informed, tiered system of supports broadened beyond traditional MTSS models to address students' academic, behavioral, *and* socio-emotional needs within one framework (Lane, Oakes, and Menzies, 2014). These models offer several potential benefits, some of which we discuss here. First, Ci3T models are intended to support schools in building transparent, efficient, practical, and collaborative structures compromised of evidence-based practices at each level of prevention, with data-informed decision-making guiding movement throughout this cascade of supports (Cook and Tankersley, 2013; Lane, Oakes, and Menzies, 2014). These models provide explicit roles and responsibilities for all stakeholders (students, faculty and staff, parents, and administrators) for each domain (academic, behavior, and social), with clear procedures for teaching and reinforcing all Tier 1 elements as well as clear procedures for monitoring treatment integrity, social validity, and student performance. Throughout the year-long planning process, Ci3T leadership teams coordinate resources, eliminate redundancies, and foster strong collaborations between general educators, special educators, and parent communities. Coupled with high-quality professional learning and sustained district support, Ci3T models have the potential to support professionals in collaborating using data-informed practices to enhance instruction and establish positive, productive, safe, and even joyful learning environments (Lane, Oakes, and Menzies, 2014; Sugai and Horner, 2015).

Second, Ci3T models provide structures for clarifying expectations for all stakeholders and increasing the likelihood of equitable access to available supports for all students. By defining roles and responsibilities in each domain, expectations are clear for current and future school employees, as is the assistance they will receive in meeting their responsibilities. For example, as part of fully installing PBIS, educators and parents will need high-quality learning opportunities to understand how this is more than praise and popsicles. The shaping of behavior is theoretically grounded in applied behavior analysis, which has decades of research underlying its behavioral principles (Horner and Sugai, 2015). In addition, the full scope of supports and movement between levels of prevention are transparent using data-informed procedures, rather than subjective techniques, decreasing the likelihood of overlooking students requiring more than Tier 1 efforts. It is simply too much pressure to expect teachers to work in isolation of the larger school context to determine which students need additional assistance for meeting academic, behavior, and social skill goals (Lane, Oakes, Menzies, and Harris, 2013).

Third, Ci3T models may provide an effective structure for meeting the search and serve requirements specified in IDEA (2004). As mandated by IDEA, school must have procedures for determining students who might be eligible for special education services. For students with persistent and intensive needs for whom evidence-based practices implemented with integrity and sufficient intensity, a referral to a multi-disciplinary team may be warranted, although we are not advocating for schools to delay identification if a special education referral is necessary. Documented evidence as to what has been attempted across the cascade of supports provides additional information to multi-disciplinary teams as they collaborate to determine special education eligibility.

Finally, in this challenging economic and political climate when the value of public education is called into question, it is important for school systems to move forward with the goal of building effective, efficient systems and structures for students to be college and career ready. By attending to students' academic, behavior, and social skill needs we optimize the probability of students developing the full set of skills needed to become self-determined in their behavior: setting goals, negotiating personal relationship, responding to challenges with grace, and enjoying the lives they choose.

Summary

The intent of this chapter was to introduce the Ci3T model of prevention to professional development and technical assistance providers, school-site leaders, and researchers committed to meeting students' academic, behavioral, *and* social needs using a comprehensive, integrated, efficient, and transparent systemic approach. Each level of prevention: Tier 1, 2, and 3, is comprised of evidence-based practices to (a) prevent learning and behavioral challenges from occurring and (b) respond effectively when such challenges present themselves. After describing the Ci3T model of prevention and distinguishing it from other tiered systems, we focused on the utility of behavior screening data analyzed with other data collected as part of regular school practices. We illustrated how to use behavior screening data to inform instruction (e.g., Tier 1 efforts, teacher-delivered supports, and Tier 2 and Tier 3 supports for students according to individual needs) with attention to measures of treatment integrity and social validity. We closed with a discussion of educational implications of the Ci3T model, noting benefits (e.g., transparency, communication, coordinated resources, and efficient collaboration) and considerations (e.g., scheduling for successful implementation, responsive high-quality professional learning, and resource allocations).

References

Baer, D. M., Wolf, M. M., and Risley, T. R. (1968). Some current dimensions of applied behavior analysis. *Journal of Applied Behavior Analysis*, *1*, 91–97. doi: 10.1901/jaba.1968.1-91.

Bradshaw, C. P., Waasdorp, T. E., and Leaf, P. J. (2012). Effects of school-wide positive behavioral interventions and supports on child behavior problems. *Pediatrics*, *130*, e1136–e1145. doi: 10.1542/peds.2012-0243.

Briere, D. E., Simonsen, B., Sugai, G., and Myers, D. (2015). Increasing new teachers' specific praise using a within-school consultation intervention. *Journal of Positive Behavior Interventions*, *17*, 50–60. doi: 10.1177/1098300713497098.

Colvin, G. and Scott, T. M. (2014). *Managing the cycle of acting-out behavior in the classroom* (2nd ed.). Thousand Oaks, CA: Corwin Press.

Connect with Kids Network (2016). *Connect with Kids*. Atlanta, GA: Author.

Cook, B. and Tankersley, M. (Eds.). (2013). *Effective practices in special education*. Boston, MA: Pearson.

Crone, D. A., Hawken, L. S., and Horner, R. H. (2010). *Responding to problem behavior in schools: Behavior education program*. New York: The Guilford Press.

Drummond, T. (1994). *The Student Risk Screening Scale (SRSS)*. Grants Pass, OR: Josephine County Mental Health Program.

Elliott, S. N. and Gresham, F. M. (2008a). *Social Skills Improvement System (SSiS) – Performance Screening Guide*. San Antonio, TX: PsychCorp Pearson Education.

Elliott, S. N. and Gresham, F. (2008b). *Social Skills Improvement System (SSiS) – Classwide Intervention Program*. San Antonio, TX: PsychCorp Pearson Education.

Farmer, T. W., Irvin, M. J., Motoca, L. M., Brooks, D. S., Leung, M-C., and Hutchins, B. C. (2013). Externalizing and internalizing behavior problems, peer affiliations, and bullying involvement across the transition to middle school. *Journal of Emotional and Behavioral Disorders, 23*(1), 3–16. doi: 10.1177/1063426613491286.

Forness, S., Freeman, S., Paperella, T., Kauffman, J., and Walker, H. (2012). Special education implications of point and cumulative prevalence for children with emotional and behavioral disorder. *Journal of Emotional and Behavioral Disorders, 20*(1), 4–18.

Fuchs, L.S., Fuchs, D., and Compton, D. (2010). Rethinking response to intervention at middle and high school. *School Psychology Review, 39*, 22–28.

Goodman, R. (2001). Psychometric properties of the Strengths and Difficulties Questionnaire (SDQ). *Journal of the American Academy of Child and Adolescent Psychiatry, 40*, 1337–1345. doi: 10.1097/00004583-200111000-00015.

Horner, R. H. and Sugai, G. (2015). School-wide PBIS: an example of applied behavior analysis implemented at a scale of social importance. *Behavior Analysis in Practice, 8*(1), 80–85. doi:10.1007/s40617-015-0045-4.

Individuals with Disabilities Education Improvement Act of 2004, 20 U.S.C. 1400 *et seq.* (2004). (Reauthorization of Individuals with Disabilities Act 1990).

Kamphaus, R. W. and Reynolds, C. R. (2015). *Behavior assessment system for children – Third edition (BASC-3): Behavioral and emotional screening system (BESS)*. Bloomington, MN: Pearson.

Kilgus, S. P., Chafouleas, S. M., Riley-Tillman, T. C., and von der Embse, N. P. (2013) *Social, Academic, and Emotional Behavior Risk Screener©: Teacher Rating Form*. Columbia, MO: University of Missouri.

Lane, K. L. (2009). *Comprehensive, Integrated Three-tiered Model of Prevention: Treatment Integrity Teacher Self-Report and Direct Observation Tool*. Unpublished instrument. Nashville, TN: Vanderbilt University. Retrieved from www.ci3t.org/measures.

Lane, K. L., Carter, E. W., Jenkins, A., Dwiggins, L., and Germer, K. (2015). Supporting comprehensive, integrated, three-tiered models of prevention in schools: Administrators' perspectives. *Journal of Positive Behavior Interventions, 17*, 209–222. doi: 10.1177/1098300715578916.

Lane, K. L., Kalberg, J. R., Bruhn, A. L., Driscoll, S. A., Wehby, J. H., and Elliott, S. (2009). Assessing social validity of school-wide positive behavior support plans: Evidence for the reliability and structure of the Primary Intervention Rating Scale. *School Psychology Review, 38*, 135–144.

Lane, K. L. and Menzies, H. M. (2009). *Student Risk Screening Scale for Early Internalizing and Externalizing Behavior (SRSS-IE)*. Screening scale.

Lane, K. L., Menzies, H. M., Ennis, R. P., and Oakes, W. P. (2015). *Supporting Behavior for School Success: A Step-by-Step Guide to Key Strategies*. New York: The Guilford Press.

Lane, K. L., Menzies, H. M, Oakes, W. P., and Kalberg, J. R. (2012). *Systematic screenings of behavior to support instruction: From preschool to high school*. New York: The Guilford Press.

Lane, K. L., Oakes, W. P., Cantwell, E. D., and Royer, D. J. (2016). *Building and installing comprehensive, integrated, three-tiered (Ci3T) models of prevention: A practical guide to supporting school success* (interactive eBook). Phoenix, AZ: KOI Education.

Lane, K. L., Oakes, W. P., Ennis, R. P., and Hirsch, S. E. (2014). Identifying students for secondary and tertiary prevention efforts: How do we determine which students have Tier 2 and Tier 3 needs? *Preventing School Failure, 58*, 171–182. doi: 10.1080/1045988X.2014.895573.

Lane, K. L., Oakes, W. P., Lusk, M. E., Cantwell, E. D., and Schatschneider, C. (2016). Screening for intensive intervention needs at the secondary level: Directions for the future. *Journal of Emotional and Behavioral Disorders, 24*, 159–172. doi: 10.1177/1063426615618624.

Lane, K. L., Oakes, W. P., and Menzies, H. M. (2010). *Schoolwide Expectations Survey for Specific Settings*. Unpublished instrument. Nashville, TN: Vanderbilt University. Retrieved from www.ci3t.org/measures.

Lane, K. L., Oakes, W. P., Menzies, H. M., and Harris, P. J. (2013). Developing comprehensive, integrated, three-tiered models to prevent and manage learning and behavior. In T. Cole, H. Daniels, and J. Visser (Eds.). *The Routledge international companion to emotional and behavioural difficulties* problems (pp. 177–183). New York: Routledge.

Lane, K. L., Oakes, W. P., Swogger, E., Schatschneider, C., Menzies, H. M., and Sanchez, J. (2015). Student risk screening scale for internalizing and externalizing behaviors: Preliminary cut scores to support data-informed decision making. *Behavioral Disorders, 40,* 159–170.

Lane, K. L., Royer, D. J., Messenger, M. L., Common, E. A., Ennis, R. P., and Swogger, E. D. (2015). Empowering teachers with low-intensity strategies to support academic engagement: Implementation and effects of instructional choice for elementary students in inclusive settings. *Education and Treatment of Children, 38,* 473–504. doi: 10.1353/etc.2015.001.

Lane, K. L. and Walker, H. M. (2015). The connection between assessment and intervention: How does screening lead to better interventions? In B. Bateman, M. Tankersley, and J. Lloyd (Eds.) *Enduring issues in special education: Personal perspectives.* (pp. 283–301). New York: Routledge.

McIntosh K. and Goodman, S. (2016). *Integrating multi-tiered systems of support: Blending RTI and PBIS.* New York: The Guilford Press.

Oakes, W. P., Lane, K. L., Cantwell, E. D., and Royer, D. J. (2017). Systematic screening for behavior in K–12 settings as regular school practice: Practical considerations and recommendations. *Journal of Applied School Psychology.* Manuscript in review.

Oakes, W. P., Lane, K. L., and Ennis, R. P. (2016). Systematic screening at the elementary level: Considerations for exploring and installing universal behavior screening. *Journal of Applied School Psychology, 32,* 214–233. doi: 10.1080/15377903.2016.1165325.

Pearson Education Reading Street™: Author.

Shogren, K. A., Wehmeyer, M. L., and Lane, K. L. (2016). Embedding interventions to promote self-determination within multitiered systems of supports. *Exceptionality.* doi: 10.1080/09362835.2015.1064421.

Snyder, F. J., Flay, B. R., Vuchinich, S., Acock, A., Washburn, I. J., Beets, M., and Li, K. (2010). Impact of the Positive Action program on school-level indicators of academic achievement, absenteeism, and disciplinary outcomes: A matched-pair, cluster randomized, controlled trial. *Journal of Research on Educational Effectiveness, 3,* 25–55.

Stormont, M. and Reinke, W. (2009). The importance of precorrective statements and behavior-specific praise and strategies to increase their use. *Beyond Behavior, 18,* 26–32.

Sullivan, A. L. and Bal, A. (2013). Disproportionality in special education: Effects of individual and school variables on disability risk. *Exceptional Children, 79,* 475–494.

Umbreit, J., Ferro, J., Liaupsin, C., and Lane, K. (2007). *Functional behavioral assessment and function-based intervention: An effective, practical approach.* Upper Saddle River, NJ: Prentice Hall.

Vaughn, S. and Fletcher, J. M. (2012). Response to intervention with secondary school students with reading difficulties. *Journal of Learning Disabilities, 45*(3), 244–256. doi: 10.1177/0022219412442157.

Wagner, M., Friend, M., Bursuck, D., Kutash, K., Duchnowski, A. J., Sumi, W., and Epstein, M. (2006). Educating students with emotional disturbances: A national perspective on school programs and services. *Journal of Emotional and Behavioral Disorders, 14,* 12–30.

Watson, R. (2015). Kansas State Department of Education Annual Conference. Kansas City, KS.

Walker, H. M., Forness, S. R., and Lane, K. L. (2014). Design and management of scientific research in applied school settings. In B. Cook, M. Tankersley, and T. Landrum (Eds.). *Advances in learning and behavioral disabilities* (vol. 27, pp. 141–169). Bingley, UK: Emerald.

Walker, H. M., Severson, H. H., and Feil, E. G. (2014). *Systematic screening for behavior Disorders (SSBD) technical manual: Universal screening for PreK–9* (2nd ed.). Eugene, OR: Pacific Northwest Publishing.

Yudin, M. (2014). *PBIS: Providing opportunity.* A keynote address presented at the National PBIS Leadership Forum: PBIS Building Capacity & Partnerships to Enhance Educational Reform. Rosemont, IL.

SECTION II

Roles and Responsibilities in the RTI Process

INTRODUCTION TO SECTION II

Erica Lembke

In this section, articles are provided that address the key people who influence and make decisions within the Response to Intervention process. For an RTI process to function effectively and efficiently, it is important to engage all stakeholders and utilize their input. The articles in this section address contributions to, and engagement in, the RTI process from the perspective of pre-service teachers; school psychologists and problem-solving teams; administrators; and parents and students. Brownell and her colleagues discuss critical issues to consider as we prepare general and special education teachers to serve as implementers of RTI in their buildings. This chapter addresses evidence-based practices in teacher preparation that should be merged with RTI content and delivered in engaging ways in college courses and field experience. In the second article, Sims and his colleagues discuss effective practices in problem-solving around student data. Specifically, their chapter presents a model for utilizing the problem-solving model as a way to utilize data and make decisions about individual students. The resources in this chapter will be immediately valuable to teacher teams in buildings. In the third chapter, Billingsley and her colleagues address the crucial role of the administrator in the implementation of an RTI model. Drawing from extensive work that she and her colleagues have engaged in, Billingsley provides models and evidence for administrator development of and involvement in an RTI or MTSS system, including capacity building. Finally, Conoyer and her co-authors discuss potential models of parent and student involvement, and review the limited literature in these areas. Next, they describe the results from studies completed by the author team that addressed parent and student involvement in the RTI process. These studies occurred with elementary students and their parents, primarily. Three studies were conducted with parallel methods, but unique samples, and results from these studies are utilized to support effective methods for parent and student involvement.

Overall, this chapter will provide evidence-based practices in working with pre- and in-service teachers, with administers, with parents, and with students as schools develop and implement MTSS.

6

PROBLEM SOLVING WITHIN AN RTI FRAMEWORK

Roles and Functions of Effective Teams

Wendy M. Reinke, Wesley Sims, Daniel Cohen,
and Keith C. Herman

School-based, problem solving teams (PSTs) have been in place since the late 1970s (Inverson, 2002). PSTs tend to share many commonalities including makeup, processes, and desired outcome. PSTs are a group of educational or psycho-educational service providers working collaboratively through a problem-solving process to address an identified problem facing a student or students in the school setting. Though the specific steps in the PST processes may differ, generally PSTs identify a problem, identify possible interventions, implement an intervention, and evaluate the effects (Deno, 2002). An example of how PSTs have evolved can be found in the recent shift within education to an emphasis on prevention, early intervention, and data-based decision-making that has resulted in wide-spread adoption of Response to Intervention (RTI) or multi-tiered systems of support (MTSS) models of service delivery in schools (Dowd-Eagle and Eagle, 2014). This shift away from a focus on diagnosis and special education placement to intervention planning with the goal of maintaining students in the general education curriculum to the greatest extent possible has led to advances in PST models. The purpose of this chapter is to discuss the roles, functions, and processes of effective PSTs within an RTI/MTSS framework.

History

Multidisciplinary teams were mandated as decision making bodies for special education entitlement in 1975 following the signing of P.L. 94–142. This act changed dramatically the way schools provide educational services to children with disabling conditions. Some important components of P.L. 94–142 included requiring public schools to evaluate children with disabilities, and subsequently creating an individualized educational plan with parent input and from a least restrictive environment (LRE) perspective. The tenets on which PL 94 142 was based may have been in large part a response to the segregating practices of educational entities towards children with disabilities and minority groups. A LRE perspective seeks to combat this directly by stating that educators should make every effort to limit the removal from, or changes to, the typical educational environment and experiences for children with disabilities. The multidisciplinary team approach provided consideration of different perspectives from a diverse group of stakeholders, including parents as part of the decision-making process. These teams focused on a diagnostic perspective where processes were initiated to determine whether a child met criteria for a disability and therefore was eligible for special education services. Eligibility for special education services was determined by whether a student's ability was discrepant from performance. The process generally yielded one solution: placement in a special education program.

The limited options for solutions caused some special educators and school psychologists to recommend revisions to the role and function of multidisciplinary teams. In fact, very early on, Bergan and Caldwell (1967) were arguing that school psychologists must shift their attention away from serving students as diagnosticians and instead improve child welfare by facilitating the implementation of effective intervention practices by teachers through behavioral consultation and the problem-solving model. In the early 1980s, pre-referral intervention teams emerged as a recommended mechanism to guide provision of supplemental supports to struggling students not currently eligible for special education services (Burns and Symington, 2002). The goal of these pre-referral teams in the early years of their formation was to support children experiencing difficulties in school until they could begin receiving special education. These teams presumed that inevitably an evaluation to determine eligibility for special education services would occur, at which time the child would be found eligible to receive these services. Interestingly, although the teams developed and provided intervention, this intervention did not seek to solve an identified problem, but rather to manage the problem in the regular education setting until the evaluation process could be completed and the student could be transitioned to a placement in a special education setting. In short, the pre-referral teams existed to fill a temporal gap between regular and special education service provision (Burns and Symington, 2002). It should also be noted that pre-referral teams were guided by special education staff and special education practices. In these teams, regular educators often met with special educators functioning similarly to consultants, to develop pre-referral interventions the teacher as a consultee would implement (Burns and Symington, 2002; Rosenfeld and Gravois, 1996).

Despite the focus on pre-referral interventions, several limitations persisted with regard to the functionality and ability for PSTs to foster effective solutions when operating within a medically based discrepancy model (Fletcher, Coulter, Reschly, and Vaughn, 2004; Meyer, 2000). In such models, in order for an individual to access supplemental services, a significant discrepancy must exist between the individual's actual performance and his or her expected performance. This is to say an individual must deviate significantly, usually lagging behind, before receiving treatment (Meyer, 2000). A diagnosis-driven, discrepancy approach to service neglects a prevention or early intervention approach to service delivery, which are hallmark features of RTI/MTSS approaches. A discrepancy model often fails to account for environmental factors that contribute to deficits in performance. There are a variety of factors including, but not limited to, a lack of exposure to effective instruction, socioeconomic disadvantage, assessment bias, personal bias, or inappropriate normative comparison groups that could explain deficits in skills or performance (Kovaleski and Prasse, 2004). A discrepancy model also focuses solely on a significant deficit from normative or expected functioning. The discrepancy model is structured so that in order to access any specialized services an individual must be identified as having a disorder (O'Donnell and Miller, 2011). Individuals with disabilities can receive support, those without disability diagnoses do not receive support. In the school setting disordered functioning has traditionally equated to a performance delay of two to three years, academically. This is to say that in a discrepancy model, educators would be required to wait for a student's failure to grow to the equivalent of a 2- to 3-year gap before specialized supports could be provided (Reynolds and Shaywitz, 2009). This illustrates how the discrepancy model could easily be described very aptly as the wait-to-fail model (O'Donnell and Miller, 2011; Reynolds and Shaywitz, 2009).

The growing emphasis on alternative prevention and early intervention spurred the evolution of tiered models of service delivery and brought the evolution of PSTs in schools forward (Fletcher et al., 2004; Jiménez, 2010). An interest in prevention and early intervention, as well as the belief in an alternative means by which to identify children with learning disabilities, began to grow within education and special education. This evolution culminated in revisions to federal special education guidelines (e.g. IDEA, 2004). Since the reauthorization of IDEA 2004, which states that special education eligibility can be determined due to non-responsiveness to evidence-based interventions in addition to traditional methods, RTI/MTSS models have become increasingly relevant to school-based practices (Fuchs and Fuchs, 2006). The distinction between these models and previous service delivery models is the use of a problem-solving approach when implementing interventions for students, particularly students who have not been identified as eligible for special education services. A problem-solving approach goes beyond provision of interim or transitional pre-referral services in hopes of preventing or remediating problematic functioning. An RTI/MTSS approach allows school professionals to function within an intervention framework rather than a psychometric eligibility framework (Gresham, 2008). Integration of scientific methods like those inherent in a problem-solving approach, is an essential tenet of effective school practices (Galloway and Sheridan, 1995).

Educators have relied heavily on teams to implement the problem-solving activities that make up RTI/MTSS models. As the overall service delivery model has moved from discrepancy to RTI/MTSS, several shifts within practice have occurred. First, pre-referral intervention teams have begun to emphasize data, particularly formative data, to guide decision making (Brown-Chidsey and Andren, 2012; Deno, 2005). Second, as supplemental service delivery expanded beyond those delivered by special educators, the responsibility for intervention activities has shifted to make intervention a more regular education-oriented initiative (Hazelkorn, Bucholz, Goodman, Duffy, and Brady, 2010). This shift to use of a data-based problem-solving approach has required educators to expand their training and practices to include those necessary for RTI/MTSS activities. The evolution of special education services delivered through Individualized Education Plans allowed special educators to become more familiar with concepts including, but not limited to, formative assessment, goal setting, data-based decision-making, differentiated instruction, and alternative instructional approaches. Two methods dominated attempts to develop the knowledge and skills needed to implement RTI/MTSS service delivery for in-service general and special educators. These approaches included in-service professional development trainings and school-based PSTs (Burns and Symington, 2002; Danielson, Doolittle, and Bradley, 2007). The team approach allowed educators with varied skills and expertise to support the process and to assist schools in improving service delivery in the educational setting to address diverse student needs (Bahr, Whitten, Dieker, Kocarek, and Manson, 1999).

Problem Solving Models

Though the origins of the problem-solving approach can be traced to Greek philosophy's first attempts to analyze observed phenomena, within the field of education, problem-solving likely originated in behavioral consultation (Bergan, 1977). The application of behavioral consultation to education grew out of an increase in the number and severity of problems experienced in schools. Behavioral consultation provided an indirect service using problem-solving logic, including defining the problem(s) the client faced, formulating and implementing a plan(s) to address the problem, and evaluating the goal attainment and plan effectiveness (Bergan, 1977; Kratochwill and Bergan, 1978). Though the problem-solving process can and should be broken into numerous explicit, easily executed steps, a synthesis of problem-solving literature suggests there are four general steps that make up problem-solving, including: problem identification, problem analysis, plan implementation, and plan evaluation (Fuchs et al., 2003). The steps within PSTs bring science to practice. The PST approach mirrors the scientific method and is grounded in the use of data to predict and control identified outcomes. These four steps can be processed within PSTs using these four questions: 1) what is the problem, 2) why is the problem happening, 3) what can be done about the problem, and 4) did the intervention work (Tilley, 2008).

Interpretation of how best to implement the general guidelines referenced above in the applied school setting has resulted in numerous PST structures and formats. A few models have distinguished themselves by a particular emphasis on creating an explicit framework for the systematic collection and evaluation of data. Deno and colleagues (1985) are frequently credited as the pioneers of a problem-solving approach through the development and validation of curriculum-based measurement (CBM). Data collected using CBM facilitated the application of advancement of RTI/MTSS processes for academic difficulties. Data obtained via CBMs allowed educators to define problems and make data-based decisions regarding intervention effectiveness, as well as determine desired or appropriate levels of response. Deno (2012) noted that CBM provided a technically adequate approach for taking a more functional problem-solving approach to the prevention and solution of educational problem. Deno's model was grounded in the belief that interventions with students should be viewed as hypothesis testing. While evidence-based practices should be used, there can be no absolute certainty about their effectiveness with a given student(s) until formative data-collection is collected and analyzed. The problem-solving process then becomes an on-going series of experiments conducted by teams of educators and driven-by data.

Building from Deno's model (2012), Newton and colleagues (2012a) developed the Team Assisted Problem Solving model (TIPS) for application in tier 2 behavior teams embedded within the Positive Behavioral Interventions and Supports (PBIS) paradigm. Specifically, the TIPS model uses Office Disciplinary Referral data in a manner that is analogous to Deno's application of CBM data, and has well-defined procedures for using data in a team decision-making context that are provided to team participants using a set structured training modules. A multiple baseline single case design study (Todd et al., 2011) and a randomized wait-list trial (Newton et al., 2012b) both found that the implementation of TIPS resulted in high levels of integrity to the TIPS model, but did not shed light on the nature of the model's impact on student outcomes.

Problem Solving Teams within an RTI/MTSS framework

Frequently, PSTs organize and execute the components of RTI/MTSS tiered service delivery models. As noted previously, RTI/MTSS can be described as a general problem-solving process where a student progresses through increasingly intensive interventions based on her response to prevention or intervention efforts (Burns, Riley-Tillman, and VanDerHeyden, 2012). Ideally, this approach is driven by data-based decision-making to identify and support students based on their individual needs (Stormont, Reinke, Herman, and Lembke, 2012). Each tier of prevention or support represents an increase in the intensity, frequency, duration, and/or magnitude of intervention, or a decrease in the number of students included in the intervention. The goal of this progression is specific toward addressing students' needs through more focused or intensive interventions as determined by data (Lane, Kalberg, and Menzies, 2009). The focus is on student progression up (non- or poor response to intervention) and regression back down (positive response to intervention) through each of the tiers, rather than diagnostic categorization of a within-child problem. Through data-based decision-making, as interventions are determined to be ineffective, the intensity, duration, or specificity of the intervention increases, thus moving students through successive tiers.

In RTI/MTSS models, data-based decision-making looks like a decision to continue with the current level of support (stay on current tier), modify current support slightly (stay on current tier, but change support slightly), change the level of support to something more intensive (move to the next tier), change level of support to something less invasive (move to the previous tier), or refer for formal evaluation to determine eligibility for special education. The final option occurs after a student has progressed through all tiers of support without appropriate improvement. PSTs guide collection of baseline and progress monitoring data, evidence-based intervention identification and selection, monitoring of implementation fidelity, and organization of data.

Tilly (2008) documents the evolution of the use of PSTs within a three-tiered RTI/MTSS model. The initial Heartland problem-solving approach utilized a four-level framework. The first level consisted of consultation between a teacher and parent. This level 1 problem-solving occurred when a teacher or parent brought forward concerns about an individual child's performance. The teacher and parent worked together through the problem-solving process to determine the nature of the problem and devised strategies that might be effective. Level 2 occurred if the level 1 problem-solving process was not effective and there was a need for additional resources. Thus, level 2 was labeled consultation with other resources which include, but are not limited to, time, money, instructional materials, instructional approaches, tangible reinforcers, and individuals. Typically, the level 2 meetings included one or more additional individuals with specialized knowledge and additional information about the problem, redefining the problem if necessary, and creation of a new plan to address the problem are developed. Should level 2 not meet the needs of the student, level 3 was employed which included consultation with the extended problem-solving team. The distinction between level 2 and 3 were predominantly that related service personnel with specialized expertise and techniques were members of the level 3 PST. At level 3 the team would review all information collected form level 1 and 2, examine whether the problem was accurately identified, a more systematic use of data to determine the nature, severity, and etiology, and an explicitly articulated thinking process were used for problem analysis. Finally, should level 3 not be effective, the team would acknowledge that special education resources may be warranted to address the students' educational problems (level 4).

The issue that arose for the Heartland's PST approach was that it was designed to work for one student at a time (Tilly, 2008). The authors found four major challenges emerged to using this PST model within a three-tiered RTI/MTSS framework: 1) solving problems one at a time was not efficient when many children have similar educational problems, 2) there was no way to proactively respond to entire curricular and instructional programs that were creating educational problems, 3) individual teachers were not able to implement more than two interventions with high fidelity and as such this was problematic when classrooms with more than two students needed specific individualized interventions based on the PST process, and 4) because the problem-solving process was still reactive (i.e., teacher-referred problems) many teachers perceived the process as the new way to get students into special education, and in some situations this would undermine the implementation of interventions in the general education classroom. Based on these challenges, the shift toward the possibility of developing a PST process that allows for the problem-solving process to work with all students, not only those who struggle, evolved. Thus, while the science behind the problem-solving process was not altered, the ability to implement data-based group-level intervention and examination of the curriculum impact on student performance were incorporated into the model.

School-Wide Tiered PST Approach within RTI/MTSS

Given the lessons learned and the need for more efficient and effective practices to ensure no children are left behind, a three-tiered school-wide model of prevention and intervention has been recommended (Simmons, Kame'enui, and Good, 2002; Sugai, Horner, and Gresham, 2002). Ideally this three-tiered model employs universal screening at the first tier to identify students struggling academically or behaviorally (McIntosh, Reinke, and Herman, 2010). Teachers still have the ability and responsibility to refer students who they are concerned about in the three-tiered RTI/MTSS model. Universal screening simply provides an additional mechanism to assist with the process. The universal screening data gives important information about potential problems with the core academic instruction, as well as students who are in need of better instruction in behavioral expectations. For instance, if more than 20% of students are struggling in a particular area within the school, then revisions to curriculum or instructional practices may be warranted. Thus, tier 1 of the model uses data to determine whether school-wide, grade-level, or class-wide prevention or intervention efforts are needed. Having universal supports in place are critical if we are to use school resources wisely and to successfully find those students truly in need of additional supports (Stormont, et al., 2012).

At tier 2, supplemental instruction and/or interventions are employed for students who struggle despite universal supports being in place. Even with effective core curriculum and instruction, there will be students who continue to struggle. Within the three-tiered model approximately 10–15% of students may need additional supports (Stormont, et al., 2012). Tier 2 will use the PST to identify students in need of more intensive supports. The PST may choose to gather additional data on these students to guide what type of intervention or support is provided. All students who receive additional supports within this tier would also be progress-monitored to determine if the intervention is effective. If adequate improvements are not made (approximately 5% of students), these students will move into tier 3 and be provided with more intensive individualized supports. Ongoing progress monitoring occurs at tier 3 as well.

Advantages to PSTs within an RTI/MTSS framework

There are several advantages to implementing RTI/MTSS models using PSTs in schools. First, PSTs are inherently advantageous to service provision given they are in theory, and often in practice, collaborative (Bahr, et al., 1999). Regular education teachers, administrators, special educators, supplemental support specialists, and other specialty areas are frequently represented in PSTs. This combination of professionals with diverse experiences, training, expertise, and perspectives allows for more effective problem-solving. PSTs allow for consistency in problem-solving activities. PSTs can engage in the same problem-solving framework to identify and respond to difficulties. Ideally, the composition of the PSTs is held constant. This allows for increased efficiency in execution of problem-solving activities through repetition and practice by the core PST members.

Second, a PST approach allows for a diffusion of PST responsibilities across participants. In contrast to more traditional consultation models, PSTs can rely on more individuals to conduct problem-solving activities. The team-based problem-solving model can provide an efficient means of delivering intervention. A team approach allows service provision to exceed the limits by which a single service provider may be constrained. For example, an intervention targeting grief following a suicide of a family member, is likely be beyond the scope skills of a reading specialist, however, a school psychologist or school counselor is likely have some training or experience with this topic.

Third, of particular importance to determining whether a student is progressing within a tier is evaluating the fidelity to which the interventions within each tier are implemented. The PSTs can incorporate evaluation of treatment fidelity within the model to ensure that lack of progress is not due to lack of intervention fidelity. School psychologists and other service providers collaborating on the PSTs are bound by the ethical principles of integrity, fidelity, and responsibility to those they serve (APA, 2002). Employment of PSTs has also been identified as a means to facilitate change as education attempts to embrace an RTI/MTSS approach (Kovaleski, 2002). The team structure allows for members to support and learn from each other and face resistance to change as a group (Fuchs and Fuchs, 1996; Kovaleski, 2002).

A fourth advantage of a team-based problem-solving approach is the neutralizing effect it has on bias due to student characteristic such as race, religion, socioeconomic status, neighborhood, gender, or familial history (Fuchs, Mock, Morgan, and Young, 2003). Teams allow a variety of members to hold each other to objective analysis and actions, and address salient issues involved with the disproportional representation of minority students in discipline referrals, pre-referral interventions, and special education services (Harris-Murri, King, and Rostenberg, 2006; Skiba et al., 2008).

Team Structure

Given the collaborative nature of PSTs, the efficiency and effectiveness of these teams is highly influenced by the composition of team members. Several factors should be considered when building a PST, including: skills and expertise of members, attitude towards RTI/MTSS, and personal and professional demeanor or character traits. In addition to these individual factors, systemic factors such as confounding roles and responsibilities for members should be considered, particularly when selecting or assigning a PST facilitator(s). Typically, a PST is composed of six to eight school personnel members, who include an administrator, a general education representative, special educator, school psychologist, and other school mental health providers, such as a school counselor. Ensuring that individuals with both behavioral and academic intervention expertise are included is useful, particularly given the common co-occurrence of behavioral and academic problems for students who struggle (Reinke, Herman, Petras, and Ialongo, 2008).

Though collaborative, arguably the most important member of the PST is the facilitator. Commonly, facilitators might include the administrator, counselor, lead teacher, school psychologists, or behavior support specialist. Successful facilitators should have: administrative support, knowledge of general problem-solving processes, understanding of specific school or district RTI/MTSS and PST processes, extensive understanding of the use and interpretation of data, and good organizational and communication skills.

The roles and functions of team members vary across PST models. Ideally, cases presented to the team are brought through a process in which universal screening data help to identify students struggling in comparison to their peers. Teachers may also bring cases to the team to review based on specific data they gather in the classroom. These cases are then reviewed within the context of the problem-solving process, with the PST facilitator guiding the process. Some teams utilize time keepers and note takers to support the process. Effective teams use data to identify a problem(s), assign team members to gather additional data, facilitate monitoring of student progress, and suggest or implement interventions. Action plans for who will be responsible and what will be accomplished are completed with a specific plan for follow-up to determine whether the plan was effective for the student and what modifications are needed.

Despite use in schools for over three decades, in the absence of external, research-oriented oversight and maintenance, PSTs often remain inefficient and ineffective (Burns and Symington, 2002; Prasse, 2006). For example, it is not uncommon for a large portion of meeting time to be spent identifying a problem with little to no time on intervention planning. Additionally, following these meetings, fidelity of implementation is often left unchecked, resulting in inconsistent, unreliable intervention implementation (McNamara and Hollinger, 2000). Thus, PST models that provide more explicit guidance in the process may be needed. Many schools develop their own forms and procedures based on the RTI/MTSS model utilized in their district. A PST model, aptly named "PST 1–2–3" (Sims, 2008; www.pst123.com) or its 3-meeting cycle used to execute problem-solving processes, was developed to provide explicit guidance to teams with inefficient or ineffective PST processes. Guided by prevailing PST research and theory (see Bahr et al., 2006, 1999; S. Deno, 2002; Kovaleski, 2002), this PST format was developed in an applied setting to address common struggles experienced by school-based PSTs. The following provides a description of this model and how it can be used within the RTI/MTSS framework.

PST 1–2–3

PST 1–2–3 (Sims, 2008; www.pst123.com) provides explicit yet flexible guidance for educators as they engage in problem-solving and data-based decision-making activities to address student difficulties within tiered service delivery models. PST 1–2–3 was developed to address the ineffectiveness of typical problem-solving teams and, while grounded in school-based consultation theory (Bergan, 1977; Bergan and Kratochwill, 1990; Deno, 2005; Erchul and Martens, 2010), also draws from practical, real-world experiences in the application of these processes to team practices. PST 1–2–3 was structured through the use of agendas, repetition and consistency, time limits, and deemphasizing of needed prior training or experience in a manner that sought to limit the impact of some common barriers to collaborative problem-solving efforts, such as resistance, inconsistency, poor training, and lack of skill (see Gonzalez, Nelson, Gutkin, and Shwery, 2004; Gutkin and Hickman, 1990; MacLeod, Jones, Somers, and Havey, 2001). Since initial pilot implementation in 2008, PST 1–2–3 has been refined through incorporating additional research and theory, feedback from users, and outcomes for students. PST 1–2–3 is based on a simple technique used by professions to eliminate human error, given that no matter the training or education, on any given day, our intelligence, or training can fail, if only momentarily. To combat this human condition, physicians, engineers, pilots, and others use checklists to increase execution of processes and procedures essential to success (see Berenholtz et al., 2004; Lin et al., 2012). The PST 1–2–3 process applies a checklist-structured, consistent problem-solving model and incorporates function-based problem definition and intervention selection in addressing difficulties exhibited by students in any subject area and at any grade or support level. The model allows team members to work through the problem-solving process in an organized, structured manner while limiting traditional in-service training time by facilitating understanding through support, practice, and frequent repetition. This process allows repetition of the same processes and procedures within RTI/MTSS service delivery models across all tiers and is designed to be used to address system, building, group, or individual level problems. At the student level, the process is consistent for behavior as well as academic difficulties. This consistency in process is designed to promote fluency in problem-solving practices. The primary emphasis of PST 1–2–3 is to promote collaborative problem analysis and problem-solving while downplaying the individual, expert-driven approach to intervention inherent in a diagnosis-driven medical model of service delivery (see Brown-Chidsey and Andren, 2012).

In keeping with a collaborative, collectivist, and non-expert driven problem-solving approach, PST 1–2–3 meetings serve as organizational tools for activities to be executed following meetings. The underlying rationale for this approach is that meetings themselves do not address problems; the treatment component are the actions carried out following the meetings. Teams work through steps similar to those identified earlier, including functional problem definition, baseline data collection, intervention selection, progress monitoring, implementation fidelity checks, and data-based decision in a very structured, organized, and efficient manner. This model uses a three-meeting cycle, occurring over a six- to eight-week period to address identified problems in schools. Each meeting follows a specific agenda that results in explicit actions, roles, and responsibilities for some or all team members that will be completed. The following describes the specific roles, functions, and processes across the three-meeting cycle for PST 1–2–3.

The PST 1–2–3 process follows a three-meeting cycle that establishes problem solving as a linear process, which is a critical component. For quality problem-solving, some steps must occur in order for later steps to be completed effectively. For example, problem identification, definition, and analysis must occur to guide baseline and progress monitoring assessment as well as intervention selection. Without baseline and formative data collection that reliably and accurately assesses a targeted problem, reliable data-based decisions cannot occur. Problem-solving is time bound and linear, which requires planning, organization, forethought, and commitment for success. Possibly the most glaring component of this process that is often conducted out of sequence can be seen in the decision-making associated with a problem-solving process. It is imperative that this decision occur after all of the components essential to high-quality, informed data-based decision making have been completed.

Of course, while critical, temporal sequence of process execution is meaningless without correct execution of the steps of a problem-solving process. Describing each of the components of a problem-solving process in detail is beyond the scope of this chapter, but the complex and varied nature of individual steps further illustrates the advantage of taking a team approach. Including individuals with varying areas of expertise allows teams to draw on this expertise for problem-solving process activities such as problem analysis, data collection, and intervention research. For example, the importance of appropriately identifying and analyzing a presenting problem(s) cannot be overemphasized. This step in the process is the foundation on which subsequent actions will be launched. Appropriately identifying and analyzing a problem from a function-based perspective is critical in determining how baseline and progress monitoring data will be collected. Similarly, interventions will be selected based on the problem identification and analysis steps in the problem-solving process. Think of a situation where a math intervention would be implemented for a student with reading concerns. Though exaggerated, such a mismatch between intervention and problem is possible when a problem is not identified and analyzed appropriately. A more nuanced example is one that may be more common in schools than we might think. Numerous children each day receive some manner of behavior support for not keeping hands and feet to themselves. While on the surface these supports may seem appropriate, for some, it may not be that simple. When inappropriate behavior manifests itself in an attempt to avoid academic tasks, a behavior support plan may not be the most appropriate course of intervention. Through analysis of the problem, a team could determine that remediation of the deficient academic skills via academic-oriented interventions, and the problematic behavior may be eliminated. This is to say, if educators give the student the skills

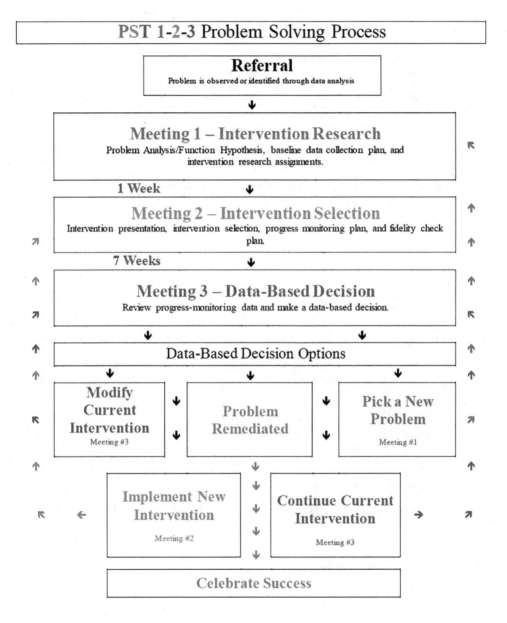

Figure 6.1

needed to be more successful in the academic tasks he or she is attempting to avoid with negative behavior, the need to engage in the negative behavior will be decreased, if not eliminated. Another glaring example of the importance of correctly completing steps in the problem-solving process is seen in the collection of baseline and progress-monitoring data. In order to make informed decisions regarding a student's response to an intervention, educators

Meeting # 1 Facilitator Agenda

Begin by assigning/reviewing the roles of:

Timekeeper	Scheduler	Focus Monitor
Secretary or Recorder	Facilitator	Engaged Participants
Case manager – If not the facilitator	Data Manager	Fidelity Monitor

Check boxes as tasks are completed

1. Strengths – 2 minutes ☐
- Query the teacher/team to determine the student's strengths

2. Function-based Problem Definition – 7 minutes ☐
- Query the teacher/team to determine the most pressing problem
- Use supplemental interview/questionnaire if necessary
- Generate a hypothesis for the function of the problem?

3. Baseline Data Collection Procedure – 5 minutes ☐
- Query the team to determine a way the identified problem area can be measured quantifiably
- Use supplemental guide if necessary

4. Intervention Research Assignments – 3 minutes ☐
- Solicit 3 volunteers to research interventions for the identified problem
- Classroom observation assignment if necessary
- Follow up RE: Function discussion if needed

5. Responsibility Assignment – 2 minutes ☐
- Review team member responsibilities
  - Baseline data
  - Intervention research
  - Additional responsibilities

6. Schedule Meeting #2 – 1 minute ☐
- Discuss with team the amount of time needed to complete the baseline data collection and intervention research activities
- Schedule next meeting based on amount of time needed
- Should be no more than 2 weeks from meeting #1

7. Complete Meeting #1 section of the PST 1-2-3 Intervention Guide ☐
- Fill in student information
- Fill in date for Meeting #1
- Complete questions for Meeting #1 ONLY

Figure 6.2

Considering Function When Analyzing Student Difficulties

Academic	Behavior
Acquisition • The student has not been taught the desired skills • The student has not learned the desired skill • The student has not had enough help doing the task • The task is too hard for the student (developmentally inappropriate) • The student has not rehearsed the skill enough (for mastery) Fluency • Student can do the task, but not at an appropriate rate • Student has not had enough practice of a learned skill (for efficiency) Generalization • The student is unable to apply learned skill in new context	Obtain/Seeking • Behavior results in student getting positive or negative attention/tangible • Power struggles are negative attention Escape/Avoid • Behavior results in avoidance of something/someone/task/demand Acquisition • The student has not been taught the desired behavior • The student has not learned the desired behavior • The student has not had enough help doing the task • The behavior is too hard for the student (developmentally inappropriate) • The student has not rehearsed the behavior enough (for mastery) Fluency • Student can do the behavior, but not at an appropriate frequency, duration, or latency • Student has not had enough practice of a learned behavior (for efficiency) Generalization • The student is unable to apply learned behavior in new context

Adapted from the Evidence Based Intervention Network
EBI Network developed by Chris Riley-Tillman, Ph.D.
www.ebi.missouri.edu
PST 1-2-3 materials and forms created by Wesley A. Sims

Figure 6.3

must have data that reliably and accurately measures a problem in question. Educators need data representing performance prior to and during intervention implantation. Progress-monitoring data should occur over a period that allows for a trend to be established within a student's performance. Data should be organized graphically to facilitate this decision-making process.

Roles and Responsibilities within PST 1–2–3

Members of the PST team will hold specific roles and responsibilities. These roles include *facilitator, scheduling coordinator, case manager, time keeper, record keeper/note taker, focus monitor, intervention researcher, intervention implementer, data collector, data manager, fidelity monitor, and active participant(s)*. These roles and responsibilities for PST 1–2–3 members can be divided into three categories, before a meeting, during the meeting, and after the meeting.

Before-meeting activities are conducted by three personnel, *schedule coordinator, facilitator,* and *case manager*. The PST 1–2–3 process beings with scheduling. This process follows a three-meeting cycle over a nine-week period. The PST 1–2–3 team keeps a master calendar with all meeting times. When an initial issue is referred to the PST, the scheduling coordinator identifies the next available opening on the schedule. The *scheduling coordinator* schedules the second PST 1–2–3 meeting a week after the initial meeting and the third PST 1–2–3 meeting seven weeks after the second meeting. The scheduling coordinator then communicates the meeting times to team members. This communication includes inviting parents if the meeting is for an individual student. If the meeting is in regard to a system, grade level, or group issue,

Problem Solving Team – Intervention Guide

Student: _____   Teacher: _____
Grade: _____   Case Manager: _____

Meeting #1 – Date:

1. What are this student's strengths?

2. What is the Function-based Problem Definition identified problem(s)?

3. What is the primary area of intervention focus?

4. How will baseline data be collected?

    a. By whom?

    b. When?

5. Who are the individuals responsible for doing intervention research (If behavior, classroom observations and interest inventory)?

6. Has the parent/EDM been notified of this concern? Yes / No

7. Date parent/EDM was contacted: _____ By whom: _____

Meeting #2 – Date:

7. What is the intervention that was selected?

8. Goal statement incorporating baseline data:

9. Who will be responsible for implementing/conducting the intervention?

10. How often will the intervention be conducted? Intervention Schedule:

Monday	Tuesday	Wednesday	Thursday	Friday

Figure 6.4

including parents may not be appropriate. Technology has proven effective in making the scheduling and communication of meetings more efficient. The *facilitator* ensures that appropriate forms and meeting materials are organized and ready for the meeting. As the process progresses, *case managers*, members of the team assigned to specific students, would contact team members with responsibilities as a reminder to prepare for the upcoming meeting, providing an additional layer of accountability for team members.

In regard to the seven-week implementation period noted above, different processes may advocate other time periods. The PST 1–2–3 rationale for a seven-week minimum before

Intervention Fidelity Check

Observer: _____   Date: _____

Location: _____   Time: _____

Student: _____   Implementer: _____

1. Intervention implementer is person noted on "Intervention Guide."	YES	NO
If no, why?		
2. Intervention occurring at time noted on "Intervention Guide."	YES	NO
If no, why?		
3. Intervention activity is consistent with description noted on "Intervention Guide."	YES	NO
If no, why?		
4. Intervention lasted the length of time noted on the "Intervention Guide."	YES	NO
If no, why?		
5. Was this intervention session atypical in any way from other intervention sessions?	YES	NO
If yes, explain.		

Additional comments/observations…

_____

_____

_____

_____

Figure 6.5

reconvening to make a data-based decision regarding intervention effectiveness is simple. PST 1–2–3 was developed to combat a frequent occurrence within RTI/MTSS implantation in which educators abandon an intervention after a short period of time. Often, when a problem (most often behavioral, but academic issues also) was not remediated after days of implementation, educators appeared quick to abandon it in favor of some alternate support service (often special education). If the implementation period is stated flatly and consistently, there should be less debate over how long a given intervention should be implemented. This seven-week period was also not selected arbitrarily. When initially developed, some state RTI/MTSS guidelines outlined criteria for eligibility for special education services using an RTI approach that required a minimum of two interventions, delivered over a minimum of 12 weeks (see dese.mo.gov; gadoe.org). Beyond governmental guidelines, a six-week intervention implementation period allows time for a reliable trend to emerge in performance following initial positive response often seen in behavior improvement plans, regression following this positive response, extinction bursts, and implementation integrity issues associated with intervention efforts.

Responsibilities during meetings are fulfilled by a *facilitator, record keeper/note taker, time keeper, focus monitor, and engaged participants*. The facilitator serves as a guide through the meeting agenda. PST 1–2–3 asks facilitators to present agenda items in sequence and check them off as they are completed. In instances where meetings get bogged down, the facilitator moves the process forward through questions or guidance. Team members are committed to being actively engaged at all times, thus all members, but particularly those who do not have another explicitly stated job, are assigned the role of *engaged participant*. This further supports the indication that everyone on the team has a specified job. Another important responsibility within meetings is completed by the *record keeper/note taker*. This person completes the paperwork and records associated with the process, including completing the PST 1–2–3 Intervention Guide, which aligns with meeting agendas. This form is not meant to replace notes taken by other participants, but serves as a final, permanent record of meeting activities. The person that ensures the team adheres to time allotted to agenda items, the *time keeper*, is also an extremely important member of the PST 1–2–3 team. This person notes when work on an agenda item begins and warns team members when allotted time is about to expire. Similarly, the *focus monitor* redirects discussion should team members get off topic. Despite the importance of staying focused on completing problem-solving process in a timely, progressive manner, teams frequently get sidetracked. For instance, it is easy for team members to use this meeting as an opportunity to vent their frustration. Team members find themselves in such situations frequently, and not

Meeting # 3 Agenda

Check boxes as tasks are completed

1. Restate Problem/Goal – 1 minutes ☐

2. Restate Intervention – 2 minutes ☐

3. Intervention Fidelity Check – 2 minutes ☐

4. Report Progress Monitoring Data – 4 minutes ☐

5. Discuss Progress Monitoring Data – 5 minutes ☐

6. Make a Data Based Decision – 5 minutes ☐

7. Reschedule Next Meeting – 1 minute ☐

8. Complete Meeting # 3 section of PST Intervention Guide ☐

Figure 6.6

PST 1-2-3 **Data-Based Decision Making**

Based on the trend analysis of the graphed baseline and progress-monitoring data, make a data-based decision about next steps.

Problem Remediated – Celebrate Success!

Continue Current Intervention – Reconvene in six weeks for another meeting #3.

Modify Current Intervention – Reconvene for another meeting #2 (one week) or #3 (six weeks) as needed.

Implement New Intervention – Assign research duties and reconvene in one week for another meeting #2.

Pick a New Problem – Reconvene in one week for another meeting #1.

Consider a Referral for Evaluation to Determine Eligibility for Special Education Services
If team has progressed through multiple interventions and **data** does not indicate sufficient progress.

Figure 6.7

interrupting and getting these discussions back on track can have terrible consequences for problem solving-efforts. This is why a *focus monitor* is critically important to PST processes.

In later meetings, (i.e. the second and third meeting) in which data is being discussed and goals are being developed, additional roles are represented. A *data-manager* for example, would be responsible for presenting baseline and/or progress-monitoring data to the team. Also, in meetings occurring further along in the overall process, the *case manager* might also play a role in communicating information to the team about occurrences outside the meetings.

Since meetings are only the organizational tool for activates occurring between meetings, the roles and responsibilities of individuals after or before meetings will determine the ultimate success or failure of this or any PST process. Specific roles between meetings include *intervention researcher, intervention implementer, data collector, data manager, fidelity monitor, case manager, and scheduling coordinator.* Following the PST meeting the *data-manager* would have the responsibility of ensuring that data is collected, organized, and entered into a graph for dissemination. The greatest distinction between PST 1–2–3 and other PST formats is the separation of the first several steps of a problem-solving process into multiple meetings. This separation results in the inception of an important role on the team, *intervention researcher.* PST 1–2–3 developers frequently experienced initial meetings in which educators were expected to come into the meeting having identified the problem and collected baseline data. Team members would then "brainstorm" evidence-based interventions. Rarely was this approach successful. Often these ideas, while well-intentioned and possibly useful in addressing the problem, were more commonly used practice, rather than evidence-based practice. This inevitably created frustration and resentment towards team members that attempted to redirect team practices to analyze problems deeper, collect new baseline data, and questioned the evidence base of proposed interventions. In the PST 1–2–3 approach, meeting 1 focuses on problem identification, function-based problem analysis, baseline data collection method, and intervention research assignments. In the subsequent meeting 2, *intervention researchers*, typically at least three, present interventions they researched and believe will address the identified problem. This explicitly stated role and the activity associated with it illustrates the critical emphasis of engaging in evidence-based practice.

One advantage of a team-based approach to any activity is that responsibilities can be distributed across team members. The role of *intervention researcher* can and should be assumed by multiple team members over time. With guidance (e.g. where and how to do intervention research) from more experienced and knowledgeable team members, rotation of this responsibility facilitates the ability to do intervention research in other less knowledgeable and experienced others. An additional advantage to the inclusion of this meeting division and intervention research role is seen in the increase in awareness of evidence-based practices. This process advocates for three intervention researchers to bring one intervention option each to the second meeting. From these three interventions, one intervention will be selected. Though only one of the three will be implemented with the present issue, team members have been exposed to three evidence-based practices that may be useful in the future.

The idea of thoughtful, collaborative, and accountable data collection is emphasized within the first PST 1–2–3 meeting. The more collaborative this process is, the higher the likelihood that appropriate data-collection and intervention research and selection will occur. Collaborative, function-based analysis of problems allows multiple individuals with varied experience and expertise to provide multiple perspectives as to the underlying cause of the apparent problem(s). To clarify, a function-based analysis of problems is not meant to indicate a functional behavior assessment (FBA) or functional analysis (FA), though in some cases these approaches may be appropriate. A function-based problem analysis denotes a perspective in which team members consider underlying causes of behavior (e.g. obtain, avoid, acquisition, fluency, generalization) consistent with an FBA or FA approach. Research demonstrates adoption of this approach increases the likelihood of desirable outcomes for student difficulties (Reinke, Stormont, Clare, Latimore, and Herman, 2013).

It is difficult to say which role or responsibility is most critical within PST processes as they are so interconnected and interdependent, but many would argue the role of *intervention implementer* is the likely choice. Team members, particularly the *case manager, facilitator, intervention researchers*, and others should support the *intervention implementer* in accumulation of resources needed to implement the intervention as outlined by the evidence base supporting its use. This support should also include teaching and modeling of intervention components, scripting, and implementation supports as needed. This support should be ongoing throughout the intervention implementation period, ideally, a minimum of six weeks.

An additional role within this process, which serves to support the *intervention implementer*, is that of *fidelity monitor*. There is a growing body of work around the importance of implementation fidelity along with the varying ways by which to assess this important construct (see Burns, Peters, and Noell, 2008; McNamara and Hollinger, 2000; Sanetti and Reed, 2012). Ultimately, implementation fidelity will impact the data-based decision made regarding the effectiveness of intervention efforts. If the role of *fidelity monitor* is viewed as supportive, this role can be viewed as serving to identify and address factors that influence effective intervention implementation.

To ensure implementation fidelity in the applied setting, teams should consider the skills and abilities of team members, time and resources, and available assessment tools. Teams should begin their assessment efforts by creating intervention protocols that include checklists and implementer scripts. *Fidelity monitors* can use these protocols to evaluate implementation and work with an implementer(s) to provide supplemental support should implementation issues arise.

Case Example using PST 1–2–3

Consider this example of a successful implementation of the PST 1–2–3 process. Christopher was a 10 year, 8 month-old fifth grade student at a rural Midwestern elementary school. This elementary school did not employ any specific screening procedures to identify children to the building's PST. Students exhibiting reading concerns were referred to supplemental reading interventions similar to Title I reading programs. No specific procedures were in place for intervention efforts in the event of non-response to intervention efforts. Christopher was therefore referred to the PST for disruptive classroom behavior. In keeping with established procedures, the teacher emailed the PST facilitator and schedule coordinator. The schedule coordinator scheduled three meetings for Christopher. The facilitator gathered the appropriate meeting forms in preparation for the first PST 1–2–3 meeting, including the facilitator's packet and participants' agendas. The scheduling coordinator worked with the teacher to ensure the parent/guardian(s) were invited to the meeting.

In the first meeting the team worked through each of the PST 1–2–3 meeting 1 agenda items: 1) Student Strengths – 2min., 2) Function-based Problem Definition – 7 min., 3) Baseline Data Collection Procedure – 5 min., 4) Intervention Research Assignments – 3 min., 5) Responsibility Assignments – 2 min., 6) Schedule Meeting 2 – 1 min., and 7) Complete Meeting # 2 section of PST 1–2–3 Intervention Guide.

The PST 1–2–3 team was composed of the following members: School Psychologist – Facilitator, fourth grade teacher – Schedule Coordinator, fifth grade teacher – Record Keeper, fifth grade teacher – Referring Teacher, Special Educator – Focus Monitor, Reading Specialist – Time Keeper, and one additional special education teacher, a third grade teacher, the building administrator, Speech-Language Pathologist, and the parent – Engaged Participants. The team met every Tuesday immediately following school, typically from 3:30 to 4:15. Each meeting one to two problems were discussed. The team identified kindness, creativity, achievement in all subjects, and being social as Christopher's strengths. Christopher's teacher was asked to describe the problem behavior. The classroom teacher stated that Christopher asks questions at inappropriate times during whole-group discussion, calls out answers, asks seemingly inane question during independent work periods, starts an excessive number of conversations with her and at inappropriate times, gets out of his seat to talk to her at inappropriate times, and wanders around the classroom following the teacher. The teacher stated that these behaviors interfere with the teacher's ability to monitor other students and interrupts instructional activities. The teacher indicated the behaviors in question begin when Christopher enters her classroom and persist until the end of the day. She reported that when redirected, Christopher complies, but returns to the behavior after a brief period. The teacher stated that she did not believe the behavior was malicious or willful. This discussion led the team to the hypothesis that Christopher's behavior likely functioned to obtain attention from the teacher. Next, the team discussed baseline data collection options. After a brief discussion, the teacher agreed that she could tally each time Christopher attempted to interact with her. The school psychologist agreed to serve as the data-manager for this activity. The team discussed collecting frequency data until the next meeting in one week. The teacher was asked if she needed additional clarification for this procedure, which she declined, and the discussion moved on. Next, the facilitator solicited three volunteers from the team to conduct intervention research. The reading specialist, a third-grade teacher, and the school psychologist agreed to research interventions. The facilitator briefly reviewed some resources for behavioral interventions. The team then reviewed who was responsible for activities and what those activities were before the schedule coordinator reminded everyone that the next meeting would occur at the same time and location in one week. It was determined that the facilitator would act as the case manager for this child as the meeting occurred at a time when there were few kids in the PST process.

Following the meeting the record keeper completed the first section of the PST 1–2–3 Intervention Guide. The record keeper also sent an email reminder to team members outlining responsibilities for those who have responsibilities. The school psychologist (data manager) created a simple tally sheet for the teacher to use to collect frequency data. The teacher began using the tally sheet the day following the first meeting. The day before meeting two, the school psychologist fulfilled the responsibilities of the data manager by collecting the tally sheets from the teacher and calculating the average number of times Christopher initiated an inappropriate interaction with the teacher.

The following week the team reconvened to work through the PST 1–2–3 meeting 2 agenda: 1) Restate Problem/Report Baseline Data – 1 minute, 2) Intervention Presentations – 6 minutes, 3) Intervention Selection – 4 minutes, 4) Develop Problem Statement and SMART Goal – 2 minute, 5) Progress Monitoring Plan – 2 minute, 6) Responsibility Assignment – 4 minutes, 7) Schedule Meeting # 3 – 1 minute, and 8) Complete Meeting # 2 section of PST Intervention Guide. The meeting began by reviewing the identified problem, initiation of interactions with the classroom teacher at inappropriate times with goal of obtaining teacher attention. The school psychologist reported that on average this behavior occurs at a rate of 14 times per day. Next, the intervention researchers presented possible interventions. The reading specialist presented Check-In, Check-Out (Campbell and Anderson, 2011). The third grade teacher presented a Daily Behavior Report Card intervention (Volpe and Fabiano, 2013). The school psychologist presented non-contingent reinforcement. Each researcher briefly described the time and resources needed to implement the identified interventions, the source of the intervention, and the steps followed to implement the intervention. After a discussion of the interventions, the teacher expressed willingness to implement and preference for non-contingent reinforcement. The team then discussed a goal for the target behavior. Given the uniqueness of this behavior and the assessment tool used to assess this behavior, normative information was not available to support this process. The team ultimately determined that a drop of two inappropriate interaction attempts per week over the next 6-weeks was reasonable. A goal was established based on this decision. The progress monitoring plan was also brief after selecting an assessment procedure that was easily repeated for formative assessment. The team then reviewed post-meeting responsibilities. This discussion included soliciting volunteers to assess implementation fidelity. The school psychologist agreed to meet with the teacher the following morning to discuss specifics of implementing non-contingent reinforcement. The teacher agreed to continue frequency tallies for initiation of interactions at inappropriate times. An administrator and fifth grade teacher agreed to conduct observations of the teacher's use of non-contingent reinforcement. The school psychologist agreed to continue to serve as the data manager. The schedule coordinator confirmed the next meeting in six weeks. The meeting concluded as the record keeper completed the Meeting #2 section of the PST 1–2–3 Intervention Guide.

Following the meeting, the record keeper emailed team members with reminders of responsibilities and the date of the next meeting. The school psychologist met with the teacher the following morning to ensure the teacher understood implementation steps as well as data collection procedures. Over the next six weeks, the teacher was observed a total of eight times by fidelity monitors. During each these observations, the teacher was observed using non-contingent reinforcement with Christopher. Each Monday morning, the data manager collected tally sheets from the teacher and inputted data into an excel spreadsheet to create a chart.

After six weeks, the team reconvened for the third meeting in the PST 1–2–3 cycle. Agenda items included: 1) Restate Problem/Goal – 1 min., 2) Restate Intervention – 2 min., 3) Intervention Fidelity Check – 2 min., 4) Report Progress Monitoring Data – 4 min., 5) Discuss Progress Monitoring Data – 5 min., 6) Make a Data Based Decision – 5 min., 7) Reschedule Next Meeting – 1 min., and 8) Complete Meeting # 3 section of PST Intervention Guide.

The facilitator/case manager began the meeting by revisiting the identified problem and associated SMART goal. Next, the teacher was asked to restate the intervention. Fidelity monitors presented information gained from their fidelity checks and the teacher was asked to elaborate on this information. The teacher stated that she had no difficulty implementing the intervention beyond the initial discomfort of forcing herself to modify her behavior. Fidelity was determined to be acceptable. The data manager then presented a chart graphing daily rates of Christopher's rates of interaction initiations at inappropriate times. This graphic representation included a goal and trend line. The trend line showed a steady decrease over the time period shown on the graph. Though this data did not indicate the behavior had been completely extinguished, it suggested a dramatic decrease in frequency. This progress monitoring data suggested that the target behavior now occurred between 0 and 3 times per day. The team discussed this data briefly including the apparent trend of the data and apparent current occurrence rate. This discussion carried over into making a data-based decision. Possible decisions included: 1) Continue Current Intervention – Reconvene in six weeks for another meeting #3, 2) Modify Current Intervention – Reconvene for another meeting #2 (one week) or #3 (six weeks) as needed, 3) Celebrate Success – Problem Remediated, 4) Implement New Intervention – Assign research duties and reconvene in one week for another meeting #2, or 5) Pick a New Problem – Reconvene in one week for another Meeting #1. After a brief discussion, the teacher reported, as the data indicted, the problem had decreased dramatically. She expressed a desire to continue the intervention in its current form for an additional six weeks. The meeting concluded with the team revisiting responsibility assignments and scheduling another Meeting #3 in six weeks.

Implications for Practice

The use of PSTs in schools has occurred for several decades (Burns and Symington, 2002). Over the course of time a great deal has been learned and PSTs have evolved to meet the needs of teams using an RTI/MTSS model. While PSTs within an RTI/MTSS framework hold great promise, schools may benefit from models such as the PST 1–2–3 to support and guide the process. PST models such as the PST 1–2–3 that have forms and procedures that can improve the fidelity to the problem-solving process may be useful to schools for improving outcomes for their students. Future research may want to focus on the use of PST to improve team processes with an eye toward whether improvements in the process lead to more effective outcomes for students. One potential way to support teams in following the PST process with integrity is through performance feedback (Burns et al., 2008). Performance feedback could be provided to the team following a meeting as well as to those individuals implementing the selected interventions. Prior research has shown that performance feedback can be quite effective for changing behaviors of school practitioners (Burns, et al., 2008l Reinke, Merrell, and Lewis-Palmer, 2008). More research in systems-level consultation and ways to improve the PST process in schools is needed.

Further, while PSTs can be effective in helping schools provide and monitor interventions for students who need additional supports, there continue to be areas for improvements. First, preservice training for teachers and ancillary school professionals who may be part of a PST would be beneficial. Coursework for preservice teachers on the types of academic and behavioral assessments produce useful data within a PST context would increase the effectiveness of teams in schools. Training in school-wide models that use universal screening data for academics and behaviors within a preservice context could potentially reduce resistance to gathering and using these data in the schools. Second, providing in-service training and ongoing support to PST team members on gathering and using data within a three-tiered RTI/MTSS model may increase the effectiveness of PST teams. Here again, future research might focus on consultation with PST teams that provides feedback to improve the process.

Conclusion

RTI/MTSS models focus on prevention and early intervention. This focus on prevention and early intervention not only benefits the students whose problems are prevented or remediated early, but also allows more efficient or concentrated application of support services devoted to students whose problems could not be prevented or remediated. Using PSTs within schools implementing these-tiered models of support holds immense promise for ameliorating academic and behavior problems for students before they become entrenched and difficult to improve. PSTs offer a scientific approach that uses data to inform interventions. This approach can be employed across all tiers, including universally to identify school-level, grade-level, and classroom-level areas for intervention. Using PSTs within an RTI/MTSS context, rather than one student at a time, will lead to greater impact over time and improve the outcomes for large numbers of students in a building. Schools using models such as the PST 1–2–3 to support and guide the process will be more likely to stay true to the PST process, leading to better outcomes for their students. As schools move toward RTI/MTSS models, the concurrent formation of PSTs that map onto these models will be important. PSTs that are true to the scientific problem-solving process that clearly define the roles and responsibilities of team members will produce the greatest impact and likely sustain over time.

Resources for PST Processes

PST 1–2–3 Materials: www.pst123.com.
The Evidence-based Intervention Network: www.ebi.missouri.edu.
The National Center for Intensive Interventions: www.ncii.org.
Intervention Central: www.interventioncentral.org.
Team Initiated Problem Solving Model: www.pbis.org/training/tips.
Kratochwill, T. R., Elliott, S. N., and Callan-Stoiber, K. (2002). Best practices in school-based problem-solving consultation. *Best Practices in School Psychology IV, 1,* 583–608.
Tilly, W. D. (2008). The evolution of school psychology to science-based practice: Problem solving and the three-tiered model. *Best Practices in School Psychology V, 1,* 17–36.

References

Bahr, M. W., Walker, K., Hampton, E. M., Buddle, B. S., Freeman, T., Ruschman, N., . . . and Littlejohn, W. (2006). Creative problem solving for general education intervention teams: A two-year evaluation study. *Remedial and Special Education, 27*(1), 27–41.

Bahr, M. W., Whitten, E., Dieker, L., Kocarek, C. E., and Manson, D. (1999). A comparison of school-based intervention teams: Implications for educational and legal reform. *Exceptional Children*. Retrieved from http://psycnet.apa.org/psycinfo/2000–15736–004.

Berenholtz, S. M., Pronovost, P. J., Lipsett, P. A., Hobson, D., Earsing, K., Farley, J. E., . . . and others. (2004). Eliminating catheter-related bloodstream infections in the intensive care unit. *Critical Care Medicine, 32*(10), 2014–2020.

Bergan, J. R. (1970). A systems approach to psychological services. *Psychology in the Schools*. Retrieved from http://psycnet.apa.org/psycinfo/1971–21811–001.

Bergan, J. R. (1977). *Behavioral consultation*. Columbus, OH: Merrill.

Bergan, J. R., and Kratochwill, T. R. (1990). *Behavioral consultation and therapy*. Plenum Press. Retrieved from http://doi.apa.org/psycinfo/1990–98136–000.

Brown-Chidsey, R., and Andren, K. J. (2012). *Assessment for Intervention: A Problem-solving Approach*. New York: Guilford Press.

Burns, M. K., Peters, R., and Noell, G. H. (2008). Using performance feedback to enhance implementation fidelity of the problem-solving team process. *Journal of School Psychology, 46*(5), 537–550. Retrieved from http://doi.org/10.1016/j.jsp.2008.04.001.

Burns, M. K., Riley-Tillman, T. C. and VanDerHeyden, A. M. (2012). *RTI applications: Academic and behavioral interventions* (Vol. 1). New York: Guilford Press.

Burns, M. K., and Symington, T. (2002). A meta-analysis of prereferral intervention teams: Student and systemic outcomes. *Journal of School Psychology, 40*, 437–447.

Campbell, A., and Anderson, C. M. (2011). Check-in/Check-out: A systematic evaluation and component analysis. *Journal of Applied Behavior Analysis, 44*, 315–326.

Danielson, L., Doolittle, J., and Bradley, R. (2007). Professional development, capacity building, and research needs: Critical issues for response to intervention implementation. *School Psychology Review, 36*(4), 632.

Deno, S. (2002). Problem solving as best practice. *Best Practices in School Psychology IV, 1*, 37–56.

Deno, S. L. (2005). Problem-solving assessment. *Assessment for Intervention: A Problem-Solving Approach*, 10–40.

Dowd-Eagle, S., and Eagle, J. (2014). Team-based school consultation. In W. P. Erchul and S. M. Sheridan (Eds.), *Handbook of research in school consultation*. (pp. 450–472) New York: Routledge.

Erchul, W. P., and Martens, B. K. (2010). *School consultation: Conceptual and empirical bases of practice*. Springer Science & Business Media. Retrieved from https://books.google.com/books?hl=en&lr=&id=MmxSrqamrM8C&oi=fnd&pg=PR5&dq=school+consultation+erchul+martens+2010&ots=Je3dT9xJ3L&sig=figv1SZHYs2qArfdH2FEhSMClKs.

Fletcher, J. M., Coulter, W. A., Reschly, D. J., and Vaughn, S. (2004). Alternative approaches to the definition and identification of learning disabilities: Some questions and answers. *Annals of Dyslexia, 54*(2), 304–331.

Fuchs, D., and Fuchs, L. S. (1996). Consultation as a Technology and the Politics of School Reform Reaction to the Issue. *Remedial and Special Education, 17*(6), 386–392.

Fuchs, D., Mock, D., Morgan, P. L., and Young, C. L. (2003). Responsiveness-to-intervention: Definitions, evidence, and implications for the learning disabilities construct. *Learning Disabilities Research & Practice, 18*(3), 157–171.

Gonzalez, J. E., Nelson, J. R., Gutkin, T. B., and Shwery, C. S. (2004). Teacher resistance to school-based consultation with school psychologists a survey of teacher perceptions. *Journal of Emotional and Behavioral Disorders, 12*(1), 30–37.

Gresham, F. M. (2008). Best practices in school psychology. In *Best practices in diagnosis in a multitier problem-solving approach*. (Vol. 2, pp. 281–294)

Gutkin, T. B., and Hickman, J. A. (1990). The relationship of consultant, consultee, and organizational characteristics to consultee resistance to school-based consultation: An empirical analysis. *Journal of Educational & Psychological Consultation, 1*(2), 111.

Harris-Murri, N., King, K., and Rostenberg, D. (2006). Reducing disproportionate minority representation in special education programs for students with emotional disturbances: Toward a culturally responsive response to intervention model. *Education and Treatment of Children, 29*, 779.

Hazelkorn, M., Bucholz, J. L., Goodman, J. I., Duffy, M. L., and Brady, M. P. (2010). Response to intervention: General or special education? Who is responsible? In *The Educational Forum*. (Vol. 75, pp. 17–25) Taylor & Francis. Retrieved from www.tandfonline.com/doi/abs/10.1080/00131725. 2010.528552.

Jiménez, J. E. (2010). Response to intervention (RTI) model: A promising alternative for identifying students with learning disabilities? *Psicothema*, *22*(4), 932–934.

Keller-Margulis, M. A. (2012). Fidelity of implementation framework: A critical need for response to intervention models. *Psychology in the Schools*, *49*(4), 342–352.

Kovaleski, J. F. (2002). Best practices in operating pre-referral intervention teams. Retrieved from http://psycnet.apa.org/psycinfo/2006–03715–042.

Kovaleski, J. F., and Glew, M. C. (2006). Bringing instructional support teams to scale implications of the pennsylvania experience. *Remedial and Special Education*, *27*, 16–25.

Kovaleski, J., and Prasse, D. P. (2004). Response to instruction in the identification of learning disabilities: A guide for school teams. *National Association of School Psychologists (NASP) Communique*, *32*(5). Retrieved from http://sc-boces.org/english/IMC/Focus/Guide-for-School-Teams%20.pdf.

Kratochwill, T. R., and Bergan, J. R. (1978). Training school psychologists: Some perspectives on a competency-based behavioral consultation model. *Professional Psychology*, *9*, 71.

Lane, K. L., Bocian, K. M., MacMillan, D. L., and Gresham, F. M. (2004). Treatment integrity: An essential – but often forgotten – component of school-based interventions. *Preventing School Failure: Alternative Education for Children and Youth*, *48*, 36–43. http://doi.org/10.3200/PSFL.48.3.36–43.

Lin, D. M., Weeks, K., Bauer, L., Combes, J. R., George, C. T., Goeschel, C. A., . . . and others. (2012). Eradicating central line-associated bloodstream infections statewide the Hawaii experience. *American Journal of Medical Quality*, *27*, 124–129.

MacLeod, I. R., Jones, K. M., Somers, C. L., and Havey, J. M. (2001). An evaluation of the effectiveness of school-based behavioral consultation. *Journal of Educational & Psychological Consultation*, *12*, 203–216.

McIntosh, K., Reinke, W.M., and Herman, K.C. (2010). School-wide analysis of data for social behavior problems: Assessing outcomes, selecting targets for intervention, and identifying need for support. In G. Peacock, R. Ervin, E. Daly, and K. Merrell (Eds.), *Practical handbook of school psychology: Effective practices for the 21st Century*. (pp. 135–156) New York: Guilford Press.

McNamara, K., and Hollinger, C. L. (2000). Fidelity of problem-solving implementation and relationship to student performance. *School Psychology Review*, *29*, 443–461.

Meyer, M. S. (2000). The ability–achievement discrepancy: Does it contribute to an understanding of learning disabilities? *Educational Psychology Review*, *12*, 315–337.

Newton, J. S., Horner, R. H., Todd, A. W., Algozzine, R. F., and Algozzine, K. M. (2012). A pilot study of a problem-solving model for team decision making. *Education & Treatment of Children (West Virginia University Press)*, *35*, 25–49.

O'Donnell, P. S., and Miller, D. N. (2011). Identifying students with specific learning disabilities: School psychologists' acceptability of the discrepancy model versus response to intervention. *Journal of Disability Policy Studies*, *22*, 83–94.

Prasse, D. P. (2006). Legal supports for problem-solving systems. *Remedial & Special Education*, *27*, 7–15.

Pronovost, P., Needham, D., Berenholtz, S., Sinopoli, D., Chu, H., Cosgrove, S., . . . others. (2006). An intervention to decrease catheter-related bloodstream infections in the ICU. *New England Journal of Medicine*, *355*, 2725–2732.

Reinke, W. M., Stormont, M., Clare, A., Latimore, T., and Herman, K. C. (2013). Differentiating tier 2 social behavioral interventions according to function of behavior. *Journal of Applied School Psychology*, *29*, 148–166.

Reinke, W.M., Herman, K.C., Petras, H., and Ialongo, N. (2008). Empirically-derived subtypes of child academic and behavior problems: Co-Occurrence and distal outcomes. *Journal of Abnormal Child Psychology*, *36*, 759–777

Reynolds, C. R., and Shaywitz, S. E. (2009). Response to intervention: Ready or not? Or, from wait-to-fail to watch-them-fail. *School Psychology Quarterly*, *24*, 130.

Rosenfeld, S., and Gravois, T. (1996). *Instructional consultation teams: Collaborating for change*. New York: Guilford Press. (ED394260).

Sanetti, L. M. H., and Reed, F. D. D. (2012). Barriers to implementing treatment integrity procedures in school psychology research: Survey of treatment outcome researchers. *Assessment for Effective Intervention*, 1534508411432466.

Sims, W. A. (2008). PST 1–2–3. Unpublished document. Retrieved from www.pst123.com.

Skiba, R. J., Simmons, A. B., Ritter, S., Gibb, A. C., Rausch, M. K., Cuadrado, J., and Chung, C.-G. (2008). Achieving equity in special education: History, status, and current challenges. *Exceptional Children*, *74*, 264–288.

Tilly, W. D. (2008). The evolution of school psychology to science-based practice: Problem solving and the three-tiered model. *Best Practices in School Psychology V*, *1*, 17–36.

Volpe, R. J., and Fabiano, G. A. (2013). *Daily behavior report cards: An evidence-based system of assessment and intervention.* New York: Guilford Press.

7

LEADERSHIP AND MULTI-TIERED SYSTEMS OF SUPPORT

Bonnie Billingsley, James McLeskey, and Jean Crockett

Leadership is a critical component in establishing and maintaining multi-tiered systems of support (MTSS) (Hamilton, 2010; Putnam, 2008; Richter, Lewis, and Hagar, 2012), yet there is little research specifically addressing the actions of effective leaders, or the conditions that support them as they establish these frameworks (Richter et al., 2012). Although the professional literature refers to the importance of administrative support (Forman, Olin, Hoagwood, Crowe, and Saka, 2009; Pinkelman, McIntosh, Rasplica, Berg, and Strickland-Cohen, 2015), additional guidance is needed to link what is known about educational leadership with its application to school-wide approaches to academic learning and behavioral support.

We focus on leadership in this discussion to illustrate how educational leaders might build the capacity to implement MTSS frameworks as a systematic strategy for improving student achievement in their schools. We begin our discussion by reviewing the concept of tiered systems and their alignment with recent trends in educational policy and school reform. We then examine what is known about leading instructional change in schools and guiding the adoption, implementation, and sustainability of MTSS. We center our discussion within a framework linking school leadership with student learning to illustrate the actions leaders can take to drive change toward more powerful and equitable learning opportunities for all students.

Providing Support for All Students

MTSS is a comprehensive system encompassing the school-wide prevention models of Response to Intervention (RTI) and Positive Behavioral Interventions and Supports (PBIS). MTSS is not a program (i.e., it does not embody specific goals, objectives, and outcomes), but rather it is a framework for delivering a continuum of evidence-based practices across increasingly intensive tiers of support. The MTSS framework emphasizes frequent progress monitoring and collaborative decision-making to help teachers recognize and respond rapidly to students' academic and behavioral needs. Essentially MTSS is a systems change model that requires educators to work differently by preventing academic failure through better instruction, and by proactively supporting students' social and behavioral competencies (Kansas State Department of Education, n.d.)

Shifts in federal policy and school reform toward improving student outcomes help to explain the expansion of the MTSS approach. The use of tiered systems has increased since the 1997 and 2004 reauthorizations of the Individuals with Disabilities Education Act (IDEA). IDEA 1997 mentioned the use of positive behavioral interventions and supports to prevent behavioral problems and to encourage good behavior. IDEA 2004 authorized states to use early intervention services and a student's response to academic instruction to distinguish children with disabilities who need special education from those who struggle to learn because of poor instruction. Impetus to improve outcomes for all learners was generated through the provisions of the Elementary and Secondary Education Act, authorized in 2001 as the No Child Left Behind Act, as well as through whole-school improvement models incorporating the use of research-validated approaches to meet the needs of all students, with or without disabilities (Bateman and Linden, 2006).

Now, more than 40 states endorse the adoption of MTSS to address school-level problems, as well as to provide increasingly intensive instruction to individuals and small groups of students (National Center for Learning Disabilities, 2011). However, implementing complex, multi-leveled, school-wide systems remains relatively untested and successful implementation depends on adequate resources, valid assessments, effective interventions, and highly trained professionals (Bineham, Shelby, Pazey, and Yates, 2014). What we do know about implementing RTI and PBIS suggests effective leadership is an essential component if MTSS is to meet its promise in structuring the delivery of equitable and powerful instruction: "When the administrator is actively involved in adopting the model and sends the message through ongoing meetings and discussions that it is a school priority, there is a greater chance of success" (Haager and Mahdavi, 2007, p. 260).

What We Know about Leading Change in Schools

Educational leaders drive change by influencing others and mobilizing action to achieve shared goals and desirable outcomes (Leithwood and Riehl, 2005). Fullan (2005) underscored the importance of leadership by describing it as the longest lever available for enabling and sustaining systemic change. Change in schools, however, is typically hampered by immutable structures dating from the nineteenth century, before equity and personalized learning were part of the purpose of schooling (Ogawa, 2015; Tyack, 1974). As educational leaders grapple with policies reforming public education to improve the achievement of all learners, new approaches to organizational theory call for redesigning, rather than reforming public schools. New understandings about institutions suggest establishing fundamental change in schools requires the design of new systems and social networks that allow more personalized and equitable opportunities to learn for a wide diversity of students (Ogawa, 2015). Consequently, leading fundamental change in today's schools requires deep understanding of both learning and the contexts in which learning occurs (Ogawa, Crain, Loomis, and Ball, 2008).

Leadership for Learning

Only within the past two decades have organizational scholars studied the links between leadership and learning, viewing instructional leadership as shared work that relies on the interactions of teachers and administrators across school, district, and state levels (Louis, Leithwood, Wahlstrom, and Anderson, 2010). Viewed from this perspective, leadership that drives change in schools extends beyond the actions of a single leader to include relationships and interactions with others and the actions they take to improve instruction (Knapp, Honig, Plecki, Portin, and Copland, 2014).

What we know about leadership for learning is based primarily on evidence from surveys, and descriptive narratives and case studies of leaders' characteristics, and school and district programs and procedures (Louis et al., 2010; Robinson, Lloyd, and Rowe, 2008). Most quantitative evidence comes from correlations between leaders' characteristics and students' standardized test scores (Robinson, et al. 2008). Several meta-analyses (Leithwood, Louis, Anderson, and Wahlstrom, 2004; Marzano, Waters, and NcNulty, 2005; Robinson, et al. 2008) show modest correlations between leadership actions (e.g., communicating clear goals, providing resources and support, and aligning priorities) and students' academic and social outcomes. Evidence also supports learning-focused supports for parents, and professional development for educators emphasizing collaborative inquiry and evidence-based instruction (Leithwood, Patten, and Jantzi, 2010; Marzano et al., 2005; Robinson et al., 2008). Knowledge about leadership and the central role it plays in school improvement has been expanded through these studies, but less is known about establishing conditions that support new systems of teaching and learning, especially for children from historically underserved groups (Ogawa, 2015). In the educational leadership literature, students who struggle to learn (e.g., students with disabilities, English language learners) are typically considered from the broad perspectives of diversity, equity, and social justice. Although these are important considerations, they do not address the learning and leadership challenges experienced by school leaders in providing effective instruction for these students (Elfers and Stritikus, 2013).

Implementation of Systems for Teaching and Learning

The knowledge base informing learning-focused leadership has expanded over the past two decades alongside knowledge grounded in the learning sciences about the importance of evidence-based instructional practices (Cook and Smith, 2012) and professional learning to enact high quality instruction (Deshler and Cornet, 2012). There is evidence to suggest the strong influence school principals have on whether and how teachers implement desirable interventions (Burkhauser, Gates, Hamilton, and Ikemoto, 2012; McIntosh, Kelm, and Delabra, 2016), and the essential role of school and district leadership teams in the implementation and sustainability of effective instructional practices using MTSS frameworks (Sugai, O'Keefe, Hormer, and Lewis, 2012). The presence of administrative support for MTSS is described as an enabler, and its absence as a barrier, to the adoption and implementation of evidence-based practices. Supportive administrators are described as being visibly engaged in the adoption process and using their managerial skills to assist with the implementation of support systems (Forman, et al., 2009; Lembke, Garman, Deno, and Stecker, 2010; Pinkelman et al., 2015). Unsupportive administrators, in contrast, typically fail to manage staff resistance or recruit staff to engage in MTSS. They are also described as displaying passive resistance themselves by verbally supporting the use of evidence-based practices but failing to follow-through with implementing core features (Dulaney, Hallam, and Wall, 2013; Pinkelman, et al., 2015).

Despite the demands of parents and teachers for effective instructional supports, MTSS frameworks have not been widely adopted or implemented consistently by school leaders (Dulaney et al., 2013; Maier, Pate, Gibson, Hilgert, Hull, and Campbell, 2016; Pinkelman, et al., 2015). Whole-school reforms are challenging, and evidence suggests administrators find systems such as MTSS difficult to implement (Sansosti, Noltemeyer, and Goss, 2010). Using multi-tiered systems substantially changes the ways teachers have typically addressed the needs of struggling learners (Bineham et al., 2014), and MTSS may be perceived as being less compatible with customary practices than previously adopted approaches (Elfers and Stritikus, 2013). Some scholars suggest the limited uptake, and the limited attention paid to MTSS in leadership preparation and professional development programs, is exacerbated by the scarcity of experimental research showing the relative advantage of implementing tiered approaches over past practices (Bineham et al. 2014). Much of what is known about leadership for MTSS can be found in practice journals, state reports, and implementation blueprints providing examples to illustrate successful leadership actions across schools and districts (see resources at www.rti4success.org/related-rti-topics/implementation-evaluation).

Managing change is one of the most difficult tasks any leader can undertake and innovative systems such as RTI and PBIS work best in schools where conditions are in place to support and sustain their growth (Sugai et al., 2012). Evidence suggests MTSS is more likely to be successfully implemented in schools with principals who are proactively and positively engaged in encouraging their staff to work effectively and efficiently while meeting their needs and inspiring them to work toward a common purpose (Maier et al., 2016). In the face of both technical and adaptive demands, leaders at the front-line of implementation also need support from others if the use of multi-tiered systems is to be successful. This support might come from school-district leaders, school personnel, and community stakeholders, in crafting a common vision that matches school needs with district priorities and developing feasible school-wide action plans with measurable outcome goals for continuous improvement (Sugai et al. 2012). In the following section we consider the relevance of four empirically-grounded leadership dimensions to adopting, implementing, and sustaining tiered systems to support student learning.

Core Leadership Tasks and MTSS

Leithwood, Harris and Hopkins (2008) identified four core leadership practices from a comprehensive review of literature on successful school leadership, concluding that almost "all successful leaders draw on the same repertoire of basic strategies" (p. 29) (see Table 7.1 for a list of four core leadership practices and subareas). These four core leadership practices include, "building vision and setting direction, understanding and developing people, redesigning the organization, and managing the teaching and learning programme" (p. 29).

At the same time leaders need to understand the core elements of an effective MTSS model. For example, Lembke et al. (2010) identified eight core elements of an effective RTI Model. These include:

Administrative and staff support

Establishment of school-based problem-solving teams

Selection of an evidence-based, formative assessment system that includes screening and progress monitoring

Examination of the core academic program currently in place to make sure it is meet the needs of the majority of students

Team analysis of school-wide data and placement of students in tiered instructional groups

Identification of interventions for Tiers 2 and 3 and a schedule for implementation of the tiered interventions

Determination of how fidelity of treatment for Tiers 1–3 will be assessed

Determination of professionals who will monitor the progress of students in Tiers 2 and 3 on a frequent basis, including by setting goals, collecting data, implementing data-decision rules, and making changes in instruction.

(p. 363)

Table 7.1 Four Core Leadership Practices

Building Vision and Setting Direction
- Shared vision
- Fostering acceptance of group goals
- Demonstrating high-performance expectations

Understanding and Developing People
- Providing individualized support and consideration
- Fostering intellectual stimulation
- Modeling appropriate values and behaviors

Redesigning the Organization
- Building collaborative cultures
- Restructuring and reculturing the organization
- Building productive relations with parents and the community
- Connecting the school to its wider environment

Managing the Teaching and Learning Program
- Staffing the teaching program
- Providing teaching support
- Monitoring school activity
- Buffering staff against distractions from work

Source: Leithwood, Harris, and Hopkins, 2008

Both knowledge of key leadership practices (Leithwood et al., 2008) and an understanding of core elements of MTSS systems provide a foundation for leaders as they plan and implement MTSS in schools. We incorporate examples of specific practices used by researchers, leaders, and practitioners at state, district and school levels to provide insight into the work of establishing multi-tiered systems at different organizational levels.

Building Vision and Setting Direction

The initiation and implementation of complex change requires that leaders engage stakeholders in ways that build motivation and facilitate a commitment toward a shared direction in the organization (Fullan, 2015; Robinson et al., 2008). The establishment of shared goals is essential and Leithwood and colleagues emphasized the importance of collective ownership to the long-term success of the school's direction. They make clear the importance of setting direction in "crafting and revising the school's direction, so that ownership of the direction becomes widespread, deeply held and relatively resistant to the vagaries of future leadership succession" (Leithwood et al., 2008, p. 31).

Given the mission of schools, the vision needs to be firmly rooted in instructional improvement that benefits all students. Teachers will be "motivated by goals" they find personally compelling and "challenging but achievable" (Leithwood et al., 2008, p. 507). A critical skill for district and school leaders is developing a collective vision that engages stakeholders' interest in and commitment to using effective practices. Working with staff in ways that help them understand the core elements of multi-tiered systems and what these decision-making frameworks offer (e.g., improved achievement, strong research base, opportunity for locally based norms, communication with parents) are important first steps. If district leaders and principals understand and can help teachers understand and implement effective decision-making frameworks, they should be more likely to commit to using these practices. An understanding of how multi-tiered frameworks help students achieve important goals may also help to create a moral commitment, which can act as a motivator for change (Fullan, 2015).

State and district leaders also have roles in developing MTSS systems. A key role for these leaders is facilitating a shared vision and a language to communicate about such systems (Batsche, 2014). Helping stakeholders understand the essential elements of MTSS is essential to fostering clarity among all involved in planning and implementing these initiatives. State and district leaders should consider providing a definition of multi-tiered systems of support to guide others. An example is Florida's definition of multi-tiered systems of supports:

> an evidence-based model [emphasis added] of schooling that uses data-based problem-solving to integrate academic and behavioral instruction and intervention. The integrated instruction and intervention is delivered to students in varying intensities (multiple tiers) based on student need. "Need-driven" decision-making seeks to ensure that district resources reach the appropriate students (schools) at the appropriate levels to accelerate the performance of all students to achieve and/or exceed proficiency.
>
> *(Florida's Multi-Tiered System of Supports,*
> *as cited in Batsche, 2014, p. 189)*

Illinois involved numerous stakeholder groups in providing leadership for RTI in the state, including the Illinois Educational Association, Illinois Alliance of Special Education, Illinois Association of School Administrators, among others. Colorado developed an implementation rubric to help leaders in building consensus. At the school level, the rubric explicitly states the need for leaders to work toward "creating a clear vision and commitment to the RTI process." At the beginning (emerging) level, school leaders and staff are expected to discuss "how RTI could fit within their school, and develop a common understanding and definition of RTI." As RTI develops, school leaders "share a vision of collaboration and commitment to creating positive outcomes" and "create momentum for implementation" (www.cde.state.co.us/sites/default/files/documents/rti/downloads/pdf/rubrics_school.pdf, p. 3).

Even with well-planned and thoughtful change processes that involve a broad group of stakeholders, leaders should expect to encounter skepticism and resistance to tiered models, and leaders need to consider participants' perspectives as new programs are initiated and implemented. For example, stakeholders should be encouraged to raise questions, express concerns, and share what they see as problems or challenges as MTSS is introduced. The adoption of multi-tiered systems will require leaders, special and general educators, reading specialists, school psychologists, and others to do things differently and they may challenge and question changes. Although some may agree with multi-tiered systems in principle, a frequently raised concern is how to incorporate elements of MTSS into the school day. For example, staff with already full schedules may wonder how they will find time to incorporate assessment probes, additional interventions, and collaborative time (Bilton, 2011). Others may see MTSS systems as unnecessarily delaying referrals for formal assessment that are a part of the IEP process (Bilton, 2011). Some may be concerned about how a changing focus on school and classroom data may affect them. As Elliott (2008) emphasized, staff need to understand that data will not be used in a punitive way, rather it will allow "for a laser-like focus on the use of personnel, existing resources and delivery of professional development" (p. 6). Taking time to address concerns at all stages of the change process is important to garnering stakeholders' commitment to MTSS.

Understanding and Developing People

Developing a vision and shared meaning regarding MTSS provides an important foundation for successful school change. Once teachers understand what MTSS is and why it is important for this change to occur (i.e., improved instruction in their classrooms and improved outcomes for students), the initial motivation is provided for them to begin to engage in the complex process of school change. The next aspect of change is to determine how MTSS will be structured and supported within the local school, and to ensure that teachers and other involved professionals have the necessary knowledge and skills to successfully support the implementation of MTSS in their classrooms. In this section we discuss the role of the principal in making sure that teachers are well prepared to implement an MTSS model, while in the subsequent section we describe the principal's role in redesigning the school to support MTSS.

Leithwood and colleagues (2008) contend that the principal plays a key role in developing people and ensuring that they are motivated and well prepared for the demands of their classrooms. The active engagement of the principal in capacity building assures that teachers and other professionals receive the support they need to be well prepared to implement MTSS and to meet the learning needs of students in their classrooms. Key components of the principal's role in achieving these outcomes include ensuring the provision of high quality individual support for teacher development, fostering intellectual stimulation for teachers, and modeling appropriate values and behavior.

Teachers must do their work in different ways and use different skills (e.g., collecting and using student data for decision-making) to assure that MTSS is successful when it is implemented in their school (Mellard, Prewett, and Deshler, 2012). This requires that the principal and school district administrators work to support the development of teachers and other professionals to successfully implement and support the various aspects of MTSS (Sansosti and Noltemeyer, 2008). In particular, teachers must understand the 'big picture' regarding MTSS and why changes are occurring in how they do their work, and also develop skills so that they can implement new components of MTSS, including screening, student progress monitoring, tiered interventions, and using data for decision-making (Bilton, 2011; Mellard et al., 2012).

To prepare teachers for the demands of MTSS, leaders must assure that high quality professional development is provided. Research has shown that teachers more frequently learn to use skills in their classrooms if professional development: 1) is aligned with the demands of the teacher's work; 2) provides the teacher with an understanding of the conceptual foundations of the strategy or practice (e.g., why is this strategy important, what are the expected outcomes); 3) involves active learning including observations and feedback from coaches; 4) provides collective participation with others that allow the opportunity to discuss the practice and evaluate its effectiveness; and 5) is delivered in a supportive context (e.g., with administrative support) that provides professional development for a sufficient time for the teacher to learn to use the practice in the classroom (Brownell, Billingsley, McLeskey, and Sindelar, 2012; Desimone, 2009; McLeskey 2011).

This type of professional development differs substantially from that typically provided by a local school district or state department of education, which is often limited in scope, provides only a general overview of MTSS, and does not provide feedback or the necessary support to address the issues that are important to a particular teacher or school (Frigmanski, 2014; Skalski and Romero, 2011). To provide high quality professional development, the principal needs to work with school staff on a plan for addressing this need. These plans often include the development and use of experts within the school to provide support to teachers and other professionals (National Center on Intensive Intervention, 2013), as well as teachers engaging collaboratively in professional development activities (e.g., professional learning communities) that support the learning of new skills (Waldron and McLeskey, 2010).

The principal also plays a key role after MTSS is implemented, as continuing professional development is needed to support the effective implementation of MTSS, and to make sure that MTSS is sustained over time. This professional development provides teachers with on-going support as they identify new skills that are needed related to MTSS. In addition, once MTSS is implemented teachers will need coaching support as they engage in the complex and unpredictable work of problem solving, data use, and applying new skills in their classrooms (Mellard et al., 2012; Waldron, Parker, and McLeskey, 2014). The principal may provide this coaching support in some schools (Mellard et al., 2012), while in other settings a designated MTSS coach could do this work. In general, the principal plays a key role in ensuring that this high quality professional development is made available for teachers in a timely fashion.

As principals provide the supports to build teacher capacity using high quality professional development, they also have the opportunity to engage in activities that demonstrate respect and trust for teachers' perspectives and expertise, and provide teachers with intellectual stimulation. For example, high quality professional development and coaching engage the teacher as an active partner when new skills are learned and used in the classroom (Pugach, Blanton, Correa, McLeskey, and Langley, 2009). When this type of professional development is employed, the perspective of the teacher regarding how practices are implemented in the classroom is respected, and the teacher is actively engaged with coaches and other professionals in determining how MTSS will be implemented. The principal thus demonstrates respect for the teacher's expertise while actively engaging the teacher as a partner in this complex and intellectually demanding work.

Finally, the use of high quality professional development and coaching provide the principal with opportunities to model values and behaviors that support MTSS. For example, research has shown that it is critically important that principals actively engage in professional development activities to support school change (Elmore, 2004; Robinson et al., 2009). This involvement in professional development can include learning about new practices along with teachers, or, for principals who have expertise related to MTSS, providing coaching to teachers as MTSS is being implemented. This engagement in professional development as an active participant or provider of PD models the principal's support for MTSS, and also indicates the importance that the principal attaches to the success of MTSS. This level of principal involvement in instructional leadership is important to student outcomes (Robinson et al., 2008), and also serves to support and motivate teachers' engagement in developing the necessary skills to make MTSS successful.

Redesigning the Organization

Fullan (2011) has noted that technical forms of school change are relatively straightforward to implement, as they entail the application of what we already know. In contrast, adaptive changes are more complex and require changes in the beliefs of teachers and other professionals, the implementation of new classroom practices (i.e., curriculum and instruction), and new roles and responsibilities for teachers and other professionals. MTSS is an adaptive change that requires extensive change on the part of teachers and other stakeholders (Mellard et al., 2012). To support this type of complex change, principals, teachers and other stakeholders must engage in redesigning the organization "to establish workplace conditions that will allow staff members to make the most of their motivations and capacities" (Louis et al., 2010, p, 68). These authors go on to suggest that there is little reason to improve the skills of teachers and increase their motivation for implementing complex change (such as MTSS) "if working conditions will not allow their effective application" (p. 69). Leithwood et al. (2008) note that this change also should address building a collaborative culture, and connecting the school to the wider environment (e.g., parents and community).

Preliminary evidence from sites that are implementing MTSS suggests that many difficulties are occurring which could be addressed by redesigning the organization through systematic school change. This includes problems such as less than satisfactory teacher motivation because of lack of understanding of MTSS and lack of skills to successfully support implementation; lack of perceived administrative support; and difficulties with scheduling time for different MTSS activities (e.g., team meetings, data collection, delivering interventions, providing ongoing professional development and coaching) (Bilton, 2011; Frigmanski, 2014; Mellard et al., 2012; Sansosti et al., 2010; White, Polly, and Audette, 2012). Redesigning the school provides the opportunity to use resources more efficiently, schedule the school day to make MTSS activities a high priority, and redesign teacher roles to ensure time to engage in new activities related to MTSS.

Research on both school change and implementing MTSS has revealed that a key component supporting success is the active involvement of the principal as a collaborative partner with teachers and other stakeholders in planning the change (Fuchs and Deshler, 2007; Fullan, 2011; Kashima, Schleich, and Spradlin, 2009; McLeskey and Waldron, 2006; Sansosti and Noltemeyer, 2008; Spiegel, 2009; White et al., 2012). Lembke et al. (2010) described how one principal indicated that some elements were not negotiable (e.g., employing a core reading program based on research). However, other core elements of RTI "were decided by the administrator and staff collectively, such as the particular reading program and interventions to be used" (p. 363). Research on school change further suggests that a systematic change process is needed to address complex, adaptive change in a school such as MTSS (Fullan, 2015; McLeskey and Waldron, 2006). This should include steps such as the following:

Developing a team to plan MTSS. The team should include a group of well-respected administrators, teachers, and other professionals. Included among team members should be individuals who are well informed about different aspects of the MTSS process and school change. Lembke et al. (2010) suggest that teams "organize their meetings around a structured routine that allows them to accomplish their goals in the time allotted) (p. 364).

Examining the school to identify strengths that could be built on to support MTSS, as well as challenges that need to be addressed.

Examining other schools with similar demographics that have successfully implemented MTSS. This step is useful to illustrate to teachers and other professionals that it is possible to implement MTSS successfully, and to give them ideas about different components of MTSS that might be useful in their school. They also have the opportunity to discuss with other professionals the details regarding how change occurred when MTSS was implemented.

Develop a plan for MTSS. This plan should address the key components of MTSS (i.e., screening, student progress monitoring, tiered interventions, and using data for decision-making), and what needs to be done to redesign the school to make the plan successful. Determining the types of professional development that will need to be provided before implementing MTSS, as well as continuing professional development after MTSS is implemented should be included in this plan. The plan should be shared with the entire school community for review, feedback, and revision. Finally, the plan should include how the MTSS process will be evaluated and changed as part of continuous improvement once it has been implemented.

Provide professional development to build capacity for implementing the plan. This professional development should be tailored to the particular school and individual needs of teachers. Furthermore, the professional development should continue as the plan is implemented to further enhance teacher skills, and to support the development of new skills as they are identified.

Implement the plan. The most important work of the team implementing MTSS occurs after the plan is implemented. As with any complex change, unexpected difficulties will arise once the MTSS plan is implemented, and the plan must be adjusted to address these difficulties.

As Fullan (2011) has stated, "The effective change leader actively participates as a learner in helping the organization improve" (p. 5). As MTSS is implemented, the principal is often the change leader, and her involvement is critical to ensuring that the MTSS implementation will be successful. This involvement includes active participation and leadership as the plan is developed, as well as when the plan is examined and improved after implementation.

Another role of the principal throughout this change process is making sure that the school redesign includes structures that support and nurture collaboration. The principal has the opportunity to engage in several activities that begin to build a collaborative structure in the school. These activities include modeling and supporting "new forms of interaction and professionalism surrounding activities such as joint problem solving, data sharing and analysis, shared decision making, and distributed leadership" (Waldron and McLeskey, 2010, p. 59). Research has revealed that the development of a collaborative culture in the school leads to "trust and respect among colleagues, improved professional satisfaction, improved instructional practices, better outcomes for all students, and school change that is maintained over time" (Waldron and McLeskey, 2010, p. 59).

The process of redesigning a school to support MTSS also provides the opportunity to connect the school to the broader environment, including parents and other community members. The principal can make sure that this occurs by engaging parents and community members in different aspects of the school change process, and ensuring that they are informed about the changes that are being made. This builds support for the use of MTSS among parents and community members, and may also provide sources of additional resources that may be used to support MTSS.

Managing the Teaching and Learning Program

District and school leaders need to be personally involved in efforts to improve teaching and monitor learning by "planning, coordinating, and evaluating teaching and teachers" (Robinson et al., 2008) (p. 635). The active and visible presence of principals as active managers in the instructional program conveys that teaching and learning are key priorities in the school. Hamilton (2010) also emphasized the importance of the principal's role in RTI because s/he is the one who is responsible for helping to adapt the multi-tiered framework to a unique and changing context. As Hamilton states: "The adaptation for each case requires strategies based on leadership and management knowledge and skills adapted to the situation" (p. 8).

More specifically, principals are critical to creating an infrastructure of support for RTI and "must operate as real-time, contributing members of the RTI team by supervising the fidelity of instructional practices, orchestrating assessment efforts, and orchestrating assessment efforts" (Putnam, 2008, p. 14–15). In a discussion of Oregon's RTI effort, Putnam provides examples of two principals, one who provided a high level of operational involvement in leading the RTI process, while the second principal provided broad, but not direct support. In the school where there was a high level of principal involvement, benchmark scores improved dramatically over three years; however, in the school with a less involved principal, RTI did not develop. Putnam concluded that the differences between the districts was related to the leadership provided in the RTI process.

In implementing multi-tiered systems, an essential aspect is assuring that necessary personnel are available to plan, implement and evaluate the effectiveness of new practices. Recruiting and hiring highly effective teachers, ideally those with expertise in evidence-based practices and progress monitoring, is an initial step in creating a strong instructional staff. Even after multi-tiered systems are established and professional development and coaching have been provided, staff turnover can weaken educational programs, as expertise is lost and new staff must be prepared for their roles.

Staff roles also must be clarified, determining the extent to which teachers, school psychologists and related services personnel will participate across the tiers of instruction. Making decisions about staff roles is critical to assure that all key responsibilities are addressed at each tier and to make sure that each individual has the preparation for, and time for, their assigned roles. Of key importance is understanding and coordinating the roles of general and special educators as they work together in multi-tiered systems As an example, "some schools use their specialized teaching staff including special education teachers, Title I teachers, and reading specialists to assist general educators in implementing Tier 2 interventions, while these specialists provide only Tier 3 interventions and support at other school sites" (Richards, Pavri, Golez, Canges, and Murphy, 2007, p. 59). If general education teachers are primarily responsible for Tiers 1 and 2, they may initially need support in selecting appropriate interventions. Special educators may feel burdened if they take on too many responsibilities in Tiers 1 and 2, given their responsibility to serve students with disabilities (Richards et al., 2007). The roles of school and district leaders should also be clarified so all involved know the extent of support that they can expect from their supervisors.

Managing complex change requires engaging stakeholders in setting goals for a multi-tiered framework and bringing together key stakeholders to make key decisions and implement the school plan. Although multi-tiered instruction means that instruction and interventions are provided in varied levels of intensity, Batsche (2014) pointed out the challenge in operationalizing tiered instruction in practice as there is not a consensus about intensity across states, districts and schools. As Batsche pointed out, one of the challenges in supporting multi-tiered systems is defining tiers in terms of time and intensity of instruction. For example,

> 'How much time should a student get in Tier 2?,' 'How long do I have to keep them in Tier 2 (or Tier 3) until I can refer to special education?,' 'Can we call Tier 2 'RTI Time?' and 'Is Tier 2 the standard protocol approach and Tier 3 the problem-solving approach?' are asked frequently and clearly indicate that a common understanding of a multi-tiered system of supports has yet to be achieved. In reality, tiers of instruction and intervention do not exist as finite entities with clear lines of demarcation.
>
> *(p. 188)*

In implementing MTSS, leadership also need to work with staff to make decisions about the coordination, schedules and resources needed in each of the three tiers to minimize inevitable frustration, especially during the early stages of implementation. Some schools manage the process by having coordinators for varied responsibilities (e.g., managing data, interventions) (Gerzel-Short and Wilkins, 2009). For example, Gerzel-Short and Wilkins (2009) provide a detailed account of the scheduling, resources and team responsibilities in carrying out screening for all grade levels in the school:

Some schools might have to schedule benchmarking several days, depending on the number of team members and the number of students at the school. For example, in a K–5 school of about 300 students, benchmarking can take roughly five-and-a-half hours. After the benchmarking is complete, the team leader checks each booklet by classroom so that students who were absent during benchmarking are identified. Because the booklets are reused for all three universal screenings, the team leader maintains the booklets and other benchmarking materials in a safe place.

(p. 110)

Leaders also have responsibility for monitoring and assessing the impact of MTSS systems. As Lembke and colleagues (2010) stated, to operate well, these "models must be dynamic and open to changes in procedures when the goals for the models are not being achieved," (p. 372). Setting up specific plans and structures to determine the impact of MTSS on student learning is a critical consideration, as well as gathering data about fidelity of implementation, replication and improvement of systems. Table 7.2 provides questions that districts and school teams should consider as they work toward improving students outcomes and improving MTSS in their schools.

Finally, leaders need to be aware of the many practical resources and tools available online about varied aspects of multi-tiered systems (e.g., MTSS systems, core instruction, assessment tools, schedules for assessment, criteria for determining which students need Tier 2 and 3 assistance). These resources are provided through credible websites such as the National Center for Student Progress Monitoring, the National Center on Intensive Intervention, the RTI Action Network, and PBIS.org.

Table 7.2 Evaluation Questions for Multi-Tiered Systems

Context
- What are/were the goals and objectives for multi-tiered MMTSS implementation?
- Who provided support for MTSS implementation?
- Who received support during MTSS implementation?

Input
- What professional development was part of MTSS implementation support?
- Who participated in the professional development?
- What was the perceived value of the professional development?

Fidelity
- To what extent was MTSS implemented as designed?
- To what extent was MTSS implemented with fidelity?

Impact
- To what extent is MTSS associated with changes in student outcomes?
- To what extent is MTSS associated with changes in academic performance, dropout rates and other areas of schooling?

Replication, Sustainability, and Improvement
- To what extent did MTSS implementation improve capacity for the state/region/district to replicate MTSS practices, sustain MTSS practices, and improve social and academic outcomes for students?
- To what extent did MTSS implementation change educational/behavioral policy?
- To what extent did MTSS implementation affect systemic educational practice?

Source: Adapted from Algozzine, Horner, Sugai, Barrett, Dickey, Eber, Kincaid, Lewis, and Tobin, 2010 (p. i)

Summary and Conclusions

In this chapter we examined four dimensions of educational leadership and applied them to the implementation of tiered systems designed to support more equitable and effective opportunities to learn for a diversity of students. We acknowledged the limitations of the empirical research base informing leadership for MTSS, and expanded our sources to include examples of successful approaches found in implementation reports and state blueprints. To ensure that our information was grounded empirically, we drew largely from the knowledge base supporting educational leadership, and centered our discussion around a validated set of core leadership dimensions that link with student learning—building a vision and setting direction, understanding and developing people, redesigning the organization, and managing the teaching and learning program (Leithwood et al., 2008; Louis et al., 2010).

This examination prompted us to reflect on the ways in which MTSS alters business as usual in schools by requiring redesigning of instruction in ways that feature high fidelity use of evidence-based practices, and highly collaborative data-based interactions about learning and teaching. From this amalgam of knowledge we derived several conclusions about strengthening the connections between leadership and MTSS through cross-disciplinary networks, leadership preparation, and guidance grounded in the learning and organizational sciences.

Creating Change through Cross-disciplinary Networks

Fundamental changes to instructional design and delivery, such as those involved in adopting and implementing MTSS, require educational leaders to have a deep understanding of learning, as well as the contexts in which learning occurs (Ogawa et al., 2008). Yet, in preparing this analysis, we were struck by the scarcity of published research specifically addressing educational leadership in the implementation of tiered supports such as RTI and PBIS. This gap in the knowledge base threatens the establishment and sustainability of systemic instructional change. We support the creation of cross-disciplinary networks comprised of scholars who study learning and those who study leadership to examine new designs, and to study the organizational conditions that support innovative approaches to teaching and learning (Ogawa, 2015). Understanding these conditions is a much-needed area for future research at the intersection of educational leadership and MTSS.

Learning to Lead Systems of Teaching and Learning

Of special concern is the need to bring cross-disciplinary understandings to the preparation of leaders about redesigning schools for a diversity of students who struggle to learn (Burch, Theoharis, and Rauscher, 2010; Crockett, 2012). Evidence suggests the actions of educational leaders are influenced by the content and delivery of their preparation programs (Orr, 2011), but the implications of pedagogical practices are rarely addressed (Furman and Shields, 2005) despite their direct influence on student learning. Understanding how and from whom aspiring leaders are learning about the ways in which different children learn and the importance of effective approaches to teaching them; redesigning schools to support teaching and learning; establishing orderly learning environments; and collaborating with parents and community partners to support student learning are fruitful areas for future research in leadership preparation (Orr, 2011; Osterman and Hafner, 2009). We suggest grounding professional preparation in both the learning and organizational sciences would equip aspiring leaders to address the complexities of establishing systems to support effective teaching and learning.

Guiding Leadership for MTSS

Unfortunately, despite the value of using evidence-based instructional practices, the infrastructure in schools does not foster the adoption of multi-tiered systems to support their use (Sugai et al., 2012). To provide direction to those engaged in leading MTSS efforts, we conclude our discussion by summarizing several ideas to guide the successful implementation of tiered systems of academic and behavioral support. We incorporated Sugai's and his colleagues' (2012) advice for school leaders, grounded in the science of learning and implementation, within Leithwood's and his colleagues' (2008) four dimensions of organizational leadership that link with student learning in offering the following guidance:

Building vision and setting direction. Leadership for MTSS requires talented and effective principals who understand and effectively communicate the strong links between academic instruction, academic engagement, and safe and supportive cultures for teaching and learning. Effective principals also influence the use of high-fidelity practices and cultivate conditions in their schools to support effective learning environments.

Understanding and developing people. Effective leaders analyze and prioritize the influence of competing policies, their own learning histories and those of their staff members, as well as the characteristics of their neighborhoods and communities. Effective principals understand that leadership for MTSS also requires talented teachers, and they are mindful of adult learning principles and the stages involved in the adoption and implementation of educational change. Effective leaders also understand the importance of providing recognition for successful student achievement and effective teaching practice.

Redesigning the organization. Effective leaders create team-based, collaborative cultures without diminishing their own capacity to influence and mobilize others. They foster a school-wide culture of prevention and intervention that relies on collaborative consultation and universal screening, progress monitoring, and tiers of increasingly intensive and faithfully implemented evidence-based practices. They use student performance data as a means to assess the fidelity of implementation, as well as the effectiveness of personnel.

Managing the teaching and learning program. Effective school leaders analyze and prioritize the influence of competing policies and mandates, and understand how ignoring contextual factors could easily undermine MTSS as an effective or sustainable model. They consistently consider the educational benefits for students in making their decisions, and in managing the high-fidelity implementation of evidence based practices by teachers, as well as the conditions that support effective environments for teaching and learning.

In sum, providing effective leadership for MTSS requires knowledge about learning, as well as knowledge about the contexts in which learning occurs. Scholars in both the learning and organizational sciences can strengthen the empirical research base informing leadership and MTSS by joining forces across disciplines to study tiered systems and ways to prepare educational leaders to drive change toward more powerful and equitable learning opportunities for their students.

References

Algozzine, B., Horner, R. H., Sugai, G., Barrett, S., Dickey, S. R., Eber, L., . . . and Kincaid, D. (2010). *Evaluation blueprint for school-wide positive behavior support.* Eugene, OR: National Technical Assistance Center on Positive Behavior Interventions and Support. Retrieved from www.pbis.org.

Bateman, B. D., and Linden, M. A. (2006). *Better IEPs: How to develop legally correct and educationally useful programs.* Verona, WI: Attainment Company.

Batsche, G. (2014). Multi-tiered system of supports for inclusive schools. In J. McLeskey, N. L. Waldron, F. Spooner, and B. Algozzine (Eds.), *Handbook of research and practice for inclusive schools* (pp. 183–196). New York: Routledge.

Bilton, L. (2011). Exploring the concerns of teachers and principals implementing response to intervention in a pilot project: Where policy and practice collide. Unpublished doctoral dissertation. Knoxville, TN: University of Tennessee.

Bineham, S. C., Shelby, L., Pazey, B. L., and Yates, J. R. (2014). Response to intervention: Perspectives of general and special education professionals. *Journal of School Leadership, 24*, 230–252.

Brownell, M., Billingsley, B., McLeskey, J., and Sindelar, P. (2012). Teacher quality and effectiveness in an era of accountability: Challenges and solutions in special education. In J. Crockett, B. Billingsley, and M.L. Boscardin (Eds.). *The handbook of leadership & administration for special education* (pp. 260–280). New York: Routledge.

Burkhauser, S., Gates, S. M., Hamilton, L. S., and Ikemoto, G. S. (2012). *First-year principals in urban school districts*. Santa Monica, CA: RAND Corporation.

Burch, P., Theoharis, G., and Rauscher, E. (2010). Class size reduction in practice: Investigating the influence of the elementary school principal. *Educational Policy, 24*, 330–358.

Cook, B. G., and Smith, G. J. (2012). Leadership and instruction: Evidence-based practices in Special Education. In J. B. Crockett, B. S. Billingsley, and M. L. Boscardin (Eds.), *Handbook of leadership and administration for special education*, pp. 281–296. New York: Routledge.

Crockett, J. B. (2012). Developing educational leaders for the realities of special education in the 21st century. In J. B. Crockett, B. S. Billingsley, and M. L. Boscardin, (Eds.). *Handbook of leadership and administration for special education* (pp. 52–66). New York: Routledge.

Deshler, D. D., and Cornett, J. (2012). Leading to improve teacher effectiveness: implications for practice, reform, research, and policy. In J. B Crockett, B. S. Billingsley, and M. L. Boscardin (Eds.), *Handbook of leadership and administration for special education* (pp. 239–259). New York: Routledge.

Desimone, L. (2009). Improving impact studies of teachers' professional development: Toward better conceptualizations and measures. *Educational Researcher, 38*, 181–199.

Dulaney, S. K., Hallam, P. R., and Wall, G. (2013). Superintendent perceptions of multi-tiered systems of support (MTSS): Obstacles and opportunities for school system reform. *AASA Journal of Scholarship & Practice, 10*(2), 30.

Elfers, A. M., and Stritikus, T. (2013). How school and district leaders support classroom teachers' work with English language learners. *Educational Administration Quarterly, 50*(2), 305–344.

Elliott, J. (2008). Response to intervention: What & why? *School Administrator, 65*(8), 10–12, 14–16, 18.

Elmore, R. F. (2004). *School reform from the inside out: Policy, practice, and performance*. Cambridge, MA: Harvard Education Press.

Forman, S. G., Olin, S. S., Hoagwood, K. E., Crowe, M., and Saka, N. (2009). Evidence-based interventions in schools: Developers' views of implementation barriers and facilitators. *School Mental Health, 1*, 26–36. doi: 10.1007/s12310–008–9002–5.

Frigmanski, T. (2014). Administrators as change agents in implementing MTSS: Beliefs, skills, and challenges. Unpublished doctoral dissertation. Kalamazoo, MI: Western Michigan University.

Fuchs, D., and Deschler, D. (2007). What we need to know about responsiveness to intervention (and shouldn't be afraid to ask). *Learning Disabilities Research & Practice, 22*(2), 129–136.

Fullan, M. (2005). *Leadership and sustainability: System thinkers in action*. Thousand Oaks, CA: Corwin.

Fullan, M. (2011). *Change leader*. San Francisco, CA: Jossey-Bass.

Fullan, M. (2015). *The new meaning of education change* (5th Ed.). New York: Teachers College.

Furman, G. C., and Shields, C. M. (2005). How can educational leaders promote and support social justice and democratic community in schools? In W. A. Firestone and C. Riehl (Eds.), *A new agenda for research in educational leadership* (pp. 119–137). New York: Teachers College Press.

Gerzel-Short, L., and Wilkins, E. A. (2009, Spring). Response to intervention: Helping all students learn. *Kappa Delta PI Record, 45*(3), 106–110. Retrieved from http://vnweb.hwwilsonweb.com/hww/jumpstart.jhtml?recid=0bc05f7a67b1790ecf0bfd9f78899d292958f1747b59c5cfebb7ead324cf9c5aa6cce8837f95ebf7&fmt=H.

Haager, D., and Mahdavi, J. (2007). Teacher roles in implementing intervention. In D. Haager, J. Klingner, and S. Vaughn (Eds.), *Evidence-based reading practices for Response to Intervention* (pp. 245–263). Baltimore, MD: Paul H. Brookes.

Hamilton, J. L. (2010). The campus principal and RTI Implementation. *National Forum of Educational Administration and Supervision Journal, 27*(4), 1–9.

Kansas State Department of Education. (n.d.). *Leadership role in the effective implementation of MTSS: Challenges and solutions.* Kansas Technical Assistance System Network, www.ksdetasn.org.

Kashima, Y., Schleich, B., and Spradlin, T. (2009). *The core components of TRI: A closer look at leadership, parent involvement, and cultural responsibility.* Bloomington, IN: Center for Evaluation and Policy Analysis.

Klinger, J. K., and Edwards, P. A. (2006, January/February/March). Cultural considerations with response to intervention models. *Reading Research Quarterly, 41*(1), 108–117.

Knapp, M. S., Honig, M. I., Plecki, M. L., Portin, B. S., and Copland, M. A. (2014). *Learning-focused leadership in action: Improving instruction in schools and districts.* New York: Routledge.

Leithwood, K., Harris, A., and Hopkins, D. (2008). Seven strong claims about successful school leadership. *School Leadership and Management, 28*(1), 27–42.

Leithwood, K., Louis, K.S., Anderson, S., and Wahlstrom, K. (2004). *How leadership influences student learning.* Published by the Center for Applied Research and Educational Improvement, University of Minnesota, Minneapolis, MN, and Ontario Institute for Studies in Education at the University of Toronto. Retrieved from www.wallacefoundation.org/knowledge-center/school-leadership/key-research/Documents/How-Leadership-Influences-Student-Learning.pdf.

Leithwood, K., Patten, S., and Jantzi, D. (2010). Testing a conception of how school leadership influences student learning. *Educational Administration Quarterly, 46*(5), 671–706.

Leithwood, K. A., and Riehl, C. (2005). What do we already know about educational leadership? In W. A. Firestone and C. Riehl (Eds.), *A new agenda for research in educational leadership,* (pp. 12–27). New York: Teachers College Press.

Lembke, E.S., Garman, C., Deno, S.L., and Stecker, P.M. (2010). One elementary school's implementation of Response to Intervention (RTI). *Reading & Writing Quarterly, 26*(4), 361–373, doi: 10.1080/10573569.2010.500266.

Louis, K., Leithwood, K., Wahlstrom, K., and Anderson, S. (2010). *Investigating the links to improved student learning: Final report of research findings.* Minneapolis, MN: University of Minnesota.

McIntosh, K., Kelm, J. L., and Canizal Delabra, A. (2016). In search of how principals change: A qualitative study of events that help and hinder administrator support for school-wide PBIS. *Journal of Positive Behavior Interventions, 18,* 100–110. doi: 10.1177/1098300715599960.

McLeskey, J. (2011). Supporting improved practice for special education teachers: The importance of learner centered professional development. *Journal of Special Education Leadership, 24*(1), 26–35.

McLeskey, J., and Waldron, N. (2006). Comprehensive school reform and inclusive schools: Improving schools for all students. *Theory into Practice, 45*(3), 269–278.

Maier, M. P., Pate, J. L., Gibson, N. M., Hilgert, L., Hull, K., and Campbell, P. C. (2016). A quantitative examination of school leadership and Response to Intervention. *Learning Disabilities Research & Practice, 31*(2), 103–112.

Marzano, R. J., Waters, T., and McNulty, B. A. (2005). *School leadership that works: From research to results.* Alexandria, VA: ASCD.

Mellard, D. F., Prewett, S., and Deshler, D. D. (2012). Strong leadership for RTI success. *Principal Leadership, 12*(8), 28–32.

National Center for Learning Disabilities. (2011). *Multi-tier system of supports: Aka Response to intervention.* www.ncld.org/wp-content/uploads/2011/05/MTSS-brief-in-LJ-template.pdf.

National Center on Intensive Intervention (2013). *Implementing intensive intervention: Lessons learned from the field.* Washington, DC: U.S. Department of Education, Office of Special Education Programs.

Ogawa, R. T. (2015). Change of mind. *Journal of Educational Administration, 53*(6), 794–804. doi: http://dx.doe.org/10.1108/JEA-06-2014-0064.

Ogawa, R. T., Crain, R., Loomis, M., and Ball, T. (2008). CHAT/IT: Towards conceptualizing learning contexts in formal organizations. *Educational Researcher, 93,* 269–292.

Orr. M. T. (2011). Pipeline to preparation to advancement: Graduates' experiences in, through, and beyond leadership preparation. *Educational Administration Quarterly, 47,* 114–172.

Osterman, K. F., and Hafner, M. M. (2009). Curriculum in leadership preparation: Understanding where we have been in order to know where we might go. In M. D. Young, G. M. Crow, J. Murphy, and R. T. Ogawa (Eds.), *Handbook of research on the education of school leaders* (pp. 269–317). New York: Routledge.

Pinkelman, S. E., McIntosh, K., Rasplica, C. K., Berg, T., and Strickland-Cohen, M. K. (2015). Perceived enablers and barriers related to sustainability of school-wide positive behavioral interventions and supports. *Behavioral Disorders, 40*(3), 171–183.

Pugach, M., Blanton, V., Correa, V., McLeskey, J., and Langley, L. (2009). *The role of collaboration in supporting the induction and retention of new special education teachers.* (Technical paper, National Center to Improve Policy and Practice in Personnel Preparation (NCIPP)). Gainesville, FL: University of Florida.

Putnam, D. L. (2008). Guiding RTI system implementation: The Oregon experience. *School Administrator*, *65*(8), 14–15.

Richards, C., Pavri, S., Golez, F., Canges, R., Murphy, J. (2007). Response to intervention: Building the capacity of teachers to serve students with learning difficulties. *Issues in Teacher Education*, *16*(2), 55–64.

Richter, M. M., Lewis, T. J., and Hagar, J. (2012). The relationship between principal leadership skills and school-wide positive behavior support: An exploratory study. *Journal of Positive Behavior Interventions*, *14*(2), 69–77.

Robinson, V., Lloyd, C., and Rowe, K. (2008). The impact of leadership on student outcomes: An analysis of differential effects of leadership types. *Educational Administration Quarterly*, *44*, 635–674. doi:10.1177/0013161X08321509.

Sansosti, F., and Noltemeyer, A. (2008). Viewing response-to-intervention through an educational change paradigm: What can we learn? *The California School Psychologist*, *13*, 55–66.

Sansosti, F. J., Noltemeyer, A., Goss, S. (2010). Principals' perceptions of the Importance and availability of response to intervention practices within high school settings. *School Psychology Review*, *39*, 286–295.

Skalski, A., and Romero, M. (2011). Data-based decision making. *Principal Leadership*, *11*(5), 12–16.

Spiegel, A. E. (2009). Principal leadership characteristics that influence successful implementation of response-to-intervention. (Doctoral dissertation). Retrieved from ProQuest Dissertations and Theses database. (UMI No. 754057881)

Sugai, G., O'Keefe, B. V., Hormer, R. H., and Lewis, T. J. (2012). School leadership and School-wide Positive Behavior Support. In J. B Crockett, B. S. Billingsley, and M. L. Boscardin (Eds.), *Handbook of leadership and administration for special education* (pp. 297–314). New York: Routledge.

Tyack, D. (1974). *The one best system: A history of American urban education.* Cambridge, MA: Harvard University Press.

Waldron, N., and McLeskey, J. (2010). Establishing a collaborative school culture through comprehensive school reform. *Journal of Educational and Psychological Consultation*, *20*(1), 58–74.

Waldron, N., Parker, J., and McLeskey, J. (2014). How are data systems used in inclusive schools? In J. McLeskey, N.L. Waldron, F. Spooner, and B. Algozzine (Eds.), *Handbook of effective inclusive schools: Research and practice* (pp. 155–166). New York: Routledge.

White, R., Polly, D., and Audette, R. (2012). A case analysis of an elementary school's implementation of response to intervention. *Journal of Research in Childhood Education*, *26*, 73–90.

8

PREPARING GENERAL AND SPECIAL EDUCATION PRESERVICE TEACHERS FOR RESPONSE TO INTERVENTION

A Practice-Based Approach

Mary T. Brownell, David Chard, Amber Benedict,
and Ben Lignugaris/Kraft

Nationally, most states are implementing some form of Response to Intervention (RTI) to identify and serve students who struggle socially and academically (IDEA National Assessment Implementation Study, Institute for Education Sciences (IES), 2011). Zirkel (2011) found that 46 states had language about RTI and its use in preventing and intervening in academic problems in their laws or guidelines, and 35 of these states had language about approaches to preventing and intervening in behavior problems. Further, the IDEA National Assessment Implementation Study (IES, 2011) indicated that 49 states had some type of RTI commission, task force, or internal working group – suggesting that nearly every state was interested in promoting RTI approaches. State leaders also recognize the need to prepare their teachers for working within an RTI framework. In 40 states there are organized trainings on RTI, and in 37 states technical assistance is provided to school districts or schools interested in or engaged in implementing RTI (IES, 2011).

In light of the broad implementation of RTI nationally, this chapter addresses issues related to the preparation of general and special education teachers for working within an RTI framework. Specifically, we discuss the approaches states are taking to implement RTI, the demands common RTI approaches place on general and special education teachers, current barriers to preparing these teachers to work within an RTI framework, and how we might use the science on learning to strengthen teacher preparation for RTI.

Implementation of RTI and Teachers

AN RTI approach for delivering instruction requires different demands of general and special education teachers, as well as preparation to address these demands. Nearly all states, or at least districts within those states, are using some approach to RTI or Multi-tiered Systems of Support (MTSS) to prevent and intervene in instruction, and many states are using a similar approach to intervene in behavior. The RTI or MTSS approaches states use include similar components; (a) use of scientifically based interventions specifically targeted to the needs of individual students, (b) continuous monitoring of student progress, (c) opportunities for students to respond to instruction or implementation of behavioral strategies, (d) intensity of instruction or behavioral support is increased as students move through tiers, and (e) monitoring to ensure that research-based strategies are implemented with integrity. Additionally, more intensive instruction must be coordinated with core or tier 1 instruction if students are to receive coherent instruction that enables them to access the general education curriculum.

Structure of RTI and Need for Instructional Coordination

RTI is a tiered instruction and intervention framework where students with disabilities and students who are at-risk receive a combination of core (tier 1) instruction and tier 2 or 3 supplemental intervention from different teachers implementing different instructional programs (Brownell et al., 2012). Successfully implemented tier 1 instruction depends on general education teachers effectively enacting evidence-based academic strategies, and establishing a positive classroom climate for each learner while simultaneously providing appropriate, evidence-based, small group tier 2 supplemental instruction for students who require additional behavior or academic support. Frequent data collection and analysis are necessary to ensure students are making adequate progress. Students who are non-responsive to tier 2 instruction are then referred to tier 3 for interventions. Tier 3 instruction should be research-based and individualized according to student need identified through ongoing data collection. The individualized nature of tier 3 instruction is analogous to the concept of specially designed instruction required in the Individuals with Disabilities Education Act. As a result, scholars argue that special education teachers should deliver tier 3 instruction (e.g., Brownell, Sindelar, Kiely, and Danielson, 2012; Fuchs, Fuchs, and Compton, 2012).

Increased instructional support provided in tiers 2 and 3 should be coordinated, to the extent possible, with the skills, strategies, and instructional pace occurring during tier 1 instruction (Johnson, Mellard, Fuchs, and McKnight, 2006). Coordinated instruction between tiers, especially in mathematics and literacy, is important because it increases at-risk learners, and students with learning disabilities exposure to targeted content and practice opportunities, increasing the probability that these students will master the targeted content and improve their overall achievement in reading and mathematics (Fuchs et al., 2008; Wonder-McDowell, Reutzel, and Smith, 2010). Moreover, if instruction at tiers 2 and 3 is not coordinated with tier 1instruction, then students may not receive the type of instruction that will enable them to meaningfully access the general education curriculum.

Demands RTI Place on Teachers

To improve the academic achievement of students in RTI frameworks, general and special education teachers must have knowledge of reading and math curricula, and interventions in these areas. They also must have the skills needed to interpret data collected on academic and behavioral performance, and have the collaborative skills to problem solve about students and coordinate instructional efforts (Benedict et al., 2013; Brownell et al., 2012). Effective coordinated instruction across tiers requires general and special educators to develop collective understandings and skills for enacting evidence-based academic and behavioral instruction.

More specifically, general education teachers must deliberately consider the needs of *each* learner and differentiate classroom instruction accordingly (Hughes and Dexter, 2008). The ability to differentiate depends on a deep knowledge of the curriculum, an understanding of how to enact that curriculum using evidence-based strategies, and knowledge of individual learners' strengths and needs (Brownell et al., 2012). To provide tier 2 instruction, general education teachers will also need to understand how to intensify instruction, manage the classroom while providing small group instruction, and collect progress monitoring data to determine if students are making adequate gains.

To provide tier 3 instruction, special education teachers must have deep knowledge of reading, writing, mathematics, and behavior change strategies, knowledge of the general education curricula, the skills to assess students' specific strengths and needs, and evidence-based interventions that will help students with disabilities access the general education curriculum. Additionally, special education teachers must have the collaboration and communication skills needed to plan tier 1 and 2 instruction with their general education colleagues. (Fuchs, Fuchs, and Compton, 2012). Moreover, they must know to craft instruction that is explicit and systematic, and affords students frequent opportunities to respond and practice with corrective feedback (Lignugaris/Kraft and Harris, 2014).

Although general education teachers also need to craft explicit, systematic instruction that provides students with multiple learning opportunities, special education teachers need to have a more nuanced understanding of these instructional principles to create intensive instruction that is targeted to a student's individualized learning needs (Lignugaris/Kraft and Harris, 2014). Further, special education teachers must create motivating, carefully scaffolded practice opportunities that provide students with disabilities with the support required to learn particular concepts, strategies, and skills (Gersten et al., 2009). We acknowledge that both general and special education teachers must tailor their instruction to students' interests and ensure that content and presentation is developmentally appropriate. Special educators, however, are focused on individualized and clinical problem-solving that typically involves an intensive iterative cycle of individualized assessment, instructional planning, and evidence-based instruction (Lignugaris/Kraft and Harris, 2014). Obviously, the knowledge and skill required to implement, in a coordinated fashion, such well-designed, tailored instruction requires considerable knowledge and skill on the part of both general and special education teachers, and there are many barriers to acquiring it.

Barriers to Developing Teachers Who Can Participate in RTI Frameworks

Currently, there are two primary barriers that prevent teacher preparation programs from adequately preparing teachers to be successful in an RTI framework. The first of these barriers involves state regulation and policies that limit strong teacher development. The second barrier focuses on teacher education approaches that impede the development of effective teachers.

Policies that Limit Strong Teacher Development

Despite federal efforts to encourage multi-tier systems of support, authority for teacher licensure remains with state education agencies. For the most part, state licensure standards and program approval processes are based on what content someone is permitted to teach. Requirements for meeting these standards are generally global and satisfied by successfully completing a list of courses (Geiger, Mickelson, McKeown, Barton, Kleinhammer-Tramill, and Steinbrecher,

2014). In some cases, preservice teachers may complete these courses across several universities or programs within a state, with no coordination among the courses in the teacher candidates' programs of study (e.g., state sponsored alternative teacher preparation programs). Among these courses preservice general education teachers typically complete a course on exceptional learners which focuses characteristics of students with disabilities and skills related to adapting and differentiating instruction (Dove Jones, and Messenheimer-Young, 1989; Fender and Fiedler, 1990). The content on differentiation is often generic, to cover the full range of students with disabilities, and teachers are expected to apply the content to a broad range of students. Specifically, within the same course, global state standards often result in combining all students who struggle academically, including students from communities of poverty, students who are culturally and linguistically diverse, as well as students with disabilities. Consequently, preservice general education teachers are rarely taught to evaluate how an identified intervention contextually fits the skills, cultural values of those who implement the intervention (i.e., general educator, special educator, paraeducator, and parents), or the needs of children who benefit from the intervention.

Further, state regulated program approval processes often do not require that teachers demonstrate knowledge of research-based practices and how to adjust research-based interventions so they are responsive to the needs of students with disabilities (Goldrick, Sindelar, Zabala, and Hirsch, 2014). The approval processes often do not require that preservice general educators have experience with students with disabilities within an RTI framework in which teachers are required to coordinate their efforts. Rather, as new general education teachers begin their first teaching position, districts and schools must ensure that there is adequate time and support provided for professionals to learn how to coordinate instruction within the context of an effective school framework.

In special education, the licensure systems and subsequent program approval processes are typically too broad to result in focused preparation. Special education licenses are often intended to certify teachers to serve students with disabilities in a K-12 system (Geiger et al., 2014). The result is that programs for preparing special education teachers are typically too broadly focused to provide teachers with sufficient opportunities to acquire the knowledge and skills needed to design instruction to meet the unique needs of their students (Greenberg, McKee, and Walsh, 2013). Specifically, the knowledge and skills needed for serving students with disabilities in an RTI system have not been developed with sufficient practice and feedback to ensure quality of implementation (Lewis and Thomas, 2014).

Teacher Education Approaches that Limit Effective Teacher Development

Teacher education programs situated in institutions of higher education often suffer from identity confusion and time limitations. Faculty members are rewarded with tenure for studying issues that are academically meaningful, but often are not focused on topics that directly impact teacher development (Ball and Forzani, 2009). Teacher education programs often encourage or reinforce ideas about the history, context, or importance of education without directly teaching the "high leverage" instructional behaviors that help teachers find success with their students.

The experiences that are more likely to support teachers' practice in either general or special education rely on extended collaborative adult learning experiences that promote the development of professional skills and competence. An example of an extended collaborative experience might be when a student is having difficulty interacting with peers appropriately in small groups. Often new general education teachers might employ a negative consequence system with daily routines of moving a student's clothespin from the green zone (i.e., positive consequences) to the red zone (i.e., negative consequences). Based on observations and a trusting, collegial relationship with the general education teacher, a special education teacher might see that the student lacks the social skills needed to work with peers and uses this as an opportunity to teach the social skills and self-regulation behaviors (e.g., initiating conversation, turn taking) that will promote success during group work. The special educator might model the behaviors explicitly and give the student an opportunity to practice those behaviors with feedback. Subsequently, the general and special education teachers need to observe and assess the success of the intervention when the student is next given the opportunity to use her new skills in a group setting. And finally, the teachers need to discuss additional options or adjustments to the classroom environment or the instructional intervention that will help the student succeed. This process is formative, and requires a tremendous degree of professionalism, collaboration, and knowledge of behavior interventions. To develop the knowledge and skills necessary for teachers to enter the classroom equipped to support student success at this level requires ample opportunities to analyze evidence of student need, explore research-based practices that are likely to be successful, and most importantly opportunities to practice in a "low stakes" environment to develop the confidence and competence in their practice.

Improving Teacher Preparation for RTI

To acquire the research-based knowledge and skills for implementing RTI, novice teachers must participate in initial preparation programs that enable them to acquire the knowledge and skill to participate successfully in RTI. In the major sections that follow, we first discuss the essential knowledge and skill that general and special education teachers need to learn to participate, as novice teachers, in RTI. Next, we examine the research base that can inform how teacher educators might move to a more practice-based approach to teaching preservice teachers the essential knowledge and skills to teach effectively. Finally, we conclude with a practice-based approach to teaching general and special education candidates to coordinate tiered instruction within an RTI framework.

Developing a Core Curriculum: Essential Knowledge and Skills

Teacher education programs that prepare general and special education preservice teachers are often no more than 2 years in length – a short period of time for preparing teachers who are competent to teach students with disabilities. A focus on practices fundamental to effective teaching and collaboration for improving the learning of students with disabilities, as opposed to the broad coverage of content and skills that current state licensure systems often promote, is foundational to developing novice general and special education teachers who can teach and coordinate their instruction within an RTI framework. Identifying the essential content and skills needed to work successfully in an RTI context is critical to promoting the deep learning that results in more effective instruction within an RTI framework. For professionals to develop the sort of situated knowledge needed for problem-solving in authentic settings, they need focused learning situations (e.g., Zeiser, Taylor, Rickles, Garet, and Segeritz, 2014). General and special education teachers also need these opportunities if they are to develop the sophisticated knowledge and skills we expect them to have for RTI.

High Leverage Practice and High Leverage Content

Recently, teacher education scholars in general education have argued for a core curriculum in teacher education (e.g., Ball and Forzani, 2011). This core curriculum provides the foundation for a practice-based approach to teacher education where preservice teachers learn the fundamentals of effective instructional practice. These are high leverage practices and content absolutely essential to effective instructional interactions in classrooms and effective collaboration with colleagues.

High leverage practices (HLP) are those practices teachers use regardless of content or grade level taught. They are based on the available research on instruction and collaboration (Ball and Forzani, 2011). Ball and her colleagues (Ball and Forzani, 2011; Ball, Sleep, Boerst, and Bass, 2009; Forzani, 2014) identify 19 HLPs that can be systematically taught in teacher education programs. These HLPs include some practices that are established as important for the effective education of students with disabilities. For instance, Ball and her colleagues list explicit instruction and communication with parents as practices that should be deliberately taught and practiced in different courses and field experiences in teacher education. Grossman and McDonald (2008) suggest that once HLPs are identified, teacher educators can create sequences of well-structured practice opportunities to develop competence with the HLP. Ball and Forzani (2011) suggest that HLPs should be the foundation for a teacher education curriculum.

To work within an RTI framework, general and special education teachers will need to acquire HLPs across three domains. They will need to learn pedagogies of assessment and analysis, instructional enactment, and collaboration that results in program coordination. The Council for Exceptional Children, in collaboration with the Center for Effective Educator Development, Accountability, and Reform, has identified 22 practices fundamental to promoting learning in students with disabilities that should provide a foundation for our teacher education programs (McLeskey et al., 2017). For instance, general and special education teachers need to understand how to collect and analyze progress-monitoring data, and they must have the skills to enact explicit teaching or guided, interactive practice though we recognize that the differences in what general and special education teachers learn about these HLPs need to be tailored to their roles. General educators need to learn how to apply HLP's in the context of teaching large groups of students, in terms of both assessment, and instructional differentiation. In contrast, special educators need to learn how to apply HLP's in the context of intensive individualized instruction, assessment, and differentiation. HLPs that focus on coordination of instruction and collaboration with families include the ability to coordinate instructional goals, negotiate approaches in the classroom, or demonstrate active listening when working with families and colleagues. Although collaboration is often a focus of special education teacher education programs and a small group of exemplary general education teacher preparation programs (Brownell, Ross, Colon, and McCallum, 2005), it is not a topic that is addressed or practiced consistently across general education teacher preparation programs.

Of course, teaching is not content free. Preservice teachers cannot simply learn to implement pedagogical practices, such as explicit instruction, without understanding how practices such as explicit teaching change depending on the content. For instance, explicit instruction looks somewhat different when applied to teaching decoding patterns versus when it is applied to teaching the conceptual underpinnings of decimals. Thus, preservice teachers must learn to use HLPs to teach critical content effectively. Critical content includes the big ideas of curriculum or those topics that are fundamental to adequate achievement in a content area (e.g., fractions and whole number operations), and both special and general education teachers will need to know how to teach students with disabilities this content using HLPs. Special education teachers will need to know more highly structured, evidence-based approaches that are specific to content (e.g., schema-based strategy instruction, or a cognitive strategy for decoding multisyllabic words), or improving students' social behavior (e.g., social problem solving to mediate aggressive behavior). Essential content knowledge and content specific pedagogical knowledge may be referred to as High Leverage Content (HLC; e.g., Gersten et al., 2009; Wanzek, Wexler, Vaughn, and Ciullo, 2010).

Ball, Grossman, and others argue that teacher educators must focus on HLPs and HLCs and be able to assess candidates' acquisition of them, as there are limits to what preservice teachers can learn about practices that support content acquisition (Ball, Sleep, Boerst, and Bass, 2009; Grossman and McDonald, 2008). Though measures are not currently available, efforts are underway by Educational Testing Services (ETS) and the University of Michigan to assess HLPs and HLCs. Eventually, however, if we are to build an evidence-based curriculum for teaching students with disabilities, those HLPs and HLCs that have the most impact on novice general and special education teachers' instruction will need to be taught and assessed consistently across programs. HLPs and HLCs needed to teach within an RTI framework may be one component of the core teacher education curriculum for preparing general and special education teachers.

Creating Practice-Based Approaches to Teacher Education

Once a core curriculum for teacher preparation is articulated, teacher educators must consider effective ways of teaching the core curriculum to their candidates. Unfortunately, the research base informing teacher education practice is limited, and there is almost no research to inform teacher educators working to prepare general and special education preservice teachers to teach and coordinate their efforts in an RTI framework. Research findings from cognitive science and behavioral science, however, support the use of specific pedagogical practices, field experiences, and practice-based approaches to prepare preservice teachers for success in an RTI framework. These pedagogies and approaches to field experience can help both general and special education preservice teachers learn HLPs and HLC.

Research from the Science on Learning and Effective Collaboration

Researchers in cognitive and developmental psychology provide the key elements needed to develop competent skills and strategies with military personnel, athletes, musicians, and doctors (e.g., Ericsson, 2014). For adults to successfully implement complex skills and strategies, they must learn information in situations that reflect those they will encounter as independent professionals – simply observing expert performance is woefully insufficient (Ericcson, 2008). Repeatedly, researchers demonstrate the importance of practice, particularly "deliberate practice" or the practice of essential skills and strategies that are the basis for highly effective performance (Ericsson, 2009; Ritter, Anderson, Koedinger, and Corbett, 2007). The features of effective, deliberate practice include distributed learning opportunities, retrieval practice, interleaved and varied practice, coaching and feedback, and analysis and reflection.

Distributed Learning Opportunities

Distributed practice is more effective than massed practice during the knowledge and skill acquisition process. Distributed practice allows some forgetting to occur and actually strengthens memory as learners attempt to recall information. When preservice teachers have the opportunity to revisit instructional routines they acquire in coursework or practical settings that feature RTI skills, such as analyzing student data and drawing conclusions, they relearn that information in ways that may help them consolidate it in memory (Cepeda, Pashler, Vul, Wixted, and Rohrer, 2006; Moulton, Dubrowski, MacRae, Graham, Grober, and Reznick, 2006; Russ-Eft, 2002).

Retrieval Practice

Retrieval practice involves mentally rehearsing how to solve a problem or perform a task, and requires that learners are actively involved in remembering something they learned previously (Karpicke and Blunt, 2011; Roediger, Agarwal, McDaniel, and McDermott, 2011; Roediger and Karpicke, 2006). For instance, preservice teachers can be encouraged to plan in detail how they will enact specific, effective instruction routines within RTI settings. Such precise planning enables preservice teachers to mentally rehearse how they will apply a particular instructional routine to a specific instructional context.

Interleaved and Varied Practice

Interleaved and varied practice involves implementing two or more strategies or routines at once, and practicing those strategies in different contexts and under different conditions (Dunlosky, Rawson, Marsh, Nathan, and Willingham, 2013; Taylor and Rohrer, 2010); such practice is believed to help professionals learn to recognize patterns in their environment and employ the appropriate response. For instance, teacher educators might teach preservice teachers how to use a think aloud summarization strategy that includes modeling that strategy for students followed by guided practice. They might also teach preservice teachers a related strategy for solving word problems using schemas. Preservice teachers are then placed in practice contexts in which they must discriminate when and how to use each practice. Although this may be challenging initially for novice teachers (Brown, Roediger, and McDaniel, 2014), over time effective teachers learn that instructional strategies must be adjusted to fit different content and with practice become more adept making these adjustments (Kornell and Bjork, 2008; Rohrer and Pashler, 2010).

Coaching and Feedback

Coaching and feedback focused on the key components of effective performance are essential to help adult learners identify what effective performance looks like and feels like when they are engaging in it (Ericsson, 2009; Kellogg and Whiteford, 2009). According to Ericsson, coaching and feedback is what makes practice deliberate and ultimately effective in increasing performance. For teaching, key components of performance and foundational knowledge are HLPs and content specific pedagogies (or HLC). Without some knowledge of the fundamental features of effective performance, learners are not likely to develop the ability to analyze and reflect on their performance, skills that are essential in developing expertise.

Analysis and Reflection

To improve their performance independently, a learner must identify deficits in how they are approaching and enacting a task and consider how to rectify those deficits. In research on beginning special education teachers, Bishop and colleagues (2010) found that accomplished teachers were those who were more likely to reflect on or analyze their performance to determine how it could be improved, and identify resources that could help them improve. Similarly, Brownell et al. (2014) found that teachers who capably analyzed their instruction were those who easily integrated practices learned in a professional development effort, as compared to teachers who simply implemented a strategy occasionally.

Although these five elements of deliberate practice are discussed separately (e.g., distributed learning opportunities, retrieval practice, interleaved and varied practice, coaching and feedback, and analysis and reflection), they often occur simultaneously or depend on one another. For instance, practice opportunities should focus on HLP and HLC, and preservice teachers should have some vehicle for securing feedback on their performance. Without feedback, they cannot ascertain the critical elements of effective performance and thus, cannot analyze how well they engaged or adapted an identified practice. Further, practice opportunities should be varied and attempt to help preservice teachers interleave skills. By engaging in varied practice opportunities that allow preservice teachers to interleave HLPs and HLCs, they have opportunities to experience differences in applying HLP and HLC, and how they must adjust them to a variety of educational contexts. Finally, preservice teachers must have opportunities to engage in distributive practice where the problems and situations they must address change in complexity; otherwise, they will not learn to recognize the key features of situations in which a skill or strategy is needed to address a particular problem. In the sections that follow, we examine some of the pedagogical practices that have at least limited research and incorporate the critical elements of effective, deliberate practice described above. Additionally, we highlight one program that is attempting to embrace some of these pedagogical practices while demonstrating how they foster general and special education teachers' capacity to coordinate their instruction.

Pedagogical Practices that Align with the Science on Learning

Finding powerful ways to create practice opportunities is challenging because teacher education is conducted largely in inauthentic settings – either in university classes or online – and these settings are not the best vehicles for helping preservice teachers develop the conditional knowledge needed for teaching. Further, school-based settings, places where novice teachers need to apply their knowledge, are often of inconsistent quality. In the narrative that follows, we examine ways that teacher educators might focus their efforts on the HLPs and HLCs that comprise effective teaching and collaboration, and strategies for promoting such performance without total dependence on high quality clinical settings. These strategies align with the science we have about effective, deliberate practice, and can be used to help general and special education preservice teachers acquire the HLPs and HLCs needed to work effectively in RTI or multi-tiered systems of support settings. Importantly, most of the strategies are not specific to planning and executing tiered instruction; thus, we conclude the section on field experiences by discussing one strategy that provides general and special education teachers with deliberate opportunities to practice implementing coordinated, tiered instruction.

Creating Practice Opportunities within Coursework

Although research on pedagogical practices in teacher education is limited in scope and fragmented in nature, there are approaches that embrace principles we identified from the science on learning. These approaches are considered approximations of practice (Grossman and MacDonald, 2008). Other professions use approximations of practice to improve professional learning (e.g. role play in training clinical psychologists), and teacher educators may also consider doing so. In the following section, we will demonstrate how microteaching, video models, case-based instruction using technology, and virtual simulations provide general and special education teachers with opportunities to retrieve knowledge and procedural skill undergirding HLPs and HLCs, interleave HLPs and content HLCs, analyze and reflect on instruction, and promote skills needed to coordinate instruction.

Microteaching

In microteaching, preservice teachers individually plan lessons that feature a specific instructional practice or small set of practices. They then implement the lessons with peers in a university classroom. Microteaching provides preservice teachers with opportunities to rehearse how they plan to present lesson content, rehearse how to enact those lessons with students, and then analyze and reflect on their performance after teaching lessons. This simplifies the teaching-learning process and gives preservice teachers an opportunity to analyze, discuss, and reflect on their prospective lesson with peers prior to engaging children (Kamman, McCray, and Brownell, 2014). Through a microteaching process, preservice candidates have opportunities to demonstrate how they might adapt HLPs (e.g., planning, explicit instruction, engaging practice) to a range of content areas, and retrieve and use knowledge they have acquired in coursework.

Microteaching is a training approach used in a broad range of fields, including clinical psychology where students role-play using certain therapeutic techniques, instructional interventions in physical therapy training where novices learn to do such things as test for a range of motion, and preservice teacher preparation (Grossman and MacDonald, 2008; Horn, 2005). The available research has produced mixed results (Grossman, 2005), with some studies showing that microteaching does not enable preservice teachers to transfer skills to classroom settings (e.g., Copeland, 1975), and other studies demonstrating that it does under certain conditions (e.g., Copeland, 1977). Further, other scholars criticize microteaching for creating views of instruction that are inconsistent with a more complex understanding of teaching and making instructional decisions (e.g., Bell, 2007).

Although concerns about the efficacy of microteaching are valid, there might be conditions under which it might be effective, particularly when it is organized according to principles from the science on learning. For instance, microteaching can be used intermittently (distributed practice) in and across coursework to help preservice teachers practice HLCs and HLPs. Additionally, if preservice teachers have opportunities to plan, analyze, and revise their microteaching collaboratively, they might acquire more knowledge about what effective practice looks like, have opportunities to retrieve what they are learning in coursework, and more effectively analyze their instruction and the instruction of their peers (Fernandez, 2010; Fernandez and Robinson, 2006).

Microteaching, however, cannot replace the need to practice in authentic settings, as these opportunities will be essential to knowledge and skill transfer. For example, when preservice teachers have opportunities to practice instructional strategies learned using microteaching, in authentic settings, such as in virtual simulations or real classrooms, preservice teachers demonstrate stronger application of their learning than when they did not have these opportunities (Copeland, 1977; Dawson and Lignugaris/Kraft, 2013). More research is necessary on the efficacy of microteaching. In the meantime, however, microteaching can be constructed according to the principles acquired from the science on learning to be one viable way to engage preservice teachers in deliberate practice using HLPs and HLCs prior to entering a classroom-based field experience.

Video Models

In some studies researchers in general and special education use video models to improve preservice and in-service teachers' knowledge of, and skill in, implementing effective instruction. These researchers show that when preservice and in-service teachers are asked to analyze video models, they can acquire needed knowledge and instructional skill (Brunvand and Fishman, 2006–2007; Ely et al., 2014; Ely et al., 2015; Powell, Diamond, and Koehler, 2010; Prior and Bitter, 2008). Brunvand and Fishman used videos of inquiry science instruction to help preservice teachers learn to recognize common student misconceptions and use of inquiry-based instructional strategies. Preservice teachers in one of the video treatment groups also were provided scaffolds that focused their attention on specific aspects of the video in a sequential manner. Preservice teachers in the scaffolded and non-scaffolded groups identified student misconceptions and use of inquiry-based instructional strategies more frequently than teachers in a comparison group.

Ely and colleagues (2014) completed both pilot and experimental studies where they investigated the impact of Content Acquisition Podcasts (CAPs) and video modeling on preservice special education teachers' knowledge of an evidenced-based vocabulary practice and their ability to implement the practice. The CAPs introduced preservice and practicing teachers to the knowledge they needed to enact the vocabulary intervention, such as how to select appropriate words for vocabulary instruction and create a student-friendly definition. The video model was produced using Brunvand's (2010) video production principles, which address the importance of highlighting critical information, such as how the teacher is thinking while implementing a portion of the vocabulary intervention, and eliminating extraneous thinking. Preservice teachers in the CAP plus video modeling condition made significant gains in their knowledge of the intervention, and their ability to implement steps of the intervention compared to peers who simply read about the intervention. These two studies and others suggest that video modeling may be one way to help preservice teachers learn how to analyze teaching and learning to discern its essential features, and improve their ability to analyze instruction.

Case-Based Instruction Using Technology

Case-based instruction has long been a popular pedagogy in teacher education (see Shulman, 1992) and other disciplines, such as business, psychology and medicine (e.g., Mayo, 2004; Merseth, 1991). Depending on how it is constructed, case-based instruction provides preservice teachers opportunities to develop their ability to apply their knowledge to classroom contexts (Grossman, 2005). For instance, case-based instruction can provide preservice teachers important opportunities to analyze teaching and learning, a foundational principle from the science on learning. Specifically, cases can help preservice teachers analyze problems that occur in complex settings, analyze information about students and make instructional decisions, or analyze instruction. The degree to which case studies help teachers develop the skills of analysis, however, is difficult to ascertain because cases are constructed so differently across studies (Grossman, 2005), and because the measures vary greatly across available research.

Despite these limitations, Dieker and colleagues (2014), in a review of research on case-based instruction involving technology, suggest that such cases can help preservice teachers practice key skills of analysis and develop implementation knowledge. For example, Anderson and Lignugaris/Kraft (2006) used video cases to help elementary preservice teachers develop their behavior analytic skills. Preservice teachers were taught to analyze antecedents and consequences of a target student's behavior using a structured approach, and identified a positive action teachers could take to change the student's behavior. Results from the study showed that preservice teachers improved their ability to analyze student behaviors as a result of participating in the video case instruction. Beck, King, and Marshall (2002) used an experimental design to assess the impact of video cases on preservice teacher learning. Preservice teachers created cases by editing videos of their mentor teachers and selected segments of their instruction that reflected specific aspects of the teaching learning process (e.g., specific teaching strategies or evidence of student learning). Preservice teachers who participated in developing the video cases outperformed their peers in the control group (who only observed in classrooms) in terms of their ability to identify, interpret, and analyze evidence of effective teaching.

These examples suggest that case-based instruction, particularly those involving videos, might be useful in helping preservice teachers develop an understanding of effective instruction, how concepts and strategies can be addressed at each of the instructional tiers, and an ability to analyze tiered instruction. They might help preservice teachers learn to analyze and draw conclusions based on students' responsiveness to instruction. All of these skills may increase preservice teachers' ability to analyze and reflect on their own instruction and analyze and make decisions about student data, though further research is needed to substantiate these linkages.

Creating Practice Opportunities in the Field

Practice in university courses alone is insufficient to ensure that preservice teachers enact the HLP and HLC required in schools that use an RTI approach. Carefully scaffolded practice opportunities are needed to help preservice teachers learn to employ their skills in increasingly complex instruction and behavioral contexts such as schools that employ RTI and other multi-tiered systems of support (Lewis and Thomas, 2014; Lignugaris/Kraft and Harris, 2014). There are several strategies that can be scaffolded to help preservice teachers apply their skills in increasingly complex settings. Each approach incorporates principles from the science on learning; that is, teachers learn to interleave skills, retrieve knowledge of content and routines as they teach it to students, distribute their learning over multiple sessions, and receive feedback on their learning.

Tutoring

Working one-on-one with a student or several students allows teachers structured opportunities to enact HLPs and HLCs in an authentic setting that is constrained in terms of the complexity often present in a classroom that includes many students, often with diverse instructional needs, engaged in a variety of tasks. Several researchers describe carefully structured tutoring experiences in which teacher candidates learn to apply knowledge they have acquired about HLPs and HLCs in coursework, and analyze student data and teaching effectiveness for students who likely would receive tier 2 or tier 3 instruction. These structured experiences have consistently produced positive changes in preservice teachers (e.g., Al Otaiba, 2005, 2012; Spear-Swerling, 2009; Spear-Swerling and Brucker, 2003, 2004).

Spear-Swerling (2009) developed a structured tutoring routine in which preservice special education teachers learned how to teach concepts acquired in a language arts methods course to struggling readers. Preservice teachers used a structured lesson plan that supported planning for, and providing instruction in, reading and spelling of phonetically regular words and irregular words, fluency, oral reading of text with comprehension, and listening comprehension. Teacher candidates received support for implementing the lesson plan during their language arts methods course, where they learned about activities they could use, and during debriefing that occurred after instruction. Teacher candidates implemented the tutoring routines in approximately eight sessions. The first and last sessions were devoted to assessing their tutees to determine if tutees' targeted language arts skills were improving. In three separate studies, the tutoring routine combined with coursework had a significant effect on gains on preservice teachers' knowledge of the structure of language, and tutees made progress from pre to post assessments (Spear-Swerling, 2009; Spear-Swerling and Brucker, 2003, 2004).

Other researchers achieved somewhat similar findings when implementing structured tutoring experiences in reading and mathematics with special and elementary education teacher education candidates (Al Otaiba, 2005, 2012; Maheady, Mallette, and Harper, 1996; Saddler and Staulters, 2008). Al Otaiba and colleagues, in two different studies, showed that a structured approach to learning to teach reading structured through tutoring was effective in improving preservice teachers' knowledge of words, their ability to use their knowledge during instruction, and tutees' reading achievement. Additionally, in the 2012 study, they used a randomized control experimental design to investigate whether a structured comprehensive approach to tutoring in reading was preferable to one that focused exclusively on teaching meaning. Results favored the structured comprehensive approach. Preservice teachers demonstrated stronger gains in their knowledge of the structure of language and felt more prepared to teach reading than those in the approach that focused primarily on teaching meaning. Quantitative analysis of preservice teachers' lesson logs revealed that those who participated in the structured comprehensive tutoring approach applied more evidence-based reading strategies and were more likely to select activities that matched lesson objectives than those in the meaning-focused approach. Additionally, the students of preservice teachers in the comprehensive tutoring approach made stronger gains on the DIBELS Nonsense Word Fluency measure than students of preservice teachers in the meaning-focused approach.

Virtual Simulations

The use of virtual environments is one teacher preparation strategy gradually gaining ground in the field of teacher education (e.g., Clarke, 2013; Dieker et al., 2013). This emerging body of research draws on the extant literature in the area of simulation – an industry standard for training in business, medicine, aviation, and the military. In this approach, 3D online worlds are used to simulate the role of the field experience for teacher candidates, increasing preservice educators' opportunities to practice teaching before instructing in front of a live student audience (Clark, 2013). Second Life and fully developed simulators are two virtual approaches to providing teacher candidates an immersive online field experience.

Second Life (SL) is a collaborative, internet-based multi-user environment where participants interact through the use of avatars. Avatars are 3D characters within the virtual environment whose appearance and behavior are controlled by the user (http://secondlife.com/shop/learn/). Kim and Blakenship (2013) investigated how SL could be used to help preservice teachers learn to provide instruction to English Language Learners (ELLs). The researchers created a virtual SL second grade classroom that included a Spanish-speaking student. Preservice teachers were expected to provide inclusive instruction in social studies based on what they learned in their coursework. The preservice teachers planned four lessons with their peers and then enacted the lessons through their avatar with the virtual ELL learner online. Preservice teachers recognized that the SL virtual environment provided opportunities to practice designing and delivering instruction prior to facing the challenges of instructing second language learners in a real classroom. They also indicated however, that the SL virtual environment was inauthentic and they experienced many difficulties interfacing with the software.

A second approach to virtual instruction is the use of a fully developed immersive simulator. Researchers at the University of Central Florida developed an avatar-based simulation classroom, TLE TeachLivE™, to provide general and special education preservice teachers opportunities to hone instructional practice within a virtual world (Dieker, Hynes, Hughes, and Smith, 2008). Described as a mixed-reality lab, preservice teachers physically enter a classroom (including white boards, instructional materials, desks) populated by a student group of avatars. The characteristics of the students (e.g., typically developing, struggling readers, behavior difficulties, gifted at science), taken on by the avatars, vary based on the learning objectives of the teacher educator guiding the preservice teachers' experience (Dieker, Straub, Hynes, Hughes, and Hardin, 2014). The preservice teachers then interact within the TLE TeachLivE™ lab as if it were an authentic classroom setting. Preservice teachers are responsible for designing and enacting whole-group and small group instruction, modeling, reteaching, error correction, and even redirecting misbehavior. In a recent study of 134 teachers randomly assigned to TLE TeachLive™ or a control group, Dieker and colleagues (2014) found participants using the TLE TeachLivE™ for a short time period changed one critical instructional behavior and that the effective strategies acquired within the lab transferred to teachers' middle school mathematics classrooms, as demonstrated by academic improvement of their students on the National Assessment of Educational Progress (NAEP).

The attractiveness of mixed reality and other types of virtual simulations is that they can be designed to provide special and general education preservice teachers opportunities to practice the HLPs and HLCs they will need in tiered instruction, and help them understand how instruction can be intensified as they move across tiers of instruction.

Coursework Aligned with Field Experiences

Studies of small and whole group field placements that are crafted to align closely with knowledge and values taught in program coursework demonstrate the potential of such experiences for improving general and special education teacher candidates' knowledge, understandings, and classroom practices (e.g., Alexander, Lignugaris/Kraft, and Forbush, 2007; Cooper and Neismith, 2013; Maheady, Jabot, Rey, and Michielli-Pendl, 2007). Sequenced field-experiences that begin with structured tutoring, followed by structured opportunities to practice teaching small groups of learners, and then internships with an entire class, provide preservice teachers repeated opportunities to practice applying knowledge and skills acquired through coursework in increasingly complex settings.

Moyer and Husman (2006) qualitatively examined differences between teacher candidates participating in a field experience that was well aligned with their methods course in elementary mathematics and those that were not designed specifically to align with coursework. In the well-aligned experience, teacher candidates participated in coursework at the school site where they were simultaneously participating in a field experience. Teachers in the school worked collaboratively with the university for several years and were currently implementing ideas from the mathematics methods course into their classrooms. Analysis of classroom observations and teacher candidates' written reflections revealed that those in the aligned field experience described how students were learning mathematics, how student learning was an indicator of their teaching, and how they might respond to students' needs; whereas, teacher candidates in the other field placements focused more on classroom management concerns and did not seem concerned about how students were learning as a result of their instruction.

In special education, Alexander, Lignugaris/Kraft, and Forbush (2007) used a highly structured field experience aligned with an online math methods course to help teacher candidates learn how to apply what they learned previously about direct instruction principles to teaching mathematics. The online course helped preservice teachers plan mathematics lessons using direct instruction principles. Supplemental readings combined with three course modules about teaching mathematics to students with disabilities were used to develop teacher candidates' knowledge and skill. In addition, teacher candidates were presented with two data-based cases describing students' mathematics performance. Initially, course instructors guided the preservice teacher's analysis of the case studies helping them apply their knowledge of assessment and direct instruction to mathematics. Preservice teachers then completed a case independently and received corrective feedback. This experience was followed by a practicum placement where the preservice teachers applied their newly acquired knowledge and received feedback from field supervisors three to five times over a ten-week period. A multiple probe design across the three course modules showed changes in teachers' knowledge and classroom application of their knowledge. Additionally, students with disabilities made substantive gains on pre- to post-test measures. Taken together, these studies lead to the conclusion that carefully sequenced and aligned field-experiences, coupled with feedback, promote teacher candidates' capacity for effectively implementing HLPs and HLCs needed for the different tiers of instruction.

Coaching or Performance Feedback

Coaching or performance feedback is essential if professionals are to develop an understanding of the features of expert performance. In special education, there is evidence that special education teachers can improve aspects of their instruction when provided coaching or performance feedback. In three separate reviews, researchers described a number of studies in which coaching and performance feedback helped preservice candidates improve their implementation of explicit instruction, peer assisted learning strategies, and reinforcement of appropriate student behaviors (Cornelius and Nagro, 2014; Kretlow and Bartholomew, 2010; Scheeler, Ruhl, and McAfee, 2004), all instructional practices that can be used across instructional tiers. Moreover, Kretlow, and Bartholomew (2010) identified eight studies in which researchers reported improved student academic engagement (n = 6) or literacy outcomes (n = 2).

For coaching and performance feedback to be effective, several essential features are needed to help preservice teachers learn instructional practices. In their review, Kretlow and Bartholomew (2010) found that in successful studies, preservice and in-service teachers had access to initial interactive, small group training in order to learn about the instructional practice. This initial training was then followed by observations of preservice and in-service teachers using the practice, demonstrations of how to use the practice in classrooms, and feedback on their implementation efforts. Feedback from coaches was provided in multiple ways, including: a) collaboratively evaluating video recordings of lessons with teachers; b) providing teachers with corrective feedback that focused lesson strengths and occasions where instruction might be improved; and c) providing in vivo feedback. Further, performance feedback was most effective when it was immediate, the content was constructive (Scheeler et al., 2004), and the focus was on implementing specific evidence-based practices with fidelity (Cornelius and Nagro, 2014).

Coaching and performance feedback, delivered face-to-face, is not always a cost-effective option. One effective solution to this challenge is bug-in-ear technology. Bug-in-ear (BIE) coaching allows supervisors to provide immediate feedback, and with a video feed, BIE coaching may be delivered from a remote location (Scheeler, Bruno, Grubb, and Seavey, 2009). Feedback deemed as effective in studies using BIE coaching shares features similar to effective feedback provided face-to-face. Effective BIE feedback is instructional, meaning that feedback focuses on the teacher's use of specific, predetermined teaching behaviors (e.g., think pair share). Coaches encourage teachers, praising specific behaviors related to correct implementation, and coaches provide corrective feedback to help teachers understand the errors they made and how they might be corrected (e.g., By responding to her off-task behavior, you have inadvertently reinforced it. Next time, consider using proximity control to get her back on task). Finally, coaches question teachers to obtain clarification about practices preservice teachers employ. Scheeler and colleagues (2009; Scheeler, Ruhl, and McAfee, 2004; Scheeler, McAfee, Ruhl, and Lee, 2006) used this approach successfully in several studies to promote desired teaching behaviors, such as using specific praise and effective error correction, as well as increasing teachers' use of evidence-based practices, such as completing three term contingency trials. Additionally, preservice teachers who received immediate feedback through BIE coaching learned skills more quickly than when they were provided delayed feedback. Further, in several studies researchers established that preservice teachers maintain practices acquired through BIE coaching (e.g., Goodman, Brady, Duffy, Scott, and Pollard, 2008; Rock, Schumacker, Gregg, Howard, Gable, and Zigmond, 2014; Scheeler, McKinnon, and Stout, 2012). Thus, coaching, particularly BIE coaching, enables preservice teachers to identify and implement the features of effective instructional practices used in tiered instruction, but researchers have not established the degree to which coaching improves their capacity for analyzing their instruction.

Improving Preservice Teachers' Coordinated Instruction

The pedagogical practices and field experience strategies discussed thus far incorporate principles from the science on learning, and have limited evidence suggesting they may be effective in improving preservice teacher knowledge and practice. None of these approaches, however, directly address the issue of how to help preservice general and special education teachers learn to coordinate their instruction within a multi-tiered system of support. Lesson study is one practice-based approach that is uniquely structured, because of its use of collaborative planning and analysis of instruction, to help preservice general and special education teachers learn to coordinate evidence-based instruction within an RTI instructional framework.

Lesson Study

In lesson study, teachers engage in a collaborative process to analyze instructional practice (Stewart and Brendefur, 2005). Complete lesson study cycles engage teams of teachers in: (a) analyzing student data, academic standards, and curriculum to develop learning goals; (b) collaborative planning aimed at designing lessons that achieve learning goals; (c) teaching, observing, and debriefing about lesson's content and enactment; and (d) collaboratively revising lessons based on lesson analysis (Hiebert et al., 2007; Lewis, Perry, Hurd, and O'Connell, 2006; Takahasi and Yoshida, 2004). Like the other two field-based approaches, lesson study embraces several key principles from the science on learning, including opportunities to engage in retrieval practice when teaching, and receive feedback on teaching. Additionally, preservice teachers have opportunities to develop their skill in analyzing and reflecting on instruction when they observe and debrief about instruction.

Teacher educators have used lesson study to provide preservice teachers with opportunities to apply what they are learning in coursework (Sims and Walsh, 2009). In a few studies, researchers investigated how lesson study impacts teachers' knowledge of instructional planning and analyzing instruction (Sims and Walsh, 2009; Wentworth and Monrow, 2011). There is little research, however, on how lesson study can impact teachers' knowledge of student learning, classroom practice, and collaborative skills.

Sims and Walsh (2009) required teachers to plan collaboratively using a lesson planning template, provided them a protocol to facilitate their analysis and discussion of observed lessons (i.e., the Observation and Evidence Worksheet), and integrated expert feedback. They found that preservice teachers increased their ability to analyze instructional practices and lesson features. For example, the authors noted that preservice teachers increased the number of specific comments about lesson features (e.g., organization and flow) and effective instructional practices (e.g., questioning strategies) by more than 300 percent.

Lesson study was also used to help general and special education teachers learn about and coordinate evidence-based instruction within an RTI framework for students with disabilities. Benedict (2014) examined the discourse of fourth- and fifth-grade general and special education teachers using an expanded lesson study approach. The teachers learned how to plan and analyze tiered instruction collaboratively and improve their knowledge and skill for enacting multisyllabic word study instruction. Teachers participated in workshops focused on advanced word study instruction and coordinating instruction for struggling readers and students with learning disabilities served in an RTI framework. As part of the professional development experience, teachers learned how to use a planning framework that helped them focus on coordinating instruction across the three tiers of RTI. Analysis of teachers' discourse during lesson study planning sessions revealed improved understanding of how to support individualized word study instruction across instructional tiers. Students' post-test scores on morphological knowledge also improved based on a researcher created morphological measure. This is one of the few lesson study experiments in which researchers examined the impact of lesson study on student performance. More research is needed to better understand the impact that lesson study can have on preservice candidates' knowledge for teaching, instructional practice, instructional coordination, ability to analyze instruction, and ultimately, student performance.

Taking a Programmatic Approach to Practice

Practice-based approaches that draw on the science of learning and are scaffolded over time, will likely improve teacher candidates' ability to use HLPs and HLCs. Further, the power of these practices for designing effective instruction for students with disabilities likely will be strengthened, if they are applied within exemplary system frameworks such as RTI and Positive Behavior Interventions and Supports (PBIS) (Lewis and Thomas, 2014).

In this section, we describe a practice-based pilot program at Utah State University that enabled general and special education teacher candidates to develop essential knowledge and skills needed for tiered instruction.

Preparing Teachers within Multi-tiered Systems of Support at Utah State University

Teacher residency programs were initially established in response to the longstanding challenges of how to recruit, prepare and retain teachers in high-need urban schools (e.g., Berry, Montgomery, Curtis, Hernandez, Wutzel, and Snyder, 2008; Papay, West, Fullerton, and Kane, 2011). In these programs, teacher residents typically are paid a stipend while earning their masters degree and learning to teach as an "apprentice" to a mentor teacher. In contrast to traditional teacher preparation, courses in residency programs are designed to support features of the residency experience. Since the resident does not have full responsibility for a group of children, they focus on learning to teach and apply the pedagogy taught in classes. In exchange for the stipend, residents may have to commit to teaching in the district for 3 or 4 years following program completion.

These programs embrace, at least in concept, a practice-based approach to teacher education. Unlike most traditional programs that focus largely on content, residency programs focus on practice (Sanchez, 2010). Although these programs have not been evaluated extensively, an evaluation of the Boston Teacher Residency (BTR) program shows that the program produced positive results over time (Papay et al., 2011). BTR is a practice-based preparation program in which candidates teach alongside a mentor teacher for one year, while taking coursework leading to an initial teaching license. Papay and colleagues (2011) found that candidates prepared through BTR were more likely to teach in areas of high need (e.g., math and science) than other novice teachers. Moreover, they improved their skills quickly, surpassing the effectiveness of veteran teachers by their fourth or fifth year's teaching (Papay et al., 2011).

At Utah State University, faculty developed a pilot residency-based preparation model to prepare teachers to work within high-need schools (Ross and Lignugaris/Kraft, 2015). Students who completed the program earned an elementary education and special education certification. This pilot program was uniquely different from other residency programs because it featured undergraduate preservice teachers rather than masters-level preservice teachers. In addition, faculty focused on integrating teachers into schools that used model multi-tiered systems of support, a blend of RTI and PBIS. The three preservice teachers who volunteered to participate in the pilot program were hired by the school district as para-educators. They worked in the schools for two years, implementing evidence-based practices in tier 1 (general education curriculum), tier 2 (supplementary language arts and math, and coordinators for the Check-in Check-out behavior support program), and tier 3 (intensive special education services) settings.

During year 1, participants worked 17.5 hours per week as tier 2 interventionists, 5–6 hours per week in small groups of students with mild/moderate disabilities on tier 3 language arts or math interventions, and their remaining time in inclusive tier 1 classrooms with a mentor teacher. In addition, they participated in teacher team meetings at one or more grade levels. Coursework to support their tier 1, 2 and 3 experiences was provided in the evening two days a week. During year 2, participants were hired as full-time interns and placed in general education inclusive classrooms. The participants completed a student teaching portfolio similar to preservice teachers on a traditional preparation track, university supervisors conducted observations, and the teachers were assigned a school-based mentor who met with them regularly to discuss student data and challenges.

There were several distinct advantages of this residency program. First, preservice participants learned to apply their instructional skills within an evidence-based school-wide system. Since these teachers worked in each support tier, they acquired a deeper understanding of tiered support systems than teachers who did not have this preparation. Second, participants in this pilot program became highly invested in their school, and the children with whom they worked. They learned first-hand the workings of grade level team meetings and how these communities of practice can help students, and how these system might not function as intended so students might not receive the support they need to succeed. Third, and perhaps most importantly, they improved their instruction compared to veteran teachers. On three outcome variables, students' opportunities to respond, positive interactions, and academic engaged time, preservice teachers in the program outperformed veteran teachers in schools in which they were being mentored.

Although the advantages of residency programs are great, there are several barriers to scaling-up implementation of this pilot program. These include finding enough paid positions so the preservice teachers can devote full-time to learning their craft and how to effectively support teachers within these residency systems. A second barrier is identifying schools that are implementing tiered systems of support with sufficient integrity to serve as model professional development settings. Each year more states are scaling up implementation of statewide tiered systems of support, so finding willing participant schools should become easier in the future. A final barrier to scaled up implementation is the high demand that this preparation program had on the program participants. This demand may be reduced through re-evaluating the course content and schedule to establish leaner, more efficient supporting coursework while enhancing the residency experience. Overall, this novel approach to teacher preparation includes the critical elements of "deliberate practice" needed to produce highly effective educators. This includes learning *focused* on key practices and how to apply these practices within a tiered system of support framework, *distributed opportunities to rehearse and practice skills,* opportunities to *interleave* or apply multiple classroom practices concurrently to establish sophisticated practice routines often found in experienced teachers, and *feedback* so teachers develop the skills needed to independently *analyze and reflect* on their practice.

Conclusions and Some Next Steps

Preparing preservice general and special education teachers to educate students within an RTI framework requires opportunities to learn HLPs and HLCs as well as opportunities to apply them within increasingly complex settings. Practice opportunities that are structured according to what we know about the science of learning hold potential for helping preservice general and special education teachers acquire the knowledge and skill they need to provide evidence-based instruction. For example, engaging teacher candidates in well-structured tutoring experiences seems to improve both their knowledge and instructional practice, increasing their ability to promote student learning. Strategies such as tutoring along with many of the strategies described in this chapter provide practice opportunities that are not fully dependent on the quality of instruction currently provided in schools, a serious and substantial barrier to improving preservice teachers' instructional practice.

Despite the promises of practice-based approaches reviewed in this chapter, more rigorous research is needed to establish their efficacy. We need to examine these practices in isolation and in combination. Ultimately, we will need to understand their cumulative impact in order to structure effective practice-based teacher education approaches that ensure preservice general and special education teachers have the knowledge, instructional skill, and collaborative skill needed to coordinate evidence-based instruction in an RTI framework. Accumulating this research, however, will not be easy. Currently, there are no federal funding sources for examining the impact of teacher education pedagogies on preservice teachers enrolled in preparation programs. The U.S. Department of Education, Institute for Education Sciences only funds research on teacher education that can be connected directly to student outcomes. Student achievement gains, while important, are difficult to use as metrics of preservice teacher progress. Teacher preparation candidates who are currently in programs cannot easily provide student data that can be associated with their instructional efforts. Moreover, preservice teachers are often in practical settings for limited time periods, working within different subject areas, and working with different grade levels of students; under these three conditions it may be challenging to make connections between preservice teachers and their k-12 students' achievement (see Sindelar et al., 2010, and Lignugaris/Kraft et al., 2014 for further discussion of this point).

To address the lack of research on teacher preparation, Lignugaris/Kraft, Sindelar, McCray, and Kimerling (2014) suggest that teacher education researchers collaborate across institutions to implement and conduct research on teacher education innovations. Doing so would enable teacher educators to garner large sample sizes and demonstrate that practices have some external validity. Further, by collaborating, teacher education researchers may be able to accumulate research, a step needed for building an evidence base on teacher education practice. Of course, accumulating a solid teacher preparation research base also depends on valid and reliable measurement of proximal outcomes, such as teacher knowledge and instructional practice (Sindelar, Brownell, and Billingsley, 2010). Quantitative measures of these two outcome variables are essential for determining if preservice teachers are making progress on valued outcomes and comparing findings across studies. Further they are likely better metrics of progress, can be comparable across programs, and the act of creating such measures requires teacher educators to define the knowledge and instructional practices that are of greatest importance to teach (i.e., HLCs and HLPs). For instance, the knowledge surveys used in tutoring studies described in this chapter were comparable, and have been linked to improved student achievement in reading in elementary and prekindergarten studies.

Until we establish more research-based knowledge about teacher preparation for working within an RTI framework, teacher educators can use the science of learning to identify, develop, and implement promising practice opportunities. In organizing practice-based strategies, teacher educators should be deliberate in aligning them with HLPs and HLCs taught in coursework and in sequencing them across the program to ensure that they provide rigorous, distributed practice. Further, considerable attention should be given to how preservice general and special education teachers have opportunities to learn to plan for and implement coordinated instruction across the tiers; simply practicing in isolation will not help them acquire the collaborative skills they need to implement effective RTI instruction or positive behavioral supports. As teacher educators, we need to act now to ensure our preservice teachers have sufficient high-quality practice opportunities. We cannot afford to wait for the science of teacher education to catch up.

References

Alexander, M., Lignugaris/Kraft, B., and Forbush, D. (2007). Online mathematics methods course evaluation: Student outcomes, generalization, and pupil performance. *Teacher Education and Special Education, 30*, 199–216. doi: 10.1177/088840640703000401.

Al Otaiba, S. (2005). How effective is code-based reading tutoring in English for English learners and preservice teacher-tutors? *Remedial and Special Education, 26*, 245–254. doi: 10.1177/07419325050260 040701.

Al Otaiba, S., Lake, V. E., Greulich, L., Folsom, J. S., and Guidry, L. (2012). Preparing beginning reading teachers: An experimental comparison of initial early literacy field experiences. *Reading and Writing, 25*, 109–129. doi: 10.1007/s11145-010-9250-2.

Anderson, D. H. and Lignugaris/Kraft, B. (2006). Video-case instruction for teachers of students with problem behaviors in general and special education classrooms. *Journal of Special Education Technology, 21*(2), 31.

Ball, D. L. and Fornazi, F. M. (2011). Building a common core for learning to teach. *American Educator, 35*(2), 17–21, 38–39.

Ball, D. L. and Forzani, F. M. (2009). The work of teaching and the challenge for teacher education. *Journal of Teacher Education, 60*(5), 497–511.

Ball, D. L., Sleep, L., Boerst, T. A., and Bass, H. (2009). Combining the development of practice and the practice of development in teacher education. *The Elementary School Journal, 109*, 458–474.

Beck, R. J., King, A., and Marshall, S. K. (2002). Effects of videocase construction on preservice teachers' observations of teaching. *The Journal of Experimental Education, 70*(4), 345–361.

Bell, N.D. (2007). Microteaching: What is that is going on here? *Linguistics and Education*, *18*, 24–40. doi:10.1016/j.linged.2007.04.002.

Benedict, A. (2014). Learning together: Teachers' evolving understandings during ongoing collaborative professional development. (Doctoral dissertation, University of Florida.) Retrieved from ProQuest Dissertations and Theses. (Accession Order No. in process.)

Benedict, A., Parks, Y., Brownell, T. M., Lauterbach, A. A., and Kiely, M. T. (2013). Using lesson study to align elementary literacy instruction within the RTI framework. *Teaching Exceptional Children*, *45*(5), 22–31.

Berkeley, S., Bender, W. N., Peaster, L. G., and Saunders, L. (2009). Implementation of response to intervention: A snapshot of progress. *Journal of Learning Disabilities*, *42* (1), 85–95.

Berry, B., Montgomery, D., Curtis, R., Hernandez, M., Wurtzel, J., and Snyder, J. (2008). *Creating and sustaining urban teacher residencies: A new way to recruit, prepare, and retain effective teachers in high-needs districts.* Chapel Hill, NC: The Aspen Institute and Center for Teaching Quality.

Bishop, A. G., Brownell, M. T., Menon, S., Galman, S., and Leko, M. (2010). Understanding the influence of personal attributes, preparation, and school environment on beginning special education teachers' classroom practices during reading instruction. *Learning Disability Quarterly*, *33*(2), 75–93.

Bradley, M. C., Daley, T., Levin, M., O'Reilly, F., Parsad, A., Robertson, A., and Werner, A. (2011). IDEA National Assessment Implementation Study. Final Report. NCEE 2011–4027. National Center for Education Evaluation and Regional Assistance.

Brown, P. C., Roediger III, H. L., and McDaniel, M. A. (2014). *Make it stick.* Cambridge, MA: Harvard University Press.

Brownell, M. T., Lauterbach, A. A., Benedict, A. E., Bettini, E. A., Murphy, K., and Stephens, J. (2012). Preparing teachers to effectively deliver reading instruction and behavioral supports in response to intervention frameworks. In *Advances in learning and behavior disabilities* (Vol. 25, pp. 247–277).

Brownell, M. T., Lauterbach, A. A., Dingle, M. D., Boardman, A. G., Urbach, J. F., and Leko, M. M. (2014). Individual and contextual factors influencing special education teacher learning in Literacy Learning Cohorts. *Learning Disability Quarterly*, *37*, 31–44.

Brunvand, S. (2010). Best practices for producing video content for teacher education. *Contemporary Issues in Technology and Teacher Education*, *10*, 247–256.

Brunvand, S. and Fishman, B. (2006–2007). Investigating the impact of the availability of scaffolds on preservice teacher noticing and learning from video. *Journal of Educational Technology Systems*, *35*(2), 151–174. doi:10.2190/L353-X356-72W7–42L9.

Cepeda, N. J., Pashler, H., Vul, E., Wixted, J. T., and Rohrer, D. (2006). Distributed practice in verbal recall tasks: A review and quantitative synthesis. *Psychological bulletin*, *132*(3), 354.

Clarke, L. (2013). Virtual learning environments in teacher education: A journal, a journey. *Technology, Pedagogy and Education*, *22*(1), 121–131. doi: http://dx.doi.org/10.1080/1475939X.2012.731632.

Connor, C. M., Alberto, P. A., Compton, D. L., and O'Connor, R. E. (2014). Improving Reading Outcomes for Students with or at Risk for Reading Disabilities: A Synthesis of the Contributions from the Institute of Education Sciences Research Centers. NCSER 2014–3000. National Center for Special Education Research.

Cooper, S. and Nesmith, S. (2013). Exploring the role of field experience context in preservice teachers' development as mathematics educators. *Action in Teacher Education*, *35*(3), 165–185. doi: 10.1080/01626620.2013.770376.

Copeland, W. D. (1975). The relationship between microteaching and student teacher classroom performance. *The Journal of Educational Research*, *68*, 289–293.

Copeland, W. D. (1977). Some factors related to student teacher classroom performance following microteaching training. *American Educational Research Journal*, *14*, 147–157.

Cornelius, K. E. and Nagro, S. A. (2014). Evaluating the evidence base of performance feedback in preservice special education teacher training. *Teacher Education and Special Education*, *37*, 133–146. doi:10.1177/0888406414521837.

Danielson, L. and Zumeta, R. Discussion about states' hybrid approach to Response to Intervention (personal communication, January 5, 2015).

Dawson, M. Lignugaris/Kraft, B.(2013). TLE TeachLivE™ vs. role-play: Comparative effects on special educators' acquisition of basic teaching skills. In A. Hayes, S. Hardin, L. Dieker, C. Hughes, M. Hynes, and C. Straub. *Conference Proceedings for First National TeachLivE Conference.* Paper presented at First National TeachLivE Conference: Orlando, FL, University of Central Florida.

Dieker, L. A., Rodriguez, J. A., Lignugaris, B., Hynes, M. C., and Hughes, C. E. (2013). The potential of simulated environments in teacher education: Current and future possibilities. *Teacher Education and*

Special Education: The Journal of the Teacher Education Division of the Council for Exceptional Children, 37(1), 21–33. doi: 10.1177/0888406413512683.

Dieker, L. A., Straub, C., Hughes, C. Hynes, M. C., and Hardin, S. E. (2014). Learning from virtual students. *Educational Leadership, 71*(8), 54–58.

Dieker, L., Hynes, M., Hughes, C., and Smith, E. (2008). Implications of mixed reality and simulation technologies on special education and teacher preparation. *Focus on Exceptional Children, 40*(6), 1.

Dunlosky, J., Rawson, K. A., Marsh, E. J., Nathan, M. J., and Willingham, D. T. (2013). Improving students' learning with effective learning techniques: promising directions from cognitive and educational psychology. *Psychological Science in the Public Interest, 14*(1), 4–58. doi: 10.1177/1529100612453266.

Ely, E., Pullen, P., Kennedy, M., and Williams, M. C. (2015). A multi-media tool to deliver professional development of vocabulary instruction. *Journal of Special Education Technology, 30*, 59–72.

Ely, E., Pullen, P., Kennedy, M., Hirsch, S. E., and Williams, M. C. (2014). Use of instructional technology to improve teacher candidate knowledge of vocabulary instruction. *Computers & Education, 75*, 44–52. doi: 10.1016/j.compedu.2014.01.013.

Ericsson, K. A. (2009). Enhancing the development of professional performance: Implications from the study of deliberate practice. In K. A. Ericsson (Ed.), *Development of professional expertise* (pp. 449–469). New York: Cambridge University Press.

Ericsson, K. A. (2014). *The road to excellence: The acquisition of expert performance in the arts and sciences, sports, and games.* Florence, KY: Psychology Press.

Fernandez, M. L. (2010). Investigating how and what prospective teachers learn through microteaching lesson study. *Teaching and Teacher Education, 26*(2), 351–362.

Fernandez, M. L. and Robinson, M. (2006). Prospective teachers' perspectives on microteaching lesson study. *Education, 127*(2), 203–217.

Forzani, F. (2014). Understanding "core practices" and "practice-based" teacher education: Learning from the past. *Journal of Teacher Education, 65*(4), 357–368.

Fuchs, D., Mock, D., Morgan, P. L., and Young, C. L. (2003). Responsiveness-to-intervention: Definitions, evidence, and implications for the learning disabilities construct. *Learning Disabilities Research and Practice, 18*(3), 157–171.

Geiger, W. L., Mickelson, A., McKeown, D., Kleinhammer-Tramill, J., and Steinbrecher, T. (2014). Patterns of licensure for special education teachers. In McCray, M. T. Brownell, and B. Lignugaris/Kraft (Eds.), *Handbook of research on special education teacher preparation* (pp. 30–46). New York: Routledge.

Gersten, R., Beckmann, S., Clarke, B., Foegen, A., Marsh, L., Star, J. R., and Witzel, B. (2009). Assisting Students Struggling with Mathematics: Response to Intervention (RTI) for Elementary and Middle Schools. NCEE 2009–4060. What Works Clearinghouse.

Gersten, R., Chard, D. J., Jayanthi, M., Baker, S. K., Morphy, P., and Flojo, J. (2009). Mathematics instruction for students with learning disabilities: A meta-analysis of instructional components. *Review of Educational Research, 79*(3), 1202–1242.

Goldrick, L., Sindelar, P., Zabala, D., and Hirsch, E. (2014). The Role of State Policy in Preparing Educators to Meet the Learning Needs of Students with Disabilities. (Document No. PA-1). Retrieved from University of Florida, Collaboration for Effective Educator, Development, Accountability, and Reform Center website: http://ceedar.education.ufl.edu/tools/literature-syntheses/.

Goodman, J. I., Brady, M. P., Duffy, M. L., Scott, J., and Pollard, N. E. (2008). The effects of "bug-in-ear" supervision on special education teachers' delivery of learn units. *Focus on Autism & Other Developmental Disabilities, 23*, 207–216.

Greenberg, J., McKee, A., and Walsh, K. (June 1, 2013). Teacher Prep Review: A Review of the Nation's Teacher Preparation Programs. Retrieved from SSRN: http://ssrn.com/abstract=2353894 orhttp://dx.doi.org/10.2139/ssrn.2353894.

Grossman, P. (2005). Research on pedagogical approaches. In M, Cochran-Smith and K. M. Zeichner (Eds.), *Studying teacher education* (pp. 425–476). Mahwah, NJ: Lawrence Erlbaum.

Grossman, P. and McDonald, M. (2008). Back to the future: Directions for research in teaching and teacher education. *American Educational Research Journal, 45*, 184–205.

Hiebert, J., Morris, A. K., Berk, D., and Jansen, A. (2007). Preparing teachers to learn from teaching. *Journal of Teacher Education, 58*(1), 47–61.

Horn, I. (2005). Learning on the job: A situated account of teacher learning in highschool mathematics departments. *Cognition and Instruction, 23*, 207–236.

Hughes, C. A. and Dexter, D. D. (2008). Selecting a scientifically based core curriculum for Tier 1. Retrieved March 10, 2010 from www.rtinetwork.org.

Jones, S. D. and Messenheimer-Young, T. (1989). Content of special education courses for preservice regular education teachers. *Teacher Education and Special Education: The Journal of the Teacher Education Division of the Council for Exceptional Children, 12*(4), 154–159.

Kamman, M. L., McCray, E. D. and Brownell, M. T. (2014*). Teacher education pedagogy: What we know about preparing effective teachers.* Unpublished manuscript.

Karpicke, J. D. and Blunt, J. R. (2011). Retrieval practice produces more learning than elaborative studying with concept mapping. *Science, 331*, 772–775. doi: 10.1126/science.1199327.

Kellogg, R. T. and Whiteford, A. P. (2009). Training advanced writing skills: The case for deliberate practice. *Educational Psychologist, 44*, 250–266. doi: org/10.1080/00461520903213600.

Kim, D. and Blankenship, R. J. (2013). Using second life as a virtual collaborative tool for preservice teachers seeking English for speakers of other languages endorsement. *Journal of Educational Computing Research, 48*(1), 19–43.

Klingner, J., Brownell, M., Mason, L. H., Sindelar, P. T., Benedict, A., with Griffin, C., Lane, K., Israel, M., Oakes, W. P., Menzies, H. M., Germer, K. and Park, Y. (2016). Teaching students with special needs in the new millennium. In D. H. Gitomer and C. A. Bell (Eds.). *Handbook of research on teaching* (5th Edition) (pp. 63–716). Washington, DC: American Education Research Association.

Kornell, N. and Bjork, R. A. (2008). Learning concepts and categories is spacing the "enemy of induction"? *Psychological Science, 19*(6), 585–592.

Kretlow, A. G. and Bartholomew, C. C. (2010). Using coaching to improve the fidelity of evidence-based practices: A review of studies. *Teacher Education and Special Education, 33*, 279–299. doi: 10.1177/0888406410371643.

Lewis, C., Perry, R., Hurd, J. and O'Connell, M. (2006). Teacher collaboration: Lesson study comes of age in North America. *Phi Delta Kappan, 88*(4), 273–281.

Lewis, T. and Thomas, C. N., (2014). Educator preparation within the context of school-wide positive behavior and academic supports. In P. Sindelar, E. D. McRay, M. T. Brownell and B. Lignugaris/Kraft (Eds.). *Handbook of research on special education teacher preparation.* New York: Routledge.

Lignugaris/Kraft, B. and Harris, S. (2014). Teacher preparation: Principles of effective pedagogy. In P. Sindelar, E. D. McRay, M. T. Brownell, and B. Lignugaris/Kraft (Eds.). *Handbook of research on special education teacher preparation.* New York: Routledge.

Lignugaris/Kraft, B., Sindelar, P. T., McCray, E. D., and Kimerling, J. (2014). The "wicked question" of teacher education effects and what to do about it. In P. T. Sindelar, E. D. McCray, M. T. Brownell, and B. Lignugaris/Kraft (Eds.). *Handbook of research on special education teacher preparation* (pp. 461–471). New York: Routledge.

Maheady, L., Jabot, M., Rey, J., and Michielli-Pendl, J. (2007). An early field-based experience and its impact on pre-service candidates' teaching practice and their pupils' outcomes. *Teacher Education and Special Education, 30*, 24–33. doi: 10.1177/088840640703000103.

Maheady, L., Mallette, B., and Harper, G. F. (1996). The pair tutoring program: An early field-based experience to prepare preservice general educators to work with students with special learning needs. *Teacher Education and Special Education, 19*(4), 277–297.

Mayo, J. A. (2004). Using case-based instruction to bridge the gap between theory and practice in psychology of adjustment. *Journal of Constructivist Psychology, 17*(2), 137–146.

Mcleskey, J., Barringer, M.D., Billingsley, B., Brownell, M., Jackson, D., Kennedy, M., Lewis, T., Maheady, L., Rodriquez, J., Scheeler, M. C., Winn, J. and Ziegler, D. (2017). *High leverage practices in special education.* Arlington, VA: Council for Exceptional Children and CEEDAR Center.

Merseth, K. K. (1991). The early history of case-based instruction: Insights for teacher education today. *Journal of Teacher Education, 42*(4), 243–249.

Moulton, C., Dubrowski, A., MacRae, H., Graham, B., Grober, E., and Reznick, R. (2006). Teaching surgical skills: What kind of practice makes perfect? *Annals of Surgery, 244*, 400–409. doi: 10.1097/01.sla.0000234808.85789.6a.

Moyer, P. S. and Husman, J. (2006). Integrating coursework and field placements: The impact on preservice elementary mathematics teachers' connections to teaching. *Teacher Education Quarterly, 33*, 37–56.

Myers, J. (2013). Creating reflective practitioners with preservice lesson study. *International Journal of Pedagogies and Learning, 8*(1), 1–9.

Papay, J. P., West, M. R., Fullerton, J. B., and Kane, T. J. (2011). Does practice-based teacher preparation increase student achievement? Early evidence from the Boston teacher residency. NBER Working Paper Series, 17646. National Bureau of Economic Research.

Powell, D. R., Diamond, K. E., and Koehler, M. J. (2010). Use of a case-based hypermedia resource in an early literacy coaching intervention with pre-kindergarten teachers. *Topics in Early Childhood Special Education, 29,* 239–249.

Prior, C. R. and Bitter, G. C. (2008). Using multimedia to teach inservice teachers: Impacts on learning, application, and retention. *Computers in Human Behavior, 24,* 2668–2681.

Ritter, S., Anderson, J. R., Koedinger, K. R., and Corbett, A. (2007). Cognitive tutor: Applied research in mathematics education. *Psychonomic Bulletin & Review, 14*(2), 249–255. doi: 10.3758/BF03194060.

Rock, M. L., Schumacker, R. E., Gregg, M., Howard, P. W., Gable, R. A., and Zigmond, N. (2014). How are they now? Longer term effects of eCoaching through online bug-in-ear technology. *Teacher Education and Special Education.* Advanced online publication. doi: 10.1177/0888406414525048.

Roediger, H. L. and Karpicke, J. D. (2006). The power of testing memory: Basic research and implications for educational practice. *Perspectives on Psychological Science, 1*(3), 181–210.

Roediger, H. L., Agarwal, P. K., McDaniel, M. A., and McDermott, K. B. (2011). Test-enhanced learning in the classroom: Long-term improvements from quizzing. *Journal of Experimental Psychology: Applied, 17*(4), 382–395. doi: 10.1037/a0026252.

Rohrer, D. and Pashler, H. (2010). Recent research on human learning challenges: Conventional instructional strategies. *Educational Researcher, 39,* 406–412. doi: 10.3102/0013189X10374770.

Ross, S. and Lignugaris/Kraft, B. (2015). Multi-tiered systems of support preservice residency: A pilot undergraduate teacher preparation model. *Journal of the National Association for Alternative Certification, 10,* 3–20.

Russ-Eft, D. (2002). A typology of training design and work environment factors affecting workplace learning and transfer. *Human Resource Development Review, 1*(1), 45–65.

Saddler, B. and Staulters, M. (2008). Beyond tutoring after-school literacy instruction. *Intervention in School and Clinic, 43,* 203–209. doi: 10.1177/1053451207310341.

Sanchez, C. (2010). Programs train teachers using medical school model. National Public Radio Special Series. Retrieved from www.npr.org/templates/story/story.php?storyId=125854975

Scheeler, M. C., Bruno, K., Grubb, E., and Seavey, T. L. (2009). Generalizing teaching techniques from university to K-12 classrooms: Teaching preservice teachers to use what they learn. *Journal of Behavioral Education, 18,* 189–210. doi: 10.1007/s10864-009-9088-3.

Scheeler, M. C., McAfeem J. K., Ruhl, K. L., and Lee, D. L. (2006). Effects of corrective feedback delivered via wireless technology on preservice teacher performance and student behavior. *Teacher and Special Education, 29*(1), 12–25. doi: 10.1177/088840640602900103.

Scheeler, M. C., McKinnon, K., and Stout, J. (2012). Effects of immediate feedback delivered via webcam and bug-in-ear technology on preservice teacher performance. *Teacher Education and Special Education, 35*(1), 77–90. doi: 10.1177/0888406411401919.

Scheeler, M. C., Ruhl, K. L., and McAfee, J. K. (2004). Providing performance feedback to teachers: A review. *Teacher Education and Special Education, 27,* 396–407.

Shulman, L. S. (1992). Toward a pedagogy of cases. In J. H. Shulman (Ed.). *Case methods in teacher education* (pp. 1–30). New York: Teachers College Press.

Sims, L. and Walsh, D. (2009). Lesson study with preservice teachers: Lessons from lessons. *Teaching and Teacher Education, 25,* 724–733.

Sindelar, P., Brownell, M., and Billingsley, B. (2010). Special education teacher education research: Current status and future directions. *Teacher Education and Special Education: The Journal of the Teacher Education Division of the Council for Exceptional Children, 33*(1), 8–24. doi: 10.1177/0888406409358593.

Spear-Swerling, L. (2009). A literacy tutoring experience for prospective special educators and struggling second graders. *Journal of Learning Disabilities, 42,* 431–443. doi:10.1177/0022219409338738.

Spear-Swerling, L. and Brucker, P. O. (2003). Teachers' acquisition of knowledge about English word structures. *Annals of Dyslexia, 53,* 72–103.

Spear-Swerling, L. and Brucker, P. O. (2004). Preparing novice teachers to develop basic reading and spelling skills in children. *Annals of Dyslexia, 54,* 332–364. doi: 10.1007/s11881-004-0016-x.

Stewart, R. A. and Brendefur, J. L. (2005). Fusing lesson study and authentic achievement: A model for teacher collaboration. *Phi Delta Kappan, 86*(9), 681–687.

Takahashi, A. and Yoshida, M. (2004). Lesson-Study Communities. *Teaching Children Mathematics, 10*(9), 436–437.

Taylor, K. and Rohrer, D. (2010). The effects of interleaved practice. *Applied Cognitive Psychology, 24,* 837–848. doi: 10.1002/acp.1598.

Vaughn, S., Gersten, R., and Chard, D. J. (2000). The underlying message in LD intervention research: Findings from research syntheses. *Exceptional Children, 67*(1), 99–114.

Wanzek, J., Wexler, J., Vaughn, S., and Ciullo, S. (2010). Reading interventions for struggling readers in the upper elementary grades: A synthesis of 20 years of research. *Reading and Writing, 23*(8), 889–912. doi: 10.1007/s11145-009-9179-5.

Wentworth, N. and Monroe, E. E. (2014). Inquiry-based lessons that integrate technology: their development in elementary mathematics teacher education. *Computers in the Schools: Interdisciplinary Journal of Practice, Theory, and Applied Research, 13*(9), 263–277. doi: 10.1080/07380569.2011.620938.

Zeiser, K., Taylor, J., Rickles, J., Garet, M., and Segeritz, M. (2014). Evidence of deeper learning outcomes. Report #3 Findings from the Study of Deeper Learning: Opportunities and Outcomes. Washington, DC: American Institutes for Research.

Zirkel, P. A. (2011). State laws and guidelines for RTI: Additional implementation features. *National Association of School Psychologists, 39*(7), 30–32.

9

PARENT AND STUDENT INVOLVEMENT IN RESPONSE TO INTERVENTION MODELS

*Sarah Conoyer, Erica S. Lembke, Sarah Owens,
Daniel Cohen, and Heather M. Campbell*

As initiatives that incorporate tiered models of intervention have increased, focus has turned from teacher implementation to involvement of other stakeholders such as administrators, students, parents, and outside agencies. Perhaps most significant among these, but least documented, is parent and student involvement.

Parent involvement in education can have a positive impact on academic achievement, and some efforts by educators to involve parents appear to be worthwhile (Anderson and Minke, 2007). Despite this, a simple and comprehensive definition of beneficial involvement is elusive due to the large degree of variability in how researchers have operationalized the construct (Fan and Chen, 2001), and therefore it is challenging to make broad determinations about the impact of parental involvement as a broad construct. Given that particular forms of parental involvement have varying effects, it is necessary to isolate specific forms of involvement and evaluate them individually.

Early literature on communication with parents of children in special education focused largely on Parent–Teacher conferences. Kroth (1978) outlined a set of several elements necessary for conferences, including location, active listening, collecting information, and time management. Ostensibly, these efforts were focused primarily on building rapport with the parent. Stephens, Blackhurst and Magliocca (1982) developed a more data-focused approach to conferencing that included the following steps: 1. define objectives; 2. review data; 3. select specific data for parents to review and prepare it in manner that can be easily interpreted; 4. develop a plan. This approach reflects the attitude that data should play a primary role. In spite of the strong emphasis on conferences in early work in the area of parent-teacher communication, it represents a small subset within the variety of ways in which parents can be involved in their child's education.

Despite the dearth of recent literature on parent-teacher communication for children with special needs, contemporary methods of engaging parents to contribute to their child's educational experience across a variety of populations have received significant attention.

A systematic review of evidence-based methods of home-school collaboration by Cox (2005) found that the most effective approaches were those that either included parents as partners in intervention activities or provided parents with data about student progress.

In their model describing the process of parental involvement, Walker and colleagues (2005) describe four constructs impacting on parents' degree of involvement, including:

> (1) parental role construction, or parents' beliefs about what they should do in the context of their child's education; (2) parental self-efficacy in helping the child succeed in school, or how much parents believed they could improve children's school outcomes; (3) parents' perceptions of general invitations for involvement from the school; and (4) perceptions of general invitations for involvement from the child.
>
> *(p. 87)*

Parental impressions of efforts on the part of the school to engage them is a particularly important aspect of the model for educators, given that it represents the most direct pathway to promote involvement by school personnel.

In a study conducted by Seitsinger and colleagues (2008), a scale was developed to document school and teacher efforts to engage parents. Subsequently, the validated scale was used in conjunction with surveys and school records to assess the relationship between parent and student perceptions of the quality of parent-school interactions as well as student achievement, with specific teacher/school engagement practices using a sample of 2,584 teachers, 83,844 students, and roughly 45,000 parents. Results indicate that efforts to engage parents are perceived as high-quality contact and associated with student achievement. This relationship was particularly significant in the case engagement efforts that involve parents in activities directly associated with student academic experience, and practices in which data are provided.

In a Response to Intervention (RTI) model, where key elements include screening students using a reliable and valid tool, implementing evidence-based core instruction and intervention, ongoing monitoring of student progress, and data-based decision making in school-based teams, the importance of relaying information to parents in an easy-to-understand manner is critical.

One potential source of data that can be used to provide parents with information about their child's academic progress is curriculum-based measurement (CBM; Deno, 1985). CBM involves the use of brief standardized assessment measures that utilize stimulus items derived from classroom materials. CBM provides outcome measures that broadly predict academic performance (Deno, 2003). CBM generates a stream of formative data that can be graphed and used to appraise academic proficiency, provide performance feedback, and evaluate the effectiveness of an intervention within a multi-tiered, problem-solving framework. As an example of the breadth of use, for the 2012–2013 school year, schools in the United States paid to assess 4.2 million students using AIMSweb, one web-based version of CBM. Although the use of CBM continues to develop as a widespread practice for generating a stream of data regarding student performance, there is no indication that standard practices have been developed or implemented in applied settings to communicate CBM data to parents, despite the assertion by Deno (2003) that such a practice is worthwhile. This gap is further evidenced by the complete absence of suggestions regarding the communication of CBM data in a relatively recent article focused on promoting parent involvement in a high-profile special education practice journal (Staples and Diliberto, 2010).

Walker and colleagues (2005) hypothesize that parents influence student behavior through reinforcement, modeling, and instruction. In reference to providing CBM data to parents, it appears that reinforcement would be the primary mechanism through which data feedback could enhance student achievement. Specifically, through the periodic distribution of student data, parents can promote current behaviors when progress is being made, or encourage alternative, more adaptive behaviors when progress is absent or insufficient. To our knowledge, there is only one example in the research literature regarding the provision of CBM data to parents. Shin and colleagues (1993) provided parents with CBM data for special education students to evaluate the impact of such data on parent attitudes regarding student reintegration into general education. Study results indicated that providing such data had no impact on parent attitudes, however this experiment represents a highly limited application of this form of school-parent communication. As CBM continues to proliferate through educational systems, further study is necessary to identify the impact of providing progress-monitoring data to parents and to highlight optimal procedures.

Why Should School Leaders Educate and Involve Parents in the RTI Process?

In the past 20 years, there has been an increased interest in research and policy surrounding why and how families influence children's achievement in schools. There has also been a growing focus on how families and schools can work together to create successful outcomes for students (Cox, 2005). Legislation has also impacted the recent development of home-school collaboration (No Child Left Behind Act). Schools are attempting to identify ways that allow parents to play an active role in their child's education. These methods or activities are usually labeled as parent involvement or home-school collaboration (Cox, 2005; Fann and Chenn, 2001).

As mentioned previously, there is literature to support parent involvement in other school-wide initiatives, but very little is published on the involvement of parents in Response to Intervention (RTI) models. Some type of RTI model is currently implemented in all states, so it is likely that parents will be exposed to the model. For more detail on implementation by states, see Zirkel (2012). Elements of effective RTI models typically include universal screening of students in academic areas, progress monitoring of students at risk, implementation of evidence-based core instruction, selection and implementation of intervention targeted to student need, and most importantly, data-based decision making by teachers and teams (Lembke, Garman, Deno, and Stecker, 2010; Lembke, McMaster, and Stecker, 2009)

How Can It Happen?

Parent involvement could occur within each of these elements or aspects of RTI. For instance, in the area of screening, data can be shared with parents by email or in person. At open house in the fall, teachers can help parents to understand what the graphed data means. Schools can set the expectation that teachers will present parents with results of screening at each face-to-face conference. In the area of progress monitoring, the same types of involvement and communication with parents might occur, but on a more frequent basis.

Our author team completed three small, parallel exploratory studies to examine the effectiveness of sharing CBM data with parents—one with high school students and two with elementary students. The purpose of the studies was to examine the effects of sharing CBM data with parents on students' academic outcomes and to survey parents regarding their perceptions of the data sharing. Two research questions were posed: 1) What are the effects of sharing CBM data with parents on their students' academic outcomes; and 2) how do parents perceive the CBM data sharing, based on a survey?

Method

Two studies were conducted across three sites as a part of the current study. Across all three sites, procedures remained constant. Specifically, across sites, participating students were assessed weekly using curriculum-based measurement (CBM) to monitor progress in the area of reading (oral reading fluency, comprehension). All parents received the "regular" assessment information: weekly, formative updates on the academic progress of their children, including comments on student attendance, homework completion, and class participation. Parents of students in treatment conditions were sent assessment information in the form of visual representation (a line graph) in addition to 'regular' assessment methods. In addition, brief surveys were distributed to all parents upon study completion; the return rate was ranged from 86–100% across the two studies. The instrument, consisting of 7–8 questions (depending on condition), was designed to determine whether or not receiving a graph of student reading CBM scores provided parents with a more accurate picture of student progress than just the narrative parent reports. The explanation of the graphed data was shared with parents at conferences. The survey was mailed home along with the final, summative report and the CBM graphs for the parents for all students (the parents of students in treatment groups had received graphs weekly throughout the study). The survey included items on: parent perceived improvement in reading throughout the duration of the study; how much the child improved in reading; and perceived usefulness and acceptability of the CBM graphs in parent understanding of progress. Letter grades were not given to any students; rather instructors provided a narrative assessment of student progress.

Across sites, variations were noted in demographics and procedures to reflect age and specific needs of students. Variations are detailed below.

Study 1

Participants and Setting

Participants in the study were 30 high school students (57% female and 43% male) from two urban and one rural high school in the Midwest. Students ranged in age from 15–18 years old and 100% qualified for the free/reduced lunch program. Fifty-three percent (53%) of the students were Asian American, 27% African American, 13% Caucasian, 3% American Indian, and 3% Hispanic/Latino. Fifty-six percent (56%) of the participants were non-native English speakers who did not speak English at home. Students were enrolled in a six-week summer, residential pre-college enrichment program designed to increase the number of first-generation and low-income students attending college. Also participating in the study were the parents of the high school students.

During the six-week summer program, participants received daily 30 minutes of silent, sustained reading time, and 80 daily of English/Language Arts instruction. Students also received intensive instruction in math and science as well as on-campus residential programming designed to simulate a college-going environment. All parents also received a summative report at the end of the program, including comments on student attendance, pre- and post-test scores by subject area, student strengths, and whether or not the student met the expectations of each course.

Procedures

At the beginning of the pre-college program, all students completed three baseline maze passages, which were counterbalanced across student. Based on median maze scores, students were matched and parents were randomly assigned to either the control or experimental condition. Parents in the control condition received only the "regular" assessment information produced by the pre-college program instructors. Parents in the experimental condition received the "regular" assessment information as well as a copy of their child's CBM maze graph and an explanation of how to read the graph at the end of the pre-college program.

All students completed a weekly, three-minute maze passage administered by the researcher in a large-group session. In the maze passage, the first sentence was left intact and then every seventh word was deleted. The correct word and two distractor choices appeared in place of the deleted word; the student chose which word best fit the sentence. The maze measures were scored by a trained pre-college program employee according to number of correct maze choices and number of correct minus incorrect maze choices. To ensure that scorer drift did not occur, the researcher scored every tenth sample and inter-scorer agreement was calculated by dividing the smaller score by the larger score, and multiplying by 100. Inter-scorer agreement across samples was 100%. The same employee graphed the baseline maze scores, generated a goal line based on one maze choice per week improvement, and then subsequently graphed each student's maze scores weekly. Students did not see their graphs during the pre-college program, but they did see examples of CBM graphs and were taught how to read them so they could help their parents should they need assistance. The same maze passages used as baseline passages were also given to students at the end of the summer program as the last data points on the CBM graphs.

Data from the surveys were analyzed using descriptive statistics. Statistical comparisons of responses between the parents in the control and experimental conditions were conducted using the Pearson chi square test.

Study 2

Participants and Setting

This study took place across two elementary school sites. Demographics are presented separately for each site.

SITE 1

Site 1 was an elementary school in a community of about 100,000 in a mid-sized city in the Midwest. The school district had a total enrollment of 13,777. The elementary school where the data were collected had 320 enrolled students from kindergarten to fifth grade. Forty-eight percent of students at the school were from diverse cultural backgrounds other than Caucasian and fifty-five percent received free and reduced lunch. Participants in the study included 8 elementary school students (50% female and 50% male) who were randomly divided evenly into control and treatment groups.

75% of the students were Caucasian, 12.5% African-American, and 12.5% Asian American. All students received special education services; six students were eligible for services as students with intellectual disabilities, one student was eligible as a student with a learning disability, and one student was eligible in the area of autism. Students and their parents participated in the study for seven weeks and received individualized special education services in the area of reading.

During the seven weeks, parents of students in the treatment condition received assessment information that included weekly graphs of student performance, comments on student attendance, homework completion, and class participation. Parents of students in the control condition received all information except for the weekly graphs. Letter grades were not given, rather the instructor provided a narrative assessment of student progress.

Site 2 included 10 elementary school students (nine female and one male) from one urban school in the upper Midwest. The original sample had three additional students, all male, who did not complete the study. Students ranged in grade level from kindergarten to fifth grade. There were approximately 650 students total at the elementary with 46% African American, 22% Hispanic, 5% Asian/Pacific Islander, 23% Caucasian, and the remainder identifying as bi-racial. Participants in the study included 12 elementary school students (nine female and three male) who were randomly divided evenly into control and treatment groups.

All students received special education services in a resource setting, with the majority receiving direct instruction in reading standard treatment protocols. Students and their parents participated in the study for four weeks.

During the four weeks, parents of students in the treatment condition received assessment information that included weekly graphs of student performance, comments on student attendance, homework completion, and class participation. Parents of students in the control condition received all information except for the weekly graphs. Letter grades were not given; rather the instructor provided a narrative assessment of student progress.

Procedures

At the beginning of the study, at both Site 1 and Site 2, three baseline oral reading fluency passages from the AIMSweb system were administered to each student. Based on the scores, students were matched and parents were randomly assigned to either the control or experimental condition. Parents in the control condition received only the "regular" assessment information that the teacher would typically send home. Parents in the experimental condition received the "regular" assessment information as well as a copy of their child's CBM reading graph and an explanation of how to read the graph.

All students completed a weekly, one-minute oral reading passage, which was individually administered by the teacher. The measure was administered and scored by the classroom teacher, who had been trained on administration by an expert (one of the co-authors of the study). To determine a baseline starting point, the median of the first three weekly scores was selected. A goal was set for each student based on the AIMSweb normative data and then each student was subsequently given a weekly oral reading measure, which was scored and graphed by the teacher. The graphed data was sent home with the students in the treatment group weekly. The students in the control group were able to view their graphs if they wished, but these were not sent home to their parents. At the conclusion of the study, a median was again calculated from the final three data points collected.

Data from the surveys were analyzed using descriptive statistics. Statistical comparisons of responses between the parents in the control and experimental conditions were conducted using the Pearson chi square test.

Results

Study 1

In Study 1, the students in the control and experimental groups had quite similar results (see Table 9.1 for descriptive statistics). Pre-test median scores on the Maze task were 27.86 correct choices for the experimental group and 26.14 correct choices for the control group. Post-test median scores were 40.98 for the experimental group and 36.89 for the control group, for a

Table 9.1 Descriptives from Reading Outcome Measures

	Study 1: Maze		Study 2: Oral Reading Fluency	
	Experimental	Control	Experimental	Control
Baseline Median	27.86	26.14	62.80	57.63
Post-test Median	40.98	36.89	73.00	62.38
Gain	13.09	11.21	10.20	4.75

Note: Study 1 Means = number of correct choices selected. Study 2 Means = words read correctly

gain of 13.9 correct choices for the experimental group and 11.21 correct choices for the control group. English test grades (based on a total of 75 points per test) were also collected for each group and mean points for the experimental group were 20.54 and 19.37 for the control group. There were no differences in the median of their maze baseline scores (p = .485), the medians of their maze post-test scores (p = .194), the gains from maze pre- to post-test scores (p = .397), their teacher-made pre-test scores in English (p = .657), their teacher-made post-test scores in English (p = .317), their gains from pre- to post-test English scores (p = .812), or their Gates MacGinitie total scores (p = .706).

Although 100% of the students in both groups demonstrated gains in their English post-test scores, and 92% of the control group and 93% of the experimental group improved in their CBM maze scores, parent perceptions of reading gains in the two groups were significantly different (χ^2 = 6.88, p = .032). While 100% of the experimental parents believed that their children improved in reading over the summer, only 64% of the control parents believed their children demonstrated gains in reading. The parents in the experimental group tended to be more accurate in their assessment of their students' progress in reading (χ^2 = 6.72, p = .010); only 21% of the control group but 69% of the experimental group were accurate in their assessment of their students' reading progress over the summer.

Study 2

Due to small sample sizes, data for all students at both sites was combined for the analysis. For 10 students total in the experimental group and 8 students total in the control group, initial performance on the students' median of their initial three CBM data points was not significantly different (p = .754). The baseline median for students in the experimental group was 63 words read correctly and 58 for the control group. Following implementation of the intervention, the mean rate of growth for words read correctly (pre to post) was 10.2 (*SD*, 10.13) for the experimental group and 4.75 (*SD*, 9.63) for the control group. While this difference was not statistically significant (p = .264), there is a substantial difference in scores on outcome measures for the experimental group as compared to the control group.

Survey results indicated that perceptions did not differ between parents in experimental and control conditions. Across questions inquiring about student improvement, ease of interpretation and usefulness of graphs and teacher comments, communication between parents and children, and expected future impact of feedback on reading performance, results were virtually identical. In addition, only half of parents in the experimental group felt that graphs were more useful than teacher comments.

While the sample size for both studies was small, the implementation of the study across two sites, with two age groups, in varying programs (one summer school and one special education during the year) leads to initial findings that can be replicated. Curriculum-based measurement data is often highlighted for its use of indicators, 'pictures of student performance,' and utility for communicating so it is important that all stakeholders are considered. At the end of this chapter, the letter that went home to parents and the graph that accompanied the letter are included. The teachers met with the parents either after school or at conferences to discuss the graph in person, but then the letter went home with the graph the first time it was sent. Communicating with parents using terms that are straightforward and easy to understand is important, and providing visuals with accompanying descriptions can be even more powerful. Previous research has documented the effects of using graphed data to communicate with teachers (Fuchs, Deno, and Mirkin, 1984) and similar principles of data sharing can be applied to use with parents, as was piloted in this study.

Student Involvement

Federal policy in special education (IDEA) specifically calls for not only parental involvement in educational planning but also student involvement in the special education process, especially for students in transition periods. This call for student involvement is in reference to special education but mirrors researcher and literature's quest for student involvement in the general education setting as well. Within a response to intervention framework, many opportunities present for an increase in student engagement within the tiered system.

Why Is It Important?

Student involvement can embody a variety of activities. It is an activity that is highly sought after and within a tiered system has been shown to promote overall engagement and academic achievement levels (Brookhart, Moss, and Long, 2009).

How Can It Happen?

Literature highlights a myriad of methods by which teachers can increase student involvement in a tiered framework. For example, McCurdy, and Shapiro (1992) demonstrated that self-monitoring reading levels through means of goal-setting and graphical performance feedback demonstrates large gains in achievement in some students. Within a tiered framework where formative assessment and progress monitoring occur frequently, opportunities to both set academic goals and monitor performance levels is a natural way to increase student involvement in the response to intervention process. Researchers suggest that in addition to increased achievement levels, student involvement in formative assessment increases overall ownership for performance, which is critical to student engagement levels (e.g., Brookhart, Moss, and Long, 2009). While not yet examined empirically, students may play an active role in home-school communication. For example, as the field continues to expand data presentation and sharing with parents, students can play an active role in deciphering progress to parents via visual graphs of performance. Goal setting, self-monitoring, and interpreting formative assessments are just examples of actions in which students can be included in educational planning and decision-making. The field has long since abandoned the notion that students are passive recipients of their education; rather, they play a vital role in the tiered systems and decision-making within. Very little literature documents the manner in which students are involved in the response to intervention process, and therefore, do not formally evaluate barriers to inclusion. One may posit that student involvement through formative assessment is not often employed due to time constraints or materials.

Parent Involvement in National Initiatives

When considering large-scale national initiatives that are currently affecting many schools, the Individuals with Disabilities Education Act (IDEA) and Positive Behavioral Interventions and Supports (PBIS) serve as prominent examples.

IDEA was first authorized in 1975 under the name, the Education for All Handicapped Children Act and was most recently reauthorized in 2004 where it was referred to as the Individuals with Disabilities Education Improvement Act. IDEA has four main objectives, including guaranteeing all students have free and appropriate education, supporting states in providing early intervention services for infants and toddlers, evaluating the effectiveness of current special education programs, and supporting parents and teachers in meeting the needs of children with disabilities (Heward, 2009).

With regard to parent involvement, IDEA emphasizes a parent's right to participate in making decisions related to their child's disability. Specifically, parents have the right to attend meetings and participate in making decisions related to determining if their child has a disability, whether their child is receiving a free and appropriate education, what intervention services their child will receive if they qualify to receive an IEP, and where their child will be placed (Center for Parent Information and Resources, 2016). Ultimately, IDEA mandates that parents have the right to be involved throughout the process of evaluating for special education eligibility and associated service delivery; however, such involvement is not a requirement.

PBIS, a school-wide program designed to promote positive student behaviors is another national initiative that contains supports associated with parent involvement. When evaluating the implementation adequacy of PBIS in the field, among many criteria, existing programs are graded in terms of how well "parents have been informed about PBIS" (Bradshaw et al., 2009, p. 158), and to what degree "parents are involved in PBIS related activities, programs, and/or services" (Bradshaw et al., 2009, p. 159).

In addition to broad guidelines, some targeted approaches for involving parents in PBIS have been developed. For example, the organization that facilitates PBIS state-wide in New Hampshire has developed a set of practices designed to support parental involvement, which includes creating linkages with organizations that represent children and families, defining family friendly school environments with input from a variety of stakeholders, on-going assessment of how schools are fostering and maintaining school environments that support families, and a mechanism for developing and implementing acting plans based on ongoing evaluation findings (Muscott et al. 2008).

Also, researchers have identified ways in which school infrastructure designed to support PBIS can be utilized to implement interventions that support home environments. Reinke, Splett, Robeson and Offutt (2009) make the case for integrating the Family Check-up, an evidence-based intervention that promotes effective family-based behavior management, within a school-wide PBIS context. They note that, "the multilevel framework of PBIS can effectively guide the need for additional services to students and families. Spanning prevention efforts to include home and school could be accomplished by integrating current psychological practices within the PBIS model" (Reinke, Splett, Robeson, and Offutt, 2009, p. 37).

Importance of Home School Collaboration

Home-school collaboration is an important topic to address when considering parent and student involvement in RTI frameworks. Cowan, Swearer, and Sheridan (2004), define home school collaboration as "a reciprocal dynamic process that occurs among systems (e.g., families, communities, partnerships), schools/classrooms, and/or individuals (e.g., parents, educators, administrators, psychologists) who share in decision making toward common goals and solutions related to students" (p. 201). According to Elser et al. (2008), home-school collaboration is fundamentally promoting positive relationships between families and schools. The National Association of School Psychologists (NASP; 2005) defines home-school collaboration, as a partnership involving families, educators, and community members that work together to support students' education and mental health needs. Much research has identified that home-school collaboration has an impact on many parts of student life, and research indicates that parental involvement has had positive impacts on student achievement.

A meta-analysis conducted by Fann and Chen (2001) indicated that parental involvement increases academic achievement around 30 percent. They discussed that parental expectations for students' educational achievement appeared to have the strongest connection with academic achievement. Whereas, Algozzine, Daunic, and Smith (2010) indicate that parent involvement improves more than academics; other areas include motivation, decreased absenteeism, increased self-confidence, and higher graduation rates.

Theoretical Framework

Two theories attempt to illustrate the interaction between the family, the school, and communities and how this interaction affects a child's development and learning. First, Christenson (2003) applies Bronfenbrenner's systems ecological theory as a rationale for how the mesosystem of the family and school influence each other and ultimately impact the child's learning. Many evidence-based interventions recognize the need for an ecological systems approach that incorporates the contexts of school, family, and the community when considering academic, behavioral, and overall development of students (Christenson, 2003). In this manner, schools are incorporating the family system, though there seems to be a more direct approach to involve the family in the RTI process. A more in-depth discussion of how Christenson's model applies specifically to RTI is discussed in the Family–School RTI Model section.

Table 9.2 Resources for Family Involvement in RTI

Source	Types of Information	Link
Wisconsin RTI Center	Response to Intervention and Family Engagement Online Module	www.wisconsinrticenter.org/parents-and-family/understanding-rti/femodule.html
National Center for Response to Intervention	Parent FAQs, Brief Overviews of components of RTI for families, Webinars	www.rti4success.org/resources/family-resources
Colorado Department of Education	Family and Community Partnering: "On the Team and at the Table" Toolkit	www.cde.state.co.us/rti/FamilyCommunityToolkit.htm
National Association of School Psychologists	Klotz, M.B. and Canter, A. (2007) *Response to Intervention: A Primer for Parents* (Resource). Bethesda, MD: National Association of School Psychologists	www.ldonline.org/article/15857/

A second theory, the overlapping spheres of influence, identifies the family, the school, and the community as three overlapping spheres of influence in the development of a child's learning (Epstein, 1995). Epstein describes the student as the center focus of the model and the main goal is to use partnerships between the family, school, and community to engage, motivate, and guide the student to success. She identifies six types of caring and involvement that have developed by educators and families at the elementary, middle, and high school levels. Each type of involvement provides different practices and challenges for implementation that can lead to various outcomes for students. These six types of involvement can guide the development of a partnership program; these include: Parenting, Communicating, Volunteering, Learning at Home, Decision Making, and Collaborating with Community.

These two theories outlined by Christenson (2003) and Epstein (1995) have often been used as guidance for incorporating parent involvement into the RTI framework. (Kashima, Schleich, and Spradlin, 2009; Reschly, n.d.). Parental involvement is more often considered to be a key component of the RTI framework due to the critical role that the family plays in academic success. It appears that the problem-solving process within an RTI framework provides an opportunity to incorporate all of the six types of involvement outlined by Epstein, especially communication, collaboration, and data-based decision-making. While parents are heavily involved in special education decision-making, the RTI frameworks may provide more opportunities for parents and students to be involved in general education decision making.

Partnerships with Culturally Diverse Parents

Currently, there are no empirically validated frameworks that specifically target the promotion of involvement of parents from culturally and linguistically diverse backgrounds. In spite of the lack of existing programs, there is a significant unmet need. Lee and Bowen (2006) found that African American and Latino parents have lower involvement at school compared to White parents. However, when minority parents had high levels of school involvement, it was associated with increased student achievement.

A major factor in explaining low involvement among culturally diverse parents is the existence of multiple barriers to participation, including perception of power imbalances, logistical issues, lack of knowledge regarding rights, absence of bilingual school professionals, and misunderstandings that arise from cultural differences (Greenan, Powers, and Lopez-Vasquez, 2001). Future work in the area of partnerships must focus on removing barriers to involvement commonly experienced by parents from non-dominant cultural groups.

Characteristics of Effective Partnerships within an RTI Model

Making Parents Aware of RTI

Given the literature that indicates that communicating with parents is important and enhances student achievement (Anderson and Minke, 2007; Cox, 2005) it is critical to examine points in the curriculum when data can be easily shared. As CBM data is collected, scored, and graphed, an efficient way to communicate with parents is to share the graph with them via email or send home in paper format. Prior to this, providing parents with the key features of the graph is important.

As schools around the country continue to implement multi-tiered systems of support for academics, data-based decision-making remains an integral component and one that schools are focusing on for grade-level general education teams as well as special education teams.

What is sometimes missing is the link to parents. Teams may wonder how and what to share with parents. Training on what the graphed data is communicating could occur at open house, back to school night, or during conferences. A more detailed explanation might be provided in a letter home. Not lost in the planning for sharing data should be helping students to clearly understand their own graphed data so that they can communicate about it with their parents. Teachers should consider how sharing of data can lead to stronger relationships with parents and should set a goal for themselves to share data with parents more often, paired with a clear explanation.

Family–School RTI Model

Reschly (n.d.) proposes a "Family–school RTI Model," which associates levels of parent involvement with each tier of intervention. For example, she shares that Tier 1 may include the three components that are essential when building positive home-school collaboration include: attitudes, atmosphere, and action (Christenson, 2003).

Attitudes are the how or whether parents and schools work together. Christenson (2003) adds that partnerships are more than merely an activity and but an attitude that encompasses the values and perceptions of the partnership. By establishing and communicating the purpose of the RTI model with parents, it may assist in the communication of an attitude that the school is providing services for all learners. Further involving parents in the RTI process may change their attitude towards the school in general, especially if they feel their involvement is vital to the student's success.

The second component, an atmosphere or climate of trust, means that effective communication and joint decisions must be established. Atmosphere, similarly to attitude, is something that cannot be developed from one interaction or meeting, Christenson (2003) explains it must be fostered by continuous communication. In addition to caretakers, students need to be educated on how they can conduct communication between their families and their schools (Epstein, 1995). Communication is a major element in effective home-school collaboration (Algozzine et al., 2010). Without two-way communication, it is very difficult to maintain a positive relationship (Cox, 2005).

Wanat (2010) interviewed twenty parents about home-school relationships within a school district. Parents shared that teachers need more training on how to speak to parents. Wanat adds that parents also expressed the want for more frequent and specific communication about student progress. Atmosphere allows parents and educators to have conversations about the expectations, actions, and values of context of the family and the school. An RTI framework provides an avenue to provide more specific feedback regarding student progress. Providing more information regarding student data in parent friendly terms may assist parents in becoming more actively involved in student progress monitoring and motivating students to increase their skills.

The third component, Action, focuses on strategies that build shared responsibility for a student's learning. Christenson (2003) describes that actions differ from merely involvement activities and should aim to increase parental responsibility for learning. Increased parental responsibility is a common theme in the literature regarding the effectiveness of home-school collaboration (Algozzine et al., 2010; Cox, 2005). These actions include supporting families and helping to improve teacher-parent communication. Similar to Epstein (1995) Christenson also endorses the need for family–school action teams. These family–school action teams can empower family members to be advocates for their child's needs and education and perhaps participate in more system level activities (Algozzine et al, 2010).

By inviting parents to be a part of problem-solving meetings, schools may be able to achieve this ideal of family–school action teams. Since problem-solving teams are comprised of general education teachers, administrators, school psychologists, school counselors, and other relevant personnel, it becomes a one-stop-shop for parents to access information and also provide additional insight into academic and behavioral concerns. Bringing parents and possibly students to the problem-solving team meetings create an attitude that the student's progress is important and the atmosphere that assistance is going to be put into action with the input of the parent and student.

At Tiers 2 and 3, Reschly (n.d.) indicates that communication and collaborative problem-solving activities intensify but vary based on the student needs, family context, and school context. Multiple sources suggest that using methods such as conjoint behavioral consultation (Sheridan and Kratochwill, 2007) can assist in the problem-solving process between schools and families (Reschly, n.d.; Manz and Mano, 2014).

Barriers and Solutions to Parent and Student Involvement

Elser et al. (2008) provide examples of both structural and psychological barriers that may hinder home-school collaboration. Economic constraints, time, employment, and lack of resources continue to be structural barriers for families. Elser and colleagues add that only communicating in a time of crisis, whether the school or the family initiate the conversation, can ultimately work against the creation of a working partnership. These challenges reinforce the need for constant communication and positive experiences and opportunities created by both the school and family to maintain a helpful and encouraging environment for the student. By making parents active partners in the RTI process, schools that include families in an RTI and data-based decision-making process may increase positive communication. Furthermore, parents and students may feel as though they are actively involved in the learning and intervention process.

However, there are barriers specific to the RTI process that schools are cautioned to consider when encouraging parent participation. Byrd (2011) explains that parents often need to be educated about the RTI process, the purpose, and the intended outcomes. RTI can be a complex system and often involve a plethora of educational jargon and terminology, which is often overwhelming. He suggests providing information about concepts such as tiers as well as the problem-solving model will be necessary. This can be done through promotional materials, such as a handout including key terms that is presented to a parent prior to the start of a problem-solving meeting. Byrd also shares that since RTI can sometimes lead to a special education referral, it gives the parent an opportunity to be involved in multiple decisions based on progress. This allows the parent to realize that educational decisions do not have to be "one time" and programming can change based on educational needs, which is helpful in both general education as well as special education (Byrd, 2011).

Ways to Get Parents and Students Involved

This section will provide some ideas for how to include parents and students in the RTI process. First, we will introduce ways to make parents active partners at Tiers 1 and Tiers 2 and 3. Then we will discuss some ways to involve students considering strategies specifically for the elementary and secondary levels, and provide examples in the appendix.

Parent Strategies

First, at Tier 1 consider what parents know or do not know about the RTI process. This may include conducting a Needs Assessment to determine what information parents need or want. This can be completed either via paper and pencil or electronically through online survey platforms such as Google Forms or Survey Monkey. Consider asking parents which topics they feel they need more information on and how they may want to access that information, for example a workshop, online, or at a PTA meeting (See appendix, Colorado Department of Education, 2009).

Tier 1. Once you have established what parents in your district need regarding the RTI process, decide ways that could allow parents to access that information. Some examples may include:

- hosting an RTI Parent Night;
- having an online presentation that parents can access that includes interactive glossary, intro video, as well as family engagement activities.

School psychologists and administrators can work with creating "talking points or scripts" for parent teacher conferences. An example is provided in Manz and Mano (2014).

Tiers 2 and 3. At these levels parents are more involved with the problem-solving process. As educational decision makers, they play key roles in data-based decision making, team meetings, and collaborative intervention development. Some strategies to include parents at this stage are as follows:

- add parent engagement/partnering to existing RTI referral form;
- consider creating an RTI partner packet that explains key terms, roles and responsibilities, and key stakeholders as well as including other educational materials;
- develop an invitation to problem solving meetings (can get home info this way as well);
- provide informational handouts – consider a FAQ about your school or district's RTI process;
- conjoint behavioral consultation actively involves parents, teachers, and the school psychologist and if developmentally appropriate the student can also be involved in the development of the intervention.

(Sheridan and Kratochwill, 2007)

Student Strategies

A few ways to consider involving students in the RTI process would be collaboratively setting academic goals, outlining student responsibilities in school (i.e. being prepared, doing homework, and attending school, and finally making students active participants by graphing progress-monitoring data). Requiring upper elementary and secondary students to graph their progress allows them to self-monitor their data. This gives students a way to self-regulate their own academic behaviors (Gunter, Miller, Venn, Thomas, and House, 2002). Technologies such as Google Sheets could be used to have students enter data into individual graph templates that can be shared with multiple users (i.e. teachers and parents) in real time. Furthermore, providing students with a graph template would easily allow a student to be instructed on how to enter data independently.

Conclusion and Next Steps in Enhancing Parent and Student Involvement in RTI

While student and parent involvement in the RTI process has not necessarily been well-researched or well-articulated in the literature, there are many connect points that can be easily made. There is also a great opportunity for research in this area in the future. Teachers, school teams, and administrators need to consider the best way to connect with parents and students around critical topics in RTI, such as data sharing, and build these topics into already-existing structures. Conferencing with parents and students becomes an opportunity to share and discuss data or have student-led conferencing; with students showing their own graphed data. Weekly reports to parents include an overview of what was done as part of tiered intervention that week, along with the student's graphed data. Following progress monitoring each week for students in Tier 3, students email their graphs in portable document format to their parents, while whoever conducted the progress monitoring emails the graph to the rest of the instructional team. The importance of fostering conversation that is guided by data, and including parents and students as valued partners in the RTI process, should be a goal that each building sets as part of their annual development. With the use of evidence-based practices and data-based decision-making as such critical pieces in a student's school experience, these can only be enhanced with parent and student involvement.

References

Anderson, K. J., and Minke, K. M. (2007). Parent involvement in education: Toward an understanding of parents' decision making. *Journal of Educational Research, 100*, 311–323. doi: 10.3200/JOER.100. 5.311-323.

Algozzine, B., Daunic, A. P., and Smith, S. W. (2010). *Preventing problem behaviors: Schoolwide programs and classroom practices.* Thousand Oaks, CA: Corwin.

Bradshaw, C. P., Debnam, K., Koth, C. W., and Leaf, P. (2009). Preliminary validation of the implementation phases inventory for assessing fidelity of schoolwide positive behavior supports. *Journal of Positive Behavior Interventions, 11*(3), 145–160.

Brookhart, S. M., Moss, C. M., and Long, B. A. (2009). Promoting student ownership of learning through high-impact formative assessment practices. *Journal of Multidisciplinary Evaluation, 6*(12), 52–67.

Byrd, E. S. (2011). Educating and involving parents in the response to intervention process: The school's important role. *Teaching Exceptional Children, 43*(3), 32–39.

Christenson, S. L. (2003). The family–school partnership: An opportunity to promote the learning competence of all students. *School Psychology Quarterly, 18*(4), 454–482.

Colorado Department of Education (2009). *Family and community partnering: "On the team and at the table" toolkit.* Denver, CO: Author.

Cox, D. D. (2005). Evidence-based interventions using home-school collaboration. *School Psychology Quarterly, 20*(4), 473–497.

Cowan, R. J., Swearer, S. M., and Sheridan, S. M. (2004) Home–school collaboration. *Encyclopedia of Applied Psychology, 2*, 201–208.

Deno, S. L. (2003). Developments in curriculum-based measurement. *Journal of Special Education, 37*, 184–192.

Deno, S. L. (1985). Curriculum-based measurement: The emerging alternative. *Exceptional Children, 52*, 219–232.

Epstein, J. L. (1995). School/family/community partnerships: Caring for the children we share. *Phi Delta Kappan, 76*, 701–712.

Esler, A. N., Godber, Y., and Christenson, S. L. (2008). Best practices in supporting school–family partnerships. In A. Thomas and J. Grimes (Eds.), *Best practices in school psychology V.* (917–1120). Bethesda, MD: National Association of School Psychologists.

Fan, X. T., and Chen. M. (2001). Parental involvement and students' academic achievement: A meta-analysis. *Educational Psychology Review, 13*(1), 1–22.

Fuchs, L. S., Deno, S. L., and Mirkin, P. K. (1984). Effects of frequent curriculum-based measurement on pedagogy, student achievement, and student awareness of learning. *American Educational Research Journal, 21,* 449–460.

Geenen, S., Powers, L. E., and Lopez-Vasquez, A. (2005). Barriers against and strategies for promoting the involvement of culturally diverse parents in school-based transition planning. *Journal for Vocational Special Needs Education, 27*(3), 4–14.

Gunter, P. L., Miller, K. A., Venn, M. L., Thomas, K., and House, S. (2002) Self-graphing to success: Computerized data management. *Teaching Exceptional Children, 35*(2), 30–34. doi:10.1177/0040059902 03500204.

Heward, W. L. (2009*). Exceptional children, an introduction to special education* (9th ed.). Upper Saddle River, NJ: Pearson Education.

Kashima, Y., Schleich, B., and Spradlin, T. (2009). The Core Components of RTI: A Closer Look at Leadership, Parent Involvement, and Cultural Responsivity. Special Report. Center for Evaluation and Education Policy, Indiana University.

Kroth, R. (1978). Parents – Powerful and necessary allies. *Teaching Exceptional Children, 10,* 88–90. doi: 10.1177/004005997801000309.

Lembke, E. S., Garman, C., Deno, S. L., and Stecker, P. (2010). One elementary school's journey to response to intervention (RTI). *Reading and Writing Quarterly, 26,* 361–373.

Lembke, E. S., McMaster, K., and Stecker, P. M. (2009). The prevention science of reading research within a response-to-intervention model. *Psychology in the Schools, 47*(1), 22–35.

Manz, P. H., and Mano, J. C. (2014). Best practices in reducing barriers to parent involvement. In P. L. Harrison and A. Thomas (Eds.), *Best practices in school psychology: System level services* (pp. 467–477). Bethesda, MD: National Association of School Psychologists

McCurdy, B. L., and Shapiro, E. S. (1992). A comparison of teacher-, peer-, and self-monitoring with curriculum-based measurement in reading among students with learning disabilities. *The Journal of Special Education, 26*(2), 162–180.

Muscott, H. S., Mann, E. L., and LeBrun, M. R. (2008). Positive behavioral interventions and supports in New Hampshire: Effects of large-scale implementation of schoolwide positive behavior support on student discipline and academic achievement. *Journal of Positive Behavior Interventions, 10,* 190–205.

National Association of School Psychologists (2005). *Home–school collaboration* (Position Statement). Bethesda, MD: Author.

Reinke, W. M., Splett, J. D., Robeson, E. N., and Offutt, C. A. (2009). Combining school and family interventions for the prevention and early intervention of disruptive behavior problems in children: A public health perspective. *Psychology in the Schools, 46*(1), 33–43.

Reschly, A. L. (n.d.). Schools, families, and Response to Intervention. RTI Action Network. Retrieved from www.rtinetwork.org/essential/family/schools-familes-and-rti.

Sheridan, S. M., and Kratochwill, T. R. (2007). *Conjoint behavioral consultation: Promoting family–school connections and interventions.* Springer Science & Business Media.

Seitsinger, A. M., Felner, R. D., Brand, S., and Burns, A. (2008). A large-scale examination of the nature and efficacy of teachers' practices to engage parents: Assessment, parental contact, and student-level impact. *Journal of School Psychology, 46,* 477–505. doi: 10.1016/j.jsp.2007.11.001.

Shinn, M. R., Habedank, L., and Good, R. H. (1993). The effects of classroom reading performance data on general education teachers' and parents' attitudes about reintegration. *Exceptionality, 4,* 205–228.

Staples, K. E., and Dilberto, J. A. (2010). Guidelines for successful parent involvement: Working with parents of students with disabilities. *Teaching Exceptional Children, 42,* 58–63.

Stephens, T. M., Blackhurst, A. E., and Magliocca, L. A. (1982). *Teaching mainstreamed students.* New York: Wiley.

Walker, J. M. T., Wilkins, A. S., Dallaire, J. R., Sandler, H. M., and Hoover-Dempsey, K. V. (2005). Parental involvement: Model revision through scale development. *The Elementary School Journal, 106,* 85–104.

Zirkel, P. (2012). The legal dimension of RTI: Part II – State laws and guidelines. RTI *Action Network.* Online at http://rtinetwork.org/learn/ld/the-legal-dimension-of-rti-part-ii-state-laws-and-guidelines.

Appendix

Sample Parent Letter and Graph

Date

Parents of students in Mrs. Smith's class,

For the next six weeks, you will receive a graph that shows how well your child is doing in reading, in addition to the weekly report that you usually receive.

The graph shows several things:

1. The **starting point** for your child's reading ability:

    • Your child read three passages at the beginning of the year that were one-minute each. These three scores form the starting point of your child's reading ability.

2. The **progress** your child has made since the beginning of the year:

    • Each week, Mrs. Smith has your child read aloud for one minute and then she graphs how many words your child read correctly.

3. A **goal** for your student's reading progress:

    • The line that you see extending from the start of the year until the end of the year is the goal that Mrs. Smith set for your child. When it looks like your child is not making progress towards his/her goal, Mrs. Smith changes her instruction to help your child do better in school.

Please take some time each week to look at the reading graph and the other information in the weekly report, and discuss it with your child. At the end of the six weeks, you will receive a survey to complete regarding the graphs and information that you have been receiving.

There is a sample graph on the back of this paper that might help you to understand your child's graph.

Thank you for your support and your participation! If you have any questions, please ask Mrs. Smith.

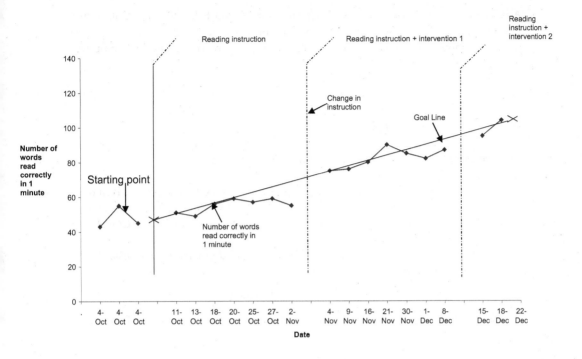

Sample Problem-Solving Team Meeting Invitation

RTI Family and Community Engagement Module/Colorado Department of Education, June 2009

Dear _____,   Date: _____

Our school is committed to supporting student success. If a student experiences difficulty in academics or behavior, it is important for schools and families to work together. You are invited to participate in the planning, implementation, and monitoring of your child's interventions. Your participation as a team member provides essential information about your child. Thank you for partnering with us. Please communicate with us at any time.

As a follow-up to our previous conversation, we would like to invite you to a team meeting on _____ at _____ in _____. The purpose of this team meeting is to share information about _____ and discuss how we can work collaboratively with you to provide school and home support. Staff members who work with your child will be at the meeting, as well as others who can help in planning for success. If there is anyone you would specifically like to attend from school or elsewhere, please let us know. If this time won't work for you, we will try to reschedule, or we will find a time to share information so that we have your input and ideas.

Attached is a home information form. This information can help the school staff in learning more about how you see your child. We will be contacting you before the meeting to review this information with you and answer any questions you may have about this team partnering process.

Sincerely,

Position: Phone: Email:

Attachments: Home Information Form, Brochure with Insert

> *Source: Adapted from Cherry Creek Schools. (2006).* Response to Intervention RTI/Problem-Solving Process: Essentials. *Greenwood Village, CO: Author*
>
> *(Colorado Department of Education, 2009)*

Sample Family Sharing Sheet

RTI Family and Community Engagement Module/Colorado Department of Education, June 2009.

It is important that schools and families partner for student success. In teaming, it is helpful for teachers to know about students and their families' views about school. Please complete this sheet and return to me. It is suggested that students and family members complete this together. Individual comments can be put in the labeled boxes. Please contact me with any questions or input at any time. I look forward to working with you this year. Thank you. _____, Teacher

I can be reached at: _____

Student: _____Family Member(s): _____Date: _____

1. What does your student like about school?

2. What are your student's successes in school?

3. What are your student's challenges in school?

4. Does your student feel liked and accepted at school? If not, why not?

5. What are some of your student's interests, activities, and hobbies?

6. What does your student feel is his/her greatest talent or skill?

7. Does your student enjoy reading? _____math? _____writing? _____other (please identify)? _____

8. What challenges does your student have in reading? _____ math? _____writing? _____ other (please identify)?_____

9. Describe how your student does homework.

Student Comments:

What else would you like me to know about you this year?

What suggestions do you have for our class?

Other thoughts?

Family Comments:

What else would you like me to know about you or your student?

Please share your goals for your student's school year.

Please tell me the best way to contact you.

(Colorado Department of Education, 2009)

Partnering Survey and Needs Assessment

Our school is developing new ways to support our teachers and families in working together. We are trying to coordinate home and school learning. This survey was developed to gather data about family–school-community partnering beliefs and practices from all stakeholders who support our students. Please answer questions from the perspective of your specific role. The **Beliefs and Needs** section is for all respondents. There are separate **Practice** sections for school/community staff and family members – please only answer the section that is appropriate for you. A brief **Needs Assessment** asks about what would be helpful to you. We welcome your comments. All this information will be used to plan our partnering activities.

Please Check Information that Relates to Your Role with Students:

Educator: _____ **Position:** _____

Family Member: _____ **Student Grade Level(s):** _____

Community Resource: _____ **Affiliation:** _____

Name (Optional): _____ **Date:** _____

I would like to participate on a family–school community partnering committee at our school. My contact information is as follows (name, email or phone or address):

(Colorado Department of Education, 2009)

RTI Family and Community Engagement Module/
Colorado Department of Education, June 2009

Adapted from the Following Sources

Vosler-Hunter, R. W. (1998). *Changing roles, changing relationships: Parent-professional collaboration on behalf of children with emotional disabilities.* Portland, OR: Portland State University, Research and Training Center on Family Support and Children's Mental Health.

Bryan, J.B, and Pelco, L. (2006). *School psychologist involvement in partnerships survey (SPIPS).* Williamsburg, VA: William and Mary School of Education.

National Center for Special Education Accountability Monitoring. *Parent survey – special education. Version 2.0.* Retrieved May 9, 2008, from www.monitoringcenter.lsuhsc.

Thanks to the family members, professionals, and graduate students who provided input as to this survey's content.

(Colorado Department of Education, 2009)

For Family Members And School Staff/Community Resources

Beliefs (What I Think . . .)

I . . .	*N/A*	*Strongly Disagree*	*Disagree*	*Unde-cided*	*Agree*	*Strongly Agree*
1. Believe that families and schools share responsibility for a student's education.	0	1	2	3	4	5
2. Believe that students should see their teachers and families working together in relation to their everyday school experiences and learning.	0	1	2	3	4	5
3. Believe that schools and families each have areas of expertise/information to share in supporting student success.	0	1	2	3	4	5
4. Believe teachers and family members should communicate regularly about both positive events and concerns.	0	1	2	3	4	5
5. Believe that I have the skills/training to work as a partner in supporting school success for students.	0	1	2	3	4	5
6. Believe that teachers and family members should share concerns when either sees a student beginning to struggle or becoming discouraged.	0	1	2	3	4	5
7. Believe that teachers and family members should each have responsibilities for student planning and interventions when concerns are identified.	0	1	2	3	4	5
8. Believe that students should be partners in home-school communication and in intervention planning.	0	1	2	3	4	5
9. Am confident in my ability to develop and maintain family–school partnerships in my specific role (as staff, family member, or community resource).	0	1	2	3	4	5
10. Know about the Response to Intervention (RTI) process in my school.	0	1	2	3	4	5

Source: Colorado Department of Education, 2009

For Family Members

Practices (What I Do . . .)

I . . .	N/A	Not at All	Rarely	Sometimes	Frequently	Very Frequently
1. Participate in problem solving with teachers when there are academic or behavior concerns, then assist with setting goals and developing a plan.	0	1	2	3	4	5
2. Have resources, training and support to help me with the following: encouraging my child in school; providing resources, time and space for homework; talking to my child about school and learning.	0	1	2	3	4	5
3. Use information from home when I discuss my child's progress, needs, problems, and possible solutions with the school.	0	1	2	3	4	5
4. Know the following for my student's school, classes and activities: rules, how progress is reported, and homework expectations for students and families.	0	1	2	3	4	5
5. Communicate regularly (two-way) with teachers for positive reasons, routine matters, progress updates, and concerns if needed.	0	1	2	3	4	5
6. Share my student's strengths, challenges, interests, and attitudes about school with the teachers.	0	1	2	3	4	5
7. Ask teachers what I can do to support my student's learning in our home or through the community.	0	1	2	3	4	5
8. Have visits in my home from school staff.	0	1	2	3	4	5
9. Feel valued and respected by teachers and school staff.	0	1	2	3	4	5
10. Visit my child's school.	0	1	2	3	4	5
11. Participate with teachers in the Response to Intervention (RTI) problem-solving process.	0	1	2	3	4	5

Source: Colorado Department of Education, 2009

For School Staff And Community Resources

Practices (What I Do . . .)

I . . .	N/A	Not at All	Rarely	Moderately	Frequently	Very Frequently
1. Include families in problem solving when there are academic or behavioral concerns; then set mutual goals, monitor progress, review and revise plan with families as needed.	0	1	2	3	4	5
2. Provide resources, training and support to help families with the following: encouraging their child in school; accessing resources, time and space for homework; talking to their child about school and learning.	0	1	2	3	4	5
3. Use data points from multiple sources when I discuss a child's progress, needs, problems, and possible solutions.	0	1	2	3	4	5
4. Share with families the following: school, class, and activity rules; how progress is reported; homework expectations for students and families.	0	1	2	3	4	5
5. Ask each family to share about student's strengths, challenges, interests, and attitudes about school.	0	1	2	3	4	5
6. Communicate regularly (two-way) with families of all my students for positive reasons, routine matters, progress updates, and concerns if needed.	0	1	2	3	4	5
7. Ask parents what they need to actively support student learning in the home and partner with the school or the community.	0	1	2	3	4	5
8. Visit families in their homes.	0	1	2	3	4	5
9. Reach out to families with cultural, language, gender, socioeconomic, and learning differences.	0	1	2	3	4	5
10. Invite families to come to school.	0	1	2	3	4	5
11. Participate with families in the Response to Intervention (RTI) problem-solving process.	0	1	2	3	4	5

Source: Colorado Department of Education, 2009

For Family Members, School Staff, Community Resources
Needs Assessment (*What Would Be Helpful to Me . . .*)

I would like more information and/or training on the following topics:

- ❑ RTI
- ❑ Creating learning opportunities at home
- ❑ Parenting classes
- ❑ Teacher–family communication strategies
- ❑ Family volunteering opportunities at home or school
- ❑ Involving families in school decision-making
- ❑ Teachers and families working together when a student is struggling
- ❑ School-community partnering
- ❑ Area community resources
- ❑ Conflict resolution strategies for teachers and families
- ❑ Homework strategies
- ❑ Communication with other families
- ❑ Other – Please identify

The best time for me to attend workshops or trainings is:

- ❑ Weekday mornings (before school)
- ❑ Weekday afternoons (after school)
- ❑ During school day
- ❑ Weekday evenings
- ❑ Saturdays
- ❑ Online
- ❑ Written workbooks, materials
- ❑ Other – Please identify

Please share any comments or questions regarding how our school can best support families, teachers, and community resources working together in coordinating student school success.

(Colorado Department of Education, 2009)

SECTION III

RTI/MTSS in Elementary Grades

INTRODUCTION
TO SECTION III

Jeanne Wanzek

The authors of the chapters in this section provide pertinent research and practical guidelines for the implementation of RTI/MTSS in the elementary grades. They examine key topics in assessment and instructional implementation in math, reading, and writing, while addressing the theoretical and empirical evidence to guide decision-making. Importantly, these chapters also identify critical areas of implementation that require further study to effectively meet the needs of students with academic difficulties at the elementary level.

In Chapter 11, "Combining Reading Comprehension Instruction with Cognitive Training to Provide Intensive Intervention to At-Risk Students," Doug Fuchs, Samuel Patton, Lynn Fuchs, Jennifer Gilbert, Meagan Walsh, Nicole Lute, Loulee Yen Haga, Peng Peng, and Amy Elleman discuss an intensive intervention that incorporates reading skill and strategy instruction as well as the integration of cognitive training. The authors present a research base for considering intensive interventions, the theoretical and empirical basis for the development of a comprehensive reading intervention for students with specific reading comprehension deficits, and the results of a study of the effects of implementing the intensive intervention. Fuchs and colleagues urge us to broaden our conceptualizations of intensive interventions and the complexities of implementing multi-tier frameworks.

In Chapter 14, "Building a Growth Mindset within Data-Based Individualization: A Case Study of Two Students with Reading Disabilities Learning to Learn," Stephanie Al Otaiba, Francesca Jones, Dawn Levy, Brenna Rivas, and Jeanne Wanzek describe a data-based individualization process for intensive reading interventions at the upper elementary level. Al Otaiba and colleagues address current issues in intensive intervention, the process for implementing data-based individualization in reading intervention, and the role of student mindset, motivation, and engagement in reading intervention. The role of growth mindset in student learning has received increased attention in recent years, but there is limited research on its relationship with instruction and intervention. Al Otaiba and colleagues further explore issues in data-based instruction and growth mindset in a study of two fourth grade students with reading disabilities who have not responded to previously implemented standard reading interventions.

In Chapter 12, "Evidence-Based Writing Intervention: Three Tiers of Instruction for Elementary Students," Linda Mason, Nancy Mamlin, and Kalin Stewart address the implementation of RTI/MTSS in writing. Mason, Mamlin, and Kalin provide key information on the identification of students with writing difficulties as well as recommended practices for elementary writing instruction. Recognizing that recent national and state standards have set high expectations for elementary students' writing progression, the authors carefully review the literature for classroom writing instruction and supplemental writing interventions. They identify the strength of evidence for various writing instructional practices at all levels of the RTI/MTSS process.

In Chapter 13, "Supporting the Mathematics Learning of Elementary Students within a Multi-Level Framework," Sarah Powell, Sarah Benz, and Suzanne Forsyth address the structure and implementation of RTI/MTSS in elementary mathematics. Although many elementary schools have established processes for RTI/MTSS implementation in reading, the processes in mathematics are often less defined. Powell, Benz, and Forsyth provide detailed descriptions of evidence-based practices and the underlying research in core, classroom mathematics instruction as well as mathematics intervention of varying intensities. They also highlight instructional programs that incorporate these evidence-based practices. Furthermore, the authors provide an overview of the tools needed to make key instructional decisions throughout the RTI/MTSS process for students with mathematics difficulties.

In Chapter 10, "Progress Monitoring in the Elementary Grades," Nathan Clemens, Oscar Widales-Benitez, Jade Kestian, Corey Peltier, Ana D'Abreu, Ahmarlay Myint, and Joshua Marbach address the issues of progress monitoring, or formative assessment, across content areas within an elementary RTI/MTSS system. Clemens and colleagues identify and describe commonly used measures for monitoring progress along with the research base and technical adequacy of the measures. In doing so, the authors provide a basis for selecting measures for varying purposes as well as an understanding of the assessment questions in need of further work or research. The process for effective progress monitoring is as important as the selection and knowledge of the measure. Clemens and colleagues discuss the key features of the progress monitoring process and the relevant research supporting its use.

10

PROGRESS MONITORING IN THE ELEMENTARY GRADES

Nathan H. Clemens, Oscar Widales-Benitez, Jade Kestian, Corey Peltier, Ana D'Abreu, Ahmarlay Myint, and Joshua Marbach

Progress Monitoring in the Elementary Grades

An important aspect of supplemental intervention for academic skills difficulties is the use of progress monitoring (i.e., formative assessment), which involves frequent and ongoing assessment to indicate when effective programs should continue, or to signal the need to alter instruction when progress is below expectations. Research has demonstrated that a systematic process for adjusting instruction based on students' progress results in superior achievement over students whose teachers do not use such a process (Denton et al., 2010; Mathes et al., 2005; Stecker, Fuchs, and Fuchs, 2005). Additionally, some form of frequent progress monitoring is recommended for all elementary students who are considered at risk for academic difficulties or who are receiving supplemental intervention (Gersten et al., 2008).

In the late 1970s, Stanley Deno and colleagues at the University of Minnesota developed curriculum-based measurement (CBM), a framework designed to allow special education teachers to repeatedly monitor students' progress toward individual educational goals using brief and efficient samples of performance (Deno, 1985; 2003; Deno and Mirkin, 1977; Fuchs, 2004). Early CBM development sought simple and brief measures that could be used to estimate overall *general outcomes* in academic achievement. For example, Deno, Mirkin, and Chiang (1982) found that the rate at which students read aloud from their reading textbook (i.e., passage reading fluency) correlated closely with their performance on standardized measures of overall reading achievement. The use of these brief, rate-based probes became what is now known as CBM.

Subsequent research indicated that teachers who used CBM were more realistic about their students' progress, demonstrated greater structure in their teaching, and were more aware of their students' progress (Fuchs, Deno, and Mirkin, 1984; Shinn and Hubbard, 1992). Research also revealed that when teachers used CBM frequently with a set of systematic decision rules, students displayed stronger academic gains over students monitored less frequently with more traditional forms of assessment (e.g., unit-end tests) or without a set of decision rules (Fuchs and Fuchs, 1986; Fuchs, Fuchs, and Hamlett, 1989; Stecker et al., 2005).

Originally, CBM measures were developed by the user and were specific to the curriculum of instruction. A process for sampling content from the students' textbook or instructional materials was used to create a set of measures, or *probes*. For example, Deno and Mirkin (1977) and Shapiro (1989) described a process for sampling text from a basal reader in order to create reading CBM probes. As another example, a teacher might sample math computation problems across an instructional period (or school year) to develop a set of math CBM probes.

Research subsequently indicated that it was not necessary that CBM probes come from a specific curriculum of instruction (see Fuchs and Deno, 1994). In fact, Fuchs and Deno (1994) suggested that the use of generic CBM probes that were created independent of the curriculum held several advantages, including the ability to better control the difficulty level of the content, the ability to use the measures across different curricula, and a lower possibility that students would be familiar with the content in the probes. This led to the creation and publication of CBM tools for different academic areas and grade levels. Today, there are several publishers that offer access to CBM tools as well as web-based software options for storing data and generating reports, including AIMSweb, The Dynamic Indicators of Basic Early Literacy Skills (DIBELS), easyCBM, and FastBridge.

The purpose of this chapter is to discuss the methods and procedures for monitoring progress in the elementary grades (i.e., kindergarten to grade 5), with a focus on the CBM framework. We will provide an overview of common and contemporary measures for monitoring progress (as well as some new, lesser-known, or non-CBM forms of measurement, such as computer-adaptive tests), an overview of the research behind the measures and their technical adequacy, and unanswered questions that may exist. We conclude the chapter by discussing key features of the progress monitoring process, including goal-setting, frequency of measurement, and decision-rules, as well as areas in which empirical research is lacking.

This chapter is by no means an exhaustive review of the research behind CBM, which could fill several chapters. Additionally, wherever possible we discussed the measures from an agnostic standpoint with regard to publishers of CBM tools. Readers interested in greater detail on measures from specific publishers as well as progress monitoring procedures are directed to the resources maintained by the National Center on Intensive Intervention (www.intensiveinterven tion.org), and the references cited throughout the chapter.

Progress Monitoring of Early Literacy Skills

Early literacy represents a set of foundational, prerequisite skills that facilitate reading development. Early literacy skills such as alphabetic knowledge (i.e., knowledge of letter names and sounds), and phonological awareness (i.e., the ability to identify and manipulate sounds in words) provide critical building blocks for students to learn to decode unknown words, and following instruction and practice opportunities, develop the ability to read words quickly as if by sight (Ehri, 2005). Accurate and efficient word recognition facilitates the ability to read connected text accurately and fluently, which in turn facilitates reading text for understanding.

Examples of common early literacy CBMs are aligned with basic early literacy skills, and most commonly administered with students in kindergarten and first grade (or later grades for students with severe reading difficulties). Phonemic segmentation tasks measure students' skills at segmenting orally presented words into phonemes, which is a sophisticated skill within the phonological awareness construct. For example, the examiner may say the word "pancake" which could be segmented into the phonemes "/p/", "/æ/", "/n/", "/k/", "/eɪ/", "/k/" for a total score of six phonemes. Phonemic segmentation tasks are typically scored in terms of the number of correct phonemes or unique sound segments the student is able to orally identify within one minute, and in theory, students that are able to segment at a more fine-grained phoneme level should earn higher scores reflecting their more sophisticated grasp of phonemic awareness.

Letter Naming Fluency (LNF) and Letter Sound Fluency (LSF) are common measures of alphabetic knowledge and indices of how quickly students can identify names and sounds from their printed forms. Both measures utilize a list of randomly ordered letters. On LNF, students are asked to identify the names of as many letters as possible within one minute. LSF is administered the same way, only students are asked to identify the sound each letter makes. Both measures are scored in terms of the number of correct letter names or sounds identified, respectively.

Word Reading Fluency (WRF; also known as Word Identification Fluency) and Nonsense Word Fluency (NWF) are tasks that involve reading lists of real or pseudowords, respectively. WRF measures are scored in terms of the number of words read correctly in one minute. NWF measures typically award credit for the number of sounds the student correctly identifies within each word either in isolation, through a process of "sounding out," or in reading the whole word by blending the sounds together. Further, some forms of NWF also award credit for the number of words read correctly as whole units.

Early Literacy Measures: Technical Adequacy and Research Base

Several studies have evaluated the reliability and validity of early literacy CBMs. Studies have typically observed adequate alternate forms and test-retest reliability (Fuchs, Fuchs, and Compton, 2004; Goffreda, and DiPerna, 2010). Additionally, studies of the criterion-related validity of scores collected at one point in time (i.e., point estimates) have generally observed the measures to be moderately to strongly predictive of reading skills measured by other more comprehensive tests of reading achievement (e.g., Clemens, Shapiro, Wu, Taylor, and Caskie, 2014; Fuchs et al. 2004; Speece, Mills, Ritchey, and Hillman, 2003; Stage, Sheppard, Davidson, and Browning, 2001).

While reliable scores and the ability to predict reading outcomes are basic indices of technical adequacy, this evidence is not sufficient to understand which measures are best for monitoring progress. To be useful for monitoring progress, measures should also be sensitive to growth over time, rate of growth on the measure (i.e., "slope") should be associated with important academic outcomes, and the data should inform instructional decision-making (Fuchs, 2004).

Unfortunately, far fewer studies have investigated the technical properties of early literacy measures when administered on a progress monitoring basis. Evidence that exists indicates that although the measures are sensitive to growth, slope on LSF measures is more indicative of later reading outcomes than growth on LNF and PSF (Ritchey and Speece, 2006; Clemens et al., 2016). Research also suggests that slope on WRF measures is a better predictor of later reading success compared to other measures, such as NWF (Clemens et al., 2014; Clemens et al., 2016; Fuchs et al., 2004). However, researchers have barely scratched the surface in investigating questions pertaining to early literacy CBMs. Studies have not investigated questions regarding how frequently early literacy skills should be measured, procedures for setting goals, or the degree to which teachers use early literacy CBM and whether progress monitoring affects student growth. Studies have rarely compared the validity of slopes on early literacy CBMs; existing studies indicate somewhat stronger validity for measures of LSF and WRF over other measures in predicting subsequent reading outcomes (Clemens, Keller-Margulis, Scholten, and Yoon, 2016; Fuchs et al., 2004; Ritchey and Speece, 2006), however more research is needed.

Few studies have worked specifically with low-achieving students, which is ironic given that CBM was originally intended for students with academic difficulties. Furthermore, the validity and utility of early literacy CBMs may be, in part, dependent on the developmental level of the children being assessed, and more research is necessary to determine if some measures are more useful for monitoring progress of students at different stages of literacy acquisition. In summary, several early literacy CBM's have good evidence of reliability and validity and show promise for monitoring progress in reading acquisition, but continued research is needed to inform their use for instructional decision making and supporting decisions for supplemental interventions.

Progress Monitoring of Reading Skills

Passage Reading Fluency (PRF)

Reading fluency refers to reading connected text smoothly, accurately, and with little conscious effort. Fluent reading frees cognitive resources that can then be devoted to understanding what is read, therefore reading fluency is considered to be a necessary (but not sufficient) prerequisite of reading comprehension (Fuchs, Fuchs, Hosp, and Jenkins, 2001). Early CBM research found that measuring students' rate of reading connected text aloud was a simple and efficient metric, and one that was highly indicative of overall reading achievement (Deno et al., 1982). Subsequently, passage reading fluency (PRF) became one of the most prominent forms of CBM.

Depending on the publisher, PRF may be referred to as Oral Reading Fluency, Passage Reading, or CBM-Oral Reading (CBM-R), but all forms generally follow the same administration and scoring procedures: Students read a passage of text aloud for one minute, while the examiner marks three-second hesitations as well as misread, omitted, and transposed words. The final score is the number of words read correctly in one minute.

PRF: Technical Adequacy and Research Base

PRF has been the most widely studied CBM measure, with an extensive research base that supports its reliability on a test-retest and alternate-forms basis, as well as the criterion-related validity of point estimates in predicting overall reading skills on a concurrent and longitudinal basis (Fuchs et al., 2001; Shinn, Good, Knutson, Tilly, and Collins, 1992; see also meta analyses by Reschly, Busch, Betts, Deno, and Long, 2009; Wayman, Wallace, Wiley, Ticha, and Espin, 2007).

Despite the evidence for the basic technical adequacy of PRF static scores, more recent work has revealed questions about available PRF probe sets, decision rules, and the accuracy of PRF for instructional decision-making. Although some natural score variability is expected on any assessment, a student's performance on two different PRF probes from the same grade level passage set have been observed to fluctuate significantly due to differences in passage difficulty, which has negative implications on teachers' ability to make accurate instructional decisions (Ardoin and Christ, 2009; Christ, Zopluoglu, Long, and Monaghen, 2012). Christ et al. (2012) emphasized the importance of choosing high-quality, equivalent passages in order to decrease the standard error in performance, which is difficult to accomplish with a passage set. Further discussion on these topics is presented at the end of this chapter.

CBM Maze

The Maze task was designed to provide an alternative to PRF as an index of overall reading achievement that could be administered to students on a group basis. A Maze task typically consists of a passage of text in which words have been removed at a fixed interval (e.g., every seventh word) and replaced by a set of answer choices. Students read the passage silently, and upon arriving at each blank, circle the answer choice that best completes the sentence. One of the appealing aspects of the Maze task is that it can be administered on a group basis and thus make data collection more efficient. Additionally, in contrast to PRF measures, Maze tasks have somewhat greater face validity on the part of teachers as indices of overall reading achievement and comprehension (Fuchs, Fuchs, and Maxwell, 1988).

Maze: Technical Adequacy and Research Base

Although some educators perceive Maze measures to be more indicative of reading comprehension than PRF, studies have indicated that maze measures tend to demonstrate equivalent or lower criterion-related validity of overall reading achievement and comprehension compared to PRF (e.g., Ardoin, Witt, Suldo, and Connell, 2004; Fuchs et al., 1988; Graney, Martinez, Missal, and Aricak, 2010). Nevertheless, research offers support for the use of Maze as a progress monitoring tool in elementary school. Shin, Deno, and Espin (2000) evaluated the technical properties of a CBM Maze task when administered once per month across a school year with students in second grade. The study revealed acceptable alternate-forms reliability and sensitivity to growth. Slope in Maze scores was also predictive of year-end reading achievement measured on a standardized test of reading comprehension. Further, Jenkins and Jewell (1993) reported that the correlation between PRF and reading comprehension measures tended to decline between Grades 2 to 6, however correlations between Maze and reading comprehension remained stable across the grades, suggesting that Maze may be more suitable for upper elementary-aged students.

Multiple Choice Reading Comprehension (MCRC)

More recently, multiple-choice comprehension (MCRC) measures have emerged as options for monitoring reading progress (Park, Irvin, Lai, Alonzo, and Tindal, 2012). On an MCRC measure, the student silently reads a passage and completes a series of multiple choice questions that assess for literal and inferential understanding. The measure is scored in terms of the number of questions answered correctly.

MCRC: Technical Adequacy and Research Base

A series of publisher-conducted studies has demonstrated adequate and acceptable levels of reliability and moderate to strong criterion-related validity of MCRC measures for Grades 2–5 (see Anderson et al., 2014). However, these measures are relatively new and little research has been conducted outside of the publishers. Also unclear is their sensitivity to growth, and whether MCRC measures improve in their predictive validity of reading comprehension outcomes over PRF measures (something Maze measures have not been able to do). Initial evidence toward this end was provided by Baker et al. (2015), who found that PRF and MCRC were comparably predictive of 7th and 8th graders' reading outcomes on a state accountability assessment (and more powerfully predictive when considered together), but this work is needed with elementary-aged students. Additionally, issues of form effects and passage equivalence that impact PRF measures are also likely to affect MCRC measures.

Progress Monitoring of Vocabulary Knowledge

Vocabulary knowledge is a relatively underappreciated aspect of reading achievement and interventions, which is unfortunate given how important vocabulary is for reading comprehension as well as the development of basic reading skills (Senechal, Oullette, and Rodney, 2006). Similarly, vocabulary is an underappreciated area of progress monitoring compared to other academic skills. However, promising frameworks for vocabulary CBM exist.

Vocabulary Matching

The most common form of vocabulary CBM that has been studied is vocabulary matching tasks, in which a set of words are listed on the left side of the page, and a set of definitions (including some distractor definitions) are listed on the right side (e.g., Espin, Busch, Shin, and Kruschwitz, 2001; Espin et al., 2013). Working independently, students complete the task by matching the words on the left with the appropriate definition on the right. Measures are typically timed for 5–6 minutes, and the number of correctly matched definitions represents the student's score.

A challenge to monitoring progress in vocabulary rests in the necessary specificity of the assessments. Vocabulary can represent a vast base of knowledge, and it is extremely difficult (if not impossible) to create efficient assessments that reliably reflect generalized vocabulary knowledge. For this reason, vocabulary CBM has often been applied to content areas such as science and social studies, where a more specific corpus of important vocabulary terms can be identified. A typical procedure for developing CBM vocabulary matching measures starts by selecting important terms from the course textbook (often the vocabulary terms from the glossary), teacher notes, and other class materials that will be taught across a period of time (Borsuk, 2010; Espin et al., 2013). Probes can be created by randomly sampling sets of words from this list, and when administered on a regular basis can provide teachers with insight into students' development of vocabulary knowledge important for the class. To date, vocabulary matching measures have been studied primarily with middle school students, although the procedure is the same for elementary-aged students.

Another challenge to CBM vocabulary matching measures is that they depend on accurate decoding of both the target word and the answer choices. Therefore, poor decoding skills may obscure accurate assessment of vocabulary knowledge. Educators who wish to monitor poor readers' progress in vocabulary knowledge might consider reading the items aloud as the students complete them (which has demonstrated similar technical adequacy to taking the measures independently; see Borsuk, 2010; Espin et al., 2001).

Vocabulary Matching: Technical Adequacy and Research Base

Vocabulary matching CBMs are fairly reliable and valid (Beyers, Lembke, and Curs, 2013; Espin et al., 2001; Espin et al., 2013; Espin, Shin, and Busch, 2005; Mooney, McCarter, Schraven, and Callicoatte, 2013). Vocabulary matching measures have demonstrated moderate to strong corrections with standardized measures of vocabulary or content knowledge in social studies (Espin et al. 2001), and science (Espin et al., 2013). Social studies and science vocabulary matching tasks have also shown sensitivity to growth on a progress monitoring basis, and rates of improvement on these measures have been shown to be predictive of students' grades in their social studies or science courses, as well as performance on tests of relevant content knowledge (Borsuk, 2010; Espin et al., 2005; Espin et al., 2013). As indicated earlier, most work with vocabulary matching measures has been conducted with students in middle school, and although the measures could easily be extended to upper or lower grades, work is needed to evaluate their technical properties with other age groups.

Multiple Choice Vocabulary Measures

More recently, efforts have been made to develop progress monitoring measures of more general vocabulary knowledge that are not tied to a particular curriculum or specific content area. Multiple choice vocabulary measures (Anderson et al., 2014) have been developed for Grades 2–8, in which the student selects a word or phrase that means the same as a target word from a set of answer choices.

Multiple Choice Vocabulary: Technical Adequacy and Research Base

Multiple choice vocabulary measures have demonstrated adequate internal consistency and overall reliability in Grades 2–8 (Wray, Alonzo, and Tindal, 2014). The measures have also demonstrated moderate correlations with standardized assessments of vocabulary and reading comprehension in Grades 2–5 (Lai, Alonzo, and Tindal, 2013), and factor analyses in Grades 3–7 indicated that performance on the multiple-choice vocabulary measures was associated with overall reading achievement (Anderson et al., 2014).

However, multiple choice vocabulary measures have not been investigated with regard to their sensitivity to growth, or the degree to which slope is related to overall growth in vocabulary or reading comprehension. Additionally, given that these measures were developed using a general set of vocabulary terms, progress monitoring results may be difficult to interpret if students never had the opportunity to learn the specific vocabulary terms in the assessment (which would be reflected as no growth on the measure).

Dynamic Indicators of Vocabulary Skills (DIVS)

Efforts have been made to extend CBM vocabulary measures downward to pre- and early elementary school. The Dynamic Indicators of Vocabulary Skills (DIVS, Parker, 2000) include two subtests designed to measure vocabulary knowledge for preschool and kindergarten students: Picture Naming Fluency, in which students name as many picture tiles representing common nouns as they can in one minute; and Reverse Definition Fluency, in which students are read a series of definitions and asked to name a word described by the definition. Vocabulary content for the DIVS was derived from common nouns found in kindergarten and first grade reading materials (Parker, 2000). Both subtests are individually administered and do not require the student to read.

DIVS: Technical Adequacy and Research Base

Limited research has investigated the technical properties of the DIVS measures. Extant studies support the reliability, criterion-related validity, and screening accuracy of the measures with preschool students (Marcotte, Clemens, Parker, and Whitcomb, 2016; Marcotte, Parker, Furey, and Hands, 2013). However, no studies to date have evaluated the technical properties of the

DIVS or its sensitivity to growth when administered on a progress monitoring basis. It is also unclear if the adequate reliability and validity properties observed in the published studies of preschool students will extend to low-achieving students in elementary school.

In summary, important advancements have occurred in the area of vocabulary CBM, however more work is needed to validate their use for progress monitoring, particularly with elementary students. Vocabulary is a critical aspect of reading proficiency and knowledge acquisition, and monitoring vocabulary acquisition may be a key indicator for students receiving supplemental intervention services for reading comprehension and/or achievement in the content areas. The emergence of tools in this previously overlooked area is encouraging.

Progress Monitoring in Spelling

Spelling CBM is an underutilized method of monitoring progress relative to reading and math CBM. Unfortunately, this underutilization is likely due to misperceptions among educators that spelling is an isolated, compartmentalized skill, and less acknowledgement of the important interrelationship between spelling and decoding skills, especially for younger students and struggling readers (Ehri, 2000). Spelling assessment can offer unique insight into students' literacy skills and provide another source of information on their phonemic awareness, letter-sound correspondence, knowledge of letter combinations or common letter-sound patterns, and morphological awareness (Oullette and Senechal, 2008). Thus, monitoring progress in spelling can help inform students' development of important foundational reading skills.

Little variation has been observed in administration and scoring procedures for CBM spelling, and a standard procedure is described in more detail by Hosp, Hosp, and Howell (2007). Spelling probes consist of a set of words that are available through CBM providers (e.g., AIMSweb), or probes can be developed based specifically on words sampled from the curriculum of instruction. In administering CBM spelling, the teacher orally dictates a list of words at a standardized pace (one word every 10 seconds for first- and second-grade students, and one word dictated every seven seconds for grades 3 and up) while the students spell the words on a numbered sheet of paper. Twelve words per list are typical for grades 1 and 2, and 17 words are common for grades 3 and up. Scoring spelling CBM can involve simply tallying the number of words spelled correctly (WSC), however, this approach obscures important information about the students' approach to spelling and underlying literacy skills. Consider Student A, who spells the word picture as "pikchur," compared to Student B who spells it as "qwtbb." Using WSC scoring, both students would receive a score of zero, however Student A is clearly at a different stage of literacy acquisition and is using phonological and alphabetic information to approximate a spelling. To account for these differences, the correct letter sequences (CLS) scoring approach can be used, which involves awarding one point for each correctly sequenced pair of letters, including points for correct initial and final letters. Using CLS in this example, pikchur would be awarded three points, whereas qwtbb would result in a score of zero. Thus, CLS provides credit when a student's spelling is a close approximation, and is more sensitive to individual differences in spelling and literacy skills.

Additional work has extended progress monitoring in spelling downward to kindergarten. Ritchey (2008) developed a kindergarten spelling progress monitoring task which uses only three-letter phonetically regular (i.e., "decodable") words such as cat, top, and sit. Five words are dictated per administration and the measure is untimed. Students' responses can be scored for WSC, CLS, or *correct sounds*, an additional scoring approach that provides credit for a phoneme represented by a correct letter or a phonologically permissible alternative (e.g., spelling [k] instead of [c]).

Spelling: Technical Adequacy and Research Base

The research base on the technical properties of spelling CBM is limited. Evidence indicates reliability for spelling CBM using WSC or CLS scoring approaches across grade levels (Shinn, 1989), however, studies of criterion-related validity are more rare. Ritchey (2008), Ritchey, Coker, and McGraw (2010) and Clemens et al. (2016) investigated the use of spelling measures with kindergarten students and observed moderate correlations with reading and literacy assessments on a concurrent and predictive basis, however scoring methods that are more sensitive to approximate spellings (e.g., CLS and correct sounds spelling) demonstrated greater validity in predicting reading and literacy skills than scores based on whole words.

A limited number of studies have investigated spelling measures on a progress monitoring basis. Across grade levels, research indicates that spelling CBM is sensitive to growth (Clemens et al., 2016; Fuchs, Fuchs, Hamlett, and Walz, 1993; Ritchey et al., 2010), slope on CLS scoring is more discriminative among lower and higher achievers compared to WSC (Fuchs et al., 1993), and slope that is measured using scoring metrics such as CLS and correct sounds is more predictive of spelling and literacy outcomes than slope in WSC among kindergarten students (Clemens, Smith, and Gamez, 2013). Additionally, Fuchs, Fuchs, Hamlett, and Allinder (1991) found that when teachers conducted skills analysis of their students' spelling scores in addition to monitoring progress, students demonstrated greater growth in spelling over students whose teachers that did not conduct skills analysis.

Future research should continue to investigate how progress monitoring in spelling can provide information not only in regard to students' spelling skills, but on their overall acquisition of reading and literacy skills. Additionally, consideration of new scoring metrics may offer greater sensitivity to growth and additional insight on early literacy skills. For example, the Spelling Sensitivity Score (Masterson and Apel, 2010) was designed to quantify growth in linguistic knowledge and to be sensitive to changes in spelling skills. Using this metric, each word is segmented by "elements" (i.e., phonemes, juncture changes, or affixes), and each element is awarded 0 to 3 points based on the accuracy or phonological plausibility of students spelling of each segment.

Progress Monitoring of Early Numeracy

Similar to the ways in which early literacy skills are foundational to subsequent reading achievement, early numeracy skills have been identified that are related to the acquisition and development of formal mathematics. The concept of early numeracy is sometimes described as an understanding of numbers or "number sense" (Clarke, Baker, Smolkowski, and Chard, 2008), a term that can be broadly defined as an understanding of numerical relationships and of the meaning of numbers (Malofeeva, Day, Saco, Young, and Ciancio, 2004). Embedded in this definition is an understanding of various concepts related to quantity, one-to-one correspondence, and relationships between numbers.

While a variety of measures exist for the progress monitoring of early numeracy concepts, four measures in particular have received the most attention: Oral Counting (OC), Number Identification (NI), Quantity Discrimination (QD), and Missing Number (MN). These measures were originally developed into CBM measures by Clarke and Shinn (2004) and Clarke et al. (2008). In the OC task, students are asked to count from 1 to as high as they can before making a mistake. In the NI measure, students read from a list of randomly ordered numbers and identify as many as possible within one minute. QD is also a one-minute task and asks students to attend to sets of paired random numbers and identify the larger number in the pair. In the MN measure, students have one minute to respond to a set of number sequences identifying what number is missing from the sequence (e.g., 4 __ 6). The position of the missing number varies across the sequences. The missing number may be the first, second, or third in the sequence.

Early Numeracy Measures: Technical Adequacy and Research Base

Several studies have investigated the reliability, validity, and growth rates of the four early numeracy indicators with students in kindergarten and first grade (Clarke et al., 2008; Lembke and Foegen, 2009; Martinez, Missal, Graney, Aricak, and Clarke, 2009). Across studies, similar levels of reliability have been observed, with each measure having demonstrated at least adequate (or stronger) alternate-forms and/or test-retest reliability across studies, and few differences between the different measures. Analyses of concurrent and predictive validity have also been fairly consistent across studies. Although all measures have been observed to be correlated with mathematics skills assessed on other measures, QD and MN have tended to be the strongest predictors of subsequent mathematics outcomes. Studies have also investigated the measures in terms of their sensitivity to growth, as well as the degree to which growth is associated with subsequent mathematics performance. Overall, studies indicate that growth tends to be slow, in some cases less than one correct point gained every four weeks or more (Lembke and Foegen, 2009). Slow growth on the measures complicates their utility for monitoring students' progress across relatively short-term periods (e.g., 6–8 weeks) if students growth very little during this time period. Rate of growth is also dependent on the measure and grade level. NI and OC measures tend to show more growth (but that must be balanced with the evidence of weaker validity compared to QD and MN). For example, Baglici, Codding, and Tryon (2010) observed that OC and MN measures demonstrated observable growth in kindergarten but not first grade, but on the other hand, QD evidenced observable growth in first grade but not kindergarten. Research that examined the relation of growth to overall mathematics outcomes indicates QD to be the superior predictor (Clarke et al., 2008).

In summary, evidence supports the reliability and validity of early numeracy progress monitoring measures, and offers evidence of their sensitivity to growth. QD appears to be a stronger measure overall compared to the others. However, additional work is needed. It does not appear that studies have focused on subsets of students with low early numeracy and mathematics skills, and instead have studied populations representing the full range of learners. Work with struggling students is important as they are the primary population for whom progress monitoring is used. Additionally, the slow rate of growth observed on early numeracy CBMs requires further investigation of their utility for ongoing instructional decision making.

Progress Monitoring in Mathematics Computation

Fuchs (2004) described two approaches for constructing progress monitoring assessments across academic areas, and these different methodologies have been most notably applied to progress monitoring measure development in mathematics (Foegen, Jiban, and Deno, 2007). A *robust indicators* approach to constructing progress monitoring measures involves the identification of a fairly specific skill or task that is highly correlated and indicative of overall performance in that academic domain, similar to how passage reading fluency is regarded as a robust indicator of overall reading achievement. In mathematics, a student's accuracy and fluency in solving simple computation problems (i.e., math facts) is indicative of overall mathematics computation achievement (Christ, Scullin, Tolbize, and Jiban, 2008), therefore serving as a robust indicator of math computation skills.

A *curriculum sampling* approach, on the other hand, involves constructing progress monitoring probes using problem types that are representative of the curriculum of instruction and/or grade level standards. For example, a fourth-grade math curriculum might target several skill areas including multi-digit multiplication and division; comparison, addition, and subtraction of fractions; and analysis of geometric figures. Thus, the creation of a set of progress monitoring measures using a curriculum sampling approach would involve identifying a large set of items that sample from across these skill areas, randomly sampling equal sets of problems, and creating probes with an equal distribution of problem types on each probe.

The decision on whether to use a robust indicators or curriculum-sampling approach depends primarily on the type of information a teacher wishes to gather to inform instruction. Robust indicators provide an index of general mathematics achievement that is less dependent on the curriculum of instruction and thus easier to generalize across students and settings. Measures from a curriculum sampling approach will be highly sensitive to growth in the skills taught in the instruction or intervention curriculum and may be more appropriate for measuring students' performance towards a set of specific mathematics goals during a relatively short period of time.

Regardless of the approach taken to construct the measures, math computation CBMs are typically timed so that fluency can be determined. Administration of the measures varies from two to six minutes depending on the grade level and specific measure. Measures can be administered on a whole-class, small group, or one-on-one basis, but are all completed independently by students. Scoring measures can vary based on the specific guidelines established by the assessment. Items are either scored by counting the number of correct digits in the answer or the item as a whole. Other measures might award a predetermined set of points depending on the established difficulty of each item.

Math Computation Measures: Technical Adequacy and Research Base

In their literature review of mathematics CBM, Foegen et al. (2007) reviewed 15 studies that measured math computation skills. Of these 15 studies, seven used a curriculum sampling approach to construct measures, five used a robust indicators approach, and three used both approaches. The reliability coefficients across the computation measures were relatively high. Overall, studies that used a robust indicators approach reported the measures were reliable across the four basic operations (i.e., addition, subtraction, multiplication, division). Only two studies (Espin, Deno, Maruyama, and Cohen, 1989; Thurber, Shinn, and Smolkowski, 2002) that used a robust indicators approach measured criterion validity; these studies reported moderate correlations between basic facts and other measures of mathematics achievement.

Overall, the Foegen et al. (2007) review indicated that studies that used a curriculum sampling approach to measure math computation reported moderate to strong reliability. Additionally, computation measures developed with this approach tended to demonstrate stronger criterion-related validity compared to robust indicators measures, a result likely owing to the greater range of skills assessed on curriculum-sampled measures.

An additional review conducted by Christ et al. (2008) revealed that CBM computation measures demonstrated weak criterion-related validity to overall mathematics outcomes unless the criterion assessment measured computation skills more specifically. The authors also suggested that the criterion validity for CBM computation measures should be interpreted with caution because overall mathematics achievement includes language demands and spatial reasoning, which are not typically measured by computation probe. Additionally, consideration should be given to the amount of time allotted for students to complete computation CBMs. If multiple skills are being measured, Christ et al. (2008) suggested increasing the duration (i.e., 4- to 14-minutes) to gain a larger sample of student performance. However, shorter durations (i.e., 1- to 2-minutes) are acceptable when measuring a single skill or a narrow range of skills.

CBM math computation measures developed under a curriculum sampling and robust indicators approach demonstrate similar technical properties in terms of their reliability and validity (Foegen et al., 2007), however, research is needed to identify differences in the performance of the measures when administered on a progress monitoring basis, especially with students with math difficulties.

Additional research is also needed on user-generated CBMs. Websites are available that allow teachers to generate CBM math computation probes based on specific problem types or grade level. Strait, Smith, Pender, Malone, Roberts, and Hall (2015) evaluated the reliability of four parallel, randomly generated CBMs with sixth-grade students, finding moderate test-retest and alternate-forms reliability across the measures. However, studies have not contrasted the technical adequacy of user-generated measures versus commercially available CBMs, and more research is needed to evaluate their use with students in earlier grades.

Additional areas of future research might investigate new forms of computation assessment that can inform students' development of pre-algebraic skills. Assessments of pre-algebraic reasoning have emerged that use *open equations* (e.g., $4 + \_\_ = 10$; Powell, 2007), as well as progress monitoring assessments that include algebra and pre-algebraic tasks extending down to grade 2 (Alonzo, Lai, and Tindal, 2009). Because algebra has been identified as a gateway skill that facilitates achievement in more complex mathematics (National Mathematics Advisory Panel, 2008), algebra and pre-algebra skills are becoming increasingly more prevalent in mathematics standards and instruction. Therefore, it will be important to identify tools for monitoring students' progress in pre-algebraic skills.

Progress Monitoring in Mathematics Concepts and Problem-Solving

In the elementary grades, mathematics concepts and problem-solving CBM tasks involve the application of knowledge in areas such as greater than/less than, measurement, money, word problems, interpreting charts, and basic geometry (Fuchs, Fuchs, and Zumeta, 2008). CBMs used to monitor progress in math concepts and applications have primarily used a curriculum sampling approach (Foegen et al., 2007).

The research review by Foegen et al. (2007) identified studies that evaluated the use of progress monitoring measures in the area of concepts and problem-solving. Although there were far fewer studies that evaluated measures of this type compared to computation measures, results revealed generally acceptable reliability for progress monitoring purposes. The MBSP Concepts and Applications probes (Fuchs, Hamlett, and Fuchs, 1998) tended to demonstrate slightly stronger reliability compared to measures specifically focused on word problems (e.g., Jitendra, Sczesniak, and Deatline-Buchman, 2005). The review further identified a strong level of criterion-related validity associated with concepts and problem-solving assessments in relations to standardized tests of math problem solving and overall achievement.

Additional research has been conducted on measures of word problem solving with third grade students (Jitendra, Dupuis, and Zaslofsky, 2014; Leh, Jitendra, Caskie, and Griffin, 2007). These studies administered measures on a bi-weekly basis across 12–16 weeks and found that although growth was evident on the measure, growth rates were slow and not significantly different between low-achieving and average-achieving students. However, Jitendra et al. (2014) observed that slope on the measure was predictive of year-end achievement on a test of overall mathematics achievement. Thus, word problem-solving measures show potential as progress monitoring tools, particularly in terms of their predictive validity, however educators should consider that slow growth rates will require a greater number of weeks in order to have the data needed to inform instructional decisions.

In summary, evidence supports the use of CBM concepts and problem-solving measures, but more work is needed, particularly when measures are administered for the purpose for progress monitoring. The work of Jitendra and colleagues has been important for moving this area forward. Future work should continue to investigate growth rates on concepts and problem-solving measures, whether progress monitoring data informs instructional decisions, and the extent to which students demonstrate improved growth as a result. Additionally, researchers might seek to identify robust indicators that link elementary concepts and problem-solving skills with achievement in secondary grades.

Progress Monitoring in Written Expression

Students with disabilities in the area of written expression often experience difficulties in a number of areas such as handwriting, spelling, planning, and composition (Fletcher, Lyon, Fuchs, and Barnes, 2007). Consequently, students with writing difficulties generate far less output and produce shorter and less interesting writing products, commit more spelling and grammatical errors, and show far less elaboration compared to students with average achievement in writing (Graham, Harris, and Larsen, 2001). Therefore, progress monitoring in written expression attempts to capture aspects related to writing productivity, spelling, and grammatical accuracy.

The traditional approach to CBM in written expression involves obtaining a sample of writing under a timed condition. The student is provided with a "story starter" which may be a picture or 1–2 sentences designed to engage interest, for example, "*One day I woke up and could not believe what I saw in front of my house. It was . . .*". The student is given one minute to think of a story, and three minutes to write. The student's writing sample can then be scored using several different metrics, including total words written (TWW; a tally of the total number of words written within the time limit regardless of spelling or grammatical accuracy), words spelled correctly (WSC; the number of correct spellings in the student's written product), and correct writing sequences (CWS; a tally of the number of adjacent pairs of words that are correct in terms of spelling, punctuation, grammar, and syntax). More detail on these scoring methods is provided by Hosp et al. (2007). Traditional CBM writing approaches were subsequently expanded to include other tasks, such as word and sentence dictation, or sentence-writing tasks (McMaster, Parker, and Jung, 2012). Other scoring methods have emerged (see McMaster and Espin, 2007) however it is not clear how often these approaches are used in practice.

Written Expression CBM: Technical Adequacy and Research Base

Research on CBM in written expression has been reviewed by McMaster and Espin (2007) and McMaster et al. (2012). Across the studies of CBM in writing, reliability indices generally reveal weak to moderate test-retest and alternate forms reliability, suggesting a good deal of variation in students' scores between administrations. Validity evidence indicates a broad range of correlations with other standardized tests of written expression and literacy, with larger correlations evident for students in earlier grade levels, a factor likely due to sensitivity of the scoring metrics to production. In later elementary school and beyond, when composition, creativity, and writing quality become more prominent areas for characterizing students' writing achievement, the CBM fluency-based indicators of production and grammatical accuracy lose some of their ability to reflect overall skills in written expression. Findings of the reviews also suggested that correct minus incorrect writing sequences may function as better indicators of writing for older students.

Reviews on CBM written expression (McMaster and Espin, 2007; McMaster et al., 2012) revealed that CBM writing indices are sensitive to growth, however very little research has investigated CBM writing measures on a frequent basis, and several questions remain regarding the degree to which slope of improvement is indicative of growth in overall writing achievement. Toward this end, McMaster, Du, Yeo, Deno, Parker, and Ellis (2011) administered CBM writing tasks on a weekly basis with first grade students and found that slopes stable enough for decision-making were possible after 8–9 data points. Girls demonstrate stronger CBM writing performance compared to boys (consistent with other work in written expression), although it is less clear whether rates of growth over time differ among girls and boys (e.g., Fearrington et al., 2013; Malecki and Jewell, 2003; Parker, McMaster, Medhanie, and Silberglitt, 2011).

Recent work has sought to address the limitations of the focus on mechanics in CBM writing, to capture more qualitative and complex aspects of students' writing on a progress monitoring basis (Casey, Miller, Stockton, and Justice, 2016; Sturm, Cali, Nelson, and Staskowski, 2012). Initial evidence from this work is encouraging, but more research is needed to determine their validity and utility as progress monitoring tools.

Computer-Adaptive Progress Monitoring Assessments

The idea for administering progress monitoring assessments on computers is not new (e.g., Fuchs and Fuchs, 1992), and today, most major publishers of CBM tools offer computer-based options for administering and/or scoring CBM assessments (which are often parallel to their paper-based versions). However, recent technological advances and greater availability of computing power in schools has given rise to computer-*adaptive* assessments (CATs). CATs are not CBMs, and unlike traditional forms of assessment, CATs continually adjust the difficulty of items based on the performance of the individual taking the test. For example, the CAT may present increasingly difficult items as the examinee continues to respond correctly, and increasingly easier items as the examinee responds incorrectly. Theoretically, this methodology is designed to provide a more precise estimate of ability across a larger amount of content, but in a shorter amount of time compared to a traditional paper-based assessment. CATs are available from various publishers in the areas of reading, early literacy, and mathematics, such as the Measures of Academic Progress (Northwest Evaluation Association, 2016), STAR 360 (Renaissance, 2016), and aReading (FastBridge Learning, 2016). Some have been marketed as options for replacing paper-based progress monitoring measures (Renaissance Learning, 2009).

Research to date on the technical properties of CATs in comparison to paper-based CBMs or when administered for progress monitoring are extremely limited. In elementary grades, a mathematics CAT was slightly more predictive of student performance on a year-end state mathematics proficiency exam compared to CBMs of computation and concepts/applications (Shapiro, Dennis, and Fu, 2015; Shapiro and Gebhart, 2012), although the differences were not large. In the area of early literacy, recent studies indicate that although a CAT administered in kindergarten was predictive of reading skills at the end of kindergarten and first grade, the CAT generally did not improve in the prediction of reading outcomes over the paper-based measures, and in some cases demonstrated weaker predictive validity compared to one-minute paper-based measures such as word identification fluency (Clemens et al., 2015; 2016).

Furthermore, Clemens et al. (2015) compared the intercepts and slopes generated by an early literacy CAT to those from common paper-based CBMs of early literacy in predicting reading outcomes at the end of kindergarten and first grade. Results indicated equal or weaker predictive strength for the CATs for both intercept and slope in predicting kindergarten and first grade reading outcomes compared to most of the paper-based CBMs, such as letter sound fluency and word identification fluency.

Characteristics of CATs suggest the need for caution when considering their use for progress monitoring. First, some publishers do not recommend administration in greater frequency than once per month, and in some cases, not more frequent than four times per year, which has obvious implications on the ability for teachers to obtain frequent feedback on student growth. Second, Shapiro et al. (2015) raised a concern regarding the high standard error of measurement (SEM) of some CATs relative to their low rates of growth, meaning that progress would need to be monitored for at least three months before slope exceeded the SEM in order to permit confidence in interpreting slope for instructional decision-making. Third, given the adaptive nature of the assessment, not all students may see items in all skill areas contained in the CAT, yet the software might estimate subscale scores even though students were never exposed to content in those skill areas. Fourth, it is not clear if CATs provide information that is useful for instructional planning or identifying when intervention changes should be made.

In summary, CATs represent an interesting advancement in academic assessment. However, the lack of research on their technical properties with elementary-aged students and questions about their utility for instructional decision-making suggests the need for caution when considering these measures for progress monitoring purposes.

Goal Setting, Frequency of Assessment, and Decision Rules in Progress Monitoring: General Recommendations and Unanswered Questions

Goal-Setting

When monitoring student progress using a CBM approach, decisions regarding when to maintain or change intervention programs are often based on students' progress toward a particular target or "goal." After a goal has been set, a line can be drawn on a graph connecting the students' baseline data point with the goal, thus providing a goal or "aim" line, which reflects the rate of growth the student should demonstrate to achieve the goal within the time frame. Because instructional decisions are often based on the student's observed rate of growth (or slope) relative to the target growth rate, goal-setting is an important aspect of progress monitoring.

There are several approaches to goal setting, and further detail is provided by the National Center on Intensive Intervention (2012). *Benchmark* goal setting methods utilize target scores established for specific progress monitoring measures that predict a greater likelihood of success in that academic area in subsequent grades or assessments, whereas *norm-referenced* goal setting uses normative data provided by the publisher of the progress monitoring tool to select a target score associated with a desired level of achievement. For example, a student receiving additional support in reading may currently have scores that place him at the eleventh percentile relative to same-grade peers for that time of year. One objective of an intervention would be to improve the student's reading skills and thus *close the gap* with his peers. Therefore, the teacher might use a target score associated with the twenty-fifth percentile (i.e., lower bound of the average range) by the end of the school year.

Benchmark and norm-referenced goals are simple and straightforward to understand, and do not require calculation. However, they may not always be the best choice, especially when students demonstrate very low achievement, in which case the benchmark or norm-referenced targets may require an unrealistic rate of growth to attain (National Center on Intensive Intervention, 2012). Thus, this method of goal setting may be appropriate for students who are achieving below the average range but whose performance is not severely discrepant from their peers. For students with more significant performance deficits, one of the following methods may be more appropriate.

The *rate of improvement* method involves calculating a greater rate of improvement than that demonstrated by students on a normative basis in order to yield a target rate of improvement. Typically, this process involves multiplying normative growth rates by a value between 1.5 and 2 to reflect greater growth associated with more intensive intervention (National Center on Intensive Intervention, 2012). Multiplying the targeted rate by the number of weeks that progress will be monitored yields the target amount of growth, which is then added to the student's baseline score to yield the progress monitoring goal score. The rate of improvement method requires calculation and may be prone to error when used in practice, however when implemented correctly, the method holds advantages in reflecting a target that is based on evidence of typical rates of growth, but is more ambitious consistent with the goal of supplemental intervention supports to close achievement gaps.

The *intra-individual framework* method of goal setting uses the student's current rate of improvement and targets a more ambitious growth rate (National Center on Intensive Intervention, 2012). In short, the student's weekly rate of growth across at least eight recent data points is multiplied by 1.5 or greater (to reflect a greater rate of growth targeted by more intensive intervention), which is then multiplied by the number of weeks in the upcoming progress monitoring period. The product is added to the students' baseline score, resulting in the student's progress monitoring goal. This method is individualized for the student (like the nature of specialized services), however, it requires current progress monitoring data for the student which may not always be available.

To date, methods of progress monitoring goal setting have been more the subject of training materials and expert recommendations, and less the subject of empirical research. Evidence suggests that setting ambitious goals offers advantages in improving teachers' responsiveness to data and improving students' achievement (Fuchs, Fuchs, and Hamlett, 1989; Jenkins and Terjeson, 2011). However, research has not compared goal-setting methods in terms of their ease of use by teachers, how well they are understood, whether their use results in appropriately ambitious targets, or the impact of goal-setting methods on the frequency of instructional changes or improved student achievement. Until research provides greater guidance in this area, educators should select a goal setting method based on consideration of the individual needs of their students and their comfort level in determining a goal accurately.

Frequency of Assessment and Number of Data Points

Recommendations on how frequently progress monitoring assessment should occur have varied, but in general they have ranged from two times per week to at least once per month. Assessment should be frequent enough to provide timely feedback on student progress; however, frequency must be balanced with practical and logistical constraints. Frequency of measurement also has implications for decisions based on students' rate of growth (i.e., slope). More data points allow for greater confidence that a student's slope is reflective of their "true" rate of growth and not overly influenced by measurement error of the measures. Although CBM probe sets were designed to be as equivalent in difficulty as possible, a high degree of variability in difficulty has been observed in some published PRF CBM probe sets (Ardoin and Christ, 2009). Thus, monitoring progress with a probe set that varies more in difficulty would require more data points (and more weeks of data collection if data are collected less frequently) in order to have confidence that the student's trendline is accurately reflective of his/her rate of growth.

Studies of PRF CBM measures with students in middle elementary school have recommended 6–10 data points before making instructional decisions (Christ and Silberglitt, 2007; Shinn, Good, and Stein, 1989), and more recent work has recommended upwards of 13 data points or more (Christ, Zopluoglu, Monaghen, and Van Norman, 2013). When progress monitoring is less frequent, probe sets are less well controlled for difficulty, and conditions associated with the progress monitoring assessment sessions are less stable, more data points are needed (Ardoin and Christ, 2009). On the other hand, considering progress monitoring data in terms of how often it prompts teachers to make instructional changes, Jenkins and Terjeson (2011) observed that assessment as infrequent as once every eight weeks may be sufficient for generating data needed for making instructional decisions. Unfortunately, most of the research on measurement frequency has been conducted with CBM passage reading fluency measures with students in middle elementary school, and more work is needed on measures in other academic areas, as well as with students of different ages and skill levels. For example, no research to date has evaluated the number of data points needed before making decisions based on early literacy progress monitoring data. Work is sorely needed in these areas.

Decision Rules

Research suggests that it is not sufficient to just monitor progress; the real benefits in improved student achievement are realized when teachers use a structured set of decision rules to evaluate students' data on an ongoing basis (Stecker et al., 2005). In general, decisions based on progress monitoring data might include those that continue a current intervention plan, change instruction (i.e., increase or decrease intensity, alter or add components, or alter other aspects of instruction), or increase a goal.

There are two primary frameworks for making decisions based on progress monitoring data (Ardoin, Christ, Morena, Cormier, and Klingbeil, 2013; National Center on Intensive Intervention, 2012). *Point rules* involve examining the student's most recent 3–4 consecutive data points in relation to the goal line (Mirkin, Deno, Tindal, and Kuehnle, 1982; Stecker and Lembke, 2011). When those data points fall below the student's goal line, it suggests that an instructional change should be made to improve performance. On the other hand, all data points above the goal line indicate that the current intervention program is successful, and the teacher can either continue implementing until the goal is met (at which point the goal might be raised or intervention might be reduced in intensity, depending on continued needs).

Slope rules involve comparing the "steepness" of the student's slope to the goal line. A trendline that is flat or less steep than the goal line suggests an instructional change is needed, whereas a trendline that follows the goal line with the same degree of steepness indicates the current program is working as planned (and intervention may continue until the goal is met). A trendline that is steeper than the goal line suggests the need to raise the goal or consider reducing the intensity of the intervention if achievement goals have been met.

Very little research has compared the point and slope rule methods in terms of their effects on progress monitoring procedures and outcomes. Jenkins and Terjeson (2011) found that slope tended to generate greater responsiveness of teachers to progress monitoring data compared to point rules, but student outcomes were not evaluated. In their comprehensive review of CBM passage reading fluency research, Ardoin et al. (2013) reported that no studies have empirically investigated the accuracy of instructional decisions that are made using point or slope decision rules, or their outcomes on student achievement.

Additional questions remain regarding the use of slope for decision-making purposes. Some research indicated that slope did not aid in the prediction of students' reading outcomes over the predictive effects of the most recent score (Al Otaiba et al., 2011; Schatschneider, Wagner, and Crawford, 2008) unless students were in the early stages of skill development or the progress monitoring measure was well-aligned with the outcome measure (Tolar, Barth, Fletcher, Francis, and Vaughn, 2014). These findings question the importance of slope, particularly when it is used to predict future achievement. Recently, Mark Shinn suggested during a panel discussion (Ysseldyke, Shinn, Betts, and Clemens, 2016) that a student's most recent data are perhaps most important for understanding his or her current instructional needs, whereas slope is affected by all data points in the set, including data collected several weeks or months before (which may have little relevance to current achievement). Future research should compare point versus slope decision rules, and investigate the overall importance of slope for instructional decision-making.

Overall Summary and Conclusions

Many options exist for monitoring students' progress across academic skill areas, and progress monitoring is considered an important part of intervention support systems. Although the uses of CBM measures have increased over the years to include universal screening, establishing group norms, predicting state accountability test achievement, and informing high-stakes decisions such as special education eligibility identification (Deno, 2003), CBM tools are perhaps best suited for their original role: providing timely feedback on students' progress in order to make instructional adjustments that maximize student growth. As revealed in this chapter, our work in progress monitoring is far from finished. More research is needed on the technical adequacy and utility of measures for monitoring progress on an ongoing basis (especially with low-achieving students), goal-setting methods, the amount of data that are needed for reliable decisions, and ideal rule frameworks for decision-making. Additional work in these areas will improve educators' ability to make data-driven decisions and improve instruction for students who are most in need.

References

Al Otaiba, S., Folsom, J. S., Schatschneider, C., Wanzek, J., Greulich, L., Meadows, J., . . . and Connor, C. M. (2011). Predicting first-grade reading performance from kindergarten response to tier 1 instruction. *Exceptional Children*, 77(4), 453–470.

Alonzo, J., Lai, C., and Tindal, G. (2009). *The development of K-8 progress monitoring measures in mathematics for use with the 2% and general education populations: Grade 4 (Technical Report No. 0902)*. Eugene, OR: Behavioral Research and Teaching.

Anderson, D., Alonzo, J., Tindal, G., Farley, D., Irvin, P. S., Lai, C. F., . . . and Wray, K. A. (2014). *Technical manual: easyCBM*.

Ardoin, S. P., and Christ, T. J. (2009). Curriculum-based measurement of oral reading: Standard errors associated with progress monitoring outcomes from DIBELS, AIMSweb, and an Experimental Passage Set. *School Psychology Review*, 38(2), 266–283.

Ardoin, S. P., Christ, T. J., Morena, L. S., Cormier, D. C., and Klingbeil, D. A. (2013). A systematic review and summarization of the recommendations and research surrounding curriculum-based measurement of oral reading fluency (CBM-R) decision rules. *Journal of School Psychology*, 51(1), 1–18.

Ardoin, S. P., Witt, J. C., Suldo, S. M., and Connell, J. E. (2004). Examining the incremental benefits of administering a maze and three versus one curriculum-based measurement reading probes when conducting universal screening. *School Psychology Review, 33*(2), 218–233.

Baglici, S. P., Codding, R., and Tryon, G. (2010). Extending the research on the tests of early numeracy: Longitudinal analyses over two school years. *Assessment for Effective Intervention, 35*(2), 89–102.

Baker, D. L., Biancarosa, G., Park, B. J., Bousselot, T., Smith, J. L., Baker, S. K., . . . and Tindal, G. (2015). Validity of CBM measures of oral reading fluency and reading comprehension on high-stakes reading assessments in Grades 7 and 8. *Reading and Writing, 28*(1), 57–104.

Beyers, S. J., Lembke, E. S., and Curs, B. (2013). Social studies progress monitoring and intervention for middle school students. *Assessment for Effective Intervention, 38*(4), 224–235. doi: 10.1177/15345084 13489162.

Borsuk, E. R. (2010). Examination of an administrator-read vocabulary-matching measure as an indicator of science achievement. *Assessment for Effective Intervention, 35*(3), 168–177.

Casey, L. B., Miller, N. D., Stockton, M. B., and Justice, W. V. (2016). Assessing writing in elementary schools: Moving away from a focus on mechanics. *Language Assessment Quarterly, 13*(1), 42–54.

Christ, T. J., Scullin, S., Tolbize, A., and Jiban, C. L. (2008). Implications of recent research: Curriculum-based measurement of math computation. *Assessment for Effective Intervention, 33*, 198–205. doi: 10.1177/ 1534508407313480.

Christ, T. J., and Silberglitt, B. (2007). Estimates of the standard error of measurement for curriculum-based measures of oral reading fluency. *School Psychology Review, 36*(1), 130.

Christ, T. J., Zopluoglu, C., Long, J. D., and Monaghen, B. D. (2012). Curriculum-based measurement of oral reading: Quality of progress monitoring outcomes. *Exceptional Children, 78*(3), 356–373.

Christ, T. J., Zopluoglu, C., Monaghen, B. D., and Van Norman, E. R. (2013). Curriculum-based measurement of oral reading: Multi-study evaluation of schedule, duration, and dataset quality on progress monitoring outcomes. *Journal of School Psychology, 51*(1), 19–57.

Clarke, B., Baker, S., Smolkowski, K., and Chard, D. J. (2008). An analysis of early numeracy curriculum-based measurement: Examining the role of growth in students; outcomes. *Remedial and Special Education, 29*(1), 46–57.

Clarke, B., and Shinn, M. R. (2004). A preliminary investigation into the identification and development of early mathematics curriculum-based measurement. *School Psychology Review, 33*(2), 234–248.

Clemens, N. H., Hagan-Burke, S., Luo, W., Cerda, C., Blakely, A., Frosch, J., . . . and Jones, M. (2015). The predictive validity of a computer-adaptive assessment of kindergarten and first-grade reading skills. *School Psychology Review, 44*(1), 76–97.

Clemens, N. H., Keller-Margulis, M. A., Scholten, T., and Yoon, M. (2016). Screening assessment within a multi-tiered system of support: Current practices, advances, and next steps. In S. R. Jimmerson, M. K. Burns, and A. M. VanDerHeyden (Eds.), *Handbook of Response to Intervention* (pp. 187–213). New York: Springer.

Clemens, N. H., Shapiro, E. S., Wu, J., Taylor, A. B., and Caskie, G.L. (2014). Monitoring early first-grade reading progress: A comparison of two measures. *Journal of Learning Disabilities, 47*(3), 254–270.

Clemens, N. H., Smith, P. J., and Gamez, B. A. (2013, February). *Assessing Spelling in Kindergarten: Why and How-To.* Paper presented at the 2013 Convention of the National Association of School Psychologists, Seattle, WA.

Clemens, N. H., Soohoo, M., Wiley, C. P., Hsiao, Y., Estrella, I., Allee-Smith, P. J., and Yoon, M. (2016). Advancing stage 2 research on measures for monitoring kindergarten reading progress. *Journal of Learning Disabilities, 51*, 85–104.

Deno, S. L. (1985). Curriculum-based measurement: The emerging alternative. *Exceptional children, 52*(3), 219–232.

Deno, S. L. (2003). Developments in curriculum-based measurement. *The Journal of Special Education, 37*(3), 184–192.

Deno, S. L., and Mirkin, P. K. (1977). *Data-Based Program Modification: A Manual.* Reston: Council or Exceptional Children.

Deno, S. L., Mirkin, P. K., and Chiang, B. (1982). Identifying valid measures of reading. *Exceptional Children, 49*(1), 36–45.

Denton, C. A., Nimon, K., Mathes, P. G., Swanson, E. A., Kethley, C., Kurz, T. B., and Shih, M. (2010). Effectiveness of a supplemental early reading intervention scaled up in multiple schools. *Exceptional Children, 76*(4), 394–416.

Ehri, L. C. (2000). Learning to read and learning to spell: Two sides of a coin. *Topics in Language Disorders*, *20*(3), 19–36.

Ehri, L. C. (2005). Learning to read words: Theory, findings, and issues. *Scientific Studies of Reading*, *9*(2), 167–188.

Espin, C. A., Busch, T. W., Lembke, E. S., Hampton, D. D., Seo, K., and Zukowski, B. A. (2013). Curriculum-based measurement in science learning: Vocabulary-matching as an indicator of performance and progress. *Assessment for Effective Intervention*, *38*(4), 203–213. doi: 10.1177/1534508413489724.

Espin, C. A., Busch, T. W., Shin, J., and Kruschwitz, R. (2001). Curriculum-based measurement in the content areas: Validity of vocabulary-matching as an indicator of performance in social studies. *Learning Disabilities Research & Practice*, *16*(3), 142–151.

Espin, C. A., Deno, S. L., Maruyama, G., and Cohen, C. (1989, April). *The Basic Academic Skills Sample (BASS): An instrument for the screening and identification of children at risk for failure in regular education classrooms*. Paper presented at the annual meeting of the American Educational Research Association, San Francisco.

Espin, C. A., Shin, J., and Busch, T. W. (2005). Curriculum-based measurement in the content areas: Vocabulary matching as an indicator of progress in social studies learning. *Journal of Learning Disabilities*, *38*(4), 353–363.

FastBridge Learning (2016). *aReading*. Available: www.fastbridge.org/areading.

Fearrington, J. Y., Parker, P. D., Kidder-Ashley, P., Gagnon, S. G., McCane-Bowling, S., and Sorrell, C. A. (2014). Gender differences in written expression curriculum-based measurement in third-through eighth-grade students. *Psychology in The Schools*, *51*(1), 85–96.

Fletcher, J., Lyon, G., Fuchs, L., and Barnes, M. (2007). *Learning disabilities: From identification to intervention*. New York: Guilford Press.

Foegen, A., Jiban, C., and Deno, S. (2007). Progress monitoring measures in mathematics a review of the literature. *The Journal of Special Education*, *41*(2), 121–139.

Fuchs, L. S. (2004) The past, present, and future of curriculum-based measurement research. *School Psychology Review*, *33*(2), 188–192.

Fuchs, L. S., and Deno, S. L. (1994). Must instructionally useful performance assessment be based in the curriculum? *Exceptional Children*, *61*(1), 15–24.

Fuchs, L. S., Deno, S. L., and Mirkin, P. K. (1984). The effects of frequent curriculum-based measurement and evaluation on pedagogy, student achievement, and student awareness of learning. *American Educational Research Journal*, *21*(2), 449–460.

Fuchs, L. S., and Fuchs, D. (1986). Effects of systematic formative evaluation: A meta-analysis. *Exceptional Children*, *53*(3), 199–208.

Fuchs, L. S., and Fuchs, D. (1992). Identifying a measure for monitoring student reading progress. *School Psychology Review*, *21*, 45–58.

Fuchs, L. S., Fuchs, D., and Compton, D.L. (2004). Monitoring early reading development in first grade: Word identification fluency versus nonsense word fluency. *Exceptional Children*, *71*(1), 7–21.

Fuchs, L. S., Fuchs, D., and Hamlett, C. L. (1989). Effects of instrumental use of curriculum-based measurement to enhance instructional programs. *Remedial and Special Education*, *10*(2), 43–52.

Fuchs, L. S., Fuchs, D., Hamlett, C. L., and Allinder, R. M. (1991). The contribution of skills analysis to curriculum-based measurement in spelling. *Exceptional Children*, *57*(5), 443–452.

Fuchs, L. S., Fuchs, D., Hamlett, C. L., and Walz, L. (1993). Formative evaluation of academic progress: How much growth can we expect? *School Psychology Review*, *22*(1), 27–48.

Fuchs, L. S., Fuchs, D., Hosp, M. K., and Jenkins, J. R. (2001). Oral reading fluency as an indicator of reading competence: A theoretical, empirical, and historical analysis. *Scientific Studies of Reading*, *5*(3), 239–256.

Fuchs, L. S., Fuchs, D., and Maxwell, L. (1988). The validity of informal reading comprehension measures. *Remedial and Special Education*, *9*(2), 20–28. doi: 10.1177/074193258800900206.

Fuchs, L. S., Fuchs, D., and Zumeta, R. O. (2008). A curricular-sampling approach to progress monitoring: Mathematics concepts and applications. *Assessment for Effective Intervention*, *33*(4), 225–233.

Fuchs, L. S., Hamlett, C. L., and Fuchs, D. (1998). *Monitoring basic skills progress: Basic math concepts and applications*. Austin, TX: Pro-Ed.

Gersten, R., Compton, D., Connor, C. M., Dimino, J., Santoro, L., Linan-Thompson, S., and Tilly, W.D. (2008). *Assisting students struggling with reading: Response to Intervention and multi-tier intervention for reading in the primary grades. A practice guide*. (NCEE 2009–4045). Washington, DC: National Center for Education Evaluation and Regional Assistance, Institute of Education Sciences, U.S. Department of Education.

Goffreda, C. T., and DiPerna, J. C. (2010). An empirical review of psychometric evidence for the dynamic indicators of basic early literacy skills. *School Psychology Review, 39*(3), 463.

Graham, S., Harris, K. R., and Larsen, L. (2001). Prevention and intervention of writing difficulties for students with learning disabilities. *Learning Disabilities Research & Practice, 16*(2), 74–84.

Graney, S. B., Martinez, R. S., Missall, K. N., and Aricak, O. T. (2010). Universal screening of reading in late elementary school: R-CBM versus CBM maze. *Remedial And Special Education, 31*(5), 368–377.

Hosp, M. K., Hosp, J. L., and Howell, K. W. (2007). *The ABCs of CBM: A practical guide to curriculum-based measurement. Practical intervention in the schools series.* New York: Guilford Publications.

Jenkins, J. R., and Jewell, M. (1993). Examining the validity of two measures for formative teaching: Reading aloud and maze. *Exceptional Children, 59*, 421–432.

Jenkins, J., and Terjeson, K. J. (2011). Monitoring reading growth: Goal setting, measurement frequency, and methods of evaluation. *Learning Disabilities Research & Practice, 26*(1), 28–35.

Jitendra, A. K., Dupuis, D. N., and Zaslofsky, A. F. (2014). Curriculum-based measurement and standards-based mathematics: Monitoring the arithmetic word problem-solving performance of third-grade students at risk for mathematics difficulties. *Learning Disability Quarterly*, 0731948713516766.

Jitendra, A. K., Sczesniak, E., and Deatline-Buchman, A. (2005). An exploratory validation of curriculum-based mathematical word problem solving tasks as indicators of mathematics proficiency for third graders. *School Psychology Review, 34*, 358–371.

Lai, C., Alonzo, J., Tindal, G., and University of Oregon. (2013). easyCBM Reading Criterion Related Validity Evidence: Grades 2–5. Technical Report #1310. *Behavioral Research and Teaching.*

Leh, J. M., Jitendra, A. K., Caskie, G. L., and Griffin, C. C. (2007). An evaluation of curriculum-based measurement of mathematics word problem-solving measures for monitoring third-grade students' mathematics competence. *Assessment for Effective Intervention, 32*(2), 90–99. doi:10.1177/153450840703 20020601.

Lembke, E., and Foegen, A. (2009). Identifying early numeracy indicators for kindergarten and first-grade students. *Learning Disabilities Research & Practice, 24*(1), 12–20.

Malecki, C. K., and Jewell, J. (2003). Developmental, gender, and practical considerations in scoring curriculum-based measurement writing probes. *Psychology in the Schools, 40*(4), 379–390.

Malofeeva, E., Day, J., Saco, X., Young, L., and Ciancio, D. (2004). Construction and evaluation of a number sense test with head start children. *Journal of Educational Psychology, 96*(4), 648–659.

Marcotte, A. M., Clemens, N. H., Parker, C., and Whitcomb, S. A. (2016). Examining the classification accuracy of a vocabulary screening measure with preschool children. *Assessment for Effective Intervention*, 1534508416632236.

Marcotte, A. M., Parker, C., Furey, W., and Hands, J. L. (2013). An examination of the validity of the dynamic indicators of vocabulary skills (DIVS). *Journal of Psychoeducational Assessment*, 073428291349 8849.

Martinez, R. S., Missall, K. N., Graney, S. B., Aricak, O. T., and Clarke, B. (2009). Technical adequacy of early numeracy curriculum-based measurement in kindergarten. *Assessment for Effective Intervention, 34*(2), 116–125.

Masterson, J. J., and Apel, K. (2010). The spelling sensitivity score: Noting developmental changes in spelling knowledge. *Assessment for Effective Intervention, 36*(1), 35–45.

Mathes, P. G., Denton, C. A., Fletcher, J. M., Anthony, J. L., Francis, D. J., and Schatschneider, C. (2005). The effects of theoretically different instruction and student characteristics on the skills of struggling readers. *Reading Research Quarterly, 40*(2), 148–182.

McMaster, K., and Espin, C. (2007). Technical features of curriculum-based measurement in writing: A literature review. *Journal of Special Education, 41*(2), 68–84.

McMaster, K. L., Du, X., Parker, D. C., and Pinto, V. (2011). Using curriculum-based measurement for struggling beginning writers. *Teaching Exceptional Children, 44*(2), 26–34.

McMaster, K. L., Du, X., Yeo, S., Deno, S. L., Parker, D., and Ellis, T. (2011). Curriculum-based measures of beginning writing: Technical features of the slope. *Exceptional Children, 77*(2), 185–206.

McMaster, K. L., Parker, D., and Jung, P. (2012). Using curriculum-based measurement for beginning writers within a response to intervention framework. *Reading Psychology, 33*(1–2), 190–216.

Mirkin, P., Deno, S., Tindal, G., and Kuehnle, K. (1982). Frequency of measurement and data utilization as factors in standardized behavioral assessment of academic skill. *Journal of Behavioral Assessment, 4*(4), 361–370.

Mooney, P., McCarter, K., Schraven, J., and Callicoatte, S. (2013). Additional performance and progress validity findings targeting the content-focused vocabulary matching. *Council for Exceptional Children, 80*(1), 85–100.

National Center on Response to Intervention (2012). *Using academic progress monitoring for individualized instructional planning*. Available: www.intensiveintervention.org/sites/default/files/Academic_Progress_Monitoring-updated.pdf.

National Mathematics Advisory Panel (2008). *Foundations for success: The final report of the National Mathematics Advisory Panel*. Washington, DC: U.S. Department of Education.

Northwest Evaluation Association (2016). *Measures of Academic Progress*. Available: www.nwea.org/assessments/map.

Park, B. J., Irvin, P. S., Lai, C. F., Alonzo, J., and Tindal, G. (2012). *Analyzing the reliability of the easy CBM reading comprehension measures: Grade 5* (Technical Report No. 1204). Eugene, OR: Behavioral Research and Teaching, University of Oregon.

Ouellette, G. P., and Sénéchal, M. (2008). A window into early literacy: Exploring the cognitive and linguistic underpinnings of invented spelling. *Scientific Studies of Reading, 12*(2), 195–219.

Parker, C. (2000). Identifying technically adequate measures of vocabulary for young children at risk for reading disabilities. Unpublished doctoral dissertation, University of Oregon, Oregon.

Parker, D. C., McMaster, K. L., Medhanie, A., and Silberglitt, B. (2011). Modeling early writing growth with curriculum-based measures. *School Psychology Quarterly, 26*(4), 290–304.

Powell, S. R. (2007). *Open Equations* (assessment). Available from S. R. Powell, Box 228 Peabody, Nashville, TN, 37203.

Renaissance (2016). *STAR 360*. Available: www.renaissance.com/products/assessment/star-360.

Renaissance Learning. (2009). *With the right information, you can help your students shine like stars* (product brochure). Wisconsin Rapids, WI: Author.

Reschly, A. L., Busch, T. W., Betts, J., Deno, S. L., and Long, J. D. (2009). Curriculum-based measurement oral reading as an indicator of reading achievement: A meta-analysis of the correlational evidence. *Journal of School Psychology, 47*(6), 427–469.

Ritchey, K. D. (2008). The building blocks of writing: Learning to write letters and spell words. *Reading & Writing, 21*(1/2), 27–47. doi:10.1007/s11145-007-9063-0.

Ritchey, K. D., Coker, D. J., and McCraw, S. B. (2010). A comparison of metrics for scoring beginning spelling. *Assessment for Effective Intervention, 35*(2), 78–88.

Ritchey, K. D., and Speece, D. L. (2006). From letter names to word reading: The nascent role of sublexical fluency. *Contemporary Educational Psychology, 31*(3), 301–327.

Schatschneider, C., Wagner, R. K., and Crawford, E. C. (2008). The importance of measuring growth in response to intervention models: Testing a core assumption. *Learning and Individual Differences, 18*(3), 308–315.

Sénéchal, M., Ouellette, G., and Rodney, D. (2006). The misunderstood giant: On the predictive role of early vocabulary to future reading. *Handbook of Early Literacy Research, 2*, 173–182.

Shapiro, E. S. (1989). *Academic skills problems: Direct assessment and intervention*. New York: Guilford Press.

Shapiro, E. S., Dennis, M. S., and Fu, Q. (2015). Comparing computer adaptive and curriculum-based measures of math in progress monitoring. *School Psychology Quarterly, 30*(4), 470.

Shapiro, E. S., and Gebhardt, S. N. (2012). Comparing computer-adaptive and curriculum-based measurement methods of assessment. *School Psychology Review, 41*(3), 295.

Shin, J., Deno, S. L., and Espin, C. (2000). Technical adequacy of the maze task for curriculum-based measurement of reading growth. *The Journal of Special Education, 34*(3), 164–172.

Shinn, M. R. (Ed.) (1989). *Curriculum-based measurement: Assessing special children*. New York: Guilford Press.

Shinn, M. R., Good, R. H., Knutson, N., Tilly, W. D., and Collins, V. L. (1992). Curriculum-based measurement of oral reading fluency: A confirmatory analysis of its relation to reading. *School Psychology Review, 21*(3), 459–479.

Shinn, M. R., Good III, R. H., and Stein, S. (1989). Summarizing trend in student achievement: A comparison of methods. *School Psychology Review, 18*(3), 356–370.

Shinn, M. R., and Hubbard, D. D. (1992). Curriculum-based measurement and problem-solving assessment: Basic procedures and outcomes. *Focus on Exceptional Children, 24*(5), 1–20.

Speece, D. L., Mills, C., Ritchey, K. D., and Hillman, E. (2003). Initial evidence that letter fluency tasks are valid indicators of early reading skill. *The Journal of Special Education, 36*(4), 223–233.

Stage, S. A., Sheppard, J., Davidson, M. M., and Browning, M. M. (2001). Prediction of first-graders' growth in oral reading fluency using kindergarten letter fluency. *Journal of School Psychology, 39*(3), 225–237.

Stecker, P. M., Fuchs, L. S., and Fuchs, D. (2005). Using curriculum-based measurement to improve student achievement: Review of research. *Psychology in the Schools, 42*(8), 795–819.

Stecker, P. M., and Lembke, E. S. (2011). *Advanced Applications of CBM in Reading (K-6): Instructional Decision-Making Strategies Manual.* National Center on Student Progress Monitoring.

Strait, G. G., Smith, B. H., Pender, C., Malone, P. S., Roberts, J., and Hall, J. D. (2015). The reliability of randomly generated math curriculum-based measurements. *Assessment for Effective Intervention, 40*(4) 247–253.

Sturm, J. M., Cali, K., Nelson, N. W., and Staskowski, M. (2012). The Developmental Writing Scale: A new progress monitoring tool for beginning writers. *Topics in Language Disorders, 32*(4), 297–318.

Thurber, R. S., Shinn, M. R., and Smolkowski, K. (2002). What is measured in mathematics tests? Construct validity of curriculum-based mathematics measures. *School Psychology Review, 31*(4), 498–513.

Tolar, T. D., Barth, A. E., Fletcher, J. M., Francis, D. J., and Vaughn, S. (2014). Predicting reading outcomes with progress monitoring slopes among middle grade students. *Learning and Individual Differences, 30*, 46–57.

Wayman, M. M., Wallace, T., Wiley, H. I., Ticha, R., and Espin, C. A. (2007). Literature synthesis on curriculum-based measurement in reading. *The Journal of Special Education, 41*(2), 85–120. doi: 10.1177/00224669070410020401.

Wray, K. A., Alonzo, J., and Tindal, G. (2014). *Internal Consistency of the easyCBM Vocabulary Measures Grades 2–8* (No. 1406). Technical Report.

Ysseldyke, J., Shinn, M., Betts, J., and Clemens, N. H. (2016). *Psychometric and practical comparison of CBM and CAT assessments.* Symposium presented at the 2016 Convention of the National Association of School Psychologists, New Orleans, LA.

11

COMBINING READING COMPREHENSION INSTRUCTION WITH COGNITIVE TRAINING TO PROVIDE INTENSIVE INTERVENTION TO AT-RISK STUDENTS

Douglas Fuchs, Samuel Patton III, Lynn S. Fuchs, Jennifer Gilbert, Meagan Walsh, Nicole Lute, Loulee Yen Haga, Peng Peng, and Amy Elleman

This research was conducted by staff from the National Center on Accelerating the Academic Achievement of Students with Severe and Persistent Learning Disabilities, which is funded by Grant No. R324D130003 from the National Center on Special Education Research, Institute for Educational Sciences. We thank Wen Zhang Tracy, Nicole Davis, Emma Hendricks, and Wooliya Kim for their guidance concerning curriculum development, and we thank the administrators in the Metro-Nashville Public Schools and the classroom teachers of the children in our study for their interest and support.

In this paper, we describe the on-going development of a comprehensive reading comprehension program to be delivered by tutors in one-to-one sessions to third- and fourth-grade children at-risk for school failure. We are developing a comprehensive program because reading for understanding requires the use of multiple skills and strategies (e.g., Edmonds et al., 2009; Gajria, Jitendra, Sood, and Sacks, 2007; Gersten, Fuchs, Williams, and Baker, 2001). The program is comprehensive in two ways. First, it aims to teach a relatively large set of skills and strategies. Second, it integrates this teaching with cognitive training because many with poor comprehension also demonstrate weak cognitive abilities, such as working memory, that are strongly associated with understanding text (e.g., Cain, 2006). In the following, we characterize our reading comprehension program as intensive intervention, partly because of its relative comprehensiveness, and describe a recently completed randomized control trial of its effects. But first, we contextualize intensive intervention by discussing its relationship to Responsiveness to Intervention (RTI). We define *intensive*, assert that it is infrequently conducted in schools, and explain why this is a mistake.

RTI Purposes and Outcomes

Purposes

RTI (a.k.a. Multi-Tier System of Supports, or MTSS) first appeared in federal law in the 2004 reauthorization of the Individuals with Disabilities Education Act (IDEA). As defined in the statute, its purpose was twofold: to provide a more defensible method of disability identification and to strengthen general education's capacity to prevent or mitigate disabilities and the learning problems of children without disabilities (e.g., D. Fuchs and Fuchs, 2006). Regarding its second aim, RTI was regarded (a) as a means of providing help to at-risk children in a timely manner, and (b) as a necessary system of service delivery—with multiple tiers of increasingly intensive data-based intervention—that would increase general education's capacity to accommodate greater academic diversity and to simultaneously decrease its dependence on special education (cf. D. Fuchs, Fuchs, and Stecker, 2010).

Outcomes

Many school districts across the nation have implemented RTI for a decade or longer. Educators in these districts have worked diligently to make it work. Yet, large numbers of children with and without disabilities continue to perform very poorly. There are multiple sources of evidence of this poor performance (e.g., National Assessment Governing Board, 2015; www.nagb.org/newsroom/naep-releases/2015-reading-math-tuda.html). The federal government has recently expressed its concern in this regard. The Office of Special Education Programs (OSEP) in the U.S. Department of Education wrote in the Federal Register (Individuals with Disabilities Act, March 26, 2014):

> To date . . . the [Education] Department's primary focus of monitoring has been on States' compliance with substantive and procedural requirements. Unfortunately, we have not seen significant improvement in results for children with disabilities (e.g., performance on assessment, graduation rate, and early childhood outcomes. [W]e need to balance the focus of our accountability system on both ensuring compliance and improving results. [Thus, OSEP] is reconceptualizing its IDEA accountability system [by introducing Results Driven Accountability, or RDA].

The persistently poor academic achievement of many students with and without disabilities raises questions about the efficacy of RTI-as-educational-reform. In the past ten years or so, several states and school districts have conducted evaluations of RTI. The evaluations do not provide evidence that RTI strengthens academic achievement. For example, in the early 2000s, the Iowa State Department of Education conducted a study of 11 RTI schools and 11 demographically similar non-RTI schools in Heartland Area Educational Agency (Ikeda, Rahn-Blakeslee, and Allison, 2005). In each of the 22 study schools, and across nine consecutive years, Ikeda et al. obtained fourth grade reading and math scores of students without disabilities on state-mandated tests. Ikeda et al. reported, "On the majority of measures, RTI [schools] did not differ significantly from comparison schools" (p. 2). See Ikeda and Gustafson (2002) and Marston, Muyskens, Lau, and Canter (2003) for additional RTI evaluations with similar results.

Some believe that practitioners' admirable intent to use RTI to strengthen service delivery has been undercut by both its inherent complexity and practitioners' inaccurate implementation of its multiple components. In 1996–1997, Telzrow, McNamara, and Hollinger (2000) conducted a statewide evaluation in Ohio of Intervention Based Assessment (IBA), a team approach to pre-referral intervention and a forerunner of RTI. They wrote, "Ohio's [IBA problem-solving implementation] was frequently inconsistent and below desired levels of fidelity" (p. 457); and, "The [data] suggest that reliable implementation of problem solving approaches in schools remains elusive" (p. 458).

By contrast, when researchers have implemented key RTI components (such as Tier 2 intervention), they have typically done so with strong fidelity and have frequently obtained impressive results (cf. Al Otaiba, Allor, Werfel, and Clemens, 2016). We believe it is safe to assume that researchers tend to conduct RTI with greater accuracy and completeness than practitioners because their focus is likely to be more single-minded than that of practitioners whose professional responsibilities often take them in different directions at the same time. This presumed difference in accuracy of implementation no doubt contributes significantly to researchers' positive RTI-related results. But it would be a mistake to think that accuracy of implementation is the only, or most important, difference between researchers' and practitioners' use of RTI, and that it is the only explanation for researchers' more impressive efforts.

Treatment Intensity

Quantitative Differences

Researchers also tend to use RTI interventions of greater intensity (e.g., Wanzek and Vaughn, 2009). This usually means more sessions of greater duration for longer periods of time. It isn't unusual for researchers to report that their interventions were conducted four days per week for 20 weeks, with each session lasting 45 minutes. This sums to 60 hours of instruction, which is often delivered in groups of two to four students. Practitioner-delivered implementations often pale in comparison with respect to these numbers.

A case in point: We recently completed a study of a first-grade tutoring program, which we conducted in 15 schools. These schools offered tutoring programs of their own, both during and after school hours. A sizable minority of our study participants received this tutoring in addition to the tutoring we provided. Whereas this suggested multiple treatment effects and a serious confounding of our evaluation effort, teachers in these schools reported that the additional tutoring was delivered inconsistently and infrequently. From mid-October when our tutoring began to late-May when our post-treatment testing was completed, teachers estimated that children in the two versions of our treatment program and control students were tutored an average of 5.07 hours, 6.36 hours, and 10.87 hours, respectively, by school and non-school personnel who weren't part of our project. Although this information came from teachers in only 15 schools, we suspect it is representative of many more schools (cf. D. Fuchs et al., 2016).

Qualitative Differences

We have been discussing intensity of intervention in terms of quantity: More instructional sessions with more time per session across more weeks. But intensity of intervention may have an important, albeit infrequently recognized, quality dimension, too. We make this point by discussing intervention in Tiers 2 and 3 in RTI frameworks.

An unheralded achievement in the last decade has been the development of many Tier 2 instructional programs that have accelerated the reading and math performances of many at-risk students. Most of these programs are based on standard treatment protocols (D. Fuchs, Mock, Morgan, and Young, 2003), which, when conducted by researchers, are delivered to small groups of students who meet frequently with tutors who are rigorously trained to implement explicit, systematic instruction. Despite their overall, or general, effectiveness, none of these programs have been shown to work for all participants (e.g., Gilbert et al., 2013; O'Connor and Fuchs, 2013; Vaughn et al., 2010). Put another way, efficacy studies of these Tier 2 programs have consistently revealed sizable subgroups of children who did not benefit from them. These children tend to have very serious learning problems. Recognition grows that such children do not need more of the same. Helping these students may require a qualitative, not quantitative, change in instruction. One uniquely different approach is data-based individualization (DBI; e.g., Deno and Mirkin, 1977).

DBI is a highly specialized, prototypical Tier 3 intervention. It doesn't come with scripts printed in a manual. Rather, it denotes individualized instruction: The DBI instructor must be capable of using formative assessments to judge the efficacy of an intervention—whether and when it needs to be modified or exchanged for a different one to continue to boost student performance. Moreover, the instructor must be a storehouse of instructional approaches; a master of mixing and matching curricula; a motivator who can establish and maintain student engagement as she leads a child through an iterative, often weeks-long, search for how to accelerate the student's academic progress (e.g., Lemons, Kearns, and Davidson, 2014; Powell and Stecker, 2014).

Beyond a need for deep knowledge in assessment, instruction, and curricula, successful DBI instructors are intelligent, knowledgeable, experienced, and tenacious, and possess a high tolerance for ambiguity (see D. Fuchs, Fuchs, and Vaughn, 2014). There aren't many such teachers in today's schools, in good measure because colleges and universities may no longer see themselves in the business of preparing such professionals.

Another approach to intensive intervention, also qualitatively different from conventional Tier 2 intervention, is the use of instructional protocols that are much more comprehensive and complex than typical standard protocols. We are currently developing two versions of a complex, comprehensive program with which to strengthen the reading comprehension of poor readers in the intermediate grades. The first version of the program aims to teach multiple skills and strategies on which good reading comprehension depends. A second version combines the teaching of many skills and strategies with the training of cognitive abilities, like working memory, which presumably support the use of these skills and strategies. We do not regard our program as in competition with DBI. Rather, we see it as a potentially useful Tier 3 intervention alternative. More about this later.

Developing a Comprehensive Reading Comprehension Program

Teaching children to read for understanding is a pivotal goal of early education. This is because reading *without* understanding often causes frustration and an eventual avoidance of reading, which in turn reduces opportunities to become a more skilled reader (e.g., Morgan and Fuchs, 2007; Stanovich, 1986). Whereas many students require little from teachers to develop useful comprehension skills, others will develop these skills only if they participate in intensive instruction. Following is discussion of a study in which we investigated whether combining reading comprehension instruction and cognitive training would improve understanding among at-risk students when compared to similar children participating in the same comprehension instruction without the cognitive training; in cognitive training without the comprehension instruction; or in a control group. In the following, we describe our sample as demonstrating specific reading comprehension deficits (S-RCD). We then discuss these deficits, the rationale for our three treatment conditions, and the study's design.

Three Explanations of S-RCD

According to the Simple View of Reading, reading comprehension partly depends on word recognition, especially in the early grades (e.g., Juel, Griffith, and Gough, 1986). For a majority of poor readers, reading problems are caused by poor word recognition skills (e.g., Hulme and Snowling, 2009). However, there are also children who read words and sentences accurately and fluently at an appropriate level for their age, but who fail to understand much of what they read. These children are sometimes identified as children with S-RCD. An estimated 10–15% of primary school-aged children have S-RCD (Lerväg and Aukrust, 2010; Nation and Snowling, 1997; Stothard and Hulme, 1992; Yuill and Oakhill, 1991). A growing literature suggests that it is caused by deficits in comprehension skills and strategies (e.g., vocabulary and inference-making; Oakhill, Berenhaus, and Cain, 2015) and cognitive abilities (e.g., working memory; Cain, 2006; De Beni and Palladino, 2000; Yuill, Oakhill, and Parkin, 1989). There are at least three ways of thinking about these deficits as causes of S-RCD.

Hypothesis 1

A first hypothesis is that weak comprehension skills and strategies are necessary and sufficient explanations of reading comprehension problems (e.g., Hulme and Snowling, 2011). Comprehension *skills* often include vocabulary development because it is a strong predictor of reading comprehension (e.g., Carrol, 1993; de Jong and van der Leij, 2002; Roth, Speece, and Cooper, 2002), and because children with S-RCD often demonstrate deficits in this area (e.g., Catts, Adolf, and Ellis-Weismer, 2006; Nation, Cocksey, Taylor, and Bishop, 2010). Comprehension *strategies* refer to such procedures or routines as self-monitoring for understanding, recognizing text features, generating and answering questions, and summarizing text. Use of these and other strategies often distinguishes students with good comprehension from those with poor comprehension (National Reading Panel, 2000).

Hypothesis 2

A second hypothesis is that inadequate cognitive abilities are necessary and sufficient causes of reading comprehension problems (e.g., Cain, 2010). Working memory (WM) is considered especially important in this regard. This is because children are believed to rely on WM to remember previously learned information while simultaneously integrating incoming information as they progress through a passage (e.g., Carretti, Borella, Cornoldi, and De Beni, 2009; Cain, Oakhill, and Bryant, 2004). If true, cognitive training that strengthens WM can also strengthen reading comprehension.

Indeed, recent evidence is consistent with this belief. Peng and Fuchs (2015) conducted a modest study of whether the training of verbal WM improves this cognitive process and listening comprehension among first-grade children with both decoding and comprehension deficits. The first graders were randomly assigned to three groups: WM training with a rehearsal strategy, WM training without a rehearsal strategy, and controls. After a short but intensive training period, both training groups improved performance on trained verbal WM tasks and on passage listening comprehension relative to controls. Although Peng and Fuchs (2015) did not directly measure reading comprehension, and focused on children with both decoding and comprehension deficits, their findings suggest that training verbal WM may improve comprehension among children with S-RCD.

Hypothesis 3

A third hypothesis is that neither deficits in comprehension skills/strategies nor weak cognitive abilities are sufficient to explain S-RCD children's performance. According to this view, skills, strategies, and cognitive abilities all contribute to comprehension problems. A corollary of this perspective is that comprehension instruction and cognitive ability training should both be important components in efforts to address comprehension problems (e.g., Eason and Cutting, 2009; Peng and Fuchs, 2015).

In support of this hypothesis, we invoke cognitive load theory and long-term memory theory. According to both, children use WM to learn, but learning is most efficient when long-term memory is also involved in the process (e.g., Ericsson and Kintsch, 1995; Sweller, van Merrienboer, and Paas, 1998). More specifically, to comprehend written text, children use WM to hold information from the text. But they must also retrieve from long-term memory relevant information *not* in the passage. By integrating information from WM and long-term memory, children can develop understanding. Long-term memory retrieval requires a good vocabulary and background knowledge, as well as comprehension strategies to help children decide when and what information to retrieve. Based on this view, comprehension instruction can strengthen vocabulary, background knowledge, and strategies to access long-term memory; working memory training can strengthen the processing of information in text. In short, combining comprehension instruction and WM training may create additive—even perhaps synergistic—effects on reading comprehension for children with S-RCD. To date, there has been an absence of randomized control trials examining the efficacy of this combined approach to address reading comprehension in children with S-RCD.

Study Aim

In this study, we randomly assigned third and fourth grade children with S-RCD to four study groups: reading comprehension instruction (RC), WM training (WM), combined reading comprehension and WM training (RC[WM]), and controls. Our hypotheses were that, first, in comparison to controls, the three treatment conditions would strengthen children's reading comprehension performance and, second, that these treatment conditions would be differentially effective such that RC[WM] would show greater improvement on reading comprehension than either the RC or the WM group.

Methods

Participants

Selection of children and their assignment to study conditions. In the fall of the 2014–2015 school year, third and fourth grade teachers from 11 schools in a large urban public school district in the Southeastern United States were asked to nominate students for possible participation in our study. Specifically, we were interested in children with adequate word reading but poor reading comprehension, because the intent of our intervention was to teach comprehension, not word reading. We asked the teachers *not* to nominate students with disruptive behavior, poor attendance, or limited English proficiency. Limited English proficiency was defined as scores below Advanced Proficiency on the district's annual language assessment.

We obtained written consents from the parents of 309 of the 394 nominated students (78%). We screened these 309 students on the Phonemic Decoding and Sight Word subtests of the *Test of Word Reading Efficiency, Second Edition* (TOWRE; Torgesen, Wagner, and Rashotte, 1999); Understanding Spoken Paragraphs subtest of the *Clinical Evaluation of Language Fundamentals, 4th edition* (CELF; Semel, Wiig, and Secord 2003); and the Vocabulary and Matrix Reasoning subtests of the *Wechsler Abbreviated Scales of Intelligence* (WASI; Wechsler, 2011). For study inclusion, students had to achieve scores above the 32nd percentile at third grade or 25th percentile at fourth grade on the Sight Word Efficiency subtest. We used different percentiles at the two grades because there was an inadequate number of students with word reading scores at or above the 30th percentile in fourth grade. In addition to this word-reading criterion, students were required to score at or below the 50th percentile on the CELF, and to achieve T-scores on the Matrix Reasoning or Vocabulary subtests of the WASI that were greater than or equal to 37. The word reading criterion eliminated 75 students; the oral comprehension criterion eliminated another 105. Nine more students did not meet the WASI cut-offs. In combination, these criteria reduced our sample to 120 children— children with adequate word reading and relatively poor oral comprehension, who were not intellectually disabled.

An equal number of the 120 students was randomly assigned to four study conditions: reading comprehension alone (RC), RC with an embedded WM component (RC[WM]), WM training alone (WM), and controls. During implementation of the study, four students moved, reducing our sample to 116 (3% attrition).

Demographics and pretreatment reading performance. These 116 children were racially, ethnically, and socioeconomically diverse. The demographics of the sample, organized by grade and treatment condition, are displayed in Table 11.1. There were no statistically significant differences by study condition on these variables.

The sample's pretreatment performance on standardized measures of word reading was (by design and in accord with expectations) in the average-to-below-average range. The mean percentile score for the sample was 41.53 (*SD* = 20.18) on TOWRE Sight Word Efficiency. By contrast, the mean percentile score on the CELF was 21.11 (*SD* = 14.53). The sample's averaged percentile score was 32.87 on the Passage Comprehension subtest of the *Woodcock Johnson III* (WJ III; Woodcock, McGrew, and Mather, 2001), 31.82 on the Reading Comprehension Test of the *Gates–MacGinite–4* (Gates; MacGinite, MacGinite, Maria, Dreyer, and Hughes, 2000), and 31.18 on the Reading Comprehension subtest of the *Wechsler Individual Achievement Test, 3rd edition* (WIAT; Wechsler, 2009). There were no statistically significant differences between study groups on the screening or pretreatment tests. Table 11.1 displays pretreatment scores by grade and study condition.

Measures

Reading comprehension. To generate a factor score for reading comprehension, three (just mentioned) measures were administered: WJ III Passage Comprehension (Woodcock et al., 2001); WIAT Reading Comprehension (Wechsler, 2009); and Gates (MacGinite et al., 2000). On the WJ III, students read passages silently and identify missing words. Testing is discontinued after six consecutive errors. On the WIAT, students read passages (aloud or silently) that are

Table 11.1 Demographic Variables and Screening and Pretreatment Scores by Grade and Condition

Variable	RC Grade 3 #	RC Grade 3 %	RC Grade 4 #	RC Grade 4 %	RC/WM Grade 3 #	RC/WM Grade 3 %	RC/WM Grade 4 #	RC/WM Grade 4 %	WM Grade 3 #	WM Grade 3 %	WM Grade 4 #	WM Grade 4 %	Control Grade 3 #	Control Grade 3 %	Control Grade 4 #	Control Grade 4 %
Demographics																
Free/Reduced Lunch	17	89.5	5	55.6	20	90.9	6	75.0	16	79.2	4	57.1	16	76.2	6	66.7
Not Free/Reduced Lunch	2	10.5	4	44.4	2	9.1	2	25.0	5	23.8	3	42.9	5	23.8	2	22.2
Race																
Black/Afican American	6	31.6	4	44.4	5	22.7	4	50.0	4	19.1	1	14.3	5	23.8	4	44.4
Caucasian	1	5.3	3	33.3	4	18.2	1	12.5	2	9.5	2	28.6	4	19.1	4	44.4
Hispanic	7	36.8	1	11.1	8	36.4	1	12.5	7	33.3	1	14.3	2	9.5	0	0.0
Other (including missing)	5	26.3	1	11.1	5	22.7	2	25.0	8	38.1	3	42.9	10	47.6	1	11.1
Sex																
Female	9	47.4	4	44.4	13	59.1	3	37.5	5	23.8	2	28.6	8	38.1	2	22.2
Male	9	47.4	5	55.6	7	31.8	4	50.0	14	66.7	4	57.1	8	38.1	6	66.7
Missing	1	5.3	0	0.0	2	9.1	1	12.5	2	9.5	1	14.3	5	23.8	1	11.1
	M	SD	M	SD	M	SD	M	SD	M	SD	M	SD	M	SD	M	SD
Screening Measures																
CELF-4 USP Percentile	17.0	9.6	25.3	18.8	19.7	12.4	22.6	21.1	18.2	10.9	21.6	10.9	25.7	16.3	23.6	22.0
TOWRE-2 SWE Percentile	41.8	18.0	34.0	18.2	46.2	18.7	26.6	12.7	49.1	21.6	26.4	24.2	45.2	20.5	35.9	17.5
WASI2-MR T	44.1	7.6	47.4	44.9	44.0	7.5	46.3	5.3	42.4	7.5	39.0	11.0	42.6	7.9	45.3	45.0
WASI2-V T	44.2	5.1	6.2	8.9	46.3	7.5	43.6	8.8	47.0	8.8	42.9	7.0	42.8	7.2	7.7	6.6
Pre-Treatment Measures																
Gates %ile	35.2	11.5	43.2	15.0	38.1	10.5	41.0	12.9	35.2	11.5	41.3	16.7	40.9	8.7	38.5	13.1
WJ-PC SS	91.0	6.5	96.9	7.2	91.5	8.4	90.9	6.4	91.0	6.5	92.0	6.8	93.7	6.5	95.2	4.5
WIAT SS	91.9	5.3	93.7	6.3	92.6	6.2	91.0	5.5	91.9	5.3	87.4	7.6	94.0	6.1	94.1	6.8
WMTB LR RS	8.2	2.7	12.7	1.9	9.8	3.1	10.0	3.7	9.0	3.0	11.9	3.6	8.9	3.5	10.4	4.7
WMTB BDR RS	10.7	4.4	9.1	4.6	11.0	3.8	12.5	1.9	10.0	2.7	8.9	5.4	10.3	3.0	13.6	3.8

Note: CELF Listening Comprehension is Clinical Evaluation of Language Fundamentals-4 (Semel, Wiig, and Secord, 2003) – Understanding Spoken Paragraphs. TOWRE Sight Word Efficiency is Test of Word Reading Efficiency–2 (Torgesen, Wagner, and Rashotte, 2012) Sight Word Efficiency. WASI 2 is Wechsler Abbreviated Scale of Intelligence II (Wechsler, 2011) Matrix Reasoning and Vocabulary. Gates is Gates MacGinitie Reading Tests (MacGinitie, MacGinitie, Maria, and Dreyer, 2000). WJ-PC is Woodcock Johnson III Tests of Achievement (Woodcock, McGrew, and Mather, 2001) Passage Comprehension. WIAT is Wechsler Individual Achievement Test (3rd ed.) (Wechsler, 2009) Reading Comprehension. WMTB is Working Memory Test Battery for Children (Pickering & Gathercole, 2001) Listening Recall and Backward Digit Recall.

grouped by grade level, range in difficulty, and represent a variety of genres. Testers then read questions to the students, who are permitted access to the just-read texts while answering. Students read passages and answer questions at their assigned grade level, unless they fail to meet a minimal threshold score on the first passage. If this threshold is not attained, the tester administers passages at the preceding grade level. Our third of three reading comprehension measures was the Gates. It is a 35-minute, paper and pencil, multiple-choice test that is administered in small groups. Students read short passages and answer questions about them.

Working memory span. WM span was assessed with two measures: Listening Recall and Backward Digit Recall subtests of the *Working Memory Test Battery for Children* (WMTB; Pickering and Gathercole, 2001). For Listening Recall, the child listens to a series of short sentences, judges the veracity of each, responds with a yes or no, and then recalls the final word of each sentence in the sequence, from first to last. There are six trials at each set size (one to six sentences per set). The score is the number of trials recalled correctly. We modified the administration of this subtest by lowering the floor; that is, we changed its discontinue rule. Testing was discontinued when the child incorrectly answered four items in a set, rather than the standard three items. In addition, contrary to directions in the manual, we gave feedback to the children on the first three test items. Backward Digit Recall asks the child to recall a set of numbers in backwards order. Again, there are six trials in each set size. The score is the number of trials recalled correctly. We modified the standard administration of this subtest, too, by discontinuing it when a child incorrectly answered four items. We provided feedback if the student gave the numbers in forward order instead of backwards order.

IQ. The two-subtest form of the abbreviated WASI (Wechsler, 2011) consists of *Vocabulary*, which requires students to identify pictures and define words and *Matrix Reasoning*, for which students select one of five options that best completes a visual pattern.

Word reading. The Sight Word Efficiency test of the TOWRE (Torgesen et al., 1999) is time-limited (45 seconds) and requires students to read as many sight words as possible from a list of words that increases in difficulty.

Oral comprehension. The first of two measures of oral comprehension was the Understanding Spoken Paragraphs subtest of the CELF (Semel et al., 2003). The second was the Oral Comprehension subtest of the WJ III (Woodcock et al., 2001). On the CELF, the tester reads a paragraph from a story and asks five questions that collectively assess literal and inferential comprehension. On the WJ III, the tester reads a series of sentences. Students supply a one-word answer to complete them. Testing is discontinued after six incorrect answers.

Treatment Conditions

All students in RC, RC[WM], and WM conditions participated in 42 tutoring sessions (three times per week for 14 weeks). They and their tutors worked one-to-one for 25 minutes in each of the 42 sessions, which totaled 17.5 instructional hours. Tutors used scripted lessons to promote treatment fidelity. They were required to become familiar with the scripts but were told not to read from them. Experience indicates that reading from scripts to children works against their active engagement. Before each session, tutors expressed their expectations for student behavior. They also used a point system to encourage careful listening, hard work, and respectful behavior.

Students advanced through the lessons at their own pace. As a result, some covered more content than others. The median number of lessons completed by students across the three treatment conditions was 19 (range: 15 to 22 lessons). On average, one lesson required two sessions to complete. There was not a statistically significant difference in lesson coverage between the RC and RC[WM] conditions.

We used social studies and biography texts that were selected from three content areas: animals, ancient Egypt, and civil rights. Social studies and biography texts were selected because they typically adhere to a narrative structure, with which incoming third grade students would be familiar. The texts were adapted or created specifically for the project. Cohmetrix and Lexile scores were calculated for each and were used to order the texts so that their level of difficulty increased gradually.

Reading comprehension (RC). Participants received direct instruction in evidence-based strategies that were meant to strengthen comprehension of informational text. Emphasis was placed on increasing reading fluency, identifying key facts and main ideas, and drawing accurate inferences. Children in both RC and RC[WM] conditions were taught to use these and other comprehension strategies before, during, and after reading texts. In early lessons, tutors prompted the use of the strategies; in later lessons, children were encouraged to apply them independently.

Tutoring sessions always began with a review of the lesson's purpose. Also, before reading the day's text, tutors directed students through several activities meant to 'prime' their understanding. They were asked to identify the author's purpose. They predicted what they would likely learn from the text by combining author's purpose with their scan of text features. They were encouraged to connect background knowledge to text content. And finally, they and their tutors discussed unfamiliar words. They then read aloud and, as they read, tutors circled key words and phrases. The students then used these key words during their retell of what they read; in their identification of the main idea; and during reciprocal questioning (see below). Students were also taught to decide if an answer to a question was "in" or "out" of the text. They were reminded that answers in the text were associated with factual questions, or text-based inference questions. Answers out of text were connected to elaborative inference questions. These activities are described below.

Students identified the *author's purpose* for each text by using context clues (e.g., title) to determine if it was biographical or descriptive in nature. Then they skimmed the text and used a Text Feature Checklist to discuss key informational *text features*. Examples of common text features included title, section headings, and bolded and italicized print. Students practiced identifying the author's purpose and text features to predict what they would learn.

The tutor identified and defined *vocabulary* words likely to be unfamiliar. The tutors gave concise definitions, using student-friendly language, high-frequency words, and examples.

To encourage *fluency-building*, students were presented with summary paragraphs from previously read text. The tutors first read these paragraphs to the students to model fluent reading. Then, students and tutors read the same passage together. Finally, the students read the passage alone with encouragement to read quickly, carefully, and with expression. Tutors timed student's reading while correcting reading errors. If an error was made, the tutor pointed to the word in the text and said, "This word is _____. What's the word?" Points were awarded for improvements in speed, accuracy, and prosody.

Reciprocal questioning was conducted following the reading of each paragraph to check for student understanding. During earlier sessions, tutors asked questions and students answered. The questions were meant to focus the students' attention on important content to assist with main idea creation. In later sessions, students guessed the tutors' questions and produced their own questions based on the text.

Tutors and students followed a 'paragraph shrinking' strategy to identify the *main idea* of a passage. They were taught that a main idea statement is brief and expresses only the most important idea in a paragraph; it does not include supporting details. They learned a three-step process to make main idea statements: (a) name the most important who or what; (b) tell the most important thing about who or what; and (c) say the main idea in as few words as possible.

Students were given strategies to answer three types of comprehension questions: *factual questions, text-based inference questions*, and *elaborative inference questions*. Students were told that answers to factual questions and text-based inference questions are stated explicitly in the text. They were taught a Key Word strategy to answer them. The Key Word strategy had four steps: identify the key word in the question; find it in the text; read one to two sentences before and after it; and answer the question. Because (by definition) answers to elaborative inference questions are based on information beyond or outside of the text, students were taught an "In or Out" strategy. When faced with an elaborative inference question, they were taught to find the most important word or phrase in such a question and to activate relevant background knowledge by 'brainstorming' about what they already knew about it.

Reading comprehension with embedded working memory (RC[WM]). Students in the RC[WM] condition had the same RC instruction, but with two exceptions. They participated in *main idea complex span* and *cloze recall* activities. The purpose of main idea complex span and cloze recall was to strengthen WM and reading comprehension simultaneously. The two activities required students to process text and complete tasks while storing information in their WM for later use. Although these activities were designed to mimic complex span tasks typically used in "domain general" WM training, they had the additional purpose of highlighting important information in the text.

For main idea complex span, students read several paragraphs in a lesson, created a main idea statement for each, and recalled these statements in correct sequence from earliest to most recent. If they failed to do so, the tutor presented the main idea statements in correct order and asked the student to try again. Students were asked to recall the main idea statements from passages read in the current session, even if they had begun reading the text in a previous one. The tutor awarded points for correct recall and effort.

Once each session, students participated in the second activity distinguishing the RC[WM] condition—cloze recall. Students re-read a paragraph from the text with five to seven semantically or grammatically important words removed. Beside each of the five to seven blanks caused by the removal of these words were two word options. As the children read, they chose one of the two words to go in the blank. After reading the paragraph, the tutors removed the text and the students were asked to recall in order the words they selected. As with main idea complex span, the tutor presented the correct words in proper sequence when the student could not, and then gave the student another opportunity to do so. Points were awarded for correct recall and effort.

Working memory (WM). Domain general WM sessions were different from RC and RC[WM] sessions. Students were not taught explicit reading strategies. They did not read expository texts. Instead they completed activities addressing three dimensions of WM believed to be closely associated with reading comprehension: complex span, updating, and inhibition. During each session, students completed 15 minutes of complex span activities and 5 minutes of updating. The remaining 5 minutes was spent on inhibition activities.

During *complex span* activities students first remember a word or number while attempting a distractor task; then a different word or number when doing a second distractor task. Then they are asked to recall the words or numbers in order. An adaptive rule was used to further challenge their WM. If they correctly recalled all items in a trial, the next trial would include one more item to recall. If students were unable to recall the words or numbers in order, they were given another chance. If they were still unsuccessful, the next trial would have one less item. Four kinds of complex span activities were used: listening span, reading span, calculation span, and operation span.

To train students in *updating*, two versions of "N-back" activities were used: 2-back and 3-back. Students were presented with a stack of cards, arranged in a predetermined sequence. They were asked to tell whether the face card was the same card as presented two (or three) cards before. Depictions on the cards varied across sessions. Sometimes they showed colors; other times shapes or numbers. In later tutoring sessions, students had to judge if a word on a card was in the same category as the word on a card two (or three) back. Students completed three one-minute trials per session. After each session, tutors emphasized accuracy over speed when awarding points. Students were encouraged to make fewer errors during each trial.

In *inhibition* activities, students had to inhibit a presumed first response. These activities were adapted from those developed by Stroop (1935). At first, students were shown words printed in various colors. They were asked to name the *color* of the word, rather than to read the word. In a second activity, students named the number of digits on a card instead of reading the number. A third activity required students to switch between naming the number of digits and the *color* of a word. The final and most challenging activity asked students to alternate between reading a word and naming the color of the word.

Procedures for Testing, Tutoring, and Determining Implementation Fidelity

Research assistants (RAs) were trained to administer measures during four two-hour training sessions. Before testing students, the RAs had to demonstrate fidelity greater than 95% on administering and scoring tests. Their administration and scoring accuracy was determined by a project coordinator as she acted as a student in a mock testing situation. The project coordinator simultaneously used a detailed checklist to record the RAs' performance. Prior to post-testing, the RAs participated in a four-hour refresher session to review administration and scoring procedures. The RAs never tested the children they tutored and were blind during testing to the children's study condition.

In an additional four-hour training session, the RAs learned to use the scripted tutoring lessons and were coached more generally on how to tutor effectively. Prior to their first session with children, they had to show 90% or greater procedural fidelity for all three treatment conditions (RC, RC[WM], and WM). They did this while tutoring a project coordinator who was acting as a student in a mock session and who was simultaneously recording the tutors' performance on a checklist. During the 14-week treatment, the RAs attended weekly staff meetings where they were encouraged to ask questions about treatment implementation and related issues.

The RAs were observed three times—one time during implementation of each of three treatment conditions—by a project coordinator using a procedural checklist. Averaged RA fidelity across treatment conditions was 93% at Time 1, 96% at Time 2, and 96% at Time 3. In addition to these "live" observations, the RAs recorded all of their sessions on audiotape. For each RA, 20% of these recorded sessions were analyzed for procedural fidelity by someone other than the RA conducting the tutoring. Averaged fidelity was 91%, 93%, and 93% for RC, RC[WM], and WM conditions, respectively. To assess inter-observer agreement (IOA), another RA listened to the same sessions. IOA was 82% for RC; 82% RC[WM]; and 78% for WM.

Data Collection and Data Analysis

Data collection. To avoid familiarity effects, participants were tested by unfamiliar RAs at both pre- and post-testing (e.g., D. Fuchs and Fuchs, 1986). Students were assessed on screening measures in late August through mid-September, and pre-treatment testing took place from early September to mid-October. Post-treatment testing occurred in March. All testing occurred in school classrooms, hallways or libraries. Each session lasted about 45 minutes. Scripted protocols were used to ensure tests were administered consistently. All testing sessions were audiotaped. Completed assessment protocols were double-scored. Scoring differences were resolved by a third party. The data were double-entered and discrepancies were resolved to ensure accuracy.

Data analysis. The research question directing our analysis was whether any of the treatment conditions produced superior scores in reading comprehension or WM compared to controls. We hypothesized that the three treatment groups would demonstrate improvements in reading comprehension to various degrees, with students in the RC[WM] condition outperforming the other conditions. Data analysis proceeded in four steps. The first step was to generate domain-specific factor scores, pre- and post-treatment Reading Comprehension and pre- and post-treatment WM. Reading Comprehension scores were regression-based factor scores resulting from the following three measures: Gates normal curve equivalent score (MacGinitie et al., 2000); WIAT standard score (Wechsler, 2009); and WJ III standard score (Woodcock et al., 2001). WM scores were regression-based factor scores based on raw scores from the Listening Recall and Backward Digit Recall subtests of the WMTB (Pickering and Gathercole, 2001).

Second, we ran unconditional multilevel models, separately by outcome and grade, to describe the proportion of variance associated with each level of clustering: school, classroom, and student/error. The proportion of variance attributable to between-school differences in Reading Comprehension was .01 in grade 3 and 0.14 in grade 4 whereas the proportion attributable to between-classroom differences was .09 in grade 3 and .00 in Grade 4. For WM, none of the variance in either grade was attributable to between-school or between-classroom differences. Nonetheless, classroom and school random effects were retained in all models for consistency. The third step in our analysis was to estimate conditional multilevel models by including three dummy variables (leaving control as the comparison condition) along with the pre-treatment score of the relevant post-treatment outcome. Models were estimated separately by grade and outcome. The generic form of the final equation was:

$$\text{Posttreatment score}_{ijk} = \gamma_{00} + \gamma_{01} * \text{Pretreatment score}_{ijk} + \gamma_{02} * D\_WM_{ijk} +$$
$$\gamma_{03} * D\_RC_{ijk} + \gamma_{04} * D\_WMRC_{ijk} + u_{0k} +$$
$$r_{0jk} + e_{ijk} \tag{1}$$

All models were estimated using the mixed command in Stata 14.1. Following each model run, residuals were checked for normality and homoscedasticity. Assumptions were upheld in all models. Hedges *g* effect sizes (*ESs*) were calculated from model fixed effects according to the formula provided in What Works Clearinghouse Procedures and Standards Handbook (U.S. Department of Education, 2013), which includes a correction for small-sample sizes. Results are discussed first in terms of reading comprehension; then, WM.

Table 11.2 Multilevel Model Results for Posttreatment Reading Comprehension by Grade

	Grade 3 (n = 83)				Grade 4 (n = 33)			
	Estimate	SE	t	p	Estimate	SE	t	p
Fixed Effect								
Intercept, γ_{00}	−0.30	0.15	−2.04	.042	0.01	0.26	0.03	.975
Pre-treatment Reading Comprehension, γ_{01}	0.66	0.08	8.66	<.001	0.80	0.13	6.21	<.001
D_WM, γ_{02}	0.05	0.20	0.24	.807	0.37	0.36	1.01	.310
D_RC, γ_{03}	0.29	0.21	1.35	.177	0.44	0.33	1.31 ·	.189
D_RCWM, γ_{04}	0.33	0.20	1.62	.105	0.47	0.35	1.35	.178
Random Effect								
School (τ_u)	0.00				0.03			
Classroom (τ_u)	0.02				0.00			
Student/Error (σ^2)	0.42				0.49			

Note: Reading Comprehension Factor is based on Gates-MacGinitie-Reading Comprehension normal curve equivalent score, Wechsler Individual Achievement Test-Reading Comprehension standard score, and Woodcock-Johnson III-Passage Comprehension standard score. D_WM = dummy variable comparing working memory training to control. D_RC = dummy variable comparing reading comprehension training to control. D_RCWM = dummy variable comparing working memory embedded in reading comprehension training to control.

Results

Results for the reading comprehension models are provided in Table 11.2. Controlling for pretreatment reading comprehension, as well as classroom and school effects, no statistically significant differences were detected between any of the treatment conditions and control on posttreatment reading comprehension. This was true in both grades three and four. Our relatively small samples and low statistical power no doubt played a role in these outcomes. Nevertheless, moderate *ESs* were detected (see Figure 11.1). In grade three, the two treatment conditions that included reading comprehension instruction (RC and RC[WM]) had larger ESs than controls, *ESs* = 0.30 and 0.40, respectively. In grade four, all three treatment conditions had greater ESs than controls: *ES* = 0.33 for WM, *ES* = 0.40 for RC, and *ES* = 0.45 for RC[WM].

Findings for the WM models are listed in Table 11.3. As with the reading comprehension models, no statistically significant differences were obtained between treatments and controls on the WM outcome, after accounting for pretreatment WM and clustering effects. These analyses were also affected by low power. *ESs* in Figure 11.1, however, show that WM training alone was associated with notable effects in grade three (*ES* = 0.36) and grade four (*ES* = 0.24). The embedded WM training (RC[WM]) effects on the WM outcome were inconsistent across grades with negative effects in grade three (*ES* = −0.31); small positive effects in grade four (*ES* = 0.17). The RC condition had negligible effects on WM across the two grades.

Overall, our descriptive data suggest, however tentatively, that instructing students in reading comprehension boosted reading comprehension performance with little transfer to WM performance. WM training strengthened WM performance and, additionally, seemed to improve reading comprehension in grade three. Combining the reading comprehension instruction with WM training by embedding the latter in the former produced the largest *ESs* in reading comprehension in grades three and four, but resulted in inconsistent *ESs* in WM.

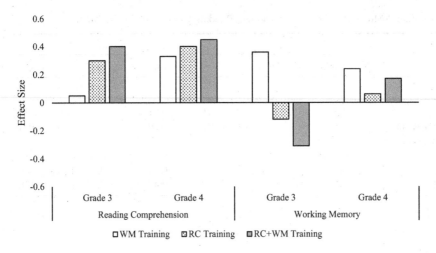

Figure 11.1

Table 11.3 Multilevel Model Results for Posttreatment Working Memory by Grade

	Grade 3 (n = 83)				Grade 4 (n = 33)			
	Estimate	SE	t	p	Estimate	SE	t	p
Fixed Effect								
Intercept, γ_{00}	−0.07	0.18	−0.40	.688	0.11	0.33	0.32	.750
Pre-treatment Working Memory, γ_{01}	0.56	0.10	5.76	<.001	0.44	0.16	2.76	.006
D_WM, γ_{02}	0.35	0.25	1.40	.162	0.30	0.48	0.63	.530
D_RC, γ_{03}	−0.12	0.26	−0.46	.648	0.07	0.44	0.17	.869
D_RCWM, γ_{04}	−0.25	0.25	−1.00	.316	0.20	0.46	0.45	.654
Random Effect								
School (τ_u)	0.00				0.00			
Classroom (τ_u)	0.00				0.00			
Student/Error (σ^2)	0.66				0.87			

Note: Working Memory Factor is based on Working Memory Test Battery (WMTB)-Listening Recall raw score and WMTB-Backward Digit Recall raw score. D_WM = dummy variable comparing working memory training to control. D_RC = dummy variable comparing reading comprehension training to control. D_RCWM = dummy variable comparing working memory embedded in reading comprehension training to control.

Discussion

Third- and fourth-grade low-performing readers participated in a unique study in which we compared two versions of a reading comprehension program—one with and one without embedded WM training—against each other, against WM training without comprehension instruction, and controls. No statistically significant differences were obtained between these four conditions on post-treatment reading comprehension performance when controlling for pre-treatment comprehension performance. However, at both grades three and four, moderately large *ESs* were detected. In grade three, the two treatment conditions that included reading comprehension instruction (i.e., RC and RC[WM]) outperformed controls, *ESs* = 0.30 and 0.40, respectively. In grade four, children in all three treatment conditions demonstrated stronger reading comprehension than controls at posttreatment: *ESs* = 0.33 for WM; 0.40 for RC; and 0.45 for RC[WM].

When considering these inferential and descriptive findings, it is important to remember several features of the study. First, study participants were weak readers. At study entry, they had a mean percentile score of 41.53 on the TOWRE Sight Word Efficiency test; and mean percentile scores of 32.87, 31.82, and 31.18 on the WJ III, Gates, and WIAT comprehension tests, respectively. We and they had to make up a lot of ground. Second, our treatments were delivered in three 25-minute sessions per week for 14 weeks, totaling 17.5 hours—not a brief implementation period, but not a lengthy one either (cf. Wanzek et al., 2013); probably considerably more intensive than what many schools provide their poorer readers—and not just in terms of intervention hours, but in terms of the quality of the treatments and the fidelity with which they were conducted. But more weeks of treatment than the 14 weeks we provided, or longer tutoring sessions, would have permitted the children in our study greater opportunity (a) to read connected text and practice application of reading comprehension skills and strategies, and (b) to strengthen their WM.

A third study feature to keep in mind is that we used only commercially published, normative, "far-transfer" tests of reading comprehension to gauge program effects. There are at least two ways of thinking about this fact. As indicated by Wanzek, Wexler, Vaughn, and Ciullo (2010), few evaluations of reading comprehension interventions developed for intermediate-grade struggling readers have relied on such far-transfer measures. So, in this sense, our study was relatively unique. But, in another sense, our exclusive reliance on far transfer tests was a mistake because they mapped poorly onto our comprehension instruction. That is, many of the comprehension skills and strategies we attempted to teach were simply not assessed by our far-transfer comprehension measures. It is reasonable to wonder whether these tests may have underestimated instructional effects. Although we believe far-transfer measures have an important role to play in evaluating the effects of programs such as ours, we also believe that near- and mid-transfer measures may have a more important role. We recognize that this may be an unconventional view, one consequence of which is that there are few guidelines to follow when developing valid near- and mid-transfer measures of reading comprehension.

We believe that the RC and RC[WM] groups' seemingly superior (but not statistically significant) reading comprehension performance across grades three and four (*ESs* = .30 to .45) justify a conclusion that our reading program has promise for weak readers in third and fourth grades. This judgement is based partly on a recent synthesis of efficacy studies of reading comprehension interventions conducted with students in grades four to twelve (Scammacca, Roberts, Vaughn, and Stuebing, 2016). The mean *ES* across these studies was .19 on standardized, norm-referenced tests. Whereas our *ESs* are superior to this mean, they are still too modest to suggest that our program has practical value-added. In short, we're not ready for prime time but we seem to be on the right track.

These preliminary findings are consonant with a view that more comprehensive approaches to reading comprehension instruction are generally more effective than less comprehensive ones (e.g., Elleman, Lindo, Morphy, and Compton, 2009; Gajria et al., 2007; Gersten et al., 2001; Edmonds et al., 2009). As already described, our RC component called for the instruction of many skills and strategies such as fluency-building, identifying main ideas, making text-based and elaborative inferences, and so forth.

In the same vein, our more complex, if not more comprehensive, RC[WM] group of children seemed to do better than the RC-only group on reading comprehension performance

(*ESs* = .40 versus .30 in favor of RC[WM] at third grade; *ESs* = .45 versus .40 at fourth grade; also see Figure 11.1). Why might this be so? Did embedded WM training strengthen WM that in turn supported reading comprehension? Or were our embedded WM activities really reading comprehension activities that strengthened comprehension in different and supplemental ways? One embedded WM activity was main idea complex span. Its purpose was to strengthen WM and reading comprehension simultaneously. It required the RC[WM] students to read several paragraphs in a lesson, create a main idea statement for each, and recall these statements in correct sequence from earliest to most recent. If they failed to do so, the tutor presented them in correct order and then asked the students to try again.

At fourth grade, the WM group's posttreatment reading comprehension performance seemed better than that of controls (*ES* = 0.33). This (statistically non-significant) finding was unexpected because the WM group, as well as the control group, did not get reading comprehension instruction. Yet, our WM group's apparent superiority over controls would probably be expected by those who believe in domain-general effects of WM training: Strengthening it is like strengthening a muscle that facilitates more impressive performance across many disparate academic domains (see Peng and Fuchs, 2016, for extended discussion of a domain-general perspective).

An alternative explanation of our fourth-grade WM group's performance on comprehension outcomes is that the training inadvertently strengthened the group's *attention* rather than or in addition to WM. (Attention is widely acknowledged as closely related to WM; see Miller et al., 2014). In this scenario, the children then applied their stronger attention to posttreatment performance. Put differently, WM training—embedded or not in reading comprehension instruction—may have improved children's attention and primed them for stronger posttreatment performance. An important aim of future research may be to better understand the relationships between WM and attention. If the reading comprehension program inadvertently fortified children's attention and primed them for a more impressive posttreatment performance, then maybe the reported *ESs* overestimate the importance of the reading comprehension program. This prompts the question, "how might we parse the possible strengthening of cognitive abilities from program effects on comprehension skills and strategies?"

We have reported on our implementation and evaluation of two versions of a reading comprehension program for third- and fourth-grade low-performing readers. We have described both versions of the program as relatively comprehensive and intensive; and we have argued for the importance of such programs in schools serving children and youth with serious learning problems. At the same time, we have expressed the belief that a factor contributing to the apparent difficulty many educators experience with RTI implementation is the inherent complexities of the multi-tier framework. This includes the complexity of related interventions. We are unhappy to say that, for now, this is a conundrum researchers and practitioners must try to solve together if we are to help children and youth with serious learning problems.

References

Al Otaiba, S., Allor, J., Werfel, K.L., and Clemens, N. (2016). Critical components of phonemic awareness instruction and intervention: Recommendations for teacher training and for future research. In R. Schiff and R.M. Joshi (Eds.), *Interventions in learning disabilities: A handbook on systematic training programs for individuals with learning disabilities* (pp. 9–27). AG Switzerland: Springer.

Cain, K. (2006). Children's reading comprehension: The role of working memory in normal and impaired development. In S. J. Pickering (Ed.), *Working memory and education* (pp. 61–91). San Diego, CA: Academic Press.

Cain, K. (2010). *Reading development and difficulties*. Chichester, UK: Wiley-Blackwell.

Cain, K., Oakhill, J., and Bryant, P. (2004). Children's reading comprehension ability: Concurrent prediction by working memory, verbal ability, and component skills. *Journal of Educational Psychology, 96*(1), 31–42. http://dx.doi.org/10.1037/0022-0663.96.1.31.

Carretti, B., Borella, E., Cornoldi, C., and De Beni, R. (2009). Role of working memory in explaining the performance of individuals with specific reading comprehension difficulties: A meta-analysis. *Learning and Individual Differences, 19*(2), 246–251. doi: 10.1016/j.lindif.2008.10.002.

Carroll, J. B. (1993). *Human cognitive abilities: A survey of factor-analytic studies*. Cambridge, UK: Cambridge University Press.

Catts, H. W., Adolf, S. M., and Ellis Weismer, S. (2006). Language deficits in poor comprehenders: A case for the simple view of reading. *Journal of Speech, Language, and Hearing Research, 49,* 278–293. doi: 10.1044/1092-4388(2006/023).

De Beni, R., and Palladino, P. (2000). Intrusion errors in working memory tasks: Are they related to reading comprehension ability? *Learning and Individual Differences, 12*(2), 131–143. doi: 10.1016/S1041-–6080(01)00033-4.

de Jong, P. F., and van der Leij, A. (2002). Effects of phonological abilities and linguistic comprehension on the development of reading. *Scientific Studies of Reading, 6*(1), 51–77. doi: 10.1207/S1532799 XSSR0601_03.

Deno, S. L., and Mirkin, P. K. (1977). *Data-based program modification: A manual*. Minneapolis, MN: Leadership Training Institute for Special Education.

Eason, S. H., and Cutting, L. E. (2009). Examining sources of poor comprehension in older poor readers: Preliminary findings, issues, and challenges. In R. K. Wagner, C. S. Schatschneider, and C. Phythian-Sence (Eds.), *Beyond decoding: The behavioral and biological foundations of reading comprehension* (pp. 263–283). New York: Guilford.

Edmonds, M. S., Vaughn, S., Wexler, J., Reutebuch, C., Cable, A., Tackett, K. K., and Schnakenberg, J. W. (2009). A synthesis of reading interventions and effects on reading comprehension outcomes for older struggling readers. *Review of Educational Research, 79,* 262–300.

Elleman, A. M., Lindo, E., Morphy, P., and Compton, D.L. (2009). The impact of vocabulary instruction on passage-level comprehension of school-age children: A meta-analysis. *Journal of Research on Educational Effectiveness, 2*(1), 1–44.

Ericsson, K. A., and Kintsch, W. (1995). Long-term working memory. *Psychological Review, 102*(2), 211–245.

Fuchs, D., Elleman, A. M., Fuchs, L. S., Peng, P., Kearns, D. M. Compton, D. L., . . ., Miller, A. C. (2016). *A randomized control trial of explicit instruction with and without cognitive training to strengthen the reading comprehension of poor readers in first grade*. Manuscript submitted for publication.

Fuchs, D., and Fuchs, L.S. (1986). Test procedure bias: A meta-analysis of examiner familiarity effects. *Review of Educational Research, 56,* 243–262.

Fuchs, D. and Fuchs, L. S. (2006). Introduction to response to intervention: What, why, and how valid is it? *Reading Research Quarterly, 41,* 93–99.

Fuchs, D., Fuchs, L. S., and Stecker, P. M. (2010). The "blurring" of special education in a new continuum of general education placements and services. *Exceptional Children, 76*(3), 301–323.

Fuchs, D., Fuchs, L. S., and Vaughn, S. (2014). What is intensive instruction and why is it important? *Teaching Exceptional Children, 46*(4), 13–18.

Fuchs, D., Mock, D., Morgan, P. L., and Young, C. L. (2003). Responsiveness-to-intervention: Definitions, evidence, and implications for the learning disabilities construct. *Learning Disabilities Research & Practice, 18*(3), 157–171.

Gajria, M., Jitendra, A. K., Sood, S., and Sacks, G. 92007). Improving comprehension of expository texts in students with LD: A research synthesis. *Journal of Learning Disabilities, 40,* 210–227.

Gersten, R. Fuchs. L. S., Williams, J. P., and Baker, S. (2001). Teaching reading comprehension strategies to students with learning disabilities: A review of research. *Review of Educational Research, 71,* 279–320.

Gilbert, J. K., Compton, D. L., Fuchs, D., Fuchs, L. S., Bouton, B., Barquero, L. A., and Cho, E. (2013). Efficacy of a first-grade responsiveness-to-intervention prevention model for struggling readers. *Reading Research Quarterly, 48*(2), 135–154.

Hulme, C., and Snowling, M. J. (2011). Children's reading comprehension difficulties nature, causes, and treatments. *Current Directions in Psychological Science, 20*(3), 139–142. doi: 10.1177/096372141140 8673.

Individuals with Disabilities Education Act; Request for Information on the Use of Results Data in Making Determinations Under Sections 616(d)(2) and 642 of the IDEA, 79 Fed. Reg. 16778 (March 26, 2014).

Ikeda, M., and Gustafson, J. K. (2002). Heartland AEA 11's problem solving process: Impact on issues related to special education (Research Report No. 2002–01). Johnston, IA: Heartland Area Education Agency 11.

Ikeda, M. J., Rahn-Blakeslee, A. R., and Allison, R. (2005). *Effects of response-to-intervention on special education placement and student achievement.* (Research Rep. No. 2005–2001). Johnston, IA: Heartland Area Education Agency 11.

Juel, C., Griffith, P. L., and Gough, P. B. (1986). Acquisition of literacy: A longitudinal study of children in first and second grade. *Journal of Educational Psychology, 78*(4), 243–255. http://dx.doi.org/10.1037/0022-0663.78.4.243.

Lemons, C. J., Kearns, D. M., and Davidson, K. A. (2014). Data-based individualization in reading: Intensifying interventions for students with significant reading disabilities. *Teaching Exceptional Children, 46,* 20–29.

Lervåg, A., and Aukrust, V. G. (2010). Vocabulary knowledge is a critical determinant of the difference in reading comprehension growth between first and second language learners. *Journal of Child Psychology and Psychiatry, 51*(5), 612–620. doi: 10.1111/j.1469-7610.2009.02185.x.

MacGinitie, W. H., MacGinitie, R. K., Maria, K., and Dreyer, L. G. (2000). *Gates-MacGinitie Reading Tests (Level 4, Form S).* Rolling Meadows, IL: Riverside.

Marston, D., Muyskens, P., Lau, M., and Canter, A. (2003). Problem-solving model for decision making with high-incidence disabilities: The Minneapolis experience. *Learning Disabilities Research & Practice, 18*(3), 187–200.

Miller, A. C., Fuchs, D., Fuchs, L. S., Compton, D., Kearns, D., Zhang, W., . . . and Kirchner, D. P. (2014). Behavioral attention: A longitudinal study of whether and how it influences the development of word reading and reading comprehension among at-risk readers. *Journal of Research on Educational Effectiveness, 7*(3), 232–249.

Morgan, P. L., and Fuchs, D. (2007). Is there a bidirectional relationship between children's reading skills and reading motivation? *Exceptional Children, 73*(2), 165–183. doi: 10.1177/001440290707300203.

Nation, K., and Snowling, M. (1997). Assessing reading difficulties: The validity and utility of current measures of reading skill. *British Journal of Educational Psychology, 67*(3), 359–370. doi: 10.1111/j.2044-8279.1997.tb01250.x.

Nation, K., Cocksey, J., Taylor, J. S., and Bishop, D. V. (2010). A longitudinal investigation of early reading and language skills in children with poor reading comprehension. *Journal of Child Psychology and Psychiatry, 51*(9), 1031–1039. doi: 10.1111/j.1469-7610.2010.02254.x.

National Assessment Governing Board (2015): www.nagb.org/newsroom/naep-releases/2015-reading-math-tuda.html.

National Reading Panel, National Institute of Child Health and Human Development, Nation Institutes of Health. (2000). Report of the national reading panel: Teaching children to read: An evidence-based assessment of the scientific research literature on reading and its implications for reading instruction: Reports of the subgroups. Retrieved from: www.nichd.nih.gov/publications/pubs/nrp/documents/report.pdf

Oakhill, J., Berenhaus, M. S., and Cain, K. (2015). Children's reading comprehension and comprehension difficulties. In A. Pollatsek and R. Treiman (Eds.), *The Oxford handbook of reading.* New York: Oxford University Press.

O'Connor, R., and Fuchs, L. S. (2013). Responsiveness to intervention in the elementary grades: Implications for early childhood education. In V. Buysse, E. Peisner-Feinberg, and Cantler (Eds.) *Handbook of response to intervention (RTI) in early childhood education* (pp. 41–56). Baltimore, MD: Brookes.

Peng, P., and Fuchs, D. (2015). A randomized control trial of working memory training with and without strategy instruction effects on young children's working memory and comprehension. *Journal of Learning Disabilities.* Advance online publication. doi: 10.1177/0022219415594609.

Pickering, S., and Gathercole, S. (2001). *Working Memory Test Battery for Children.* London: The Psychological Corporation.

Powell, S. R., and Stecker, P.M. (2014). Using data-based individualization to intensify mathematics intervention for students with disabilities. *Teaching Exceptional Children, 46,* 31–37.

Roth, F. P., Speece, D. L., and Cooper, D. H. (2002). A longitudinal analysis of the connection between oral language and early reading. *The Journal of Educational Research*, *95*(5), 259–272. doi:10.1080/00220 670209596600.

Semel, E., Wiig, E. H., and Secord, W. A. (2003). *Clinical evaluation of language fundamentals* (4th ed.). Toronto: Psychological Corporation.

Stanovich, K. E. (1986). Matthew effects in reading: Some consequences of individual differences in the acquisition of literacy. *Reading Research Quarterly*, *21*, 360–407. www.jstor.org/stable/747612.

Stothard, S. E., and Hulme, C. (1992). Reading comprehension difficulties in children. *Reading and Writing*, *4*(3), 245–256. doi: 10.1007/BF01027150.

Stroop, J. R. (1935). Studies of interference in serial verbal reactions. *Journal of Experimental Psychology*, *18*, 643–662.

Sweller, J., Van Merrienboer, J. J., and Paas, F. G. (1998). Cognitive architecture and instructional design. *Educational Psychology Review*, *10*(3), 251–296. doi: 10.1023/A:1022193728205.

Telzrow, C. F., McNamara, K., and Hollinger, C. L. (2000). Fidelity of problem-solving implementation and relationship to student performance. *School Psychology Review*, *29*(3), 443–461.

Torgesen, J. K., Wagner, R. K., and Rashotte, C. A. (2012). *Test of word reading efficiency* (2nd ed.). Austin, TX: PRO-ED.

U.S. Department of Education, Institute of Education Sciences, What Works Clearinghouse. (2013, March). *What Works Clearinghouse: Procedures and Standards Handbook* (Version 3.0). Retrieved from: http://whatworks.ed.gov.

Vaughn, S., Cirino, P. T., Wanzek, J., Wexler, J., Fletcher, J. M., Denton, C. D. . . . and Francis, D. J. (2010). Response to intervention for middle school students with reading difficulties: Effects of a primary and secondary intervention. *School Psychology Review*, *39*(1), 3–21.

Wanzek, J., and Vaughn, S. (2009). Students demonstrating persistent low response to reading intervention: Three case studies. *Learning Disabilities Research and Practice*, *24*,151–163.

Wanzek, J., Vaughn, S., Scammacca, N., Metz, K., Murray, C., Roberts, G., and Danielson, L. (2013). Extensive reading interventions for older struggling readers: Implications from research. *Review of Educational Research*, *83*, 163–195.

Wanzek, J., Wexler, J., Vaughn, S., and Ciullo, S. (2010). Reading interventions for struggling readers in the upper elementary grades: A synthesis of 20 years of research. *Reading and Writing*, *23*, 889–912.

Wechsler, D. (2009). *Wechsler individual achievement test* (3rd ed.). San Antonio, TX: Psychological Corporation.

Wechsler, D. (2011). *Wechsler Abbreviated Scale of Intelligence* (2nd ed.). New York: Harcourt Brace & Company.

Woodcock, R. W., McGrew, K. S., and Mather, N. (2001). *Woodcock-Johnson III tests of achievement*. Itasca, IL: Riverside.

Yuill, N., and Oakhill, J. (1991). *Children's problems in text comprehension: An experimental investigation*. Cambridge, UK: Cambridge University Press.

Yuill, N., Oakhill, J., and Parkin, A. (1989). Working memory, comprehension ability and the resolution of text anomaly. *British Journal of Psychology*, *80*(3), 351–361. doi: 10.1111/j.2044-8295.1989.tb02325.x.

12

EVIDENCE-BASED WRITING INTERVENTION

Three Tiers of Instruction for Elementary Students

Linda H. Mason, Nancy Mamlin, and Kalin Stewart

Recent initiatives for improving academic outcomes for all students, such as the recommendations for a Response to Intervention (RTI) model for identification of specific learning disabilities within the reauthorization of the Individuals with Disabilities Education Improvement Act of 2004 (P.L. 108–446) and standards such as the Common Core State Standards (National Governors Association Center for Best Practices & Council of Chief State School Officers [NGACBP], 2010), have prompted attention to students' writing in both assessment and intervention literature. Within the context of RTI, schools are expected to conduct school-wide screening of students' writing performance; teachers are expected to deliver evidence-based classroom instruction with increasing levels of intensity and provide continuous progress monitoring of students' writing with specific attention to intervention effectiveness (Johnson, Mellard, Fuchs, and McKnight, 2006). Within the context of standards (NGACBP, 2010), elementary students are expected to (a) write persuasive text, informative text, and narrative text; (b) write with clarity and cohesion to meet task, purpose, and audience; (c) plan and revise, edit, or rewrite; (d) use technology for production, publication, and collaboration; (e) write both shorter and longer responses to demonstrate understanding of subject matter; (f) use and integrate multiple sources while avoiding plagiarism; (g) gather evidence from text to support writing; and (h) write in both short and extended time frames. In addition, given the specificity of initiatives and the "shared responsibility" within schools (NGACBP, p. 4), all teachers should understand how formative writing assessment for process skills and written expression can be used to inform instruction that ensures students' progress towards meeting standards across the three tiers of instruction in RTI (Graham, Harris, and Hebert, 2011a, 2011b; Mason and Mong Cramer, 2014).

Results from the 2007 and 2011 National Assessment of Educational Progress Report Cards indicate an impasse in writing achievement, with 74% of eighth grade and 65% of twelfth grade students not meeting proficient writing skill levels (National Center for Education Statistics, 2012; Salahu-Din, Persky, and Miller, 2008). Clearly, many students will require additional scaffolding, intense intervention, and a wider array of learning opportunities to meet the demands for performance standards (Wixson and Lipson, 2012). Unfortunately, given the paucity of research in early writing screening and early elementary writing intervention (Berninger, Nielsen, Abbott, Wijsman, and Raskind, 2008), there has been little discourse in framing writing assessment and instruction within an RTI model (Saddler and Asaro-Saddler, 2013). In this chapter, we begin by setting the context for RTI with a brief summary of what is currently known about school-based assessment for establishing students' writing performance and for identifying writing difficulties. Next, we (a) highlight recommended practices for elementary writing instruction, as noted in the What Work Clearinghouse practice guide for elementary students (Graham, Bollinger, et al., 2012), (b) summarize intervention research for writing mechanics and written expression, and (c) review key research findings for whole class instruction (i.e., Tier I instruction), and for small group and individualized instruction (i.e., Tier II and Tier III instruction).

Evaluation of Writing Performance

Accurate evaluation of students' writing process skill mastery and writing skill application during written expression, for instructional, diagnostic, and remediation purposes, should drive classroom instruction (Huot and Neal, 2006), and is critical within the context of RTI. Due to the subjectivity within writing assessment and the lack of scientifically validated assessment for early writing, assessment should include both quantitative and qualitative measures (Tindal and Parker, 1991). In persuasive writing, for example, the number of words correctly sequenced in each sentence (quantitative) and the strength of persuasive arguments written (qualitative), are important for evaluating students' opinion writing. In addition, assessment should consider the relationship of oral language processing (i.e., grammar and vocabulary), transcription (i.e., handwriting/word processing and spelling fluency), and short- and long-term memory skills for effective written expression at the sentence, paragraph, and essay level (Berninger and Abbott, 2010; Fletcher, Lyon, Fuchs, and Barnes, 2007; Olinghouse, 2008). Kim, Al Otaiba, Sidler, and Gruelich's (2013) study with 527 first grade students highlights the complexity of writing for young children; in their study, language, literacy, and attention were found differentially related to outcomes in writing quality and conventions. Given the complexity of writing, formative and summative assessment is recommended for assessing various aspects of the writing process. Graham et al. (2011a, 2011b) recommend that formative assessment be used to help improve students' writing, and to apply best practices for any assessment of classroom writing.

Formative assessment measures, such as curriculum-based measurement (CBM), that examine core writing components such as fluency, syntactic maturity, vocabulary, content, and writing mechanics (e.g., transcription skills and sentence development) should occur frequently (Benson and Campbell, 2009; Coker and Ritchey, 2010). However, commonly used CBM writing measures such as Story Prompts vary in criterion validity for students across the elementary grade levels (Deno, Mirkin, and Marston, 1980; Gansle, Van Der Heyden, Noell, Resetar, and Williams, 2006). CBM task measures for transcription and text writing skills have shown promise for more fully capturing students' writing (e.g., Lembke, Deno, and Hall, 2003; Ritchey and Coker, 2014); however, due to findings of low specificity in accurately identifying students in need of intervention, combining CBM measures (e.g., Story Prompts; task measures) is recommended for screening and classification purposes.

Assessment that examines ability to write short (e.g., writing a few sentences or paragraphs) and extended responses (e.g., writing multiple paragraphs) across a variety of tasks (e.g., report writing in science, letter writing in social studies) are valid for benchmarking developmental and/or grade levels and provide evidence of students' process skill application specific to genre and task, and can provide evidence for what students need in terms of intervention (Sermis, Burstein, and Leacock, 2006). These written expression assessments provide formative information and are used frequently in summative assessment. Specific writing tasks (e.g., students' ability to write simple, compound, and complex sentences; CCSS L.3.2b, NGACBP, 2010) can be assessed systematically within the context of sentence, paragraph, and essay writing instruction. Assessment rubrics are often used to inform instruction by evaluating a student's ability to demonstrate writing skills and ability to express ideas in writing by (a) including genre-specific primary traits, (b) writing an organized text, and (c) attending to audience and task purpose (Mason and Mong Cramer, 2014). In addition, overall writing quality can be assessed holistically by comparing a student's writing to a model or anchor paper (Olinghouse and Santangelo, 2010).

Recommendations for Writing Instruction at the Elementary Level

Elementary schools are responsible for educating children from approximately ages five to 12. Naturally, recommendations for practice may look different for five-year-olds than for fifth-graders. It is expected that teachers and other practitioners will take into account the developmental nature of instruction and make adjustments in terms of emphasis and content. For a practice to be recommended there needs to be consistent positive results when experimentally tested (Graham, Bollinger, et al., 2012). This implies that high-quality research has been conducted by either experimental, quasi-experimental, or single-subject research designs, and published in peer-reviewed professional journals. In the area of writing, four recommendations for classroom practice, writing mechanics, and written expression have been identified and are highlighted in the following sections. See the following on-line resources for more detailed explanation and supporting research: *Teaching elementary school students to be effective writers: A practice guide* (Graham, Bollinger, et al., 2012) and *Evidence-based practices for writing instruction* (Troia, 2014). We review each recommendation, noting the level of evidence as found by Graham, Bollinger, et al. (2012), then, summarize research recommendations for writing mechanics and written expression intervention.

Four Practices

Four practices for the elementary classroom are recommended to support students' writing performance (Graham, Bollinger, et al., 2012; Troia, 2014). Each practice, noted in order of evidence strength, is described in the context of Tier I classroom instruction with recommendations for Tier II and Tier III intervention.

Teach Students the Writing Process

Instruction in (a) the various processes of writing (planning, drafting, sharing, evaluating, editing, and publishing) and (b) providing genre-specific instruction is recommended and has strong support in the research literature for all instructional tiers (Graham, McKeown, Kiuhura, and Harris, 2012). Teaching students strategies within a writing process framework that includes planning, composing, revising, and editing facilitates student writing in each writing process component (e.g., Harris, Lane, Driscoll, et al., 2012). Explicit strategy instruction for each of the three writing genres (narrative, informative, and persuasive) has been tested in multiple studies – for example, Harris, Graham, and Mason (2006) and Graham, Harris, and Mason

(2005) performed intervention studies for small group and individualized instruction as required for Tier II and Tier III intervention. In these studies of young struggling writers in second and third grade, researchers examined the effects of strategy instruction for narrative writing (e.g., writing stories) and persuasive writing (e.g., writing an opinion writing). A generalizable organizing strategy, POW (**P**ick ideas, **O**rganize using the genre-specific strategy, **W**rite and say more), was taught along with the genre-specific strategies for using story grammar (WWW, What=2, How=2: **W**ho is the main character, **W**here, **W**hen, **W**hat does the character what to do, **W**hat happens next, **H**ow does the story end, **H**ow does the character feel?) and for writing an opinion (TREE: **T**opic sentence, **R**easons: three or more, **E**xplanations, **E**nding). The combination of POW with genre specific strategies enhances students' opportunities to see strategy use across the writing process components and genres.

Help Students with the Technical Aspects of Writing

A moderate amount of evidence has been established for providing instruction in handwriting (e.g., Graham, Harris, and Fink, 2000), spelling (e.g., Berninger et al., 2002), sentence construction (e.g., Saddler and Graham, 2005), and word processing (Jones, 1994). For students who are receiving Tier II and Tier III intervention, some of these technical aspects can be particularly difficult, and may hinder progress in other aspects of writing (Graham and Harris, 2005). By establishing writing benchmarks and goals, as well as appropriate scaffolding of explicit instruction, these difficulties can be mitigated. When technology is used, students need explicit instruction. For example, keyboarding (i.e., typing) needs to be taught, and students need to be shown how to effectively use the tools provided by word processing software (e.g., spellcheck, grammar check).

Provide Adequate Time for Writing

For elementary students in first- through fifth-grade, most recommend that at least an hour each day is spent writing; 30 minutes a day is recommended for kindergarteners (Graham, Bollinger, et al., 2012; Troia, 2014). This includes time available for free writing as well as writing across curricular areas. Writing time has minimal evidence (see Berninger et al., 2006 for evidence); however, it is rational to believe that students need time to learn and practice writing skills to develop writing fluency and confidence in their writing abilities. Aside from the specific time set aside each day for explicit writing instruction, students need to be given opportunities to practice their writing skills in authentic writing tasks throughout the school day. Teachers should therefore explicitly plan for and provide supplemental daily writing opportunities for students who have been identified as needing Tier II and Tier III writing intervention. As noted by Graham, Bollinger, et al., writing time alone does not support improved outcomes; instruction must also be provided.

Help Students View Themselves as Writers

A supportive environment increases students' self-confidence, and helps them see themselves as writers (Graham, Bollinger, et al., 2012; Troia, 2014). Both independence and inter-dependence of students as writers creates an environment where all learners are engaged in the writing process. Although this recommendation has minimal support in the literature, Graham, Bollinger, et al. (2012) note, "The panel believes, however, that the practices described in this recommendation are an integral component of effective writing instruction" (p. 35).

When teaching the writing process, there are several opportunities for teachers to help students view themselves as writers. First, students can be given a choice in writing—for example, a choice of two or more writing prompts. Providing choice gives students more opportunity for personalizing their response within the context of the writing task (MacArthur, Schwartz, and Graham, 1991). Next, collaborative writing (i.e., shared writing with a peer or small group of peers), a best practice for students in all tiers of instruction, supports students' positive writing outcomes (Troia and Graham, 2002; Yarrow and Topping, 2001). In addition, the use of peer feedback in sharing, evaluating, and editing fosters a community of writers (e.g., MacArthur et al., 1991). As students move to the publishing stage, they can come to see themselves as having something of value to share with a larger audience, whether that is the whole class, the whole school, or another form of publication that reaches a wider audience.

Intervention for Writing Mechanics

The use of technology has mitigated some of the issues with writing mechanics, specifically for handwriting and spelling, that previous generations of students may have faced; however, this does not indicate that reliance on technology is the answer for all students at any Tier level. In a survey about classroom instruction for handwriting, primary-grade teachers reported spending 70 minutes per week on handwriting instruction (Graham, Harris, et al., 2008). However, these teachers also reported feeling inadequately prepared for teaching handwriting, and therefore may not have used best practices in their instruction. Best practice for teaching handwriting includes teaching students (a) how to hold a pencil correctly and (b) how to form letters correctly and fluently (Denton, Cope, and Moser, 2006; Graham et al., 2000). It is also important to provide handwriting instruction to students to help alleviate the negative effects of poor transcription on writing abilities (Graham and Harris, 2005).

For students who struggle with writing, spelling is the most common difficulty and one of the hardest to remediate (Moats, 2009). Unfortunately, results of survey research indicated that 42% of primary-grade teachers were found to use few if any adaptations in their spelling instruction for students who were weaker in spelling (Graham, Morphy, et al., 2008). Research-based recommendations for spelling instruction include the use of a multisensory approach, teaching frequently used words, and teaching students to use known rules to generate possible spellings (Mason and Benedek-Wood, 2014).

Less skilled writers tend to produce short, simple sentences with frequent grammatical errors (Graham and Harris, 2005). When teaching proper sentence construction to students, explicit instruction is recommended. Teachers need to provide instruction according to the student's developmental level regarding proper syntax, mechanics, and variety of structures. Integrating reading and writing instruction can be particularly useful in this area, as reading a variety of genres can serve as models for writers at any level (Graham, Bollinger, et al., 2012). Students also benefit from sentence-combining instruction, where students are taught how to combine two simple sentences into one sentence through writing and revising (Saddler and Graham, 2005).

Intervention for Written Expression

While there are several intervention approaches for improving students' written expression, strategy instruction has the largest researched database across grade levels (Graham, McKeown, et al., 2012). One approach, Self-Regulated Strategy Development (SRSD), has been identified as an EBP (e.g., Baker, Chard, Ketterlin-Geller, Apichatabutra, and Doabler, 2009). SRSD instruction includes an explicit focus on teaching self-regulation procedures (e.g., goal setting, self-monitoring, self-instruction, and self-reinforcement) to support students' use of writing strategies (Graham, Harris, and McKeown, 2013). SRSD improves students' writing performance through teaching these strategies and embedding aspects of self-efficacy and knowledge on how to complete a specific writing task (Graham et al., 2005). SRSD instruction is meant to increase motivation through embedded aspects of self-efficacy and knowledge on how to complete the specific writing task. In SRSD instruction, six stages for strategy acquisition are emphasized: developing background knowledge, discussing the strategy, modeling the strategy, memorization

Table 12.1 SRSD: Stages for Strategy Acquisition

Stage	Description
Develop Background Knowledge	The teacher develops students' background knowledge and any necessary preskill needed for the writing task and/or self-regulation procedures. When teaching opinion writing, for example, the teacher discusses related vocabulary and concepts such as the parts of an opinion (e.g., reasons and explanation).
Discuss It	The teacher discusses how the strategies and self-regulation procedures help students with their writing. The teacher discusses each strategy step and how and when to use the strategies. For example, when teaching opinion writing, the teacher will introduce and discuss the strategy steps used to develop and argument. Anchor papers are read and strategy parts located. After introducing the targeted strategies, the teacher and student make a commitment and set goals to learn and use the strategy. At this time, the students' current performance can be reviewed.
Model It	The teacher models how to complete each step of the strategy and how to apply the self-regulation procedures by "thinking aloud" while completing the writing task. The purpose of a "think aloud" model is to show students how a skilled writer thinks, plans, and writes throughout the writing process. The teacher models self-instructions for setting goals, organizing notes, constructing a response, self-monitoring performance, evaluating performance, and using self-reinforcement. Positive self-instructions such as "This strategy will help me" and "Did I use all of the steps" support writing productivity, whereas negative self-instructions, such as "I can't write" and "I don't know how to write," interfere with the writing process. After the teacher models, students develop a personal list of self-instructions.
Memorize It	Students begin working on memorizing the strategy mnemonic and strategy steps as soon as they are introduced. The teacher provides students with mnemonic charts and other materials to support memorization in the beginning, but these supports are gradually faded over time. The teacher provides practice opportunities for memorization, for example, by asking students to recite steps at the beginning and/or end of class. For students experience memory difficulties, the teacher may decide to continue the use of supports.
Support It	The teacher provides scaffolded support so that students will be successful in applying the targeted strategies and self-regulation procedures. Opportunities for writing with guided support are critical when students are learning strategies; lessons should be repeated as many times as necessary. The teacher monitors students' performance and gradually fades support while students monitor and graph their performance.
Independent Performance	The teacher fades support completely and provides opportunities for students' independent practice in writing. During this stage, the teacher should continue to monitor student performance to ensure that students continue to use strategies and self-regulation procedures effectively. This stage should include plans for maintaining and generalizing the strategies and self-regulation procedures across content-areas.

of the strategy, support and collaborative practice, and finally independent practice of the strategy (Graham and Harris, 1993). See Table 12.1 for Six Stages of SRSD Instruction. Teaching the writing process and helping students view themselves as writers are addressed in all SRSD stages and self-regulation procedures.

Research focused on providing writing instruction at each tier of RTI is highlighted next. Specifically, we describe evidence-based interventions that examined instruction in randomized controlled trial (RCT) experimental studies.

Evidence-Based Practice for Tier I Intervention

Tier I interventions in elementary school are generally focused on remediating any potential skill deficits during the early stage of a student's writing development as a universal prevention measure. Tier I instruction emphasizes the use of evidence-based practices to prevent academic problems from occurring. Within Tier I instruction, writing progress is monitored frequently, and students who do not respond adequately to Tier I instruction are referred to Tier II intervention. There is a paucity of research examining the effects of evidence-based intervention within Tier I instruction for writing mechanics, with just one study related to handwriting instruction. However, research in Tier I written expression is emerging with promising results for teacher professional development.

Handwriting

In 2013, Ohl et al. examined the effectiveness of a 10-week Tier I intervention program for improving fine motor and visual–motor skills with general education kindergarten students. Six schools, with two teachers at each school, participated ($n = 113$ students). Classrooms were randomly assigned to the Specialized Teaching and Enhancement of Performance Skills for Kindergarteners (STEPS–K) program intervention group or to a control condition. The STEPS–K program was developed in collaboration with general education kindergarten teachers to promote the fine motor and visual–motor skills needed for achieving benchmarks in the kindergarten curriculum. This program has three main components: (a) direct instruction, in which an occupational therapist leads in collaboration with the classroom teacher, for ten 30-minute lessons once a week for ten consecutive weeks; (b) a classroom center focused on the fine motor activities introduced in the ten lessons; and (c) consultation between the occupational therapist and teacher throughout the ten-week instructional period. After the intervention, neither group demonstrated improvement in pencil grip; however, the intervention group, when compared to the control group, demonstrated significant gains in fine motor skills (Effect Size: $ES = 0.34$) and visual-motor integration ($ES = 0.24$). Although the intervention proved to be effective, Ohl and colleagues (2013) note these limitations: (a) the short instructional time may have influenced the noted small effect size gains and (b) functional performance (i.e., handwriting) was not measured.

Written Expression

Only a few experimental studies have examined Tier I writing instruction – Harris, Lane, Driscoll, et al. (2012) examined the effects of Tier I instruction for students with behavioral challenges, and Harris, Lane, Graham et al. (2012) and Mason et al. (2017) examined the effect of practice-based professional development for class-wide Tier I instruction. In Harris, Lane, Driscoll, et al. (2012), the effects of SRSD instruction (see Table 12.1 for instructional procedures) for second- and third-grade general education classes were evaluated. Nine teachers were randomly assigned to teaching story writing with the POW + WWW, What =2, How = 2, and 11 teachers were assigned to teach opinion writing with the POW + TREE strategies. Thirty-five second-grade and 21 third-grade students at moderate or high risk for behavioral challenges participated in this RCT study; these students were matched for comparison with a group of students without behavioral challenges. After instruction, students receiving SRSD story and opinion writing instruction improved in the number of genre specific elements written (*ES* = .78 and .54 respectively) and writing quality (*ES* = .51 to 1.15 respectively). No effects were found for the number of words written. Harris and colleagues reflected that gains for students at risk for behavioral difficulties were not as strong as effects for similar students participating in Tier II instruction (e.g., Lane et al., 2011), and suggest that future study compare the effects of whole-class and small group instruction.

Practice-Based Professional Development (PBPD)

Professional development for SRSD writing instruction has also been examined. PBPD for SRSD writing instruction extends prior models of professional development, increasing the likelihood that classroom teachers will apply instruction with fidelity over time. Eight critical components are included in PBPD for SRSD writing instruction, teaching teachers (a) the value of written expression, (b) procedures for developing written expression, (c) evidence-based principles for instruction and assessment of written expression, (d) procedures for differentiation, (e) how to provide opportunities for scaffolded practice in teaching, (f) procedures for sustainability, (g) procedures for in-school and district leadership, and (h) the feasibility of the model.

In an RCT study (Harris, Lane, Graham et al., 2012), 12–14 hours of PBPD for SRSD with second- and third-grade teachers was found effective for Tier-I whole-class instruction. Two strategies were taught: POW + WWW, What = 2, How = 2 for story writing and TREE for opinion writing. After 24 instructional class sessions, students increased the number of elements in their stories (*ES* = 1.82) and opinion essays (*ES* = 2.02). In a second PBPD for SRSD Tier I study, Mason et al. (2017) evaluated the effects of PBPD + consultation for SRSD for POW + TREE opinion writing with 19 fifth- and sixth-grade teachers in four U.S. states (*n* = 564 students). Matched teacher-pairs were assigned either to SRSD treatment or to control. Five hours of face-to-face PBPD, followed by two hours of virtual consultation, were provided. Significant effects for students in treatment, when compared to students in control, were noted for the number of words written (*ES* = .47) and total number of elements written (*ES* = .90).

The results of the two PBPD studies highlight the feasibility and the effectiveness of SRSD for Tier I instruction. The lower effects of the second study (Mason et al., 2017) point to the importance of sufficient time for teacher training.

EBPs for Tiers II and III Writing Instruction

Tiers II and III provide additional support in writing instruction to students who have been identified as struggling writers through screening or class-wide progress monitoring. The recommended group size for Tier II supplemental writing instruction is four to eight students, with ten to 15 weeks of 20 to 40 min weekly sessions (Saddler and Asaro-Saddler, 2013). Tier III writing instruction generally includes groups of one to four students with longer, more individualized instruction than Tier II. It is critical that Tier II and Tier III interventions are provided as early as possible so that students achieve parity with their grade-level peers. In the following sections we describe evidence-based instruction for handwriting, spelling, sentence writing, and composition that can be appropriate for Tier II and Tier III intervention. These interventions have been proven to be effective in small-group settings and within RTI settings with elementary-aged students.

Handwriting Instruction

As with Tier I instruction, few studies have investigated the effects of small group handwriting instruction. In a pre-RTI RCT study (Graham et al., 2000), 19 first grade students who were identified through screening as needing additional handwriting instruction (15 minutes, three times a week for nine weeks) received individual instruction in writing lowercase manuscript letters. Students were taught letter naming, matching letters with their symbols, and practicing writing each letter. Students receiving handwriting instruction out-performed 19 peers in a control group in handwriting and written expression skills, and demonstrated long-term gains (ES = 1.39 for alphabet production; ES = 0.94 for number of letters written correctly; ES = 1.46 number of letters copied correctly per minute).

In one of three RCT for individualized instruction with first-grade students, Berninger et al. (2006) evaluated the effects of constant instructional time for orthographic and motor skills (i.e., fine motor finger skills), followed by direct instruction in letter formation (combined treatment) compared to direct instruction in letter formation alone. Fourteen first grade students met the inclusion criteria and were randomly assigned to one of the conditions. Each treatment was delivered to individual students in ten sessions. Slope differences indicated that students in the combined treatment had faster growth in writing words from memory with accuracy, while students receiving only letter formation demonstrated faster growth in letter writing speed and speed in copying from text. In a second follow up study with different students, 20 first-grade students were randomly assigned to motor training + pencil training or orthographic training + pencil writing. After individualized instruction, no significant differences were noted between treatments. A third study evaluated the effects of Decoding + Handwriting compared to Decoding Only, with seven and six (respectively) first-grade students. Again, there were no differences noted in treatment after individualized instruction.

Spelling Instruction

Although spelling may be the strongest area of need for improving students' writing abilities, as noted previously, experimental research has been limited to studies investigating the effects of supplemental individualized and small group instruction. In a study with first-grade students, Graham and Harris (2005) provided explicit spelling instruction to student pairs with a focus on improving writing skills. Students randomly assigned to treatment received three 20-minute lessons a week for 16 weeks. Students were taught sound and letter combinations, spelling patterns, and common words of each spelling pattern. Students receiving the intervention made significant gains in spelling with effect sizes ranging from 0.66 to 1.05. Students also demonstrated improvements in sentence construction (ES = 0.78).

In two RCT studies, Berninger, Winn, et al. (2008) evaluated the effects of a combined spelling and composition intervention. In the first study, students in fourth to sixth grade (n = 22) and students in seventh to ninth grade (n = 19) who qualified for small group Tier III instruction (based on their diagnosis of dyslexia and non-response to prior intervention) were randomly assigned to either a morphological spelling instruction condition (i.e., emphasis on teaching students how to become aware of word parts to change the meaning of the base word) or an orthographic instruction condition (i.e., words were learned focusing on the specific spelling). The students worked in small groups of six to 12 students and participated in a writer's workshop for two hours a day for 14 consecutive weekdays during the summer. All students received composition instruction for one hour a day. In addition, randomly assigned students received an hour of orthographic spelling instruction; the remaining students received an hour of morphological spelling instruction. The orthographic spelling treatment taught students how to use specific strategies for spelling by teaching visualization and sequencing. The morphological treatment focused on students creating correct spellings of base words and learning spelling rules. Both groups demonstrated significant improvement in spelling pseudowords (ES = 0.40) and real words (ES = 0.20), as well as demonstrating improvements in composition (ES = 0.21). The group receiving morphological treatment improved more on spelling pseudowords (ES = 0.20), while the group receiving orthographic treatment improved more in their rate of phonological decoding, ES = 0.14. Authors noted that students in grades seven to nine improved significantly more across measures.

In the second Berninger, Winn, et al. (2008) study, fourth- to sixth-grade students with dyslexia and non-responsive to prior intervention received small group (n = 6 to 12) Tier III instruction in writing were randomly assigned either to an explicit written language treatment focused on phonological working memory and decoding, or to a nonverbal control group receiving virtual reality-based instruction, as well as a control group of strong readers who received the nonverbal treatment. Twenty-four students participated in a science report-writing workshop, with 12 students receiving the language treatment and 12 students receiving nonverbal control treatment in small group settings. Students in the language-based treatment group received grapheme-phoneme correspondence instruction; phonological skill instruction; note-taking strategies; and teacher, peer, and computer assistance in writing reports. The nonverbal control group received interactive, virtual-reality instruction on orca whales to improve scientific problem solving and report writing. Both the language-based and nonverbal treatment groups demonstrated significant increases in pseudoword spelling skills (ES = 0.18), note-taking (ES = 0.36), and composition (ES = 0.32). The small effect size gains for the students with dyslexia in the two Berninger, Winn, et al. (2008) studies may illustrate the pervasive spelling difficulties of this student population.

Oral and Written Language Instruction

Though there is limited research in the area of oral and written language instruction, one study by Hooper et al. (2013), evaluated the effects of The Process Assessment of the Learner (PAL) writing program (Berninger and Abbot, 2003). PAL is a commercially available, three-tiered program that targets students in grades K-6, with a focus on oral and written language. Each tier is associated with the RTI instructional model. In 2016, the program cost $540.10 for a reading and writing kit for ten students. Effects of PAL were examined in the study with students in second grade after their placement into a Tier II treatment group; these students had completed a first-grade assessment with scores in the lower 25th percentile in written expression (Hooper et al., 2013). The study included a control group of 67 students at grade level, and 138 students who were in the at-risk group, of which 69 received treatment and 70 did not receive treatment. The treatment group spent 25 minutes a day, twice a week, for 12 weeks receiving the intervention. The PAL lesson plans, adapted to meet the time constraints of the school setting, focused on subword level writing, whole word writing, handwriting, and composition. Results indicated that students receiving the Tier II treatment, when compared to at-risk students in control, had increased their writing skills immediately following the intervention (*ES* = 0.14) and at the follow-up assessment in third grade (*ES* = 0.42). Authors noted additional research was needed to determine if more time in intervention would have increased student performance. Notably, the most at-risk students responded positively to the PAL treatment, with large effect sizes appearing at the third-grade follow-up (*ES* = 0.83), suggesting that students with lower writing performance made greater gains and had a greater need for intervention.

Sentence Combining Instruction

Students receiving Tier II and III writing intervention need assistance in sentence construction, one of the major writing processes. Saddler and Graham (2005) investigated the effects of sentence combining in a RCT study with fourth-grade students who qualified for receiving supplemental instruction. Students received their regular, Tier I writing instruction in a Writer's Workshop model classroom. The students assigned to the sentence-combining training worked in pairs, receiving supplemental instruction for 25 minutes, three times a week for ten weeks. The intervention lessons were broken into five units of six lessons each. The first unit focused on combining small sentences into a compound sentence using but, and, or because. The second unit focused on adding adverbs or adjectives from one sentence into the other. The third and fourth units focused on adding different types of clauses. The fifth unit focused on combining skills from units 2 through 4 to create better sentences. Instruction was scaffolded through teacher modeling, guided practice, and independent practice. The students assigned to the comparison group received grammar instruction focused on the parts of speech. All students completed progress-monitoring assessments throughout the intervention or comparison instruction. When the assessments from sentence-combining progress monitoring were averaged, students in the sentence-combining intervention were more likely to produce a correctly written sentence (*ES* = 1.31). Students in the sentence combining treatment also demonstrated greater benefits when they were given the opportunity to revise their stories in an effort to increase writing quality (*ES* = 0.64); there was no effect of revision for students in the comparison group. Students in the sentence-combining intervention also increased the number of sentence combining revisions completed (*ES* = 0.69). Sentence combining taught in a small group setting, as in this study, was effective in improving elementary students' writing performance.

Written Expression Instruction

Prior study has evaluated the quality of SRSD interventions (see Table 12.1 for instructional stages), establishing this approach as an evidence-based practice for small group Tier II and Tier III intervention (e.g., Baker et al., 2009; Graham, McKeown, et al., 2012). SRSD is well suited for Tier II and Tier III intervention in writing because it is a flexible approach that is easily individualized based on students' needs, the writing genre, the writing prompt/task, or other factors.

Two RCT studies investigated the effects of SRSD small group instruction for the POW + WWW, What = 2, How = 2 story writing strategy and the TREE opinion writing strategy. In the first study (Graham et al., 2005), third-grade students were randomly assigned to receive SRSD instruction, assigned to receive SRSD plus peer support, or assigned to a comparison group. Students who received SRSD or SRSD with peer support instruction spent more time writing persuasive and story-writing compositions (*ES* = 2.15 and 1.83 respectively) than the comparison group, included more elements (*ES* = 1.79 and 1.76 respectively), and wrote better quality papers (*ES* = 2.80 and 2.14 respectively). In a second study with second-grade students (Harris et al., 2006), similar effects were noted. Students who received SRSD or SRSD with peer support instruction spent more time writing persuasive and story-writing compositions (*ES* = .94 and 1.41 respectively) than the comparison group, included more elements (*ES* = 1.52 and 1.68 respectively), and wrote better quality papers (*ES* = .87 and 1.31 respectively).

Lane and colleagues also investigated the effects of SRSD instruction for Tier II writing instruction for 44 second-grade students with challenging behavior (Lane et al., 2011). Students were individually taught three to four times a week in 30-minute sessions over three to four-and-a-half weeks. Students receiving SRSD made greater gains in elements, length, and quality when writing opinion essays (*ES* > 1.10). Similar gains were noted for story writing, with students who received SRSD making greater gains than controls for elements and quality (*ES* > 1.10); a moderate effect size was noted for story length (*ES* = .58).

Practice-Based Professional Development (PBPD)

The effects of PBPD for Tier II story writing instruction with second-grade teachers was examined by Harris, Graham, and Adkins (2015). Twelve to 14 hours of PBPD was delivered in two days; researchers also observed teachers once in every three lessons and provided consultation. Teachers provided an average of 6.3 hours of instruction to small groups of students. Results indicated large gains in story quality and number of elements at post-test and maintenance (*ES* = 0.89 − 1.65).

Writing about Text

Studies have also examined SRSD related to students' writing about text they have read. SRSD instruction for the TWA (Think before reading, think While reading, and think After reading) and PLANS (Pick goals, List ways to meet goals, And make Notes, and Sequence notes) strategies has been found to be beneficial to students' informational text reading and writing (Mason, Snyder, Sukhram, and Kedem, 2006). In a RCT study, Mason, Dunn Davison, Hammer, Miller, and Glutting (2012) investigated the effectiveness of small group TWA + PLANS instruction compared to a reading-only intervention group (TWA) and a control group in a RCT study with 77 fourth-grade students. Students had been identified by their principal and teachers as having difficulty with reading comprehension and writing and had scores in the lowest range (i.e., below proficiency, < 138 out of 200 possible points) in both reading and writing on their third-grade state achievement test given in the previous year. Findings indicated that a significant difference in favor of the TWA + PLANS intervention was reported compared to the TWA-only intervention and the control group on written information units (*ES* = 0.53, *ES* = 1.11, respectively). Students who received the TWA + PLANS intervention outperformed students in the control condition on a measure of writing quality (*ES* = 1.15). On reading outcomes, significant differences were reported between the TWA + PLANS group compared to the control group on an oral information unit measure (*ES* = 0.59) and the passage comprehension subtest of the Test of Reading Comprehension-III (*ES* = 0.55).

Conclusion

Two over-arching themes are noted in our synopsis of writing instruction for RTI. First, explicit evidence-based instruction, specifically SRSD instruction for the writing process, is effective at all tier levels and effective for all genres. We caution that reviewed studies maintain strong experimental control in terms of fidelity of instruction. Results could be attenuated with any change in instructional procedures. In addition, time for teacher training and time for instructional delivery appeared to have an impact on the magnitude of effects of an intervention. In practice, we would hope schools and teachers would consider the importance of time for writing instruction.

References

Baker, S. K., Chard, D. J., Ketterlin-Geller, L. R., Apichatabutra, C., and Doabler, C. (2009). Teaching writing to at-risk students: The quality of evidence for self-regulated strategy development. *Exceptional Children*, 75, 303–318.

Benson, B. J., and Campbell, H. M. (2009). Assessment of student writing with curriculum-based measurement. In G. A. Troia (Ed.), *Instruction and assessment for struggling writers* (pp. 337–357). New York: Guilford Press.

Berninger, V. W., and Abbot, S. P. (2003). *Process assessment of the learner (PAL) research-based reading and writing lessons*. San Antonio, TX: Pearson.

Berninger, V. W., and Abbott, R. D. (2010). Listening comprehension, oral expression, reading comprehension, and written expression: Related yet unique language systems in grades 1, 3, 5, and 7. *Journal of Educational Psychology*, 102, 635–651.

Berninger, V. W., Nielsen, K. H., Abbott, R. D., Wijsman, E., and Raskind, W. (2008). Writing problems in developmental dyslexia: Under-recognized and under-treated. *Journal of School Psychology*, 46, 1–21.

Berninger, V., Rutberg, J., Abbott, R., Garcia, N., Anderson-Youngstrom, M., Brooks, A., and Fulton, C. (2006). Tier 1 and tier 2 early intervention for handwriting and composing. *Journal of School Psychology*, 44, 3–30.

Berninger, V., Vaughan, K., Abbot, R., Begay, K., Coleman, K. B., Curtin, G., . . . and Graham, S. (2002). Teaching spelling and composition alone and together: Implications for the simple view of writing. *Journal of Educational Psychology*, 94, 291–304.

Berninger, V. W., Winn, W. D., Stock, P., Abbott, R. D., Eschen, K., Lin, S., . . . and Nagy, W. (2008). Tier 3 specialized writing instruction for students with dyslexia. *Reading and Writing*, 21, 95–129.

Coker, D. L., and Ritchey. K. D. (2010). Curriculum-based measurement of writing in kindergarten and first grade: An investigation of production and qualitative scores. *Exceptional Children*, 76, 175–193.

Deno, S. L., Mirkin, P., and Marston, D. (1980). *Relationships among simple measures of written expression and performance on standardized achievement tests* (Vol. IRLD-RR-22). Minneapolis, MN: University of Minnesota.

Denton, P. L., Cope, S., and Moser, C. (2006). The effects of sensorimotor-based intervention versus therapeutic practice on improving handwriting performance in 6- to 11-year-old children. *American Journal of Occupational Therapy*, 60, 16–27.

Fletcher, J. M., Lyon, G. R., Fuchs, L. S., and Barnes, M. A. (2007). *Learning disabilities: From identification to intervention*. New York: Guilford Press.

Gansle, K. A., Van Der Heyden, A. M., Noell, G. H., Resetar, J. L., and Williams, K. L. (2006). The technical adequacy of curriculum-based and rating-based measures of written expression for elementary school students. *School Psychology Review*, 35, 435–450.

Graham, S., Bollinger, A., Booth Olson, C., D'Aoust, C., MacArthur, C., McCutchen, D., and Olinghouse, N. (2012). *Teaching elementary school students to be effective writers: A practice guide* (NCEE 2012- 4058). Washington, DC: National Center for Education Evaluation and Regional Assistance, Institute of Education Sciences, U.S. Department of Education.

Graham, S., and Harris, K. R., (1993). Self-regulated strategy development: Helping students with learning problems develop as writers. *The Elementary School Journal*, 94, 169–182.

Graham, S., and Harris, K. R. (2005). Improving the writing performance of young struggling writers: Theoretical and programmatic research from the Center on Accelerating Student Learning. *The Journal of Special Education*, 39, 19–33.

Graham, S., Harris, K., and Fink, B. (2000). Is handwriting causally related to learning to write? Treatment of handwriting problems in beginning writers. *Journal of Educational Psychology*, 94, 660–686.

Graham, S., Harris, K. R., and Hebert, M. (2011a). *Assessing Writing*. Report prepared for the Carnegie Corp. of New York.

Graham, S., Harris, K., and Hebert, M. A. (2011b). Informing writing: The benefits of formative assessment. A Carnegie Corporation time to act report. Washington, DC: Alliance for Excellent Education.

Graham, S., Harris, K. R., and Mason, L. (2005). Improving the writing performance, knowledge, and self-efficacy of struggling young writers: The effects of self-regulated strategy development. *Contemporary Educational Psychology*, *30*, 207–241.

Graham, S., Harris, K. R., Mason, L., Fink-Chorzempa, B., Moran, S., and Saddler, B. (2008). How do primary grade teachers teach handwriting? A national survey. *Reading and Writing: An Interdisciplinary Journal*, *21*, 49–69.

Graham, S., Harris, K. R., and McKeown, D. (2013). The writing of students with LD and a meta-analysis of SRSD writing intervention studies: Redux. In L. Swanson, K. R. Harris, and S. Graham (Eds.), *Handbook of learning disabilities, 2nd ed.* (pp. 105–138). New York: Guilford Press.

Graham, S., McKeown, D., Kiuhara, S., and Harris, K. R. (2012). A meta-analysis of writing instruction for students in the elementary grades. *Journal of Educational Psychology*, *104*, 879–896.

Graham, S., Morphy, P., Harris, K.R., Fink-Chorzempa, B., Saddler, B., Moran, S., and Mason, L. (2008). Teaching spelling in the primary grades: A national survey of instructional practices and adaptations. *American Educational Research Journal*, *45*, 796–825.

Harris, K. R., Graham, S., and Adkins, M. (2015). Practice-based professional development and self-regulated strategy development for Tier 2, at-risk writers in second grade. *Contemporary Educational Psychology*, *40*, 5–16.

Harris, K. R., Graham, S., and Mason, L.H. (2006). Self-regulated strategy development for 2nd grade students who struggle with writing. *American Educational Research Journal*, *43*, 295–340.

Harris, K. R., Lane, K. L., Driscoll, S. A., Graham, S., Wilson, K., Sandmel, K., . . . and Schatschneider, C. (2012). Tier 1, teacher-implemented self-regulated strategy development for students with and without behavioral challenges. *The Elementary School Journal*, *113*, 160–191.

Harris, K. R., Lane, K. L., Graham, S., Driscoll, S. A., Sandmel, K., Brindle, M., and Schatschneider, C. (2012). Practice-based professional development for self-regulated strategies development in writing: A randomized controlled study. *Journal of Teacher Education*, *63*, 103–119.

Hooper, S. R., Costa, L. J. C., McBee, M., Anderson, K. L., Yerby, D. C., Childress, A., and Knuth, S. B. (2013). A written language intervention for at-risk second grade students: A randomized controlled trial of the process assessment of the learned lesson plans in a tier 2 response to intervention (RTI) model. *Annals of Dyslexia*, *63*, 44–64.

Huot, B., and Neal, M. (2006). Writing assessment: A techno-history. In C. MacArthur, S. Graham, and J. Fitzgerald (Eds.), *Handbook of writing research* (pp. 417–432). New York: Guilford Press.

Individuals with Disabilities Education Improvement Act (IDEA) of 2004. Pub. L. No. 108–446, 20 U.S.C. § *et seq.*

Johnson, E., Mellard, D. F., Fuchs, D., and McKnight, M. A. (2006). *Responsiveness to Intervention (RTI): How to Do It.* [RTI Manual]. New York: National Research Center on Learning Disabilities.

Jones, I. (1994). The effect of the word processor on the written composition of second-grade pupils. *Computers in the Schools*, *11*, 43–54.

Kim, Y. S., Al Otaiba, S., Sidler, J. F., and Gruelich, L. (2013). Language, literacy, attentional behaviors, and instructional quality predictors of written composition for first graders. *Early Childhood Research Quarterly*, *28*, 461–469.

Lane, K. L., Harris, K., Graham, S., Driscoll, S., Sandmel, K., Morphy, P., . . . and Schatschneider, C. (2011). Self-regulated strategy development at tier 2 for second-grade students with writing and behavioral difficulties: A randomized controlled trial. *Journal of Research on Educational Effectiveness*, *4*, 322–353.

Lembke, E., Deno, S. L., and Hall, K. (2003). Identifying an indicator of growth in early writing proficiency for elementary school students. *Assessment for Effective Intervention*, *28*, 23–35.

MacArthur, C., Schwartz, S., and Graham, S. (1991). Effects of a reciprocal peer revision strategy in special education classrooms. *Learning Disabilities Research & Practice*, *6*, 201–210.

Mason, L. H., and Benedek-Wood, E. (2014). Writing instruction for the inclusive classroom. In J. McLeskey, N.L. Waldron, F. Spooner, and B. Algozzine (Eds.). *Handbook of research and practice for effective inclusive schools* (pp. 247–260). Danvers, MA: Routledge.

Mason, L., Dunn Davison, M., Hammer, C., Miller, C., and Glutting, J. (2012). Knowledge, writing and language outcomes for a reading comprehension and writing intervention. *Reading & Writing, 26,* 1133–1158.

Mason, L. H., and Mong Cramer, A. (2014). Linking classroom assessment to written language interventions. In S. G. Little and A. Akin-Little (Eds.), *Academic assessment and intervention* (pp. 241–251). Danvers, MA: Routledge.

Mason, L. H., Mong Cramer, A., Garwood, J. D., Varghese, C., Hamm, J., and Murray, A. (2017). The efficacy of SRSD instruction for developing writers with and without disabilities in rural schools: A randomized controlled trial. *Rural Special Education Quarterly, 36,* 168–179.

Mason, L. H., Snyder, K. H., Sukhram, D. P., and Kedem, Y. (2006). TWA + PLANS strategies for expository reading and writing: Effects for nine fourth-grade students. *Exceptional Children, 73,* 69–89.

Moats, L. (2009). Teaching spelling to students with language and learning disabilities. In G. A. Troia (Ed.), *Instruction and assessment for struggling writers* (pp. 269–289). New York: Guilford.

National Center for Education Statistics (2012). *The Nation's Report Card: Writing 2011* (NCES 2012–470). Institute of Education Sciences, U.S. Department of Education, Washington, D.C.

National Governors Association Center for Best Practices & Council of Chief State School Officers. (2010). *Common Core State Standards.* Washington, DC: Author.

Ohl, A. M., Graze, H., Weber, K., Kenny, S., Salvatore, C., and Wagreich, S. (2013). Effectiveness of a 10-week Tier-1 response to intervention program in improving fine motor and visual–motor skills in general education kindergarten students. *American Journal of Occupational Therapy, 67,* 507–514.

Olinghouse, N. G. (2008). Student- and instruction-level predictors of narrative writing in third-grade students. *Reading and Writing, 21,* 3–26.

Olinghouse, N. G., and Santangelo, T. (2010). Assessing the writing of struggling learners. *Focus on Exceptional Children, 43,* 1–16.

Ritchey, K. D., and Coker, D. L. (2014). Identifying writing difficulties in first grade: An investigation of writing and reading measures. *Learning Disabilities Research & Practice, 29,* 54–65.

Saddler, B., and Asaro-Saddler, K. (2013). Response to Intervention in writing: A suggested framework for screening, intervention, and progress monitoring. *Reading & Writing Quarterly, 29,* 20–43.

Saddler, B., and Graham, S. (2005). The effects of peer-assisted sentence-combining instruction on the writing performance of more and less skilled young writers. *Journal of Educational Psychology, 97,* 43–54.

Salahu-Din, D., Persky, H., and Miller, J. (2008). *The nation's report card: Writing 2007* (NCES 2008–468). National Center for Education Statistics, Institute of Education Sciences, U.S. Department of Education, Washington, DC.

Sermis, M. D., Burstein, J., and Leacock, C. (2006). Application of computer in assessment and analysis of writing. In C. MacArthur, S. Graham, and J. Fitzgerald (Eds.), *Handbook of writing research* (pp. 187–207). New York: Guilford Press.

Tindal, G., and Parker, R. (1991). Identifying measures for evaluating written expression. *Learning Disabilities Research & Practice, 6,* 211–218.

Troia, G. (2014). *Evidence-based practices for writing instruction* (Document No. IC-5). Retrieved from University of Florida, Collaboration for Effective Educator, Development, Accountability, and Reform Center website: http://ceedar.education.ufl.edu/tools/innovation-configuration/.

Troia, G., and Graham, S. (2002). The effectiveness of a highly explicit, teacher-directed strategy instruction routine: Changing the writing performance of students with learning disabilities. *Journal of Learning Disabilities, 35,* 290–305.

Wixson, K. K., and Lipson, M. Y. (2012). Relations between the CCSS and RTI in literacy and language. *The Reading Teacher, 65,* 387–391.

Yarrow, F., and Topping, K. (2001). Collaborative writing: The effects of metacognitive prompting and structured peer interaction. *British Journal of Educational Psychology, 71,* 261–282.

13

SUPPORTING THE MATHEMATICS LEARNING OF ELEMENTARY STUDENTS WITHIN A MULTI-LEVEL FRAMEWORK

Sarah R. Powell, Sarah A. Benz, and Suzanne R. Forsyth

Multi-level frameworks for supporting the learning of students with and without disabilities have become prevalent in schools over the last two decades. Academic multi-level frameworks may be referred to as multi-tier systems of support (MTSS) or response-to-intervention (RTI). All terms describe a framework for providing appropriate levels of support for the individual needs of elementary students. In this chapter, we use the term *multi-level framework* (D. Fuchs, Fuchs, and Compton, 2012) and highlight research and practices about the framework in the area of elementary mathematics.

Typical Multi-level Framework

Schools utilize multi-level frameworks for several reasons. Some schools use a multi-level framework to identify students with a specific learning disability (Hauerwas, Brown, and Scott, 2013), whereas some schools may use a multi-level framework to provide necessary instructional supports to all students. Other schools use a multi-level framework to provide supports to all students *and* identify students with learning disabilities. Regardless of the reason for implementation of such a framework, research indicates improved outcomes for students at-risk for mathematics disability (MD) when educators implement multi-level frameworks (e.g., Clarke, Doabler, et al., 2014; L. S. Fuchs, Fuchs, Craddock, et al., 2008), although more research is necessary to understand the validity of such efforts (Turse and Albrecht, 2015). There is no universal multi-level framework, but the most common framework involves three levels of support (L. S. Fuchs and Fuchs, 2002).

At Level 1 or primary prevention, all students receive high-quality, evidence-based instruction in the general education mathematics classroom. Every student in the classroom participates in a screening assessment, and results from this assessment reveal to educators which students may be at-risk for developing MD (D. Fuchs and Fuchs, 2006). These students who are suspected to be at-risk continue receiving mathematics instruction in the general education classroom. Using a brief, reliable, and valid progress-monitoring tool, educators actively monitor the progress of the suspected at-risk students to determine whether these students make adequate growth and meet adequate benchmarks (D. Fuchs et al., 2012). Students who do not show adequate progress and meet benchmarks require additional support, which occurs at Level 2 of a multi-level framework (Mellard, Stern, and Woods, 2011).

At secondary prevention (i.e., Level 2), students at-risk for MD receive high-quality, evidence-based instruction in small-group settings. This small-group intervention should both supplement and complement primary prevention instruction (L. Fuchs, Fuchs, Craddock, et al., 2008). That is, students should receive both Level 1 instruction and Level 2 intervention to receive a double dose of mathematics support. Level 2 intervention typically relies on a standardized intervention package (Powell and Fuchs, 2015). During secondary prevention, progress monitoring continues frequently (e.g., weekly) to check the progress of students at Level 2 as they receive intervention (Mellard et al., 2011). Students who demonstrate adequate response and meet benchmarks cease participation in Level 2 intervention and return to receive mathematics instruction at Level 1 only. Students who do not meet benchmarks or show adequate response move to receive the next level of intervention, Level 3. No student should receive Level 2 services continually. That is, Level 2 intervention is used to decide whether the student's needs are best met in Level 1 instruction or require Level 3 intervention.

At Level 3, also called tertiary prevention, students receive high-quality, evidence-based intervention that is individualized for the student's needs and provided one-to-one. Some educators call Level 3 intensive intervention (D. Fuchs, Fuchs, and Vaughn, 2014; Powell and Stecker, 2014), and it may occur in or outside of special education (D. Fuchs et al., 2012). Approximately 5% of students show inadequate response to Levels 1 and 2 and require some form of tertiary support (Zumeta, 2015), with more intensive and focused mathematics instruction. Level 3 intervention typically relies on a standardized intervention package that is intensified based on the individual needs of the student, but in some cases intervention materials may be generated from a collection of evidence-based practices (Powell and Fuchs, 2015). In Level 3, educators set goals and monitor progress using progress-monitoring tools to understand if students are on track to meet these goals or whether an intensification of intervention is required. Educators also use progress monitoring to determine whether students may be able to exit Level 3 intervention and return to Level 1 instruction.

Throughout the levels of a multi-level framework, instruction is provided by highly qualified general education teachers, special education teachers, mathematics specialists, interventionists, paraprofessionals, and other trained personnel. Typically, general education teachers provide Level 1 instruction and the other aforementioned personnel provide intervention at Levels 2 and 3, but every school may have different arrangements for a multi-level framework. Regardless, all instruction should be rooted in evidence-based practices (i.e., effective practices that emerge from multiple, high-quality research studies; Cook et al., 2015) and all practices should be implemented with fidelity (O'Donnell, 2008). Throughout this chapter, we refer to any person responsible for instructional delivery or decision making within a multi-level framework as an *educator*.

A vital component across levels is data-based decision making, with assessment occurring at every level. Progress-monitoring tools should be sensitive to change over time and administered frequently enough to make timely decisions (Ysseldyke, Burns, Scholin, and Parker, 2010). Progress-monitoring data is used across the multi-level framework to make decisions about movement among levels based on student response. For example, data helps educators decide which students need Level 2 intervention, which students benefit from Level 2 intervention, or which students require Level 3 intervention. In Level 3, progress-monitoring data also informs decisions about instructional changes and adaptations to the individualized intervention (Powell and Stecker, 2014). In this chapter, we provide educators with a glimpse into evidence-based practices (Cook and Cook, 2013) for instruction at Levels 1, 2, and 3 to help increase educator knowledge about multi-level frameworks in mathematics. We focus less on the assessment component, because assessment is covered in other chapters of this handbook.

Level 1 Mathematics Instruction

Within a multi-level framework, the goal of Level 1 instruction is to provide high-quality, whole-class instruction on the core mathematics curriculum. This instruction is coupled with systematic screening and progress monitoring in order to detect MD and to remediate accordingly with Level 2 or Level 3 interventions. The ideal Level 1 mathematics program combines a standards-based curriculum and evidence-based instruction to provide a high-quality learning environment for all students. In this section, we discuss three evidence-based practices that researchers have demonstrated to be effective components of Level 1 mathematics instruction: *explicit instruction*; *conceptual understanding and procedural understanding* taught in tandem; and *peer tutoring*. Then, we highlight three Level 1 instructional programs that feature some combination of these evidence-based practices. Finally, we discuss decision making within Level 1 instruction.

Evidence-Based Practices at Level 1

Explicit instruction is a systematic instructional approach in which ambiguity regarding the roles of the educator and students is minimized (Archer and Hughes, 2011). That is, the educator's role in designing and leading instruction is transparent. Explicit instruction is essential for teaching foundational concepts and procedures in an effective and efficient manner (Doabler et al., 2015), and it has proven necessary for students with MD (Gersten et al., 2009). With explicit instruction, the educator first explains the expectation for learning. Then, the educator highlights important details of the concept or procedure and provides precise instruction by modeling a concept or procedure. Next, students practice the concepts or procedures with the educator, and then students practice independently. During explicit instruction, the role of the educator is to provide feedback and connect newly learned concepts to previously learned material (Miller and Hudson, 2007). Researchers consider techniques systematic and explicit when educators demonstrate a specific strategy for tackling a concept or procedure, which students use in subsequent independent work.

Conceptual knowledge is having an understanding of mathematics concepts, and students must develop conceptual understanding to be able to link mathematical relationships (Rittle-Johnson, Star, and Schneider, 2015). For example, students must learn two concepts related to subtraction: subtraction as taking away (e.g., "There are 5 dinosaurs, and you take away 3. How many do you have left?") and subtraction as comparison (e.g., "If you have 5 dinosaurs, and I have 3 dinosaurs. What's the difference between our dinosaurs?"). Understanding these concepts of subtraction will help students in problem-solving scenarios and with understanding higher-level mathematics.

Researchers also suggest that a successful whole-class mathematics curriculum should provide opportunities to build *procedural fluency*, while incorporating activities to develop conceptual understanding (VanDerHeyden and Allsopp, 2014). For example, building procedural fluency with subtraction involves developing automaticity with subtraction facts (e.g., $8 - 5 = 3$; $14 - 8 = 6$) and fluency with subtraction computation (e.g., $45 - 19$; $204 - 173$). Procedural fluency predicts success of learning related to mathematics; however, educators should always provide an explanation (i.e., tie procedures to the concepts) of why the procedure works to provide a solution (Wu, 1999). Therefore, it is not necessary for educators to focus first on procedural skill development and then on conceptual understanding, but educators should develop conceptual and procedural understanding in tandem.

Peer tutoring is a strategy that involves pairing two students together to learn or practice an academic task. Research suggests that utilizing peer tutoring increases both student motivation and achievement (Light and Littleton, 1999). Peer tutoring can be used to reinforce mathematics facts, computational skills, or mathematics concepts (L. S. Fuchs et al., 1997). Peers can be of the same or different ability level, although research supports pairing stronger mathematics students with students who struggle with mathematics (L. S. Fuchs, Fuchs, Yazdian, and Powell, 2002). Peer tutoring increases students' response opportunities, feedback, and time on-task (Maheady, Harper, and Mallette, 2001). Using peer tutoring gives all students an opportunity to practice and verbalize mathematics skills. In order to effectively implement peer tutoring in the classroom, students must be trained to work in a pair team. Students must learn the process and benefits of peer tutoring, how to ask for help, how to offer help, and how to follow highly structured procedures.

Examples at Level 1

Early Learning in Mathematics (ELM; Chard et al., 2008) is a Level 1 kindergarten program that supports mathematics learning through explicit instruction, developing conceptual knowledge, and establishing fluency. ELM utilizes instructional scaffolding to promote the mathematics learning of all students. Researchers have demonstrated the efficacy of ELM through several rigorous studies (e.g., Chard et al., 2008; Clarke, Baker, et al., 2014; Doabler et al., 2015). For example, Clarke et al. (2011) determined that kindergarten students who participated in ELM made greater gains from pre- to post-test than students who did not participate in the focused program. Importantly, students with lower mathematics performance at pretest (i.e., students at-risk for MD) demonstrated greater gains than students not at-risk for MD with an effect size (ES) of 0.24.

ELM contains 120 lessons of 45 min each and consists of four to five math activities within one of the following content areas: numbers and operations, measurement, vocabulary, or geometry. The first activity is educator led and reviews or introduces a mathematical skill. The second activity allows for practice on the lesson's skill. The third activity provides practice on the same skill but from another content area, building conceptual understanding. Finally, the last activity is a pencil-and-paper review of the lesson and ends with a note that goes home to the parent or guardian about the mathematics covered in the lesson (Clarke et al., 2014). Throughout every lesson, ELM incorporates principles of *explicit instruction*, such as educator modeling, student practice with educator feedback, and making explicit connections for students. ELM also directly connects mathematical *concepts and procedures*.

Another evidence-based Level 1 intervention is Peer Assisted Learning Strategies (PALS) Math (L. S. Fuchs et al., 1997; L. S. Fuchs et al., 2002). This intervention is a whole-class *peer-tutoring* program that systematically provides opportunities for students to work in partnership on computation and applied problems. In the early elementary grades, a typical lesson comprises *explicit modeling* by the educator followed by peer coaching and practice. In the late elementary grades, the explicit modeling and practice occurs at the partner level. Several research teams have demonstrated the efficacy of PALS (e.g., Codding, Chan-Iannetta, George, Ferreira, and Volpe, 2011; L. S. Fuchs et al., 2002) and the effectiveness of mathematics peer tutoring in general (e.g., Maheady and Gard, 2010). In each of these studies, students who participated in PALS demonstrated significantly stronger outcomes at post-test than students who did not participate in PALS. For example, Codding et al. (2011) noted ESs of 0.29 to 0.42 for kindergarten students who participated in two active PALS conditions over a third control condition.

PALS Math is implemented two or three days a week for approximately 20 to 30 minutes a session. Therefore, PALS Math is a complement to the core mathematics curriculum but not the entire curriculum. PALS Math has two procedures: coaching and practice. During coaching, students work on problems in a prescribed area. One peer uses a question sheet to guide (i.e., coach) the other peer. The question sheet helps the coach walk their partner step-by-step through different types of math problems, therefore, helping the partner establish procedural fluency. The coach clarifies misconceptions by helping the partner understand the connection between the mathematical *concepts and procedures*. Throughout the lesson, the students switch roles and the same process is repeated for the other peer. During practice, students work independently on a mixed review of problems.

Available in several intervention packages (e.g., L. S. Fuchs et al., 2014; Jitendra et al., 2007), schema instruction is another instructional method that can be utilized within Level 1. With schema instruction, students solve word problems by identifying the problem schema, representing that schema through a diagram or equation, and solving the word problem (Powell, 2011). Schema instruction relies heavily on explicit teaching of conceptual and procedural knowledge related to word problems (Jitendra and Hoff, 1996). Schema instruction is well-researched in the elementary grades, and this type of word-problem instruction has a "strong" level of evidence as designated through What Works Clearinghouse (Gersten et al., 2009). For example, after implementing schema instruction in second-grade classrooms, Fuchs et al. (2010) noted significant gains from pre- to post-test over students in the control classrooms (ES = 0.46).

Schema instruction teaches a student to employ a set of problem-solving steps (i.e., a procedure) when given a word problem. *Explicit instruction* is used to introduce each step to students. First, the student reads the word problem. The student then identifies the problem type (i.e., schema) and uses a schematic diagram or an equation to represent the problem. Then, the student solves the word problem by solving the equation and checks for accuracy (L. S. Fuchs et al., 2009; Jitendra and Hoff, 1996; Xin, Jitendra, and Deatline-Buchman, 2005). Schemas focus on helping students understand the *conceptual underpinnings* of the word problem, and the problem-solving *procedures* assist students in solving the problem. In some iterations of schema instruction (e.g., L. S. Fuchs et al., 2010; L. S. Fuchs et al., 2014), the intervention uses *peer tutoring* to help students practice word-problem solving using schemas.

We present these Level 1 studies to demonstrate how the same evidence-based practices are incorporated into multiple evidence-based Level 1 programs. To determine how well students respond to this evidence-based instruction within a multi-level framework, educators should use progress-monitoring tools for decision making.

Decision Making Within Level 1

Any multi-level framework, whether used to provide appropriate instruction to all students or to also identify students with learning disabilities, must have an embedded assessment component for decision making. At Level 1, educators should use a two-stage assessment process (Mellard et al., 2011). A universal screening assessment should be administered to all students to determine which students might be at-risk for MD. This universal assessment might be a progress-monitoring measure, a high-stakes assessment administered within the school, or another type of assessment. Regardless, the universal assessment should provide holistic information on a student's mathematics profile and be able to identify students at-risk for not meeting grade-level expectations. The second stage involves ongoing progress monitoring of the suspected students at-risk for MD to determine whether these students require additional (i.e., Level 2) intervention. Students demonstrating adequate progress and meeting benchmarks with Level 1 instruction only remain in Level 1 instruction, and students without adequate progress begin to receive supplemental Level 2 intervention.

Level 2 Mathematics Intervention

Within a typical multi-level framework, Level 2 intervention occurs in a small-group setting within or outside of the general education classroom. The physical location of the Level 2 intervention does not matter (e.g., conference room, library, hallway, table in general education classroom), but the content of the intervention must be substantially different from instruction within Level 1. Students referred to Level 2 intervention have demonstrated, through lack of adequate progress in Level 1 instruction, the need for additional support and are at-risk for MD. If Level 2 intervention is simply more of the same, students may continue to fall behind on grade-level expectations. Ideally, it is best that students in Level 2 intervention continue to receive Level 1 instruction to allow for a double dose of mathematics (e.g., L. S. Fuchs, Fuchs, Craddock, et al., 2008; Hunt, 2014; Jitendra et al., 2013).

In evidence-based Level 2 interventions, small groups typically consist of groups of three to five students (Clarke, Doabler, et al., 2014; Dennis, 2015; Swanson, Lussier, and Orosco, 2015). These small groups meet for a substantial amount of time. For example, researchers have implemented Level 2 intervention for 12 weeks, five times a week for 30 minutes a session (Jitendra et al., 2013); five months, three times a week for 20 minutes a session (Clarke et al., 2016); or 19 weeks, four times a week for 25 minutes a session (D. P. Bryant et al., 2011). Each of these examples demonstrates that Level 2 intervention is implemented consistently during the school week for a substantial amount of time across several months. In this section, we highlight Level 2 evidence-based practices that should be integral to any Level 2 intervention. Then, we feature Level 2 interventions with these components. Finally, we discuss decision making within Level 2.

Evidence-Based Practices at Level 2

Level 2 intervention is an extension of Level 1 instruction; therefore, several effective practices can be employed at both levels. For example, research-based Level 2 interventions employ the principles of *explicit instruction* (Pool, Carter, Johnson, and Carter, 2012). Intervention lessons typically follow the format of educator modeling, guided practice (i.e., educator and student work on problems together), and independent practice (i.e., student works problems with educator feedback). The content continues to focus on teaching *conceptual and procedural understanding* in tandem. Using peer tutoring as a Level 2 intervention, however, is not usually feasible, as the students are grouped in small groups for targeted intervention with too few peers for peer practice.

Additionally, several research-based Level 2 interventions incorporate a *fluency* activity to help students with automaticity of mathematics facts or computation (e.g., Powell, Fuchs, et al., 2015). Level 2 interventions also utilize *multiple representations* to help students develop a deeper conceptual understanding of mathematics. For example, L. S. Fuchs, Schumacher, et al. (2013) used both fraction tiles and fraction circles to reinforce concepts related to fractions. In a similar manner, Clarke et al. (2016) and D. P. Bryant et al. (2011) employed visual representations to reinforce early numeracy concepts. Researchers emphasize the role of *feedback* within Level 2 intervention and how feedback is delivered to students (Clarke, Doabler, et al., 2014). Finally, researchers incorporate a *behavioral component* for effective Level 2 implementation (D. P. Bryant et al., 2011; Powell, Fuchs, et al., 2015). This behavioral component helps students maintain on-task behaviors and promote self-regulation during the lesson.

Examples at Level 2

Clarke, Doabler, et al. (2014) developed a kindergarten Level 2 intervention called ROOTS that focused on improvement of early numeracy skills. To demonstrate the importance of Level 2 intervention implemented alongside Level 1 instruction, ROOTS students also received the ELM mathematics instruction we highlighted at Level 1 (Chard et al., 2008). During ROOTS, students work on kindergarten specific standards related to counting and cardinality, number operations, and place value. The ROOTS intervention incorporates *explicit instruction* in all lessons by modeling important *concepts* and providing guided practice within each lesson. Practice focuses on establishing *procedural fluency*. Students use *multiple representations*, such as number lines, ten frames, base-10 blocks, and tally marks, to learn core kindergarten mathematics skills as the tutors provide timely academic *feedback* on student responses. ROOTS is comprised of 50 lessons implemented three times a week in small groups. Each lesson lasts approximately 20 minutes. Students who participated in this Level 2 intervention demonstrated improved mathematics learning on a standardized mathematics assessment over students who did not participate in ROOTS with an ES on a standardized mathematics assessment of 0.38.

With a focus at first grade, D. P. Bryant et al. (2008) implemented a Level 2 intervention for 23 weeks, four times per week at 20 minutes each session. Students work on a variety of mathematics skills, such as counting, number relationships, comparison, place value, and addition and subtraction concepts. D. P. Bryant et al. (2008) employed *explicit instruction* principles in every lesson by having tutors model *concepts and procedures*. Tutors use *multiple representations* to boost mathematics understanding. Examples of representations include base-10 blocks, number lines, hundreds charts, and counters. Students learn explicit strategies for addition and subtraction facts and used a "fast facts" activity to build *fluency*. Tutors provide *feedback* through specific correction on errors. Tutors also employ a *behavioral component* in which students received stickers for listening, responding, and sitting in a chair. The post-test scores of students who participated in this Level 2 intervention were significantly higher than expected based on a regression-discontinuity analysis, which indicated promise for this intervention.

At fourth grade, L. S. Fuchs et al. (2013) developed an evidence-based Level 2 intervention focused on understanding fractions. This intervention was delivered in small groups of three students during 36 lessons lasting 30 minutes each. The content of the intervention focuses on representing, comparing, and ordering fractions. *Multiple representations* of number lines, fraction tiles, and fractions circles help students connect *conceptual and procedural* knowledge. Each lesson involves a tutor using elements of *explicit instruction*, such as modeling, guided practice, and independent practice. Students develop *fluency* with fractions through a "Speed Game." Tutors provide *feedback* throughout the lesson and on an independently solved review at the end of the lesson. To help with on-task behavior, tutors use a *behavioral component*, utilizing checkmarks at sporadic intervals for listening, working hard, and following directions. After several checkmarks, students earn imitation money to buy prizes. Students who participated in this Level 2 intervention demonstrated significant gains from pre- to post-test over students in a control conditions, with ES ranging from 0.29 to 2.50.

Even though these interventions focused on developing different mathematical skills across a variety of grade levels, the intervention elements were quite similar. All interventions incorporated the Level 1 instruction evidence-based practices of *explicit instruction* and developing *conceptual and procedural knowledge* simultaneously. Level 2 interventions promoted strong procedural skill with *fluency* practice. Conceptual understanding was developed using *multiple representations*. Each educator provided *feedback* to students; this feedback was both affirmative and corrective. Interventions also integrated a *behavioral component* to assist with attention and motivation. To determine whether interventions, with these embedded components, help improve the mathematical performance of students receiving Level 2 intervention, educators must make timely decisions using assessment data.

Decision Making Within Level 2

Ideally, assessment within Level 2 should be conducted using progress-monitoring tools (e.g., D. P. Bryant et al., 2011). The collected data helps teams make decisions about movement among levels (Lembke, Hampton, and Beyers, 2012). That is, educators use data to determine whether students return to Level 1 (i.e., demonstrated adequate growth and met benchmarks in Level 2) or require intensive instruction in Level 3 (i.e., did not meet growth or benchmark expectations). Even though many schools keep students in Level 2 even after deciding the student has not demonstrated adequate growth or meets benchmarks, we suggest that Level 2 is only a temporary setting. It is used to help students catch up to their grade-level peers (i.e., Level 1) or to understand when individualized, intensive intervention (i.e., Level 3) is appropriate.

Level 3 Mathematics Intervention

Even under ideal conditions in Level 1 instruction and Level 2 intervention using evidence-based practices, approximately 5% of students struggling in mathematics will fail to show growth in targeted mathematics skills (L. S. Fuchs, Fuchs, and Compton, 2012; Zumeta, 2015). These students require a more intensive Level 3 intervention using structured, individualized, and data-driven methods (B. R. Bryant et al., 2016). This is particularly critical in the elementary grades because students who lag behind in early numeracy skills tend to continue to struggle in mathematics throughout their school careers (Geary, Hoard, Nugent, and Bailey, 2012). In this section on Level 3 intervention, we discuss evidence-based practices that should be included in Level 3 mathematics intervention. Then, we provide examples of specific interventions with these components. Finally, we review decision making and provide methods for intensification within Level 3.

Evidence-Based Practices at Level 3

As previous instructional methods at Levels 1 and 2 have proven unsuccessful for this group of students, there are broad changes that must be considered for Level 3 intervention (Powell and Fuchs, 2015). At the most basic level, significant adjustments should be made to the dosage of the intervention, the educator to student ratio, the collection and use of data, and the intervention itself (Harlacher, Nelson Walker, and Sanford, 2010; Hunt and Little, 2014; Powell and Fuchs, 2015).

Dosage refers to the time and frequency of the intervention and should be intensified for Level 3 intervention by increasing at least one of the following: the number of sessions per week, the length of the sessions, or the duration (i.e., number of weeks) of the intervention. For a Level 3 intervention, the educator ratio should also be reduced as much as possible, ideally to one-on-one instruction (Dennis, 2015).

Data collection is essential for the success of Level 3 intervention (L. S. Fuchs, Fuchs, Powell, et al., 2008) and may differ slightly from previous levels. Although assessment is important across all levels in a multi-level framework, it is crucial to success for Level 3 intervention. At this level, data informs the critical concepts or procedures that need to be targeted, whether mastery of a mathematics concept or procedure has been achieved, when to move to the next concept or procedure, and whether the intervention is impacting achievement on grade-level standards (Ciullo, SoRelle, Kim, Seo, and Bryant, 2011). For each student, the intervention team must first consider what student strengths and weaknesses have been documented during work at the previous levels of instruction and supplement this knowledge with quantitative and qualitative assessment data to reveal any foundational deficits or gaps in skills. These gaps will be targeted when individualizing the intervention plan (Hunt and Little, 2014; Powell and Fuchs, 2015). Additionally, daily and cumulative checks as well as formal progress-monitoring measures should be used to inform instruction and to track progress in closing the instructional gap with grade-level peers (Ciullo et al., 2011).

Rather than depend on a standardized intervention protocol, similar to those described in the Level 2 intervention section and which may not always be available, educators may need to individualize the material to meet the unique needs of the learner (Hunt and Little, 2014). After determining the critical skills to be addressed, the educator must determine whether there is an available Level 2 intervention that has been validated for use with students with MD and whether it can be individualized to meet the needs of the Level 3 intervention student (Powell and Fuchs, 2015). If there is no available Level 2 intervention to adapt, an educator may have to develop a scope and sequence for the student to address specific needs.

In addition to these adaptations designed to individualize and intensify the intervention, there are several fundamental components to Level 3 interventions which, when used together, provide a strong network of support for struggling learners: *explicit instruction, scaffolded instruction, conceptual and procedural knowledge building, repeated practice, review,* and a *behavioral component* (L. S. Fuchs, Fuchs, Powell, et al., 2008). Many of these are the same components of previous levels of support; however, for Level 3 intervention, educators implement these components with greater intensity. We discuss this intensity in the decision-making paragraph of this section.

As stated previously, *explicit instruction* involves the educator directly stating what the student needs to learn using precise language (L. S. Fuchs, Fuchs, Powell, et al., 2008). It includes a combination of attributes, such as modeling while thinking aloud about strategies, using multiple examples, and specific and immediate feedback on student work, whether affirmative or corrective (Jayanthi, Gersten, and Baker, 2008). Explicit instruction is not only educator talk; it also involves engaging the student in an interactive discussion regarding thinking through the problem-solving steps for problem solution (Powell and Fuchs, 2015). At Level 1 instruction, some of the interactive communication process occurs with peers; at Level 2 intervention, it occurs in a small group with educator feedback. At Level 3 intervention, this verbal discussion of concepts occurs with the student and educator in a one-on-one setting, which allows immediate affirmative or corrective feedback at a more precise and individualized level.

Another critical component of intensive intervention is *scaffolded instruction*, which is a structured frame of guidance with slowly fading supports. Scaffolded instruction may be employed at Level 1 or 2, but it is vital at Level 3 because students require varying support from the teacher. Within Level 3, the daily learning objectives need to be divided into smaller, carefully sequenced, understandable pieces, depending on the needs of the particular student (Powell and Fuchs, 2015). Secondly, if multiple steps need to be learned, mnemonic devices, written charts, or graphic organizers could be helpful in automating sequential steps. Third, it is important to use simpler examples at the beginning of learning a new concept, while slowly increasing the level of difficulty. Even the explicit instruction component can be scaffolded as the tutor moves slowly from explaining their own thought process, to asking the student what he or she thinks should be the next steps, to the student explaining the way a problem should be solved, and why.

For students at Level 3 intervention, a strong *conceptual basis tied with procedures* remains an essential component of instruction (L. S. Fuchs, Fuchs, Powell, et al., 2008). To start, the educator should connect ideas to previous knowledge and mastered prerequisite skills are a good starting point. The use of *multiple representations* can be effective by using tangible manipulatives and pictures or computerized "virtual" manipulatives to represent abstract numbers and symbols. By choosing manipulatives not explored at previous levels of instruction, conceptual understandings will be broadened (Powell and Fuchs, 2015).

Cumulative spiraling *review* is another indispensable element of successful Level 3 intervention (L. S. Fuchs, Fuchs, Powell, et al., 2008). To promote automaticity and to prevent forgetfulness in using acquired skills, all previously learned facts, concepts, and procedures need to be reviewed. More frequent reviews are required when a new skill is learned, while slowly increasing the time between addressing the same skill as the student demonstrates the ability to retrieve it and apply it over time. The data from this systematic review informs the next steps of intensive intervention (Ciullo et al., 2011).

Lack of *fluency* in mathematics facts is a well-documented feature of persistent MD (e.g., Geary et al., 2012); therefore, the Level 2 intervention activities focusing on fluency should be continued or incorporated at Level 3 intervention. Repeated review of mathematics facts, procedures, and strategies is essential for building fluency and developing automaticity. Having these skills builds confidence, increases speed, and allows the student to devote less working memory to very basic skills so that he or she can devote attention to the more complex attributes of a problem (Andersson, 2008; L. S. Fuchs, et al., 2009). Fluency activities at Level 3 could be intensified above and beyond Level 2 by focusing on a select set of fluency facts, by using manipulatives alongside fluency activities, or providing more specific feedback on fluency errors.

As in Level 2 intervention, Level 3 interventions should include a *behavioral component*. Students with persistent MD often have attention difficulties as well (Cirino, Fletcher, Ewing-Cobbs, Barnes, and Fuchs, 2007). Students at Level 3 have already worked at Levels 1 and 2 without making significant progress and can become frustrated and discouraged without a reward component built into their intervention. Having a behavioral system to monitor behavior may help students focus their attention and remain motivated to work on a subject (i.e., mathematics) that can often be overwhelming.

Examples of Level 3 Interventions

At Level 3 intervention, educators can start with an intervention designed for Level 3 intervention and delivered one-to-one. If a Level 3 intervention program is not available, tutors may select a Level 2 intervention program and intensify that intervention to a Level 3 intervention (Powell and Stecker, 2014). In some situations, tutors may create their own intervention package for Level 3. The first two options use or build upon existing evidence-based practices, which is a better route for most educators. We provide examples of all three options.

A typical Level 3 intervention is administered individually. For example, Galaxy Math (L. S. Fuchs et al., 2013) was delivered one-to-one over a period of 16 weeks, 3 sessions per week at 30 min per session. Students who participated in the Galaxy Math intervention with speeded practice focused on *fluency* demonstrated superior outcomes to students who did not receive intervention, with ESs of 0.69 and 0.87 on calculation outcomes. The program uses *explicit instruction* and *multiple representations* to increase *conceptual and procedural* understanding of numeracy skills including numbers, comparison, counting, place value, and addition and subtraction. At the end of each lesson, students participate in a speeded practice activity where they answer fact flash cards for 90 seconds and have two opportunities to beat the score from the first round. This speeded practice increases student *fluency*. Also in each lesson, students work on a *review* of previously learned materials. Embedded throughout each lesson is a *behavioral component* in which students earn stickers for exemplar behavior. After several stickers, the students select a small toy prize.

In other instances, an educator may select a Level 2 intervention program to use as a platform for developing a Level 3 intervention (Powell and Fuchs, 2015). For example, if a student required additional instruction on setting up and solving word problems, the educator might start with Pirate Math (Powell, Fuchs, et al. 2015). The second-grade version of Pirate Math targeted addition and subtraction word-problem skills and was designed for a small group of students. Under experimental conditions, Pirate Math students outperformed control students (ES = 1.31), which helps to establish Pirate Math as an evidence-based practice. Daily components of the program include a warm-up *fluency* practice activity on mathematics facts. The structured lesson comprises of *explicit instruction* to model setting up and solving word problems by *schema*. Educators model a word problem; then students work on word problems with the educator, and finally students solve word problems alone with educator *feedback*. In this way, intervention is *scaffolded*. Every lesson includes a word-problem sorting activity, where the student focuses on the *conceptual underpinnings* of the word problem. The student practices word-problem *procedures* in a daily *review*. A *behavioral component* is embedded within each lesson as students earned gold coins for on-task behavior. Earning a certain number of coins permits the student to pick a small prize from a treasure chest. An educator may use the Pirate Math small-group materials but adapt the program for a Level 3 student's needs. That is, perhaps the student requires more practice with *multiple representations* to understand the action within word problems or the student needs additional practice and review opportunities. By starting with a Level 2 intervention platform, an educator has a set of materials and can adapt the lessons from the platform to meet the unique needs of a student in need of Level 3 intervention.

In some cases, a Level 3 individual intervention or an adaptable Level 2 small-group intervention may not be available. In these instances, educators must create a scope and sequence of Level 3 instruction and assemble a set of materials for the intervention. The evidence-based practices of instruction in Level 1, 2, and 3 within a multi-level framework can guide educators when creating an individualized intervention for a student. For example, all lessons should include the major principles of *explicit instruction*, in which the educator models *concepts and procedures* and the student has multiple opportunities for practice. Instruction is *scaffolded* as the educator should provide more intensive support initially and lessen that support as the student becomes more confident and skilled with the mathematics task. *Feedback*, both positive and corrective, should be provided when necessary, and a *behavioral component* should be incorporated to help with motivation and attention. To learn whether the individualized components benefit a student receiving Level 3 intervention, assessment data helps inform decision making about intensity of the intervention.

Decision Making Within Level 3

At Level 3, data collection using progress-monitoring tools is vital so educators can make timely decisions about whether the Level 3 intervention is improving the mathematics understanding of the student. If, after a period of weeks, students do not demonstrate adequate growth with the Level 3 intervention, the educator must make an instructional change to the intervention. Powell and Stecker (2014) describe this as intensifying the intervention. Principles for intensification include: breaking down problems into *smaller steps*; ensuring the educator use *precise language* with a focus on explicit instruction of mathematics vocabulary terms; *repeating language* consistently throughout a lesson and the course of the intervention; asking the *student to explain* their reasoning to catch gaps in conceptual and procedural understanding; incorporating more *modeling* of concepts and procedures; using different *manipulatives*; providing the student with *worked examples* and discussing such example; providing opportunities for *repeated practice* throughout intervention; using *error correction* procedures when necessary; *fading support* as students do not require such intensity; building *fluency*; and *moving on* when appropriate.

Summary

Many schools have well-established frameworks for multi-level support in reading (Lembke, Garman, Deno, and Stecker, 2010), but fewer schools have established protocols for a multi-level framework in mathematics. As mathematics skill in the elementary grades is a significant predictor of mathematics performance in high school (Siegler et al., 2012) and as high-school mathematics performance sets the stage for post-secondary access and success (Lee, 2012) as well as adulthood outcomes (Dougherty, 2003), it is absolutely necessary to provide every student with access to appropriate mathematics instruction and intervention. One method for providing equitable access may be through a multi-level framework.

When designing a mathematics multi-level framework, educators must first select a reliable and valid progress-monitoring tool. The National Center on Intensive Intervention (www.intensiveintervention.org) provides useful information about different progress-monitoring measures to help educators with the decision-making process about assessments. Educators must also ensure that the Level 1 instructional program is evidence-based. The What Works Clearinghouse (ies.ed.gov/ncee/wwc/) can aid educators in determining which programs have strong evidence of impacting mathematics learning. When specific evidence-based interventions are not available, educators should rely on evidence-based practices. These are not necessarily packaged interventions, but they are strategies and practices that have shown promising evidence across a number of studies (Hughes, Powell, Lembke, and Riley-Tillman, 2016).

After the progress-monitoring measure is selected and the Level 1 instruction program is in place, it is time for educators to create an outline for multi-level instruction. As explained in this chapter, progress-monitoring growth (or lack of) determines whether students require Level 2 intervention. Level 2 intervention comprises small-group, evidence-based intervention coupled with progress monitoring. At Level 2, progress-monitoring data helps educators determine whether students return to Level 1 or proceed to Level 3. At Level 3, specific mathematics IEP goals are set, and interventions are selected or designed to meet these goals. Educators use progress-monitoring to determine whether the individual instruction at Level 3 is appropriate; in some cases, educators may need to intensify intervention.

A multi-level framework requires the participation of a team of educators who will implement instruction, administer assessments, and make decisions about movement among levels (Hoover, 2011). By implementing a multi-level framework, educators meet the needs of all students and make decisions about supplemental support in a timely fashion. This effort will likely improve the mathematics outcomes for a range of students.

References

Andersson, U. (2008). Mathematical competencies in children with different types of learning difficulties. *Journal of Educational Psychology, 100,* 48–66. doi: 10.1037/0022-0663.100.1.48.

Archer, A. L., and Hughes, C. A. (2011). *Explicit instruction: Effective and efficient teaching.* New York: The Guilford Press.

Bryant, D. P., Bryant, B. R., Gersten, R. M., Scammacca, N. N., Funk, C., Winter, A., Shih, M., and Pool, C. (2008). The effects of tier 2 intervention on the mathematics performance of first-grade students who are at risk for mathematics difficulties. *Learning Disability Quarterly, 31,* 47–63.

Bryant, B. R., Bryant, D. P., Porterfield, J., Dennis, M. S. Falcomata, T., Valentine, C., Brewer, C., and Bell, K. (2016). The effects of a tier 3 intervention on the mathematics performance of second grade students with severe mathematics difficulties. *Journal of Learning Disabilities, 49,* 176–188. doi: 10.1177/0022219414538516.

Bryant, D. P., Bryant, B. R., Roberts, G., Vaughn, S., Pfannenstiel, K. H., Porterfield, J., and Gersten, R. (2011). Early numeracy intervention program for first-grade students with mathematics difficulties. *Exceptional Children, 78,* 7–23.

Chard, D. J., Baker, S. K., Clarke, B., Jungjohann, K., Davis, K. L. S., and Smolkowski, K. (2008). Preventing early mathematics difficulties: The feasibility of a rigorous kindergarten mathematics curriculum. *Learning Disability Quarterly, 31,* 11–20.

Cirino, P. T., Fletcher, J. M., Ewing-Cobbs L., Barnes, M. A., and Fuchs, L. S. (2007). Cognitive arithmetic differences in learning disability groups and the role of behavioral inattention. *Learning Disabilities Research and Practice, 22,* 25–35. doi: 10.1111/j.1540–5826.2007.00228.

Ciullo, S., SoRelle, D., Kim, S. A., Seo, Y., and Bryant, B. R. (2011). Monitoring student response to mathematics intervention: Using data to inform tier 3 intervention. *Intervention in School and Clinic, 47,* 120–124. doi: 10.1177/1053451211414188.

Clarke, B., Baker, S. K., Smolkowski, K., Doabler, C. T., Strand Cary, M., and Fien, H. (2014). Investigating the efficacy of a core kindergarten mathematics curriculum to improve student mathematics learning outcomes. *Journal of Research on Educational Effectiveness, 8,* 303–324. doi: 10.1080/19345747. 2014.980021.

Clarke, B., Doabler, C. T., Cary, M. S., Kosty, D., Baker, C., Fien, H., and Smolkowski, K. (2014). Preliminary evaluation of a tier 2 mathematics intervention for first-grade students: Using a theory of change to guide formative evaluation activities. *School Psychology Review, 43,* 160–177.

Clarke, B., Doabler, C. T., Smolkowski, K., Baker, S. K., Fien, H., and Cary, M. S. (2016). Examining the efficacy of a tier 2 kindergarten mathematics intervention. *Journal of Learning Disabilities, 49,* 152–165. doi: 10.1177/0022219414538514.

Clarke, B., Smolkowski, K., Baker, S. K., Fien, H., Doabler, C. T., and Chard, D. J. (2011). The impact of a comprehensive Tier 1 core kindergarten program on the achievement of students at risk in mathematics. *The Elementary School Journal, 111,* 561–584. doi: 10.1086/659033.

Codding, R. S., Chan-Iannetta, L., George, S., Ferreira, K., and Volpe, R. (2011). Early number skills: Examining the effects of class-wide interventions on kindergarten performance. *School Psychology Quarterly, 26,* 85–96. doi: 10.1037/a0022661.

Cook, B. G., Buysse, V., Klingner, J., Landrum, T. J., McWilliams, R. A., Tankersley, M., and Test, D. W. (2015). CEC's standards for classifying the evidence base of practices in special education. *Remedial and Special Education, 36,* 220–234. doi: 10.1177/0741932514557271.

Cook, B. G., and Cook, S. C. (2013). Unraveling evidence-based practices in special education. *The Journal of Special Education, 47,* 71–82. doi: 10.1177/0022466911420877.

Dennis, M. S. (2015). Effects of tier 2 and tier 3 mathematics interventions for second graders with mathematics difficulties. *Learning Disabilities Research and Practice, 30,* 29–42. doi: 10.1111/ldrp. 12051.

Doabler, C. T., Baker, S. K., Kosty, D. B., Smolkowski, K., Clarke, B., Miller, S. J., and Fien, H. (2015). Examining the association between explicit mathematics instruction and student mathematics achievement. *The Elementary School Journal, 115,* 303–333. doi: 10.1086/679969.

Dougherty, C. (2003). Numeracy, literacy and earnings: Evidence from the National Longitudinal Survey of Youth. Economics of Education Review, 22, 511–521. doi: 10.1016/S0272-7757(03)00040-2.

Fuchs, D., and Fuchs, L. S. (2006). Introduction to response to intervention: What, why, and how valid is it? *Reading Research Quarterly, 41,* 93–99. doi: 10.1598/RRQ.41.1.4.

Fuchs, D., Fuchs, L. S., and Compton, D. L. (2012). Smart RTI: A next-generation approach to multilevel prevention. *Exceptional Children, 78,* 263–279. doi: 10.1177/001440291207800301.

Fuchs, D., Fuchs, L. S., and Vaughn, S. (2014). What is intensive instruction and why is it important? *Teaching Exceptional Children, 46,* 13–18. doi: 10.1177/0040059914522966.

Fuchs, L. S., and Fuchs, D. (2002). Principles for the prevention and intervention of mathematics difficulties. *Learning Disabilities Research and Practice, 16,* 85–95. doi: 10.1111/0938-8982.00010.

Fuchs, L. S., Fuchs, D., and Compton, D. L. (2012). Intervention effects for students with comorbid forms of learning disability: Understanding the needs of non-responders. *Journal of Learning Disabilities, 46,* 534–548. doi: 10.1177/0022219412468889.

Fuchs, L. S., Fuchs, D., Craddock, C., Hollenbeck, K. N., Hamlett, C. L., and Schatschneider, C. (2008). Effects of small-group tutoring with and without validated classroom instruction on at-risk students' math problem solving: Are two tiers of prevention better than one? *Journal of Educational Psychology, 100,* 491–509. doi: 10.1037/0022-0663.100.3.491.

Fuchs, L. S., Fuchs, D., Hamlett, C. L., Phillips, N. B., Karns, K., and Dutka, S. (1997). Enhancing students' helping behavior during peer tutoring with conceptual mathematical explanations. *The Elementary School Journal, 97,* 223–250. doi: 10.1086/461863.

Fuchs, L. S., Fuchs, D., Powell, S. R., Seethaler, P. M., Cirino, P. T., and Fletcher, J. M. (2008). Intensive intervention for students with mathematics disabilities: Seven principles of effective practice. *Learning Disability Quarterly, 31,* 79–92.

Fuchs, L. S., Fuchs, D., Yazdian, L., and Powell, S. R. (2002). Enhancing first-grade children's mathematical development with peer-assisted learning strategies. *School Psychology Review, 31,* 569–583.

Fuchs, L. S., Geary, D. C., Compton, D. L., Fuchs, D., Schatschneider, C., Hamlett, C. L., . . . and Changas, P. (2013). Effects of first-grade number knowledge tutoring with contrasting forms of practice. *Journal of Educational Psychology, 105,* 58–77. doi: 10.1037/a0030127.

Fuchs, L. S., Powell, S. R., Cirino, P. T., Schumacher, R. F., Marrin, S., Hamlett, C. L., . . . and Changas, P. C. (2014). Does calculation or word-problem instruction provide a stronger route to pre-algebraic knowledge? *Journal of Educational Psychology, 106,* 990–1006. doi: 10.1037/a0036793.

Fuchs, L. S., Powell, S. R., Seethaler, P. M., Cirino, P. T., Fletcher, J. M., Fuchs, D., Hamlett, C.L., and Zumeta, R. O. (2009). Remediating number combination and word problem deficits among students with mathematics difficulties: A randomized control trial. *Journal of Educational Psychology, 101,* 561–576. doi: 10.1037/a0014701.

Fuchs, L. S., Schumacher, R. F., Long, J., Namkung, J., Hamlett, C. L., Cirino, P. T., . . . and Gersten, R. (2012). Improving at-risk learners' understanding of fractions. *Journal of Educational Psychology, 105,* 683–700. doi: 10.1037/a0032446.

Fuchs, L. S., Zumeta, R. O., Schumacher, R. F., Powell, S. R., Seethaler, P. M., Hamlett, C. L., and Fuchs, D. (2010). The effects of schema-broadening instruction on second graders' word-problem performance and their ability to represent word problems with algebraic equations: A randomized control study. *The Elementary School Journal, 110,* 440–463. doi: 10.1086/651191.

Geary, D. C., Hoard, M. K., Nugent, L., and Bailey, D. H. (2012). Mathematical cognition deficits in children with learning disabilities and persistent low achievement: A five year prospective study. *Journal of Educational Psychology, 104,* 206–223. doi: 10.1037/a0025398.

Gersten, R., Beckmann, S., Clarke, B., Foegen, A., Marsh, L., Star, J. R., and Witzel, B. (2009). *Assisting students struggling with mathematics: Response to Intervention (RTI) for elementary and middle schools* (NCEE 2009–4060). Washington, DC: National Center for Education Evaluation and Regional Assistance, Institute of Education Sciences, U.S. Department of Education.

Harlacher, J. E., Nelson Walker, N. J., and Sanford, A. K. (2010). The "I" in RTI: Research-based factors for intensifying instruction. *Teaching Exceptional Children, 42*(6), 30–38. doi: 10.1177/004005991004200604.

Hauerwas, L. B., Brown, R., and Scott, A. N. (2013). Specific learning disability and response to intervention: State-level guidance. *Exceptional Children, 80,* 101–120.

Hoover, J. J. (2011). Making informed instructional adjustments in RTI models: Essentials for practitioners. *Intervention in School and Clinic, 47*, 82–90. doi: 10.1177/1053451211414193.

Hughes, E. M., Powell, S. R., Lembke, E. S., and Riley-Tillman, T. C. (2016). Taking the guesswork out of locating evidence-based practices for diverse learners. *Learning Disabilities Research and* Practice, *31*(3), 130–141. doi: 10.1111/ldrp.12103.

Hunt, J. H. (2014). Effects of a supplemental intervention focused in equivalency concepts for students with varying abilities. *Remedial and Special Education, 35*, 135–144. doi: 10.1177/074193251350778.

Hunt, J. H., and Little, M. E. (2014). Intensifying interventions for students by identifying and remediating conceptual understandings in mathematics. *Teaching Exceptional Children, 46*, 187–196. doi: 10.1177/0040059914534617.

Jayanthi, M., Gersten, R., and Baker, S. (2008). *Mathematics instruction for students with learning disabilities or difficulty learning mathematics: A guide for teachers.* Portsmouth, NH: RMC Research Corporation, Center on Instruction.

Jitendra, A. K., Griffin, C. C., Haria, P., Leh, J., Adams, A., and Kaduvettoor, A. (2007). A comparison of single and multiple strategy instruction on third-grade students' mathematical problem solving. *Journal of Educational Psychology, 99*, 115–127. doi: 10.1037/0022-0663.99.1.115.

Jitendra, A. K., and Hoff, K. (1996). The effects of schema-based instruction on the mathematical word-problem-solving performance of students with learning disabilities. *Journal of Learning Disabilities, 29*, 422–431. doi: 10.1177/002221949602900410.

Jitendra, A. K., Rodriguez, M., Kanive, R., Huang, J.-P., Church, C., Corroy, K. A., and Zaslofsky, A. (2013). Impact of small-group tutoring interventions on the mathematical problem solving and achievement of third-grade students with mathematics difficulties. *Learning Disability Quarterly, 36*, 21–35. doi: 10.1177/0731948712457561.

Lee, J. (2012). College for all gaps between desirable and actual P–12 math achievement trajectories for college readiness. *Educational Researcher, 41*, 43–55. doi: 10.3102/0013189X11432746.

Lembke, E. S., Garman, C., Deno, S. L., and Stecker, P. M. (2010). One elementary school's implementation of response to intervention (RTI). *Reading and Writing Quarterly, 26*, 361–373. doi: 10.1080/10573569.2010.500266.

Lembke, E. S., Hampton, D., and Beyers, S. J. (2012). Response to intervention in mathematics: Critical elements. *Psychology in the Schools, 49*, 252–272. doi: 10.1002/pits.21596.

Light, P. L., and Littleton, K. (1999). *Social processes in children's learning.* Cambridge, UK: Cambridge University Press.

Maheady, L., Harper, G. F., and Mallette, B. (2001). Peer-mediated instruction and interventions and students with mild disabilities. *Remedial and Special Education, 22*(1), 4–15. doi: 10.1177/074193250102200102.

Maheady, L., and Gard, J. (2010). Classwide peer tutoring: Practice, theory, research, and personal narrative. *Intervention in School and Clinic, 46*, 71–78. doi: 10.1177/1053451210376359.

Mellard, D. F., Stern, A., and Woods, K. (2011). RTI school-based practices and evidence-based models. *Focus on Exceptional Children, 43*(6), 1–15.

Miller, S. P., and Hudson, P. J. (2007). Using evidence-based practices to build mathematic competence related to conceptual, procedural, and declarative knowledge. *Learning Disabilities Research and Practice, 22*(1), 47–57. doi: 10.1111/j.1540-5826.2007.00230.x.

O'Donnell, C. L. (2008). Defining, conceptualizing, and measuring fidelity of implementation and its relationship to outcomes in K-12 curriculum intervention research. *Review of Educational Research, 78*, 33–84. doi: 10.3102/0034654307313793.

Pool, J. L., Carter, G. M., Johnson, E. S., and Carter, D. R. (2012). The use and effectiveness of a targeted math intervention for third graders. *Intervention in School and Clinic, 48*, 210–217. doi: 10.1177/1053451212462882.

Powell, S. R. (2011). Solving word problems using schemas: A review of the literature. *Learning Disabilities Research and Practice, 26*, 94–108. doi: 10.1111/j.1540-5826.2011.00329.x.

Powell, S. R., and Fuchs, L. S. (2015). Intensive intervention in mathematics. *Learning Disabilities Research and Practice, 30*, 182–192. doi: 10.1111/ldrp.12087.

Powell, S. R., Fuchs, L. S., Cirino, P. T., Fuchs, D., Compton, D. L., and Changas, P. C. (2015). Effects of a multitier support system on calculation, word problem, and pre-algebraic learning among at-risk learners. *Exceptional Children, 81*, 443–470. doi: 10.1177/0014402914563702.

Powell, S. R., and Stecker, P. M. (2014). Using data-based individualization to intensify mathematics intervention for students with disabilities. *Teaching Exceptional Children, 46*(4), 31–37. doi: 10.1177/0040059914523735.

Rittle-Johnson, B., Schneider, M., and Star, J. R. (2015). Not a one-way street: bidirectional relations between procedural and conceptual knowledge of mathematics. *Educational Psychology Review, 27,* 587–597. doi: 10.1007/s10648-015-9302-x.

Siegler, R. S., Duncan, G. J., Davis-Kean, P. E., Duckworth, K., Claessens, A., Engel, M., . . . & Chen, M. (2012). Early predictors of high school mathematics achievement. *Psychological Science, 23,* 691–697. doi: 10.1177/0956797612440101.

Swanson, H. L., Lussier, C. M., and Orosco, M. J. (2015). Cognitive strategies, working memory, and growth in word problem solving in children with math difficulties. *Journal of Learning Disabilities, 48,* 339–358. doi: 10.1177/0022219413498771.

Turse, K. A., and Albrecht, S. F. (2015). The ABCs of RTI: An introduction to the building blocks of response to intervention. *Preventing School Failure, 59,* 83–89. doi: 10.1080/1045988X.2013.837813.

VanDerHeyden, A., and Allsopp, D. (2014). *Innovation configuration for mathematics* (Document No. IC-6). Retrieved from University of Florida, Collaboration for Effective Educator, Development, Account-ability, and Reform Center website: http://ceedar.education.ufl.edu/tools/innovation-configuration/.

Wu, H. (1999). Basic skills versus conceptual understanding. *American Educator, 23*(3), 14–19.

Xin, Y. P., Jitendra, A.K., Deatline-Buchman, A. (2005). Effects of mathematical word problem-solving instruction on middle school students with learning problems. *The Journal of Special Education, 39,* 181–192. doi: 10.1177/00224669050390030501.

Ysseldyke, J., Burns, M. K., Scholin, S. E., and Parker, D. C. (2010). Instructionally valid assessment within response to intervention. *Teaching Exceptional Children, 42,* 54–61. doi: 10.1177/00400599100420 0406.

Zumeta, R. O. (2015). Implementing intensive intervention: How do we get there from here? *Remedial and Special Education, 36,* 83–88. doi: 10.1177/0741932514558935.

14

BUILDING A GROWTH MINDSET WITHIN DATA-BASED INDIVIDUALIZATION

A Case Study of Two Students with Reading Disabilities Learning to Learn

Stephanie Al Otaiba, Francesca Jones, Dawn Levy, Brenna Rivas, and Jeanne Wanzek

The research reported here was supported by the Institute of Education Sciences, U.S. Department of Education, through Grant R324A130262 to Vanderbilt University. The opinions expressed are those of the authors and do not represent views of the Institute or the U.S. Department of Education.

The purpose of this chapter is to describe and extend the limited literature on response to intervention (RTI) or multi-tiered systems of support (MTSS) for upper-elementary struggling readers. In the first section of the chapter, we explain RTI for struggling readers at this level, and synthesize the small but growing body of research that has provided intensive intervention to students who have not adequately responded to earlier intervention. We also describe a data-based individualized process for intensifying interventions for students with the most persistent reading difficulties. In the second section, we describe how developing an academic growth mindset may enhance students' motivation and reading engagement. This process involves training students to understand that intelligence and reading ability are not fixed, but malleable, and therefore can be improved, or grown through hard work and practice (e.g., Dweck, 2006).

In the third section, we describe an exploratory case study of two fourth grade students with reading disabilities who had not adequately responded to a widely implemented standard intervention provided in the context of a large experimental study. We explain the context of this larger study, then describe how we developed and implemented an intensive intervention combining elements of a growth mindset training with a data-based instruction (DBI) intensive, small group reading intervention with these two students. As we analyzed our results, we employed Dweck's (2006) mindset model of achievement motivation as a theoretical lens to describe and analyze the beliefs these children held about their reading ability, and the challenges they faced in a low-performing school. In the final section, we discuss implications for designing DBI reading interventions that support both the cognitive and psycho-social needs of students who have demonstrated significant and persistent reading difficulties in standardized interventions and suggest directions for future research about RTI implementation.

Challenges for Poor Readers in the Upper Elementary Grades: RTI and the Promise of Data-based Individualization

Nearly a third of fourth-graders in the United States read below basic levels of proficiency (National Assessment of Educational Progress, 2015) and 65% cannot read at a proficient level. Poor reading is linked to academic problems, risk of drop out, and un-or underemployment (Francis, Shaywitz, Stuebing, Shaywitz, and Fletcher, 1996; National Center for Educational Statistics, 2004; 2006; Shaywitz, 1996). The recently passed Every Student Succeeds Act (ESSA, 2015) emphasizes the need to support struggling readers by providing increasingly intensive intervention through RTI or MTSS. The Institute for Education Sciences practice guide for RTI at the primary grades, authored by Gersten and colleagues (2009), synthesized the existing research and found relatively strong evidence in the primary grades for standard tier 2 interventions for students below grade level benchmarks. Researchers have reported that RTI decreases the proportion of students found eligible for special education (e.g., O'Connor, Harty, and Fulmer, 2005; Wanzek and Vaughn, 2011).

To date, there has been very limited RTI research conducted in the upper elementary grades. When Wanzek and colleagues (Wanzek, Wexler, Vaughn and Ciullo, 2010) synthesized the research on supplemental interventions for struggling readers in the upper elementary grades, they located a relatively small number of studies ($n = 24$), only nine of which were experimental studies. The largest effects, ranging from moderate to large, were found for the few studies that implemented multi-component interventions. Of note, none of the studies examined more intensive interventions provided for students who demonstrated insufficient response to previous reading interventions.

There remains relatively limited research to guide more intensive (tier 3) interventions for early and upper elementary students who did not adequately respond to tier 2 interventions (Al Otaiba and Fuchs, 2002; Gersten et al., 2009; Lam and McMaster, 2014). What follows is a brief summary of the extant research that includes tier 2 and tier 3 interventions. The first team of researchers, Vaughn and her colleagues, conducted a series of studies (Vaughn et al., 2009; Vaughn, Wanzek and Fletcher, 2007; Wanzek and Vaughn, 2009) in which students with persistent reading problems were provided increasingly intensive standard interventions from first to third grade (roughly 500 students participated). In light of the association of poor reading achievement, academic failure, and poor post-school outcomes (NCES, 2004; 2006), Vaughn and colleagues cautioned that students who did not respond to these standard interventions would require ongoing intensive interventions that were closely guided by individual students' data.

In an in-depth case study, Wanzek and Vaughn (2009) described three third-grade students who were the least responsive to the standardized interventions that were delivered in first and second grade. In fall of first grade, the intervention was in groups of four to six students and was provided daily. In spring of first grade, they received a double dose or 60 minutes a day. In fall of second grade, intervention was in groups of three students for 50 minutes per day and in spring of second grade, intervention was one to one for 50 minutes per day. Then in third grade the intervention was one to one for 50 minutes per day. The number of intervention sessions varied by student. Carlos received 142 sessions in first grade, 98 sessions in second grade, and 94 in third grade. Ella received 145, 81, and 87, respectively and Ada received 95, 101, and 94 sessions, respectively. When he finished intervention, Carlos achieved standard scores of 98, 100, and 93 on word identification, word attack and passage comprehension, indicating he was reaching grade level performance, albeit with relatively low comprehension. Ada's standardized scores were lower: 85, 88, and 83 for word identification, word attack and passage comprehension, indicating she was roughly a standard deviation behind her peers. Similarly, Ella scores were 88, 96, and 87 for word identification, word attack and passage comprehension. Relative to the DIBELS benchmark for end of third grade oral reading fluency of 110 words correct per minute, Ada read only 28 and Carlos read 63; Ella had scores only in the fall, but she read only 19 words correct per minute, which was far behind the benchmark of 77. The authors highlighted the need for additional research on robust individualized interventions for students in special education with the most persistent learning difficulties.

Similarly, a second research team led by Denton (Denton, Fletcher, Anthony, and Francis, 2006) provided intensive tier 3 intervention to two groups of second-graders; one group had not responded to a generally successful year-long tier 2 standard protocol intervention, which also included teacher-supported tier 1, core classroom reading instruction (Mathes et al., 2005), and a second group of students consisted of classmates with similarly low reading scores. Denton and colleagues found large individual differences in response, with some students demonstrating little or no growth in the tier 3 reading intervention. She and her colleagues argued that tier 3 interventions for students with the most intractable reading problems will require something other than a standard protocol approach, suggesting research on a more data-based, individualized intervention.

Data-Based Individualized Interventions

Findings from the series of studies on RTI implementation reinforce the need to consider a DBI process for intensifying tier 3 reading interventions for students who have not responded adequately to well-implemented and generally effective standard protocol reading interventions (see also Danielson and Rosenquist, 2014; Fuchs, Fuchs, and Vaughn, 2014; Lemons, Kearns, and Davidson, 2014). Lemons et al. recommend that the DBI process involves several steps, including (1) administering diagnostic assessments as needed; (2) selecting and implementing an intensive standard protocol intervention that is consistent with the students' needs; (3) evaluating students' progress on reading skills being taught; (4) intensify or modify the intervention based on students' needs; (5) repeat as needed. For example, let's assume that Thomas is a fourth-grader with very weak comprehension, who has not demonstrated adequate progress despite receiving a standard tier 2 small-group intervention. His interventionist noted that Thomas lacked the ability to decode multi-syllabic words and was a very dysfluent reader, but the intervention was focused primarily on comprehension. She would then assess his decoding and fluency and determine what additional intervention components would build those skills. She would continue to monitor his progress and adjust to add more components, or withdraw them, as needed. Additional ways to individualize might be to reduce the size of his intervention group, to increase the amount of time he received intervention, or to ensure Thomas was practicing on texts that were at his independent reading level.

Yet another way Thomas' teacher might think about individualizing intervention may relate to informal observation data related to his lack of engagement or motivation to practice. Research has shown that poor readers often lack motivation to read and often have a diminished sense of self-efficacy (e.g., Guthrie and Davis, 2003; Quirk, Schwanenflugel, and Webb, 2004; Wigfield and Eccles, 1992). A recent study conducted at first grade supports the need for individualized reading interventions to also target engagement, self-efficacy, and motivation. Greulich et al. (2014) used a mixed methods approach to explore differences between first-graders who did and did not respond to tier 2 or tier 3 intervention (see also Al Otaiba et al., 2014 for a description of the randomized control trial). Findings from qualitative observations of intervention sessions indicated that inadequate responders, in contrast to adequate responders, demonstrated physical and verbal task avoidance when interventionists asked them to perform skills that were difficult for them; namely to blend, segment, and decode words. This avoidance behavior never occurred when their interventionists read to them during dialogic reading, a task that only required them to listen and respond to comprehension questions. In addition, inadequate responders shut down when receiving corrective feedback and frequently displayed emotions of hopelessness and shame about their poor reading. In contrast, their peers who demonstrated adequate response were less likely to avoid difficult tasks and did not demonstrate emotions of hopelessness or shame.

Developing an Academic Mindset

Reading interventions for struggling readers do not routinely support motivation and engagement (e.g., Quirk, Schwanenflugel, and Webb, 2004). One potential strategy for improving students' motivation and engagement comes from work about students' mindsets by Dweck and colleagues (e.g., Dweck, 1999; Dweck and Leggett, 1988), suggesting that students hold implicit theories of intelligence, effort, and ability that influence how tenaciously they respond to academic challenges, which in the present chapter relates to students with persistent reading problems. In her book, *Mindset: The New Psychology of Success* (2006), Dweck built on her earlier studies (e.g., Dweck, 1999; Dweck and Leggett, 1988) and hypothesized that students who hold a *fixed mindset* believe that an individual's IQ and academic ability are pre-determined and are, therefore, not malleable. Thus, individuals with a fixed mindset do not perceive that grit, perseverance, or effort impact academic learning, so they give up or avoid difficult tasks. Moreover, this fixed mindset is consistent with a view that if one does not learn something easily, it is because one is not intelligent. Success is viewed as the result of talent or an innate ability. In contrast, individuals with a *growth mindset* believe that intelligence and academic ability are dynamic and can be changed and developed through practice; further corrective feedback can contribute to growth. To individuals with a growth mindset, success is the result of grit, perseverance, or sustained effort and practice, and failure is an integral part of developing one's abilities and growth. A recent meta-analysis (Burnette, O'Boyle, Van Epps, Pollack, and Finkel, 2013) revealed that having a growth mindset significantly predicted, albeit weakly, three aspects of self-regulation: goal setting that involves learning rather than performance ($r = .18$), goal operating that involves mastery rather than helplessness ($r = .23$), and goal monitoring that involves positive expectations rather than negative emotions ($r = .16$).

There is a growing body of research indicating that older students (mostly adolescent and college-aged) who endorse the growth mindset do believe that their intelligence and academic ability can be developed through effortful and challenging work (e.g., Hong, Chiu, Dweck, Lin, and Wan, 1999; Yeager and Dweck, 2012; Yeager and Walton, 2011); students who embody the growth mindset earned higher grades (e.g., Henderson and Dweck, 1990). This mindset may be particularly important for minority students (e.g., Yeager and Walton, 2011). It also appears important for students in upper elementary, in light of findings from a recent study (Petscher, Al Otaiba, Wanzek, Rivas, and Jones, 2017). Petscher and colleagues found that fourth-graders' growth mindset (including their theory of intelligence, learning goals, and effort beliefs with regard to general intelligence and to reading, specifically) contributed to their end of year reading comprehension, controlling for their initial basic reading skills. Furthermore, having a growth mindset was more strongly associated with reading for students with weaker reading skills.

Findings from a growing body of training studies have suggested students' mindset can be influenced. Within this body of training studies two major types of interventions have been used to date. The first type of intervention is the web-based workshop *Brainology*™, which includes roughly eight 30-minute sessions that teach students that intelligence can be changed and that their brains will grow like muscles. Blackwell, Trzesniewski, and Dweck (2008) conducted a randomized control trial to examine the effects of *Brainology*™ on middle school students; participating seventh-graders demonstrated significantly higher grades in math than controls who received study skill training.

The second type of intervention, tested in four experimental studies, provided the same type of message but in a briefer training format for students in high school or college (e.g., Aronson, Fried, and Good, 2002; Good, Aronson, and Inzlicht, 2003; Paunesko, Walton, Romero, Smith, Yeager, and Dweck, 2015). Training involved reading materials about the malleability of intelligence and also required students to mentor or to write a letter to a struggling younger student about the importance of having a growth mindset. Across the studies, relative to controls, participating students had significantly greater increases in grade point averages (Aronson et al., 2002; Good et al., 2003, were less likely to drop out (Paunesko et al., 2015), and had higher end of year GPAs (Paunesku et al., 2015). Notably, Aronson et al. found the effect was slightly stronger for African American students and Paunesko et al. (2015) found that the intervention was significant for at-risk students (although this relation was not moderated by race or gender).

Exploratory Case Study

We were motivated to conduct the present case study out of concern for two students who were receiving intervention as part of a larger study in which we screened all fourth-grade students in 10 schools in two southern states (one urban district and three rural districts) to identify those who scored at or below the 30th percentile on the reading comprehension subtest of the Gates-MacGinitie Reading Test – 4th Ed. (MacGinitie, MacGinitie, Dreyer, and Hughes, 2006). Once identified, the 221 participants were randomly assigned within schools to a treatment group or to a typical school services group. In the treatment group students received daily 30-minute sessions of reading intervention provided by research staff in addition to the tier 1 core reading program. Students received intervention in small groups of four to seven students throughout the school year. The intervention, *Passport to Literacy*, is a widely-used multi-component intervention addressing word study, vocabulary, text reading, and comprehension. Overall, the treatment yielded small effects (ES = 0.14–0.28) on standardized measures of comprehension, but no effects on word reading or fluency measures (Wanzek et al., in press).

By late November, it became apparent for two students that the reading comprehension activities were far beyond their independent reading levels. Both had fourth-grade oral reading fluency (ORF) scores that hovered in the 11–19 words correct per minute (wcpm), far below the 110 wcpm benchmark for risk; they demonstrated the lowest level and slowest growth trajectory among any students in the treatment group. Further, similar to characteristics of inadequate responders in the Greulich et al. study (2014), interventionists and observers expressed concern that both of the students had begun to demonstrate more off-task behavior, more embarrassment, more avoidance, less engagement, and less motivation. Their interventionist tried making modifications; for example, she pulled these two students prior to daily intervention and previewed the vocabulary words and read the lesson stories aloud to them. She pre-taught the spelling words and helped them practice words and sentences they would be asked to read aloud in the group. However, they still could not keep up in the group setting and their off-task behavior escalated.

Our research team, in consultation with the classroom teacher and the students' guardians, withdrew them from the larger study and began this case study with one overarching research question: Is it feasible and promising to combine growth mindset training within a DBI reading intervention process?

Case Study Methods

Participants

The participants were two fourth-grade African American students; Peter and Bianca (pseudonyms), who had just been identified in late fall as having unspecified reading disabilities and began receiving special education (resource room setting). According to their classroom teacher, neither had previously received any intervention from the school, although Bianca had repeated third grade. Both students had the same general education teacher and the same special education resource teacher. They attended a high need elementary school serving 430 students (preschool through fifth grade) located in a high-poverty, urban area of a large southern city in which 97% of students qualified for free or reduced lunch. Notably only 43.4% of the fourth-graders passed the statewide reading exam the year prior to our intervention.

For the case study, we selected an interventionist who was the most experienced member of the research team. She had a Master's degree in reading and writing, nearly a decade of classroom experience, and had served as a teacher on a prior research project. Further, she had experience teaching the intensive standard protocol intervention we selected to be consistent with the students' needs. She also had extensive experience with progress monitoring and with modifying instruction to meet the instructional needs of students and was capable of implementing instructional changes to benefit Peter and Bianca.

Diagnosing Students' Initial Reading Skills

To measure students' initial reading skills, we conducted diagnostic assessments and progress monitoring measures (see Methods section). Bianca's standard scores were two or more standard deviations below grade level norms. Her standard scores were 60, 63, 68, and 69 on the Woodcock Johnson III (WJ-III; Woodcock, McGrew, and Mather, 2001) letter word identification, passage comprehension, word attack and picture vocabulary subtests, respectively. On the Test of Oral Word Reading Efficiency (TOWRE, Torgesen, Wagner, and Rashotte, 1999), she scored a 55 and 60 for sight word and phonemic decoding fluency, respectively. She read only 12 words per minute on the Dynamic Indicators of Basic Early Literacy Skills (DIBELS; Good and Kaminski, 2002) fourth grade ORF measure. Furthermore, on the criterion-referenced Diagnostic Assessment of Reading (DAR, Roswell, Chall, Curtis, and Kearnes, 2005), she knew her consonants (but confused b and d) and short vowel sounds, but could not read any words with silent-e, vowel diagraphs, diphthongs, -r controlled vowels, or any multi-syllabic words.

Peter performed at a slightly higher level, particularly on vocabulary, but was also dysfluent in his reading. His standard score equivalents on the WJ-III (Woodcock et al., 2001) letter word identification, passage comprehension, word attack, and picture vocabulary subtests were 74, 60, 73, and 103, respectively. He scored 55 and 56, respectively on the sight word fluency and phonemic decoding fluency subtests of the TOWRE (Torgesen et al., 1999). Similar to Bianca, he read only 11 words correct per minute on the DIBELS (Good and Kaminski, 202) fourth grade ORF. The DAR (Chall et al., 2005) results revealed he knew 17 consonants and the short vowel sounds, read only a few words with silent-e, and like Bianca, he could not read any vowel digraphs, diphthongs, -r controlled vowels, or any multi-syllabic words. As a result of the two students' performance on these measures, it was determined that they were at a beginning reading level across all measures.

DBI Intervention: Combining Growth Mindset and Reading

The Reading DBI Intervention

The students' pre-test scores revealed a need to improve their basic word reading and fluency, so as a starting point, we selected *Early Interventions in Reading* (*EIR*; Mathes, Torgesen, Wahl, Menchetti, and Grek, 1999; Mathes et al., 2005) as the intensive intervention that would be most closely matched with the students' reading needs. *EIR* is a standard commercially available curriculum that has a strong evidence base for students in first grade. Each lesson includes: phonemic awareness, alphabetics and phonics, and fluency. The interventionist administered the *EIR* placement test and both students' performance indicated they should begin on Lesson 21. Across the 14-week intervention, students completed 28 lessons (two lessons per week during four 30-minute sessions). Fidelity of implementation of EIR was monitored using a fidelity checklist used in previous studies (Mathes et al., 2005); the interventionists' average fidelity score was high (97%).

Following typical DBI procedures, other intervention components were added as the interventionist and the research team met weekly to consider Bianca and Peters' progress-monitoring data and informal observations by the interventionist. Four intervention components were added in phases. The first component was goal setting and student self-graphing, which was selected based on prior research (e.g., Hattie, 2009) and because it connected well to the mindset aspect of the intervention (described below) by helping students recognize the relation between improved reading scores and their own hard work. Each week students were encouraged to increase their personal goal over their prior week's results by two words per measure. After each assessment, the students were given time to shade in their new results on a graph.

The second component was high-frequency sight word flashcard training beginning with the pre-primer – first grade Dolch word list. This was selected as a result of observations of students' lack of fluency on these words and that they required more practice on sight words than was part of *EIR*. Flashcards were practiced once or twice at the beginning of each lesson. The interventionist used mindset terminology as she praised the students' hard work and related this to their increasing scores. The third component was developed after it was noted that the students routinely confused the letters /b/ and /d/. The interventionist taught the students to form the letter "b" with their left-hand thumb and forefinger, and "d" with their right-hand forefinger and thumb whenever they were to read a word with a "b" or "d" and weren't sure which letter it was. This was used as needed. The fourth component was essentially related to the second component; namely once the students mastered the pre-primer – first grade DOLCH words, we added second grade DOLCH words. These four extra components are represented in the graphs of progress monitoring in the Results section in Figures 13.1 and 13.2.

Mindset Training

To specifically address students' off-task behavior and to improve their engagement and motivation, we embedded elements of *Mindset* (Dweck, 2006) throughout the intervention. During the first week with the students and prior to beginning the DBI reading intervention, the interventionist read an excerpt from *Mindset* that was about the growth mindset, that the brain can grow and develop, and that reading effort and practice can improve reading performance. During reading intervention, the interventionist used praise for effort that improved their performance (trying hard, persisting, staying engaged). In addition, once a week, she read aloud to Bianca and Peter from the book *Portraits of African-American Heroes* (Bolden, 2003). She selected a total of six four-page biographies of African American heroes, including Martin Luther King, Jr., Fredrick Douglas, W.E.B. Du Bois, Thurgood Marshall, Ben Carson, Malcolm X, and Shirley Chisholm. She also read from *Barack Obama Working to Make a Difference* (Brill, 2006). These biographies were consistent with the growth mindset in that the main characters overcame adversity and challenges through hard work and perseverance. After the interventionist read each biography, she led discussions by eliciting background knowledge, and asking open-ended questions. She explicitly linked these books thematically and directly back to mindset, while also making direct connections to the students' own hard work during intervention sessions.

Data Sources and Data Collection Procedures

Student Progress Monitoring Measures

The interventionist administered three, one-minute curriculum-based measurement progress-monitoring measures to determine responsiveness to various intervention elements within *EIR* and to guide individualization of the intervention. She administered the Word Identification Fluency (WIF) task (Fuchs, Fuchs, and Compton, 2004) to assess students' fluent reading of first grade sight words. In this task, students read from an array of 50 first-grade sight words (randomly selected from a high-frequency word list). To assess students' fluent reading of low frequency CVC words (e.g., lid), she administered a measure created by Burns and colleagues, also named the Word Identification Fluency task (Press Research Team, 2014). Then to assess oral reading fluency growth weekly, she administered first grade DIBELS ORF (Good and Kaminski, 2002).

Observations of Instruction

To describe the quality of Tier 1 and special education reading instruction, on two occasions trained team members observed the students' Tier 1 instruction and then, on three occasions, listened to audiotapes of the students' special education reading instruction. The low-inference Instructional Content Emphasis Instrument-Revised was used (ICE-R; Edmonds and Briggs, 2003), to code the content (e.g. phonemic awareness, phonics, comprehension) and group size for instruction (e.g., whole class, small-group). Student engagement was coded using a three-point rubric (3 = high engagement, 1 = low engagement) and the overall quality of instruction was coded with a four-point rubric ranging from weak (rating of 1) to excellent (rating of 4). Global instructional quality included the teacher's use of direct and explicit language, modeling, opportunities for practice, specific feedback, monitoring and encouragement of engagement, scaffolding of tasks, and pacing. Interrater reliability over 95% was established as part of the larger study (See Wanzek et al., in press).

Mindset Coding

In addition to the ICE-R instructional coding, members of the research team coded the special education intervention recordings to address the nature of instruction and whether the teachers' instructional language was consistent with a fixed or a growth mindset. Coders noted the teacher statements of growth to support or, conversely, correction or frustration. A consensus was achieved, but no formal inter-rater reliability was calculated. The intention was to describe the instructional context that these students experienced.

Field Notes

The DBI interventionist kept field notes following each lesson that described the school environment, the instructional components, and the aspects of instruction related to fixed vs. growth mindset. During her lessons she would note any moments or statements of failure or success that the students made. Further, two doctoral students trained in qualitative research observed the DBI intervention instruction and collected field notes. Specifically, they described the instructional activity and noted any statements of struggle, frustration, growth, or success by the students or teacher. Further, they described both the instructional setting and learning environment in their observation.

Data Analysis

We used several strategies to improve the reliability and validity of the study (e.g. LeCompte and Schensul, 1999; Strauss and Corbin, 1998). We also applied the quality indicators suggested for qualitative research in special education (Brantlinger, Jimenez, Klingner, Pugach, and Richardson, 2005) to strengthen confidence in the findings. For example, during the study the research team met frequently for member-checking and participant debriefing. An important aspect of qualitative research is the use of multiple forms of data in order to support the credibility and accuracy of the data and in order to triangulate findings.

We took several steps to analyze this data. We first examined the progress-monitoring graphs created through the data-based individualization process to describe the students' progress. Next, we reviewed data from the ICE-R observations, and field notes about instruction and intervention. This step also involved checking in with the research team (i.e., member-checking and theory-checking). Then we began to code data, which involved analyzing and discussing specific cases examples and non-examples of fixed and growth mindset among co-authors to validate the coding process (Denzin, 1996). During this coding process, one theme the team noted was that the chaotic home and school environments may contribute to both the mindset and the responsiveness of students, and so we coded examples of *chaos in general education* and *chaos in special education*. We also noted another theme, that there were initial differences in mindset language depending upon whether students were engaged in intervention or were being assessed (*growth in intervention; growth in assessment; fixed in intervention, fixed in assessment*). Therefore, we noted instances when fixed vs. growth mindsets were embedded in these assessment or instruction contexts (i.e., axial coding; Strauss and Corbin, 1998). Another theme was that the interventionist seemed to scaffold, or to hold a growth mindset for the students (*holding a growth mindset for the students*). Finally, a cross-case analysis was used to examine patterns of differences across the two students. Two members of the research team coded all the data independently and in the rare instances of disagreement, results were compared, discussed, and re-coded.

Results

Our primary research question asked whether it was feasible and promising to combine growth mindset training within a DBI reading intervention process. We describe findings for both the students' mindsets and their progress monitoring on reading measures to examine their response to intervention. We initiated our results with the overall theme that emerged of challenges within the school and classrooms related to chaos and criticism. Next, we describe the feasibility and promise of our intervention that combined growth mindset and DBI reading components by examining three themes for each student: how they reacted to the challenges of chaos and criticism, how they reacted to challenges during assessment and a description of their trajectories and growth on the progress monitoring, and how they reacted to challenges during the DBI intervention.

Challenges: Chaos and Criticism

One of the pervasive themes that emerged from the coding of the field notes and observations was the level of school and classroom chaos that Peter and Bianca experienced. The research team had documented in their field notes that there were students unsupervised in the hallways, teachers frequently yelling at students and a very high noise level throughout the school. The interventionist frequently had trouble finding the students for intervention because they might be in a different classroom.

The team also reported that the initial classroom teacher, observed only during the first ICE-R observation, had health issues that led to frequent absences. She was often late to school or absent altogether and, in these instances her class was either divided among other classrooms, or an aide would substitute if there was no certified substitute. In their fieldnotes, the interventionist and the fidelity of implementation observer reported that the substitutes who then stepped in were of varied quality and that a lack of classroom management was a persistent issue for all of them. The classroom teacher's instruction, as documented through the ICE-R observation in the fall, was generally good quality (3 out of 4) and student engagement was high (3 out of 3). However, she did not provide any word study or phonics instruction, which were areas of instruction needed by Bianca and Peter. During her observation, she spent 31 (out of 56) minutes on comprehension activities and 14 minutes on text reading activities, which consisted of a student reading aloud while the other students followed along; the remaining 11 minutes were spent doing transitional or non-academic activities. During the second ICE-R observation in the spring, there was a long-term substitute teacher, who was observed for a 34-minute instructional period; he spent 29 minutes on comprehension activities and the rest in transitional, non-academic activities. He received an instructional quality rating of 4 and student engagement remained high at 3, which is not consistent with the general chaos that was observed.

The ICE-R observations of the special education teacher indicated she also received fairly good scores on all three occasions, despite the chaos generally observed in her resource room. Her quality of instruction ratings averaged a 3 and student engagement was a 2.5. During the first observation, she provided 29 minutes of instruction; phonics predominated (25 minutes), with the remaining minutes devoted to comprehension activities. During the second observation, she taught for 46 minutes (25 minutes of phonics instruction, 19 minutes of text reading, and three min of non-academic activity). During the third observation, she provided 50 minutes of instruction (37 minutes of phonics, four minutes of text reading, and nine minutes of non-academic activities).

However, the ICE-R was not designed to capture the quality of interactions between the teacher and students, the warmth and sensitivity of the teacher, or the occurrence of positive feedback. The coding of audiotapes for growth and fixed mindset revealed that the special education teacher was highly critical of both Peter and Bianca. For example, she frequently expressed exasperation about their low academic performance and behavior.

Bianca: Challenges, Chaos, and Criticism

The interventionist's field notes suggest that the chaos of the school and classroom was associated with Bianca's mood when she came for intervention sessions. In times of the greatest chaos, she would come to the intensive intervention in this study unsettled and insecure. She would often act out and it was difficult to get her to sit and engage to receive instruction. For example, one day a team member noted that Bianca refused to work at the onset of the session, but then she responded to praise for her subsequent effort. The initial coding suggested Bianca did not have a growth mindset. However, the fieldnotes revealed over time that she had more of a growth mindset than initially hypothesized. For example, she enjoyed discussing the brain as a muscle that one can exercise and grow like other muscles.

BIANCA: CHALLENGE DURING ASSESSMENT

As the interventionist's field notes described, when initially given an assessment, Bianca put her head on the table and sighed and then simply guessed at the answers without trying to read the material. But after the interventionist encouraged her to work her hardest even if she did not know the answers, she persisted on the next few assessments and stayed engaged. As the weeks went on, however, her growth mindset was more independent, and she did not need any prompts to do her best work on her assessments and kept trying even if the tasks were difficult. During one observation, it was noted that she asked to do a test over because there was a lot of noise in the hallway that distracted her and she wanted to do her best.

Bianca's reading growth was steady. Her initial fourth grade ORF was only 12; hence we monitored her progress on first grade ORF; her scores on the first grade ORF averaged 23 wpm during baseline. We considered one word a week improvement as an ambitious goal (Fuchs and Fuchs, Hamlett, Walz, and Germann, 1993). During the last phase of intervention, her correct ORF words per minute increased to an average of 49 (see Figure 14.1). This represents a growth of 1.85 words per week over 14 weeks of intervention. Her scores on the WIF averaged 21 at baseline and increased to 35 for the final phase of intervention, which represents growth of one word per week. However, on the decoding WIF (Press Research Team, 2014), she only read one more word at post-test than she did at baseline. Overall, this is strong growth, but clearly despite the intervention, she was still not on grade level and showed no improvement in terms of standardized test scores on any of the measures.

When analyzing the promise and feasibility of the DBI intervention, two components were associated with the steepest improvement in her scores. The goal setting and self-graphing intervention had students graph their scores and track progress toward self-selected goals. Bianca's scores increased from 26 to 34 wcpm on the ORF measure during this phase. Further, sharp improvement was observed with the introduction of the b/d strategy where she was given a specific tool (hand signs) to distinguish between the letters b/d with a jump from 24 to 42 wcpm on the ORF measure. Scores showed steady but slow progress and may continue to progress with continued consistent participation in the intervention.

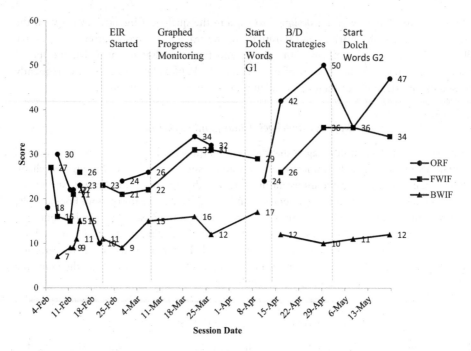

Figure 14.1

BIANCA CHALLENGES: INTERVENTION

During the reading intervention, Bianca was embarrassed when she made mistakes and did engage in some avoidance behaviors such as eye rubbing and playing with her jewelry. When faced with a challenging task she would sometimes state, "this is too hard." However, the coding from the interventionist's field notes revealed this was not her most frequent response. More often, she would work harder to master tasks that challenged her. For example, Bianca asked to take home a list of Dolch sight words to practice. She also asked if she could bring her ORF story and graph to show her mom and teacher. On another occasion, when she was practicing fluency, she was proud of herself for reading well and asked to read the story again. And in yet another example, when she was told their reading session could end early she said, "No! I want to continue the lesson!" Bianca continued to exert effort, recognize that deliberate practice was paying off, and she began to be more persistent as the observations and field notes revealed.

Peter Challenges: Chaos and Criticism

Initially, based on his participation in small group instruction for the larger study, the research team thought Peter might have more of a growth mindset during the reading intervention. This was because, despite his struggles and the chaos in the school, he was polite, seemed happy and was respectful. However, once the data from the case study were coded and themes emerged, it was evident that he did not like trying tasks when he thought he would fail. Because he did not act out or get visibly upset, this pattern was not initially clear but he had developed skills of avoidance, such as constantly asking off-topic questions so he would not have to complete tasks. Also, when Peter failed, he would quietly shut down and withdraw from tasks rather than act out. This was consistent in his classroom, too. While others would act out and misbehave, he would withdraw. During the mindset intervention time, where students read biographies of individuals who had to overcome great odds, Peter was very engaged and eager to hear about the success of others. In particular, the interventionist noted that he asked to reread about Malcolm X and then was able to recall many details.

PETER CHALLENGES: ASSESSMENT

Evidence supported that, initially, Peter had a very fixed mindset, especially towards assessment. He had anxiety about any assessment activity and expected failure whenever he was faced with a test; this was compounded when the assessment was timed. He had to be encouraged by his teacher to even continue to complete an assessment at the outset of the study. For several tests, Peter simply replied, "I don't know" for every item. However, as the interventionist supported his growth mindset, he became more positive about the tests and viewed them as a challenge he could overcome. As the study progressed, field notes revealed that Peter attacked assessment with a more positive attitude. In particular, one intervention component that was particularly helpful in helping his mindset towards assessment was when he graphed his progress monitoring results. The interventionist's field notes reported that Peter was very excited about graphing his scores and wanted to keep setting the goals higher. Similar to Bianca, this component was associated with the steepest improvement in Peter's first grade ORF scores (see Figure 14.2); he increased from 16 to 35 wcpm, and eventually to 37.5 wcpm for an average growth of 1.05 words per week. His WIF scores averaged 21.6 words during baseline and grew to 30 wcpm for an average growth of .64 words a week. Scores on the decodable WIF (Burns) averaged 4.4 at baseline and grew to 10.5 at the end of the intervention for an average growth of .43 words a week. Overall, he made good growth on these proximal progress monitoring measures,

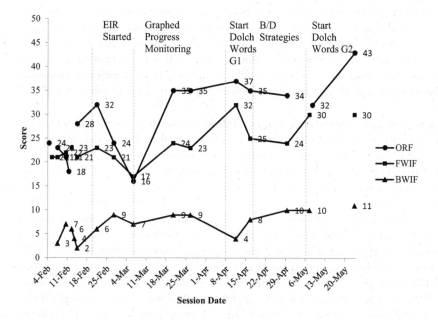

Figure 14.2

but clearly despite the intervention, he was still not on grade level and, like Bianca, Peter showed no improvement in terms of standardized test scores on any of the measures.

PETER CHALLENGES: INTERVENTION

Peter's initial mindset towards reading seemed to be fixed. During one observation, the interventionist noted that Peter continued to reject the notion that his reading abilities could improve. Peter believed that a single error made the entirety of his effort unsuccessful and saw little value in his efforts when they did not result in a perfect outcome. Peter was unable to admit shortcomings and was frustrated when faced with challenges.

Peter required the interventionist to hold the growth mindset for him and to continuously scaffold his growth towards that mindset. Initially this scaffold was not enough. Early in the reading intervention, he stated, "I'm not very good at reading." However, a month later, when asked what he does if he's stuck on a word, Peter stated, "Sound it out." When asked, "What happens if you can't sound it out?" he replied, "You ask someone to help you." This represented a new attitude of persisting through a challenge and not simply giving up. Encouragingly, by the end of the intervention he would even ask for harder books as he became more confident in challenging himself and his newfound abilities.

Implications and Directions for Future Research About RTI

Our findings add to the growing debate regarding whether older students with such weak initial skills should participate in a less intensive tier 2 intervention prior to receiving the most robust DBI and resources schools can offer. It is hard to fathom that these students had not been eligible for special education or early intervention before fourth grade, given their very weak reading performance. As with all case studies, our findings can contribute by guiding designs for future intensive DBI in reading, providing some preliminary evidence of the promise of embedding mindset training into intervention, but no causal conclusions can be made. Our field notes indicated that the students appeared to enjoy the program. Further, field notes revealed students gradually learned to attribute their own growth to effort and practice on the DBI components. Across time, the interventionist reported fewer instances of avoidance, hopelessness, and shame that initially characterized our students. These negative characteristics had been shown to distinguish inadequate vs. adequate responders in the Greulich et al (2014) study.

Although promising, the intervention was not sufficient to accelerate our students to reach grade level expectations on standardized measures. However, the students did demonstrate growth on first grade oral reading fluency (reaching 50 and 43 wcpm, respectively) and on their sight word reading fluency (reaching 36 and 30 wcpm, respectively). They did not increase their ability to fluently read CVC decodable low frequency words.

Our findings are similar to Wanzek and Vaughn's case study (2009), which found that despite very intensive intervention, only one of the three participants demonstrated average word reading standard scores and none of the children met oral reading fluency benchmarks. Our students received approximately 73 total sessions (ranging from 30 minutes in tier 2 to 45 minutes in tier 3), which is less than in the Wanzek and Vaughn (2009) case study in which students could receive up to 94 50-minute one-to-one sessions across third grade. Denton and colleagues (2006) also provided more intensive intervention than we were able to in this study; delivering over 80 sessions across 120 hours of tier 3 intervention, but still, only half the students demonstrated growth of at least a half a standard deviation on the WJII-Basic Reading

Skills (Woodcock et al., 2001; word attack and letter word identification). Thus, findings from these studies emphasize the need for intensive and sustained intervention; more research is needed to explore the efficacy of more robust interventions, including those with psycho-social supports as well as academic components. Having a growth mindset across time may help students have the grit to persist even when reading remains very challenging.

References

Al Otaiba, S. and Fuchs, D. (2002). Characteristics of children who are unresponsive to early literacy intervention: A review of the literature. *Remedial and Special Education, 23*, 300–316.

Al Otaiba, S., Connor, C. M., Folsom, J. S., Wanzek, J., Greulich, L., Schatschneider, C., and Wagner, R. K. (2014). To wait in tier 1 or intervene immediately: A randomized experiment examining first grade response to intervention (RTI) in reading. *Exceptional Children, 81*(1) 11–27. doi: 10.1177/00144 02914532234.

Aronson, J., Fried, C., and Good, C. (2002). Reducing the effects of stereotype threat on African American college students by shaping theories of intelligence. *Journal of Experimental Social Psychology, 38*, 113–125.

Boldon, (2003). *Portraits of African-American heroes.* New York: Dutton.

Blackwell, L., Trzesniewski, K., and Dweck, C. S. (2008). Implicit theories of intelligence predict achievement across an adolescent transition: A longitudinal study and an intervention. *Child Development, 78*, 246–263.

Brantlinger, E., Jimenez, R., Klinger, J., Pugach, M., and Richardson, V. (2005). Qualitative studies in special education. *Exceptional Children, 71*(2), 195–207.

Brill, M. T. (2006). *Barack Obama: Working to make a difference.* Minneapolis, MN: Millbrook Press.

Burnette, J. L., O'Boyle, E. H., Van Epps, E. M., Pollack, J. M., and Finkel, E. J. (2013). Mind-sets matter: A meta-analytic review of implicit theories and self-regulation. *Psychological Bulletin, 139*(3), 655–701.

Danielson, L., and Rosenquist, C. (2014). Introduction to the TEC special issue on data-based individualization. *Teaching Exceptional Children, 46*, 6–12.

Denton, C. A., Fletcher, J. M., Anthony, J. L., and Francis, D. J. (2006). An evaluation of intensive intervention for students with persistent reading difficulties. *Journal of Learning Disabilities, 39*, 447–466. doi: http://dx.doi.org/10.1177/00222194060390050601.

Denzin, N. K. (1996). *Interpretive ethnography: Ethnographic practices for the 21st century.* Thousand Oaks, CA: Sage.

Dweck, C. S. (1999). *Self-theories: Their role in motivation, personality and development.* Philadelphia, PA: Psychology Press.

Dweck, C. S. (2006). *Mindset: The new psychology of success.* New York: Random House.

Dweck, C. S., and Leggett, E. L. (1988). A social-cognitive approach to motivation and personality. *Psychological Review, 95*, 256–273.

Edmonds, M., and Briggs, K. (2003). The instructional content emphasis instrument: Observations of reading instruction. In S. Vaughn and K. L. Briggs (Eds.), *Reading in the classroom: Systems for the observation of teaching and learning* (pp. 31–52). Baltimore, MD: Brookes Publishing Co.

Every Student Succeeds Act Pub. L. 114–95.

Francis, D., Shaywitz, S., Stuebing, K., Shaywitz, B., and Fletcher, J. (1996). Developmental lag versus deficit models of reading disability: A longitudinal, individual growth curves analysis. *Journal of Educational Psychology, 88*(1), 3–17.

Fuchs, L. S., Fuchs, D., Hamlett, C.L., Walz, L., and Germann, G. (1993). Formative evaluation of academic progress: How much growth can we expect? *School Psychology Review, 22*, 27–48.

Fuchs, L. S., Fuchs, D., and Compton, D. L. (2004). Monitoring early reading development in first grade: Word identification fluency versus nonsense word fluency. *Exceptional Children, 71*(1), 7–21.

Fuchs, D., Fuchs, L. S., and Vaughn, S. (2014). What is intensive instruction and why is it important? *Teaching Exceptional Children, 46*(4), 13–18.

Good, C., Aronson, J., and Inzlicht, M. (2003). Improving adolescents' standardized test performance: An intervention to reduce the effects of stereotype threat. *Journal of Applied Developmental Psychology, 24*, 645–662.

Good, R. H., and Kaminski, R. (2002). *Dynamic Indicators of Basic Early Literacy Skills 6th Edition (DIBELS).* Eugene, OR: Institute for the Development of Educational Achievement. Retrieved from http://dibels.uoregon.edu/.

Gersten, R., Compton, D., Connor, C. M., Dimino, J., Santoro, L., Linan-Thompson, S., and Tilly, W. D. (2009). *Assisting students struggling with reading: Response to Intervention and multitier intervention for reading in the primary grades. A practice guide* (NCEE 2009–4045). Washington, DC: National Center for Education Evaluation and Regional Assistance, Institute of Education Sciences, U.S. Department of Education.

Greulich, L., Al Otaiba, S., Schatschneider,C., Wanzek, J., Ortiz, M., and Wagner, R. K. (2014). Understanding inadequate response to first grade multi-tier intervention: Nomothetic and idiographic perspectives. *Learning Disability Quarterly, 37*, 204–217. doi: 10.1177/0731948714526999.

Guthrie, J. T., and Davis, M. H. (2003). Motivating struggling readers in middle school through an engagement model of classroom practice. *Reading and Writing Quarterly, 19*, 59–85.

Hattie, J. A. C. (2009). *Visible learning: A synthesis of over 800 meta-analyses relating to achievement.* New York: Routledge.

Henderson, V. L., & Dweck, C. S. (1990). Achievement and motivation in adolescence: A new model and data. In S. Feldman and G. Elliott (Eds.) *At the threshold: The developing adolescent.* Cambridge, MA: Harvard University Press.

Hong, Y. Y., Chiu, C. Y., Dweck, C. S., Lin, D., and Wan, W. (1999). Implicit theories, attributions, and coping: A meaning system approach. *Journal of Personality and Social Psychology, 77*, 588–599.

Lam, E. A., and McMaster, K. L. (2014). Predictors of responsiveness to early literacy intervention: A ten year update. *Learning Disability Quarterly, 37*(3), 134–147. doi: 10.1177/0731948714529772.

LeCompte M. D., and Schunsul, J. J. (1999). *Designing and conducting ethnographic research.* Plymouth, UK: Alta Mira.

Lemons, C. J., Kearns, D. M., and Davidson, K. A. (2014). Data-based individualization in reading. *Teaching Exceptional Children, 46*(4), 20–29.

MacGinitie, W. H., MacGinitie, R. K., Maria, K., Dreyer, L. G., and Hughes, K. E. (2006). *Gates-MacGinitie Reading Tests* (4th ed.). Rolling Meadows, IL: Riverside Publishing.

Mathes, P. G., Denton, C. A., Fletcher, J. M., Anthony, J. L., Francis, D. J., and Schatschneider, C. (2005). The effects of theoretically different instruction and student characteristics on the skills of struggling readers. *Reading Research Quarterly, 40*, 148–182. doi: http://dx.doi.org/10.1598/RRQ. 40.2.2.

Mathes, P. G., Torgesen, J. K., Wahl, M., Menchetti, J. C., and Grek, M. L. (1999). *Proactive beginning reading: Intensive small group instruction for struggling readers.* Dallas TX: Southern Methodist University.

Mathes, P., and Torgesen, J. (2005). *Early Interventions in Reading.* Columbus. OH: SRA/McGraw-Hill.

National Assessment for Educational Progress (2015). *National assessment of educational progress.* Washington, DC: U.S. Department of Education.

National Center for Educational Statistics. (2004). *National assessment of educational progress: The nation's report card.* Washington, DC: U.S. Department of Education.

National Center for Educational Statistics. (2006). *National assessment of educational progress: The nation's report card.* Washington, DC: U.S. Department of Education.

O'Connor, R. E., Harty, K. R., and Fulmer, D. (2005). Tiers of intervention in kindergarten through third grade. *Journal of Learning Disabilities, 38*(6), 532–538. doi: 10.1177/00222194050380060901.

Paunesku, D., Walton, G. M., Romero, C. Smith, E. N., Yeager, D. S., and Dweck, C. S. (2015). Mind-set interventions are a scalable treatment for academic underachievement. *Psychological Science, 26*(6), 784–793.

Petscher, Y. Al Otaiba, S., Wanzek, J., Rivas, B., and Jones, F. (2017). The relation between global and specific mindset with reading outcomes for elementary school students. *Scientific Studies of Reading, 21*(5), 376–391, doi: 10.1080/10888438.2017.1313846.

Press Research Team (2014). *Word Identification Fluency Task.*

Quirk, M., Schwanenflugel, P., and Webb, M-Y. (2004). Do supplemental remedial reading programs address the motivational issues of struggling readers? An analysis of five popular programs. *Reading Research and Instruction, 43*(3), 1–19. doi: http://dx.doi.org/10.1080/19388070509558408.

Roswell, F. G., Chall, J. S., Curtis, M. E., and Kearns, G. (2005). *Diagnostic assessments of reading* (2nd ed.). Austin, TX: ProEd.

Shaywitz, S. E. (1996). Dyslexia. *Scientific American, 275*, 98–104.

Strauss, A., and Corbin, J. (1998). *Basics of qualitative research: Techniques and procedures for developing grounded theory* (2nd ed.). Thousand Oaks, CA: Sage.

Torgesen, J. K., Wagner, R., and Rashotte, C. A. (1999). *Test of word reading efficiency*. Austin, TX: PRO-ED.

Vaughn, S., Wanzek, J., and Fletcher, J. M. (2007). Multiple tiers of intervention: A framework for prevention and identification of students with reading/learning disabilities. In B. M. Taylor and J. E. Ysseldyke (Eds.), *Effective instruction for struggling readers, K–6* (pp. 173–195). New York: Teacher's College Press.

Vaughn, S., Wanzek, J., Murray, C. S., Scammaca, N., Linan-Thompson,S., and Woodruff, A. (2009). Response to early reading intervention: Examining higher and lower responders. *Exceptional Children*, *75*(2), 165–183.

Wanzek, J. Petscher, Y., Al Otaiba, S. Kent, S. C., Schatschneider, C., Haynes, M., Rivas, B. K., and Jones, F. J., (in press). Examining the effects of a standardized treatment for fourth graders with reading difficulties. *Journal of Research on Educational Effectiveness*.

Wanzek, J., and Vaughn, S. (2009). Students demonstrating persistent low response to reading intervention: Three case studies. *Learning Disabilities Research and Practice*, *24*(3), 151–163.

Wanzek, J., and Vaughn, S. (2011). Is a three-tier reading intervention model associated with reduced placement in special education? *Remedial and Special Education*, *32*, 167–175.

Wanzek, J., Wexler, J., Vaughn, S., and Ciullo, S. (2010). Reading interventions for struggling readers in the upper elementary grades: a synthesis of 20 years of research. *Reading and Writing*, *23*(8), 889–912. doi: 10.1007/s11145–009–9179–5.

Wigfield, A., and Eccles, J. (1992). The development of achievement task values: A theoretical analysis. *Developmental Review*, *12*, 265–310.

Woodcock, R. W., McGrew, K. S., and Mather, N. (2001). *Woodcock-Johnson tests of achievement – III*. Itasca, IL: Riverside Publishing Co.

Yeager, D. S., and Walton, D. M. (2011). Social-psychological interventions in education: They're not magic. *Review of Educational Research*, *81*(2), 267–301.

Yeager, D.S., and Dweck, C.S. (2012). Mindsets that promote resilience: When students believe that personal characteristics can be developed. *Educational Psychologist*, *47*, 1–13.

SECTION IV

RTI/MTSS in Secondary Grades

INTRODUCTION
TO SECTION IV

Michael J. Kennedy

Important differences between elementary and secondary (middle and high) schools lead to challenges in implementation of evidence-based practices associated with the response to intervention (RTI) framework at the secondary level. The differences can be structural and pedagogical. In terms of structure, middle and high schools revolve around students' core content area courses, which are taught by content experts. Little time (if any) is typically built into students' schedules to receive daily, individualized instruction such as is possible at the elementary level. A primary reason is secondary schools typically do not offer courses specifically intended to provide students with remedial instruction in reading, mathematics, or other core areas. Special education teachers are present but are often deployed in co-teaching roles within the general education (tier 1) classrooms.

Pedagogically, professionals hired to teach within secondary schools are content experts, and well-versed in teaching practices appropriate for their discipline. However, content area teachers usually only take one course during their preparation program dealing specifically with the characteristics and learning needs of students with disabilities. As a result, these professionals are not always prepared to support the unique learning needs of students with disabilities in their courses. In practice, this can mean even tier 1 evidence-based practices known to be effective for students with disabilities are not in place. Special educators who work as co-teachers in this setting are simultaneously hamstrung in many cases by their limited content knowledge. Thus, students with disabilities do not receive strong core instruction, and miss out on high-quality tier 2 and 3 instruction as well as a function of aforementioned pedagogical and structural problems.

In this section, we feature four chapters written by experts in the field of secondary level RTI. Espin, Chung, Foegen, and Campbell outline what the field has learned about curriculum-based measurement at the secondary level over the past several decades. They identify a systematic problem that becomes a theme across all chapters: Teachers are not always well-positioned to interpret and use data in an efficient and effective manner. Jitendra and Krawec provide a review of mathematics interventions, and Williams, Stevens, and Vaughn review reading interventions at the secondary level broken down across the three tiers. Both author teams highlight the need for more research in their respective fields, but simultaneously are encouraged by the quality of current research findings. Finally, Flannery, Pinkney, McGrath Kato, and Swain-Bradway discuss research on positive behavioral interventions at the secondary level. Across all chapters, the authors note the significant difficulty in implementing RTI at the secondary level stemming in part from the structural and pedagogical challenges of secondary schools. Despite the difficulties, each chapter is full of success stories in terms of interventions across the content areas that lead to positive outcomes for students with disabilities.

15

EFFECTS FROM SECONDARY INTERVENTIONS AND APPROACHES FOR THE PREVENTION AND REMEDIATION OF MATHEMATICS DIFFICULTIES

Multi-Tiered Response-to-Intervention Instructional Models

Asha K. Jitendra and Jennifer Krawec

The purpose of this chapter is to describe mathematics interventions and approaches that could be used within multi-tiered systems of support or a response to intervention (RTI) framework. We will provide information about the nature of these interventions and the settings in which they have been studied. In addition, we will discuss RTI in terms of the strength of the impact of the instructional programs or approaches on mathematics outcomes for secondary students with learning disabilities (LD) and mathematics difficulties (MD). There is a critical need for effective interventions in mathematics for secondary grades, since current data from the National Assessment of Educational Progress (NAEP, National Center for Education Statistics, 2013) indicate that 65% of students with disabilities cannot meet basic standards of mathematics competence compared to 21% of students without disabilities.

To meet the needs of students at risk for learning difficulties, many schools have implemented multi-tiered models that provide coordinated Tier 1 (prevention), Tier 2 (targeted), and Tier 3 (intensive) systems of support. Features of successful RTI implementation include universal screening to identify students at risk for learning difficulties, evidence-based instructional and intervention practices along with professional development to improve Tier 1 instruction and "to enhance the impact of Tier 2 instruction on middle school students struggling with mathematics" (Chard, 2012, p. 199). Furthermore, successful RTI implementation entails ongoing progress monitoring to evaluate the effects of instruction and intervention in improving student learning. Also critical to the success of a multi-tiered RTI model is the effectiveness of Tier 2 and Tier 3 supports.

Conceptual Framework: Content and Focus of Instructional Programs and Practices

The first part of our conceptual framework for discussing interventions to address students' mathematics difficulties involves the *content*, or focus of interventions. With the inception of the Common Core State Standards (CCSS) for mathematics (National Governors Association [NGA] Center for Best Practices, Council of Chief State School Officers [CCSSO], 2010), the emphasis is on grade-specific content standards that define what students should understand and be able to do. For example, the content standards for middle grades (6–8) include ratios and proportional relationships, number system, expressions and equations, geometry, statistics and probability, and functions. In high school, the standards include number and quantity, algebra, functions, modeling, geometry, and statistics and probability. Also critical to the CCSS are the mathematical practice standards (e.g., make sense of problems, look for and make use of structure, model with mathematics, attend to precision) that describe ways in which students should connect the practices to the content. In short, instruction should ensure that all students are achieving the high standards set by the CCSS and measured by state achievement tests.

Instructional objectives in the core classroom are based on the standards, which are the focus of Tier 1 instruction and play a key role in determining which students need extra support (Tier 2 and Tier 3 instruction) to prevent and remediate mathematics difficulties. However, the CCSS do not identify what interventions or materials are necessary to support students struggling with mathematics. Also, the standards do not specify how the grade-level content should be balanced with foundational skills to support students who have significant gaps in their prior knowledge of mathematics. Based on findings of a research synthesis on mathematics interventions for students struggling in mathematics, the U.S. Department of Education's What Works Clearinghouse (Gersten, Beckmann, et al., 2009) recommended that instructional materials focus on in-depth treatment of rational numbers in upper elementary and middle grades.

The second aspect of the conceptual framework of this chapter involves the instructional *methods* or practices that are characteristic of successful programs for students with LD and MD. A summary of several meta-analyses with regard to effective instructional practices for students with LD or at risk for MD identified key instructional characteristics that address these students' particular needs (Jayanthi and Gersten, 2011). Specifically, instructional interventions shown to be effective included the following elements: (a) explicit instruction to teach mathematical concepts and procedures (Baker, Gersten, and Lee, 2002; Gersten, Chard et al., 2009; Kroesbergen and Van Luit, 2003; Xin and Jitendra, 1999; Zhang and Xin, 2012; Zheng, Flynn, and Swanson, 2012); (b) heuristics to organize information (Gersten, Chard et al., 2009); (c) student verbalization during problem solving (Gersten, Chard et al., 2009); (d) modeling mathematical ideas using visual representations (Gersten, Chard, et al., 2009; Xin and Jitendra, 1999; Zhang and Xin, 2012); and (e) multiple exemplars and sequential patterns (e.g., concrete to abstract; easy to hard) (Gersten, Chard et al., 2009). Research has consistently validated the effectiveness of explicit and systematic instruction, which provides "models of proficient problem solving, verbalization of thought processes, guided practice, corrective feedback, and frequent cumulative review" (Gersten, Beckmann, et al., 2009, p. 6). In addition to the five instructional elements described above and outlined in Jayanthi and Gersten's (2011) review, several other instructional approaches show promise in improving the performance of students with or at risk for mathematics difficulties (Gersten, Chard, et al., 2009). These include: (a) providing students with opportunities to solve real world problems, which increase student motivation; (b) incorporating the use of formative assessments so that teachers receive ongoing feedback on student performance; and (c) providing cross-age tutoring opportunities (Gersten, Chard, et al., 2009; Baker et al., 2002).

Students who struggle in mathematics within a general education classroom may benefit from interventions that incorporate research-based instructional design elements (e.g., explicit and systematic instruction, practice/review, corrective feedback). As such, replacing the less explicit classroom curriculum with the more explicit curriculum would be considered a Tier 1 intervention that is given to all students. If most of the students in the classroom (special education or remedial) are students with LD or MD, adopting an explicit whole-classroom approach to instruction has been shown to produce positive effects when compared with a less explicit curriculum (e.g., Kelly, Gersten, and Carnine, 1990). It is important to understand that even well-designed core instruction in general education classrooms may not be sufficient to address the instructional needs of some students with LD and MD, who may need more intensive Tier 2 and Tier 3 interventions and supports.

Relevant Research and Evidence of Effectiveness of Mathematics Interventions within Secondary-Level RTI/MTSS

In this section, the focus is on studies examining Tier 1, 2, and 3 mathematics instruction and support. Due to the limited scope of this chapter, we selected randomized controlled, quasi-experimental, and single case design studies. Participants in the studies were students identified as having LD or students with MD (scored < 25th percentile in mathematics). The included studies targeted content that was appropriate for secondary grades. For example, we excluded studies of whole number computation, which are typically taught in elementary grades. Studies were not included in Tier 1 if they used a class-wide mathematics instructional program in the general education classroom, but did not discuss the findings for students with LD and MD. Similarly, studies that used a whole-classroom approach to instruction in special education or remedial classrooms were excluded since they did not meet our criterion for Tier 2 (see Targeted or Tier 2 Instruction).

The next section describes each study in terms of the participants and overall school context, as well as the nature and effectiveness of the instructional program. Table 15.1 provides a summary of implications for practice in terms of the resources necessary to implement Tier 1 and Tier 2 interventions; Table 15.2 provides a summary of implications for practice in terms of the resources necessary to implement Tier 3 interventions.

Universal or Tier 1 Instruction

The focus of Tier 1 instruction is on grade level standards-based core curriculum using instructional strategies designed to meet the needs of a majority of students. To examine how well Tier 1 core instruction can improve mathematics learning for students with LD and those with MD in general education classrooms, we examine four studies (Jitendra, Dupuis, Star, and Rodriguez, 2016; Krawec, Huang, Montague, Kressler, and de Alba, 2013; Witzel, Mercer, and Miller, 2003; Woodward and Brown, 2006). In an ongoing series of investigations, Jitendra and colleagues have examined the effects of schema-based instruction (SBI) on seventh-grade

Table 15.1 Summary Table of Implications for Practice: Tier 1 and 2 Interventions

Study	Participants; Grade	Intervention and Content; Duration; Instructional Grouping	Interventionist & Training; Fidelity of Implementation (%)	Measures	Hedges' g/PND
Tier 1					
Jitendra, Dupuis, Star, & Rodriguez (2016)	Students with mathematics and reading difficulties (scores < 25th percentile on the mathematics and reading subtests of the MCA-II), diverse participants; 7th grade	C: Typical school mathematics instruction; T: Schema-based instruction (SBI) – 21 lessons on ratio, proportion, and percent; 5 lessons per week, 45 min each across 6 weeks (Total time: 1,350 min); whole group instruction	Math teachers; 2-day training; 87.0	Experimental PPS posttests and transfer test (released items from NAEP, TIMSS and state assessments)	*Experimental immediate posttest:* SBI vs. C = 0.40 *Experimental delayed posttest (6 weeks later):* SBI vs. C = 0.42 *Experimental Transfer test:* SBI vs. C = ns
Krawec, Huang, Montague, Kressler, & de Alba (2013)	Students with LD (district identified; FCAT math score levels of 1 or 2 out of a possible 5), diverse participants; 7th & 8th grade	C: Typical school mathematics instruction; T: Cognitive strategy instruction (CSI) in word problem solving – 3 initial lessons then once-weekly practice sessions, each 40 minutes, across six months – approx. 25 lessons (Total time: 1,000 min); whole group instruction	Math teachers; 3-day training; 84.0–90.0	Experimental math problem-solving assessment– students' self report of strategies used in each step of the problem-solving process	*Experimental posttest:* CSI vs. C = 0.55
Witzel, Mercer, & Miller (2003)	Students with LD (1.5 SD discrepancy between ability and achievement) and MD (scores < the 50th percentile on state	C: Typical instruction involving abstract lessons; T: Concrete-representational-abstract sequence of instruction (CRA) – 19 lessons	Math and special education teachers; 1-day training + several follow-up meetings; 100	Experimental algebra posttest	*Experimental immediate posttest:* CRA vs. C = 0.84 *Experimental delayed posttest (3 weeks later):* CRA vs. C = 0.50

achievement test), diverse participants; NA; 6th & 7th grade	focused on algebra, with content moving from reducing expressions to solving complex equations; 50 min each of 19 lessons (Total time: 950 min); whole group instruction	Experimental Core Concept posttest; standardized CTB Terra Nova test	Middle grade teachers; training prior to beginning of the study; 100	*Experimental posttest:* TM vs. C = 1.81 *Standardized achievement test:* TM vs. C = 0.89
Woodward & Brown (2006)	Students with LD (scores, on average, at the 20th percentile on the CTB Terra Nova), NA; 6th grade	C: Standards-based mathematics curriculum; T: Transitional Mathematics (TM) curriculum covering whole number operations, number theory concepts, data analysis, measurement, and geometric concepts; daily 55 min for intervention group and 80 min daily for comparison group across the school year; whole group instruction		

Tier 2

Scheuerman, Deshler, & Schumaker (2009)	Students with LD (scores < 25th percentile on a mathematics achievement test); 6th, 7th, 8th grade	B: Typical mathematics instruction; T: Explicit Inquiry Routine (explicit content sequencing, scaffolded inquiry, and C–R–A sequence) – 10 lessons on one-variable equations;	Word problem probe (instructed and uninstructed); Concrete manipulation (CM) test; Far-generalization (FG) test; standardized KeyMath Revised (KM)	NA; NA; NA	*Word problem probe:* Instructed: PND = 100; Uninstructed: PND = 79.2; Maintenance (11 weeks later): PND = 100 for instructed and 82.1 for uninstructed problems.

continued . . . .

Table 15.1 Continued

Study	Participants; Grade	Intervention and Content; Duration; Instructional Grouping	Interventionist & Training; Fidelity of Implementation (%)	Measures	Hedges' g/PND
Tier 2					
		55 min each of 13–23 sessions (Total time: 715–1,265 min); small group instruction (3–6 students)			*CM test:* Pre: M = 38%; Post: M = 89%; Maintenance: M = 80% *FG test:* Pre: M = 21%; Post: M = 30% *Standardized achievement test:* Pretest vs. Posttest: g = 0.58
Xin, Jitendra, & Deatline-Buchman (2005)	Students with learning problems (scores 1 SD below the mean on the MAT mathematics subtest); including students with disabilities (LD, ED) and students at-risk for math failure, diverse participants; 6th, 7th, 8th grade	C: General strategy instruction on word problem solving; T: Schema-based instruction (SBI) – lessons on one-step multiplication and division word problems involving *Multiplicative Compare and Proportion* problem types, including mixed review; 12 sessions, 60 min, 3–4 times a week (Total time: 720 min); small group instruction (4–7 students)	Tutors were from the university and special education middle school teachers (n = 4); two 1-hr training sessions; 94.0	Experimental word problem solving immediate and delayed posttests (pooled 1–2 week, 3 weeks to 3 month follow-up tests) and a transfer test (items taken from commercially published tests)	*Experimental immediate posttest:* SBI vs. C = 1.87 *Experimental delayed posttests (1 wk. to 3 mo. later):* SBI vs. C = 2.78 *Experimental transfer test:* SBI vs. C = 1.09

Note: C = comparison; T = treatment; ED = emotional disorders; LD = learning disabilities; MD = mathematics difficulties; NA = not available; CTB Terra Nova, McGraw-Hill, 2002; FCAT = Florida Comprehensive Assessment Test; GMADE = Group Mathematics Assessment and Diagnostic Evaluation (Pearson Education, 2004); MAT = Metropolitan Achievement Test; MCA = Minnesota Comprehensive Assessment; NAEP = National Assessment of Educational Progress; PND = percentage of nonoverlapping data; TIMSS = Trends in International Mathematics and Science Study.

students' proportional problem-solving performance. SBI is a multicomponent intervention that is grounded in schema theory, incorporates features from the expert/novice literature, and is guided by cognitive models of mathematical problem solving (Mayer, 1999). SBI intervention includes (a) a focus on the mathematical structure of problems, (b) use of visual representations, (c) explicit problem solving and metacognitive strategy instruction, and (d) an emphasis on procedural flexibility. These components correspond with the recommendations articulated in the What Works Clearinghouse's recent research synthesis on improving students' mathematical problem-solving performance (Woodward et al., 2012) and address the mathematical practices (e.g., look for and make use of structure, model with mathematics) in the CCSS.

In a recent randomized controlled study of SBI, the focus was on a subgroup of students with MD only and both mathematics and reading difficulties (MDRD) (Jitendra et al., 2016). The authors contrasted SBI with "business as usual" mathematics instruction, in which teachers relied on the instructional activities in their district-adopted mathematics textbook to teach ratio, proportion, and percent. The study took place in six middle schools and 42 classrooms, and involved 260 students (50% were eligible for free or reduced-price lunch, 56% were minority students, 14% were English language learners, and 21% were receiving special education services) with MD and students with MDRD based on their scores (< 25th percentile) on statewide mathematics and reading achievement tests. The study examined students' responsiveness to a six-week treatment. The 21-lesson SBI program was implemented daily for 45 minutes over the course of six weeks. On a measure of proportional problem solving (comprised of released items from NAEP, TIMSS and state mathematics assessments related to the topics of ratio/rate, proportion, and percent), students with MD and MDRD in the SBI classrooms not only outperformed their counterparts in control classrooms on the immediate post-test, but also sustained the effects six weeks after the intervention.

Two randomized controlled studies focused on word problem solving (Krawec et al., 2013) and algebra skills (Witzel et al., 2003). One study (Krawec et al., 2013) utilized cognitive strategy instruction (CSI), a well-researched instructional practice (see Montague, Krawec, Enders, and Dietz, 2014) for improving the problem-solving performance of students with LD. CSI teaches cognitive processes and metacognitive skills, with students selecting and applying them to solve word problems while monitoring their strategy use. While previous studies of CSI have focused on problem-solving performance, this study examined the impact of CSI on students' knowledge of math problem-solving strategies (e.g., visualize, hypothesize, estimate). A total of 83 typically achieving students and 78 students with LD (68% were eligible for free or reduced-price lunch, 90% were minority students) participated. On a structured interview that assessed students' knowledge of word problem-solving strategies, students with LD in the treatment group reported using significantly more strategies than their counterparts in the comparison group. Also encouraging is that students with LD in the treatment group increased their strategy knowledge to a level slightly above that of their typically achieving peers in the comparison group.

In a second study (Witzel et al., 2003), the effectiveness of a concrete-representational-abstract (CRA) sequence of instruction was compared to conventional instruction for teaching algebraic transformation equations. CRA incorporates multiple representations and the graduated sequence of instruction progresses from the use of concrete manipulative materials, to visual representations, to abstract notations to solve a variety of mathematical tasks. Participants comprised 34 students with LD (evidenced 1.5 SD discrepancy between ability and achievement) and MD included in sixth- and seventh-grade general education classrooms. Following five weeks of instruction on algebra content, results showed statistically significant differences, with large effects favoring treatment students with LD and MD on solving single-variable and multiple-variable algebraic equations. These effects were maintained on follow-up measures administered three weeks after treatment ended.

To learn whether differences in curricula influence the mathematics performance of middle school students with LD (no individualized education plan in mathematics) and MD, we examine the findings from Woodward and Brown (2006). This yearlong, quasi-experimental study contrasted the effects of a curriculum (*Transitional Mathematics, Level 1*, Sopris West, 2004) that incorporated principles of effective instruction identified in the special education literature (e.g., explicit connections between topics, distributed practice of concepts and skills) with a standards-based curriculum (*Connected Mathematics Program*, Prentice Hall, 2002). Participants were six middle grade teachers and their 53 students in two intact middle schools. Results indicated statistically significant differences, with large effects favoring students in the intervention group on both proximal (Core Concepts Test) and distal measures of mathematics (CTB Terra Nova). Woodward and Brown concluded that based on the findings of this study, many of the principles discussed in the special education literature are applicable across a broad range of learners.

Targeted or Tier 2 Instruction

When students struggling in mathematics do not meet instructional objectives in their core classrooms, there is a need for Tier 2 level of instructional support. Such support might include "targeted interventions designed to help struggling students to progress consistent with grade-level expectations" (Chard, 2012, p. 199) and small group instruction in structured learning environments that present opportunities for practice with immediate high-quality feedback (Gersten et al., 2008). Tier 2 interventions are provided to students above and beyond core class instruction and may be implemented by the classroom teacher or by a specialist working outside of the classroom with small groups of students who share similar needs. Whether instruction is provided by the classroom teacher or a specialist, "the purpose remains to support the goals and objectives taught in the core classroom" (Chard, 2012, p. 200). We examine the findings from two studies that met the criterion of Tier 2 level of instructional support, with regard to providing supplemental, explicit instruction coupled with small group tutoring for students with LD and MD (Scheuerman, Deshler, and Schumaker, 2009; Xin, Jitendra, and Deatline-Buchman, 2005).

Scheuermann et al. tested the effectiveness of an Explicit Inquiry Routine (EIR) on the mathematics performance of 14 middle-school students with LD (14% were minority students) using a multiple baseline across students design. EIR consisted of a blend of instructional practices from general education and special education, such as explicit content sequencing, scaffolded inquiry, and multiple modes of illustration. Following typical instruction across varied mathematics topics in the baseline phase, students received small group EIR tutoring (three to six students) to understand and solve one-variable equations. On a progress-monitoring measure (one-variable word problem test), students' performance improved from baseline to post-test on both instructed and uninstructed problems. This improvement was substantial for instructed problems and effective for uninstructed problems. Students maintained the improved performance 11 weeks after the intervention ended. In addition, students showed improvement from pre-test to post-test on the concrete manipulation and far generalization measures. An important finding of the study was the pretest to posttest improvement for students with LD on the KeyMath Revised, a norm-referenced test of mathematics achievement.

In the second study (Xin et al., 2005), the effectiveness of SBI was compared to a general strategy instruction (GSI) for teaching word problem solving. Participants comprised 22 students

(68% were minority students) with LD (evidenced > 1 SD discrepancy between ability and achievement) and MD in grades six through eight. Students received about three to four 60-minute small group tutoring sessions per week for a total of 12 sessions in solving word problems involving proportion and multiplicative compare problems using the assigned strategy (SBI or GSI). Students in the SBI group scored on average higher than students in the GSI group, with large effects on a post-test and retention tests. Furthermore, transfer occurred to novel problems derived from standardized mathematics achievement tests.

In summary, results of Tier 1 and Tier 2 intervention studies indicate that SBI and CRA interventions led to significant improvement in students' ability to solve complex word problems and single-variable and multiple-variable algebraic equations. Students with LD receiving the CSI intervention demonstrated significantly more problem-solving strategies (e.g., paraphrase, visualize, hypothesize, estimate) compared to control group students with LD. In addition, students with LD benefitted from curricula that incorporated effective teaching practices from special education or a blend of mathematics teaching practices from both general education and special education literature.

Intensive or Tier 3 Instruction

For a small proportion of students, the supplemental small group instruction provided in Tier 2 is not sufficient to improve performance in the targeted skill area(s). These students need very intensive and formative Tier 3 interventions that usually consist of "one on one tutoring along with an appropriate mix of instructional interventions" (Gersten, Beckmann, et al., 2009, p. 5). Furthermore, Tier 3 calls for an increase in the frequency of progress monitoring to test the efficacy of interventions and to determine when changes are needed. Given that students struggling in mathematics experience decreased motivation, there is also the need for Tier 3 interventions to address motivational and behavior management issues (Gersten, Beckmann, et al, 2009).

In this section, we summarize the relevant research and evidence from a literature review of investigations that have provided Tier 3 mathematics interventions for secondary students with LD. The conceptual framework about CCSS mathematics content and instructional practices is used to describe the nature and results of Tier 3 interventions to provide an understanding of the intensity of instructional conditions that need to be in place to prevent and remediate early mathematics problems.

Instructional Content and Implementation Practices

We examined the content addressed during Tier 3 sessions and found that instruction focused on skills and concepts in four specific CCSS domains: (a) *Ratios and Proportional Relationships* (Hunt and Vasquez, 2014; Jitendra, DiPipi, and Perron-Jones, 2002), (b) *Geometry* (Cass, Cates, Smith, and Jackson, 2003; Satsangi and Bouck, 2015), c) *Expressions and Equations* (Hutchinson, 1993; Maccini and Hughes, 2000; Maccini and Ruhl, 2000; Strickland and Maccini, 2013a; Strickland and Maccini, 2013b), and (d) *The Number System* (Freeman-Green, O'Brien, Wood, and Hitt, 2015; Joseph and Hunter, 2001; Montague, 1992; Montague and Bos, 1986; Test and Ellis, 2005; van Garderen, 2007). Furthermore, we examined current practices to determine whether Tier 3 interventions at the secondary grades incorporated the key elements of effective instruction (i.e., explicit instruction, use of heuristics, student verbalization, use of visual representations, and sequenced instruction) identified by Gersten, Beckmann, et al. (2009).

Table 15.2 Summary Table of Implications for Practice: Tier 3 Interventions

Study	Design	Participants (n); Grade	Setting; Interventionist; FOI	Intervention; Duration	Domain	Dependent Measure	PND
Cass, Cates, Smith, & Jackson (2003)	Multiple probe across behaviors	Students with LD[a] (< 50% on domain test) (n = 3); 7th–10th grades	Resource room; special education teacher; 100	Manipulative instruction with geoboards; number of sessions: NA/ 15–20 min each	Perimeter and area problems involving multiplication with regrouping	Perimeter probe Skill maintenance Area probe Skill maintenance	82.1 100 84.9 100
Freeman-Green, O'Brien, Wood, & Hitt (2015)	Multiple probe across participants	Students with LD[d] (n = 6); 8th grade	Private high school for students with a specific LD or ADHD; researcher (doctoral student); 97.5	SOLVE (Study the problem and organize the facts; line up a plan; verify plan with action and evaluate answer) intervention on word problems; number and length of sessions: NA (Total time: 270 min)	Word problems involving all four operations	Word problem-solving probe Skill maintenance	100 100
Hunt & Vasquez (2014)	Multiple baseline across participants	Students with LD[a] (n = 3); 6th & 7th grade	Study room in a university tutoring clinic; researcher (certified in exceptional and mathematics education); NA	Representational intervention focusing on additive and multiplication relation, build-up, and unit rate strategies;	Ratio equivalency problems	Ratio equivalency probe	100

Hutchinson (1993)	AB design across problem types with 11 replications	Students with LD[a] (scores < 40% correct on domain test) (n = 11); 8th–10th grade	Learning disabilities resource classroom; researcher (former special education teacher); 100	15 sessions/ 25 min each (Total time: 375 min) Cognitive strategy instruction (CSI);	Algebra word problems – Relational, Proportional, and Two-variable, two equation	*Algebra problems probe:* Representation — 100; Solution — 100; Answer — 100; Skill maintenance — 100
Jitendra, DiPipi, & Perron-Jones (2002)	Multiple probe across participants	Students with LD[a] (n = 4); 8th grade	Learning support classroom; special education teacher, 100	30–34 sessions/ 40 min each (Total time: 1,200–1,360 min) Schema-based instruction;	Ratio and proportion word problems	Ratio and proportion word problem solving probe — 82.5; Skill maintenance — 100
Joseph & Hunter (2001)	Multiple baseline across participants	Students with LD[e] (n = 3); 8th grade	NA; special education teacher, 100	6–12 sessions/ 35–40 min each (Total time: 210–480 min) Strategy instruction; 24 sessions/ min per session: NA	Fraction problems involving addition and subtraction	Fraction computation probe — 95.9; Skill maintenance — 100
Maccini & Hughes (2000)	Multiple probe across participants	Students with LD[b] (> 2 years below grade level) (n = 6); 9th–12th grades	NA; researcher; 100	Concrete-representational-abstract (CRA) strategy instruction; number and length of sessions: NA	Algebra word problems involving addition, subtraction, multiplication, and division of integers	Problem representation probe — 90.5; Skill maintenance — 85.7; Problem solution probe — 73.8; Skill maintenance — 66.7

continued ...

Table 15.2 Continued

Study	Design	Participants (n); Grade	Setting; Interventionist; FOI	Intervention; Duration	Domain	Dependent Measure	PND
Maccini & Ruhl (2000)	Multiple probe across participants	Students with LD[a] (n=3); 8th grade	Conference room in school; researcher; 80.0–97.0	STAR intervention: (a) CRA, (b) general problem-solving strategies, and (c) self-monitoring strategies; number of sessions: NA/ 20–30 min each	Algebra problems involving subtraction with integers	Problem representation probe Skill maintenance Problem solution probe Skill maintenance	66.7 66.7 94.4 100
Montague (1992)	Multiple probe across participants	Students with LD[b] (n=6); 6th–8th grades	Empty classroom; researcher; fidelity not reported	CMSI; 6–13 sessions/55 min each (Total time: 330–715 min)	Word problems involving all four operations	Word problem-solving probe	88.3
Montague & Bos (1986)	Multiple probe across participants	Students with LD[a] (< grade level on WJPB math test) (n=6); 10th–12th grades	Resource room; resource teacher; fidelity not reported	CSI; 6–10 sessions; 50 min each (Total time: 300–500 min)	Word problems involving all four operations	Word problem-solving probe Skill maintenance	87.0 91.7
Satsangi & Bouck (2015)	Multiple probe across participants	Students with LD[a, b, c] (scored < 50% on domain pretest) (n = 3); 9th and 11th grades	Empty conference room in charter high school; researcher; 100	Instruction using virtual manipulatives; 5–9 number and length of sessions: NA	Area and perimeter problems	Area probe Perimeter probe Skill maintenance	100 100 100

Study	Design	Participants	Setting	Instruction	Content	Dependent measures	%
Strickland & Maccini (2013a)	Multiple probe across participants	Students with LD[a] (n = 3); 8th and 9th grades;	Office of private day school; researcher; 100	CRA; 3 lessons/ 40 min each (Total time: 120 min)	Multiplication of linear equations	Domain and lesson probe Skill maintenance	100 100
Strickland & Maccini (2013b)	Multiple probe across groups	Students with LD[b] (n = 3) and MD (n = 2); 11th grade	Private school; researcher; 100	CRA; 10 lessons/ 45 min each (Total time: 450 min)	Quadratic expressions within area problems	Domain and lesson probe Skill maintenance	100 100
Test & Ellis (2005)	Multiple probe across pairs	Students with LD[a] (n = 3) & mild disabilities (n = 3); 8th grade	Math resource classroom; researcher; 100	LAP (look at sign and denominator; ask question; pick fraction type) Fractions strategy instruction; 18–34 lessons/ 30 min each (Total time: 540–1,020 min)	Fraction problems involving addition and subtraction	Fractions probe Skill maintenance LAP strategy LAP strategy maintenance	100 100 100 100
van Garderen (2007)	Multiple probe across participants	Students with LD[b] (n = 3); 8th grade;	Quiet room in school; researcher; lesson scripts ensured fidelity	Strategic instruction in diagram generation; number of sessions: NA/ 35 min each	One step and two-step word problems involving all four operations	One- and two-step word problem solving probe Skill maintenance	66.7 66.7

Note. CMSI = cognitive and metacognitive strategy instruction; FOI = fidelity of implementation; MD = mathematics difficulties; NA = not available; [a] Identified using IQ-achievement discrepancy; [b] Met district/state eligibility criteria; [c]based on school's response-to-intervention process; [d]based on psycho-educational evaluations from an outside agency; [e]Identification method not provided.

To determine how well Tier 3 instruction can improve student understanding of ratios and proportions, we examine findings from two studies that emphasized proportional problem solving and ratio equivalency. In one of the earliest studies of SBI for secondary grade students with LD, Jitendra et al. (2002) focused on ratio and proportion word problem solving. Implemented one-on-one by a special education teacher, the 6- to 12-session intervention was very effective in improving the problem-solving performance of all four participants with LD. These gains were maintained 2.5 to 10 weeks following termination of the intervention. In a recent study, Hunt and Vasquez (2014) provided 15 sessions of explicit instruction and visual representations to teach ratio equivalency (i.e., multiplicative relation between quantities) to three middle school students with LD. Instruction emphasized a developmental trajectory of strategies (buildup, unit, and, proportional reasoning) to strengthen students' conceptual understanding of ratios through multiplicative reasoning. Results support instructional trajectories as a very effective method to increase students' performance and strategy use in solving equivalent ratios.

Five studies in this research review addressed the *Expressions and Equations* domain. While an early study of CSI conducted by Hutchinson (1993) was very effective in teaching students with LD algebraic problem solving across varying problem types (i.e., relational, proportional, and two-variable, two equation), one research team (Maccini and Hughes, 2000; Maccini and Ruhl, 2000; Strickland and Maccini, 2013a; Strickland and Maccini, 2013b) has carefully implemented a series of studies to address expectations within the *Expressions and Equations* domain. Maccini and colleagues implemented one-on-one interventions across various algebraic skills using the CRA approach. For high school students, CRA led to improvement in problem representation and the improved performance was maintained over time; however, they performed less well on problem solution (Maccini and Hughes, 2000). Eighth-grade students who received the same intervention but focused only on subtraction problems showed greater gains on problem solution than problem representation (Maccini and Ruhl, 2000). In two CRA studies (Strickland and Maccini, 2013a; Strickland and Maccini, 2013b), which addressed more complex skills of linear and quadratic equations, the intervention was found to be very effective for all students.

To learn whether manipulative materials such as concrete models and dynamic software are effective tools for teaching high school students with LD skills within the *Geometry* domain, we examine the findings from Cass et al. (2003) and Satsangi and Bouck (2015). In Cass et al., the special education teacher used geoboards to teach perimeter and area problem-solving skills. The intervention was very effective, both immediately following instruction as well as two months later. Compared to concrete materials that place cognitive load on learners when they have to manipulate numerous physical objects as well as relate the manipulations to the mathematical ideas, virtual manipulatives are known to reduce that cognitive load because manipulations are conducted on screen and facilitate the interactive analysis of complex mathematical relations. Satsangi and Bouck (2015) used the National Library of Virtual Manipulatives, an online website that allows users to create irregular shapes and determine their geometric properties, to teach the concepts of area and perimeter. Findings showed virtual manipulatives to be a very effective tool in acquiring and maintaining the concepts of perimeter and area. Furthermore, students generalized the skill of solving for "area and perimeter of static shapes" to word problems involving area and perimeter (p. 179).

The remaining studies addressed *The Number System* domain. Two studies tested the effectiveness of strategy instruction to improve eighth-grade students' proficiency in adding and subtracting fractions. In the first study by Joseph and Hunter (2001), the special education teacher provided explicit instruction along with cue cards of strategies for solving problems with like and unlike denominators. The four students with LD who participated also learned self-regulatory behaviors to facilitate cue card application. Results indicated that strategy instruction was very effective, with improved performance over that of baseline for all students. Interestingly, students who scored higher on a measure of planning ability responded more quickly to the intervention than those with lower planning scores. The second study (Test and Ellis, 2005) investigated the effectiveness of a mnemonic LAP (Look at the sign and denominator; Ask yourself the question – Will the smallest denominator divide into the largest denominator an even number of times?; Pick your fraction type) strategy on students' fraction computation skills. Similarly to Joseph and Hunter (2001), the authors used cue cards to guide students through the steps of the solving process, but differed in that the LAP strategy makes explicit three types of problems (like denominators, unlike denominators that are divisible, unlike denominators that are not divisible). Results showed the LAP strategy to be a highly effective intervention immediately following instruction, and also at a six-week follow up.

To date, four studies have focused on improving the word problem solving performance of students with LD. Montague and Bos (1986) developed and tested the effectiveness of the CSI intervention, which included explicit metacognitive prompts (self-instruction, self-questioning, self-checking) in addition to an eight-step cognitive strategy routine. The six participating high school students with LD solved two- and three-step mathematical word problems that included rational numbers. Following baseline, students received between six and ten instructional sessions. Results showed that five of the six students improved their problem-solving performance to mastery levels (i.e., 70% across four consecutive probes). In a follow-up study (Montague, 1992), the focus was on metacognitive and cognitive components in isolation before providing instruction in both components to middle school students with LD. Word problems were taken from middle school textbooks and included whole and rational numbers and one-, two-, and three-step problems. Students received explicit instruction across six to 12 sessions, which resulted in problem-solving accuracy gains. None of the students met mastery after receiving either metacognitive or cognitive instruction in isolation. However, five of the six students met mastery following instruction in both cognitive and metacognitive strategy instruction. Thus, an important finding was that instruction in both components was necessary for seventh- and eighth-graders to attain mastery.

In a related study, van Garderen (2007) investigated the effectiveness of a CSI intervention which was based on five of the eight strategies of Montague's (1992) problem-solving routine (i.e., Read, Visualize, Plan, Compute, Check). Students learned to solve one- and two-step word problems that included both whole and rational numbers. The intervention centered on visualizing, with explicit instruction in generating schematic diagrams based on problem type. Results indicated that although students improved in their ability to accurately generate schematic representations of problems, the effectiveness of the intervention in improving problem-solving accuracy was questionable.

To better understand how the SOLVE strategy (Study the problem, Organize the facts, Line up a plan, Verify your plan, Evaluate your answer) impacts students' problem solving performance, Freeman-Green et al. (2015) conducted a study with six eighth-grade students with LD. Word problems were included only after confirmation by an expert in secondary mathematics curricula that they reflected grade-level material. At the end of the intervention, students responded positively to the intervention, with all students demonstrating improvement in their problem-solving accuracy scores. The improved performance was maintained at two- and six-week follow-ups.

In addition to the emphasis on the CCSS content standards, all Tier 3 studies addressed the CCSS *Standards for Mathematical Practice*, which encompass "expertise that mathematics educators at all levels should seek to develop in their students" (NGA and CCSSO, 2010, p. 6). The interventions, which targeted skills in ratios and proportional relationships, algebra, fractions, and word problem solving, align specifically with the following CCSS *Standards for Mathematical Practice*: (1) make sense of problems and persevere in solving them, (2) reason abstractly and quantitatively, (3) model with mathematics, and (4) look for and make use of structure. Connecting the standards for mathematical practice to the standards for mathematical content is critical; these practices should be embedded within content instruction as they focus on the conceptual understanding necessary for application in mathematics (NGA and CCSSO, 2010).

Overall, Tier 3 intervention studies at the secondary grades seem to reflect the content and practice standards of the CCSS. Furthermore, all studies incorporated elements of instructional practice that have been shown to address the particular needs of students with LD. Most consistent in these Tier 3 studies were the use of explicit instruction, student verbalizations, and sequenced instruction. Regarding the Tier 3 interventions included in this research, SBI and strategy instruction based on developmental trajectories were found to be very effective in improving students' proficiency in solving ratio and proportion problems. These interventions served to bridge critical research in mathematics education and special education to effect change. Other effective interventions include CSI and CRA. The effectiveness of CSI to improve mathematical word problem solving with single- and multi-step problems was established across studies. Students with LD responded positively to CRA instruction to improve their accuracy with algebraic expressions, including one- and two-variable equations, multiplication of linear equations, and quadratic expressions.

Limitations and Future Direction

While our review of mathematics instruction across multi-tiered systems of support identified effective instruction that spanned mathematical content domains, it also highlighted several limitations of this research base. First, universal screening and identification of LD was not consistent across studies in the three tiers of support; two of the studies reviewed did not provide information on LD identification methods. As far back as 1993, Rosenberg and colleagues called for greater transparency by researchers in reporting the way by which students were identified as LD. It remains true today that "vague, shorthand phrases frequently used to describe participants in LD research (e.g., school-identified learning-disabled, state guidelines) tend to be meaningless because of the great variety of eligibility criteria, referral processes, and measurement nuances used by local school districts and state education agencies" (p. 210). Less than half of the studies included in this review provided more detail than the typical "shorthand phrases."

The second limitation is related to the use of progress-monitoring measures. With the exception of Scheuermann et al. (2009), none of the studies reviewed in Tiers 1 or 2 used progress-monitoring measures. Though pre-test/post-test assessment provides critical information on student improvement following instruction, progress monitoring highlights students' growth (or lack thereof) at a micro level and is thus more sensitive to change. In their overview of RTI, Fletcher and Vaughn (2009) make explicit that "providing effective Tier 1 instruction to all students requires ongoing professional development, screening, and *progress monitoring* [emphasis added] of students" (p. 31). Consistent and timely measurement of student growth across tiers is necessary to identify potentially struggling students prior to summative assessments. Even at the Tier 3 level where progress monitoring is standard, issues exist related to equivalency of forms. None of the studies reviewed used experimental probes that were equated across forms. Because progress monitoring measures inform educational decisions impacting students, "it is essential that alternate forms. . .are not only technically sound (i.e., reliable and valid) but also yield scores that are equivalent" (Montague, Penfield, Enders, and Huang, 2010, p. 41). Providing evidence of equated forms will strengthen findings in research and will further support the decisions that are made based on student responsiveness in practice.

Third, none of the studies in this research review addressed the high school CCSS content standards of *Functions*, *Modeling*, and *Statistics and Probability*. If students with LD are to access the general education curriculum, research-based instructional programs and strategies must exist that address their needs in these complex, higher order content areas. Notwithstanding the limitations, it is concerning that the available research on secondary mathematics interventions for students with LD or MD is not adequate to provide guidance about multi-tiered RTI implementation. Studies described in this chapter provide the basis for additional research.

One issue that warrants further research concerns the lack of coherence of interventions across tiers. In our review, only one intervention (SBI) was represented in each of the three tiers of support. Chard (2012) argues that the lack of intervention packages that systematically vary in intensity results in the "misalignment of Tier 1 and Tier 2 instruction" (p. 200), whereby students receive different instructional approaches from different programs depending on the tier. This lack of coherence is especially problematic for students with LD, who already struggle with concept and strategy generalization.

Second, there is a lack of consensus in the definition of what constitutes Tier 2 instruction in mathematics. Specifically, are studies conducted in special education classrooms using whole class instruction categorized as Tier 1 or Tier 2? Relatedly, there appears to be less clarity in the special education mathematics literature compared to reading in terms of size of groups in Tier 2. Given that mathematics is as complex as reading, it seems clear that the parameters should be the same, such that Tier 2 in mathematics would entail the same small group size as in reading to effect change. Clarification on these issues will help researchers design instruction that meets both the technical parameters and the theoretical intent of Tier 2. In this review of research, we excluded several studies conducted in special education classrooms that included a grouping ratio of more than seven students per teacher since they did not meet our criteria for Tier 2 intervention studies. This lack of intervention studies that not only provide targeted instruction over and above that of the core classroom but also present opportunities for practice with immediate high-quality feedback using small group instruction is problematic, given that Tier 2 is implemented as a means to prevent mathematics difficulties by providing instruction to meet the high standards in the secondary mathematics curriculum. Researchers should consider ways in which research-based Tier 1 instruction may be systematically modified to provide critical Tier 2 support to students not making adequate progress in the core curriculum.

Third, motivation has been shown to be a key factor in students' academic performance; Gersten, Beckmann, et al. (2009) highlighted the need for academic interventions to consider not only students' skill-related needs, but also motivational and behavioral factors that may influence performance. A parsimonious intervention that includes only those critical components necessary to bring about significant change is important for efficiency but incorporating aspects of instruction known to impact motivation and behavior (e.g., goal-setting, engagement, real life application) may actually increase the rate at which students with LD respond to the intervention. Future studies should investigate this possibility.

Conclusion

Based on our review of the 21 studies described in this chapter, mathematics interventions in multi-tiered systems of support align well with the instructional methods and practices necessary to improve the performance of students with LD and MD. However, limitations exist concerning LD identification methods, progress monitoring, and the relatively narrow range of math skills addressed in these interventions. Relatedly, several questions remain unanswered: Can proven interventions be systematically modified to fit student needs at each instructional tier? What constitutes Tier 2 instruction in mathematics? Will the addition of motivational and behavioral components help students with LD master skills more efficiently? These questions provide directions for future research on secondary interventions in mathematics for students with LD and should help in establishing clear guidelines on the implementation of RTI in this domain.

References

Baker, S., Gersten, R., and Lee, D. (2002). A synthesis of empirical research on teaching mathematics to low-achieving students. *The Elementary School Journal, 103*, 51–73.

Cass, M., Cates, D., Smith, M., and Jackson, C. (2003). Effects of manipulative instruction on solving area and perimeter problems by students with learning disabilities. *Learning Disabilities Research & Practice, 18,* 112–120.

Chard, D. J. (2012). Systems impact: Issues and trends in improving school outcomes for all learners through multitier instructional models. *Intervention in School and Clinic, 48*, 198–202.

Fletcher, J. M., and Vaughn, S. (2009). Response to intervention: Preventing and remediating academic difficulties. *Child Development Perspectives, 3*, 30–37.

Freeman-Green, S. M., O'Brien, C., Wood, C. L., and Hitt, S. B. (2015). Effects of the SOLVE strategy on the mathematical problem solving skills of secondary students with learning disabilities. *Learning Disabilities Research & Practice, 30*, 76–90.

Gersten, R., Beckmann, S., Clarke, B., Foegen, A., Marsh. L., Star, J. R., and Witzel, B. (2009). *Assisting students struggling with mathematics: Response to intervention (RTI) for elementary and middle schools* (NCEE 2009–4060). Washington, DC: National Center for Education Evaluation and Regional Services, Institute of Education Sciences, U.S. Department of Education.

Gersten, R., Chard, D. J., Jayanthi, M., Baker, S. K., Morphy, P., and Flojo, J. (2009). Mathematics instruction for students with learning disabilities: A meta-analysis of instructional components. *Review of Educational Research, 79*, 1202–1242.

Gersten, R., Compton, D., Connor, C. M., Dimino, J., Santoro, L, Linn-Thompson, S., and Tilly, W. D. (2008). *Assisting students struggling with reading: Response to intervention and multi-tier intervention for reading in the primary grades* (NCEE 2009–4060). Washington, DC: National Center for Education Evaluation and Regional Services, Institute of Education Sciences, U.S. Department of Education.

Hunt, J. H., and Vasquez, E. (2014). Effects of ratio strategies intervention on knowledge of ratio equivalence for students with learning disability. *Journal of Special Education, 48*, 180–190.

Hutchinson, N. L. (1993). Effects of cognitive strategy instruction on algebra problem solving of adolescents with learning disabilities. *Learning Disability Quarterly, 16*, 34–63.

Jayanthi, M., and Gersten, R. (2011). Effective instructional practices in mathematics for tier 2 and tier 3 instruction. In R. Gersten and R. Newman-Gonchar (Eds.), *Understanding RTI in mathematics: Proven methods and applications* (pp. 109–125). Baltimore, MD: Paul H. Brookes.

Jitendra, A. K., DiPipi, C. M., and Perron-Jones, N. (2002). An exploratory study of word problem-solving instruction for middle school students with learning disabilities: An emphasis on conceptual and procedural understanding. *Journal of Special Education, 36*, 23–38.

Jitendra, A. K., Dupuis, D. N., Star, J. R., and Rodriguez, M. C. (2016). The effects of schema-based instruction on the proportional thinking of students with mathematics difficulties with and without reading difficulties. *Journal of Learning Disabilities, 49*, 354–367.

Joseph, L. M., and Hunter, A. D. (2001). Differential application of a cue card strategy for solving fraction problems: Exploring instructional utility of the cognitive assessment system. *Child Study Journal, 31*, 123–136.

Kelly, B., Gersten, R., and Carnine, D. (1990). Student error patterns as a function of curriculum design: Teaching fractions to remedial high school students and high school students with learning disabilities. *Journal of Learning Disabilities, 23*, 23–29.

Krawec, J., Huang, J., Montague, M., Kressler, B., and de Alba, A. M. (2013). The effects of cognitive strategy instruction on knowledge of math problem-solving processes of middle school students with learning disabilities. *Learning Disability Quarterly, 36,* 80–92.

Kroesbergen, E. H., and Van Luit, J. H. (2003). Mathematics interventions for children with special educational needs: A meta-analysis. *Remedial and Special Education, 24,* 97–114.

Maccini, P., and Hughes, C. A. (2000). Effects of a problem-solving strategy on the introductory algebra performance of secondary students with learning disabilities. *Learning Disabilities Research & Practice, 15,* 10–21.

Maccini, P., and Ruhl, K. L. (2000). Effects of a graduated instructional sequence on the algebraic subtraction of integers by secondary students with learning disabilities. *Education & Treatment of Children, 23,* 465–489.

Mayer, R. E. (1999). *The promise of educational psychology Vol. I: Learning in the content areas.* Upper Saddle River, NJ: Merrill Prentice Hall.

Montague, M. (1992). The effects of cognitive and metacognitive strategy instruction on the mathematical problem solving of middle school students with learning disabilities. *Journal of Learning Disabilities, 25,* 230–248.

Montague, M., and Bos, C. S. (1986). The effect of cognitive strategy training on verbal math problem solving performance of learning disabled adolescents. *Journal of Learning Disabilities, 19,* 26–33.

Montague, M., Krawec, J., Enders, C., and Dietz, S. (2014). The effects of cognitive strategy instruction on math problem solving of middle-school students of varying ability. *Journal of Educational Psychology, 106,* 469–481.

Montague, M., Penfield, R. D., Enders, C., and Huang, J. (2010). Curriculum-based measurement of math problem solving: A methodology and rationale for establishing equivalence of scores. *Journal of School Psychology, 48,* 39–52.

National Center for Education Statistics. (2013). *The nation's report card: A first look: 2013 mathematics and reading* (NCES 2014–451). Washington, DC: U.S. Department of Education, Institute of Education Sciences. Retrieved from http://nces.ed.gov/nationsreportcard/subject/publications/main2013/pdf/2014451.pdf.

National Governor's Association Center for Best Practices & Council of Chief State School Officers (2010). *Common Core State Standards.* Washington, DC: Authors.

Rosenberg, M. S., Bott, D., Majsterek, D., Chiang, B., Gartland, D., Wesson, C. . . . and Wilson, R. (1993). Minimum standards for the description of participants in learning disabilities research. *Journal of Learning Disabilities, 26,* 210–213.

Satsangi, R., and Bouck, E. C. (2015). Using virtual manipulative instruction to teach the concepts of area and perimeter to secondary students with learning disabilities. *Learning Disability Quarterly, 38,* 174–186.

Scheuermann, A. M., Deshler, D. D., and Schumaker, J. B. (2009). The effects of the explicit inquiry routine on the performance of students with learning disabilities on one-variable equations. *Learning Disability Quarterly, 32,* 103–120.

Strickland, T. K., and Maccini, P. (2013a). The effects of the concrete–representational–abstract integration strategy on the ability of students with learning disabilities to multiply linear expressions within area problems. *Remedial & Special Education, 34,* 142–153.

Strickland, T. K., and Maccini, P. (2013b). Exploration of quadratic equations through multiple representations for students with mathematics difficulties. *Learning Disabilities: A Contemporary Journal, 19,* 61–71.

Test, D. W., and Ellis, M. F. (2005). The effects of LAP fractions on addition and subtraction of fractions with students with mild disabilities. *Education & Treatment of Children, 28,* 11–24.

van Garderen, D. (2007). Teaching students with learning disabilities to use diagrams to solve mathematical word problems. *Journal of Learning Disabilities, 40,* 540–553.

Witzel, B. S., Mercer, C. D., and Miller, M. D. (2003). Teaching algebra to students with learning difficulties: An investigation of an explicit instruction model. *Learning Disabilities Research & Practice, 18,* 121–131.

Woodward, J., Beckmann, S., Driscoll, M., Franke, M., Herzig, P., Jitendra, A., Koedinger, K. R., and Ogbuehi, P. (2012). *Improving mathematical problem solving in grades 4 through 8: A practice guide* (NCEE 2012–4055). Washington, DC: National Center for Education Evaluation and Regional Assistance, Institute of Education Sciences, U.S. Department of Education. Retrieved from htt://ies.ed.gov/ncee/wwc/publications_reviews.aspx#pubsearch/.

Woodward, J., and Brown, C. (2006). Meeting the curricular needs of academically low-achieving students in middle grade mathematics. *Journal of Special Education, 40,* 151–159.

Xin, Y. P., Jitendra, A., and Deatline-Buchman, A. (2005). The effects of mathematical word problem-solving instruction on middle school students with learning problems. *The Journal of Special Education, 39,* 181–192.

Xin, Y. P., and Jitendra, A. K. (1999). The effects of instruction in solving mathematical word problems for students with learning problems: A meta-analysis. *Journal of Special Education, 32,* 207–225.

Zhang, D., and Xin, Y.P. (2012). A follow-up meta-analysis for word-problem-solving interventions for students with mathematics difficulties. *The Journal of Educational Research, 105,* 303–318.

Zheng, X., Flynn, L. J., and Swanson, H. L. (2012). Experimental intervention studies on word problem solving and math disabilities: A selective analysis of the literature. *Learning Disability Quarterly, 36,* 97–111.

16

CURRICULUM-BASED MEASUREMENT FOR SECONDARY-SCHOOL STUDENTS

*Christine Espin, Siuman Chung, Anne Foegen,
and Heather Campbell*

Curriculum-Based Measurement (CBM; Deno, 1985) is an ongoing progress-monitoring system designed to provide educators with data that can be used to evaluate the effectiveness of instructional programs for individual students. CBM originally was designed to monitor the progress of students with severe and persistent learning difficulties (see Jenkins and Fuchs, 2012). Interventions for these students were seen as "instructional hypotheses" whose effectiveness was tested empirically via collection and inspection of progress data (Deno and Mirkin, 1977). This approach was referred to as a *problem-solving approach* (Deno and Fuchs, 1987; Deno, 2013).

At present, CBM often is used as a part of Response to Intervention (RTI)/Multi-Tiered Systems of Support (MTSS) to screen students and inform decisions about placement into tiers of instruction, or about movement from one tier to another. *Problem-solving* is an essential part of an RTI/MTSS approach, especially at Tier 3, where students with severe and persistent learning difficulties/disabilities (LD) are provided intensive, individualized interventions, and progress data are used to evaluate the effectiveness of the instruction (see Berry Kuchle, Zumeta Edmonds, Danielson, Peterson, and Riley-Tillman, 2015; www. intensiveintervention.org).

The majority of work to date on both CBM and RTI/MTSS has focused on elementary-school students (see Vaughn and Fletcher, 2012; Wayman, Wallace, Wiley, Tichá, and Espin, 2007), perhaps because the needs of these students are less complex, and the goals of instruction more clear, than for secondary-school students. However, in recent years, attention has turned to implementation of a problem-solving approach for secondary-school students with LD, and with it, the development of CBM measures for screening and progress monitoring.

Development of CBM at the Secondary-School Level: Unique Challenges

The development of CBM measures at the secondary-school level has presented unique challenges (Espin and Campbell, 2012; Espin and Tindal, 1998). One of these has been to decide *what to measure*. Decisions about what to measure depend on how "curriculum" is defined for secondary-school students with LD. For example, if curriculum is defined as the continued development of basic reading and writing skills, then CBM measures must be designed to measure progress in reading and writing. If curriculum is defined as the acquisition of content-area knowledge, then CBM measures must be designed to measure progress in content areas such as history and science. In this chapter, we outline research and development of CBM progress measures in both basic skills and content areas.

A second and related challenge has been to determine *what the long-range goals* for secondary-school students with LD should be. That is, what level of reading or writing proficiency should students with LD be expected to achieve, or how much content-area knowledge should they be expected to acquire? The answers to these questions guide and direct the development and implementation of CBM measures, and the use of the scores for instructional decision-making at the secondary-school level. To some extent such questions can be answered by linking the CBM scores to Common Core Standards to scores on state standards tests, but even here the question arises as to whether the standards set for students in general should be the standards set for individual students with LD. More research is needed on determining appropriate long-range learning goals for secondary-school students with severe and persistent learning difficulties.

Overview of the Chapter

In the following chapter, we outline research and development of CBM progress monitoring at the secondary-school level in reading, content-area learning (social studies and science), writing, and mathematics. For each area, we first describe what and how to measure, then briefly summarize the research done in the area, and finally outline future directions for research. Although the measures and procedures for administering and scoring CBM measures often differ from those used at the elementary-school level, the essence of CBM remains the same at both elementary- and secondary-school level – that is, the use of progress data to empirically test the effectiveness of interventions for students who struggle.

Reading

At the secondary-school level, the reading demands for students increase significantly, with an increase in reading complexity (Seifert and Espin, 2012), and a corresponding decrease in formal reading instruction (see NAEP data, U. S. Department of Education, 2016), creating significant challenges for students who struggle with reading. Students with severe and persistent reading difficulties might benefit from continued, systematic, intensive reading instruction throughout their middle- and high-school years (see, for example, Edmonds et al., 2009; Solis, Miciak, Vaughn, and Fletcher, 2014), and from implementation of CBM progress monitoring to evaluate the effectiveness of such instruction.

What and How to Measure in Reading

Two types of reading CBM measures have been examined at the secondary-school level: reading aloud and maze selection (Wayman et al., 2007). For reading aloud, students read aloud from a passage, and the number of words read correctly is scored. The examiner's copy of the passage includes a cumulative count of the number of words per line to aide in scoring. The time given is usually one min, although time varies across studies. Reading aloud is administered 1:1; thus, it is time consuming for monitoring large numbers of students.

For maze selection, students read silently from a passage in which every seventh word is deleted and replaced with a multiple-choice item consisting of the correct answer and two distractors. Students select words that restore meaning to the text. The time given is usually two to three minutes, although, again, time varies across studies. Either correct or correct minus incorrect choices is scored. To control for guessing, scoring stops after three consecutive incorrect choices.[1]

Rules for selecting the distractor items for the maze vary somewhat, but usually consist of selecting words that are within one letter in length of the correct word and are clearly wrong choices – that is, are semantically different from, do not rhyme with, and have a different sound and letter configuration than the correct word (Espin, Deno, Maruyama, and Cohen, 1989; L. Fuchs and Fuchs, 1992). Because maze passages are read silently, the measure can be administered to students in groups, and can be administered and scored electronically.

Both narrative and informative texts have been used to develop CBM reading passages. If informative texts are used, it is important that they do not require detailed background information to read and understand the text. Texts length varies between 300 and 800 words (depending on the time given to complete the task). Several commercial sites have reading aloud and/or maze passages available for up to Grades 8 or 9 (*AIMSweb*, www.aimsweb.com; *easyCBM* www. easycbm.com/faq.html; *DIBELS*, https://dibels.uoregon.edu). In addition, via *Intervention Central,* one can create maze passages from any text (www. interventioncentral.org).

Research on CBM in Reading

Studies have examined the technical adequacy of scores from reading aloud and maze selection as both performance level (screening) and progress (growth) measures, although the majority of studies have focused on performance level measures.

Performance Measures

To use CBM measures as performance level or screening measures in reading, the scores must reliably and validly rank-order students at a single point in time. Thus scores must have good alternate-form reliability, must positively relate to scores from criterion reading measures, and must accurately classify students as proficient or non-proficient (at-risk) in reading. In recent years, a number of studies have examined the technical adequacy of scores from reading-aloud and maze-selection measures as indicators of performance in reading for secondary-school students (Baker et al., 2015; Barth et al., 2012; Barth et al., 2014; Chung, Espin, and Stevenson, 2018; Codding, Petscher, and Truckenmiller, 2015; Decker, Hixson, Shaw, and Johnson, 2014; Denton, et al., 2014; Espin, Wallace, Lembke, Campbell, and Long, 2010; Kim, Petscher, and Foorman, 2015; McMaster, Wayman, and Cao, 2006; Silberglitt, Burns, Madyun, and Lail, 2006; Tichá, Espin, and Wayman, 2009; Tolar et al., 2012; Yeo, Fearrington, and Christ, 2012; Yovanoff, Duesbery, Alonzo, and Tindal, 2005). We summarize the results of this research below.

Alternate-Form Reliability. Alternate-form reliability coefficients for reading-aloud scores have ranged from $r = .75$ to .97 and for maze-selection from $r = .52$ to .96, with a majority of coefficients above .70. Not surprisingly, obtained reliability coefficients have been lower when the interval between repeated testing is longer (two to six months; $r = .52$ to .79, Yeo et al., 2012; Tolar et al., 2012) than when it is shorter (same day or week; $r = .69$ to .96, Espin et al., 2010; Tichá et al., 2009). Related to probe duration, obtained reliability coefficients for reading-aloud scores have been similar across time frames (1- vs. 2- vs. 3-minutes vs.

untimed; Barth et al., 2014; Espin et al., 2010; Tichá et al., 2009); however, for maze-selection scores, a small increase in obtained coefficients has been seen with increased time (2- vs. 3- vs. 4-minutes), although the significance of the differences has not been tested (Espin et al., 2010; Tichá et al., 2009).

Validity. To examine evidence for validity, correlations between CBM scores and scores on criterion measures – including a variety of standardized and state-standards tests in reading – have been examined. Correlation coefficients between CBM and criterion-measure scores have varied widely across studies, ranging from $r = .32$ to .89 for reading-aloud and from $r = .37$ to .88 for maze-selection. Coefficients have been found to be similar across administration time (for example 1- vs. 2- vs. 3-minutes) and scoring procedure (for example, correct vs. correct minus incorrect) (Barth et al., 2014; Espin et al., 2010; Tichá et al., 2009).

A small number of studies have examined the use of the CBM scores for predicting which students are "at-risk" and in need of intensive reading instruction. In many of these studies, a measure of predictive power called Area Under the Curve (AUC) has been calculated (but see, for example, Stevenson, 2015 for a different approach). AUC refers to the chance that a student is correctly classified as a proficient or non-proficient reader. AUC values range from .50 to 1.00, with .90 to 1.00 considered to be excellent, .80 to .89 considered to be good, and .70 to .79 considered to be poor (Christ, Zopluoglu, Monaghen, and Van Norman, 2013). Most studies have used scores on state-standards tests as the criterion. For reading aloud, AUC values have ranged from .58 to .87 and for maze selection from .59 to .80 (Barth et al., 2014; Decker et al., 2014; Denton et al., 2011).

Summary of Research on Performance Measures. In sum, scores from both reading-aloud and maze-selection measures have reasonable alternate-form reliability. There is some evidence for validity, however results are variable. This variability might be due to differences across studies related to factors such as the passages used, the participants included, the setting (school/district), the number of passages administered per assessment occasion, scoring procedures, etc. The influence of such factors on the validity of CBM reading measures has been investigated within studies (see Baker et al., 2015; Barth et al., 2012; Chung et al., 2018; Codding et al., 2014; Decker et al., 2014; Espin et al., 2010; Kim et al., 2015; Silberglitt et al., 2006; Tichá et al., 2009; Tolar et al., 2012), but there is a need to examine whether such factors account differences in results across studies.

Progress Measures

For measuring progress or growth in reading, it is important that scores from CBM measures accurately reflect change or improvement in reading. Thus, the scores must be sensitive to growth at a group level, sensitive to interindividual differences in growth, and there must be a positive relation between improvement in CBM scores and improvement in scores on criterion measures.

For many progress studies, growth has been based on a small number of data points. For example, Codding et al. (2015) found that the number of correct maze choices on one three-minute maze passage administered in the fall, winter, and spring of the school year to 247 seventh-graders reflected significant growth over time and interindividual differences in growth trajectories. Yeo et al. (2012) found that three one-minute reading-aloud and one three-minute maze-selection probe administered to 261 seventh- and 225 eighth-grade students in the fall, winter, spring of the school year did not contribute to the prediction of performance on a statewide reading assessment after controlling for initial status. In addition, Yeo et al. found that growth on the two measures was not correlated.

Tolar et al. (2012) and Tolar, Barth, Fletcher, Francis, and Vaughn (2014) measured students five times across the school year. They administered three to five one-minute reading-aloud and one three-minute maze-selection passage per measurement occasion to 1,343 students in Grades 6–8. Reading-aloud scores were the mean number of words read correctly across the three to five passages per occasion, and maze-selection scores were the number of correct–minus–incorrect choices. In general, results revealed that scores for both reading-aloud and maze-selection reflected growth over time, but for neither was change in scores related to growth on the criterion measures (Tolar et al., 2012; Tolar et al., 2014), although change on maze-selection scores was related to performance on a reading measure given at the start of the study (Tolar et al., 2012). McMaster et al. (2006) also measured students five times, but over a period of 13 weeks. Reading-aloud and maze-selection measures were administered to 25 English Learners (ELs) once every three weeks. Both reading-aloud and maze-selection scores reflected statistically significant growth over the 13 weeks, but standard error of estimates for both measures were large relatively to the slopes.

Only two studies involved repeated, weekly data collection of the sort seen in Tiers 2 and 3 of MTSS, and these studies were of short duration. However, see Chung et al., 2018, published since the time of this review. In Espin et al. (2010) and Tichá et al. (2009), 236 and 35 eighth-grade students (respectively) completed weekly reading-aloud and maze-selection probes over a period of 10 weeks. The reading-aloud and maze-selection probes were created from the same materials, controlling for potential differences in outcomes due to passage content. Results revealed that for reading-aloud, there was minimal or no improvement in scores across the 10 weeks, regardless of time frame (1-, 2-, or 3-minutes) or scoring procedure (total words read vs. words read correctly). For maze-selection, improvement in scores was significantly different from 0 at all time frames (2-, 3-, and 4-minutes), and improvement in maze-selection scores was related to scores on a state standards test in reading (Espin et al., 2010), to placement in reading groups, and to improvement in scores on a standardized test of reading (Tichá et al., 2009). The pattern of results did not differ across maze scoring procedure (correct vs. correct minus incorrect choices).

Summary of Research on Progress Measures. In sum, there is some evidence that scores on CBM measures reflect change over time, but it is unclear whether such changes are valid reflections of growth in reading. One factor that may affect the validity of the growth trajectories produced by scores on the CBM measures is the error associated with scores on "parallel" forms. That is, there is a great deal of variability or error associated with scores across different passages, despite the fact the passages are designed to be equivalent. The problem with passage effect has led to recent recommendations to use equated rather than raw scores in CBM progress monitoring (Betts, Pickart, Heistad, 2009; McMaster et al., 2006; Tolar et al., 2012; Tolar et al., 2014). Other factors that may affect the validity of the growth trajectories produced by CBM scores include the frequency and schedule of data collection (see Jenkins, Graff, and Miclioretti, 2009), the effects of instruction (Tolar et al., 2012; Tolar et al., 2014), the application of linear vs. non-linear growth models (Chung et al., 2018; Nese et al., 2013; Tolar et al., 2014), and the participants' level of reading and/or English-language ability (see McMaster et al., 2006; Tolar et al., 2012; Tolar et al., 2014).

Summary and Future Directions in Reading

Perhaps the most striking outcome of both the performance level and progress research in CBM reading is the inconsistency in results across studies. There is a need for additional research and/or systematic reviews and meta-analyses to examine factors that account for the inconsistency in results. Several potential factors have been mentioned in the previous section. These can be categorized as factors related to participant characteristics, measure characteristics, scoring approach, data-collection schedule, effects of instruction on growth, criterion measures selected, and the growth model applied to the data (linear vs. non-linear).

There is also a pressing need for more research on the technical adequacy of the scores as progress indicators. Specifically, there is a need for research on the technical adequacy of the growth rates produced by scores from repeated, frequent (weekly) administration of the CBM measures. Such research is time-intensive and expensive because it requires that a large number of students be monitored over an extended period of time, but the research is critical to use of CBM measures within Tiers 2 and 3 of MTSS. In these tiers, CBM measures are administered frequently (weekly or bi-weekly) so that the growth data can be used to evaluate the effectiveness of instruction and make instructional decisions in a timely fashion. Research is needed to address questions related to the effects of schedules and frequency of data collection, the error due to form effects, and the use of linear vs. nonlinear growth models, on the technical adequacy of growth rates produced by CBM measures. There is also a need for more research focused on older students. To date, the majority of research at the secondary-school level has focused on students in Grades 6–8. More research is needed focused on students in Grades 9–12.

Finally, there is a need to reflect upon the issue of what is being measured with CBM measures at the secondary-school level, and upon the nature of the research questions addressed at the secondary-school level. With regard to the issue of "what" is being measured, at the secondary-school level, maze often is referred to as a measure of "reading comprehension," however, within a CBM approach, both maze-selection and reading-aloud are designed to produce scores that serve as *indicators of general reading proficiency*, not as measures of fluency and/or comprehension (see Conoyer et al., 2016, for a more in-depth discussion of this point). Such a distinction is important in terms of both formulating research questions and using and interpreting CBM scores for decision-making.

With regard to the nature of the research questions, we wonder how important screening is at the secondary-school level. A proportionally large number of CBM studies in reading focus on use of the scores as performance or screening measures – but to what extent is it necessary to screen secondary-school students for reading difficulties? By the time students reach seventh or eighth grade, is it not clear, based on existing information, which students have reading difficulties? Do scores from CBM measures add anything to the accuracy of identification of students with reading difficulties? As an example, Denton et al. (2011) found that the best predictor of whether students would pass or fail the state standards test in reading was the previous score on the state standards test; scores from CBM measures did not improve prediction accuracy. Future research should consider whether the cost of testing a large number of students (especially with reading-aloud) three times a year outweighs the benefits associated with use of the scores to identify students at-risk.

Content-Area Learning

Students with learning difficulties often receive their content-area instruction in the general education classrooms, and are held to the same standards as peers without disabilities. Yet learning in the content areas presents significant challenges for many students with learning difficulties, not the least of which is reading large amounts of text, often from textbooks that are "inconsiderate" – that is, not well-structured, replete with specific vocabulary terms, and dense with new ideas and concepts (Armbruster and Anderson, 1988; Groves, 1995; Yager, 1983). Students with disabilities may require additional supports/interventions to succeed in their content-area classes. CBM progress monitoring can be used to help determine whether such supports/interventions are effective in helping students to learn content area material, to achieve content-area standards, and to attain passing grades on state standards tests.

What and How to Measure in the Content Areas

Various types of CBM content-area measures have been examined over the years, including reading aloud (see Espin and Deno, 1993a, 1993b; Espin and Foegen, 1996; Fewster and MacMillan, 2002), story writing (see Fewster and MacMillan, 2002), and maze-selection (see Espin and Foegen, 1996; Johnson, Semmelroth, Allison, and Fritsch, 2013; Ketterlin-Geller, McCoy, Twyman, and Tindal, 2006); however, most research has employed a vocabulary-based type of measure. The focus on vocabulary is perhaps is not surprising given the importance of *academic* or *key vocabulary* in the content-areas. Academic or key vocabulary refers to words or terms that represent specific concepts and processes within an academic area (Antonacci, O'Callaghan, and Berkowitz, 2015; Vannest, Parker, and Dyer, 2011). These concepts and terms form the basis for learning in the content areas (Vannest et al., 2011). The vocabulary-based tasks used in CBM typically involve matching key vocabulary terms with definitions; however, the specific form of the task varies from study to study. For simplicity's sake, we outline one commonly-used approach in this section (see Busch and Espin, 2003, for a detailed description of how to create and use vocabulary-matching measures).

The first step in the development of the vocabulary-matching measure is to create a pool of key terms and definitions from the glossaries of the textbooks and with teacher input. From this pool, 20 terms and definitions are randomly selected with replacement to appear on each probe. The 20 terms are listed in alphabetical order vertically on the left side of the page, and 20 definitions plus 2 distractor definitions are listed in random order on the right. Students have five minutes to match terms with definition. Scores are the number of correct matches.

Probes must be long enough so that students do *not* finish within the allotted time. This is because growth on the CBM measures is reflected in both accuracy and automaticity; thus, as students increase content-area knowledge, they more accurately and efficiently read and define key vocabulary terms. If students finish the probes before the allotted time, there is little room for growth on subsequent probes. The procedures outlined in the previous paragraph should thus be viewed as guidelines: It may be necessary to have more than 20 terms on each probe for the measures to remain sensitive to growth across an entire school year.

Research on CBM in the Content Areas

Research on CBM in the content areas has been conducted in various areas, including social studies, science, and foreign-language learning. Espin and Tindal (1998) reviewed the early work on the development of CBM measures in the content areas, thus we focus on research conducted after the time of that review, and on research conducted in the areas of social studies (including history) and science because the majority of work has been conducted in those areas (see Chung and Espin, 2013, for research on foreign-language learning). Finally, we focus on research conducted with students in Grades 6 and above (see Mooney, McCarter, Russo, and Blackwood, 2013, and Vannest et al., 2011 for studies with participants in Grade 5).

In general, the research has supported the reliability and validity of scores from vocabulary-based CBM measures as indicators of both performance and progress in the content areas. In both social studies and science, alternate-form (AF) reliabilities have varied from .58 to .87, with averages in the .70s. Combining scores across two probes has resulted in higher AF reliabilities than for single probes (r = .80 and above) (Beyers, Lembke, and Curs, 2013; Espin, Busch, Shin, and Kruschwitz, 2001; Espin et al., 2013). Espin et al. (2013) found that reliabilities of adjacent scores on weekly science probes increased across time, perhaps because the scores became more stable as students accumulated science knowledge over time. Espin et al. (2001) found a similar increase in AF reliabilities in social studies from weeks one to eight, but reliabilities then decreased from weeks nine to 11.

With regard to the validity of CBM vocabulary scores as indicators of content-area performance, correlations with scores on state standards tests and commercial standardized tests in social studies and science typically have ranged from .53 to .76, with the majority of correlations between .60 and .65 (Espin, et al., 2001; Espin et al., 2013; Beyers et al., 2013; Mooney, McCarter, Schraven, and Callicoatte, 2013; Mooney, McCarter, Schraven, and Haydel, 2010). Coefficients have been found to be similar across race, gender, SES, and exceptionality (Mooney et al., 2010; Mooney et al., 2013). Scores on the CBM vocabulary measures also have been found to relate to scores on researcher-made knowledge tests, with concurrent validity coefficients ranging from .59 to .84, and predictive validity coefficients from .66 to .67 (Espin et al., 2001; Espin et al., 2013). Finally, correlations with course grades have been found to be significant but have been somewhat lower than correlations with the standardized or research-made instruments, ranging from .57 to .65 in science (Espin et al., 2013) and .27 to .51 in social studies (Espin et al., 2001).

With regard to the sensitivity of the measures to progress or learning, and to the validity of the growth rates produced by the measures, growth on CBM vocabulary measures has been shown to be significantly different from zero, to reflect interindividual differences in growth rates, and to be significantly related to disability status, SES, scores on standardized/state tests, course grades, and improvement in scores on research-made knowledge tests (Beyers et al., 2013; Borsuk, 2010; Espin et al., 2013; Espin, Shin, and Busch, 2005; Mooney et al., 2013). The amount of observed growth has varied from study to study. Espin et al. (2013) and Espin et al. (2005) found growth rates of .63 matches per week in science and .65 in social studies respectively, whereas Beyers et al. (2013) found growth rates of only .15 matches per week in social studies.

Growth rates may vary with the type of probe used. For example, Mooney et al. (2013) found that growth was higher for probes in which terms were randomly selected from the entire pool of terms (.23 high SES and .10 low SES) than when probes included equal number of terms from the first and second half of the year (.11 high SES and .02 low SES). Espin et al. (2005) found lower growth rates when probes were read to the students than when the students read the probes themselves (.22 vs .65 matches per week). Borsuk (2010) found growth rates of .26 for probes that were read to the students, and for which students were presented a definition and asked to select the correct term from six options. Reasons for differences in growth rates across studies need to be systematically addressed in future research.

Summary and Future Directions in the Content Areas

In sum, research in the content areas has supported the technical adequacy of CBM vocabulary-based measures as indicators of performance and progress in social studies and science; however, several questions must be addressed in future research. As stated earlier, reasons for the differences in growth rates among studies should be systematically examined. Relatedly, different approaches for creating probes should be systematically compared, as was done in Mooney et al. (2013) and Espin et al. (2005). Such comparisons could examine the effects of different time frames and number of items on the technical adequacy of the measures. This research also could examine administration of the measures across an entire school year to determine whether there are floor or ceiling effects for the scores.

The most important question to be addressed in future research, however, is the question of data use for decision-making. Related to this, consideration must be given to the relatively low growth rates produced by the vocabulary measures. That is, although it is good news that a growth rate of .65 is significantly different from 0 and relates to performance and progress on criterion variables, it is unclear whether this low rate of growth will be useful in practical settings. Will teachers find the rate of progress too low to be practically useful for decision-making? There is also a need for research on whether and how content and special education teachers use the data to evaluate growth and adjust instruction.

Writing

There are two methods often used for direct writing scoring: holistic and analytic (Huot, 1990). Holistic scoring reflects a rater's general impression of the quality of a writing sample (e.g. Charney, 1984; Espin, Weissenburger, and Benson, 2004; Huot, 1990) while analytic scoring quantifies particular characteristics in writing samples (Isaacson, 1988). Although there is some evidence for the reliability and validity of holistic and analytic assessments as static measures of writing proficiency, they would be neither realistic nor appropriate for school personnel to use for general screening or regular monitoring of student writing progress in RTI/MTSS models. For example, to produce the writing samples for holistic and analytic scoring, teachers would have to dedicate approximately 30 minutes for each administration. Additionally, the restricted ranges of the rubric scores are not sensitive to incremental progress in writing proficiency.

Curriculum-based measurement in writing (CBM-W), however, is a method that could be used to screen and monitor students' writing proficiencies if the probes are technically adequate indicators of writing proficiency. That is, the CBM-W probes must provide reliable data and be valid with respect to the "standardized" writing assessments mentioned above. CBM-W measures have been used with secondary students to predict student scores on standardized tests (Diercks-Gransee, Weissenburger, Johnson, and Christensen, 2009; Espin, et al., 2008; Lopez and Thompson, 2011) and to monitor writing progress (Viel-Ruma, Houchins, Jolivette, Fredrick, and Gama, 2010; Walker, Shippen, Alberto, Houchins, and Cihak, 2005).

What and How to Measure in Writing

In CBM-W students are given a prompt to inspire their writing sample, either a picture or a narrative or expository prompt. A picture prompt should elicit a story and contain familiar images easily identifiable for students. Written prompts (either narrative or expository) often end mid-sentence to stimulate a response and should be written to be appropriate for students regardless of their backgrounds. The most challenging aspect of creating these prompts is ensuring that they are sufficiently motivating or relatable to allow for sustained student interest for the duration of the writing sample. CBM-W measures can be easily created by teachers, although there are CBM-W generators available free online (through Intervention Central www.interventioncentral.org/teacher-resources/curriculum-based-measurement-probes-writing) as well as CBM-W measures available commercially (AIMSweb www.aimsweb.com). After the prompt is shown or read to students, they are given 30 seconds to think about what they will write, and then a set amount of time in which to write (based on research, ranging from three to seven minutes).

One of the hallmarks of CBM has been the efficient administration and scoring of probes. Unfortunately, research on CBM-W consistently has revealed that long samples (up to seven minutes) and complex scoring methods are necessary to obtain a valid and reliable indicator of general writing performance for secondary students (Espin, De La Paz, Scierka, and Roelofs, 2005; Espin et al., 2000; Jewell and Malecki, 2005; McMaster and Campbell, 2008; Parker, Tindal, and Hasbrouck, 1991b; Tindal and Parker, 1989; Weissenburger and Espin, 2005). However, the five to seven minutes of CBM writing at the secondary level is more efficient than the at least 30-minute writing samples that would be required for holistic or atomistic scoring.

Research on CBM in Writing

Technical Adequacy of the Measures

Most research on CBM-W for secondary students has been on the technical adequacy of static administrations and not the use of CBM-W to monitor student progress in writing. The research focus to date has mainly been on establishing the reliability (alternate-form, inter-scorer) and validity (correlations with standardized measures of writing quality such as the TOWL-3) of CBM-W. Researchers have investigated scoring procedures, types of prompts, and writing times that produce the most technically adequate measures. Additionally, CBM-W has been investigated for the ability to predict high-stakes writing assessment scores.

Scoring procedures and time. CBM-W samples have been scored using different procedures, but those that have been shown to be technically adequate for secondary students are correct word sequences and correct minus incorrect word sequences (see McMaster and Espin, 2007 for a review of the literature). A correct word sequence (CWS) is scored between two adjacent correctly spelled words which are acceptable within the context of the sample and both syntactically and semantically correct (Videen, Deno, and Marston, 1982). Correct minus incorrect word sequences (CIWS) is the number of correct sequences minus the number of incorrect word sequences (Espin, Scierka, Skare, and Halverson, 1999). For more details on CBM-W scoring, see Hessler and Konrad (2008).

CBM-W measures have been scored using production-dependent (total words written, words spelled correctly), production-independent (percentage calculations such as %CWS), and accurate-production (CIWS) measures (Jewell and Maleki, 2005). While the production-dependent measures are easier to score and more reliable across raters, it is often the accurate-production (CIWS) and production-independent (such as %CWS) measures that are more strongly correlated with criterion measures, particularly for secondary students (Amato and Watkins, 2011; McMaster and Espin, 2007). However, when considering measures for progress monitoring, researchers have noted that the production-independent measures would likely not be as sensitive to growth as the accurate-production measures (Amato and Watkins, 2011; Malecki and Jewell, 2003; Tindal and Parker, 1989).

Considering measures that might be appropriate for progress monitoring, McMaster and Espin (2007) noted in their literature review that longer writing samples (five to seven minutes) scored using complex CBM-W procedures are required to produce technical adequacy for older students. Criterion-validity coefficients for CWS are generally higher ($r = .18$–$.65$) than those for words written ($r = .10$–$.47$) or words spelled correctly ($r = .08$–$.54$), measures that are often used with elementary students. However, for secondary students, correct minus incorrect word sequences (CIWS) has been found to have higher validity coefficients ($r = .56$–$.75$) than other scoring procedures (e.g., Espin et al., 1999; Espin et al., 2000; Jewell and Malecki, 2005; McMaster and Campbell, 2008; McMaster and Espin, 2007).

Prompt type. Prompt type (narrative, picture, and expository) for CBM-W has also been investigated, but research has not coalesced around the best prompt type. Based on the results from a study with 112 culturally and linguistically diverse middle school students, Espin et al. (2000) reported that the type of prompt (narrative or expository) did not seem to impact validity coefficients (calculated from student scores on a district writing assessment and holistic teacher ratings of student writing). However, McMaster and Campbell (2008) found that for seventh-grade students, seven minutes of student writing in response to picture prompts scored for CIWS produced significant correlations with grade point average (GPA) and the picture-based TOWL-3 ($.55$–$.67$), as did writing in response to expository ($.52$–$.68$) prompts. Narrative prompts did not produce significant correlations with the TOWL-3 at seven minutes but did with GPA ($.72$).

In contrast, Mercer, Martinez, Faust, and Mitchell (2012) found that for tenth-graders, five-minute narrative prompts scored for CWS or CIWS were more predictive of end of course assessment tests ($r = .35, .42$) than were expository prompts ($r = .29, .20$). Additionally, they found stronger correlations for five-minute narrative prompts scored for CWS and CIWS ($.40, .45$) to a tenth-grade Indiana state writing test than for expository prompts ($.36, .28$). Narrative prompts scored for CWS, CIWS, and %CWS also explained more variance on the state test than did the expository prompts.

Predictive measures. As writing tests can be used to make high stakes decisions, it is important to investigate whether or not CBM-W can predict student performance on standardized tests of writing. Espin et al. (2008) examined the reliability and validity of CBM measures in response to an expository prompt to predict scores on a statewide tenth-grade standardized writing test. Informed by the strongest CBM-W reliability and validity coefficients, researchers constructed tables of probable success using seven minutes of writing scored for CIWS.

While most of these statewide or high-stakes writing-proficiency assessments require tudents to write in response to expository prompts, researchers have also investigated the use of narrative prompt type in relation to standardized tests. Lopez and Thompson (2011) found moderately strong correlations ($.59, .67$) between three-minute narrative prompts scored for CWS and a state writing assessment for seventh- and eighth-graders. Lopez and Thompson then used the data to determine cut-scores predictive of the statewide writing assessments. Similarly, Mercer et al. (2012) found that for tenth-graders, CWS and CIWS scores from five minutes of writing in response to narrative prompts were stronger predictors of a state writing assessment than were CBM scores from samples written in response to expository prompts.

Use of CBM-W for screening in RTI/MTSS

In order to use CBM-W for screening or progress-monitoring within Response to Intervention (RTI) models and multi-tier system of supports (MTSS) frameworks, it is important to have access to benchmark scores and growth norms to help inform goal-setting and decision making.

AIMSweb (2012) makes available Grades 1–8 winter national norms for CWS (calculated from selected, representative student data in the AIMSweb database). These norms should be used with caution, particularly for secondary students, as the sample sizes for CBM-W are much smaller than those for CBM-R and CBM-M. For example, for eighth-graders, there were only 312 students in the CBM-W norming sample compared to 5,048 in CBM-R ORF and 6,095 in MAZE. Additionally, these norms only report CWS and not the more complex scoring procedure, CIWS, which has been shown to be more technically adequate for older students. Alternately, districts could establish their own CBM-W norms which would be more reflective of their student populations.

The use of CBM-W measures in RTI/MTSS models have not been investigated at the secondary level, however Ritchey and Coker (2013) examined the utility of CBM-W to screen at-risk second- and third-grade students. To test the classification accuracy of CWS, researchers created local norms using CWS scores below the 25th percentile as cutpoints. Researchers noted that these cutpoints were above the norms reported in AIMSweb (2012). While CWS scores were the most reliable in identifying students with writing difficulties, the false positive rates for second- and third-graders still ranged from 14.3% to 26.2%. Researchers urged caution for the sole use of CBM-W measures for screening due to the lack of research in CBM-W progress monitoring and the large false-positive rate.

For secondary students, there appears to be some support for the use of production-independent measures for screening in RTI/MTSS models, %CWS measures often have moderate to moderately strong validity and reliability correlations (r = .36–.73; McMaster and Espin, 2007). However, the use of %CWS for screening has not specifically been investigated.

Growth and Progress-Monitoring with CBM-W

Few researchers have investigated teachers' regular use of CBM-W scores to monitor writing progress and make data-based instructional decisions. Growth studies in CBM-W tend to report static scores over only two or three administrations of writing prompts (such as fall-winter-spring).

Growth measures. Parker, Tindal, and Hasbrouck (1991a) investigated the use of several CBM-W measures to monitor middle school students' writing progress. Participants included 54 students with learning disabilities who were asked to write for six minutes (and mark at three minutes) in response to a narrative prompt. Prompts were administered in October, January, February, and April. Scoring procedures included production-independent measures (WW, legible words written, CWS, correctly spelled words) as well as production-independent measures (%CWS, percent legible words, and the mean length of strings of correct word sequences). Measures producing moderate correlations with the TOWL and with holistic ratings included percent legible words, CWS, and the mean length of CWS (rs = .45–.75), however these correlations were not stable over the four administrations of the writing assessments. Additionally, only CWS and percent legible words produced linear trends over the four administrations. Authors urged caution in the use of any of these measures for progress monitoring and provided only tepid support for the use of percent legible words, CWS, or mean length of CWS for screening purposes.

Malecki and Jewell (2003) administered fall and spring three-minute narrative CBM-W prompts to 946 first- through eighth-graders (which included 126 middle school students). Researchers noted that while the accurate-production measure (CIWS) was significantly related to WW for elementary students, such a relationship was not significant at the middle school level providing further caution that simple production-dependent measures (including WW) were not appropriate for monitoring the writing progress of older students. And although all scoring procedures (WW, WSC, CWS, CIWS, %WSC, %CWS) produced small gains across grade levels, the production-independent measures (%WSC and %CWS) failed to differentiate among the different grade levels and thus would likely not be sensitive to growth.

Espin et al. (2005) investigated the growth in CBM-W measures of 22 seventh- and eighth-graders with a range of writing proficiencies. Data analyzed were from an existing data set in which students produced six 35-minute essays in response to an expository prompt before and then after a four-week writing intervention. Researchers randomly selected three prompts before and three prompts after the intervention for each participant and scored them for WW, CWS, and CIWS. While all scoring procedures produced strong validity coefficients with holistic and analytic ratings of writing proficiency ($r = .58-.90$), a subset of the writing samples (the first 50 words) scored for CWS and CIWS produced lower correlations ($r = .33-.59$). The 35-minute writing samples scored for CWS, CIWS, and WW produced statistically significant growth for all students, however CWS and CIWS scored on the first 50 words of the essay were only sensitive to growth for the least proficient writers. While the regular use of a 35-min writing sample for progress monitoring would be prohibitive for teachers, researchers did find support for the use of shorter writing samples scored for CWS or CIWS with less proficient writers.

McMaster and Campbell (2008) investigated the growth from fall (November) to spring (May) in CBM-W measures among third-, fifth-, and seventh-graders who were predominately culturally and linguistically diverse students. The 123 participants wrote for three to seven minutes in response to picture, narrative, and expository prompts. Prompts were scored for WW, WSC, CWS and CIWS and measures were correlated with the TOWL-3, a state writing measure (for fifth-graders), and language arts GPA (for seventh-graders). Researchers found that no measures for third-graders demonstrated technical adequacy or statistically significant growth. However, for fifth-graders, three minutes of narrative writing scored for CWS and five minutes of narrative or expository writing scored for CWS or CIWS met the above criteria. For seventh-graders, only five minutes of expository writing scored for CIWS demonstrated technical adequacy and statistically significant growth (although small at .43 CIWS gain per week) from fall to spring.

Codding et al. (2015) expanded on CBM research at the middle school level. They investigated the relationships among CBM-W, CBM-R, CBM-M, and standardized assessments in language arts (ELA) and math. They also analyzed the growth in the CBM measures fall-winter-spring. Researchers found statistically significant growth in the CBM-W measures (both CIWS and WW) and noted that students with lower fall CBM-W scores grew at higher rates than students with higher fall scores. Additionally, researchers noted that correlations between the ELA assessment and both CBM-R ($r = .65-.70$) and W ($r = .44-.55$) measures were significant and moderate, with the highest correlates produced from the spring CBM administrations (which were concurrent to the ELA assessment).

Progress monitoring. Few researchers have investigated the regular use of CBM-W to monitor secondary student writing proficiency progress. Walker, Shippen, Alberto, Houchins, and Cihak (2005) used CBM-W to investigate the effectiveness of a direct instruction writing program: *Expressive Writing* (Engelmann and Silbert, 1983) for three culturally and linguistically diverse students with learning disabilities. For 50 daily sessions, three high school students received 50 minutes of instruction. Starting with lesson 12, students wrote a practice paragraph for which the first three minutes were scored for CWS. By the end of the intervention, all participants increased their CWS throughout the program (increases of seven, eight, and 10 CWS over 39 days of instruction), and TOWL-3 scores also increased. Based on these results, the authors concluded that the *Expressive Writing* curriculum made positive impacts on writing proficiency and produced growth over a short period of time that would normally be expected for the entire academic year based on CBM-W growth norms from AIMSweb.

Viel-Ruma et al. (2010) also investigated the effectiveness of *Expressive Writing*. Six high school students (three of whom were English learners) participated in 26 consecutive lessons; after each lesson, students wrote for three minutes in response to a picture prompt. Researchers scored the prompts for CWS and noted that isolation of student errors as a result of the scoring could inform instruction. Scores were reported as percentage of CWS, and while all students showed gain scores, the slopes of the gains were low. Authors noted that percentage of CWS calculated in a short, three-minute writing sample likely lacked sensitivity to change over this short period of time and that future replications should utilize CWS or CIWS scoring of five to seven minutes of writing.

Summary and Future Research in Writing

In sum, there are data to support the technical adequacy of the following CBM-W measures for secondary students: five to seven minutes of writing (with longer samples being necessary for older students) in response to either a narrative or expository prompt scored for CIWS or CWS. Shorter writing times (as little as three minutes) may be sufficient for students producing less proficient writing, as could the use of CWS. However, due to the lack of true progress monitoring studies, it is not clear that for secondary students the use of these measures will (1) be technically adequate for universal screening in RTI/MTSS models, (2) produce statistically significant growth for use in progress monitoring, (3) be able to be used to establish national or local growth norms, or (4) be practically sensitive so teachers can use the measures for progress monitoring with secondary students. It is clear that continued research with CBM-W is needed particularly to inform RTI/MTSS models where technically adequate screening and progress monitoring measures are vital.

Mathematics

Measuring progress in secondary mathematics raises unique challenges because the curriculum becomes more divergent as students move through the middle school and high school grades. The "general mathematics" curriculum that is typical in the elementary grades and into middle school (depending on the school system) becomes differentiated as students begin coursework in algebra, geometry, and advanced topics such as trigonometry and calculus. As instruction becomes more focused on specific topics within mathematics, "general" measures of mathematics progress become less sensitive to student changes in proficiency in the instructional content. General mathematics measures developed for the elementary grades may be useful in providing sensitive indicators to track improvement in prerequisite skill gaps for secondary students but are not likely to be reflective of progress toward grade level curriculum outcomes. In this section of the chapter, we review existing measures for middle school and high school mathematics, summarize the research on the measures' technical adequacy for monitoring student progress, and identify future directions for ongoing research and measure development in secondary mathematics.

What and How to Measure in Mathematics

Options for secondary mathematics measures are relatively limited. Many tools have the elementary grades as a primary focus and may include Grade 6, but do not offer additional levels representing the typical secondary range (e.g., seven through twelve). The tools described here included measures at least through Grade 8 and had accessible information regarding their reliability, validity, and rates of growth; they are limited to two suites of tools and measures developed by Foegen and her colleagues for middle school and for algebra. Readers should note that a third suite of tools available from easyCBM (Alonzo and Tindal, 2010/2015; Anderson, et al., 2014) is not included here because space constraints do not allow for sufficient description of the system's complexity, which includes multiple mathematics tools (NCTM, CCSS) and multiple forms of the system (Lite, Teacher Deluxe, District) available through multiple sources (University of Oregon, n.d.; HMH-Riverside Publishing, n.d.).

AIMSweb

The AIMSweb (Pearson, n.d.) suite of mathematics measures includes Mathematics Computation (M-COMP; Pearson, 2012a) measures for Grades 1–8 and Mathematics Concepts and Applications (M-CAP; Pearson, 2012b) measures for Grades 2 through 8; 30 grade-level forms of each type of measure are available. Items use a constructed response format and students have between eight and ten minutes to respond. Students' responses are scored using a key; answers are judged either correct or incorrect and the number of points awarded per correct answer ranges from one to three. M-COMP content was determined with "guidance from internal and external experts" (Pearson, 2012d, p. 26). The publisher recommends using the Grade 8 forms for students in Grades 9–12 and provides national norms for Grades 9–12 based on the Grade 8 probes, although the data for these grade levels are not included in the National Norms Technical Report document (Pearson, 2012c). M-CAP content was designed to reflect the National Research Council's five strands of mathematical proficiency (Kilpatrick, Swafford, and Findell, 2001) as well as the NRC recommendation that instruction should "focus on problem-solving, logical reasoning, and application of analytical skills" (Pearson, 2012d, p. 18). The distribution of items across domains for each grade level was matched to the content blueprint for the Stanford Achievement Test, Tenth Edition (SAT10; Harcourt Educational Measurement, 2002).

STAR Math

STAR Math (Renaissance Learning, n.d.) is an assessment system that spans kindergarten through Grade 12, providing support for screening, instructional grouping, measuring student growth, and predicting performance on state standards assessments. The online assessment system uses computer adaptive assessments, with content drawn from an item bank that represents eleven domains for students in Grades 1–8 and 21 domains for students in Grades 9–12; content can be customized to align with individual states' standards. Each STAR Math assessment includes 24 items, and the assessment is untimed (though the developers note that measures usually require 20 minutes or less).

Estimation, Complex Quantity Discrimination, and Missing Number for Middle School

Foegen and her colleagues (Foegen, 2000, 2008; Foegen and Deno, 2001) have developed three types of measures for middle school mathematics with common forms that can be used across Grades 6 through 8. The 40-item Estimation measure is evenly split between computational estimation (numbers only) and contextualized estimation tasks (e.g., word or story problems), both reflecting whole and rational numbers. Eighteen parallel forms are available; students have three minutes to complete the multiple-choice items. Each of the 44 items on the Complex Quantity Discrimination measure includes two quantities (e.g., whole numbers or rational numbers and expressions involving whole numbers); students have one minute to complete items by responding with the appropriate symbol (<, >, =). The Missing Number measure also has 44 items; each is a number sequence with three positive whole numbers (up to two digits) and a blank (the position of the blank varies across items). In addition to counting sequences, and step-counting (e.g., by threes and sevens), the patterns represented also include the multiplicative relations of halving and doubling. For both the Complex Quantity Discrimination and the Missing Number measures, eight parallel forms are available, students have one minute to respond, and the total score is the number of correct responses.

AAIMS Algebra Progress Monitoring Measures

Foegen and her colleagues extended their middle school work to address beginning algebra instruction. Three types of measures were examined in the initial research (Perkmen, Foegen, and Olson, 2006a): Algebra Basic Skills, Algebra Foundations, and Algebra Content Analysis. The Algebra Basic Skills measure includes 60 items representing five types of skills for which proficiency is necessary for success in Algebra 1 (e.g., combining like terms, applying the distributive property). The 50-item Algebra Foundations measure includes some of the same skills (solving simple equations, evaluating expressions) as Algebra Basic Skills, but adds additional types of items on graphing linear equations and inequalities, as well as generalizing relations and functions. Students have five minutes to respond to the Algebra Basic Skills and Algebra Foundations measures; the total score for each is the number of items completed correctly. The Algebra Content Analysis measure reflects more advanced skills (including simplifying rational expressions, determining slopes, and solving linear systems). Each of the 16 items has four distractors and is worth up to three points; students are encouraged to show their work to earn partial credit. Teachers score the measure using a rubric that guides the process of awarding partial credit for each item type. Work currently underway is further refining these measures, as well as developing three additional measures intended to gauge students' conceptual understanding of algebra (Foegen and Dougherty, 2010).

Research on CBM in Mathematics

In this section, we discuss the evidence related to the technical adequacy of the identified measures, including reliability, criterion validity, and rates of improvement/growth on the measures over time. We report median correlation coefficients by grade level (when available) and focus on validity with respect to mathematics achievement measures for greater comparability across studies and measures. We drew our data from published studies, technical manuals, and data reported to the National Center for Intensive Intervention's (NCII's) Technical Review Committee, which are available on the Center's website (National Center on Intensive Intervention, n.d.).

AIMSweb

Data for the AIMSweb measures were drawn from the NCII website and the Technical Manual for the measures (Pearson, 2012d). Both the M-COMP and M-CAP have demonstrated high levels of reliability, with median alternate form coefficients for M-COMP of .89, .90, and .89

for Grades 6, 7, and 8, respectively and M-CAP coefficients of .86, .88, and .86 for Grades 6, 7, and 8, respectively. Median interscorer agreement rates exceeded 96% for both measures. The median M-COMP construct validity coefficient was .76 with a Grade 8 mathematics achievement measure; comparable M-CAP coefficients were .75, .76, and .71 for Grades 6, 7, and 8, respectively. Mean rates of weekly improvement were .33, .16, and .22 for the M-COMP in Grades 6, 7, and 8, respectively. Mean rates of weekly improvement were .20, .28, and .11 for the M-CAP in Grades 6, 7, and 8, respectively. Although AIMSweb recommends using the Grade 8 measures for students in high school, no technical adequacy data are reported for Grades 9–12 in either the technical manual or the national norms document available on the website.

STAR Math

Data for STAR math were drawn from the STAR Math Technical Manual (Renaissance Learning, 2015). Although numerous published studies report results of the effects of STAR Math on student achievement, we were unable to identify published studies of the measures' technical adequacy beyond the sources cited. Reliability data are reported for grade-level samples from 6 to 12. Alternate form reliability coefficients across these grade levels ranged from .72 to .80, with a median of .74. Split-half estimates ranged from .84 to .88, with a median of .87. Generic reliability, described as the "proportion of test score variance attributable to true variation in the trait the test measures" (Renaissance Learning, 2015, p. 47), ranged from .84 to .88, with a median of .87. With respect to criterion validity with mathematics achievement tests, a median concurrent validity coefficient of .64 was obtained in a meta-analysis of 276 correlations representing students across Grades 1–12. Predictive validity coefficients for students in Grades 7–12 ranged from .75 to .80, with a median of .76. STAR Math rates of improvement (e.g., growth norms) are not reported in the technical manual; these data are derived annually from user norms and reported using decile groups within each grade level for STAR Math clients through the system's website reporting interface.

Foegen and Colleagues' Middle School Measures

Data for the middle school measures developed by Foegen and her colleagues (Estimation, Complex Quantity Discrimination, Missing Number) were drawn from three published studies of students in Grades 6, 7, and 8 (Foegen, 2000, 2008; Foegen and Deno, 2001). For the Estimation measure, median alternate form reliability coefficients were .82, .72, and .80 for Grades 6, 7, and 8, respectively; test-retest coefficients for the same grades were .86, .75, and .80. Concurrent validity coefficients with a mathematics achievement measure were .55, .48, and .53 for Grades 6, 7, and 8, respectively for the Estimation measure. Mean rates of weekly improvement on Estimation were .25, .22, and .20 for Grades 6, 7, and 8, respectively. For the Complex Quantity Discrimination measure, alternate form reliability coefficients were .86, .87, and .88 for Grades 6, 7, and 8, respectively; test-retest coefficients for the same grades were .82, .82, and .86. Concurrent criterion validity coefficients for the Complex Quantity Discrimination measure and a mathematics achievement test were .53, .59, and .55 for Grades 6, 7, and 8, respectively. Mean rates of weekly improvement on Complex Quantity Discrimination were .31, .38, and .31 for Grades 6, 7, and 8, respectively. For the Missing Number measure, alternate form reliability coefficients were .69, .74, and .68 for Grades 6, 7, and 8, respectively; test-retest coefficients for the same grades were .82, .83, and .88. Concurrent criterion validity coefficients for the Missing Number measure and a mathematics achievement test were .47, .61, and .47 for Grades 6, 7, and 8, respectively. Mean rates of weekly improvement on Complex Quantity Discrimination were .16, .13, and .09 for Grades 6, 7, and 8, respectively.

Foegen and Colleagues' Algebra Measures

Data for the algebra measures developed by Foegen and her colleagues were drawn from five technical reports (Foegen and Olson, 2007a, 2007b; Perkmen, Foegen, and Olson, 2006a, 2006b, 2006c) resulting from a federally-funded project. All data were gathered in inclusive Algebra 1 courses that enrolled students in Grades 8–12. We conducted technical adequacy analyses at the course level, rather than by grade levels. Alternate-form reliability coefficients for the Algebra Basic Skills measure ranged from .49 to .93, with a median of .81. Test–retest coefficients ranged from .75 to .89, with a median of .83. Concurrent criterion validity co-efficients with an algebra test ranged from .50 to .60, with a median of .53; comparable coefficients for predictive validity ranged from .45 to .59, with a median of .56. The median weekly rate of improvement for Algebra Basic Skills ranged from .03 to .80, with a median of .34 points.

Alternate-form reliability coefficients for the Algebra Foundations measure ranged from .72 to .91, with a median of .84. Test-retest coefficients ranged from .80 to .91, with a median of .84. Concurrent criterion validity coefficients with an algebra test ranged from .56 to .73, with a median of .57; comparable coefficients for predictive validity ranged from .54 to .61, with a median of .58. The mean weekly rate of improvement for Algebra Foundations was .39 points.

Alternate-form reliability coefficients for the Algebra Content Analysis measure ranged from .48 to .94, with a median of .79. Test-retest coefficients ranged from .64 to .88, with a median of .77. Concurrent criterion validity coefficients with an algebra test ranged from .36 to .76, with a median of .58; comparable coefficients for predictive validity ranged from .30 to .63, with a median of .54. The median weekly rate of improvement for Algebra Content Analysis ranged from −0.45 to .1.54 points, with a median of .62.

Summary and Future Directions in Mathematics

Across the range of secondary mathematics measures, reliability coefficients are in the acceptable range. Criterion validity estimates are generally modest for the Foegen middle school and high school measures, but stronger for the AIMSweb and STAR Math measures. Rates of improvement are quite modest for the large majority of measures, with most in the .10 to .40 points per week range. One notable exception was the Algebra Content Analysis measure, which had a median rate of improvement of .62 points per week. This outcome is likely reflective of the limited proficiency of students with the content of the assessment as they enter an Algebra 1 course, combined with the close alignment of the measure content with the content of instruction. Given the relative comparability of the measures' technical adequacy, educators are advised to select measures that are best aligned to their instructional curriculum and most sensitive to student improvement.

Future research is needed in several areas. The majority of the measures reviewed here address general mathematics proficiency or numeracy ability, rather than course-specific content. As middle school and high school mathematics content becomes more topic-specific, this may present a challenge with respect to sufficiently sensitive measures for screening and progress monitoring; low rates of improvement are not helpful to teachers in identifying when changes in instruction are needed. In addition, there are no clear "winners" with regard to type of measure among those reviewed here. As an example, STAR Math and AIMSweb have clear advantages in reliability and criterion validity, but limited sensitivity to growth. Foegen and colleagues' Algebra Content Analysis measure had the highest rate of improvement, but more modest reliability and criterion validity. As a result, future research should examine the efficacy of using different types of measures to inform instructional decision-making. Relatively little research has examined the effects of teachers' use of the measures to guide instructional decision making on student achievement (one exception is STAR Math, which is paired with an online instructional learning system, Accelerated Math). Research of this type will produce data that can more effectively guide teachers in selecting among the available options.

Future research is also needed to extend the complexity of analyses (e.g., diagnostic accuracy, item response theory) used to examine secondary mathematics measures for screening and progress monitoring. While comparable research in the elementary grades is beginning to address these approaches, only a few of the secondary measures have similar data (which could not be addressed here due to space limitations). Finally, few options exist for high school level mathematics content. While the Foegen algebra measures offer one example of a course-specific measure, we were unable to identify any similar measures for geometry or other advanced mathematics topics. As graduation expectations in mathematics continue to increase, teachers of students with learning and behavior disabilities will have a growing need for appropriate, course-specific tools for screening and progress monitoring.

Conclusion

In recent years, much research has been done on the development of CBM measures for secondary-school students in reading, content-area learning, writing, and mathematics. Within each area, we have provided a summary of the research and suggestions for future directions. In this final section, we comment briefly on two themes that cut across the areas. The first is the need for more research on the use of the measures as progress measures. Such research is critical if the measures are to be used within a problem-solving, MTSS system at Tiers 2 and 3. The second theme is the need for more research related to teachers' use of the measures for instructional decision-making. At the elementary-school level, research has been done on teachers' use of CBM progress data for instructional decision-making (see Stecker, Fuchs, and Fuchs, 2005 for a review), but little research has been done on this topic at the secondary-school level. Such research is essential because answers to data-use questions go to the heart of CBM.

Note

1. See Hale et al. (2011) and McCane-Bowling, Strait, Guess, Wiedo, and Muncie (2014) for examples of alternative methods for creating and scoring the maze.

References

AIMSweb Pearson Education (2012). *AIMSweb National Norms Technical Documentation*. Retrieved from www.aimsweb.com/wp-content/uploads/AIMSweb-National-Norms-Technical-Documentation.pdf.

AIMSweb Pearson Education (2014). *Written Expression*. Retrieved from www.aimsweb.com/assessments/features/assessments/written-expression.

Alonzo, J., and Tindal, G. (2010/2015). *Teachers' manual for regular easyCBM: Getting the most out of the system*. Eugene, OR: University of Oregon.

Amato, J. M., and Watkins, M. W. (2011). The predictive validity of CBM writing indices for eighth-grade students. *Journal of Special Education*, *44*(4), 195–204. doi: 10.1177/0022466909333516.

Anderson, D., Alonzo, J., Tindal, G., Farley, D., Irvin, P. S., Lai, C., Saven, J. L., and Wray, K. A. (2014). *Technical manual: easyCBM* (Technical Report #1408). Eugene, OR: Behavioral Research & Teaching, University of Oregon. Retrieved from www.brtprojects.org/publications/technical-reports.

Antonacci, P. A., O'Callaghan, C. M., and Berkowitz, E. (2015). *Developing content area literacy: 40 strategies for middle and secondary classrooms* (2nd ed). Thousand Oaks, CA: Sage.

Armbruster, B. B., and Anderson, T. H. (1988). On selecting "considerate" content area textbooks. *Remedial and Special Education, 9*, 47–52. doi: 10.1177/074193258800900109.

Baker, D. L, Biancarosa, G., Park, B. J., Bousselot, T., Smith, J., Baker, S. K., . . . and Tindal, G. (2015). Validity of CBM measures of oral reading fluency and reading comprehension on high-stakes reading assessments in grades 7 and 8. *Reading and Writing: An Interdisciplinary Journal, 28*(1), 57–104. doi: 10.1007/s11145–014- 9513–4.

Barth, A. E., Stuebing, K. K., Fletcher, J. M., Cirino, P. T., Romain, M., Francis, D., and Vaughn, S. (2012). Reliability and validity of oral reading fluency median and mean scores among middle grade readers when using equated texts. *Reading Psychology, 33*, 133–161. doi: 10.1080/02702711.2012.631863.

Barth, A. E., Stuebing, K. K., Fletcher, J. M., Denton, C. A., Vaughn, S., and Francis, D. (2014). The effect of reading duration on the reliability and validity of middle school students' ORF performance. *Assessment for Effective Intervention, 40*, 53–64. doi: 10.1177/1534508414545643.

Berry Kuchle, L., Zumeta Edmonds, R., Danielson, L. C., Peterson, A., and Riley-Tillman, T. C. (2015). The next big idea: A framework for integrated academic and behavioral intensive intervention. *Learning Disabilities Research and Practice, 30*, 150–158. doi: 10.1111/ldrp.12084.

Betts, J., Pickart, M., and Heistad, D. (2009). An investigation of the psychometric evidence of CBM-R passage equivalence: Utility of readability statistics and equating for alternate forms. *Journal of School Psychology, 47*, 1–17. doi: 10.1016/j.jsp.2008.09.001.

Beyers, S. J., Lembke, E. S., and Curs, B. (2013). Social studies progress monitoring and intervention for middle school students. *Assessment for Effective Intervention, 38*, 224–235. doi: 10.1177/153450841348 9162.

Borsuk, E. R. (2010). Examination of an administrator-read vocabulary-matching measure as an indicator of science achievement. *Assessment for Effective Intervention, 35*, 168–177. doi: 10.1177/153450841037 2081.

Busch, T. W., and Espin, C. A. (2003). Using curriculum-based measurement to prevent failure and assess learning in the content areas. *Assessment for Effective Intervention, 28*, 49–58. doi: 10.1177/07372477 0302800306.

Christ, T. J., Zopluoglu, C., Monaghen, B. D., and Van Norman, E. R. (2013). Curriculum-based measurement of oral reading: Multi-study evaluation of schedule, duration, and dataset quality on progress monitoring outcomes. *Journal of School Psychology, 51*, 19–57. doi: 10.1016/j.jsp.2012.11.001.

Charney, D. (1984). The validity of using holistic scoring to evaluate writing: A critical overview. *Research in the Teaching of English, 18*(1), 65–81.

Chung, S., and Espin, C. A. (2013). CBM progress monitoring in foreign language learning for secondary school students: Technical adequacy of different measures and scoring procedures. *Assessment for Effective Intervention, 38*, 236–248. doi: 10.1177/1534508413489723.

Chung, S., Espin, C.A., and Stevenson, C. E. (2018). CBM maze-scores as indicators of reading level and growth for seventh-grade students. *Reading and Writing, 31*, 627–648. doi: 10.1007/s11145-017-9803-8

Codding, R. S., Petscher, Y., and Truckenmiller, A. (2015). CBM reading, mathematics, and written expression at the secondary level: Examining latent composite relations among indices and unique predictions with a state achievement test. *Journal of Educational Psychology, 107*, 437–450. doi: 10.1037/a0037520.

Conoyer, S. J., Lembke, E. S., Hosp, J., Espin, C. A., Hosp, M., and Poch, A. (2016). Getting more from your maze: Examining differences in distractors. *Reading & Writing Quarterly: Overcoming Learning Difficulties*. Advanced Online Publication doi: 10.1080/10573569.2016.1142913

Decker, D. M., Hixson, M. D., Shaw, A., and Johnson, G. (2014). Classification accuracy of oral reading fluency and maze in predicting performance on large-scale reading assessments. *Psychology in the Schools, 51*, 625–635. doi: 10.1002/pits.21773.

Deno, S. L. (1985). Curriculum-based measurement: The emerging alternative. *Exceptional Children, 52*, 219–232. doi: 10.1177/001440298505200303.

Deno, S. L. (2013). Problem-solving assessment. In R. Brown-Chidsey and K. J. Andren (Eds.), *Assessment for Intervention: A problem-solving approach* (pp. 10–38). New York: Guilford Press.

Deno, S. L., and Fuchs, L. S. (1987). Developing curriculum-based measurement systems for data-based special education problem solving. *Focus on Exceptional Children*, *19*(8), 1–16.

Deno, S. L., and Mirkin, P. K. (1977). *Data-based program modification: A manual*. Reston, VA: Council for Exceptional Children.

Denton, C. A., Barth, A. E., Fletcher, J. M., Wexler, J., Vaughn, S., Cirino, P. T., Romain, M., and Francis, D. J. (2011). The relations among oral and silent reading fluency and comprehension in middle school: Implications for identification and instruction of students with reading difficulties. *Scientific Studies of Reading*, *15*, 109–135. doi: 10.1080/10888431003623546.

Diercks-Gransee, B., Weissenburger, J., Johnson, C., and Christensen, P. (2009). Curriculum-based measures of writing for high school students. *Remedial and Special Education*, *30*(6), 360–371. doi: 10.1177/0741932508324398.

Edmonds, M. S., Vaughn, S., Wexler, J., Reutebuch, C., Cable, A., Tackett, K. K., and Schnakenberg, J. W. (2009). A synthesis of reading interventions and effects on reading comprehension outcomes for older struggling readers. *Review of Educational Research*, *79*(1), 262–300. doi: 10.3102/003465430832 5998.

Engelmann, S., and Silbert, J. (1983). *Expressive writing I*. Desoto, TX: SRA/McGraw-Hill.

Espin, C. A., Busch, T. W., Lembke, E. S., Hampton, D. D., Seo, K., and Zukowski, B. (2013). Curriculum-based measurement in science learning: Vocabulary-matching as an indicator of performance and progress. *Assessment for Effective Intervention*, *38*, 203–213. doi: 10.1177/1534508413489724.

Espin, C. A., Busch, T. W., Shin, J., and Kruschwitz, R. (2001). Curriculum-based measurement in the content areas: Validity of vocabulary-matching as an indicator of performance in social studies. *Learning Disabilities Research and Practice*, *16*, 142–151. doi: 10.1111/0938–8982.00015.

Espin, C. A., and Campbell, II. (2012). They're getting older ... but are they getting better? The influence of CBM on programming for secondary-school students with learning disabilities. In C. Espin, K. McMaster, S. Rose, and M. Wayman (Eds.) *A measure of success: The influence of curriculum-based measurement on education* (pp.149–164). Minneapolis, MN: University of Minnesota Press.

Espin, C. A., and Deno, S. L. (1993a). Content-specific and general reading disabilities of secondary-level students: Identification and educational relevance. *Journal of Special Education*, *27*, 321–337.

Espin, C. A., and Deno, S. L. (1993b). Performance in reading from content-area text as an indicator of achievement. *Remedial and Special Education*, *14*(6), 47–59. doi: 10.1177/074193259301400610.

Espin, C. A., Deno, S. L., Maruyama, G., and Cohen, C. (1989). *The Basic Academic Skills Samples (BASS): An instrument for the screening and identification of children at risk for failure in regular education classrooms*. Paper presented at the National Convention of the American Educational Research Association, March 1989.

Espin, C. A., De La Paz, S., Scierka, B. J., and Roelofs, L. (2005). The relationship between curriculum-based measures in written expression and quality and completeness of expository writing for middle school students. *Journal of Special Education*, *38*(4), 208–217. doi: 10.1177/00224669050380040201.

Espin, C. A., and Foegen, A. (1996). Validity of three general outcome measures for predicting secondary students' performance on content-area tasks. *Exceptional Children*, *62*, 497–514.

Espin, C. A., Scierka, B. J., Skare, S., and Halverson, N. (1999). Criterion-related validity of curriculum-based measures in writing for secondary school students. *Reading and Writing Quarterly*, *15*, 5–27. doi: 10.1080/105735699278279.

Espin, C. A., Shin, J., and Busch, T. W. (2005). Curriculum-Based Measurement in the content areas: Vocabulary matching as an indicator of progress in social studies learning. *Journal of Learning Disabilities*, *38*, 353–363. doi: 10.1177/00222194050380041301.

Espin, C. A., Shin, J., Deno, S. L., Skare, S., Robinson, S., and Benner, B. (2000). Identifying indicators of written expression proficiency for middle school students. *Journal of Special Education*, *34*(3), 140–153. doi: 10.1177/002246690003400303.

Espin, C. A., and Tindal, G. (1998). Curriculum-based measurement for secondary students. In M. R. Shinn (Ed.), *Advanced applications of curriculum-based measurement* (pp. 214–253). New York: Guilford Press.

Espin, C. A., Wallace, T., Campbell, H., Lembke, E., Long, J., and Ticha, R. (2008). Curriculum-based measurement in writing: Predicting the success of high school students on state standards tests. *Exceptional Children*, *74*(2), 174–193. doi: 10.1177/001440290807400203.

Espin, C. A., Wallace, T., Lembke, E., Campbell, H., and Long, J. (2010). Creating a progress-monitoring system in reading for middle-school students: Tracking progress toward meeting high-stakes standards. *Learning Disabilities Research and Practice, 25*(2), 60–75. doi: 10.1111/j.1540-5826.2010.00304.x.

Espin, C. A., Weissenburger, J. W., and Benson, B. J. (2004). Assessing the writing performance of students in special education. *Exceptionality, 12*(1), 55–66. doi: 10.1207/s15327035ex1201_5.

Fewster, S., and MacMillan, P. (2002). School-based evidence for the validity of curriculum-based measurement of reading and writing. *Remedial and Special Education, 23*, 149–156. doi: 10.1177/07419325020230030301.

Foegen, A. (2000). Technical adequacy of general outcome measures for middle school mathematics. *Assessment for Effective Intervention, 25*(3), 175–203. doi: 10.1177/073724770002500301.

Foegen, A. (2008). Progress monitoring in middle school mathematics: Options and issues. *Remedial and Special Education, 29*, 195–207. doi: 10.1177/0741932507309716.

Foegen, A., and Deno, S. L. (2001). Identifying growth indicators for low-achieving students in middle school mathematics. *The Journal of Special Education, 35*(1), 4–16. doi: 10.1177/002246690103500102.

Foegen, A., and Dougherty, B. (2010). Algebra screening and progress monitoring. Measurement (Goal 5) award from the Institute for Education Sciences, U.S. Department of Education. Award Number: R324A110262.

Foegen, A., and Olson, J. (2007a). *Effects of Teachers' Access to Student Data on Algebra Progress (Technical Report 15).* Ames, IA: Iowa State University, Department of Curriculum and Instruction, Project AAIMS. Retrieved from: www.education.iastate.edu/aaims/technical_reports/AAIMS%20TR15.pdf

Foegen, A., and Olson, J. (2007b). *Effects of Teachers' Engagement with Student Data on Students' Algebra Progress (Technical Report 16).* Ames, IA: Iowa State University, Department of Curriculum and Instruction, Project AAIMS. Retrieved from: www.education.iastate.edu/aaims/technical_reports/AAIMS%20TR16.pdf.

Fuchs, L. S., and Fuchs, D. (1992). Identifying a measure for monitoring student reading progress. *School Psychology Review, 21*, 45–59.

Groves, F. H. (1995). Science vocabulary load of selected secondary science textbooks. *School Sciences & Mathematics, 95*, 231–235. doi: 10.1111/j.1949-8594.1995.tb15772.x.

Hale, A. D., Henning, J. B., Hawkins, R. O., Sheeley, W., Shoemaker, L., Reynolds, J. R., and Moch, C. (2011). Reading assessment methods for middle-school students: An investigation of reading comprehension rate and maze accurate response rate. *Psychology in the Schools, 48*, 28–36. doi: 10.1002/pits.20544.

Harcourt Educational Measurement. (2002). *Stanford achievement test, tenth edition.* San Antonio, TX: Author.

Hessler, T., and Konrad, M. (2008). Using curriculum-based measurement to drive IEP's and instruction in written expression. *Teaching Exceptional Children, 41*(2), 28–37. doi: 10.1177/004005990804100204.

HMH-Riverside Publishing. (n.d.). *easyCBM.* Retrieved from: https://hmhco.com/programs/easycbm.

Huot, B. (1990). Reliability, validity, and holistic scoring: What we know and what we need to know. *College Composition and Communication, 41*(2), 201–213. doi: 10.2307/358160.

Isaacson, S. L. (1988) Assessing the writing product: qualitative and quantitative measures. *Exceptional Children, 54*(6), 528–534. doi: 10.1177/001440298805400606.

Intervention Central (n.d.). *Writing Probe Generator.* Retrieved from: www.interventioncentral.org/teacher-resources/curriculum-based-measurement-probes-writing.

Jenkins, J., and Fuchs, L. S. (2012). Curriculum-Based Measurement: The paradigm, history, and legacy. In C. Espin, K. McMaster, S. Rose, and M. Wayman (Eds.) *A measure of success: The influence of curriculum-based measurement on education* (pp. 7–26). Minneapolis, MN: University of Minnesota Press.

Jenkins, J. R., Graff, J. J., and Miglioretti, D. L. (2009). Estimating reading growth using intermittent CBM progress monitoring. *Exceptional Children, 75*, 151–163. doi: 10.1177/001440290907500202.

Jewell, J., and Malecki, C. K. (2005). The utility of CBM written language indices: An investigation of production-dependent, production-independent, and accurate-production scores. *School Psychology Review, 34*(1), 27–44.

Johnson, E. S., Semmelroth, C., Allison, J., and Fritsch, T. (2013). The technical properties of science content maze passages for middle school students. *Assessment for Effective Intervention, 38*, 214–233. doi: 10.1177/1534508413489337.

Ketterlin-Geller, L. R., McCoy, J. D., Twyman, T., and Tindal, G. (2006). Using a concept maze to assess student understanding of secondary-level content. *Assessment for Effective Intervention, 31*, 39–50. doi: 10.1177/073724770603100204.

Kilpatrick, J., Swafford, J., and Findell, B. (Eds.) (2001). *Adding it up: Helping children learn mathematics.* Washington, DC: National Academies Press, Mathematics Learning Study Committee.

Kim, Y., Petscher, Y., and Foorman, B. (2015). The unique relation of silent reading fluency to end-of-year reading comprehension: Understanding individual differences at the student, classroom, school, and district levels. *Reading and Writing: An Interdisciplinary Journal, 28,* 131–150. doi: 10.1007/s11145-013-9455-2.

Lopez, F., and Thompson, S. (2011). The relationship among measures of written expression using curriculum-based measurement and the Arizona Instrument to Measure Skills (AIMS) at the middle school level. *Reading and Writing Quarterly, 27*(1–2), 129–152. doi: 10.1080/10573561003769640.

Malecki, C. K., and Jewell, J. (2003). Developmental, gender, and practical considerations in scoring curriculum-based measurement writing probes. *Psychology in the Schools, 40,* 379–390. doi:10.1002/pits.10096.

McCane-Bowling, S. J., Strait, A. D., Guess, P. E., Wiedo, J. R., and Muncie, E. (2014). The utility of maze accurate response rate in assessing reading comprehension in upper elementary and middle school students. *Psychology in the Schools, 51,* 789–800. doi: 10.1002/pits.21789.

McMaster, K., and Espin, C. (2007). Technical features of curriculum-based measurement in writing: A literature review. *Journal of Special Education, 41*(2), 68–84. doi: 10.1177/00224669070410020301.

McMaster, K. L., and Campbell, H. (2008). New and existing curriculum-based writing measures: Technical features within and across grades. *School Psychology Review, 37*(4), 550–566.

McMaster, K. L., Wayman, M. M., and Cao, M. (2006). Monitoring the reading progress of secondary-level English learners: Technical features of oral reading and maze tasks. *Assessment for Effective Intervention, 31*(4), 17–31. doi: 10.1177/073724770603100402.

Mercer, S., Martinez, R., Faust, D., and Mitchell, R. (2012). Criterion-related validity of curriculum-based measurement in writing with narrative and expository prompts relative to passage copying speed in 10th grade students. *School Psychology Quarterly, 27*(2), 85–95. doi: 10.1037/a0029123.

Mooney, P., McCarter, K. S., Russo, R. J., and Blackwood, D. L. (2013). Examining an online content general outcome measure: Technical features of the static score. *Assessment for Effective Intervention, 38,* 249–260. doi: 10.1177/1534508413488794.

Mooney, P., McCarter, K. S., Schraven, J., and Callicoatte, S. (2013). Additional performance and progress validity findings targeting the content-focused vocabulary matching. *Exceptional Children, 80,* 85–100. doi: 10.1177/001440291308000104.

Mooney, P., McCarter, K. S., Schraven, J., and Haydel, B. (2010). The relationship between content area general outcome measurement and statewide testing in sixth-grade world history. *Assessment for Effective Intervention, 35*(3), 148–158. doi: 10.1177/1534508409346052.

National Center for Intensive Intervention. (n.d.). *Tools chart: Academic progress monitoring GOM.* Retrieved from: www.intensiveintervention.org/chart/progress-monitoring.

Nese, J. F. T., Biancarosa, G., Cummings, K., Kennedy, P., Alonzo, J., and Tindal, G. (2013). In search of average growth: Describing within-year oral reading fluency growth across Grades 1–8. *Journal of School Psychology, 51,* 625–642. doi: 10.1016/j.jsp.2013.05.006.

Parker, R. I., Tindal, G., and Hasbrouck, J. (1991a). Progress monitoring with objective measures of writing performance for students with mild disabilities. *Exceptional Children, 58,* 61–73.

Parker, R. I., Tindal, G., and Hasbrouck, J. (1991b). Countable indices of writing quality: Their suitability for screening-eligibility decisions. *Exceptionality, 2,* 1–17. doi: 10.1080/09362839109524763.

Pearson (n.d.). *AIMSweb.* www.aimsweb.com/

Pearson (2012a). *AIMSweb: Mathematics Computation Administration and Scoring Guide.* Bloomington, MN: Author. Retrieved from: www.aimsweb.com/wp-content/uploads/MCOMP_Admin_Scoring-Guide_2.01.pdf.

Pearson (2012b). *AIMSweb: Mathematics Concepts and Applications Administration and Scoring Guide.* Bloomington, MN: Author. Retrieved from: www.aimsweb.com/wp-content/uploads/M-CAP-Admin-Scoring-Guide-2.0.pdf

Pearson (2012c). *AIMSweb national norms technical documentation.* Bloomington, MN: Author. Retrieved from: www.aimsweb.com/wp-content/uploads/AIMSweb-National-Norms-Technical-Documentation.pdf.

Pearson (2012d). *AIMSweb: Technical manual.* Bloomington, MN: Author. Retrieved from: www.aimsweb.com/wp-content/uploads/aimsweb-Technical-Manual.pdf.

Perkmen, S., Foegen, A., and Olson, J. (2006a*). Reliability, criterion validity, and sensitivity to growth: Extending work on two algebra progress monitoring measures. (Technical Report 12).* Ames, IA: Iowa State

University, Department of Curriculum and Instruction, Project AAIMS. Retrieved from: www. education.iastate.edu/aaims/technical_reports/AAIMS%20TR12.pdf.

Perkmen, S., Foegen, A., and Olson, J. (2006b). *A replication study of the reliability, criterion validity and sensitivity to growth of two algebra progress monitoring measures. (Technical Report 13).* Ames, IA: Iowa State University, Department of Curriculum and Instruction, Project AAIMS. Retrieved from: www. education.iastate.edu/aaims/technical_reports/AAIMS%20TR13.pdf.

Perkmen, S., Foegen, A., and Olson, J. (2006c). *Technical characteristics of two algebra progress monitoring measures: Reliability, criterion validity, and sensitivity to growth. (Technical Report 14).* Ames, IA: Iowa State University, Department of Curriculum and Instruction, Project AAIMS. Retrieved from: www. education.iastate.edu/aaims/technical_reports/AAIMS%20TR14.pdf.

Renaissance Learning. (n.d.). *STAR Math.* www.renaissance.com/Products/Star-Assessments/Star-Math.

Renaissance Learning. (n.d.). *STAR Math* [assessment]. Wisconsin Rapids, WI: Author.

Renaissance Learning. (2015). *STAR Math™ technical manual.* Wisconsin Rapids, WI: Author.

Ritchey, K., and Coker, D. (2013). An investigation of the validity and utility of two curriculum-based measurement writing tasks. *Reading & Writing Quarterly, 29*(1), 89–119. doi: 10.1080/10573569. 2013.741957.

Seifert, K., and Espin, C. A. (2012). Improving reading of science text for secondary students with learning disabilities: Effects of text reading, vocabulary learning, and combined approaches to instruction. *Learning Disability Quarterly, 35*, 236–247. doi: 10.1177/0731948712444275.

Silberglitt, B., Burns, M. K., Madyun, N., and Lail, K. E. (2006). Relationship of reading fluency assessment data with state accountability test scores: A longitudinal comparison of grade levels. *Psychology in the Schools, 43*, 527–535. doi: 10.1002/pits.20175.

Solis, M., Miciak, J., Vaughn, S., and Fletcher, J. M. (2014). Why intensive interventions matter: Longitudinal studies of adolescents with reading disabilities and poor reading comprehension. *Learning Disability Quarterly, 37*(4), 218–229. doi: 10.1177/0731948714528806.

Stecker, P. M., Fuchs, L. S., and Fuchs, D. (2005). Using curriculum-based measurement to improve student achievement: Review of research. *Psychology in the Schools, 42*, 795–819. doi: 10.1002/pits.20113.

Stevenson, N. A. (2015). Predicting proficiency on statewide assessments: A comparison of Curriculum-Based Measures in middle school. *The Journal of Educational Research, 108*(6), 492–503. doi: 10.1080/ 0022067.2014.910161.

Tichá, R., Espin, C. A., and Wayman, M. M. (2009). Reading progress monitoring for secondary-school students: Reliability, validity, and sensitivity to growth of reading aloud and maze selection measures. *Learning Disabilities Research and Practice, 24*, 132–142. doi: 10.1111/j.1540-5826.2009.00287.x.

Tindal, G., and Parker, R. (1989). Assessment of written expression for students in compensatory and special education programs. *Journal of Special Education, 23*(2), 169–183. doi: 10.1177/00224669890230 0204.

Tolar, T. D., Barth, A. E., Fletcher, J. M., Francis, D. J., and Vaughn, S. (2014). Predicting reading outcomes with progress monitoring slopes among middle grade students. *Learning and Individual Differences, 30*, 46–57. doi: 10.1016/j.lindif.2013.11.001.

Tolar, T. D., Barth, A. E., Francis, D. J., Fletcher, J. M., Stuebing, K. K., and Vaughn, S. (2012). Psychometric properties of maze tasks in middle school students. *Assessment for Effective Intervention, 37*(3), 131–146. doi: 10.1177/1534508411413913.

University of Oregon (n.d.). *UO DIBELS data system: easyCBM Math.* https://dibels.uoregon.edu/ assessment/math.

U. S. Department of Education (2016). *The nation's report card: 2011 Reading assessments: Classroom context: Time spent on language arts.* Retrieved from: www.nationsreportcard.gov/reading_2011/context_1.aspx.

Vannest, K. J., Parker, R., and Dyer, N. (2011). Progress monitoring in grade 5 science for low achievers. *Journal of Special Education, 44*(4), 221–233. doi: 10.1177/0022466909343121.

Vaughn, S., and Fletcher, J. J. (2012). Response to intervention with secondary school students with reading difficulties. *Journal of Learning Disabilities, 45*, 244–256. doi: 10.1177/0022219412442157.

Videen, J., Deno, S. L., and Marston, D. (1982). *Correct word sequences: a valid indicator of proficiency in written expression* (Vol. IRLD-RR-84). University of Minnesota, Institute for Research on Learning Disabilities.

Viel-Ruma, K. K., Houchins, D. E., Jolivette, K., Fredrick, L. D., and Gama, R. (2010). Direct instruction in written expression: the effects on English speakers and English language learners with disabilities. *Learning Disabilities Research & Practice, 25*(2), 97–108. doi: 10.1111/j.1540-5826.2010.00307.x.

Walker, B., Shippen, M. E., Alberto, P., Houchins, D. E., and Cihak, D. F. (2005). Using the *Expressive Writing* program to improve the writing skills of high school students with learning disabilities. *Learning Disabilities Research and Practice, 20*(3), 175–183. doi: 10.1111/j.1540-5826.2005.00131.x.

Wayman, M., Wallace, T., Wiley, H. I., Tichá, R., and Espin, C. A. (2007). Literature synthesis on curriculum-based measurement in reading. *Journal of Special Education, 41*(2), 85–120. doi: 10.1177/00224669070410020401.

Weissenburger, J. W., and Espin, C. A. (2005). Curriculum-based measures of writing across grade levels. *Journal of School Psychology, 43*(2), 153–169. doi: 10.1016/j.jsp.2005.03.002.

Yager, R. E. (1983). The importance of terminology in teaching K–12 science. *Journal of Research in Science Teaching, 20*, 577–588. doi: 10.1002/tea.3660200610.

Yeo, S., Fearrington, J. Y., and Christ, T. J. (2012). Relation between CBM-R and CBM-mR slopes: An application of latent growth modeling. *Assessment for Effective Intervention, 37*(3), 147–158. doi: 10.1177/1534508411420129.

Yovanoff, P., Duesbery, L., Alonzo, J., and Tindal, G. (2005). Grade-level invariance of a theoretical causal structure predicting reading comprehension with vocabulary and oral reading fluency. *Educational Measurement: Issues and Practice, 24*, 4–12. doi: 10.1111/j.1745-3992.2005.00014.x.

17

SCHOOLWIDE PBIS IN HIGH SCHOOLS

K. B. Flannery, C. Pinkney, M. McGrath Kato,
and J. Swain-Bradway

High school educators are under mounting pressure to improve the in-school and post-school outcomes of all students. To accomplish this, high school educators must face the growing challenge to meet simultaneously the instructional and social-behavioral needs of the many at-risk and struggling students in the school system. It is not possible to deliver individualized supports or instruction to all students who fail to demonstrate proficiency. High school personnel must be efficient, effective, and cost-effective as they install systems to ensure all students are successful in meeting expected high school outcomes. To reduce the number of students in need of intensive individualized supports, some schools have developed a continuum of supports to address varying student needs. A whole-school approach requires that leadership and faculty examine and adjust the supports being offered to all students on a day to day basis. This whole school approach is implemented, monitored and adjusted so that at least 80% of the students can meet academic and social-behavioral expectations through a standard curriculum and support. Building on these standard curriculum and supports, the school can then develop a system of targeted interventions and supports that are readily available to meet the academic and social-behavioral needs of a smaller number of students, about 15%. This academic or social skills small group instruction (e.g., math, reading, anger management) provides these students with supplemental support but does not provide intensive, individually designed support. This effective but more efficient group support allows the school to free up resources to support the fewer remaining students who need intensive, individualized supports (approximately 5%).

The continuum of support described above is known as a multi-tiered system of support (MTSS) and is most often described in three levels (i.e., Tier I, Tier II, Tier III). The tiers are differentiated by the intensity of services, with each having assessment, instruction, progress monitoring, and fidelity measurement. Tier I, also known as the universal level, creates the foundation for the other tiers. It refers to schoolwide expectations, curriculum and supports provided for all students in the building as part of the day to day operations, so that most students (about 80%) can be successful in academics and social behavior (Sugai, Horner, and Gresham, 2002). With this strong foundational tier, the number of students who need additional support is reduced and therefore becomes more manageable, allowing for even more effective targeted and individual supports to be developed and delivered to students who need them.

Consider a high school of 1,200 students where 30% of the students (360) have low attendance rates. To try and develop individual or small group supports or interventions for the 360 students would be overwhelming. Instead, the school installs systems, data and practices that are delivered schoolwide and effective for 80% of the students. The Tier I supports might include re-teaching the attendance rules to students and teachers, acknowledging classrooms that achieve high rates of attendance or "most improved" over a designated period of time, etc. The key is that Tier I supports are efficiently designed to be delivered to *all* students as part of the daily operation of the school.

Tier II, also known as the targeted level, provides supplemental instruction and supports to those students who display poor response to the standard instruction provided at Tier I. At this level only some of the students (about 15%) receive instruction and support in addition to, not in place of, Tier I supports. These Tier II supports and instruction are more intense (e.g., more time, narrow focus of instruction/intervention) than Tier I but are typically provided in a small group format by a variety of staff (e.g., teacher, behavior specialist, counselor, paraprofessionals). Tier II supports are designed for a rapid response to academic and social-behavioral needs, and thus are not designed for each individual student. For example, a high school may have an algebra tutoring group or an anger management group that will accept students at any time in the term when the student has been referred for this service.

Tier III provides individualized support for students (about 5%) and is the most intensive level of supports or instruction provided. Supports at this level often require coordination and collaboration among staff as well as individuals from outside of the school. Students who receive Tier III also receive Tier I and II services. In this way, the tiers of support are layered in order to provide a continuum of supports that meets the needs of all students.

Schoolwide Positive Behavior Interventions and Supports

One such multi-tiered system of support (MTSS) being implemented in high schools is Schoolwide Positive Behavior Interventions and Supports (SWPBIS). The overarching goal of SWPBIS is to sustain a predictable, consistent, positive, and safe environment that prevents patterns of problem behaviors and promotes the academic achievement and social competence of all students (Horner et al., 2009). Schools that are implementing SWPBIS with fidelity (a) clearly define, teach, and reinforce schoolwide expectations; (b) organize practices, systems and data; (c) monitor intervention implementation to maximize student response through data-based decisions; (d) provide early access to, and differentiated levels of, support in response to student need; and (e) establish systems to sustain implementation over time (Lewis and Sugai, 1999; Sugai et al., 2010). The SWPBIS framework allows for the organization of current and new supports to prevent problems from occurring and to quickly respond to existing problems. Like any MTSS, the continuum of supports that begins with the whole school becomes more intensive and individualized based on the support a student needs (see www.pbis.org).

Four Critical Elements

SWPBIS operates as a framework that links elements critical for implementation but allows for the flexibility to adapt to the context and priorities of a school. Each of the three tiers of the MTSS continuum includes four foundational and interactive elements: outcomes, practices, systems and data (Horner, Sugai, Todd, and Lewis-Palmer, 2005). Clearly defined academic and social-behavioral *outcomes* are measured on an ongoing basis and are used to guide the schoolwide implementation process (Sugai and Horner, 2008). For high schools, the overarching outcomes might be improved graduation rates, increased scores on state benchmark tests, reduction in suspension/expulsions, etc. *Empirically supported practices* are implemented by staff and faculty to influence the behaviors of the students. These practices, whenever possible, are evidence-based practices that have clear documentation of addressing the need or problem in the indicated situation or context. *Systems* are the structures required to facilitate and support implementation of the ongoing use of practices and active data-based decision making. These include organizational and team structures, policies and guiding principles, operating routines, resources (funding and personnel), training, and administrative leadership. The focus on systems assists schools that implement SWPBIS to sustain their practices despite changing staff or administration, influx of new initiatives, and other changes.

The final element is the use of *data* to make decisions regarding effectiveness, identifying needs, and monitoring fidelity of implementation and progress toward identified outcomes. Schools establish teams of faculty and staff that collect and use both outcome and fidelity data for decision making. Though positive outcome data is the goal of any intervention, the effectiveness of the intervention is dependent on the fidelity of implementation. Fidelity data answer the question, "Did we do it?", while outcome data answers the question, "Is it working?". Program fidelity can be organized into two major categories, implementation fidelity and treatment integrity (Newcomer, Freeman, and Barrett, 2013). Implementation fidelity concerns the extent to which the systems are implemented. SWPBIS implementation fidelity is measured by tools such as the Schoolwide Evaluation Tool (SET: Horner et al., 2004) Benchmarks of Quality, (BOQ: Kincaid, Childs, and George, 2005) or the Tiered Fidelity Instrument (TFI: Algozzine et al., 2014), which can be helpful both in periodic progress monitoring and in annual evaluation of implementation at each of the tiers. These are broad summative tools that look at the data, systems and practices that are necessary to include when implementing SWPBIS supports. The TFI assesses SWPBIS implementation across the three tiers, however it may be used to evaluate the implementation of only the specific tiers addressed in a school's action plan (Algozzine et al., 2014). The TFI should be used every three to four months to inform progress toward sufficient implementation (i.e., scoring a minimum of 70–80% of points available within each tier) and to update school action plans. Treatment integrity, the extent to which interventions and supports are delivered as prescribed, should also be reviewed prior to using student outcome data for the purpose of decision making. Once fidelity is ensured, the outcome data can be examined to make decisions about next steps, or priorities in implementation. The Tier I Leadership Team examines the outcome data in an aggregate format across all students, whereas Tier II and III teams examine data for the students receiving those specific, additional supports to determine if interventions are proving effective. This use of fidelity and outcome data continues in an ongoing cycle throughout the implementation of data monitoring, problem solving, and planning to allow schools to continuously improve practices and systems in order to achieve the expected outcomes (Horner et al., 2005). It is recommended that each tier of support is evaluated annually. The results are used to make adjustments to practices or systems and outcomes are shared with school staff, district leadership, and other relevant stakeholders.

Teams

Each of the tiers implements a *team structure* that works with the staff, students and administrators to implement SWPBIS. These teams are all focused on: (a) identifying and monitoring outcomes; (b) developing systems or evidence-based practices; (c) making data-based decisions; and (d) communicating with relevant stakeholders. To have effective teams in SWPBIS there needs to be attention to the membership of the team and the efficiency of the meeting structure and organization. Though team membership and size vary across the tiers, each team includes at minimum an administrator, representatives of those impacted by decision-making (e.g., students, teachers, classified staff, security staff), an individual knowledgeable about school resources and procedures, and an individual knowledgeable about behavioral principles. Once a representative team has been identified, it is equally important for there to be clear operating procedures so that the team can function effectively and efficiently. It is recommended that the leadership team for each tier: (a) meets at least monthly, (b) has a regular meeting format/agenda, (c) takes meeting minutes, (d) has defined meeting roles, and (e) has a current action plan (Algozzine et al., 2014).

Implementation of Schoolwide Positive Behavior Support in High School

SWPBIS was developed initially in elementary and middle schools (Sugai and Horner, 2009), and currently is being implemented in over 22,000 schools across the United States, with a growing number of schools in 14 other countries (Horner, 2016). SWPBIS has been associated with improvements in office discipline referrals, attendance, academics, school climate, and teacher stress/efficacy, (e.g., Algozzine, Wang, and Violette, 2011; Bradshaw, Koth, Thornton, and Leaf, 2009; Horner et al., 2009; Ross and Horner, 2009). The implementation of SWPBIS at the high school level has been shown to impact attendance, office discipline referrals, and dropout (Bohanon et al., 2006; Flannery, Fenning, Kato, and McIntosh, 2014; Flannery, Frank, Doren, Kato, and Fenning, 2013; Freeman et al., 2015a; Freeman et al., 2015b; Morrissey, Bohanon, and Fenning, 2010; Muscott, Mann, and LeBrun, 2008). As of July 2016, there were 2,906 high schools actively engaged in implementing SWPBIS, which accounts for nearly 13% of all implementing schools (Horner, 2016).

Critical to implementation of any initiative is the attention to (a) the fidelity of the features and (b) the context for implementation (Fixsen, Naoom, Blase, Friedman, and Wallace, 2005). The features of the SWPBIS framework remain the same at the high school level, but the high school context has strong implications for how that implementation occurs. Three interconnected contextual influences that seem to be particularly important to consider when implementing SWPBIS in high schools are the size, organizational culture, and the developmental level of the students (Flannery et al., 2013; Flannery and Kato, 2016). On average, high schools are *physically larger, have more staff and students* than any other school levels. This results in a different infrastructure (e.g., departments, multiple administrators) but also may result in the availability of expanded course offerings or resources for students (e.g., tutors, student clubs). Implementation of SWPBIS requires strategic communication and professional development for these large staff and student populations.

Organizational or school culture is the shared meanings and values of the members of the organization about how the organization should function and why it exists. The values held by high school staff will need to be considered when implementing SWPBIS. For example, at the high school level there is a shift in balance of the importance of academic outcomes over social-emotional outcomes. High school teachers are trained in their content and the pedagogy for that content, with less emphasis on the social behavior of students, often not seeing the development of social behaviors as a component of a teacher's job. Another difference is that high school staff also are more likely to accept a heavily exclusionary or zero tolerance approach to addressing student problem behavior as the mainstay of the discipline system.

The third contextual variable in the high school is student-related – the *developmental level of the students*. These adolescents are at a time in their development when they want increased autonomy from adults and have greater dependence on peers; don't understand the consequences of their actions; believe they have figured it all out and that they should be part of the decision-making process (Morrison, Robertson, Laurie, and Kelly, 2002; Steinberg, 2012). Together the three contextual variables of size, organizational culture, and the developmental level of the students have a strong impact on the three systems that are foundational to the implementation of SWPBIS: leadership system, communication system, data system. Staff working to implement any initiative, including SWPBIS, must keep these three contextual influences in the forefront and plan for their impact.

Implementation Across the Tiers of Support

The features of each of the three tiers will be described below along with examples from implementing high schools. Where appropriate, the impact of the high school contextual variables will be highlighted.

Implementation of Tier I

Tier I provides highly effective core strategies designed to meet the needs of all of the students in the school and focuses on preventing problems before they occur. The practices, systems and data used at this tier are put in place to sustain a predictable, consistent, positive and safe environment that prevents patterns of problem behaviors and promotes the academic achievement and social competence of all students.

Establishing a Schoolwide Leadership Team

As mentioned earlier, there are two important features to the development of a Schoolwide Leadership Team: membership and ensuring team efficiency and effectiveness. When developing the Schoolwide Leadership Team in the high school setting, there are contextual factors to consider both in the composition of the team itself, and in the team's operating procedures. The large, diverse and content-oriented staffing in high school requires additional considerations when building a representative team. Organizationally, the staff is usually grouped into departments by content area, and most work gets communicated and rolled out through these content areas. It is common to try to build teams by including representation across every division (i.e., content areas) and adding representation from those who provide student support roles (e.g., security, special education, counseling). This can often result in more than the recommended six to eight team members, making it hard to find time to meet and accomplish the work. A couple of steps that can be taken to improve the representation on the team. First, focus on selection of members who represent three broad areas: curricular areas (at least two core content areas and one elective area), student support systems (e.g., campus security, counselors, career staff) and administration. Second, after the final selection, and each year thereafter, the team facilitator, coach and/or administrator should examine and adjust the team membership to be sure there are always individuals amongst the membership with behavioral expertise, knowledge about the school context, and the skills to examine academic and social-behavioral data on the team. Third, members of the Leadership Team need to consider it a part of their role to outreach to others in the building to ensure all faculty and staff have a "voice" and that ongoing communication is taking place. Several strategies are used by high schools to ensure that the broader faculty and staff voice is included. One strategy is to engage faculty and staff through a committee structure that works directly with the Leadership Team, with each focused on a key component (e.g., communication, acknowledgements, student involvement). Other schools have developed a standing list of faculty willing to assist, and then as needed form a *hoc* committees on specific topics. Both of these committee structures function best when they include a member from the Schoolwide Leadership Team to ensure adequate communication and connection to the schoolwide action plan.

Administrative representation is one of the most important practices in SWPBIS leadership. As with SWPBIS Leadership Teams in elementary and middle schools, it is critical to ensure the participation of the principal or vice principal as an active member. While only one of many administrators might officially be on the team in the high school, research has shown that principal support is a critical variable for implementing and sustaining evidence-based practices (Adelman and Taylor, 2011; Grissom, Loeb, and Urban Institute, 2009; McIntosh et al., 2014). Swain-Bradway, Pinkney, and Flannery (2015) identified strategies for principal leadership in high school such as: a) making weekly morning announcements, b) making announcements at staff meetings, c) sharing positive data reports, and d) distributing acknowledgements to staff. As important is that all administrators are aware of the SWPBIS efforts and support these in their work. High schools have vice principals, deans of students, department heads, etc., all of whom play a leadership role in the school. SWPBIS implementation can cut across many areas under the supervision of these different building leaders, including curriculum, discipline, school structure and finance. As a result, high schools must develop strategies to keep all individuals involved in the leadership of the school aware of the efforts and involved in the decision making related to implementation.

Finally, it is also important to consider the voice of students in the SWPBIS leadership system at the high school level. The developmental stage of high school students will result in them wanting active participation in the planning and implementation of practices. Schools who have implemented successfully have developed an approach that allows students to be active in decision-making and that supports student to student influence in implementation of practices. Leadership Teams in high schools have involved students in a variety of ways (Bohanon et al., 2012; Flannery et al., 2009; Swain-Bradway et al., 2015). Although Leadership Teams occasionally have one or more students who serve as regular members of the Team, many implementers indicate that this configuration is problematic. It is difficult to select a small number of students who are representative of the entire student body and difficult for students to be available for meetings that occur during the school day or even after school. Some schools have found more success in establishing a standing committee of students who work with the Leadership Team in developing and delivering some of the SWPBIS components (e.g., development of lessons or videos, delivery of lessons related to expectations, orientations for new students, delivery of acknowledgement to students and staff). Other schools have recruited or appointed students representative of the school population to serve on short term *ad hoc* committees focused on a specific issue or initiative (e.g., "Use another word" to reduce harassment), or focused on a specific task (e.g., developing and teaching lessons for expectations, freshmen orientation, creating a video around a specific expectation). Often these are student-initiated efforts, which makes them even more powerful. Last, some schools have worked within their existing student club infrastructure by selecting a specific club to support the development and implementation of a specific related initiative (e.g., Media club to develop a SWPBIS video) or have asked clubs to send a representative to a schoolwide *ad hoc* team. No matter how a high school organizes the inclusion of students, the selection in membership should ensure representation across the many different groups of students within the building.

Once team membership has been established, it is critical to ensure ongoing staff, administrative, and student involvement in development and implementation, as well as ongoing opportunities for professional development. The professional development will include the rationale and process for each component of their SWPBIS effort, as well as skill-building around specific interventions and strategies that can be used in the classrooms and the common areas. This schoolwide professional development is foundational for all teachers and critical for development of the Tier II and III supports.

To ensure initial staff buy–in, ongoing staff involvement, and professional development, an ongoing communication plan needs to be developed by the Team. To initially educate and build consensus among staff and students, teams need to develop processes to: (a) identify and gain agreement on the presence of a problem, (b) provide orientation to basic PBIS principles and practices, and (c) gain agreement that PBIS is a good solution to the problem. High school staff often spend more time conversing and sharing with their departmental peers than with the school staff as a whole, so it can be more effective and less disruptive to utilize the departmental structure to have these conversations. Many high schools have found that obtaining agreement on the status of schoolwide academic and social needs of all students is best accomplished through the objective sharing of schoolwide data, in graphic format by grade level or other subgroups. This illustrates the performance of all students in the school, and facilitates initial acknowledgement and agreement across staff on problem areas in the building. High schools can use both informal processes such as discussions within departmental meetings and more formal processes such as the Gallery Walk (Kennedy, Mimmack, and Flannery, 2012). The initial work of educating and gaining consensus often takes multiple conversations with the educational staff and students. Some high schools take several months to prepare and complete this process. The school should develop a plan for communication that can get information out quickly, in a format useful to the stakeholder group and with content relevant to their role in the implementation of SWPBIS.

Selecting Appropriate Interventions and Supports

Tier I has two overarching standard interventions and supports: Development and teaching of expectations, and the implementation of a consequence system – discipline and acknowledgements.

Developing and Teaching Expectations. As with any grade level, the implementation of SWPBIS at the high school level is grounded in a set of three to five positively stated schoolwide expectations. Much of the work in Tier I uses these schoolwide expectations as a foundation, so it is very important to be thoughtful and context-specific in identifying them. High schools have been more successful when they ensure these expectations are applicable in post-high school settings such as college or career, and when they go through a vetting process with students as well as staff while they are developing the set of expectations. Considering language that is applicable to both adults and students in the building will help ensure that students and staff engage and see value in the expectations. In this way, the expectations serve to impact the entire climate of the school – both for young adult students and all staff. For this reason, during development, be sure to plan and follow a vetting process to get student and staff input into the expectations. This can be done through conducting a simple survey or by targeting existing groups such as clubs or classes (students) and departmental or staff meetings (staff) in order to get feedback and ideas. Taking the time to go through such a vetting process before expectations are finalized will improve the likelihood that students and staff buy in to SWPBIS implementation.

An important part of establishing clear expectations is posting them in multiple locations around the school. In high schools, posting includes signage in classrooms and common areas (e.g., hallways, cafeterias, stairways), placement in school codes of conduct, student and staff handbooks, and on school websites, as with elementary and middle schools. High schools may also include them in student parking lots, sports fields, and community settings where students may go during off-campus lunch. This public posting provides a visual reminder of the school's commitment to these expectations, serves as an ongoing mechanism for re-teaching the expectations, and provides an opportunity to expand the level of consistency across multiple stakeholder groups.

The teaching culture in high schools is generally one that does not include a focus on social behavior. In fact, many teachers and staff in high schools believe that students should know how to behave by the time they get to high school and therefore time should not be spent on teaching students social-behavioral expectations, so it's important to provide teachers with the rationale for spending class time teaching the schoolwide expectations. It is also important to keep in mind that teaching these expectations often looks different in high schools than in the younger grades, largely because of the developmental level of the students. As mentioned earlier, high school students are young adults and want to play a role in systems that impact them. Therefore, lesson plans need to be developed in a way that is age-appropriate. Consider making time within the lesson plan for student contribution and meaningful discussion around the schoolwide expectations, including scenarios of when they are relevant and how they apply to a variety of settings and situations. It can be effective to have upperclassmen deliver the lessons to the younger classmen. This strategy provides a leadership opportunity for a set of older students and delivers the lesson in a way that is more meaningful to ninth and tenth-graders (by older peers instead of adults).

Beyond overall schoolwide expectations, high schools are also encouraged to implement agreements around classroom management and instructional strategies, such as academic expectations, grading and homework policies, and strategies that build positive student-teacher relationships. In doing so, consideration of the developmental level of students is critical. Schools will likely have a foundational set of agreements that exist schoolwide and help create a consistent, predictable, positive environment (definition of a tardy, cell phone policy, hat policy, grades updated by the 1st and 15th of each month, etc.). These agreements would need to be scaffolded to provide more structure and support to incoming ninth-graders, with the scaffolds faded as students move through high school and build behavioral and academic independence.

Along with developing a consistent set of agreements around student behavior and teacher practices, it is also imperative for high schools to review and adjust school discipline policies and procedures to be in alignment with a multi-tiered approach. Many high schools have discipline policies outlined in student and staff handbooks, but the shift when implementing a positive, tiered framework such as SWPBIS is to revise such policies to describe and emphasize proactive, instructive, and/or restorative approaches, and to implement them consistently. Doing so calls for a shift in thinking, away from more punitive disciplinary practices and zero tolerance policies, and requires that any administrator or staff member who deals with discipline in the building (deans of students, resource officers, security staff) is trained in both the rationale and specific strategies around implementing the discipline policies.

Implementing a Consequence System: Acknowledgement and Discipline. Effectively changing social or academic behavior requires a combination of both corrective feedback and acknowledgement (Hattie and Timperley, 2007; Kluger and DeNisi, 1996). Most high school discipline systems do not take this into account. First, the discipline systems that are in place tend to be punitive and are not designed as a mechanism to correct, reteach and improve problematic behavior. Instead discipline in the high school is often in the form of punishment that occurs in the absence of any active correction or teaching. Similarly, while some forms of acknowledgement systems do exist in high schools, they are typically tied to high academic standards or sports success (e.g., 100% attendance, honor roll, celebrations for sports championships). Schools need to expand these acknowledgement systems to support development of all schoolwide expectations. SWPBIS encourages schools to develop a single interconnected system – corrective feedback and acknowledgement – that is utilized to both correct and re-teach students to meet social and academic expectations, and then acknowledge them for doing so.

A key consideration in the implementation of an acknowledgement system in high schools is the language that is used. Due to the developmental age of students and the philosophical approach of many high school teachers and staff, the idea of 'rewarding' students for expected behavior is offensive. If the language is shifted to acknowledgement or recognition for a job well done, however, it becomes much more acceptable. It is critical for leadership teams to attend to such connotations when vetting their ideas with staff and students around the development of a schoolwide acknowledgement system. It can be helpful to point to real life examples of adult-oriented recognition systems (e.g., frequent flyer programs, good driver insurance discounts, customer loyalty programs) to help build support.

Schoolwide acknowledgement systems can and should have numerous ways to provide recognition. Including both group and individual formats is most effective, so that all students are a recipient of an acknowledgement in some form on a regular basis. Examples of group acknowledgements include class or grade level competitions, or group celebrations that are tied to a specific performance goal. Individual acknowledgements most commonly used are ticket systems. These can be very successful in high schools, especially if the developmental age of the students is taken into account by providing age-appropriate, tangible, and privilege recognition. Age-appropriate examples of tangible acknowledgments include coffee cards, tickets to a school event (dance, prom, play), or a free yearbook. Privilege-based acknowledgements can include things such as a fast pass at lunch, a special parking place, a great seat for the student and one guest at a school event (play, game, or concert). It is important for Teams to consider how the delivery of acknowledgement systems may vary across high school as well, as students develop and mature from ninth to twelfth grade. Systems will work best when they offer a range of options to acknowledge students.

One of the key components of any discipline system is the definitions of the problem behavior. The establishment of common definitions can often be complicated in high schools by the size and teaching culture of the staff who are expected to implement them. Simply put, it can be more difficult to get a larger group of staff to agree and be consistent than if it were a smaller group. For example, while a staff of 30 at the elementary grade level can have a range of opinions, a staff of 100 is potentially more difficult to bring to consensus. Beyond numbers, the teaching culture in high school can be highly autonomous. When clarifying and working toward a consistent use of problem behavior definitions, high schools need to use a strong communication system that may utilize the departmental structure that already exists.

Evaluation and Progress Monitoring

The types of evaluation used at the universal level are the same as at all tiers: fidelity and outcome. High schools are used to tracking outcomes; they operate on credit accrual, and graduation rates and standardized test results are at the forefront of most conversations. In high schools, the strong focus on academic achievement requires that school teams expand the focus of their data that are used to monitor outcomes and in ongoing decision-making. One way to consider data best suited for decision-making at the high school is to ensure that Leadership

Teams are examining the "ABCs" of student outcomes– Attendance, Behavior, and Course Performance. Because attendance can be such a pervasive issue in high schools, Leadership Teams can look at overall attendance rates, but it is beneficial to focus on more specific data points related to attendance (i.e., excused and unexcused absences, tardies, skips). Teams can focus their initial behavior data review on seven areas: number of office discipline referrals (ODRs) per day per month, number of ODRs per day of week, number of ODRs by student, number of ODRs by location, number of ODRs by grade, number of ODRs by type of problem behavior, and number of ODRs by time of day. It has been demonstrated that most behaviors occur in the classroom, and the most common types of behavior for this age group are tardy, skip, and defiance and disrespect (Spaulding et al., 2010). Course Performance data may include more distal measures (e.g., GPA, courses passed, graduation, state test performance) but should also consider more proximal measures (homework completion, proficiency exams, testing and study skills, time and self-management skills). Staff consistency is key to making these data reliable, so ongoing work, such as establishing and continuing to revisit teacher agreements (as mentioned earlier), is needed to ensure and maintain as much consistency as possible. Attendance data can be impacted if all staff define a tardy differently, for example. Or if grading policies vary widely, then special consideration needs to be made in selecting which course performance variables are the most useful to the Leadership Team. It is important to look across all three categories of data, at the relationship between them (e.g., attendance or skip rates for students with poor course performance) and to disaggregate by subgroups (e.g., freshmen, students' racial/ethnicity, students identified as ELL, students with disabilities) in order to ensure that outcomes are being evenly achieved by all students.

Schoolwide Leadership Teams can identify their available data, review it to establish benchmarks, and determine when to follow up on this data throughout the year. Having the identified data at the right time (i.e., prior to each Leadership Team meeting) can be a challenge in high schools (Swain-Bradway et al., 2015). High school data collection and reporting systems are not typically designed for staff to use in decision-making (Kennedy et al., 2009). Instead, administrators collect data with the purpose to report to the state, school board and public, and data are usually reported at an aggregate level. High school teams new to the process struggle in obtaining the right data at the right time for two primary reasons. First, these data are often collected and maintained by different people in different locations (e.g., district, building). In the implementation of SWPBIS in high schools, data are often entered and maintained in different computer applications and by different personnel. For example, a Leadership Team may need to collect attendance data from the attendance secretary, behavior data from the vice principal in charge of discipline, and course performance data from another staff member with expertise in accessing the school's academic data system. Second, larger enrollment at the high school level can make the simple task of working with data enormously time consuming and error prone. The large amount of academic and social behavior data that are generated on a daily basis often do not have efficient systems or strategies to integrate this information for decision-making (Bohanon, Fenning, Borgmeier, Flannery, and Malloy, 2009). To successfully use data in decision making, school teams must identify what data they need and how to get it in a timely manner (Swain-Bradway et al., 2015).

Annual evaluation of any effort by those implementing it is essential to ongoing improvement and to ensuring the effort is having the desired effects, and is worth the resources being allocated to it. The same is true for implementation of universal SWPBIS supports in high schools. At least once a year, the Leadership Team, including at least one administrator, needs to collect annual fidelity and outcome data for review, to ensure that implementation is on track and is having the desired outcomes. Annual action planning for Tier I supports can then take place to make adjustments where needed, try new strategies, celebrate successes. The fidelity data used may include evaluation tools such as the Schoolwide Evaluation Tool (SET) or the Tiered Fidelity Instrument (TFI), discussed earlier. Summative outcome data including attendance, behavior, and course performance (ABCs; discussed above), both schoolwide and by key subgroups (grade level, gender, IEP status, ethnicity groups) are valuable indicators of whether implementation is making progress toward the desired effects. It is critical for such annual evaluation to dovetail with other initiatives in the building. For example, if a building has identified increased graduation rates as a central goal, then SWPBIS implementation should be evaluated at least annually for its impact in relation to that goal. The same would be true for a school with an identified goal of improving literacy rates or overall school climate.

Conducting at least annual evaluation of Tier I implementation can also set the stage for identifying when the school is ready to begin planning for implementation of supports at Tiers II and III. While it is believed that a school must have Tier I firmly in place before implementing Tier II, as measured by a certain score on one of the fidelity measures, it is documented that it can take multiple years to implement Tier I with fidelity in high schools (Flannery et al., 2014). For this reason, while it is critical to get certain key elements of Tier I in place, many high schools see a need to address the upper tiers well before their Tier I is implemented with full fidelity.

Implementation of Tier II

Within an MTSS such as SWPBIS, it is anticipated that approximately 15% of students will need supplemental Tier II interventions and supports to consistently meet schoolwide expectations. These students often have instructional or other support needs that put them at risk for social or academic failure. To prevent or remediate this failure, schools implement a menu of targeted interventions and supports. These Tier II practices are aligned to meet the needs of the students and thus may vary from one high school to the next. Despite this variability, all Tier II interventions and supports should be: (a) implemented with similar procedures across all students, (b) continuously available with rapid access, (c) consistently applied across all settings and staff, and (d) progress monitored using valid and reliable data (Newcomer et al., 2013). One of the initial steps schools should take in implementing Tier II interventions and supports is the establishment of a strong multi-disciplinary team.

Establishing a Tier II Team

The Tier II leadership team drives the implementation of targeted interventions and supports. In addition to the standard team roles, the Tier II team responsibilities include: (a) identifying at-risk students; (b) matching those students to appropriate interventions and supports; and (c) evaluating the effectiveness of selected interventions and supports. Given this important role of managing the supplemental supports provided to at-risk students, great care should be taken in the selection of team members. Several of the recommendations for establishing the Tier II Team overlap those for selecting the Schoolwide Leadership Team (e.g., size, a systems coordinator, an administrator), however a few key considerations set this process apart.

The first consideration is that of student privacy; members of the Tier II Team are privy to sensitive student data, including grades, attendance, and discipline records. While the School-wide Leadership Team uses similar student outcomes as part of their decision-making process, these data are aggregated and typically lack identifying information for individual students.

The outcome data used by the Tier II Team necessarily include student names as well as other sensitive information such as medical or educational diagnoses. To comply with federal, state, and local statutes protecting student privacy (e.g., FERPA), it is recommended that students and family members *not* be included as standing members of the Tier II Team. Steps should be taken however, to honor the "voices" of these parties in the decision-making process by regularly soliciting their thoughts and opinions throughout implementation.

A second consideration in establishing a Tier II Team is effective communication with the Tier I and Tier III Teams. Students maintain access to Tier I interventions and supports even while receiving Tier II supports. To facilitate the sharing of data and other important information regarding at-risk students across tiers, it is important to have someone knowledgeable of those students at each meeting. For this reason, it is recommended that there be at least one representative of the Tier II Team at each of the Tier I and Tier III Team meetings. This can be accomplished via common membership across tiers (e.g., a member of the Tier II Team is also a member of the Tier I or Tier III Team) or via a rotating schedule of attendance in which a different team member attends an additional team meeting each month.

A third consideration is to include individuals with knowledge and expertise in the interventions and supports provided to at-risk students. It is recommended that team membership include the coordinators of these individual interventions or supports. Coordinators should not only have the requisite expertise, but also access to the student outcome and implementation fidelity data used to evaluate program effectiveness. The size and composition of the student body in high schools may present challenges to including all individual intervention and support coordinators on the Tier II Team. A large urban or suburban high school, for example, might have upwards of 2,000 students. Schools of this size may implement 10 or more different targeted interventions and supports, potentially resulting in a Tier II Team that is too large to effectively work together. To address this challenge, it is again recommended that high school teams employ a subcommittee structure to improve efficiency. In situations in which an intervention or support is managed by non-school personnel, such as in the case of some mentoring or juvenile justice programs, it is important to appoint a school liaison to aid in the communication process. If non-school personnel are included on the Tier II Team, it is also necessary to establish clear guidelines for the dissemination and use of identifiable student data.

A fourth and final consideration is to include at least one team member with extensive knowledge of the school schedule as well as graduation and post-secondary educational requirements. High school faculty, administrators, and the students themselves, are driven by the fact that students must meet and accrue credits in certain categories to obtain a diploma. This credit-accruing nature of high schools greatly impacts the administration of Tier II interventions and supports. At-risk students who may need additional supports must still continue to earn credits (and in some cases recover credit) toward existing requirements while participating in supplemental programs. It is essential that the Tier II Team has the requisite knowledge to schedule supports in times and locations that do not hinder student progress toward graduation. In response, some schools have worked to embed the Tier II supports into credit-bearing classes. Once membership has been decided, it is important that defined operating procedures are followed as part of the teaming process (e.g., meeting minutes, regular meetings, roles).

The Tier II Team will need to use multiple sources of data in conjunction with clear decision rules to identify and monitor at-risk students. The number of office discipline referrals (ODRs) a student has received is often a primary source of data for the purpose of decision making. Sugai, Sprague, Horner, and Walker (2000) recommend a cutoff of two to five ODRs for identifying at-risk students. McIntosh, Campbell, Carter, and Zumbo (2009) however, found that this cutoff was more accurate in identifying students with externalizing (e.g., defiance, bullying) rather than internalizing (e.g., anxiety, depression) behaviors. At the high school level it is important to not rely only on ODRs for screening and referral. Teams consider attendance and course performance as well. To better identify students with internalizing behaviors in need of targeted interventions and supports, it is recommended that schools administer a norm-referenced screening tool to all students. Screening tools such as the Social Skills Improvement System Rating Scales (Gresham and Elliott, 2008) may help the Tier II Team identify at-risk students whose support needs would not be revealed through review of ODR or other typically collected schoolwide data. The Tier II Team may use published cutoffs to establish student risk status.

In addition to ODR and screening data, the Tier II Team also uses stakeholder nominations to identify at-risk students. A written request for assistance form and process should be available to all staff, families, and students to initiate the identification process in a timely manner. In high schools, great emphasis should be placed on student self-nomination as it is developmentally appropriate for adolescents to assume more responsibility for their educational experiences. Self-nomination is of particular importance in schools not employing a system of universal screening, as it is one of only a few alternative, efficient methods of identifying at-risk students with internalizing behaviors.

Selecting Appropriate Interventions and Supports

During initial implementation of Tier II, high school personnnel often struggle to identify and implement a range of effective, targeted interventions and supports. These struggles are often attributed to a lack of available resources, and while this may be true, a school's size and organizational structure often contribute to this issue. The relatively large number of staff and departmental structure of many high schools results in a type of isolation in which many staff members, members of the Tier II Team included, are unaware of the interventions and supports already available in the school. When planning Tier II implementation, this lack of knowledge may make the selection of appropriate interventions and supports seem too daunting, as team members struggle to find the time to create needed programs. High schools, unlike the lower grades, often have a number of supports in place. Before developing new supports, it is recommended that the Tier II Team conduct an audit of existing classes, clubs, programs and other targeted supports available to students. The audit process involves soliciting school administrators (facilitated by the presence of a school administrator on the team), department heads/leads, and school or district-level community liaisons to generate a list of current interventions and supports. As part of this list, the Tier II Team should include the following information for each intervention/support: (a) program name, (b) contact person(s) and contact information, (c) program goals/outcomes, (d) how goals/outcomes are measured, and (e) program logistics (e.g., number of students served in a single group, target population, time of day, location). Engaging in such an auditing process would also allow teams to 'work smarter' by potentially combining or eliminating redundant interventions and supports, modifying existing supports to meet the students' needs, and reducing the need to develop new supports.

Available Tier II interventions and supports may look different across schools, however they should all share the following core features: (a) be delivered in small group settings (e.g., 10–15 students), (b) increase structure and predictability for students, (c) provide additional opportunities for students to practice and receive feedback on critical academic and social skills, and (d) provide increased positive student-adult interactions (Anderson et al., 2012; Newcomer et al., 2013).

Effective and efficient teaming processes should not only identify at-risk students but also allow interventions and supports to be matched to students' needs. Determining students' needs and monitoring progress may require the Tier II Team to gather information beyond the typical schoolwide data. Anecdotal records, student interviews, and simple functional behavioral assessments may assist the team in the selection of appropriate interventions and supports. Take for example a tenth-grade student who has received three ODRs from his Algebra I teacher for leaving the classroom without permission. If the Tier II Team were to simply look at frequency and type of infractions, they may conclude that the student needs anger management or social skills support. However, upon reviewing the student's academic record and speaking with some of the student's teachers, the team might discover that the student in fact needs additional academic support in math and engaged in escape maintained behavior (i.e., leaving the class without permission) when asked to solve an equation in front of the class. Such a scenario is not uncommon in high schools and underscores the importance of using multiple sources of data to attempt to identify the function of problem behavior and select appropriate interventions and supports. It also highlights the often-observed relationship between problem behavior and academic achievement (McIntosh, Horner, Chard, Boland, and Good, 2006).

Tier II Teams should engage in a formal process to select Tier II interventions that are matched to student need (e.g., function of problem behavior, skill deficits), while taking measures to improve contextual fit. Common Tier II interventions and supports with empirical evidence of their effectiveness include: (a) social skills instruction (Gresham, Sugai, and Horner, 2001), (b) organizational skills training (Anderson, Munk, Young, Conley, and Caldarella, 2008), (c) Check in-Check out (Maggin, Zurheide, Pickett, and Baillie, 2015), (d) mentoring (Bernstein, Rappaport, Olsho, Hunt, and Levin, 2009), and (e) academic support (Burns, Appleton, and Stehouwer, 2005). Though each of these supports has been effective in research settings, it is likely that some non-critical features would need to be augmented to match the values and available resources of a given high school. As an example, high school students enrolled in Check in-Check out may be assigned to common first period classes to reduce the number of teachers needed for morning check in, thereby simplifying the intervention.

As mentioned previously, Tier II interventions and supports build upon rather than supplant those provided to at-risk students in Tier I. Great care should be taken to ensure that at-risk students maintain access to the schoolwide acknowledgement system and other universal interventions and supports. Tier II intervention coordinators should also take steps to increase the likelihood that content or skills learned during the receipt of Tier II supports be generalizable to schoolwide settings. To assist this effort, a written process is followed to ensure that all relevant stakeholders are trained and coached in the aspects of intervention delivery. Content area teachers and other staff members not directly involved in the delivery of Tier II interventions and supports should be trained in how to initiate the request for assistance process, how to monitor student progress and use progress reports to inform instruction, as well as deliver effective feedback students. This system of professional development and communication is essential to getting at-risk students needed interventions and supports in a timely manner and maintaining those supports across school settings.

Evaluation and Progress Monitoring

After at-risk students have been identified and appropriate interventions and supports have been selected, the Tier II Team is tasked with evaluating Tier II systems and practices. This evaluation occurs across multiple levels, starting with student participation. The Tier II team should compare the observed or actual proportion of students receiving targeted interventions and supports to the suggested figure of 15%. When the proportion of students is significantly lower than this expected value (e.g., 5%), the Tier II Team should determine if this is the result of a lack of capacity to support additional students or a lack of student need. In most situations, only the former is cause for concern, especially in schools with a relatively high proportion (e.g., 10% or more) of students participating in individualized, Tier III supports. In such cases an action plan should be developed to strengthen the supports offered in Tiers I and II to reduce the number of students in need of Tier III supports. In schools in which the proportion of students receiving Tier II supports is much higher than 15%, the Tier II Team should work in concert with the Schoolwide Leadership Team to strengthen the existing Tier I interventions and supports to better meet the needs of all students. Student participation data should also be disaggregated by race/ethnicity, English language proficiency status, grade level, disability status, and gender to analyze potentially disproportionate need for supplemental supports across groups.

The second level of evaluation is student response to intervention. Intervention coordinators monitor student progress using schoolwide (i.e., attendance, behavior, course performance), and intervention specific student outcome data (e.g., assignments completed, use of appropriate social skills, proportion of goals met). The Tier II Team defines criteria for each intervention and support, indicating adequate progress toward meeting program goals. Utilizing these criteria, the proportion of participating students being successful can be tracked. Decision rules are then applied to student outcome data to inform whether provided supports should be continued or altered (e.g., intensified or faded) for individual students with the results of daily/weekly progress reports communicated to students' families. For example, if a student meets her intervention goals less than 80% of the time, the Tier II Team may decide that the intervention needs to be altered to better support the student.

Program fidelity is the third level of evaluation. As with all of the tiers, implementation fidelity and treatment integrity should be measured. For example, the Tiered Fidelity Inventory (TFI) allows evaluation of each tier of SWPBIS implementation, so if a school's action plan is focused only on Tier II, the team only needs to complete the Tier II section of TFI (Algozzine et al., 2014). It is also recommended that for best results, the treatment integrity of each Tier II intervention and support be direcly assessed, with a protocol put in place to ensure ongoing monitoring and review.

Finally, as with all tiers, summative evaluation is recommended at least annually to evaluate the overall effectiveness and efficiency of interventions, to make clear alterations in process and to share outcomes with school staff, district leadership, and other relevant stakeholders. Included in this evaluation are: (a) data-decision rules to identify students, (b) the range of available interventions and supports, (c) program fidelity, and (d) ongoing support to implementers (Algozzine et al., 2014).

Implementation of Tier III

Tier III supports within PBIS are highly individualized, intense, person-centered interventions that are developed by a team to improve quality of life indicators for a small proportion of students in a school, 1–5%, who are unresponsive to lower tiers of support alone. A strong foundation of: (a) practices at Tiers I and II (e.g. effective instruction and evidence-based behavior supports), (b) systems at Tier I and Tier II (e.g. professional development, teaming, leadership), and (c) data for decision-making at Tier I and II (e.g. fidelity and outcomes) ensure that highly individualized Tier III supports are tenable (Sugai et al, 2010).

Establishing a Tier III Team

There are two main teaming structures in Tier III: The Tier III Team, and Individual Student Teams. The Tier III Team ensures the systems are in place to successfully implement individualized intense interventions. Individual Student Teams are focused on an individual student and are responsible for assessing needs, developing a plan, monitoring outcomes and modifying the plan as needed for that student. Plans are created "one student at a time" to support success as defined by the student, family, teacher, and others who spend the most time with, or have the most responsibility for, the student (Eber, 2002).

Team composition at Tier III builds on the teaming structures and membership at Tiers I and II but due to the age of the student include the student and have an additional focus on transition and independence. This expanded focus will result in a broader membership including school and community members. School staff continue to participate, but the team is expanded to include members who: (a) are chosen by the individual student to ensure student voice in the development of the plan; (b) are committed to engaging students in the planning process; (c) include formal (someone who is paid to support the student; e.g., school staff, social worker, community partner) and natural supports (someone who is important and helpful to the student; e.g., peer, family member, neighbor, dating partner); and (d) link logically to the needs and strengths of the individual student. For example, if a student's transition goals include working as a mechanic, the vocational liaison or shop teacher may be a part of her individual team. The adolescent period is a time when the people and thus supports in a student's life are often changing. In developing teams these changes should be anticipated and thus the team compoisition reviewed and adjusted accordingly. This broad-based membership also requires that these teams are flexible and responsive to scheduling and meeting location needs of all members.

The composition of these teams also include person(s) with knowledge of wraparound systems of care, complex Function-Based Assessments and Behavior Support Plans, and individuals with expertise in adolescent development. Knowledge of 'typical' adolescent behaviors, and risk behaviors is critical in providing comprehensive care at Tier III. Approximately one out of five adolescents has a diagnosable mental health disorder (Schwarz, 2009) and nearly one third show symptoms of depression (Child Trends, 2014). High school-aged adolescents are also much more likely to use illicit substances (Stagman, Schwarz, and Powers, 2011) and engage in sexual activity than their elementary counterparts (Kellogg, 2009). Initial assessments, plan development and progress monitoring must cover all quality of life indicators therefore these areas of expertise are required to be part of individual teams.

Administrative engagement in the process becomes even more critical due to the coordination of resources for the individualized plan, which can include shifting staff FTE to provide supports, addressing the logistics of credit recovery, modifying student schedules, among other modifications to the daily routines at Tier I. Team operating procedures are similar to those at Tiers I and II, but require additional coordination and agreement with individuals from the school and community partnerships, such as juvenile justice, community housing, work place representatives, substance abuse prevention counselors, etc.

Last, is the provision of professional development. Because high school students are in multiple classrooms, multiple teachers need to implement an individual student's plan. Tier III teams also need to ensure that teachers receive professional development that is focused on (a) how to refer a student for Tier III supports, (b) the role of staff in the classroom in delivering and monitoring specific intervention components, and (c) critical features and contraindications for intervention components such as function-based intervention and trauma informed care.

Selecting Appropriate Interventions and Supports

Intervention plans at Tier III are multi-domain plans and can include strategies to support students in multiple environments (e.g., school, community) and across multiple needs (e.g., medical, emotional) (Eber, 2002). Tier III supports are driven by multi-domain assessments, and developed by a team of natural and formal supports. Students and their families have a leading role in the development of plans by identifying the valued outcomes that are specific and meaningful for them, and the supports that are a good 'fit' for them.

Because Tier III intervention plans are comprehensive across life domains and specific to the deficits and strengths of individual students, they often require coordination and collaboration amongst school staff as well outside agencies. To facilitate coordination of services effectively, memorandums of understanding (MOUs) are often developed between the district and external agencies that define how the external agencies will work within the school. These might include such things as how the agency staff spend their time on the school site, billing for services provided, roles on teams, and confidentiality.

Two commonly used evidence-based Tier III interventions within SWPBIS include wrap-around plans (Eber, 2002) and Complex/multi-domain Function-based Behavior Intervention Plans (Freeman et al., 2006). *Wraparound*, as defined by the Encyclopedia of Behavior Modification and Cognitive Behavior Therapy (Eber, 2002) is a philosophy of care with a defined planning process used to build constructive relationships and support networks among students and youth with emotional or behavioral disabilities and their families. Major features of wraparound are that it is community based, culturally relevant, individualized, strength based, and family centered. A robust feature of wraparound is that it is unconditional; if interventions are not achieving the outcomes desired by the team, the team regroups to rethink the configuration of supports, services, and interventions to ensure success in natural settings such as the home, school, and community. As teams problem-solve how to effectively meet students' needs, they combine supports for natural activities (e.g., child care, mentoring, making friends) with traditional interventions (e.g., behavioral interventions, specialized reading instruction, medication) (Eber, 2002). Wraparound is based on the belief that services and supports should be flexibly arranged to meet the unique needs of the students and their families, and they are not an attempt to fit a student into already existing interventions. Malloy and Cormier (2004) designed a model that expands wraparound and specifically addresses high school student's needs and developmental level. RENEW (Rehabilitation for Empowerment, Natural supports Education and Work) includes: (a) strategies to increase self-determination, (b) personal futures planning, (c) creative and individualized school-to-career planning, and (d) systemic support and consultation.

Function-Based Assessments and Behavior Support Plans (FBA-BSP) in high school use the same process as implemented for elementary-aged students, but again with (a) a focus on transition goals, (b) heavy inclusion of student voice, especially as related to rewards for using the desired, positive behaviors, and (c) special attention paid to the school/community/family collaboration necessary to address life domains. The FBA-BSP process to facilitate behavioral change is supported by over 50 years of research (Baer, Wolf, and Risley, 1968; Bijou and Baer, 1961; Skinner, 1953; Sugai et al., 2000). The Individuals with Disabilities Education Improvement Act (IDEA, 2004) places explicit requirements on IEP teams to use or consider an FBA assessment for addressing behavioral challenges, and strong arguments have been made as to their utility for students in general education (Scott et al., 2004).

The technical components of the FBA include (a) operational description of problem behavior, (b) identification of contexts where problem behavior is most likely, and (c) maintaining reinforcers (e.g., behavioral function) in these contexts. Behavior support plans (BSPs) must include or consider (a) prevention strategies, (b) teaching strategies, (c) strategies for removing rewards for problem behavior, (d) specific rewards for desired behavior, (e) safety elements where needed, (f) a systematic process for assessing fidelity and impact, and (g) the action plan for putting the support plan in place (O'Neill, Horner, Albin, Storey, and Sprague, 1990).

Evaluation and Progress Monitoring

As with the previous Tiers of support, using data for decision-making is a key component to implementing and sustaining SWPBIS (Coffey and Horner, 2012; Horner, Sugai, and Todd, 2001; McIntosh et al., 2013). The data collected at Tier III are related to the fidelity and outcomes of individualized plan for each student as well as the overall fidelity and impact of Tier III systems. The schedule for data review requires a weekly review of progress for students on Tier III interventions in order to modify plans in response to student progress or needs. Data systems may need to be adapted or modified to (a) allow for more frequent review of data, and/or (b) to include additional data on student goals across domains, such as work place, relationships, and living arrangements that are relevant for our high school aged youth. Teams also need to consider sharing outcome data with the student they are supporting to ensure continued student voice and choice in the process.

Conclusion

High schools are implementing SWPBIS, a framework for multi-tiered systems of supports designed to develop a consistent, predictable and safe school so students can succeed. The implementation in high schools is aligned with the essential elements of the framework, including development of outcomes, systems (e.g., team leadership, positive acknowledgement and discipline systems), practices (e.g., teaching expectations, rewarding appropriate behaviors, clarifying discipline policies), and data (e.g., data-based decision-making, access to multiple sources of data on attendance, behavior, course performance). Yet due to the size, organizational structure, school culture, and the developmental level of students, how this framework is implemented will be different than in the lower grades. In particular, the context of the high school impacts three systems integral to implementation – leadership, communication and data. Leadership, as with all SWPBIS schools, includes leadership teams at each tier of support. A key member of these teams is the administration representative, but it also requires the expansion of communication with and participation of others in leadership roles. Though one person is designated to support these teams it will be critical that the full 'administrative team' is aware of the direction and plans of the teams, the outcomes and the practices, so they can fully support these and integrate them into their work with the faculty, staff and students. Due to the age of the high school students it is as important to consider them as active stakeholders and develop a mechanism for them to have input into, and feedback from, this leadership team.

The second system affected by the high school context is the communication system. As mentioned earlier, a critical group to communicate with is students. Also, due to the fact that adolescents 'listen' to their peers, it is important to have them front and center in any school initiative. Have them play an active role in teaching expectations, developing the acknowledgement system, and clarifying the discipline system. High school teams also need to examine how they currently communicate and use these mechanisms to get the messages out, and to regularly update faculty, staff, students and families as to the impact and status of the implementation process.

Finally, data systems need to align with the critical outcomes of high school to include student attendance, behavior, and course performance. The use of data for decision-making is currently hampered in many high schools by the large volume of data that are generated and the tendency for these data to be managed by different people, housed in different locations, using often incompatible management systems/software. To move beyond the use of data solely for the purposes of reporting and accountability, systems will need to be developed to effectively and efficiently collect, organize, and evaluate data in a timely manner. Once established, these data systems would allow high school teams to more quickly take action in response to developing trends in student support needs and more effectively monitor progress toward identified goals.

High schools can implement a multi-tiered system of support such as SWPBIS and at the same time attend to their high school context and the faculty and students within it. The implementation of this system that addresses the needs of students with the intensity of support needed will improve outcomes for students.

References

Adelman, H., and Taylor, L. (2011). What do principals say about their work? Implications for addressing barriers to learning and school improvement. In *A Center Policy and Practice Brief* (pp. 1–22). Los Angeles, CA: Center for Mental Health in Schools.

Algozzine, R. F., Barrett, S., Eber, L., George, H., Horner, R. H., Lewis, T. J., . . . and Sugai, G. (2014). *PBIS Tiered Fidelity Inventory (TFI)*. Eugene, OR: OSEP Technical Assistance Center on Positive Behavioral Interventions and Supports.

Algozzine, B., Wang, C., and Violette, A. S. (2011). Reexamining the relationship between academic achievement and social behavior. *Journal of Positive Behavior Interventions, 13*, 3–16. doi: http://dx.doi.org/10.1177/1098300709359084.

Anderson, C. M., Lewis-Palmer, T., Todd, A. W., Horner, R. H., Sugar, G., and Sampson, N. K. (2012). *Individual student systems evaluation tool*. Eugene, OR: University of Oregon, Educational and Community Supports.

Anderson, D. H., Munk, J. H., Young, K. R., Conley, L., and Caldarella, P. (2008). Teaching organizational skills to promote academic achievement in behaviorally challenged students. *Teaching Exceptional Children, 40*, 6–13. doi: http://dx.doi.org/10.1177/004005990804000401.

Baer, D. M., Wolf, M. M., and Risley, T. R. (1968). Some current dimensions of applied behavior analysis. *Journal of Applied Behavior Analysis, 1*, 91–97. doi: http://dx.doi.org/10.1901/jaba.1987.20-313.

Bijou, S. W., & Baer, D. M. (1961). *Child development I: A systematic and empirical theory*. Englewood Cliffs, NJ: Prentice Hall.

Bernstein, L., Rappaport, C. D., Olsho, L., Hunt, D., and Levin, M. (2009). *Impact evaluation of the U.S. Department of Education's Student Mentoring Program: Final report*. Washington, DC: National Center for Education Evaluation and Regional Assistance, Institute of Education, U.S. Department of Education.

Bohanon, H., Fenning, P., Borgmeier, C., Flannery, K. B., and Malloy, J. (2009). Finding a direction for high school positive behavior support. In W. Sailor, G. Dunlap, G. Sugai, and R. Horner (Eds.), *Handbook of positive behavior support* (pp. 581–602). New York: Springer. doi: http://dx.doi.org/10.1007/978-0-387-09632-2_24.

Bohanon, H., Fenning, P., Carney, K., Minnis, M., Anderson-Harris, S., Moroz, K., . . . and Sailor, W. (2006). School-wide application of urban high school positive behavior support: A case study. *Journal of Positive Behavior Interventions and Supports, 8*, 131–145.

Bohanon, H., Fenning, P., Hicks, K., Weber, S., Thier, K., Aikins, B., . . . and Irvin, L. (2012). A case example of the implementation of schoolwide positive behavior support in a high school setting using change point test analysis. *Preventing School Failure, 56*, 91–103. doi: http://dx.doi.org/10.1080/1045988X.2011.588973.

Bradshaw, C., Koth, C., Thornton, L., and Leaf, P. (2009). Altering school climate through schoolwide positive behavioral interventions and supports: Findings from a group randomized effectiveness trial. *Prevention Science, 10*, 100–115. doi: http://dx.doi.org/10.1007/s11121-008-0114-9.

Burns, M. K., Appleton, J. J., and Stehouwer, J. D. (2005). Meta-analytic review of responsiveness-to-intervention research: Examining field-based and research-implemented models. *Journal of Psycho-educational Assessment, 23*, 381–394. doi: http://dx.doi.org/10.1177/073428290502300406.

Child Trends. (2014). Child Trends Databank: Adolescents who feel sad or hopeless. Retrieved February 16, 2016, from: www.childtrends.org/?indicators=adolescents-who-felt-sad-or-hopeless.

Coffey, J., and Horner, R. H. (2012). The sustainability of school-wide positive behavior support. *Exceptional Children, 78*, 407–422. doi: http://dx.doi.org/10.1177/001440291207800402.

Eber, L. (2002). Description of Wraparound and Case Example. From the *Encyclopedia of behavior modification and cognitive behavior therapy*, Volume 3, Issue 1, Educational Applications. Retrieved on March 22, 2010 from: www.pbis.org/common/cms/files/Newsletter/Volume3%20Issue2.pdf.

Flannery, K. B., Fenning, P., Kato, M. M., and McIntosh, K. (2014). Effects of school-wide positive behavioral interventions and supports and fidelity of implementation on problem behavior in high schools. *School Psychology Quarterly, 29*, 111–24. doi: http://dx.doi.org/10.1037/spq0000039.

Flannery, K. B., Frank, J. L., Doren, B., Kato, M. M., and Fenning, P. (2013). Implementing schoolwide positive behavior support in high school settings: Analysis of eight high schools. *The High School Journal, 96*, 267–282. doi: http://dx.doi.org/10.1037/spq0000039.

Flannery, K. B., and Kato, M. M (2016). Implementation of SWPBIS in high school: Why is it different? *Preventing School Failure: Alternative Education for Children and Youth, 61*(1), 69–79, doi: 10.1080/1045988X.2016.1196644.

Flannery, K. B., Sugai, G., and Anderson, C. (2009). Schoolwide Positive Behavioral Support in high schools: Early lessons learned. *Journal of Positive Behavioral Support, 11*, 177–185.

Freeman, J., Simonsen, B., McCoach, D.B., Sugai, G., Lombardi, A., and Horner, R. (2015a). Relationship between school-wide positive behavior interventions and supports and academic, attendance, and behavior outcomes in high schools. *Journal of Positive Behavior Interventions*. Advance online publication. doi: http://dx.doi.org/10.1177/1098300715580992.

Freeman, J., Simonsen, B., McCoach, D. B., Sugai, G., Lombardi, A., Horner, R. (2015b). An analysis of the relationship between implementation of school-wide positive behavior interventions and supports and high school attendance and dropout rates. *The High School Journal, 98*, 290–315.

Freeman, R., Eber, L., Anderson, C., Irvin, L., Horner, R., Bounds, M., and Dunlap, G. (2006). Building inclusive school cultures using school-wide positive behavior support: Designing effective individual support systems for students with significant disabilities. *Research and Practice for Persons with Severe Disabilities, 31*, 4–17. doi: http://dx.doi.org/10.2511/rpsd.31.1.4.

Fixsen, D. L., Naoom, S. F., Blase, K. A., Friedman, R. M., and Wallace, F. (2005). *Implementation research: A synthesis of the literature*. Tampa, FL: University of South Florida, Louis de la Parte Florida Mental Health Institute, The National Implementation Research Network (FMHI Publication #231).

Gresham, F. M., and Elliott, S. N. (2008). *Social skills improvement system: Rating scales*. Bloomington, MN: Pearson Assessments.

Gresham, F. M., Sugai, G., and Horner, R. H. (2001). Interpreting outcomes of social skills training for students with high-incidence disabilities. *Exceptional Children, 67*, 331–344.

Grissom, J. A., Loeb, S., and Urban Institute, N. (2009). Triangulating principal effectiveness: How perspectives of parents, teachers, and assistant principals identify the central importance of managerial skills. Working Paper 35. *National Center for Analysis of Longitudinal Data in Education Research, Retrieved from EBSCO host*. doi: http://dx.doi.org/10.3102/0002831211402663.

Hattie, J., and Timperley, H. (2007). The power of feedback. *Review of Educational Research, 77*, 81–112. doi: http://dx.doi.org/10.3102/003465430298487.

Horner, R., Quirk, C., Gandhi, A., Lemons, C., and Megert, B. (2016, August) *Updates and Current Issues Related to Multi-Tier Systems of Supports (MTSS) for Academic and Behavioral Difficulties*. Panel presentation at OSEP Project Directors Conference, Washington, DC.

Horner, R., Sugai, G., Smolkowski, K., Eber, L., Nakasato, J., Todd, A., and Esperanza, J., (2009). A randomized, wait-list controlled effectiveness trial assessing school-wide positive behavior support in elementary schools. *Journal of Positive Behavior Interventions, 11*, 133–145. doi: http://dx.doi.org/10.1177/1098300709332067.

Horner, R. H., Sugai, G., and Todd, A. W. (2001). "Data" need not be a four-letter word: Using data to improve schoolwide discipline. *Beyond Behavior, 11*, 20–26.

Horner, R. H., Sugai, G., Todd, A. W., and Lewis-Palmer, T. (2005). School-wide positive behavior support. In L. M. Bambara and L. Kern (Eds.), *Individualized supports for students with problem behaviors: Designing positive behavior plans* (pp. 359–390). New York: The Guilford Press.

Horner, R. H., Todd, A. W., Lewis-Palmer, T., Irvin, L. K., Sugai, G., and Boland, J. B. (2004). The School-wide Evaluation Tool (SET): A research instrument for assessing school-wide positive behavior support. *Journal of Positive Behavior Interventions*, *6*, 3–12. doi: http://dx.doi.org/10.1177/10983007040060010201.

Individuals with Disabilities Education Act of 2004. (IDEA 2004). Public Law 108–446, 108th Congress, Statute 2647. Retrieved from: http://idea.ed.ogv/explore.home.

Kellogg, N. D. (2009). Clinical report – the evaluation of sexual behaviors in children. *Pediatrics*, *124*, 992–998. doi: http://dx.doi.org/10.1542/peds.2009-1692.

Kennedy, M. J., Horner, R. H., McNelly, D., Mimmack, J., Sobel, D., and Tillman, D. R. (2009). Data-based decision making in high schools: Informed implementation of school-wide positive behavior support. In B. Flannery and G. Sugai (Eds.), *SWPBS Implementation in high schools: Current practice and future directions* (pp. 81–114). Retrieved from: www.pbis.org.

Kennedy, M., Mimmack, J., and Flannery K. B. (2012). Innovation in data-driven decision making within PBIS systems: Welcome to the gallery walk. *Beyond Behavior*, *21*, 8–14.

Kincaid, D., Childs, K., and George, H. (2005). School-wide Benchmarks of Quality (BoQ). Unpublished instrument, University of South Florida. Retrieved from: www.pbis.org

Kluger, A. N., and DeNisi, A. (1996). The effects of feedback interventions on performance: A historical review, a meta-analysis, and a preliminary feedback intervention theory. *Psychological Bulletin*, *119*, 254–284. doi: http://dx.doi.org/10.1037/0033-2909.119.2.254.

Lewis, T., and Sugai, G. (1999). Effective behavior support: A systems approach to proactive schoolwide management. *Focus on Exceptional Children*, *31*, 1–24.

Maggin, D. M., Zurheide, J., Pickett, K. C., and Baillie, S. J. (2015). A systematic evidence review of the check-in/check-out program for reducing student challenging behaviors. *Journal of Positive Behavior Interventions*, *17*, 197–208. doi: http://dx.doi.org/10.1177/1098300715573630.

Malloy, J., and Cormier, G. (2004). Project RENEW: Building the community's capacity to support youths' transition from school to adult life. In D. Cheney (Ed.), *Transition of secondary students with emotional or behavioral disorders: Current approaches for positive outcomes* (pp. 180–200). Arlington, VA: Council for Children with Behavioral Disorders.

McIntosh, K., Campbell, A. L., Carter, D. R., and Zumbo, B. D. (2009). Concurrent validity of office discipline referrals and cut points used in schoolwide positive behavior supports. *Behavioral Disorders*, *34*, 100–113.

McIntosh, K., Horner, R. H., Chard, D., Boland, J., and Good, R. (2006). The use of reading and behavior screening measures to predict non-response to school-wide positive behavior support: A longitudinal analysis. *School Psychology Review*, *35*, 275–291.

McIntosh, K., Mercer, S. H., Hume, A. E., Frank, J. L., Turri, M. G., and Mathews, S. (2013). Factors associated with sustained implementation of school-wide positive behavior support. *Exceptional Children*, *79*, 293–311.

McIntosh, K., Predy, L. K., Upreti, G., Hume, A. E., Turri, M. G., and Mathews, S. (2014). Perceptions of contextual features related to implementation and sustainability of school-wide positive behavior support. *Journal of Positive Behavior Interventions*, *16*, 29–41. doi: http://dx.doi.org/10.1177/1098300712470723.

Morrison, G. M., Robertson, L., Laurie, B., and Kelly, J. (2002). Protective factors related to antisocial behavior trajectories. *Journal of Clinical Psychology*, *58*, 277–290. doi: http://dx.doi.org/10.1002/jclp.10022.

Morrissey, K., Bohanon, H., and Fenning, P. (2010). Positive behavior support: Teaching and acknowledging expected behaviors in an urban high school. *Teaching Exceptional Children*, *42*, 26–35. doi: http://dx.doi.org/10.1177/004005991004200503.

Muscott, H., Mann, E., and LeBrun, M. (2008). Positive behavioral interventions and supports in New Hampshire: Effects of large-scale implementation of schoolwide positive behavior support on student discipline and academic achievement. *Journal of Positive Behavior Interventions*, *10*, 190–205. doi: http://dx.doi.org/10.1177/1098300708316258.

Newcomer, L. L., Freeman, R., and Barrett, S. (2013). Essential systems for sustainable implementation of Tier 2 supports. *Journal of Applied Psychology*, *29*, 126–147. doi: http://dx.doi.org/10.1080/15377903.2013.778770.

O'Neill, R. E., Horner, R. H., Albin, R. W., Storey, K., and Sprague, J. R. (1990). *Functional analysis of problem behavior: A practical assessment guide*. Sycamore, IL: Sycamore Publishing Company.

Ross, S. W., and Horner, R. H. (2009). Bully prevention in positive behavior support. *Journal of Applied Behavior Analysis, 42*, 747–759. doi: http://dx.doi.org/10.1901/jaba.2009.42-747.

Schwarz, S. W. (2009). *Adolescent mental health in the United States: Facts for Policymakers.* Retrieved February 16, 2016, from http://nccp.org/publications/pdf/text_878.pdf.

Scott, T. M., Bucalos, A., Liaupsin, C., Nelson, C. M., Jolivette, K., and DeShea, L. (2004). Using functional behavior assessment in general education settings: Making a case for effectiveness and efficiency. *Behavioral Disorders, 29*, 189–201.

Skinner, B. F. (1953). *Science and behavior.* New York: The Macmillan Company

Spaulding, S., Irvin, L., Horner, R., May, S., Emeldi, M., Tobin, T., and Sugai, G. (2010). School-wide social-behavioral climate, student problem behavior, and related administrative decisions: Empirical patterns from 1,510 schools nationwide. *Journal of Positive Behavior Interventions, 12*, 69–85.

Stagman, S. M., Schwarz, S. W., and Powers, D. (2011). *Adolescent substance use in the US: Facts for policymakers.* Retrieved May 25, 2016 from: www.nccp.org/publications/pdf/text_1008.pdf.

Steinberg, L. (2012). Should the sciences of adolescent brain development inform public policy? *Issues in Science and Technology, 28*. doi: http://dx.doi.org/10.1037/0003-066X.64.8.739.

Sugai, G., and Horner, R. H. (2008). What we know and need to know about preventing problem behavior in schools. *Exceptionality, 16*, 67–77.

Sugai, G., and Horner, R. H. (2009, invited). Responsiveness-to-intervention and school-wide positive behavior supports: Integration of multi-tiered system approaches. *Exceptionality, 17*, 223–237. doi: http://dx.doi.org/10.1080/09362830903235375.

Sugai, G., Horner, R. H., Algozzine, R., Barrett, S., Lewis, T., Anderson, C., . . . and Simonsen, B. (2010). *School-wide positive behavior support: Implementers' blueprint and self-assessment.* Eugene, OR: University of Oregon

Sugai, G., Horner, R. H., and Gresham, F. (2002). Behaviorally effective school environments. In M. R. Shinn, G. Stoner, and H. M. Walker (Eds.), *Interventions for academic and behavior problems: Preventive and remedial approaches* (pp. 315–350). Silver Spring, MD: National Association for School Psychologists.

Sugai, G., Sprague, J., Horner, R. H., and Walker, H. M. (2000). Preventing school violence: The use of office discipline referrals to assess and monitor schoolwide discipline interventions. *Journal of Emotional and Behavioral Disorders, 8*, 94–101. doi: http://dx.doi.org/10.1177/106342660000800205.

Swain-Bradway, J., Pinkney, C., and Flannery, K. B. (2015). Implementing schoolwide positive behavior interventions and supports in high schools: Contextual factors and stages of implementation. *Teaching Exceptional Children, 47*, 245–255. doi: http://dx.doi.org/10.1177/0040059915580030.

18

RTI IN SECONDARY SCHOOLS

Current Issues and Recommendations

Kelly J. Williams, Elizabeth Stevens,
and Sharon Vaughn

Introduction

The reauthorization of the Individuals with Disabilities Education Improvement Act (2004) incorporates a revised framework to address more efficiently individual learning needs and contribute to identifying students with learning disabilities. This revised framework is referred to as Response to Intervention (RTI). RTI is a multi-tiered system aimed at identifying students with learning and behavior difficulties early on and then assuring that they are provided with appropriate interventions to meet their learning needs. Students move through successive levels of intervention based on inadequate response to previous, less intensive interventions (Vaughn and Fuchs, 2003). Conceptually, the RTI framework is based on the following components: (a) preventing school failure, (b) providing universal screening to identify students who are at-risk, (c) using ongoing progress monitoring, and (d) providing three tiers of instructional support (Vaughn and Fletcher, 2012). As a result of these components, students are provided with research-based, high-quality instruction delivered in the general education classroom (Tier 1), thus providing assurances that students who are behind have been given opportunities to learn. Universal screening identifies students who may need more intensive instructional or behavioral support; those students receive a more intensive research-based intervention in small group settings (Tier 2) in addition to Tier 1 instruction. Data collected via ongoing progress monitoring allows educators to track individual student progress and move Tier 2 students who are minimal responders to even more intensive intervention (Tier 3); data collected may also be used for special education referrals and possible identification.

The RTI framework, which is similar to public health models, has been implemented by schools to prevent and address academic and behavioral difficulties (Vaughn and Fletcher, 2012). Because of the emphasis on early identification and prevention, the emphasis on RTI has been at the elementary level. In addition to the focus on early identification of students with learning and behavior difficulties and the emphasis on prevention of subsequent difficulties, there are other reasons why the emphasis within RTI has been at the early grades (Vaughn and Fletcher, 2012). Reading First (No Child Left Behind, 2001) provided funding for implementing research-based practices related to improved reading instruction as well as early identification of reading problems with supplemental reading interventions as needed. Thus, Reading First provided a model for early implementation of RTI-type practices. Also, there is a significantly

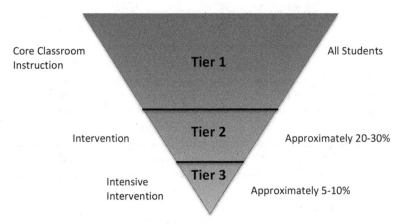

Figure 18.1 The RTI Continuum of Academic Support

larger knowledge base about research-based practices for intervening with young learners compared with students at the secondary level.

With young learners (K through third grade), the expectation is that approximately 80% of these students would respond to research-based Tier 1 reading instruction; the majority of the remaining 20% are expected to respond to effective Tier 2 instruction, leaving only those with the most severe learning needs requiring Tier 3 reading intervention (Fletcher and Vaughn, 2009). It is important to note that, while we describe RTI within a three-tier framework, many districts and states use multiple tiers of support with more intensive interventions occurring at Tier 4 or 5. Many students requiring these more intensive interventions are often identified with learning disabilities in reading.

While many of the fundamental principles of RTI are appropriate at the secondary level—e.g., use of research-based practices, implementation of intensive interventions aligned with students need—the conceptualization of RTI also has different challenges and procedures for middle and high school settings. Secondary students often have well-established, documented learning difficulties; as such, screening for learning difficulties is unnecessary and counterproductive (Reed et al., 2012). Likewise, the emphasis is on remediation rather than prevention, and students are provided with necessary, intensive interventions immediately, rather than moving through successive tiers of support. The purpose of this chapter is to explain what we know about RTI at the middle and high school levels and to define the complexities surrounding implementation. Finally, we will provide recommendations for improving this framework for secondary students and identify areas requiring further research.

Issues with Applying the Current Conceptualization of RTI to Secondary Settings Screening

Screening to identify students at-risk for academic failure does not apply in the same way in secondary settings as it has been conceptualized in elementary settings, because academic difficulties have already been documented throughout students' school experiences (Fuchs et al., 2010; Vaughn and Fletcher, 2010). The National Assessment of Educational Progress 2015 report indicates that 22% of eighth and 25% of twelfth graders did not meet grade level expectations in reading (Kena et al., 2015). Students with high-incidence disabilities do not make the adequate academic progress when compared with their general education peers

(U.S. Department of Education, 2011). These students take fewer academic courses, earn fewer credits, and have lower grade point averages than their classmates. Moreover, only 50–75% of students with learning disabilities or emotional disturbance graduate with a general education diploma or certificate (Swanson, 2008). The National Longitudinal Transition Study-2 (Wagner et al., 2006) indicates that students with disabilities have significantly lower academic achievement than their general education peers. Of these students, 21–28% drop out of school, and they are less likely to hold paid employment and more likely to have served jail time (Wagner et al., 2006). Fuchs et al. (2010) refer to these data as a public health crisis; it makes no sense to identify those students at-risk for failure when there are established mechanisms for identifying students who are already failing. Furthermore, the time and resources traditionally allocated to screening can be better spent on providing high-quality Tier 2 and 3 interventions (Vaughn and Fletcher, 2010).

Failure to Respond

Another issue with RTI at the secondary level is the application of inadequate response to intervention prior to moving to more intensive tiers of support. Because academic difficulties have previously been identified and documented, it is unnecessary to wait to provide intensive interventions to students with the greatest need (Vaughn and Fletcher, 2010). Vaughn et al. (2010) conducted a multi-year RTI study with struggling middle school readers. Students with the lowest reading achievement the first year also demonstrated the lowest RTI after three years of treatment. The RTI framework cannot ameliorate academic difficulties if secondary students are required to demonstrate failure to respond to lesser Tiers of support. When struggling readers are not fast-tracked to Tier 2 or 3, they do not receive the supplemental, intensive intervention needed to help them be successful. Furthermore, Tier 1 general education instruction may be weaker because many secondary teachers focus on content area instruction, rather than reading instruction (Brozo, 2009). This could result in students being misplaced in more intensive tiers when their needs could be met with appropriate Tier 1 instructional strategies. The overall effectiveness of the RTI framework may be diminished if too many students are referred for more intensive tiers.

What We Know about Interventions for Secondary Students

Supplemental reading interventions have positive outcomes for older struggling readers. A recent meta-analysis on reading interventions for at-risk students in grades 4 through 12 yielded a mean effect size of 0.95 across interventions, suggesting they produce strong effects on reading outcomes for adolescent readers (Scammacca et al., 2007). The overall mean effect size for standardized measures was small to moderate at 0.42. However, these studies did not address students with persistent reading difficulties who respond minimally to previously effective interventions. Nor did the studies include multi-tiered interventions like those used in RTI; most used researcher-developed outcome measures, which are typically associated with higher effect sizes. Edmonds et al. (2009) reported similar results for a meta-analysis of 13 studies conducted in grades 6–12 between 1994 and 2004. Reading comprehension and word-level interventions produced the greatest gains in reading outcomes, whereas fluency interventions did not improve reading comprehension (Edmonds et al., 2009; Scammacca et al., 2013).

More recently, Scammacca et al. (2013) updated Scammacca's 2007 meta-analysis to include results published between 2004 and 2011. Results showed a decline in effect sizes over time, with an overall mean effect size of 0.49 and a mean effect of 0.21 for standardized measures.

Reading comprehension interventions were more effective than reading fluency interventions, and there was no difference between researcher- and teacher-provided interventions. The decline in magnitude of reading intervention effects since 2004 may be a result of an increased use of standardized measures in research designs, which is typically associated with smaller effect sizes (Scammacca et al., 2013). However, it could also be a result of improved interventions provided in the comparison group. Due to implementation of RTI, lower effect sizes may indicate that the comparison condition is receiving more intensive intervention than what was provided during the previous meta-analyses. Additionally, longer interventions were associated with smaller effect sizes (Scammacca et al., 2013). One possible explanation is that shorter interventions produce a larger, immediate effect; however, it's difficult to maintain gains over time, particularly when students are assessed using distal measures, such as standardized assessments.

Research on Students Requiring Tier 3 Interventions

While the research shows that struggling readers are generally responsive to evidence-based reading interventions, less is known about inadequate responders, or students with persistent reading difficulties who respond minimally to typically effective interventions (Vaughn and Fletcher, 2010). These students may need to remain in Tier 3 intervention and continue to receive support throughout their secondary education due to the severity of their difficulties. Vaughn et al. (2012) conducted a longitudinal study with middle school students to examine response to a multi-tiered, increasingly intensive system of support for students with persistent reading difficulties. During the first year, treatment students received researcher-provided, enhanced Tier 1 instruction in the general education classroom. In year 2, students identified as inadequate responders to Tier 1 instruction received intensified intervention in an individualized or standardized format. While the treatment students outperformed the control group with a small effect size ($d = -.23$), there were no significant differences between the individualized and standardized intervention groups. In year 3, inadequate responders received a third year of intensified intervention. The treatment students outperformed the comparison group (also inadequate responders) at the end of this year, but they did not close the achievement gap with typically achieving peers. Furthermore, while the treatment group maintained steady performance throughout the intervention, the comparison group actually declined in reading measures by the end of year 3. These results suggest that minimal responders may need continued, extensive Tier 3 intervention to maintain current reading performance. Consequently, it may be unrealistic to expect these students to make accelerated reading growth, or to close the achievement gap with proficient readers (Vaughn et al., 2010).

The Complex Nature of Providing Effective Remediation for Struggling Adolescent Readers

Implementation of RTI in middle and high school settings is further complicated by the feasibility of providing effective remediation, which is more challenging than at the elementary level. For example, content area demands increase, while reading instruction decreases (Brozo, 2009; Johnson et al., 2009). Secondary teachers are viewed as experts in content area knowledge, but may be unprepared to teach literacy skills to diverse populations (National High School Center, 2010; Vaughn and Fletcher, 2010). Because teachers are focused on content-area instruction, they may not view their role as supporting academic learning in literacy.

Furthermore, students beyond grade 7 are unlikely to have a dedicated class during the school day to improve reading outcomes (Vaughn and Fletcher, 2012). In spite of this, teachers require students to use reading and writing skills regularly to access information (Johnson et al., 2009). Students use complex texts to learn concepts across the content areas and then use writing as a tool to communicate what they have learned. If reading instruction is not integrated into these content areas, students may fail to access the general education curriculum. Improving the quality of Tier 1 reading instruction is achieved across content areas and teachers, rather than in one classroom with one teacher.

Consistent Tier 2-type interventions may be more difficult to implement at the secondary level due to scheduling barriers. Students have more individualized schedules and it may be difficult to incorporate a remediation block into these schedules. Vaughn et al. (2010) described the challenge they faced with implementing Tier 2 intervention due to the transient flow of students in and out of intervention groups. Schools may not have the staffing resources necessary to provide Tier 2 intervention in such a way that accommodates every student's schedule. Students requiring Tier 3 intervention might need support with greater intensity, which can also be difficult to achieve in middle and high school settings (Torgesen et al., 2001; Vaughn and Fletcher, 2010, 2012). Schools typically allow for Tier 2 intervention groups of ten–15 students. This group size is too large for Tier 3 intervention because tutors cannot provide the intensity required, including individualizing instruction based on student needs and addressing motivation and self-confidence (Fuchs et al., 2010). Providing consistent intervention in smaller groups allows tutors manageably to individualize interventions, including providing students with more opportunities to engage and to receive targeted feedback (Vaughn and Fletcher, 2012). Addressing these scheduling barriers is critical to ensuring that all students reliably receive appropriate, consistent intervention.

In addition to the challenges with feasibility of implementing interventions at the secondary level, students' instructional needs are complex. Unlike at elementary school, where early reading problems are typically characterized by phonological processing, or word-reading difficulties, secondary students exhibit difficulties ranging from word-reading to higher level comprehension tasks (Fuchs et al., 2010). Students require extensive support in vocabulary and building background knowledge (Fuchs et al., 2010; Vaughn et al., 2012). Yet, very few studies exist that investigate how to improve reading comprehension for secondary students. Emphasizing strategy instruction in reading comprehension may be futile given the importance of these underlying difficulties in vocabulary and background knowledge (Fuchs et al., 2010; Vaughn and Fletcher, 2012). When students struggle to read, they avoid reading tasks, spending less time reading than proficient peers. Consequently, this negatively impacts vocabulary acquisition, background knowledge, and content understanding (Fuchs et al., 2010). Furthermore, weaknesses in these areas are not easily remediated, because difficulties are deeply entrenched; in other words, there won't be a one-size-fits-all program and improvement will take time. As such, given the array of student difficulties, needs must be addressed over time on an individualized basis (Vaughn and Fletcher, 2012).

Students' social/emotional and behavioral needs might negatively impact learning to read, which contributes to the challenge of remediating difficulties. The effectiveness of reading interventions may be compromised by student difficulties with attention, language development, or memory processing (Cutting and Scarborough, 2006; Hock et al., 2009). When providing interventions to secondary students, it is also important to address low motivation and self-confidence (Fuchs et al., 2010). Interventions should motivate students and garner peer approval. If peer groups dismiss intervention programs, struggling readers are unlikely to engage in the remediation process.

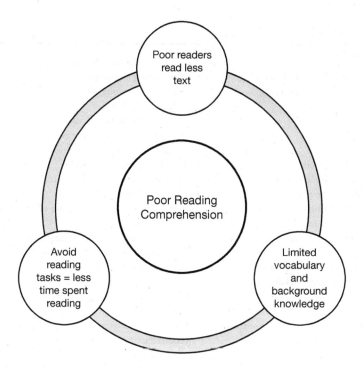

Figure 18.2 Complexity of Adolescents' Reading Problems

Recommendations for RTI at the Secondary Level

As discussed previously, the purpose of RTI at the elementary level is to prevent reading difficulties through screening, provide early interventions, and use response to intervention as a disability determinant (Johnson et al., 2009). However, this purpose shifts as students enter secondary schools. RTI at the secondary level emphasizes remediation of pre-existing difficulties and ensures all students receive adequate, research-based instruction and interventions to increase academic achievement and meet graduation requirements (Johnson et al., 2009; Pyle and Vaughn, 2012; Reed et al., 2012). The following section outlines recommendations for addressing the challenges of implementing RTI at the secondary level. Table 18.1 describes the differences in how the RTI process is conceptualized at the elementary versus secondary level.

Screening and Placement Recommendations

At the elementary level, screening is used to identify students who are at-risk for academic failure, while, at the secondary level, at-risk students have already been identified and extensive data have been collected on these students (Fuchs et al., 2010; Vaughn and Fletcher, 2010). Furthermore, reliable universal screening measures have not be developed for older, struggling readers (National High School Center, 2010). Instead of using traditional screening methods, instructional time and resources can be better spent on analyzing data from extant sources, such as state assessments, to identify students who need more intensive support (Fuchs et al., 2010; Pyle and Vaughn, 2012; Vaughn and Fletcher, 2010).

In a three-year study with struggling middle school readers, Vaughn and Fletcher (2012) used an RTI model to remediate reading difficulties. Instead of screening for at-risk students,

Table 18.1 Elementary versus Secondary RTI

RTI Component	Elementary	Secondary
Screening	• Identify at-risk students using universal screening tools.	• Use existing assessment data or teacher nomination to identify struggling students. • Conduct supplemental assessments as necessary (i.e., brief measures of fluency, decoding, or vocabulary).
Response to Intervention	• Tier 1 instruction is provided within one classroom. • Minimal Response to Intervention is required before moving to more intensive tiers.	• Tier 1 instruction should be strengthened across content areas. • Using existing data, fast-track students to the appropriate tier of interventions.
Effective interventions	• Many research-based interventions already exist. • Interventions focus on a smaller subset of reading skills (i.e., decoding). • Tier 2 and 3 intervention can be provided within existing schedules.	• These may require multi-component interventions to target needed skills. • Motivation, engagement, and attention must be addressed to provide effective Tier 2 and 3 intervention. • Schedules and/or graduation requirements may need to be changed in order to provide students intensive interventions.
Progress monitoring.	• Frequent assessment data are used to monitor Response to Intervention and adjust intervention as needed. • There is fluid movement through the tiers.	• Use curriculum based assessments less frequently to adjust intervention as needed. • Minimal responders may remain in Tier 3.

data from a state criterion referenced assessment in reading were used to identify struggling readers. This demonstrates the possibility of using this type of measure to identify at-risk students. However, when using such assessments, it is also important to consider their psychometric properties. The measure should have strong reliability and validity and each state's assessment may need to be evaluated for these properties (Pyle and Vaughn, 2012). Cut-scores may also need to be examined by the school's RTI or leadership team to determine which scores classify students as "at-risk." Another option might be to use teacher nominations to identify struggling readers. By using existing data sources or nominations, school resources can be reallocated to provide more effective instruction and interventions (Fuchs et al., 2010).

Additional brief assessments may be necessary to pinpoint specific academic difficulties (i.e., decoding multisyllabic words or reading fluency), particularly because the main focus of many state reading assessments is comprehension (Fuchs et al., 2010; Pyle and Vaughn, 2012). While it's important to limit assessment demands and conserve resources for intervention, measures of fluency, vocabulary, and decoding can be used to form more homogenous intervention groups and provide appropriately scaffolded instruction for struggling adolescent readers. The use of these additional assessments, combined with a state assessment, can be a powerful tool to identify which students may require immediate access to the most intensive levels of intervention

(Fuchs et al., 2010). For example, some students may require less intensive interventions because their reading difficulties are not as severe, while other students may need to be placed directly in the most supportive tier.

This fast-tracking of students to the appropriate tier demonstrates another departure from elementary-based RTI systems. At the elementary level, students are required to show inadequate response to Tier 1 instruction prior to moving to more intensive tiers. Secondary students have already demonstrated reading difficulties and can be placed into more or less intensive tiers based on their reading profiles and not based on inadequate response (Fuchs et al., 2010; Vaughn and Fletcher, 2010). This allows for maximum intervention benefits for students in Tiers 2 and 3 (Fuchs et al., 2010).

Effective Tier 1 Instruction

Teachers can strengthen Tier 1 instruction by implementing a schoolwide approach to RTI and using research-based practices for improving literacy across the content areas. Involving all content teachers improves the quality of instruction and facilitates a shared ownership for remediating difficulties (Fisher and Frey, 2011). Reed et al. (2012) identified seven key features of effective instruction: (1) communicate clear expectations, (2) demonstrate or model new content, (3) provide scaffolded steps and immediate corrective feedback, (4) provide follow-up instruction, (5) engage and motivate students, (6) plan for distributed practice, and (7) differentiate instruction as necessary. Professional development may be a path to improving instruction in vocabulary and comprehension, which leads to all students receiving quality Tier 1 instruction (Vaughn and Fletcher, 2012).

Vocabulary and concept learning strategies are essential for acquiring content area knowledge and facilitate acquisition of background knowledge, which improves reading outcomes (Scammacca et al., 2007). First, content area teachers select vocabulary words that relate to key concepts and are of relative importance (Alvermann et al., 2010). Teachers can choose words based on what students need to know to understand the most important ideas. Words selected may have high utility and frequency or may be those that are likely to be unfamiliar or confusing (Denton et al., 2012). Then, teachers can provide instruction and distributed practice with the vocabulary words assuring that they know the words not just "in the moment" but for long-term retention and use (Kamil et al., 2008; Reed et al., 2012). One vocabulary strategy that can be applied across content areas is semantic mapping. Semantic maps are visual diagrams that show how key words are connected and can help students define difficult vocabulary words (Alvermann et al., 2010). Teachers work with students to create semantic maps through discussion and modeling, which helps students organize important information in their memory. Another valuable strategy is the Frayer model, which is a visual representation of vocabulary that includes the word's characteristics, nonessential characteristics, examples, and nonexamples (Alvermann et al., 2010). The Frayer model (Frayer et al., 1969) helps students discriminate between the features of words and allows them to clarify their vocabulary knowledge. By strengthening vocabulary instruction, teachers can foster increased reading and content area comprehension.

Tier 1 instruction can also be enhanced through systematic comprehension skill instruction, which includes previewing, finding the main idea, summarizing, drawing conclusions, and activating or building prior knowledge (Kamil et al., 2008; Reed et al., 2012). There are many strategies for teaching students reading comprehension skills before, during, and after reading. Students benefit from multiple opportunities to practice and demonstrate knowledge of the strategies (Denton et al., 2012). Before reading, teachers set a purpose for reading, activate

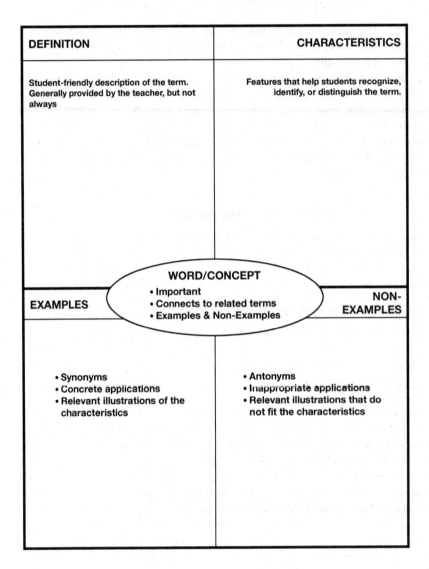

Figure 18.3 Frayer Model Example

Source: Reprinted with permission from Meadows Center for Preventing Educational Risk (2014). *Middle School Matters Institute.* Austin, TX: Author.

prior knowledge through text previewing or using semantic maps, and connect students' background knowledge to the reading selection (Klingner et al., 2015). During- and after-reading strategies should focus on deeper understanding of the text through questioning strategies, such as question–answer relationships, inferring, self-generated questions, main idea formation, and summarizing (Klingner et al., 2015). One comprehension strategy content area teachers could use is a notes log to summarize main ideas and details from a text (Reed et al., 2012). Another beneficial strategy is an anticipation guide, which helps students activate prior knowledge and form new concepts from a text (Alvermann et al., 2010).

While there are many strategies that foster vocabulary and comprehension, it is recommended that the RTI team carefully select the best practices for their school. Additionally, teachers might need professional development and training to implement these strategies (Fisher and Frey, 2011). Strong Tier 1 instruction is the basis for a comprehensive literacy program for all students (Brozo, 2009). Without this level being successfully in place, students may be inappropriately placed in Tiers 2 and 3, diluting the overall effectiveness of the RTI process.

Effective Tier 2 and 3 Interventions

Despite effective Tier 1 instruction, approximately 20% of a school's populations will require more intensive support (Reed et al., 2012). In the elementary grades, this level of support is provided to students typically in small groups as part of Tiers 2-type interventions. However, there may be reasons to move directly to more intensive interventions with students in secondary grades. It is likely that students in grades 6 and above have already experienced Tier 2-type interventions and may require more intensive interventions via increased instructional time, extended duration of the intervention, and individualized instruction using regular progress monitoring (Vaughn and Wanzek, 2014).

Providing intensive interventions for struggling adolescent readers is not always feasible, due to the complex nature of students' reading problems, school schedules, and other psychosocial factors. One way to address these factors is to design interventions that address secondary students' complex reading needs. Students' interest and motivation to learn can be increased through interventions that are engaging, responsive, and related to content areas, students' interests, lives, or current events (Brozo, 2011; Kamil et al., 2008). Teachers can implement this by allowing for student choice of text, creating social interactions that focus on comprehension, providing a range of engaging texts, and focusing on thought-provoking learning goals (Torgesen et al., 2007). Additionally, safe and supportive learning environments can help students build confidence in their skills (Kamil et al., 2008). It's important to address struggling readers' weaknesses in a way is motivating, engaging, and responsive, especially since these factors may mediate the effectiveness of the intervention (Fuchs et al., 2010).

Struggling readers also benefit from word-level interventions, which provide explicit word recognition instruction through decoding and word study (Edmonds et al., 2009; Scammacca et al., 2007). When students struggle to read with accuracy and automaticity, they cannot comprehend what they are reading (Flanigan et al., 2011). Many secondary students have difficulty reading multisyllabic words and may need instruction on syllabication, vowel patterns, and strategies for decoding unknown multisyllabic words (Denton et al., 2012). Content area instruction also includes many common roots and affixes, so is also beneficial to model morphemic analysis. This teaches students to recognize word parts such as prefixes, suffixes, and Greek or Latin roots, to decode unknown words, and to recognize relationships between words (Alvermann et al., 2010).

In addition to word-level interventions, recent research indicates that vocabulary interventions also strengthen reading comprehension (Scammacca et al., 2013). Students benefit from understanding the general and specific meanings of words, which can increase comprehension (Klingner et al., 2015). Students in Tiers 2 and 3 also benefit from the vocabulary strategies used in Tier 1 (i.e., semantic and vocabulary maps); however, instruction might need to be intensified to address individual needs by incorporating word recognition instruction and morphemic analysis. (Denton et al., 2012; Kamil et al., 2008; Klingner et al., 2015; Scammacca et al., 2007). Teachers may incorporate hands-on experiences, in-class presentation, and graphic or visual representations of words and concepts to teach meanings of new words. (Alvermann et al., 2010). Students can be taught to monitor their understanding of words and strategies for learning words (Klinger et al., 2015).

Secondary schools may also face issues with their organization, faculty, and schedule when implementing intensive interventions. In every state, there are credit requirements that stipulate which classes students need to take in order to earn a diploma. With all of the required classes, it can be difficult to find time in the schedule to supplement Tier 1 instruction. School leaders may need to alter course schedules or remove students from optional elective classes so that they have adequate time in their school day to take the necessary reading intervention classes (Reed et al., 2012). Since literacy skills are necessary to pursue postsecondary education, they need to be prioritized when establishing a student's schedule (Torgesen et al., 2007). If adequate support cannot be incorporated into the daily schedule, schools may even need to extend the school day or school year for those students. It is unlikely that a single approach to resolving reading difficulties will work for all students.

Progress Monitoring Recommendations

Progress monitoring is traditionally used to track students' progress and adjust the instruction as necessary. It serves to identify when students have met predetermined benchmarks and when they can be transitioned back to lower levels of support (Fuchs et al., 2010). Students' progress in the secondary grades differs considerably from that of younger students (e.g., early elementary grades) in that their reading problems involve more complex processes (e.g., background knowledge, vocabulary), and thus their progress is more difficult both to measure and to observe growth in (Vaughn and Fletcher, 2012). Curriculum-based measures, or other proximal measures, may provide a more accurate picture of a student's progress (Pyle and Vaughn, 2012).

Progress monitoring may indicate that some students need continued intensive support throughout their secondary education. These students may progress more slowly than grade-level peers, or their difficulties may be so great that they have difficulty keeping up with the demands of the secondary curriculum. Although RTI is typically viewed as a framework in which students move fluidly throughout the tiers as they require and respond to interventions, inadequate responders may require long-term support in the most intensive tiers and may not return to less supportive tiers. Schools should be prepared to provide the necessary staffing in order to meet these students' needs with potentially long-term interventions.

Summary

The RTI framework provides a multitiered system of supports for struggling readers. At the secondary level, this framework focuses on addressing individual learning needs through strong core instruction across content areas, as well as remediation of previously-established difficulties. Although RTI aims to address student learning needs at all levels, implementing a successful RTI model in secondary schools presents many challenges. Schools face unique issues involving screening, inadequate responders, and effective instruction and interventions throughout the tiers. We recommend adjusting the RTI framework at the secondary level by using pre-eixisting data to identify difficulties and fast-tracking students to appropriate tiers. Additionally, providing high-quality instruction and interventions to struggling adolescent readers is a complex process. This requires reorganization of school schedules, along with increased professional development for school personnel across all content areas. Reading interventions can address the unique needs of adolescents, and those students who respond minimally might need continued support throughout their secondary education. RTI has a promising future at the secondary level and schools may need to be prepared to address the aforementioned issues and recommendations to successfully implement an RTI framework.

Finally, there are some remaining questions about how to incorporate RTI at the secondary level. What should be the primary aim of the intervention, particularly with respect to inadequate responders? Should interventions address all reading skills, a targeted subset of the most important skills, or a set of functional literacy skills needed for adulthood? While research suggests struggling adolescent readers benefit from reading interventions, particularly if they've received inadequate core instruction, further research is needed to identify how we can effectively remediate difficulties for persistent struggling readers.

References

Alvermann, D. E., Phelps, S. F., and Gillis, V. R. (2010). *Content area reading and literacy: Succeeding in today's diverse classrooms.* Boston, MA: Allyn & Bacon.

Brozo, W. G. (2009). Response to intervention or responsive instruction? Challenges and possibilities of response to intervention for adolescent literacy. *Journal of Adolescent and Adult Literacy*, 53(4), 277–281. doi: 10.1598/JAAL.53.4.1

Brozo, W. G. (2011). *RTI and the adolescent reader: Responsive literacy instruction in secondary schools.* New York: Teachers College Press.

Cutting, L. E. and Scarborough, H. S. (2006). Prediction of reading comprehension: Relative contributions of word recognition, language proficiency, and other cognitive skills can depend on how comprehension is measured. *Scientific Studies of Reading*, 10(3), 277–299. http://doi.org/10.1207/s1532799xssr1003_5

Denton, C. A., Fletcher, J. M., Anthony, J. L., and Francis, D. J. (2006). An evaluation of intensive intervention for students with persistent reading difficulties. *Journal of Learning Disabilities*, 39(5), 447–466. http://doi.org/10.1177/00222194060390050601

Denton, C. A., Vaughn, S., Wexler, J., Bryan, D., and Reed, D. (2012). *Effective instruction for middle school students with reading difficulties: The reading teacher's sourcebook.* Baltimore, MD: Paul H. Brookes Publishing.

Edmonds, M. S., Vaughn, S., Wexler, J., Reutebuch, C., Cable, A., Tackett, K. K., and Schnakenberg, J. W. (2009). A synthesis of reading interventions and effects on reading comprehension outcomes for older struggling readers. *Review of Educational Research*, 79(1), 262–300.

Fisher, D. and Frey, N. (2011). Implementing TRI in a high school: A case study. *Journal of Learning Disabilities*, 46(2), 99–114. doi: 10.1177/0022219411407923

Flanigan, K., Hayes, L., Templeton, S., Bear, D. R., Invernizzi, M., and Johnston, F. (2011). *Words their way with struggling readers: Word study for reading, vocabulary, and spelling instruction, grades 4–12.* Boston, MA: Pearson.

Fletcher, J. M. and Vaughn, S. (2009). Response to intervention: Preventing and remediating academic difficulties. *Child Development Perspectives*, 3(1), 30–37. http://doi.org/10.1111/j.1750–8606.2008.00072.x

Frayer. D. A., Frederick, W. C., and Klausmeier, H. G. (1969). A schema for testing the level of concept mastery (Technical Report No. 16). Madison, WI: University of Wisconsin Research and Development Center for Cognitive Learning.

Fuchs, L. S., Fuchs, D., and Compton, D. L. (2010). Rethinking response to intervention at middle and high school. *School Psychology Review*, 39(1), 22–28.

Hock, M. F., Brasseur, I. F., Deshler, D. D., Catts, H. W., Marquis, J. G., Mark, C. A., and Stribling, J. W. (2009). What is the reading component skill profile of adolescent struggling readers in urban schools? *Learning Disability Quarterly*, 32(1), 21–38. http://doi.org/10.2307/25474660

Individuals with Disabilities Education Improvement Act of 2004, Pub. L. No. 108–446, (2006).

Johnson, E. S., Smith, L., and Harris, M. L. (2009). *How RTI works in secondary schools.* Thousand Oaks, CA: Corwin.

Kamil, M. L., Borman, G. D., Dole, J., Kral, C. C., Salinger, T., and Torgesen, J. (2008). Improving adolescent literacy: Effective classroom and intervention practices: A practice guide (NCEE #2008–4027). Washington, DC: National Center for Education Evaluation and Regional Assistance, Institute of Education Sciences, U.S. Department of Education. http://ies.ed.gov/ncee/wwc

Kena, G., Musu-Gillette, L., Robinson, J., Wang, X., Rathbun, A., Zhang, J., . . . and Dunlop Velez, E. (2015). The condition of education 2015 (NCES 2015–144). Washington, DC: U.S. Department of Education, National Center for Education Statistics. http://nces.ed.gov

Klingner, J. K., Vaughn, S., and Boardman, A. (2015). Teaching reading comprehension to students with learning difficulties. New York: Guilford Press.

Meadows Center for Preventing Educational Risk (2014). *Middle School Matters Institute*. Austin, TX: Author.

Meyer, M. S. and Felton, R. H. (1999). Repeated reading to enhance fluency: Old approaches and new directions. *Annals of Dyslexia*, 49(1), 283–306. http://doi.org/10.1007/s11881–999–0027–8

National Center for Education Statistics (2011). The nation's report card: Reading 2011 (NCES 2012–457). Washington, DC: U.S. Department of Education, Institute of Education Sciences.

National High School Center, National Center on Response to Intervention, and Center on Instruction. (2010). *Tiered interventions in high schools: Using preliminary "lessons learned" to guide ongoing discussion*. Washington, DC: American Institutes for Research.

No Child Left Behind Act of 2001, ESEA, 2001, Title 1, Part B, Subpart 1, Section 1202(c)(7)(A)(IV)(2).

Pyle, N. and Vaughn, S. (2012). Remediating reading difficulties in a response to intervention model with secondary students. *Psychology in the Schools*, 49(3), 273–284. doi: 10.1002/pits.21593

Reed, D. K., Wexler, J., and Vaughn, S. (2012). *RTI for reading at the secondary level: Recommended literacy practices and remaining questions*. New York: The Guilford Press.

Scammacca, N., Roberts, G., Vaughn, S., Edmonds, M., Wexler, J., Reutebuch, C. K., and Torgesen, J. K. (2007). Interventions for adolescent struggling readers: A meta-analysis with implications for practice. Center on Instruction. http://eric.ed.gov/?id=ED521837

Scammacca, N. K., Roberts, G., Vaughn, S., and Stuebing, K. K. (2013). A Meta-analysis of interventions for struggling readers in grades 4–12: 1980–2011. *Journal of Learning Disabilities*, 0022219413504995. http://doi.org/10.1177/0022219413504995

Swanson, C. B. (2008). Special education in America: The states of students with disabilities in the nation's high schools. Retrieved from Editorial Projects in Education Research Center website: www.edweek.org/media/eperc_specialeducationinamerica.pdf

Torgesen, J. K., Alexander, A. W., and Wagner, R. K. (2001). Intensive remedial instruction for children with severe reading disabilities: immediate and long-term outcomes from two instructional approaches. *Journal of Learning Disabilities*, 34(1), 33–58. http://doi.org/10.1177/002221940103400104

U.S. Department of Education, Institute of Education Sciences, National Center for Special Education Research. (2011). Secondary school programs and performance of students with disabilities: A special topic report of findings from the national longitudinal transition study-2 (NCSER 2012–3000). http://ies.ed.gov/ncser/pubs/20123000/pdf/20123000.pdf

Vaughn, S., Cirino, P. T., Wanzek, J., Wexler, J., Fletcher, J. M., Denton, C. D., . . . and Francis, D. J. (2010). Response to intervention for middle school students with reading difficulties: Effects of a primary and secondary intervention. *School Psychology Review*, 39(1), 3–21.

Vaughn, S. and Fletcher, J. M. (2010). Thoughts on rethinking response to intervention with secondary students. *School Psychology Review*, 39(2), 296–299.

Vaughn, S. and Fletcher, J. M. (2012). Response to intervention with secondary school students with reading difficulties. *Journal of Learning Disabilities*, 45(3), 244–256. http://doi.org/10.1177/002221 9412442157

Vaughn, S. and Fuchs, L. S. (2003). Redefining learning disabilities as inadequate response to instruction: The promise and potential problems. *Learning Disabilities Research and Practice*, 18(3), 137–146. http://doi.org/10.1111/1540–5826.00070

Vaughn, S. and Wanzek, J. (2014). Intensive interventions in reading for students with reading disabilities: Meaningful impacts. *Learning Disabilities Research and Practice*, 29(2), 46–53.

Vaughn, S., Wexler, J., Leroux, A., Roberts, G., Denton, C., Barth, A., and Fletcher, J. (2012). Effects of intensive reading intervention for eighth-grade students with persistently inadequate response to intervention. *Journal of Learning Disabilities*, 45(6), 515–525. http://doi.org/10.1177/0022219411402692

Vaughn, S., Wexler, J., Roberts, G., Barth, A., Denton, C., and Romain, M. (2010, February). Standardized versus individualized approaches to treating students with reading disabilities. Pacific Coast Research Conference, San Diego, CA.

Wagner, M., Newman, L., Cameto, R., Levine, P., and Garza, N. (2006). An overview of findings from wave 2 of the National Longitudinal Transition Study-2 (NLTS2). (NCSER 2006–3004). Menlo Park, CA: SRI International.

INDEX